D0254635

EXPLORER'S GUIDE

COASTAL MAINE

EXPLORER'S GUIDE

COASTAL MAINE

FIRST EDITION

CHRISTINA TREE & NANCY ENGLISH

THE COUNTRYMAN PRESS
A division of W. W. Norton & Company
Independent Publishers Since 1923

Maps by Erin Greb Cartography © The Countryman Press
Book design by Chris Welch
Manufacturing by Versa Press

For information about permission to reproduce selections from this book, write to Permissions,
W. W. Norton & Company, Inc., 500 Fifth Avenue, New York, NY 10110

For information about special discounts for bulk purchases, please contact
W. W. Norton Special Sales at specialsales@wwnorton.com or 800-233-4830

The Countryman Press
www.countrymanpress.com

A division of W. W. Norton & Company, Inc.
500 Fifth Avenue, New York, NY 10110
www.wwnorton.com

ISBN: 978-1-58157-331-2 (pbk.)

10 9 8 7 6 5 4 3 2 1

For lifelong explorers Liam, Tim, and Christopher Davis —C. T.

To Emma, with thanks and appreciation —N. E.

EXPLORE WITH US!

Explorer's Guide Coastal Maine covers the coast with the same format and detail that our *Explorer's Guide Maine*, currently in its 18th edition, presents the entire Pine Tree State. For this new guide we have revisited the coast and islands with an eye to focusing and expanding coverage of our favorite places and the many ways of enjoying them. For more "About this Book," see p. 32.

WHAT'S WHERE In the beginning of the book you'll find an alphabetical listing of special highlights and important information that you may want to reference quickly. You'll find advice on everything from where to buy the best local lobster to where to write or call for camping reservations and park information.

LODGING We've selected lodging places for mention in this book based on their merit alone; we do not charge innkeepers to be listed. The authors personally check as many bed & breakfasts, farms, sporting lodges, and inns as possible.

PRICES Please don't hold us or the respective innkeepers responsible for the rates listed as of press time in 2017. Some changes are inevitable. **The 8 percent state rooms and meals tax should be added to all prices unless we specifically state that it's included in a price.** We've tried to note when a gratuity is added, as it often is in high-end accommodations, but it's always wise to check before booking.

SMOKING Maine B&Bs, inns, and restaurants are now generally smoke-free, but many lodging places still reserve some rooms for smokers, and some restaurants still offer a smoking area in their outdoor seating. If this is important to you, be sure to ask when making reservations.

KEY TO SYMBOLS

- ✪ **Authors' favorites.** These are the places we think have the best to offer in each region, whether that means great food, outstanding rooms, beautiful scenery, or overall appeal.
- 💍 **Weddings.** The wedding-ring symbol appears next to lodging venues that specialize in weddings.
- 🎗 **Special value.** The blue-ribbon symbol appears next to selected lodging and restaurants that combine quality and moderate prices.
- 🐾 **Pets.** The dog-paw symbol appears next to venues that accept pets.
- ✎ **Child-friendly.** The crayon symbol appears next to lodging, restaurants, activities, and shops of special interest or appeal to youngsters.
- ♿ **Handicapped access.** The wheelchair symbol appears next to lodging, restaurants, and attractions that are partially or completely handicapped-accessible.
- ((•)) **Wireless Internet.** The wireless symbol appears next to public spaces, restaurants, and attractions that offer wireless Internet access.

RESTAURANTS In most sections please note a distinction between *Dining Out* and *Eating Out*. By their nature, restaurants included in the *Eating Out* group are generally inexpensive.

We would appreciate any comments or corrections. Please write to:

Explorer's Guide Editor
The Countryman Press
A division of W. W. Norton & Company
500 Fifth Avenue
New York, NY 10110

For more info, go to: maineguidebook.com.

You can also email tree.christina@gmail.com.

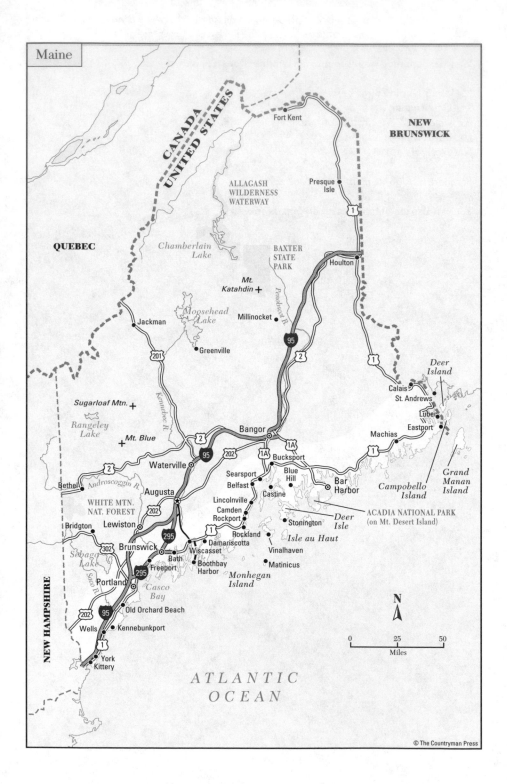

CONTENTS

MAPS

INTRODUCTION

The Maine coast is lengthier, more varied, and more accessible than most visitors assume. Kittery on Maine's southern border is officially just 211 driving miles southwest of Bar Harbor and 293 driving miles from Eastport, but the shoreline between Kittery and Eastport measures more than 4,500 miles—and some 7,000 miles if you count offshore islands.

That's more than the rest of the East Coast combined.

In contrast with much of this country's East Coast and most of the West Coast, Maine's shoreline rarely faces open ocean. With the exception of a sandy arc of land along the South Coast and a high, rocky stretch of Way Downeast headlands known as the Bold Coast—both measuring fewer than 40 miles—the shore corkscrews in and out of coves and points, winding along bays and up wide, tidal rivers. More than a dozen ragged peninsulas extend like fingers south from Rt. 1, the coastal highway, separating the bays and rivers, notched in turn with numerous coves and harbors.

In many places, islands are "hinged" to the mainland by bridges and causeways. Scientists tell us that the peninsulas and offshore islands are mountains drowned by the same glaciers that sculpted the area's many shallow, (relatively) warm-water lakes. The tides shift from high to low roughly every 12 hours; these shifts are more extreme as you move northeast, measuring a difference of 9 feet in Kittery, up to 25 feet at Eastport.

Current offshore vessels tend to be leisure crafts, fishing boats, and lobster boats, but for more than two centuries these waters were busy freight and passenger lanes. It's because visitors arrived primarily by water prior to the 1920s that summer resorts—from Popham Beach and Boothbay Harbor to Bar Harbor—are at the tips of peninsulas and hinged islands, miles from Rt. 1.

The good news: This lengthy and convoluted shoreline harbors a wide choice of places to sleep, as well as to walk and to eat within sound and sight of water. Access to coastal preserves has been dramatically increased in recent decades by both state and conservation groups.

The waters that splinter the coast ensure the distinctive character of the many relatively isolated communities. The feel as well as the shape of the coast changes as you travel northeast. The lightly settled and touristed region beyond the turnoff for Bar Harbor is a very different Maine from the heavily populated and touristed South Coast. Still, the moment you cross the southern border, you know you're in Maine. Kittery and York both have their share of coves and rocky paths, and local accents are as strong as any to be found in Eastport.

The bad news: You can't rush. The chief complaint among Maine visitors is "not enough time." The shape of the coast and the two-lane nature of Rt. 1 hobble attempts to reach Acadia National Park from points south on a summer weekend, especially a long weekend.

The key: Most visitors come to Maine for R&R. So turn off Rt. 1. Savor the salt air and the scenery in a lobster-boat–filled harbor. Slow down. Walk a shore path. Eat lobster in a real lobster pound. Talk to a local. Stroll the dock and find a windjammer or a whale watch trip, a ferry or a seagoing kayaking tour, for a chance to be out on the water.

The Authors

Chris was born in Hawaii and bred in Manhattan, came to Massachusetts to attend Mount Holyoke College, and began to work for the *Boston Globe* in 1968. Her first *Globe* travel story was on Ogunquit and she continued to chronicle Maine's growing options for visitors over the next 40 years. She is addicted to many Maines. As a toddler, she learned to swim in the Ogunquit River and later watched her sons do the same in Monhegan's icy waters. Her number two son was married on Little Cranberry Island off Mount Desert. She has sea kayaked off points from Portland to Pembroke as well as sailed whenever possible on Penobscot Bay. She values her Boston vantage point, far enough away to give her the perspective on what it means to be a visitor, yet near enough to comfortably and continually explore Maine. She launched the Explorer's Guide series in 1979 and has authored or co-authored all editions of the Maine Explorer's Guides as well as Explorer's Guides to Vermont, New Hampshire and Western Massachusetts. She continues to contribute to *Yankee Magazine*.

Born in New York City and raised in northeastern Vermont, Nancy has spent most of her life in Portland, Maine. She has heard the cry of a bobcat at night in Vermont, listened to the calls of loons on Maine lakes, and watched a red-tailed hawk pluck a pigeon for dinner in her Portland backyard. She was the restaurant reviewer for the *Maine Sunday Telegram* for more than six years. Her travel writing started in the 1970s while still an undergraduate at Vassar College, with articles in *Vermont Life* magazine. She wrote *Chow Maine*, a guide to the best restaurants, cafés, lobster shacks, and markets on the Maine coast. She has co-authored the Maine Explorer's Guide for the past seven editions.

Chris and Nancy also co-authored the three editions of the Explorer's Guides Maine Coast & Islands, which this new, far more detailed, guide is now replacing.

We are frequently asked how we manage to keep up with Maine's constant changes, and the answer is: only with the help of the many kind and knowledgeable people along the road and to those kind enough to read and comment on our updates. Chris owes special thanks for help from Carol Lord of York, Richard and Ann Moseley of Harpswell, Elizabeth Knowlten in Bath, Tom and Carolyn Church in Georgetown, Steve and Susan Plansteiner of East Boothbay, Bobby and Sherry Weare in Damariscotta, Ann Hamilton of Brooklin, Joan Yeaton in Addison, Joyce Morrell and Jan Meiners on Campobello, and Robert Godfrey in Eastport. Finally, thanks to the world's most helpful, talented, and long-suffering husband and companion on the road, former *Boston Globe* travel editor William A. Davis. Check out Chris's on-road blogs at mainemeanderings.wordpress.com.

Nancy wishes to thank all the many people who have the luck to live on the coast and are kind enough to share what they know. Karen Arel of the Ogunquit Chamber of Commerce and Chamber Vice President Frances Reed alert her to all the changes in that thriving town. Karen, retiring in the summer of 2017, will be much missed! Laura Snyder Smith at the Chamber in the Kennebunks and James Jasper at the Biddeford Saco Chamber alerted me to fine new businesses now listed here. Thanks go to Roy Kasindorf of beautiful Ullikana and Aaron Brown and Melanie Graten at the Bar Harbor Chamber of Commerce. Cynthia Crow, manager of the Southwest Harbor & Tremont Chamber, has an eagle eye for needed changes in the text. Kathleen Coleman, manager at Belfast Area Chamber, is a kind and resourceful expert; and in Rockland and Camden kudos go to the local volunteers in the visitor information centers. Sharon in Rockland was particularly attentive and full of information. Caroline Sulzer and David Walker, of Surry, are gracious hosts for every guidebook update. Thanks go to all the friendly people in Downeast Maine who took time from their busy schedules to answer questions.

Both authors are deeply grateful to Countryman Press editor Dan Crissman for his initiative, flexibility, and patience in producing this splendid new book.

History You Can See

You can experience Maine's rich history through the places that still recall or dramatize it.

The first residents of this region were the Abanaki, also known as Wabanaki, "people of the dawn." They were here for many thousands of years, judging from shell heaps and artifacts found in the Damariscotta/Boothbay and Blue Hill areas. Later pictographs can be found around Machias Bay. An excellent exhibit in the **Maine State Museum** (maine statemuseum.org) in Augusta depicts the distinct periods of this history and features the Red Paint People who flourished between 5,000 and 3,800 years ago and are said to have fished from large, sturdy boats. The **Abbe Museum** (abbemuseum.org) in Bar Harbor, showcases the cultures of Maine's Wabanaki, the less than 7,000 members of the Penobscot, Passamaquoddy, Micmac, and Maliseet tribes who live in the state.

In 1794 the Penobscots technically deeded most of Maine to Massachusetts in exchange for the 140 small islands in the Penobscot River, and in 1818 Massachusetts agreed to pay them an assortment of trinkets for the land. In 1820, when Maine became a state, a trust fund was set aside but ended up in the general treasury. The state's three reservations (two belonging to the Passamaquoddys and one to the Penobscots) were termed "enclaves of disfranchised citizens bereft of any special status."

In 1972 the Penobscots and Passamaquoddys sued to reclaim 1.5 million acres of land allegedly illegally appropriated by the state, and in 1980 they received an $80.6 million settlement, which they have since invested in a variety of enterprises. The Passamaquoddy tribe today numbers about 3,400 members, roughly divided between the reservations at **Indian Township** in Princeton and at **Sipayik**, also known as **Pleasant Point** (wabanaki.com), near Eastport, site of the **Indian Ceremonial Days**, which are held annually in mid-August to celebrate Passamaquoddy culture, climaxing in dances in full regalia. Exhibits at the **Wabanaki Culture Center** in Calais focus on Passamaquoddy history and craftsmanship.

For traces of early 17th-century settlement, see our descriptions of **Phippsburg**, **Pemaquid**, and **Augusta**. The French and Indian Wars (1675–1760), in which Maine was more involved than most of New England, are recalled in the reconstructed English **Fort William Henry** at Pemaquid and in historical markers scattered around Castine. (Baron de Saint Castine, a young French nobleman married to a Penobscot Indian princess, controlled the coastal area we now call Downeast.) A striking house built in 1760 on **Kittery Point** (see "Kittery, South Berwick, and the Yorks") and exhibits in nearby **Fort McClary** and in the **Kittery Historical** and **Naval Museum** evoke Sir William Pepperrell, credited with having captured the fortress at Louisburg from the French. The nonprofit **Old York Historical Society** museum buildings (oldyork.org) reveal Maine's brief, peaceful colonial period.

In the **Burnham Tavern** at Machias, you discover that townspeople captured a British man-of-war on June 1, 1775, the first naval engagement of the Revolution. Other reminders of the Revolution are less triumphant: At **Fort George** in Castine and in a multimedia presentation at **The Castine Historical Society**, you learn about how a substantial patriot fleet utterly disgraced itself there. Maine's brush with the British didn't end with the Revolution: **The Barracks Museum** in Eastport tells of British occupation again in 1814.

Climb the 103 steps of the **Portland Observatory** (built in 1807) and hear how Portland ranked second among New England ports, its tonnage based on lumber, the resource that fueled fortunes such as on such as those evidenced by the amazingly opulent **Colonel Black Mansion** in Ellsworth and the elegant **Ruggles House** way Downeast in Columbia

Falls. In 1820 Maine finally became a state (the 23rd), but not without a price. The mother state (Massachusetts), her coffers at their usual low, stipulated an even division of all previously undeeded wilderness, and some 10.5 million acres were quickly sold off. Vast privately owned tracts survive today as the unorganized townships.

This boundary with Canada was set only in 1842 when the Webster-Ashburton treaty ended the bloodless "Aroostook War," for which Maine raised a militia of more than 3,000 men. There were no battles but in 1844 the state built massive **Fort Knox** at the mouth of the Penobscot River (see "Bucksport/Orland Area"), just in case. Never entirely completed, it's a spooky centerpiece for a state park, particularly popular at Halloween.

The Webster-Ashburton treaty also established the illogical Maine/New Brunswick boundary line across Passamaquoddy Bay and the Bay of Fundy. That's how it happens that Campobello and Grand Manan Islands are part of Canada, not Maine. Lubec is just across a bridge from Grand Manan, fewer than 5 miles off Cutler but 00 miles south of the New Brunswick mainland.

As we note in the introduction to "Brunswick and the Harpswells," it can be argued that the Civil War began and ended in Brunswick. Unfortunately, the state suffered heavy losses: Some 18,000 young soldiers from Maine died, as Civil War monuments along the **Civil War Trail** (mainecivilwartrail.org) attest. The end of the war, however, ushered in a boom decade. Outstanding displays in the **Vinalhaven Historical Society Museum** (see "Vinalhaven, North Haven, and Matinicus") and **Deer Isle Granite Museum** in Stonington (see "Stonington and Isle au Haut") present the ways that Maine granite fed the demand for monumental public buildings throughout the country, and both schooners and Down Easters (graceful square-rigged vessels) were in great demand (see the **Penobscot Marine Museum** in "Belfast, Searsport, and Stockton Springs" and the **Maine Maritime Museum** in "Bath Area").

In the late 19th century, many Maine industries boomed, tourism included. We describe Maine's tourism history in its own sidebar because it is so colorful, little recognized, and so much a part of what you see in Maine today.

General Information

The **Maine Office of Tourism** maintains visit maine.com, the best first-stop for in-line information about travel in Maine. A phone line (1-888-624-6345) connects callers with a live knowledgeable person in a Maine Visitor Center during open hours, 8-6 in summer and 9-5.30 off-season. You can request the thick, helpful, four-season guide *Maine Invites You* (accompanied by a Maine highway map) and a brochure guide to *The Maine Art Museum Trail*. The *Guide to Inns and Bed & Breakfasts and Camps and Cottages*, a lodging guide, and *Maine Invites You* are published by the **Maine Tourism Association** (207-623-036), which also maintains a helpful vacation-planning website: mainetourism.com. This is a member-supported group that maintains well-stocked and -staffed welcome centers at its southern gateway at Kittery (207-439-1319)

Christina Tree

STATUE OF A PASSAMAQUODDY WOMEN AT THE ST. CROIX INTERNATIONAL HISTORIC SITE OUTLOOK, SOUTH OF CALAIS

TOURISM IN MAINE

We are fascinated by Maine's history in general and her tourism history in particular. It seems ironic that back in the 1920s "motor touring" was hailed as a big improvement over train and steamer travel because it meant you no longer had to go where everyone else did—over routes prescribed by railroad tracks and steamboat schedules. In Maine cars seem, however, to have had precisely the opposite effect. In summer more than 70 percent of the state's visitors follow the coastal tourist route faithfully, as though their wheels were grooved to Rt. 1.

Tourism has always been driven by images. In the 1840s Thomas Cole, Frederic Church (both of whom sketched and painted scenes of Mount Desert), and lesser-known artists began projecting Maine as a romantic, remote destination in the many papers, magazines, and children's books of the decade. While Henry David Thoreau's *The Maine Woods* was not published until 1864, many of its chapters appeared as magazine articles years earlier (Thoreau first climbed Katahdin in 1846), and in 1853, *Atlantic Monthly* editor James Russell Lowell visited and wrote about Moosehead Lake.

After the Civil War, Maine tourism boomed. Via railroad and steamboat, residents of cities throughout the East and Midwest streamed into the Pine Tree State, most toting guidebooks, many published by rail and steamboat lines to boost business. "Sports" in search of big game and big fish patronized "sporting camps" throughout the North Woods. Along the coast and on dozens of islands, hotels of every size were built, most by Maine natives. Blue-collar workers came by trolley to religious camp meetings, and the wealthy built themselves elaborate summer "cottages" on islands and around Bar Harbor, Camden, and Boothbay Harbor, and on the island of Campobello.

Developments and sophisticated landscaping transformed much of the previously ignored sandy Southern Coast. Then came World War I, coinciding with the proliferation of the Model A.

on I-95 northbound (also accessible from Rt. 1); in Yarmouth just off Rt. 1 and I-95 (207-846-0833); at the West Gardiner Service Plaza (with a shop showcasing work by the Maine Center for Craft/Maine Craft Association), I-95 exit 102/103 and I-295 exit 51; Hampden near Bangor on I-95 both northbound and southbound; Calais (207-454-7227); and Houlton (207-532-6349). There's also an information center near the New Hampshire line on Rt. 302 in Fryeburg (207-532-4792). In each chapter, we describe the local sources under *Guidance*.

AIRPORTS AND AIRLINES **Portland International Jetport** (207-774-7301); Portland is served by Delta (delta.com), United (united .com), American Airlines (AA.com), JetBlue (jetblue.com), and Southwest Airlines (south west.com) and Elite Airways (eliteairways .net), serving Orlando, Fla. **Bangor International Airport** (207-947-0384; flybangor.com) offers flights to Florida via Allegiant Air (alle giantair.com), NYC and Detroit on Delta;

American serves NYC, Philadelphia, and Washington, DC. **Hancock County-Bar Harbor Airport** (bhairport.com) near Bar Harbor, **Augusta State Airport** (augustaair port.org), and **Knox County Regional Airport** (207-594-4131) in Owls Head near Rockland are all served by Cape Air (capeair.com). **Penobscot Island Air** (penobscotislandair .net), based at Owls Head, has regular flights to the islands of Vinalhaven, North Haven, and Matinicus. **Northern Maine Regional Airport** (flypresqueisle.com) is served by Pen Air (penair.com). **Manchester, NH**, and **Boston's Logan International Airport** are both popular gateways for Maine travelers; both are served by Mermaid Transportation (gomermaid. com) to Portland. **Concord Coach Lines** (see *Bus Service*) offers express service from Logan to Portland with continuing service to Augusta, Bangor, and coastal other destinations.

AMTRAK Maine passenger service is not just back but a resounding success! Amtrak's

The 1922 founding of the Maine Publicity Bureau (the present Maine Tourism Association), we suspect, reflects the panic of hoteliers (founder Hiram Ricker himself owned three of the state's grandest hotels: the Mount Kinco House, the Poland Spring House, and the Samoset). Over the next few years, these hotels went the way of passenger service, and "motorists" stuck to motor courts and motels along Rt. 1 and a limited number of inland roads.

By the late 1960s, when Chris began writing about Maine, much of the state had all but dropped off the tourist map; in the decades since, she has chronicled the reawakening of most of the old resort areas. Whale-watching and whitewater rafting, skiing and snowmobiling, windjamming and kayaking, outlet shopping, and the renewed popularity of country inns and B&Bs, locally sourced food, brew, and spirits all continue to contribute to this reawakening.

In recent decades the extent of easily accessible waterside walks and hikes has significantly increased. The idea of preserving and maintaining outstanding landscapes—from Ogunquit's Marginal Way to the core of present-day Acadia National Park—were also an offshoot of Maine's first tourism boom. The current expansion of preserved coastal trails and preserves gives new meaning to "getting off the beaten track," whether you are in a South Coast resort area or Way Downeast.

While we can't bring back the days of the steamboat era when visitors arrived by water, ways of getting out to the coast's many rivers and bays have also significantly increased in recent years. A dozen Windjammers offer cruises, stopping at islands and small ports in Penobscot Bay, and more "tall ships" and sailing crafts, as well as a variety of excursion and charter boats and ferries, transport you out on the water and to island communities.

No figures document how many tourists summered along the Maine Coast during its first tourist boom but the current annual count (coast and inland) is 39 million. Maine is, after all, magnificent.

Downeaster (amtrakdowneaster.com) offers frequent round trips between Boston's North Station and Brunswick with stops in Wells, Old Orchard, Saco, Portland, and Freeport. More people every year are discovering the view of the shoreline you otherwise never see. Northbound, the first Maine stop is **Wells** at a regional transportation center, served by taxis and a seasonal trolley to the beach. In Saco, the station is just beyond the mighty falls (taxi service and shuttle bus). In **Old Orchard**, the stop is a short walk from the beach and lodging. The **Portland** station doubles as a stop for Concord Coach Lines and there's bus and taxi service to downtown; you can also rent a bike. In **Freeport**, the stop is right at the outlets, while the **Brunswick** station is steps from lodging, dining, and shopping and an easy walk to Bowdoin College museums. Prices are reasonable; seniors and ages 15 and under are half price, and frequent packages lure Mainers to sports and entertainment events in Boston.

AREA CODE The area code throughout Maine is 207.

BUS SERVICE **Concord Coach Lines** (1-800-639-3317; concordcoachlines.com) serves Portland, Augusta, Brunswick, Bath, Wiscasset, Damariscotta, Waldoboro, Rockland, Camden, Belfast, Searsport and Bangor. Its Boston/Portland/Bangor Express is the fastest service to eastern Maine and (we recommend it over) **Greyhound Bus Lines** (1-800-231-2222), serving Augusta, Lewiston, Waterville, Portland, and Bangor. Coastal Connector (1-800-596-2823) offers daily service year-round from Bangor Airport (stopping at both bus terminals) to Calais, with stops in Machias and Perry, along with many flag-down stops (call ahead) in between. See exploremaine.org for details about other local buses.

FERRIES The Maine Department of Transportation maintains a brilliant website (exploremaine.org) with schedules for **Maine**

State Ferry Service (1-800-491-4883) from Rockland to Vinalhaven, North Haven, and Matinicus, from Lincolnville to Islesboro, and from Bass Harbor to Swans Island and Frenchboro. They also list services to Monhegan Island, Isle au Haut, and the Cranberry Islands. Casco Bay Islands are served by **Casco Bay Lines** (cascobaylines.com) from Portland. **Quoddy Loop Ferries** (quoddyloop .com) travel from Campobello Island to the New Brunswick mainland via Deer Island, and from Black Harbor to Grand Manan.

FIRE PERMITS Maine law dictates that no person shall kindle or use outdoor fires without a permit, except at authorized campsites or picnic grounds. Fire permits in the organized townships are obtained from the local town warden; in the unorganized townships, from the nearest forest ranger. Portable stoves fueled by propane gas, gasoline, or Sterno are exempt from the rule.

LITTER Littering in Maine is punishable by a $100 fine; this applies to dumping from boats as well as other vehicles. Most cans and bottles are redeemable.

HANDICAPPED ACCESS Within this book, handicapped-accessible lodging, restaurants, and attractions are marked with a wheelchair symbol. **Maine Adaptive Sports & Recreation** offers an outstanding snow sports program, including cross-country and alpine skiing, snowshoeing, and snowboarding (maineadaptive.org). Summer programs offer paddling, golf, and cycling.

INNS AND BED & BREAKFASTS For each edition we personally inspect hundreds of inns and B&Bs. Our choices reflect both what we have seen and the feedback we receive from others; they are not paid listings. The **Maine Innkeepers Association** maintains a website of their members at maineinns.com. Also check listings at visitmaine.com and mainetourism.com.

MAPS Free state maps are available from the **Maine Office of Tourism** (1-888-624-6345) and at the state visitors information centers, but we are sad to see the way these have deteriorated in recent years. The **AAA map** to Northern New England states is a step up, and

within this book we have done our best to detail obvious destinations. Sooner or later, however, serious Maine explorers have to invest in *The Maine Atlas and Gazetteer* published by DeLorme (shopdeloreme.com). **Map Adventures** publishes excellent waterproof maps to regional hiking and bike trails (mapadventures.com).

PUBLIC BROADCASTING The **Maine Public Broadcasting Network** (mpbn.net) offers statewide television and radio. **Maine Public Television** stations are **Channel 10** in Augusta and Presque Isle, **Channel 12** in Orono, **Channel 13** in Calais, and **Channel 26** in Biddeford. Local programming includes *Maine Watch*, highlighting important issues in Maine each week. **Maine's seven public radio stations** can be found on the dial at 90.1 in Portland, 90.9 in Bangor, 91.3 in Waterville, 90.5 in Camden, 89.7 in Calais, 106.1 in Presque Isle, and 106.5 in Fort Kent. *Maine Watch* and *Maine Things Considered* highlight state news.

POPULATION 1.33 million, according to the 2014 census. It has grown 4.2 percent since 2000, enough to hold on to its two congressional representatives.

TRAFFIC AND HIGHWAY TRAVEL TIPS Maine coastal travel has its sticky wickets. By far the worst is the weekend backup at the tolls at the entrance to the Maine Turnpike (maineturnpike.com). The 109-mile toll highway (I-95) begins in Kittery. Don't be confused by the exit numbers. Rather than sequential numbering, they represent the number of miles from the New Hampshire line. Tolls are a flat rate paid when getting on—and sometimes off—the turnpike. Get E-ZPass (ezpassmaineturnpike.com) and avoid peak travel times. Note that it takes no longer to reach a Downeast than a Midcoast destination, thanks to the way the highways run. The quickest way to Rockland or Camden from points south is I-295 from Portland to Brunswick or Topsham and then coastal Rt. 1. Belfast and destinations east through the Blue Hill Peninsula, however, can be reached in roughly the same time by taking I-295 to I-95 at Augusta and Rt. 3 to coastal Rt. 1 at Belfast. You can reach Ellsworth (gateway to Mount Desert and points east) in equal time by traveling I-295 to I-95 to Bangor and then heading down Rt. 1A. For current information on road conditions and delays, dial 511. For a live voice telling you about travel conditions and construction updates, phone 1-800-675-PIKE, or check the excellent website, maineturnpike .com., which includes web cams and describes service plazas (Kennebunk, Grey, Cumberland and West Gardiner).

SEAT BELTS Seat belts are the law in Maine, and right turns on a red light are permitted—unless otherwise stated—after a stop to check for oncoming traffic. Headlights should be turned on when using windshield wipers.

WEDDINGS Every year thousands of couples, many from "away," are married in several chambers of commerce—notably York, Kennebunkport, Boothbay, and Camden, are particularly helpful. Within the book we note properties that specialize in weddings with our ring symbol ⚭.

Arts

ART Maine's landscape has drawn major artists since the mid-19th century. The **Maine Arts Commission** (mainearts.com) offers a searchable database of artists, arts organizations, and events. Also see maineartmuseums .org for the state's leading art museums. Within each chapter, we describe the best art destinations. For more about art throughout the state, pick up a current copy of the *Maine Gallery & Studio Guide*, available at most galleries.

CRAFTS *Maine Guide to Crafts and Culture*, available free from the **Maine Crafts Association** (mainecrafts.org), showcases the work of more than 300 members at the **Center for Maine Craft**, a retail store in the West Gardiner Service Plaza, accessible from both the Maine Turnpike and Rt.295. **United Maine Craftsmen, Inc.** (207-621-2818; unitedmaine craftsmen.com), sponsors a series of major shows each year. **Haystack Mountain School of Crafts** (haystack-mtn.org; see "Stonington and Isle au Haut") is a summer school nationally respected in a variety of crafts with three-week workshops mid-June through mid-September. The surrounding area (Blue Hill to Stonington) contains the largest concentration of Maine craftspeople, many with open studios. For fiber studios, farms, and galleries listed at mainefiberarts.org; a printed or online tour map is also available. **Fiber Central**, the association headquarters in Topsham (13 Main St.) mounts changing exhibits.

FILM **Northeast Historic Film** (1-800-639-1636; oldfilm.org) is based at "The Alamo," a vintage-1916 movie house in Bucksport. This admirable group has created a regional moving-image archive of films based on or made in New England that were shown in every small town during the first part of the 20th century. Request the catalog *Videos of Life in New England*. The **International Film & Television Workshops** (207-236-8581) in Rockport offer a variety of weeklong courses in various aspects of film. The **Maine International Film Festival** is a 10-day event, with more than 60 films shown in Waterville (miff .org). Portland hosts the **Maine Jewish Film Festival** (mjff.org) in mid-March. The **Camden International Film Festival** is now one of the largest. For an overview of festivals, see the **Maine Film Office** website (filminmaine.com) and the **Maine Arts Commission** site, main carts.maine.gov. There is still a functioning **drive-in** in Saco (thesacodrivein.com).

MUSIC Maine offers a wide variety of musical events, festivals, and live shows depending on your taste. **Bowdoin International Music Festival** (bowdoinfestival.org) in Brunswick is the state's most prestigious and varied chamber music series, and the **Kneisel Hall Chamber Music Festival** (kneisel.org) in Blue Hill is its oldest chamber music festival, also still outstanding. Farther Downeast the **Monteux School of Conducting in Hancock** (monteux school.org) stages frequent concerts as does **SummerKeys** (summerkeys.com) in Lubec, a program specializing in piano but welcoming of students of all levels in a variety of instruments. In the Boothbay Region, the **Lincoln Arts Festival** is a summer series of classical and choral music and the Labor Day weekend **Bluegrass Festival** at Thomas Point Beach in Brunswick caps off the summer. There is also, of course, the **Portland Symphony Orchestra** (portlandsymphony.org), which has a summertime pops series. See maineperforms.com for more information.

THEATER The **Ogunquit Playhouse** (ogun quitplayhouse.org) is among the oldest and most prestigious summer theaters in the country. Along the South Coast, also check out the **Hackmatack Playhouse** in Berwick (hackmatack.org). In Brunswick the **Maine State Music Theatre** at Bowdoin College (msmt.org) is a big draw and in Boothbay there's the **Carousel Music Theater** (carousel musictheater.org). Farther along the coast, look for the **Camden Civic Theatre** (camden civictheater.com), the **Belfast Maskers** (bel fastmaskerstheater.com), the **New Surry Theatre** in Blue Hill (newsurrytheatre.org), the **Stonington Opera House** (operahearts.org), and the **Acadia Repertory Theatre** in Somesville (acadiarep.com). Year-round venues include **The Portland Players** (portlandplay ers.org) and **Portland Stage Company** (port landstage.com), the **Camden Civic Theatre** in Camden (camdencivictheater.com), and the **City Theater** (citytheater.org) in Biddeford. See maineperforms.com.

Food & Drink

Locally produced items include venison and beeswax as well as blueberries, Christmas wreaths, smoked seafood, teas, beer, wine, maple syrup, gin, vodka, and lobster stew, to name just a few. The Maine Department of Agriculture, Conservation and Forestry (getrealmaine.com) publishes several helpful guides. The website lists farmers' markets, orchards, farm stores, and much more.

AGRICULTURAL FAIRS The season opens in late June and runs through the first week of October, culminating with the large, colorful, immensely popular **Fryeburg Fair**. Among the best traditional fairs are the **Union Fair** (late August) and the **Blue Hill Fair** (Labor Day weekend). **The Common Ground Country Fair** (third weekend in September, at the fairgrounds in Unity), sponsored by the Maine Organic Farmers and Gardeners Association (mofga.org), features organic Maine-grown food, farming techniques, dancing, and music, and draws city folk and organic gardeners from all corners of the state. For details about fairs, see the **Maine Department of Agriculture, Conservation and Forestry** website: getreal maine.com. A vibrant tradition of harness racing at Maine fairs has been reinvigorated with a small percentage of revenues earned by Hollywood Casino in Bangor.

APPLES Fall brings plenty of pick-your-own opportunities across the state, and many orchards also sell apples and cider. For a map/guide to PYO orchards, see maineapples.org. And check out **Maine Apple Sunday** throughout the state in mid-September.

BEER Maine's craft breweries already outnumber its lighthouses and seem to be multiplying by the week. The *Maine Beer Trail,* a map/guide published by the **Maine Brewers Guild** (mainebrewersguild.org) and downloadable from the site, currently lists 70 breweries that welcome visitors and offers a pass that patrons get stamped at venues, good for "gear" like hats and T-shirts. At present, there are roughly two dozen brew pubs but all the listed breweries offer tours and tastings on selective days. Greater Portland alone has a dozen breweries and the South Coast, a half dozen, the Mid Coast and Penobscot Bay area, a dozen more, including the seasonal **Monhegan Brewing**, ten miles out to sea. From Kittery to Lubec, you are never more than a short drive from a craft brewery but you don't have to drive—just hop a **brew bus**, already a popular service in the Portland and South Coast areas. We can't claim to have visited them all, but have tried to include the local brew pubs within their respective chapters.

BLUEBERRIES Maine grows 98 percent of US lowbush wild blueberries, on an estimated 64,000 acres. Few growers allow U-pick, at least not until the commercial harvest is over. (One exception is **Staples Homestead Blueberries** in Stockton Springs.) Then the public can go "stumping" for leftovers (except where posted)—but the berries might not be in the best shape. On the other hand, berrying along roads and hiking paths is a rite of summer. The **blueberry barrens**—thousands of blueberry-covered acres—spread across Cherryfield, Columbia, and Machias (site of the state's most colorful blueberry festival in August) in Washington County. For more about Maine's famous fruit, click on wildblueberries.com. **The Wild Blueberry Festival** in Machias (machiasblueberry.com) in mid-August is one of the state's most colorful events; there are also blueberry festivals in Union and Rangeley.

CHEESE Maine claims 80 licensed cheese-makers, most selling at local farmers' markets. Check mainecheeseguild.org for a map/listing and events such as **Open Creamery Day** in early October.

CRAFT DISTILLERIES In Maine, small-batch distillers are increasing in number and quality, winning awards for rums, vodkas, brandies, whiskeys, and gins. First there was **Maine Distilleries** (mainedistilleries.com), founded by brothers from an Aroostook farm who found a new use for their potatoes, winning national recognition for their Cold River Vodka and offering a tasting room in Freeport. Currently Portland is home to **Maine Craft Distilling** (mainecraftdistilling.com), **Stroudwater Distillery** (stroudwaterdistillery.com), **New England Distilling** (newenglanddistilling.com) and **In'finiti Fermentation & Distillation** and **Liquid Riot Bottling Company**. In York, **Wiggly Bridge Distillery** (wigglybridgedistillery.com) offers a small plate menu as well as tours and tastings, also a seasonal tasting room in York Beach. Housed in a Biddeford mill building, **Round Turn Distilling** (roundturndistilling.com) specializes in gin. You might also want to check out craft distillerytours.com/Maine. Few of these small batch distilleries are easy to find. Also see **Bartlett Spirits of Maine Distillery** in Gouldsboro and **Sweetgrass Farm Winery and Distillery** with its excellent apple brandy and more, in Union and also listed under *Wine*.

FARMS AND FARMERS' MARKETS The **Maine Department of Agriculture, Conservation, and Forestry**'s website (getrealmaine.com) is a terrific resource detailing farms, farmers' markets, agricultural events, and what's available season by season.

LOBSTERS Lobster is just another item on the menu elsewhere in the world, but in Maine, it's an experience. It's no secret that Maine's, clean, cold waters produce some of the world's tastiest lobster. This hard-shelled crustacean has a long body and five sets of legs, including two large front claws—one large, flat, and heavy and the other smaller, thinner. They don't like light, hiding by day and emerging at night to eat mussels, sea urchins, and crabs. Most are more than five years old by the time they are caught, because Maine regulates the minimum (also maximum) size of what can be sold. The state also prohibits catching pregnant females, and imposes trap limits and license controls. In the 1880s most lobster was canned. Currently 70 percent of what's caught by Maine lobstermen is shipped live out of state. While elsewhere its appeal may be the fanciful ways it's prepared, in Maine it's the opposite. The shorter the time between a lobster's last crawl—not in a restaurant tank but in its home waters—and your plate, the better. The preferred cooking method: 10 to 15 minutes in boiling seawater for an average-sized (1- to 1½-pound) lobster. Selecting the lobster is a bit more complicated. Choices may include a "cull" (a lobster with one claw), a "chicken" (a female, usually 1 pound, and considered to have the most delicate meat), and "hard shell" or "soft shell." Lobsters molt, usually shedding their shells in summer. The soft shell fills with seawater, which is replaced by new meat as the animal grows and the shell hardens. Which is better depends on whom you talk to. Many prefer "shedders" because the shells are easy to crack and the meat is sweet. These actually don't transport as well as the full and firmly meated "hard shells," so chances are you won't have a chance to sample one outside Maine. How to eat a lobster is a no-holds-barred experience best embarked upon (and always explained) at lobster pounds. See lobsterfrommaine.com for more, and check out the Lobster sidebars throughout this book for the best lobster pounds, shacks, and restaurants.

MAPLE SUGARING Maine produces roughly 450,000 gallons of syrup a year and the **Maine Maple Producers Association** (mainemapleproducers.com) publishes a list of producers who welcome visitors on **Maine Maple Sunday** (also known as Sap Sunday), always the fourth Sunday in March.

OYSTERS AND CLAMS Maine, like the rest of New England, produces some of the best shellfish in the world. Feasting on raw oysters is a 2,000-year-old tradition in Maine, as evidenced by heaps of empty oyster shells ("middens") still to be seen in Damariscotta. By the mid-1800s, native oyster beds had all but disappeared, but thanks to seeding methods, these sweet and salty oysters are back and the Damariscotta River estuary remains their epicenter. See the Damariscotta chapter for more about **Pemaquid Oyster Co.**, and **Glidden Point Sea Farm**. For do-it-yourselfers, state law permits shellfish harvesting for personal use only, unless you have a commercial license. But rules vary with each town, so check with the town clerk (source of licenses) before you dig, and make sure there's no red tide. Urban clam flats have been closed for decades and are unlikely to reopen. Some towns do prohibit clamming, and in certain places there is a temporary stay on harvesting while the beds are being seeded.

WINE Prohibition began in Maine, and before Bob and Kathe Bartlett could open Maine's first winery, in 1982, they had to get the law changed. Just off Rt. 1 in Gouldsboro, **Bartlett Maine Estate Winery** (bartlettwinery .com) offers tastings of its prizewinning fruit wines utilizing Maine apples, blueberries, raspberries, and honey as well as regional pears and peaches, and has added S**pirits of Maine** to its name, pear eau de vie and Calvados-style apple brandy to its labels. Currently the website mainewinetrail.com lists more than 20 visitor-friendly wineries that use hardy grapes as well as fruit. **Cellardoor Vineyard** (mainewine.com) in Lincoln offers wine tastings in their state-of-the-art restored 18th-century barn at their vineyard in Lincoln, at "The Villa," Rt. 1 in Rockport and at its glamorous tasting room in Thompson's Point in Portland. **Breakwater Vineyards** (breakwatervineyards.com) in Owls Head has planted some 3,000 vines; its tasting room commands a glorious view of Penobscot Bay. In this area also check out **Oyster River Winegrowers** (oysterriverwinegrowers.com) in Thomaston; in Union, **Sweetgrass Farm Winery and Distillery** (sweetgrasswinery .com) uses fruit to craft gins and rum as well as fruit brandies and wine, and **Savage Oakes** (savageoakes.com) produces apple and grape wines. **Blacksmiths Winery** (blacksmithwin ery.com) on Rt. 302 in South Casco produces both prizewinning grape and fruit wines. The Wine Trail brochure includes a "Passport" that can be stamped at each winery, good for prizes.

Glidden Point Oysters

DAMARISCOTTA RIVER AREA OYSTERS ARE UNUSUALLY SWEET AND SALTY

Museums

Eight of the state's museums have formed a partnership and created the **Maine Art Museum Trail** (maineartmuseums .org). **The Portland Museum of Art** (port landmuseum.org) is known for its strong collection of works by impressionist and post-impressionist masters as well as Winslow Homer, whose recently restored studio in Prout's Neck is open (by reservation through the museum) for tours. **The Farnsworth Art Museum**, with its **Center for the Wyeth Family in Maine** in Rockland (farnsworthmuseum .org), has a stellar collection of Maine art, as well as frequent special exhibits and the **Center for Maine Contemporary Art** (cmcanow .org) mounts changing exhibits. The seasonal **Ogunquit Museum of American Art** (ogun quitmuseum.org) is worth checking out; the **Colby College Museum of Art** (colby.edu/ museum) in Waterville has the largest exhibit area of any Maine museum, and exceptional quality as well (it's just off the Maine Turnpike on the way to Acadia via Bangor). The **Bowdoin College Museum of Art** (bowdoin .edu/artmuseum) is in the Brunswick chapter. The seasonal **Monhegan Art and History Museum** is also a delight. The island has drawn major artists since the mid 1800s and striking paintings are on permanent display and in the special exhibit gallery.

MUSEUMS ABOUT THE SEA The **Maine Maritime Museum** (mainemaritimemuseum .org) in Bath stands in a class by itself and should not be missed. The **Penobscot Marine Museum** (penobscotmarinemuseum.org) in Searsport is smaller but still substantial, focusing on the merchant captains and their experiences in far corners of the world, featuring yearlong special exhibits. The **Marine Resources Aquarium** in Boothbay Harbor displays regional fish and sea creatures, many of them surprisingly colorful. The stars of the show are the sharks and skates in a large touch tank. The **Mount Desert Oceanarium** (theoceanarium.com) is a commercial attraction with several locations in the Bar Harbor area.

MORE MUSEUMS Easily the most under-visited museum in the state, the outstanding **Maine State Museum** (maine statemuseum.org) in Augusta has outstanding displays on the varied Maine landscape and offers historical exhibits ranging from traces of the area's earliest people to fishing, agriculture, lumbering, quarrying, and shipbuilding. It's a great place for families. We recommend it as a way-stop for coastal travelers heading to Belfast and points farther east via Rt.3.

The **Seashore Trolley Museum** (trolley museum.org) in Kennebunkport and the **Owls Head Transportation Museum** (ohtm.org) near Rockland are family finds as well. Our favorites also include the **Peary-MacMillan Arctic Museum** at Bowdoin College in Brunswick, the **Wilson Museum** (wilsonmuseum.org) in Castine and the museum at the **Colonial Pemaquid Restoration** in Pemaquid, presenting archaeological finds from the adjacent early-17th-century settlement, is unexpectedly fascinating. Also see the **Abbe Museum** under *Wabanaki*.

Nature

BEACHES Given the rising summer temperature of the Atlantic Ocean—62 degrees in Portland and 63 degrees at Bar Harbor—swimming has become more enjoyable, but it still isn't the primary reason most folks come to the Maine coast. Still, Maine beaches (for instance at York, Wells, the Kennebunks,

Portland, Popham, and Pemaquid) can be splendid walking, sunning, and kite-flying places. At **Ogunquit** and in **Reid State Park** in Georgetown, there are also warmer backwater areas in which small children can paddle. Other outstanding beaches include 7-mile-long **Old Orchard Beach** and, nearby, state-maintained **Crescent Beach** on Cape Elizabeth, **Scarborough Beach** in Scarborough, **Ferry Beach** in Saco, and **Sand Beach** in Acadia National Park. The state-maintained freshwater beaches are on Lakes **Damariscotta, St. George, Sebec, Rangeley, Sebago,** and **Moosehead**; also on **Pleasant Pond** in Richmond. All state beaches include changing facilities, restrooms, and showers; many have snack bars. The town of **Bridgton** has several fine little lakeside beaches, while **Lake George Regional Park** (between Skowhegan and Canaan) offers sandy beaches and facilities on two shores.

BIRDING Visit mainebirdingtrail.com to download the Maine Office of Tourism free map/guide to 80 birding locations in the state or to order the full *Maine Birding Trail* (Down East Books) guide, detailing 260 places to watch and hear birds across the state. Birding festivals begin in May with **Wings, Waves and Woods** in Deer Isle and Stonington and the **Down East Spring Birding Festival** (downeastbirdfest.org) in Cobscook Bay. The **Acadia Birding Festival** on Mount Desert Island and **Aroostook State Park Birding Festival**, between Houlton and Presque Isle, are both held in June. **Maine Audubon** (207-781-2330; maineaudubon.org), based at **Gilsland Farm Audubon Center** in Falmouth, maintains a number of birding sites and sponsors nature programs and field trips year-round, including naturalist-led van tours and boat cruises to see birds and other wildlife statewide. Adirondack-style lodges alongside Sunset Pond at 1,600-acre **Borestone Mountain Audubon Sanctuary** are available for group rental. **Laudholm Farm** in Wells, **Biddeford Pool**, **Scarborough Marsh, Merrymeeting Bay**, and **Mount Desert** are also popular birding sites. **Monhegan** is the island to visit in May and September. The **Moosehorn National Wildlife Refuge** (207-454-3521) in Washington County represents the northeastern terminus of the East Coast chain of wildlife refuges and is particularly rich in bird life.

Atlantic puffins are Maine's most popular bird to watch and they are smaller than you might expect. They lay just one egg a year and were almost extinct at the turn of the 20th century, when the only surviving birds nested on either Matinicus Rock or Machias Seal Island. Since 1973 Audubon has helped reintroduce nesting on Eastern Egg Rock in Muscongus Bay, 6 miles off Pemaquid Point, and since 1984 there has been a similar puffin-restoration project on Seal Island in outer Penobscot Bay, 6 miles from Matinicus Rock. The time for viewing puffins is May through mid-August. The largest colony and the only place you are allowed to view the birds on land is **Machias Seal Island**, where visitors are permitted in limited numbers and reservations must be made far in advance with Captain **Andrew Patterson** (boldcoast.com) in Cutler. With the help of binoculars (a must), you can also view the birds from the water via tours with **Cap'n Fish** (mainepuffin.com) from Boothbay Harbor, **Hardy Boat Cruises** (hardy boat.com) from New Harbor, and the **Monhegan Boat Line** (monheganboat.com) from Port Clyde. The **Hog Island Audubon Camp** (main eaudubon.org) also offers guided boat cruises to Eastern Egg Rock. For those who can't make time to get out on the water, the **Project Puffin Visitor Center** (projectpuffin.org) in Rockland uses live-streaming mini cams and audio to provide a virtual visit with nesting puffins on Seal Island.

ISLANDS Most of Maine's 3,250 offshore islands are uninhabited. We describe those that offer ferry access—**Chebeague** and **Peaks Islands** in Casco Bay; **Monhegan**, off the Midcoast, **Vinalhaven**, **North Haven**, and **Islesboro** in Penobscot Bay and in the Downeast section **Isle au Haut** off Stonington, **Swans Island** off Mount Desert Island, **Campobello** in New Brunswick (across the bridge from Lubec), and **Grand Manan** (also in Canada). In Casco Bay the ferry also serves **Cliff Island** (summer rentals are available); **Eagle Island**, former home of Admiral Peary, is served by daily excursion boats from Harpswell and South Freeport.

Boaters of all kinds are invited to explore hundreds of island destinations—both public and privately owned—on which low-impact visitors are welcome; contact the **Maine Island Trail Association** (207-596-6456; mita

.org). MITA charges $45 ($65 per family) for membership, which brings with it a detailed annually updated guidebook and the right to land on these islands. **The Island Institute** (207-594-9209; islandinstitute.org) serves as an umbrella organization for the island communities; with the $50 membership come its publications: *Island Journal* and *Working Waterfront*.

COASTAL LAKES State parks on lakes include **Damariscotta Lake State Park** (swimming, picnicking; Rt. 32, Jefferson), Lake St. **George State Park** (swimming, picnicking, fishing; Rt. 3 in Liberty, a great stop along Rt. 3 on the way to Belfast), and **Swan Lake State Park** with swimming and picnicking north of Belfast in Swanville. Every natural body of water of more than 10 acres is theoretically available to the public for "fishing and fowling." Access is, however, limited by the property owners. **Powerboat owners** should check registration rules at www.maine.gov/ifw, also the source for obtaining a milfoil sticker as required by law of all motorized boats using Maine rivers, lakes, ponds, and streams.

MOOSE The moose, Maine's state animal, has made a comeback from near extinction in the 1930s, but thanks to a deadly Winter Tick, numbers are substantially smaller than the 76,000 recorded just a few years ago. Moose are the largest animal found in the wilds of New England. They grow to be 10 feet tall and average 1,000 pounds. The largest member of the deer family, they have a large, protruding upper lip and a distinctive "bell" or "dewlap" dangling from their muzzle or throat.

"Bull" (male) moose have long been prized for their antlers, which grow to a span of up to 6 feet. They are shed in January and grow again. Female moose ("cows") do not grow antlers, and their heads are lighter in color than the bull's. All moose, however, are darker in spring than summer, grayer in winter.

Front hooves are longer than the rear, as are the legs, the better to cope with deep snow and water. In summer they favor wetlands and can usually be found near ponds or watery bogs. They also like salt and so tend to create and frequent "wallows," wet areas handy to road salt (the attraction of paved roads).

Moose are vegetarians, daily consuming more than 50 pounds of leaves, grass, and other greenery when they can find it. In winter their diet consists largely of bark and twigs. Mating season is in mid-September until late October. Calves are born in early spring and weigh in at 30 pounds. They grow quickly but keep close to their mothers for an entire year. At best, moose live 12 years.

Your chances of spotting one are greatest in early morning or at dusk on a wooded pond or lake. If you are driving through moose country at night, go slowly, because moose typically freeze rather than retreat from oncoming headlights. The common road sign and bumper sticker reading BRAKE FOR MOOSE means just that. Be extremely wary at dusk when vision is difficult and moose are active.

PARKS AND NATURE PRESERVES Within each chapter, we describe these under *Green Space* or *To Do—Hiking*. The one not to miss is **Acadia National Park** (207-288-3338; nps .gov/acad), which occupies more than 40,000 acres offering hiking, old touring, swimming, horseback riding, canoeing, and a variety of guided nature tours and programs, as well as a scenic 27-mile driving tour. The Park also includes camping, drives, hiking and biking trails on the Schoodic Peninsula and hiking trails, also primitive camping on the island of Isle au Haut.

SCENIC HIGHWAYS AND BYWAYS Books have been written about Maine's most scenic roads. Those officially recognized as **National Scenic Byways** include the 29 miles of Rt. 1 from Sullivan to Schoodic. See exploremaine .org for ten more routes designated as **Maine Scenic Byways**. They include the 125-mile **Bold Coast Trail** between Acadia and Lubec and the 12.5 **Blackwoods Byway** (Rt.182) between Cherryfield and Franklin, a shortcut between Downeast coastal destinations with access to lakes, woods, and mountain trails.

Outdoor Activities

ATVS **Alliance Trail Vehicles of Maine** (atv maine.org) offers information about the state's all-terrain vehicle clubs and riding opportunities. Registration information and more can be found at the Department of Inland Fisheries & Wildlife website, maine .gov/ifw/atv. The 85-mile **Sunrise Trail** (sun risetrail.org) runs from Washington Juntion, east of Ellsworth, to Calais, with many access points along the way.

AMUSEMENT PARKS **Funtown/Splash-town USA** in Saco is Maine's biggest, with rides, waterslides, and pools. **Aquaboggan** (pools and slides) is also on Rt. 1 in Saco. **Palace Playland** in Old Orchard Beach is a classic, with a carousel, Ferris wheel, rides, and a 60-foot waterslide. **York's Wild Kingdom** at York Beach includes a zoo as well as an old-fashioned amusement area geared to younger children. **Seacoast Fun Park** in Windham and **Wild Acadia Fun Park** in Trenton have a waterslide or tubing slide, mini golf, and rock climbing wall. Also see *Ziplines*.

BICYCLING The excellent Maine DOT site, exploremaine.org/bike, lists tours ranging from 20 to 100 miles. With the Office of Tourism, Maine DOT has published an *Explore Maine by Bike* guide to 33 loop tours, downloadable from its site. The **Bicycle Coalition of Maine** (bikemaine.org) serves as a conduit for information about both off- and on-road bicycling throughout the state and maintains a calendar of bicycling events, including an annual **BikeMaine**. Guided multiday tours are offered by **Summer Feet Cycling** (summerfeet .net) and by **Discovery Bicycle Tours** (discov erybicycletours.com); a variety of tours are offered by **L.L. Bean** (llbean.com). Biking is popular on Swan's Island off Acadia and on islands in Casco Bay. Rt. 1 is heavily traveled, and should be avoided. Dedicated recreation paths are appearing, notably in Portland, South Portland, and Brunswick/Bath, along the Kennebec between Augusta and Gardiner, and farther north between Solon and Bingham. Bicycling also makes sense in heavily touristed resort areas in which a car can be a nuisance; rentals are available in most coastal destinations. For good biking maps of various regions, **Map Adventures** (mapadventures .com) makes very readable small maps of bike routes, stocked at most bike shops and bookstores. **Mountain biking** is particularly popular on the carriage roads in **Acadia National Park**, along the 85-mile **Sunrise Trail** (sunrise trail.org) in Hancock and Washington

Counties (also popular with ATVs), at **Sunday River Resort**, and at **Sugarloaf** and the neighboring **Maine Huts and Trails** system (mainehuts.org).

BOAT EXCURSIONS You won't know what Maine is about until you stand off at sea to appreciate the beauty of the cliffs and island-dotted bays. For the greatest concentrations of boat excursions, see "Boothbay Harbor Region," "Rockland/Thomaston Area," and "Bar Harbor and Ellsworth." Also see *Coastal Cruises*; *Ferries, in Maine* and *to Canada*; *Sailing*; and *Windjammers*.

CAMPING For camping within **Acadia National Park**, see "Acadia National Park." Note that larger RVs can now be accommodated at the Schoodic Penninsula section of the Park. For private campgrounds, the booklet *Maine Camping Guide*, published by the Maine Campground Owners Association (207-782-5874; campmaine.com), lists most privately operated camping and tenting areas. Reservations are advised for the state's 13 parks that offer camping (campwithme.com; also see *Parks, State*). We have attempted to describe the state parks with camping in detail wherever they appear in this book (see Popham Beach and Reed State Parks in the Bath Region, Damariscotta Lake, Camden, Hills Cobscook Bay). Note that state campsites can accommodate average-sized campers and trailers, but only Sebago and Camden Hills offer (up to 40-foot) trailer electric and water hookups. **Warren Island** (just off Islesboro) and **Swan Island** (just off Richmond) offer organized camping, and primitive camping is permitted on a number of islands through the **Maine Island Trail Association** (MITA; see *Islands*). Within this book, we occasionally describe outstanding private campgrounds like **Hermit Island** in Phippsburg.

CAMPS AND LEARNING PROGRAMS FOR ADULTS **Outward Bound** (1-866-476-7651; outwardboundwilderness.org) offers a variety of adult-geared outdoor adventures in Maine as well as throughout the country. **L.L. Bean** (llbean.com) offers introductions to a variety of sports with programs lasting from a couple of hours to multiday family adventures and **Outdoor Discovery Schools**. The **Hog Island Audubon Center** on Hog Island off Bremen offers programs sponsored by Audubon's Project Puffin (see "Damariscotta/Newcastle"). The **AMC** (see *Appalachian Mountain Club*) also offers weeklong "Family Camp" programs at several Maine venues including Echo Lake on Mount Desert (amcecholake.org). Photographers should check out the **Maine Media Workshops** (theworkshops.com) in Rockport. Also see *Boatbuilding* (**WoodenBoat** offers much more than boatbuilding). **Road Scholar**, formerly Elderhostel (roadscholar.org), offers sailing, birding, and cultural programs in Maine for everyone over age 50. Check out **Haystack Mountain School** under *Crafts* and arts workshops under *Artists, Art Programs, and Art Galleries*. Entries under *Music Schools* and *Sailing* also have summer programs. Potters should check out the **Watershed Center for Ceramic Arts** (watershedceramics.org) in Newcastle.

CAMPS FOR CHILDREN More than 200 summer camps are listed in the exceptional booklet published annually by the **Maine Summer Camp Association** (1-800-536-7712; mainecamps.org). Also check out **Maine Camp Experience** (mainecampexperience .com).

GOLF The **Golf Maine Association** website (golfme.com) offers information and links to its member courses. Also check out the **Maine Golf Trail** at visitmaine.com and the **Maine State Golf Association** (mesga.org). Within the book we list golf courses within each chapter. The major resorts catering to golfers are the **Samoset** in Rockport and **Sebasco Harbor Resort** near Bath.

FISHING Check out the **Maine Department of Inland Fisheries and Wildlife** at maine.gov/ifw/fishing for basics and mefishwildlife.com for licensing information and public boat-launch locations for freshwater fishing on Maine's lakes, ponds, rivers, and streams. **Registered Maine Guides** (maineguides.org) know where and how to fish, and offer frequent courses. One-day fishing licenses are available at general stores and from outfitters throughout the state; they come with a regulations book. The **Maine Department of Marine Resources** furnishes saltwater recreational fishing registry information, species information, and launch sites at maine.gov/dmr. The Maine Association of Charterboat Captains (mainechartercaptains.org) is another great resource for saltwater fishing, and visitmaine.com has extensive fishing info.

HIKING Our personal favorite hikes are along the cliffs on the island of Monhegan and at West Quoddy Light. While we list hikes within most chapters, we strongly suggest acquiring detailed trail guides. In addition to the AMC map/guide to trails on Mount Desert, we recommend investing in 50 Hikes in Coastal and Inland Maine by John Gibson from The Countryman Press, which offers clear, inviting treks up hills of every size throughout the state. The Maine Atlas and Gazetteer (DeLorme) also outlines a number of rewarding hikes. While hiking is generally associated with inland Maine and Acadia, in recent years tens of thousands of acres of dramatic shore property have been preserved, much of this traversed by coastal trails, which we have attempted to list chapter by chapter. The car-free island of Monhegan is beloved by hikers for its many dramatic trails. Maine Trailfinder (mainetrailfinder.com) is an amazing resource for hikers.

KAYAKING Sea kayaking outfitters that offer guided half-day and full-day trips, also overnight and multiday expeditions with camping on Maine islands, are too numerous to be listed here but are described within each relevant chapter. The leading outfitters are Maine Island Kayak Company (maineislandkayak.com) on Peaks Island off Portland; Maine Sport Outfitters (mainesport.com) in Rockport; H2outfitters (h2outfitters.com), based on Orrs Island, which offers an extensive array of trips both locally and around the world; Old Quarry Ocean Adventures, Inc. (oldquarry.com), in Deer Isle; Tidal Transit (207-633-7140) in Boothbay Harbor; Midcoast Kayak in Damariscotta (midcoastkayak.com); and Castine Kayak Adventures (castinekayak.com). In Washington County, Sunrise Canoe & Kayak Tours (sunrisecanoeandkayak.com) offers rentals and tours in Machias Bay. L.L. Bean offers instruction in kayaking at its Outdoor Discovery Schools (llbean.com), Rt. 1, Freeport. Inquire about their Paddle Sport Weekend. Also see maineseakayakguides.com for a listing of members

of the Maine Association of Sea Kayaking Guides & Instructors. Dorcas Miller's comprehensive Kayaking the Maine Coast: A Paddler's Guide to Day Trips from Kittery to Cobscook (The Countryman Press) is an excellent resource for kayak owners and competent kayakers. Also see the Maine Island Trail under Islands. It's a great camping resource for sea kayakers.

Sailing

WINDJAMMERS In 1936 artist Frank Swift outfitted a few former fishing and cargo schooners to carry passengers around the islands of Penobscot Bay. At the time these old vessels were moored in every harbor and cove, casualties of progress. Swift's fleet grew to include more than a dozen vessels. Competitors also prospered throughout the 1950s, but the entire windjammer fleet appeared doomed by rigorous Coast Guard licensing requirements in the 1960s. The 1970s and 1980s saw the rise of a new breed of windjammer captain. Many of those now sailing built or restored the vessel he or she commands, or acquired it from the captain who did. Members of the current, nine-member Maine Windjammer Association range from the Stephen Taber and the Lewis R. French, both originally launched in 1871, to the Heritage, launched in 1983. Passenger numbers range from the 16 aboard Shooner Ladona—a vintage 1922 racing yacht, recently rebuilt by a second-generation Windjammer owner/captain—to the three-masted 40-passenger Victory Chimes. Each vessel has its loyal following and each is distinctive; prospective passengers should examine their profiles and sailing schedules on the excellent website, sailmainecoast.com. In addition to Windjammer Association members, a Camden-based, Maine Windjammer Cruises (maineswindjammercruises.com), a fleet of three vintage vessels, offer multi-day cruises and Schooner Mary Day sails from Rockport. While many passengers these days opt for three and four-day cruises, we can attest to the beauty of six days on the water aboard Schooner American Eagle.

DAY SAILS Savor the beauty of sailing Maine waters for just an hour or two or an entire day aboard a variety of yachts and historic vessels. In their respective chapters, we describe these cruises available from Kennebunkport, Portland, Harpswell, Boothbay, Rockland, Belfast, Castine, and Bar Harbor.

YACHT RENTALS AND SAILING PROGRAMS There are a limited number of places that will rent small sailing craft, fewer that will offer lessons to adults and children alike. **Linekin Bay Resort** (linekinbayresort .com) in Boothbay Harbor is billed as the only surviving full-service sailing resort on the East Coast. Qualified sailors can rent Rhodes 19-foot sailboats, and sailing lessons are offered for those of all abilities. The **Mansell Boat Rental Company** (mansellboatrentals .com), Southwest Harbor, rents sailboats by the day or longer. **Buck's Harbor Marine** (207-326-8839), South Brooksville, rents sail- and motorboats. Inquire about sailing lessons. Learn-to-sail programs are offered by **WoodenBoat School** (woodenboatschool.com) in Brooklin, the **Camden Yacht Club** (camden yachtclub.org), which offers a junior sailing program to nonmembers, and **Bay Island Sailing School** (sailme.com) based in Rockland. **Old Quarry Ocean Adventures** (oldquarry .com) in Deer Isle rents a variety of sailboats and offers lessons. Other rentals and daysails are listed throughout the book. Also see *Windjammers*.

WHALE-WATCHING Each spring humpback, finback, and minke whales migrate to New England waters, where they remain until fall, cavorting, it sometimes seems, for the pleasure of excursion boats. One prime gathering spot is **Jefferies Ledge**, about 20 miles off Kennebunkport, and another is the **Bay of Fundy**. For listings of whale-watch cruises, see "The Kennebunks," "Portland Area," "Bar Harbor," and "Way Downeast." Lighthouses are also prime viewing spots. Whales are sighted more often than not on the ferry rides across Passamaquoddy Bay.

ZIPLINES **Monkey Trunks** in Saco, **Monkey C Monkey Do** in Wiscasset, and **Take Flight Adventures** in Kittery add maneuvering with ropes to the seasonal mix of what coastal visitors can do.

Sights to See

FORTS Maine's 20 forts are actually a fascinating lot, monuments to the state's largely forgotten history. In Kittery Point, the octagonal, 1840s **Fort McClary** tells of mid-17th century scuffles over taxes between New Hampshire and Massachusetts, and offers great island and harbor views. **Fort Knox** (see "Bucksport") is the state's grandest and offers a lively seasonal schedule of events. **Fort William Henry** at Pemaquid (see "Damariscotta/ Newcastle") is genuinely fascinating, while **Fort Edgecomb** off Rt. 1 in Edgecomb, just east of Wiscasset, is an easy hit. Also check out the earthen works that are **Fort George** in Castine, granite **Fort Popham** near Bath, **Fort Pownall** at Stockton Springs, and **Fort O'Brien**, a Revolutionary War–era earthen works in Machiasport.

LIGHTHOUSES More than 800 lighthouses still stand in the US and Michigan counts 120 to Maine's 66, including the Machias Seal Island Light, maintained by the Canadian Coast Guard. But it's Maine that they symbolize. No longer simply photogenic icons, more than a dozen lighthouse stations now invite visitors to clamber up into their tower and/or to explore their Keeper's Houses-turned-museums, welcome centers, or lodging. As lighthouses have become automated, many have been adopted by "friends." The **American Lighthouse Foundation** (light

Christina Tree

FORT McCLARY, KITTERY POINT

GOOSE ROCKS LIGHT OFF NORTH HAVEN CAN BE RENTED FOR DAY-LONG AND OVERNIGHT STAYS

housefoundation.org) serves as an umbrella organization for groups supporting nine Maine lights and their site details open hours for those at the **Owls Head**, **Rockland Breakwater**, **Pemaquid Point**, **Wood Island** (off Biddeford Pool), and **Little River Lighthouse** off Cutler (lodging offered). At **Burnt Island Light Station** in Boothbay Harbor, guides dress as lighthouse keepers from the 1950s and show visitors how life was lived on an isolated island. Also in the Boothbay area, **Cuckolds Lighthouse** is now a luxurious bed & breakfast. See the Rockland chapter for details about these and **Goose Rocks Lighthouse** (beaconpreservation.org), a freestanding "spark-plug-style" light in the Fox Islands Thorofare. Nearby, off Sprucehead, the **Whitehead Light Station** (whiteheadlightstation .org) welcomes visitors with seven guestrooms, summer workshops, and September rentals. Another popular island light is the vintage-1795 **Seguin Island Light Station** (seguinisland.org). Sited 2.5 miles off the mouth of Kennebec River, it's a 186-foot granite lighthouse on a 64-acre island. A far easier shot is **The Neddick (Nubble) Light**, just off Sohier Park in York, within camera range. True lighthouse buffs also make the pilgrimage to **Burnt Harbor Light** on Swan's Island and to **Matinicus Rock**, the setting for several

children's books. **The Keeper's House** on Isle au Haut is another B&B. **Head of Harbor Lighthouse** on the island of Campobello, accessible at low tide, is the ultimate adventure; it is also a prime whale-watching post. Descriptions of all these lights are detailed in their respective chapters. **Fort Point Light** at Stockton Springs and **Bass Harbor Head Light** at Bass Harbor are easily accessible by land. **Portland Head Light** on Cape Elizabeth, completed in 1790, automated in 1990, is now a delightful museum featuring the history of lighthouses. Other lights that feature museums are the **Marshall Point Light** at Port Clyde, **Pemaquid Point** (the lighthouse itself is now open seasonally), **Monhegan Light** on Monhegan Island, **Grindle Point** on Islesboro, and **West Quoddy Head Light** in Lubec, now part of a state park with a stunning shore path. Rockland's Gateway Visitor Center is home to the **Maine Lighthouse Museum** (mainelighthousemuseum.com).

LOBSTER-BOAT RACES The season's races (lobsterboatracing.com) represent one of the best spectator events along the Maine coast. Races begin mid-June in Boothbay Harbor, and the "World's Fastest Lobster Boat Races" are always held on Moosabec Reach between Jonesport and Beals Island on July 4. Other

IN CALAIS, THE MAINE TOURIST INFORMATION CENTER IS IN THE WABANAKI CULTURE CENTER, WITH REGIONAL AND PASSAMAQUODDY TRIBAL EXHIBITS

venues are Rockland, Stonington, Harpswell, Friendship, Winter Harbor, and Pemaquid. Participants accumulate points as they go along, and there's an awards ceremony and pig roast in late September.

Shopping

ANTIQUES A member directory listing hundreds of dealers is produced by the **Maine Antiques Dealers' Association**. The association's active website lists members as well as auctions at maineantiques.org. The 60-plus-page *Maine Antique Dealer Directory* can be ordered online.

ANTIQUARIAN BOOKS Maine is well known among book buffs as a browsing mecca. **Maine Antiquarian Booksellers** posts a directory of 50 members at mainebooksellers.org.

BOOKSTORES Full-service, independent bookstores saw a welcome increase in Portland in 2016. These are the stores that stand ready to find you the kind of book you are looking for, even if you don't know what it is. Hats off to Bar Harbor–based **Sherman's Books and Stationery**, Maine's own distinctive chain with stores in Portland, Camden, Boothbay Harbor, Damariscotta, and Freeport, where gifts add to the bottom line, supporting an extensive book selection in every shop. In Portland, find the excellent **Longfellow Books**,

along with a branch of Sherman's, and **Print**, at the bottom of Munjoy Hill, with its young owners' wonderful enthusiasm for a diverse selection of books. In Brunswick the peerless **Gulf of Maine Books**' co-owner, poet Gary Lawless, is also founder of **Blackberry Press**, which has reissued many out-of-print Maine classics. In Bath there's **Mustard Seed Bookstore** which also serves tea, and in Damariscotta **Sherman's Maine Coast Book Shop** with its cyber café. **Left Bank Books** in Belfast provides treats for your dog and gorgeous, antique and witty cards, along with a fine book selection. **Book Stacks** in Bucksport offers WiFi and coffee (also sells wine), while venerable, two-story **Blue Hill Books** draws patrons throughout East Penobscot Bay to its white-clapboard house up a side street. At the **Calais Bookshop**, Carole Heinlein presides over an oasis of print, antiquarian, as well as new books, an impressive number of which she has read. Finally, we have to mention **Dockside Books** in Stonington. It may be Maine's smallest bookstore, but it has the best view.

FACTORY OUTLETS We note individual outlet stores in their respective chapters throughout; we also describe the state's two major outlet clusters: in **Freeport** (freeportusa.com), anchored by **L.L. Bean**, and **Kittery** (thekitteryoutlets.com). **New Balance** also makes sneakers in Maine and maintains outlets in Norway and Skowhegan.

L.L. BEAN (llbean.com) was founded in 1912 by Leon Leonwood Bean. He began by selling a single product, the Maine Hunting Shoe. Ninety out of the first 100 boots sold that year fell apart but Bean refunded the purchasers' money, establishing a company tradition of guaranteed customer satisfaction still honored in L.L. Bean stores throughout the United States, Japan, and China. This Maine icon's 200,000-square-foot flagship store in Freeport is open 24 hours a day, 365 days a year. Outdoor clothing and equipment remain the company's mainstay, and they can now also be found in the Hunting and Fishing Store, the Bike, Boat & Ski Store, and the Home Store. **Outdoor Discovery Schools** and **Walk-On Adventures**, ranging from kayaking to fly-fishing get customers into action year-round. See the Freeport chapter for details.

RENYS Billed as "A Maine Adventure," and as "a part of the state's culture since 1949," Renys (renys.com) is a family-owned chain of 14 discount stores that, like hermit crabs, occupy spaces vacated by previous owners. The **Farmington** Renys fills a former music hall, the **Madison** space was an opera house, and in **Damariscotta**, Renys Underground was a bowling alley. Several Renys fill former supermarkets, and in Bath, Gardiner, Dexter, Damariscotta, and Portland the shops effectively fill the void left by small-town clothing and department stores. Listing what Renys stocks is harder than saying what it doesn't. There are linens and shoes, name-brand clothing and toys, electronics, clamming and camping gear, stationery, Maine-made products, and always surprises. Renys has recently become less about odd lots (that niche is now filled by **Marden's**, Maine's other discount chain), and more about quality, service, and good value.

Further Reading

Anyone who seriously sets out to explore Maine should read the following mix of Maine classics and guidebooks: *The Maine Woods* by **Henry David Thoreau**, first published posthumously in 1864, remains very readable and gives an excellent description of Maine's mountains. For those inspired to trace Thoreau's route, there's *The Wildest Country: Exploring Thoreau's Maine* by **Parker Huber** (AMC Books), complete with maps and color photographs of local flora and fauna. Our favorite relatively recent Maine author is **Ruth Moore**, who writes about Maine islands in *The Weir, Spoonhandle,* and *Speak to the Wind* (originally published in the 1940s and reissued by Blackberry Books, Nobleboro). The 1940s classic *We Took to the Woods* by **Louise Dickinson Rich** is now published by Down East Books in Camden. **Sarah Orne Jewett**'s classic *The Country of the Pointed Firs and Other Stories* (W. W. Norton), first published in 1896, is set on the coast around Tenants Harbor and is still an excellent read. For an overview of Maine-related poetry and prose we highly recommend *The Maine Reader: The Down East Experience from 1614 to the Present* by **David R. Godine**.

Maine has been home to the authors of many of our most beloved children's classics. **Robert McCloskey**, author of *Blueberries for Sal, Time of Wonder,* and *One Morning in Maine*, resided on an island off the Blue Hill Peninsula, which was also the summer home to **E. B. White**, known for wonderful essay collections and his ever-popular children's novels *Charlotte's Web* and *Stuart Little.* Damariscotta-based **Barbara Cooney** wrote and illustrated some 200 books, among them *Miss Rumphius, Island Boy,* and *Hattie and the Wild Waves.*

Recent classics set in Maine include **Carolyn Chute**'s *The Beans of Egypt, Maine* (1985), *Letourneau's Used Auto Parts* (1988), *Merry Men* (1994), and *The School of Heart's Content Road* (2008); and **Cathie Pelletier**'s *The Funeral Makers* (1987) and *The Weight of Winter* (1991). *Maine Speaks,* an anthology of Maine literature published by the **Maine Writers and Publishers Alliance** (mainewriters.org), contains all the obvious poems and essays and many pleasant surprises. **Linda Greenlaw**'s *The Lobster Chronicles* (2002) describes the island of Isle au Haut. It's a good read with insights into life on all Maine's surviving island communities. *The Lobster Coast* by **Colin Woodward** is a must read for anyone interested in "Rebels, Rusticators, and the Struggle for a Forgotten Frontier" (Penguin, 2004). *The Poacher's Son* and five more locally set mysteries by former *Down East* editor **Paul Doiron** (Macmillan) are all worth a read. Maine titles for all ages can be found at islandportpress.com.

Guides to exploring Maine include the indispensable *Maine Atlas and Gazetteer* (DeLorme) and, from Down East Books, *Islands in Time: A Natural and Cultural History of the Islands of the Gulf of Maine* by **Philip W. Conkling**. From AMC Books comes the serious hiker's *AMC Maine Mountain Guide*, for a selection of hiking, paddling, sea kayaking. Also check out *50 Hikes in the Maine Mountains* by **Cloe Chunn** and *50 Hikes in Coastal and Inland Maine* by **John Gibson** (both The Countryman Press). For a short, entertaining, as well as reliable history of the Maine coast, we recommend *The Lobster Coast: Rebels, Rusticators, and the Struggle for a Forgotten Frontier* by **Colin Woodward** (Penguin, 2004).

About This Book

Over the past 36 years the Maine Explorer's Guide, which appeared in its 18th edition in 2016, has introduced hundreds of thousands of people to coastal as well as inland Maine. This is the first coastal version of our big book, using its detailed format. Again for this guide we have prowled the coast and islands, visiting lodging places and restaurants as well as shops and checking out ever expanding coastal walks and things to do and sights to see, also double checking phone numbers and websites. Focusing on the coast in the book, we have divided the state's "Midcoast" region into "Midcoast" and "Penobscot Bay," reflecting more precisely the lay of the land (and water). This is also true for the state's "Acadia Area" region. We have divided it into the "Acadia Area" region and "Way Downeast" because few parts of this country differ as sharply from each other as the Acadia National Park area and the far less visited and geographically distinct "Way Downeast" region that includes Washington County and Passamaquoddy Bay. We include the New Brunswick side of the Bay because both St. Andrews and Grand Manan Island are well worth exploring.

SOUTHERN COAST

KITTERY, SOUTH BERWICK,
AND THE YORKS

OGUNQUIT AND WELLS

THE KENNEBUNKS

OLD ORCHARD BEACH, SACO,
AND BIDDEFORD

Southern Coast

Square Pond

Shapleigh

109

Acton

Mousam Lake

Emery Mills

Northeast Pond

Springvale

Sanford

East Lebanon

West Lebanon

Salmon Falls R.

South Lebanon

Rochester

16

125

Dover

NEW HAMPSHIRE

Durham

108

155

4

Great Bay

33

Portsmouth

95

Hollis Center

Waterboro Center

Salmon Falls

4

35

East Waterboro

Waterboro

202

5

Goodwins Mills

5

Saco R.

112

Lyman

111

Days Mills

Alfred

4

35

99

Exit 25

Kennebunk

109

9A

9B

9

Wells

Exit 19

Wells Beach

Moody

Ogunquit

Cape Neddick

York Beach

York Village

Exit 7

North Eliot

236

91

MAINE TURNPIKE

95

Mt. Agamenticus

S. Berwick

North Berwick

4

Berwick

9

108

16

103

101

Exit 3

Kittery

Kittery Point

RACHEL CARSON NAT'L WILDLIFE REFUGE

95

West Scarborough

1

114

9

Scarborough

Old Orchard Beach

Prout's Neck

RACHEL CARSON NAT'L WILDLIFE REFUGE

Biddeford

Exit 32

Saco

Exit 36

Biddeford Pool

208

9

Goose Rocks Beach

RACHEL CARSON NAT'L WILDLIFE REFUGE

Arundel

Kennebunkport

RACHEL CARSON NAT'L WILDLIFE REFUGE

ATLANTIC OCEAN

0   5   10
Miles

N

© The Countryman Press

SOUTHERN COAST

The smell of pine needles and salt air, the taste of lobster and saltwater taffy, the shock of cold green waves, and, most of all, the promise of endless beach—this is the Maine that draws upwards of half the state's visitors, those who never get beyond its Southern Coast. The southern Maine coast makes up just 35 of the state's 4,500 coastal miles but contains 90 percent of its sand.

The early histories of these towns differ sharply, but all have been shaped since the Civil War by the summer tide of tourists. York Village and Kittery are recognized as the oldest communities in Maine; Wells dates to the 1640s; and Kennebunkport was a shipbuilding center by the 1790s. All were transformed in the second half of the 19th century, an era when most Americans—not just the rich—began to take summer vacations, each in his or her own way.

Maine's Southern Coast was one of the country's first beach resort areas, and it catered then—as it does today—to the full spectrum of vacationers, from blue-collar workers to millionaires. Before the Civil War, Old Orchard Beach rivaled Newport, Rhode Island, as the place to be seen; when the Grand Trunk Railroad to Montreal opened in 1854, it became the first American resort to attract a sizable number of Canadians.

The ebb and flow of tourist tides wash most dramatically over this stretch of Maine, cresting on summer weekends with an influx of day trippers. Most of the big old summer hotels vanished by the 1950s, the era of the motor inns that now occupy their sites. Along Rt. 1 just a few of the 1930s-era motor courts survive, sandwiched between elaborate condo-style complexes with indoor pools and elevators. Inns and bed & breakfasts are once more an endangered species, thanks to web-based ways of finding short-term rentals and the demand for year-round homes and condo complexes. Luckily, the lay of the land—salt marsh, estuarine reserves, and other wetlands—largely limits development.

GUIDANCE **The Maine Beaches Association** (mainebeachesassociation.com) publishes a guide and maintains an umbrella website linking Southern Coast chambers.

The Maine Tourism Association's Kittery Information Center (207-439-1319; maine tourism.com) is open daily (except Christmas, Easter, and Thanksgiving), 8–6 in summer months (until 8 Fri.–Sat.), otherwise 9–5:30 (bathrooms open 24 hours daily). Maine's gatehouse in a real sense is on I-95 northbound in Kittery, with exhibits and rack cards from all Maine regions. The staffed information desk is good for local as well as statewide advice on lodging, dining, and attractions. There are also picnic tables under the pines.

KITTERY, SOUTH BERWICK, AND THE YORKS

The moment you cross the Piscataqua River, you know you are in Maine.

Kittery and York both have their share of deep coves and rocky ocean paths, and both towns claim to be Maine's oldest community. Technically Kittery wins, but York looks older... depending, of course, on which Kittery and which York you are talking about.

Kittery Point (Rt. 103), an 18th-century settlement overlooking Portsmouth Harbor, boasts Maine's oldest church and some of the state's finest early mansions. The village of Kittery itself, however, has been shattered by so many highways and rotaries that it initially seems to exist only as a gateway, on the one hand for workers at the Portsmouth Naval Shipyard and on the other for patrons of the outlet malls strung along Rt. 1. (It's worth finding **Kittery Foreside**, the southernmost corner of town; some of the area's most interesting restaurants cluster here around **Wallingford Square**.)

In the late 19th century artists and literati gathered at Kittery Point. Novelist and *Atlantic Monthly* editor William Dean Howells, who summered here, became interested in preserving the area's colonial–era buildings. Novelist Sarah Orne Jewett, a contributor to *The Atlantic*, spearheaded restoration of the magnificent 18th-century Hamilton House in her hometown, nearby South Berwick. Her friend Sam Clemens (otherwise known as Mark Twain), who summered in York, was involved in an effort, led by local preservationist Elizabeth Perkins, to buy up that town's splendid old school, church, burial ground, and abundance of 1740s homes.

In 1896 Howells suggested turning York Village's "old gaol" into a museum. At the time you could count the country's historic house museums on your fingers. The Old Gaol today is one of eight buildings belonging to the **Old York Historical Society**. Stop by the visitors center at the Remick Barn to learn about the town's multilayered history, including its origin as a Native American settlement called Agamenticus, one of many wiped out by a plague in 1616. It was settled by English colonists, but not until the mid-18th century did the present colonial village become a way-stop between Portsmouth and points east.

York is divided into so many distinct villages that Clemens once observed, "It is difficult to throw a brick . . . in any one direction without danger of disabling a postmaster." The town includes **York Village**, **York Harbor**, **York Beach**, and **Cape Neddick**—such different communities that they are sometimes referred to as "the Yorks."

York Harbor has been a low-key, high-priced retreat since the 1870s. The Stage Neck Inn is built on the site of the 19th-century, 300-room Marshall House, and several grand old summer "cottages" are part of the York Harbor Inn. York Harbor's mile-or-so-long shore path, first traced by fishermen, has been smoothed and embellished with the **Wiggly Bridge**, a graceful pedestrian suspension bridge across the river and through Steedman Woods.

Landscaping and public spaces were among the consuming interests of the 19th-century summer residents, who around the turn of the century also became interested in zoning. In *Trending into Maine* (1935) Kenneth Roberts noted York Harbor's "determination to be free of billboards, tourist camps, dance halls and other cheapening manifestations of the herd instinct and Vacationland civilization."

A York Harbor corporation was formed to impose its own taxes and keep out unwanted development. The corporation fiercely fought against the Libby Camps, a tent-and-trailer

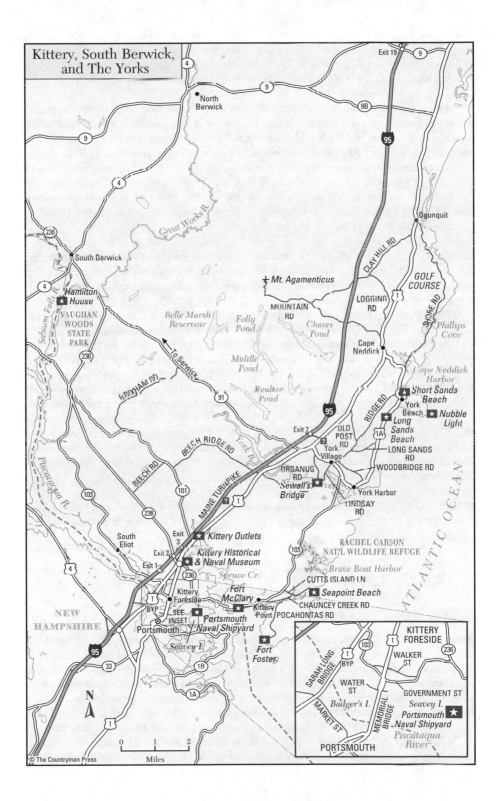

Kittery, South Berwick, and The Yorks

campground on the eastern edge of York Harbor. Roberts wrote that York Harbor was in danger of being almost completely swamped by "young ladies in shorts, young men in soiled undershirts, and fat ladies in knickerbockers." Libby's Oceanside Camp still sits on Roaring Rock Point, its trailers neatly angled along the shore. Across from it is matching Camp Eaton, established in 1923.

Beyond the campgrounds stretches mile-long **Long Sands Beach**, a magnet for surfers as well as swimmers. **Cape Neddick**, a rocky point separating Long Sands and Short Sands beaches, offers views of **"the Nubble,"** one of Maine's most photogenic lighthouses, from **Sohier Park** at its tip. At the far end of Short Sands, the Victorian village of **York Beach**, with its mostly seasonal shops and restaurants, old-style Fun-O-Rama games, bowling, and York's Wild Kingdom, evokes the 1890s "trolley era" during which a half-dozen big York Beach hotels accommodated 3,000 summer visitors, and 2,000 more guests patronized local boardinghouses. Today's lodgings are a mix of motels, condos, and cottages within walking distance of the beaches.

GUIDANCE **Greater York Region Chamber of Commerce** (207-363-4422; via the Southern Maine link, 1-800-639-2442; gatewaytomaine.org), 1 Stonewall Lane, York. Open daily, year-round. From I-95 Exit 7 (northbound) drive straight across Rt. 1 to this manned, well-stocked welcome center (restrooms).

Sohier Park Welcome Center, overlooking **Nubble Light**, York Beach. Open May–Oct. Operated by Friends of Nubble Light, primarily a gift shop with restrooms.

The Maine Tourism Association Kittery Information Center is the state's biggest and busiest. See *Guidance* in **Southern Coast** introduction. Note the rear exit to Rt. 1 in Kittery.

GETTING THERE Use I-95 Exit 1 for **Kittery Foreside** (downtown) and **Kittery Point**; exit 3 for **Kittery Outlets**; exit 7 for **The Yorks** and **Ogunquit**. You really need a car to get here.

GETTING AROUND **York Trolley Company** (207-363-9600; yorktrolley.com). Late June–Labor Day, trolleys circle all day along the beaches and around the Nubble. Inquire about special narrated tours and service to the Kittery Outlet Malls. $4 one ride around the route, $2 one way, free for 5 and under.

WHEN TO COME York Beach is highly seasonal, but this area can be appealing May through December. Thanks to the sizable year-round population, most restaurants remain open year-round. The Kittery outlets draw holiday shoppers.

✳ To See

IN KITTERY

Kittery Historical & Naval Museum (207-439-3080; kitterymuseum.com), 200 Rogers Rd. Ext. (Rt. 1, just north of the Rt. 236 rotary). Open June–Columbus Day, Wed.–Sun. 10–4. $5 adult, $3 children, $10 for a family of four. Look for the 129-foot-high flagpole, each foot commemorating a member of the USS *Thresher*, a submarine lost in 1963 during sea trials. Larger than it looks from the outside, the museum's exhibits range from ship models to a reconstructed garrison house. A film dramatizes the local area history—from a 1600s fishing settlement through a gilded resort area to the evolution of the Rt. 1 outlet mall strip.

& **Fort McClary**, Rt. 103. A state park open seasonally (grounds accessible year-round). This is a spectacular spot. Set high on a point overlooking the Isle of Shoals and the entrance to Portsmouth Harbor, the fort is a hexagonal 1846 blockhouse on a granite base. Fortifications

MUST SEE

Nubble Light (nubblelight.org), York Beach. From Rt. 1A (Long Beach Ave.), take Nubble Rd. out through the Nubble (a cottage-covered peninsula) to Sohier Park at the tip of the peninsula. The 1879 Cape Neddick Lighthouse Station is set on a small island of its own—but that's all the better for taking pictures from the park, which offers parking, restrooms, and a gift shop (also see *Guidance*).

Christina Tree

NUDDLE LIGHT

here date from 1690, an effort by Sir William Pepperell (said to be the richest man in 17th century America) to protect Massachusetts's vessels from being taxed by the New Hampshire colony. Granite blocks on the grounds evidence a plan to expand it during the Civil War.

IN YORK HARBOR AND YORK BEACH

First Parish Church, York Village. A mid-18th-century meetinghouse with a fine cemetery full of old stones with death's heads and Old English spelling.

    Sayward-Wheeler House (207-384-2454; historicnewengland.org), 79 Barrell Lane, York Harbor. Open June–Oct. 15, second and fourth Sat. of the month, 11–4; tours on the hour. $5, $4 seniors, $2.50 students. This circa-1718 house was built by a prominent resident who was locally respected despite his Tory leanings. It remained in the same family for 200 years and retains its Queen Anne and Chippendale furnishings, family portraits, and china brought back as booty from the expedition against the French at Louisburg in 1745.

Christina Tree

VIEW FROM FORT MCCLARY, KITTERY

OLD YORK HISTORICAL SOCIETY

This nonprofit group maintains several historic properties in York, open Memorial Day weekend to mid-October, Tue.-Sat. 10-5, Sun. 1-5. Admission is $5 adults for one building, $12 for all; senior, child, and family rates. It's best to pay the umbrella price and spend several hours wandering through the 18th- and 19th-century buildings scattered throughout the village. Begin at the **Old York Education Center and Remick Gallery**, attached to the vintage-1754 **Jefferds Tavern**, corner of Lindsay Rd. and York St. (parking is on Lindsay Rd.). Exhibits change but are dependably outstanding; this is also a venue for special programs and hearth cooking demonstrations. If you have time to visit only one building, pick the **Old Gaol Museum** with its dank and dismal cells and stories of luckless patrons, including women. Dating in part to 1719, this was the jail for the entire province of Maine until 1760. In the vintage-1742 **Emerson-Wilcox House Museum** on York St., you'll find period rooms and changing exhibits. The **Elizabeth Perkins House Museum**, Southside Rd. (at Sewall Bridge), is our favorite building, a 1730 house by the York River. It is filled with antiques gathered on world travels and decorative arts, and imbued with the spirit of Elizabeth Perkins, a real powerhouse behind the Colonial Revival movement in southern Maine. Nearby at 140 Lindsay Rd. are the 18th-century **John Hancock Warehouse and Wharf** and **George Marshall Store**, which was built in 1869 as a chandlery for the large schooners that once docked here; it's now a contemporary art gallery. The **York Corner School House** (1745) still retains graffiti carved into paneling by the students, and **Steedman Woods**, a nature reserve, offers views of the York River and Wiggly Bridge. Old York hosts programming year-round as well as a local historical research center in the headquarters, a former bank building at 207 York St. in the middle of York Village (207-363-1756; off-season 207-363-4974; oldyork.org).

Courtesy of The Museums of Old York

EXCURSIONS

Kittery Point, Pepperrell Cove, and Gerrish Island. From Rt. 1, find your way to Rt. 103 and follow its twists and turns along the harbor until you come to the white **First Congregational Church** and a small green across from a striking, privately owned Georgian-style house. An old graveyard overlooking the harbor completes the scene. Park at the church (built in 1730, Maine's oldest), notice the parsonage (1729), and walk across the road to the old graveyard. The magnificent neighboring house was built in 1760 for the widow of **Sir William Pepperrell**, the French and Indian War hero who captured the fortress at Louisburg from the French. Knighted for his feat, Pepperrell went on to become the richest man in New England. For a splendid view of the harbor, continue along Rt. 103 to **Fort McClary**. Four large hotels once clustered in this corner of Kittery, but today it's one of the quietest spots along the Southern Coast. At the back of the parking lot across from the general store, a seemingly forgotten tomb is inscribed with a plaque commemorating **Colonel William Pepperrell**, born in Devonshire in 1646, who died in Kittery in 1734. Just beyond you can still see the foundations of one of the former summer hotels. Turn right beyond Pepperrell Cove and follow Gerrish Island Lane to a T-intersection, then take Pocahontas Rd. (the name of another vanished hotel) to World War I–era **Fort Foster**, now a park. Also check out Chauncey Creek Lobster Pound and **Seapoint Beach**. Rt. 103 winds on by the mouth of the York River and into York Harbor.

South Berwick. A short ride north of the Rt. 1 outlets brings you to a bend in the Salmon Falls River that is anchored by a splendid 1780s Georgian mansion, restored through the efforts of Maine author Sarah Orne Jewett; a formal garden and riverside trails through the woods add to the unusual appeal of this place. From Kittery, take either Rt. 236 north from the I-95 Eliot exit or more rural Rt. 101 north from Rt. 1 at Exit 3 (turn right at its junction with Rt. 236). From York, take Rt. 91 north. Hamilton House and **Vaughan Woods State Park** are the first left after the junction of Rts. 236 and 91 (Brattle St.); follow signs. **Hamilton House** is open June–Oct. 15, Wed.–Sun. 11–4, with tours on the hour ($10 adults, $9 seniors, $5 children); grounds open every day dawn to dusk. The foursquare Georgian mansion, built in 1785 on a promontory above the Salmon Falls River, had fallen into disrepair by the time Sarah Orne Jewett (1849–1909) was growing up in nearby South Berwick; she used it as the setting for her novel *The Tory Lover* and persuaded wealthy Boston friends to restore it in 1898. **Historic New England** (207-384-2454; historicnewengland.org) also maintains the **Sarah Orne Jewett House** farther up Rt. 236, at its junction with Rt. 4 (5 Portland St.), in the middle of the pleasant village of South Berwick. It's open June–Oct., Fri.–Sun. 11–5, with tours on the hour; $8, $7 seniors, $4 students. This is another fine 1774 Georgian house. Jewett, who is best known for her classic novel *The Country of the Pointed Firs*, grew up in the clapboard house next door, now the delightful town library. Here you learn that in the mid-19th century this picturesque village was home to extensive mills. The brick **Counting House Museum** (207-384-0000) by the Salmon Falls on Main St. (Rt. 4 at the bridge) is open June–Oct., weekends 11–4. It houses the Old Berwick Historical Society collection with exhibits on 17th- through 19th-century rural life in southern Maine.

IN PORTSMOUTH, NEW HAMPSHIRE

✪ ✐ **Strawbery Banke** (603-433-1100; strawberybanke.org), 14 Hancock St. Grounds open year-round, Tyco Visitors Center (with café) open May–Oct. and for special events off-season. $20 adults, $10 ages 5–17, $50 family. In Portsmouth's oldest neighborhood, more than 40 buildings from the 17th and 18th centuries have been preserved, many restored to reflect life in three centuries for a variety of residents, from wealthy merchants and sea captains to working families and poor widows. This is a major museum, minutes across the bridge from Kittery.

FOR FAMILIES ✐ ♿ **York's Wild Kingdom** (207-363-4911; yorkswildkingdom.com), 102 Railroad Ave. York Beach. In July and Aug. the zoo is open daily 10–6 and the amusement area noon–9:30; varying hours in shoulder seasons, so call ahead to check. This is an old-fashioned amusement area and zoo with monkeys, bears, ducks, swans, a white Bengal tiger, and a number of exotic animals. You'll also find mini golf, a butterfly kingdom, and both pony and elephant rides. Zoo: $14.75 adult ages 4-10; $1 ages 3 and under. Rides: $12 all day, all ages. Combo tickets available.

✿ ✐ **Seacoast Science Center** (603-436-8043; seacoastsciencecenter.org), 570 Ocean Blvd. (Rt. 1A), Rye, NH. Open daily Mar.–Oct.; Sat.–Mon. Nov.–Feb. In nearby 135-acre Odiorne Point State Park, this is a handsome facility with kids-geared touch tanks and exhibits, tidal pool walks, and many special events. Nominal admission.

Also see ROPES COURSE and SURFING under *TO DO*

✳ To Do

BICYCLING Mount Agamenticus (see *Green Space*) is webbed with trails beloved by mountain bikers. Also **Berger's Bike Shop** (207-363-4070) in York Village.

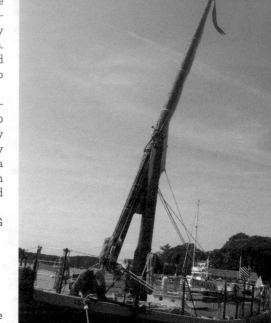
GUNDELOW CRUISES ARE OFFERED IN SEASON

BOATING Isles of Shoals Steamship Co. (603-431-5500 or 1-800-441-4620; islesof shoals.com), Portsmouth, NH. Daily cruises in-season stop at **Star Island**, site of a vast old white summer hotel that's now a Unitarian conference center. Visitors are welcome to this barren but fascinating place, webbed with walking trails. The ride on the 90-foot replica of an old steamboat takes one hour each way.

Captain & Patty's Piscataqua River Tours (207-439-8976), Town Dock, Pepperrell Rd., Kittery Point. June–Oct. 15, frequent daily departures for a tour aboard the launch *Sir William Pepperrell.*

Gundalow Co. (603-433-9505; gundalow.org), 60 Marcy St., Portsmouth, NH. The gundalow was the traditional sailing barge of the Piscataqua and other local rivers; this replica offers several daily cruises in-season.

York Harbor Marine Service (207-363-3602; yorkharbormarine.com), 20 Harris Island Rd., York. Boston whalers and other runabouts can be rented to explore the river and nearby coast.

FISHING The website **gatewaytomaine.org** lists half a dozen deep-sea fishing boats operating from York Harbor and Kittery. **Surf casting** is popular along Long Sands and Short Sands Beaches and from Sohier Park in York. **Eldredge Bros. Fly Shop** (207-363-9269; eldredgeflyshop.com), 1480 Rt. 1, Cape Neddick, is a full-service outfitter offering guided freshwater and saltwater trips.

GOLF **The Ledges Golf Club** (207-351-3000; ledgesgolf.com), 1 Ledges Dr. (off Rt. 91), York. This is a destination course for much of southern Maine: 18 holes, carts, pro shop, favored by local residents.

Cape Neddick Country Club (207-361-2011; capeneddickgolf.com), Shore Rd., Cape Neddick. Designed in the early 1900s by Donald Ross, redesigned by Brian Silva in 1998, its 18 holes feature rolling fairways integrated with ledge outcroppings and wetlands.

The Links at Outlook (207-384-4653), Rt. 4, South Berwick. An 18-hole Scottish-style course and driving range.

ROPES COURSE **Take Flight Adventures** (207-439-8838; takeflightadv.com), 506 Blue Star Memorial Highway (Rt. 1 north from Exit 3), Kittery. Open seasonally. $42.50 adults, $27.50 ages 12 and under, $37.50 students. Reserve ahead and allow two hours for the guided climbing tour, plus an extra half hour for a training session, before you hit the high ropes. They also offer zipline tours of up to two hours through the neighboring woodland.

KAYAKING The tidal York River, stretches of the Piscataqua around and above Eliot, and the Salmon Falls River (accessible from Vaughan Woods State Park in South Berwick) are particularly appealing to kayakers. **Harbor Adventures** (207-363-8466; harboradventures .com), based in York Harbor, and **Excursions** (207-363-0181; excursionsinmaine.com), based at Dixon's Campground, 1740 Rt. 1, Cape Neddick, offer guided tours and rentals.

SWIMMING ✍ **Fort Foster**, posted from Rt. 103, Kittery, is shallow a long way out and also has low-tide tidal pools with crabs and snails. Great for small children.

Long Sands, Rt. 1A, York Beach, a 1.5-mile expanse of firm sand stretching from York Harbor to Cape Neddick, backed by Rt. 1A and summer cottages, is great for walking. Metered parking the length of the beach and a bathhouse midway. Lifeguards in high

Christina Tree

SHORT SANDS BEACH

LONG SANDS BEACH, YORK BEACH

season. Popular with surfers, who have designated areas and hours. Accessed by the trolley (*Getting Around*).

Short Sands is still a substantial beach, wedged between Cape Neddick and York Beach Village, backed by Ellis Park, a green walkway with plenty of seating and changing rooms. Limited meter parking along Ocean Ave. (Rt. 1A) and in the public lot. Best to take the trolley (*Getting Around*).

York Harbor Beach is small and pebbly, but pleasant, with restrooms. Limited parking for nonresidents on Rt. 1A. This is also the entrance to York's Cliff Walk.

SURFING **Long Sands Beach** is known for its long, steady rollers; in summer an area is staked off with orange markers for swimmers; surfers use either end of the beach. **Liquid Dreams Surf Shop** (207-351-2545; liquid dreamssurf.com), 171 Long Beach Ave., rents boards and offers lessons and camps for both surfing and stand-up paddle boarding.

YORK HARBOR CLIFF PATH

✳ Green Space

PARKS **Fort Foster Park**, Kittery. Beyond Pepperrell Cove, look for Gerrish Island Lane and turn right at the T-intersection onto Pocahontas Rd., which leads, eventually, to this 92-acre town park. The World War I fortifications are ugly, but there is a choice of small beaches with different exposures (one very popular with sailboarders), extensive walking trails, and picnic facilities. Fee.

Mount Agamenticus (207-361-1102; agamenticus.org), York. Just 691 feet high but billed as the highest hill on the Atlantic seaboard between York and Florida. Views sweep down along the coast and back over hills that roll off to distant mountains. Once a ski area, now part of a 10,000-acre wooded preserve, its easiest access is from Mountain Rd. off Rt. 1 (turn at Flo's Hot Dogs). The summit is cluttered with satellite dishes and cell towers, but there are viewing platforms, especially popular for tracking hawks in spring and fall, and a new handicapped-accessible trail. Bring a picnic. Check out the new handicapped accessible summit trail.

Vaughan Woods State Park (207-384-5160), South Berwick. Seasonal. Take Old Fields Rd. off Brattle St. A 250-acre preserve on the banks of the Salmon Falls River; picnic facilities and 3 miles of nature trails. The first cows in Maine are said to have been landed here at Cow Cove in 1634.

Goodrich Park, York. A good picnic spot on the banks of the York River, accessible from Rt. 1 south; look for the entrance just before the bridge.

Hartley Mason Harbor Park, Rt. 1A, York Harbor, adjoining Harbor Beach. Created in 1998 when several classic York Harbor cottages were destroyed in accordance with the wills of their former owners, this is a great spot for a picnic.

Also see Fort McClary (*To See*).

THE WIGGLY BRIDGE IS A FAVORITE SPOT ALONG YORK HARBOR'S FISHERMAN'S WALK

WALKS Cliff Path and Fisherman's Walk, York Harbor. For more than a mile, you can pick your way along the town's most pleasant piece of shorefront. Begin at the Hancock Barn, walk east along Lindsay Rd. and left down Mill Dam Rd. to the shady Steedman Woods. Go across the **Wiggly Bridge**, a graceful pedestrian suspension bridge across a narrows through which York River funnels into the tidal mill pond. As the tides change and water rushes beneath it, the bridge is particularly wiggly. Then continue across Rt. 103, past the Sayward House, along the harbor to York Harbor Beach. Continue east from the parking circle at York Harbor Beach until the path ends at a private property line. This portion is a bit rough, and walkers are advised to keep to the path. Returning the way you've come is no hardship.

✳ Lodging

Note: This area, especially York Beach, offers many summer rentals. The big local agency in York is **seasiderentals.com**.

INNS AND RESORTS *Note:* For details about the largest local resort, **The Cliff House** resort and spa, which sits on the Ogunquit–York line, see the "Ogunquit and Wells" chapter.

⚥ ♿ 🛜 **York Harbor Inn** (207-363-5119 or 1-800-343-3869; yorkharborinn.com), York

St., Rt. 1A, York Harbor. Open year-round. Over the past decade this full-service inn has expanded to 63 rooms in six buildings, including four former York Harbor mansions. The 22-room main inn offers some reasonably priced as well as luxurious units with ocean views, and a beamed common area said to be part of a 1637 house from the Isles of Shoals. Given the inn's two popular restaurants (see *Dining Out*), however, we suggest opting for the privacy of another building. **Harbor Hill** and **Harbor Cliffs B&B**, along with **Yorkshire House**, are all within steps of the original inn. Across Rt. 1A there's waterside Hartley Mason

ONE OF FOUR FORMER YORK HARBOR MANSIONS, NOW PART OF THE YORK HARBOR INN

Park, with the beach and Cliff Walk at its base. Half a mile away two other mansions, **☙ Harbor Crest** and **Chapman Cottage**, adjoin each other. Rooms in both are also luxurious, and each building has its own character and common space. Until recently a popular inn known for its dining, Chapman Cottage still offers a delightful **Tavern**. Check the website. $289–389, from $99 off-season.

✿ ✎ ♿ (ఌ) Dockside Guest Quarters (207-363-2868 or 1-800-270-1977; docksidegq. com), 22 Harris Island Rd., York. Open late May.–late Oct. Sited on a peninsula in York Harbor, this is a gracious, family-run inn with views of fishing boats, sailing yachts, gulls, and the Boon Island Light. The Maine house forms the centerpiece of a 7-acre compound that includes four contemporary, multi-unit buildings. In all there are 25 guest rooms— including several with gas fireplaces and six apartment/suites with kitchenettes—all with private decks and water views. Breakfast is served buffet-style in the Maine House and guests have access to fishing equipment, bicycles, and boat rentals. River tours are also offered by innkeeper Eric Lusty. Two-night minimum stay during July and Aug. $155-301. Also see neighboring **Dockside Restaurant** (*Dining Out*).

♂ ♿ (ఌ) Stage Neck Inn (207-363-3850 or 1-800-222-3238; stageneck.com), 8 Stage Neck Rd., York Harbor. Open year-round, this attractive 58-room resort is sited on its own peninsula, beyond a small harbor beach. It offers water views, a formal dining room (see **Harbor Porches** in *Dining Out*), the less formal **Sandpiper Grille**, tennis courts, an outdoor pool, a small indoor pool and Jacuzzi,

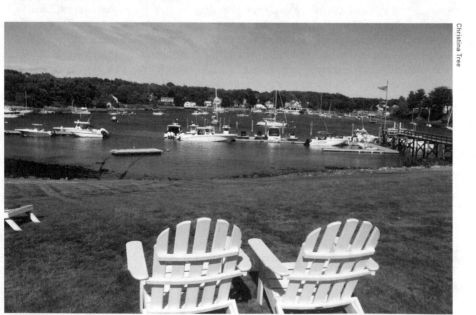

VIEW FROM DOCKSIDE GUEST QUARTERS

and a full-service spa. $286–470 per couple. B&B in high season. Geared to groups off-season. Inquire about packages.

♻ ((•)) **The Union Bluff** (207-363-1333 or 1-800-833-0721; unionbluff.com), 8 Beach St., P.O. Box 1860, York Beach. Open year-round. First opened in 1868, repeatedly renovated. There's not much of a lobby, but the elevator accesses comfortable rooms with a view of the ocean and Short Sands Beach. All three meals are served, and there's a choice between the **Union Grill** and an informal pub. The 76 units are divided among the original hotel, a three-story motel like annex with balconies, and the more recently added **Meeting House**, which also houses a function hall. $79–449.

B&B$ ((•)) **Inn at Tanglewood Hall** (207-351-1075; tanglewoodhall.com), 611 York St., York Harbor. Open year-round. A shingled 1880s summer mansion set in woods and gardens. No water views, but handy to the most dramatic stretch of the Cliff Path.

There are six nicely decorated and air-conditioned guest rooms, all with queen bed and private bath, three with gas fireplace or porch. Owners Su and Andy Wetzel serve a full breakfast, included in $185–245 in high season, otherwise $115–175.

♻ **Morning Glory Inn** (207-363-2062; morninggloryinnmaine.com), 120 Seabury Rd., York. The core of this contemporary-looking B&B is a post-and-beam cottage built more than 200 years ago on the Isles of Shoals. Banked in flower gardens and down a rural road half a mile from the ocean, Margie and Doug Mindell offer three guest rooms, each with a patio or deck, bath, TV, DVD, and mini fridge. The original cottage is now a parlor and there's also a living/dining area, library, and guest coffee bar. $245–265 June–Sept., from $195 early spring and late fall, including full breakfast.

♻ ((•)) **Bittersweet Bed & Breakfast** (207-351-3007; bittersweetbednbreakfast.com), 167 Cape Neddick Rd. Within walking distance of Short Sands Beach but handier to smaller Cape Neddick Beach, this is a 1910 farmhouse with seven guest rooms and pleasant common spaces, including a screened porch. Reasonable rates ($150 in July and August, otherwise $95) only add to the appeal. Hosts Victor and Ray are knowledgeable about dining options.

Sea Rose Inn Bed & Breakfast (207-361-4159; searoseinnmaine.com), 2 Southside Road, York. Open May–Oct. Mike and Jean are veteran B&B hosts, and this newest venture is an 1819 house in a quiet spot just off Rt. 1. There are three inviting rooms, each with quality beds (one king, two queens) and bedding, and spiffy en-suite baths. There's a parlor and deck as well as a dining room. $175–195 includes full breakfast.

IN KITTERY AND THE BERWICKS

♻ ((•)) **The Portsmouth Harbor Inn and Spa** (207-439-4040; innatportsmouth.com), 6 Water St., Kittery Foreside. Open year-round. Lynn Bowditch welcomes guests to her 1879 redbrick inn just off the Kittery green, across from the Piscataqua River and within walking distance of the theaters, shops, and restaurants of downtown Portsmouth, NH (across the bridge). Common rooms are cheerful and spacious, and the five guest rooms are carefully, imaginatively furnished; all have private bath (some with claw-foot tub), air-conditioning, ceiling fan, and cable TV/VCR (there's an extensive video library). Add to all this a day spa in the Carriage House. $175–200 in-season includes a full breakfast. From $155 off-season.

OTHER LODGING View Point (207-361-3261; viewpointhotel.com), 229 Nubble Rd., York. Office open daily in summer, selected days off-season. A nicely designed oceanfront, condominium-style complex overlooking the Nubble Lighthouse. Units have a living room,

Christina Tree

PORTSMOUTH HARBOR INN

kitchen, porch or patio, gas fireplace, phone, cable TV, CD stereo, VCR, and washer-dryer, and vary from one to three bedrooms. In summer from $320 (for a couple) with a two-night minimum; from $1,920 per week. From $169 off-season. Specials.

☎ (ᵖ) **Cutty Sark Motel** (207-363-5131 or 1-800-543-5131), 58 Long Beach Ave., York Beach. Open year-round. Location! Family owned, this is the only lodging on the beach side of the road in York Beach. The 42 rooms are housed in multistory clapboard buildings wedged into a corner of the beach, above a private lawn overlooking the ocean. All units have picture windows with a water view. Lowest rates are for rooms without AC or phones. $255–280 in-season, from $119 off-season, includes a continental breakfast in season.

☎ ♿ **The Anchorage Inn** (207-363-5112; anchorageinn.com), Rt. 1A, Long Beach Ave., York Beach. Open year-round. A total of 179 motel-style rooms, most with water views across from Long Sands Beach, a good choice for families. Facilities include indoor and outdoor pools; some rooms sleep four, some have TV, small fridge. $75–595.

☎ ♿ **Sands by the Sea & the Sea Rose Suites** (207-363-2211; sandsbythesea.com), 15 Ocean Ave., York Beach. Open May–Oct. This 60-unit 1950s motel is family run. Spanking clean and recently renovated, with a pool (with waterfall) and Short Sands Beach across the road. $209–249 in high season, from $99 in spring and fall. Inquire about condo suites and cottages.

Star Island (603-430-6272; starisland .org), Isles of Shoals. Open mid-June– mid-Sept., New England's last vast, truly authentic old-fashioned coastal resort complex sits 10 miles offshore on Star Island, one of the nine Isles of Shoals. The Unitarian-Universalist and United Church of Christ has owned the vintage-1875, five-story Oceanic Hotel since 1916 and continues to operate it as a conference center, hosting some 40 week-long and weekend programs each season. A total of 265 guests can find simple but comfortable lodging among the hotel buildings, several cottages, and "the motel" (private baths). Conference topics include photography, writing, painting, and many geared to nature and renewal.

✳ Where to Eat

DINING OUT

IN KITTERY

✪ **Anneke Jans** (207-439-0001; annekejans .net), 60 Wallingford Square. Open nightly from 5. This dramatically dark dining room creates the illusion of sitting in a theater. The drama unfolds in the well-lit kitchen, visible beyond a stainless-steel framed counter. The chefs perform well. The signature Bangs Island mussels with Great Hill blue cheese, bacon, shallots, and pommes frites ($21) beg for an encore. Entrées $18–35. Fully licensed with a wide selection of wines by the glass.

⌖ **Robert's Maine Grill** (207-439-0300; robertsmainegrill.com), Rt. 1 north. Open year-round, 11:30–8 or 9. Same ownership as Bob's Clam Hut but an upscale version with an expanded menu, including a raw bar and ranging from lobster bruschetta to seafood paella. Family-geared, this is a local favorite. Chef Craig Spinney is a stickler for not just the freshest but also the best seafood (like scallops from Winter Harbor); ditto for produce. Kids menu. Entrées $18–36.

Anju Noodle Bar (207-703-4298; anju noodlebar.com), 7 Wallingford Square. Open except Mon., noon–9:30, 10 Thu.–Sat. A sleek, inviting space with an Asian menu that includes Asian-inspired small plates such as a pork bun with kimchi mayo and rice cakes with duck confit as well as noodle dishes and a wide choice of wine and beer. Same phone/ address but tucked-in around the corner Anju's offshoot, the snug **Wallingford Dram** styles itself as a craft cocktail pub. Open 3:30–12, it features cocktails with names such as Northsea Lineman. Local and bottled beers and wines by the glass/bottle. Small plates include selections of charcuterie and Vermont cheeses.

Tulsi (207-451-9511; tulsiindianrestaurant .com), 20 Walker St. Open for dinner Tue.– Sun., also Sun. buffet–2:30. Great northern Indian food. The shrimp balchow appetizer is fiery and aromatic. Try the Kashmiri lamb curry or tandoori salmon. Entrées $14–18. Cocktail options include a blue mango martini and ginger mojito.

The Black Birch (207-703-2294; theblack birch.com), 2 Government St. Open Tue.–Thu. 3:30–10; Fri., Sat. until 11. Housed in a former post office building around the corner from Wallingford Square, this is a gastro bistro with sleek, casual decor. The bar runs the length of the room; there's an open kitchen at the back, a common table in the middle, plus individual tables. Regional craft beers and a menu that changes frequently with plenty of small plates, larger plates like fish and chips and chicken picatta. $12–17.

IN YORK

♨ Clay Hill Farm (207-301-2272, clayhill farm.com), 220 Clay Hill Rd., Cape Neddick. Open year-round for dinner but generally closed Mon. and Tue. in winter. Call for off-season hours and reservations. A gracious old farmhouse set in landscaped gardens halfway up Mount Agamenticus, with valet parking and elegant decor, the farm is geared to functions. You might begin with escargots in puff pastry, then dine on roasted half duckling or Maine-lobster-stuffed shrimp. Entrées $17–34.

♨ The York Harbor Inn (207-363-5119; yorkharborinn.com), Rt. 1A, York Harbor. Open year-round for dinner and Sunday brunch. Dine either in the pleasant dining rooms with water views or downstairs in the less formal Ship's Cellar Pub (open 11:30 AM –11 PM), evoking the paneled saloon of a luxurious sailing yacht. The menu is large, but fresh seafood is the specialty. Dinner entrées might include Yorkshire lobster supreme (lobster stuffed with a scallop-and-shrimp filling) and seafood ravioli, but there are also salads, sandwiches, and flat breads. Entrées $10–30.

The Tavern at Chapman Cottage (check for days, hours, and reserve) offers a more intimate venue with light dining in attractive inside spaces and on the terrace on skirt steak tacos or shrimp scampi pizza.

♨ Cape Neddick Inn Restaurant and Tavern (207-351-1145; capeneddickinn.com), 1273 Rt. 1, Cape Neddick, York. Open for dinner from 4 PM year-round. Originally opened in 1926, burned to the ground in 1984, and rebuilt. Both the dining room and tavern have field-stone fireplaces. A hands-down top pick among locals. Entrées $16–32. Children's menu.

✪ ♨ Dockside Restaurant & Bar (207-363-2722; dockside-restaurant.com), Harris Island Rd. off Rt. 103, York Harbor. Open for lunch and dinner late May–Oct., but check. Reservations suggested for dinner. Docking as well as parking. The view of yacht-filled York Harbor from Phil and Anne Lusty's glass-walled dining room, screened porch, and open patio is hard to beat. At lunch try the Peekytoe crab cakes, at dinner the specialties are seafood, such as drunken lobster sauté with shrimp, and roast stuffed duckling. Entrées $19.50–33. Children's menu.

The York River Landing (207-351-8430; theyorkriverlanding.com), 150 Rt. 1. Open 11–9, Fri., Sat. until 10. A large (seating 300), nicely designed, shingled and open-timbered new seafood restaurant with windows maximizing its site on the York River. A large and eclectic selection of craft beers is a specialty, but there are plenty of choices when it comes to seafood and locally raised meat. Entrees $14–34.

Harbor Porches (207-363-3850; stageneck .com/harbor-porches), Stage Neck Rd., York Harbor. Open year-round for breakfast, lunch, dinner, and Sunday brunch. Glass-walled with unbeatable ocean views, this attractive dining room has shed its white tablecloths and offers a menu with light as well as serious entrées from $11–$36.

Frankie & Johnny's Natural Food Restaurant (207-363-1909), 1594 Rt. 1, Cape Neddick. Open for dinner Thu.–Sun., closed Jan. No credit cards. BYOB. This colorful, funky place offers vegan and vegetarian dishes but also plenty of seafood and meat. It can hit the spot if you're in the mood for toasted peppercorn seared sushi-grade tuna or home-made "harvest" pasta. Daily specials. Entrées $16.75–27.75.

IN PORTSMOUTH, NH

Portsmouth, linked by three bridges to Kittery, is a destination dining town for much of this area. Herewith is a listing of our favorite dining spots there. For details please see New Hampshire: An Explorers Guide. The Black Trumpet Bistro (603-431-0887; 29 Ceres St.) with a French/Mediterranean menu is the standout. Ristorante Massimo (603-436-4000;

LOBSTER

✪ **Chauncey Creek Lobster Pier** (207-439-1030; www.chaunceycreek.com), 16 Chauncey Creek Rd., Kittery Point. Open Mother's Day–Labor Day, daily 11–8; post Labor Day–Columbus Day, daily 11–7, closed Tue. Owned by the Spinney family since the 1950s, specializing in reasonably priced lobster dinners with steamers, served inside and out on a pier on a tidal river walled by pine trees. Also available: lobster rolls, chowders, baked beans, a chicken dinner, and a raw bar. On summer weekends expect a wait. BYOB.

✪ **Cape Neddick Lobster Pound and Harborside Restaurant** (207-363-5471; capeneddick .com), 60 Shore Rd. (Rt. 1A), Cape Neddick. Open Mar.–Nov. for lunch and dinner, but call for hours in shoulder seasons. In August come early or be prepared to wait. Sited by a tidal river, this attractive building with dining inside and on a deck is a local favorite. Besides lobster and clams, the menu offers a variety of choices. Entrées $8–35.

Fox's Lobster House (207-363-2643; foxslobster.com), 8 Sohier Park Rd., Nubble Point, York Beach. Open daily in-season 11:45–9. A tourist-geared and -priced place near the Nubble, with a water view and a seafood menu.

Foster's Café & Marketplace (207-363-3255; fostersclambake.com), 5 Axholme Rd., Rt. 1A, York Harbor. Open in-season with a full menu, from hot dogs to lobster dinners, live lobster to go, inside and outside seating—but this place is all about lobster bakes for groups, at their place or yours, anywhere in the world (including the White House).

Maine Lobster Outlet (207-363-9899; mainelobsteroutlet.com), 360 Rt. 1, York (just south of Rite Aid). Open Mon.–Thu. 8-6; Fri., Sat. 8–7. If you have a way to bring home cooked lobster, this is a great resource; primarily a wholesaler, the store sells more than just lobster at a good price.

Warren's Lobster House (201-349-1630; lobsterhouse.com), 11 Water St., Kittery. A lobster-dining destination since the 1940s, known for its mammoth salad bar and lobster many ways. Also plenty of seafood and other options.

Note: At this writing lobstermen rarely get more than $4–6 per pound in high season, but in this area restaurants routinely overcharge for lobster dinners. Beware.

---

59 Penhollow St.) serves elegantly prepared Italian cuisine in a grotto-like setting. **Brazo** (603-431-0050; 75 Pleasant St.) is hip, upscale. **Cava** (603-319-1575; 10 Commercial Alley) is a sophisticated wine bar featuring a vertical garden and tapas. **Jumpin' Jay's Fish Café** (603-766-3474; 150 Congress St.) features a choice of 10 catches a day. **The Library** (603-431-5202; 401 State St.) is an atmospheric old reliable.

EATING OUT

IN KITTERY AND ALONG RT. 1 THROUGH YORK (SOUTH TO NORTH)

✪ **Beach Pea Baking Co.** (207-439-555), 59 State Rd. (Rt. 1 south), Kittery, south of the Exit 2 Kittery traffic circle. Open daily 7:30–6. The aromas alone are worth a stop. Known for artisan breads—from roasted garlic boules through country French and baguettes to focaccia and fabulous cakes—also sandwiches and salads to go or to eat in the small, cheerful dining room on the deck. Deservedly popular; parking can be a problem.

& (ꚝ) **Lil's Café** (207-703-2800; lilscafe .com), 7 Wallingford Sq., #106. Open Mon.–Fr. 6:30–5. Sat. 7–5, Sun. 7–4. A great place any time of day for a latte and ham and gruyere croissant or veggie egg wrap for breakfast through the wide blackboard choice of sandwiches (and breads) for lunch to a mid-afternoon tea and brownie break.

Wood Grill Pizza (207-439-9700), 68 Wallingford Square, Kittery. Open daily 11–9; Fri., Sat until 10. Terrific pizzas with options like "Nancy's White" (garlic spread, tomato slices, eggplant, and more) plus endless "make your own" toppings. Also salads, gluten-free options, nightly specials.

✪ **Loco Cocos Tacos** (207-438-9322; loco cocos.com), 36 Walker St. (Rt. 103), Kittery. Open daily 11–9. Cal-Mex fare, expanded from the original truck to a roomy restaurant with lounge, heated patio. A great spot for stoking after shopping, also a quick road-food hit from I-95. Tasty *enchiladas con mole*, chili, soups and salads, guacamole, cabbage slaw, four kinds of free salsa (try the green avocado sauce).

✪ **Bob's Clam Hut** (207-439-4233; bobs clamhut.com), Rt. 1 south, next to the Kittery Trading Post, Kittery. Open daily year-round, 11–9. Here since 1956 and definitely the best fried clams on the strip—some say the entire coast. The menu includes all the usual fried seafood (using "cholesterol-free oil") plus burgers and sandwiches. Order at the takeout and look for seating either inside or at the picnic tables around back.

♪ ((ᵞ)) **When Pigs Fly Wood-Fired Pizzeria** (207-438-7036), 460 Rt. 1, Kittery. Open 11:30–9 Sun.–Wed.; until 10 Thu.–Sat. Ron Siegel's nearby bakery now supplies retail outlets throughout the Northeast. This company store and 160-seat restaurant features pizza and dishes that beg for bread, like steamed mussels. Craft beers, full bar.

Stonewall Kitchen Café (207-351-2719), 2 Stonewall Lane, just off Rt. 1, beside the Chamber of Commerce, York. Open Mon.–Sat.

8–5, Sun. 9–4. Shorter hours off-season. At the Stonewall Kitchen flagship store (see *Selective Shopping*) you order from the espresso bar or deli and carry your tray to a table in the café or (weather permitting) at an outside table. Breakfast breads and house granola for breakfast; daily soups, deli sandwiches (like BLT and avocado), and salads all afternoon.

Fishermen's Dock (207-351-8100; fishermensdock.com), 674 Rt.1, York. Open 11–9. This new place fills a gap: a fish market and moderately priced restaurant with fresh, tasty seafood at reasonable prices. We lunched on a generous mixed greens salad topped with perfectly grilled salmon.

♪ **Wild Willy's Burgers** (207-363-9924), 765 Rt. 1, York. Daily (except Sun.) 11–7:30. This wildly popular family eatery features certified Angus ground chuck hand shaped daily into burgers, topped with more combinations than you thought possible.

✪ **Flo's Hot Dogs**, Rt. 1 North, Cape Neddick. Open seasonally 11–3; closed Wed. The steamed hot dogs are bargain-priced and have a loyal following. Flo has passed away, but her daughter in law Gail carries on. Go for the special relish and hold the mustard and ketchup.

LIL'S CAFÉ, WALLINGFORD SQUARE, KITTERY

CRAFT BREWS & SMALL-BATCH SPIRITS

Small breweries and distilleries are multiplying quickly in Maine, nowhere more so than in the state's southernmost coastal towns.

Tributary Brewing Co. (207-703-0093; tributarybrewingcompany.com), 10 Shapleigh Road (a half mile from I-95, exit 2 on Rt.236, beside the post office), Kittery Village. Tasting room open Wed.–Sat., 12–7; Sun.,1–5; inquire about brewery tours. Tod Mott has been a master brewer for more than two dozen years and is known as the creator of Harpoon IPA and Portsmouth Brewery's signature imperial stout. In the attractive tasting room a half dozen of the small batch beers are on tap at any one, some available in 32 oz. squealers and 64 oz. growlers. Tasting flights are $4–5 and brewery tours are $1.50. The crisp Pale Ale is always on tap and when limited bottles of Tod's famed Russian Imperial-style stout—now named "Mott The Lesser"—is released in Spring and Fall, fans stand in line for hours. Music in the tasting room is Sat., 4–6, Sun., 3–5. No food served at time of this writing.

SoMe Company Craft Brewery & Tasting Room (207-351-8162; somebrewingco.com) 1 York St., Unit 3. Open Mon.–Wed., 12–8, Thurs.–Sat. 12–9, Sun. 12–7. Squirreled away at the rear of building (look for the York County Federal Credit Union) near the Rt.1 turnoff for York Village, this is friendly inviting tasting room. On the day we stopped by the blackboard listed available brews ranging from light and tasty Old Orange Eyes to potent Whoopie Pie Stout and cask conditioned Crystal Persuasion Double Pale Ale . Local friends recommend the Agamenticus Amber Ale. The owner is Dave Rowland, Sr. and son Dave is the brewmaster. Tables inside and out, frequent live entertainment, popcorn always.

THE SoMe COMPANY TASTING ROOM IS A POPULAR YORK GATHERING SPOT

Warner Lord

Wiggly Bridge Distillery (207-363-9322; wigglybridgedistillery.com), 441 Rt. 1 (across from Hannaford's Supermarket). Open year-round, daily from noon for tours and tastings (reserve on line). This is also a father/son venture (both named Dave). Local residents and businessmen, they create and bottle small batch rum, whisky, bourbon, dry gin, sour mash, and vodka. The tasting room offers a choice of 50 cocktails as well tastings as small plates. A small tasting room at 19 Railroad Ave., York Beach is open seasonally.

Best Brew Tours (1-877-BREWSKI) offers tours of spirited destinations in Kittery, York, and Ogunquit.

IN YORK VILLAGE

✧ **Fat Tomato Grill** (207-363-5333), 241 York St. Open Tue.–Sat. 11–8, Sun.–Mon. 11–4. Basic sandwiches, multiple kinds of burgers and dogs, fried green tomatoes, kids' menu, cheap, cheerful, and handy.

IN YORK BEACH

✪ 🐾 ✧ **The Goldenrod** (207-363-2621; the goldenrod.com), Rt. 1A. Open Memorial Day–Columbus Day for breakfast, lunch, and dinner, 8 AM–9 PM. Still owned by the Talpey family, who first opened for business here in 1896. Lunch and dinner specials are served up at time-polished wooden tables in the big dining room with a fieldstone fireplace as well as at the old-style soda fountain. Their famous Goldenrod Kisses are made from saltwater taffy cooked and pulled in the windows. Usually 135 flavors of house-made ice creams. Salads and terrific club sandwiches and longtime favorites like cream-cheese-and-olive or -nuts.

Union Bluff Pub (207-363-1333), Union Bluff Hotel, 8 Beach St. Open year-round for lunch and dinner. A local favorite with a welcoming atmosphere and full sandwich and burger menu, pizzas, and dinner specials ranging from crab-stuffed haddock to filet mignon. Entrées $17.95–29.95. Full bar.

✧ **Lobster Cove** (207-351-1100), 756 York St. Open breakfast–dinner. Just west of Long Sands Beach with an upstairs deck and water views. The Talpey family, owners of The Goldenrod, have created this moderately priced eatery. No surprises, but a good dinner bet for broiled haddock or baked stuffed shrimp. Burgers all day plus a children's menu.

✧ **Sand Dollar** (207-606-0077), 2 Beach St. Open noon–12. This upstairs space in the Atlantic House is now a casual restaurant owned by the Tapley family, overlooking their iconic Goldenrod. Tables line the second floor porch as well as interior. Seafood and comfort food, piano bar and frequent music on the porch.

THE GOLDENROD, YORK BEACH

Christina Tree

ELSEWHERE

Thistle Pig (207-704-0624; thistlepig.com), 279 Main St., South Berwick. Open Thu.–Mon. 11 AM–10 PM, Sun. 10 AM–10 PM. Not so out of the way (see *Excursions*) and a local favorite for locally sourced lunch and dinner, with signature pork dishes like fried pork shoulder with Buffalo sauce.

SNACKS, TREATS, AND TAKE-HOME

Dunne's Ice Cream (207-363-1277), 214 Nubble Rd., York Beach. Seasonal, noon–9. This tidy, spanking new ice cream takeout (with restrooms), owned by Fox's Lobster House, replaces Brown's, the area's former ice cream landmark.

Terra Cotta Pasta Company (207-475-3025), Rt. 1 north, below the Kittery traffic circle. Open Mon.–Sat. 9–7, Sun. 11–5. Pick up freshly made linguine and lasagna for supper or a full-bodied sandwich for a picnic at nearby Fort McClary.

✱ Entertainment

Ogunquit Playhouse (see *Entertainment* in "Ogunquit and Wells") is the nearest and most famous summer theater. Special children's presentations.

Hackmatack Playhouse (207-698-1807; hackmatack.org), in Berwick, presents summer-stock performances most evenings; Thu. matinees.

Seacoast Repertory Theatre (603-433-3372; seacoastrep.org), 125 Bow St., Portsmouth, NH. Professional theater productions.

The Dance Hall (207-703-2085; thedancehall.org), 7 Walker St., Kittery. A venue for frequent live dance and music performances. Check the website.

✱ Selective Shopping

ANTIQUES Half a dozen antiques dealers can be found along Rt. 1 between **Bell Farm Antiques** in York and **Columbary House Antiques** in Cape Neddick. Stop in one and pick up the leaflet guide. **York Antiques Gallery** (746 Rt. 1; open daily 10–5), showcases 65 quality dealers on four floors.

ART GALLERIES **York Art Association Gallery** (207-363-4049 or 207-363-2918), Rt. 1A, York Harbor. Annual July art show, films, and workshops.

George Marshall Store Gallery, 140 Lindsay Rd., York. Open mid-June–mid-Oct., Tue.–Sat. 10–5, Sun. 1–5. Housed in an 18th-century store maintained by the Museums of Old York. Exhibits feature regional contemporary art and fine crafts.

Kittery Art Association (207-451-9384; kitteryart.org), 8 Coleman Ave., Kittery Point. Open all year, Sat. noon–6, Sun. noon–5, also March–Nov. Thu. 2:30–5. Housed in a former firehouse marked from (and just off) Rt. 103, changing shows by member artists.

IN YORK

Stonewall Kitchen (207-351-2712; stonewallkitchen.com), Stonewall Lane, Rt. 1, beside the Chamber of Commerce visitors center, York. Open 8 AM–8 PM in high season, except 9–6 Sun.; check for off-season hours. What began as a display of offbeat vinegars at a local farmers' market is now a mega specialty food business. Owners Jonathan King and Jim Stott maintain that all their products—from roasted garlic and onion red pepper jelly to raspberry peach champagne jam—still represent homemade care. Sample them in the open-kitchen-style shop, pick up free recipes, and find kitchen supplies and more. There's also a café (see *Eating Out*) and a **cooking school** with a calendar of varied classes, some taught by celebrity chefs.

Rocky Mountain Quilts (207-363-6800 or 1-800-762-5940), 130 York St., York Village. Open by appointment. Betsey Telford restores quilts and sells antique quilts (more than 450 in stock, "from doll to king"), blocks, and fabrics from the late 1700s to the 1940s.

Woods to Goods (207-363-6001; woodstogoods.com), 891 Rt. 1, York. Open daily 10–6; 10–5 off-season. Not all but many of the lamps, ship models, and other decorative items in this roadside shop are made by inmates of Maine prisons. The PRISON BLUES T-shirts and sweatshirts with the catchy line MADE ON THE INSIDE TO BE WORN ON THE OUTSIDE are produced by Oregon inmates.

IN KITTERY

SPECIAL STORES **Kittery Trading Post** (207-439-2700; kitterytradingpost.com), 301 Rt. 1, Kittery. A local institution since 1926, this sprawling store completed a major expansion in 2004 and is always jammed with shoppers in search of quality sportswear, shoes, children's clothing, firearms, outdoor books, and fishing or camping gear. The summer-end sales are legendary and many items are often discounted, but this is not an outlet store.

✪ **Sue's Seafood** (207-439-5608), 33 Old Post Rd. Sue Allen's classic seafood market is the place to pick up fish on your way home.

OUTLET MALLS **Kittery Outlets** (1-888-548-8379; thekitteryoutlets.com). Open daily year-round, mid-Mar.–Dec., Mon.–Sat. 9 AM–9 PM, Sun. 10–6; shorter hours off-season. Take I-95 Exit 3. At this writing, more than 120 discount stores within a 1.3-mile strip of Rt. 1 in Kittery represent a mix of clothing, household furnishings, gifts, and basics. All purport to offer savings of at least 20 percent on retail prices.

✳ Special Events

June–mid-October: **Gateway Farmers' Market** (gatewayfarmersmarket.org), behind the Greater York Region Chamber (see *Guidance*), Sat. 9–1 Jun.–Sept., also Thu. 9–1 in July, Aug. Many local products, crafts, produce, and food.

July: **Ellis Park Concerts** almost nightly at the gazebo at Short Sands Pavilion, York Beach. Schedule at gatewaytomaine.org. **Concerts at Hamilton House**, South Berwick (historicnewengland.org). **Sundays in the Garden Concert Series**, every Sunday in July, 5 PM at Hamilton House, South Berwick (southberwickmain.org); bring a picnic.

Late July/early August: **York Days Celebration**—flower show, church supper, concerts, square dances, parade, and sand castle contest.

August: **Summer House and Garden Tour**, York (oldyork.org), sponsored by the Museums of Old York.

Labor Day weekend: **Old York Antiques Show** (oldyork.org) fills Remick Barn, the Museums of Old York visitors center, York.

October: **Harvestfest** (the weekend after Columbus Day weekend) in York Beach (yorkharvestfest.com).

Saturday of Thanksgiving weekend: **Lighting of the Nubble, Sohier Park**, 5:45–7, with a shuttle bus from Ellis Park (207-363-1040). The famous lighthouse is illuminated in sparkling white lights for the Christmas season.

December: Christmas York **Festival of Lights Parade** (first weekend).

OGUNQUIT AND WELLS

Ogunquit and Wells share many miles of uninterrupted sand, and the line between the two towns also blurs along Rt. 1, a stretch of restaurants and family-geared lodging places. Named for the English cathedral town, Wells was incorporated in 1653 and remains a year-round community of 10,000 with seasonal cottages, condo complexes, and campgrounds strung along the beach and Rt. 1—parallel strips separated by a mile-wide swatch of salt marsh.

Ogunquit was part of Wells until 1980 but seceded in spirit long before that, establishing itself as a summer resort in the 1880s and a magnet for artists in the 1890s through the 1940s. It remains a compact, walk-around resort village clustered between its magnificent beach and picturesque Perkins Cove; these two venues are connected by the mile-long Marginal Way, an exceptional shore path. The village offers a vintage movie house and the Ogunquit Playhouse, one of New England's most famous summer theaters.

With the 1980s came trolleys-on-wheels to ease traffic at Perkins Cove and the beach. With a year-round population of 900 and thousands of rooms for rent, Ogunquit regularly draws 30,000 on summer and holiday weekends year-round. A reservation on summer weekends, or even on a weekday in August, is wise—but call the Ogunquit Chamber (listed below) if you are without one; they can usually help.

GUIDANCE **Ogunquit Chamber of Commerce** (207-646-2939; ogunquit.org), P.O. Box 2289, Rt. 1, Ogunquit (beside the Ogunquit Playhouse). Open year-round, Mon.–Fri. 10–4; more hours May to October and during events. Staff are helpful, and this large visitors center (with restrooms) is well stocked with pamphlets, including *This Week in Ogunquit* with entertainment and more. The lobby is open 24/7.

Wells Chamber of Commerce (207-646-2451; wellschamber.org), 136 Post Rd. (Rt. 1, northbound side) in Moody. Open year-round Mon.–Fri. 9–5; weekends in-season.

GETTING THERE *By car:* Coming north on I-95, take Exit 7 (York) and drive up Rt. 1 to the village of Ogunquit. Coming south on the Maine Turnpike/I-95, take turnpike Exit 19 (Wells).

By train: The **Downeaster** (1-800-USA-RAIL; amtrak.com), Amtrak's popular Boston–Portland service, makes five roundtrips daily, year-round. The Wells Transportation Center stop is at 696 Sanford Rd. (Rt. 109) near the Exit 19 tollbooth of the Maine Turnpike (I-95).

Coastal Taxi (207-229-0783; mainetaxicab.com). Friendly service available year-round.

By bus: C&J (ridecj.com) Direct bus trips to and from New York City in season.

GETTING AROUND Memorial Day–Columbus Day open-sided Ogunquit trolleys circle through the village of Ogunquit, Perkins Cove, and out Rt. 1 in Wells, stopping at the main entrance to Ogunquit Beach and at Footbridge Beach. Fare is nominal. Trolley stops are mapped, and maps are available from the chambers of commerce. They run weekends in June and daily from July 1 to Columbus Day.

PARKING Park and walk or take the trolley. In summer especially, the trolley is the easiest way to get around. There are at least seven public lots; call the chamber for rates. There is also free parking (one-hour limit) on Rt. 1 across from the Leavitt Theatre just north of

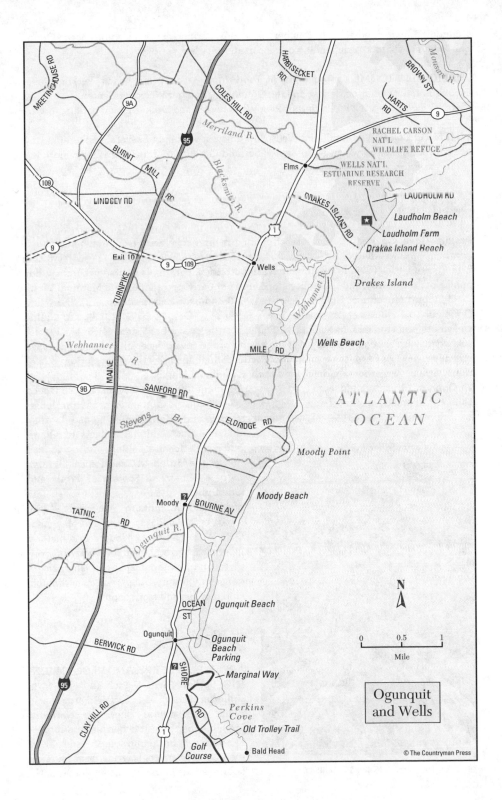

MEETINGHOUSE RD

9A

COLES HILL RD

HARRISECKET RD

BROWN ST

Mousam R.

HARTS RD

9

Merriland R.

95

BURNT MILL

109

Blacksmith R.

LINDSEY RD

RD

Elms

RACHEL CARSON NAT'L WILDLIFE REFUGE

WELLS NAT'L ESTUARINE RESEARCH RESERVE

LAUDHOLM RD

DRAKES ISLAND RD

Laudholm Beach

Laudholm Farm

Drakes Island Beach

1

Exit 10

9 109

Wells

Webhannet R.

Drakes Island

Webhannet

R.

MILE RD

Wells Beach

9B

SANFORD RD

ATLANTIC OCEAN

MAINE

Stevens Br.

ELDRIDGE RD

Moody Point

TURNPIKE

Moody

?

BOURNE AV

Moody Beach

TATNIC RD

Ogunquit R.

N

OCEAN ST

Ogunquit Beach

Ogunquit

BERWICK RD

Ogunquit Beach Parking

0   0.5   1

Mile

95

?

SHORE

Marginal Way

Ogunquit and Wells

CLAY HILL RD

RD

Perkins Cove

1

Old Trolley Trail

Golf Course

Bald Head

© The Countryman Press

Ogunquit Square or adjacent to Cumberland Farms. Parking at the main entrance to Ogunquit Beach is $10 to $30, depending on season and weather, per day.

PUBLIC RESTROOMS *In Ogunquit:* At Footbridge Beach, Main Beach, Perkins Cove, Jacob's Lot, the Dunaway Center, and the Ogunquit Chamber Welcome Center.
  In Wells: At the jetty, Wells Harbor Pier, Wells Beach, and Drakes Island parking areas.

WHEN TO COME Ogunquit and Wells slow down in winter, but several restaurants stay open through the year. Visiting in September and October or June makes for a more leisurely experience with far less traffic.

✳ To See

Perkins Cove, Ogunquit. Maine's most painted fishing cove, with restaurants and shops now housed in weathered fish shacks. It is the departure point for the area's excursion and fishing boats, based beside the famous draw-footbridge. Parking is limited in summer, but public lots are nearby, and the trolley stops here regularly, or walk here via Marginal Way.
  Ogunquit Museum of American Art (207-646-4909; ogunquitmuseum.org), Shore Rd., Ogunquit (0.4 mile west of Perkins Cove). Open May–Oct., Mon.–Sun. 10–5. $10 adults, $9 seniors and students, free under 12. Founded in 1952 and built superbly of local stone and wood, with enough glass to let in the beauty of the cove it faces, the museum displays selected paintings from its permanent collection, which includes the strong, bright oils of Henry Strater and other one-time locals such as Reginald Marsh.
  Ogunquit Heritage Museum (207-646-0296; ogunquitheritagemuseum.org), 86 Obeds Lane, Ogunquit. Open June–Sept., Tue.–Sat. 1–5. Set inside the Captain James Winn House, an 18th-century Cape with a unique Federal staircase and original paneling and flooring, this museum exhibits artifacts of Ogunquit's artistic and fishing history. It also houses the Littlefield Genealogical Library.

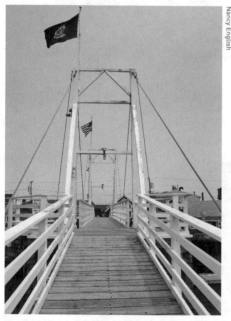
Nancy English

  ⟐ ❀ **Historical Society of Wells and Ogunquit** (207-646-4775; historicalsociety ofwellsandogunquit.org), 936 Post Rd. (Rt. 1, opposite Wells Plaza). Open mid-May–mid-Oct., Wed.–Thu. 10–4. Housed in a historic meetinghouse still used for weddings, concerts, and numerous special events; also a genealogy library, old photos, memorabilia, ship models, and a gift shop.

✳ To Do

APPLE, BLUEBERRY, AND VEGGIE PICKING Spiller Farm U-Pick (207-985-2575; spillerfarm.com), 85 Spiller Farm Lane, Wells. Pick apples (including Northern Spy), blueberries, strawberries, and more—like your own buttercup squash—and pay by the pound or piece. Hayride farm tours on fall weekends at this 130-acre 1894 farm. No

THE DRAW-FOOTBRIDGE SPANNING PERKINS COVE

credit cards. **Spillers' Farm Store** (207-985-3383), 1054 Branch Rd., Wells, does accept cards and is open year-round with farm products, Angus beef, pizza, and more.

BICYCLING **Wheels N Waves** (207-646-5774; wheelsnwaves.com), 365 Post Rd. (Rt. 1), Wells, and (207-641-2501), 161 Main St., Ogunquit. Rentals include mountain bikes, hybrids, and kids' bikes.

BOATING **Finestkind Cruises** (207-646-5227; finestkindcruises.com) offers scenic cruises and "lobstering trips." The **Bunny Clark** (207-646-2214; bunnyclark.com) offers deep-sea fishing trips from Perkins Cove.

GOLF **Merriland Farm** (207-646-0508; www.merrilandfarm.com), 545 Coles Hill Rd. (off Rt. 1), Wells. Nine-hole, par-three course on a working farm. Also a café (207-646-5040; merrilandfarmcafe.com).

MINI GOLF ✍ ♿ **Wells Beach Mini-Golf** (1-800-640-2267; wellsbeach.com), 1000 Post Rd. (Rt. 1), Wells. Open daily May 14–Oct. 14.
   ✍ **Wonder Mountain Fun Park** (207-646-9655; wondermountainfunpark.com), 270 Post Rd. (Rt. 1), Wells. Open Memorial Day–Labor Day. A human maze, two 18-hole courses—including Mountain Mania, complete with waterfalls, an arcade with skee ball and video games, and go-carts.
   ✍ **Sea-Vu Mini Golf** (207-646-7732; sea-vucampground.com) is another Rt. 1 option in Wells. 18 holes.

SEA KAYAKING **World Within Sea Kayaking** (207-646-0455; worldwithin.com), Wells. Registered Maine Guide Andrew French offers kayak and paddleboard rentals from the Ogunquit River Inn and Suites on the Ogunquit–Wells line.

SURFING **Wheels N Waves** (207-646-5774; wheelsnwaves.com), 365 Post Rd. (Rt. 1), Wells, and (207-641-2501), 161 Main St., Ogunquit. Rentals include surfboards and wet suits. A two-hour lesson with equipment is $60; it's offered year-round, but in winter generally only those 13 and older can find equipment that fits. Summer surf camps. Anyone can get on the big paddleboards; speed paddleboards offer an incredible workout.
   Liquid Dreams Surf Shop (207-641-2545; liquiddreamssurf.com). 696 Main St., Ogunquit. Learn to surf and then rent or buy your wet suit and board. $40 for the lesson on Ladies Night.

TENNIS Three public courts in Ogunquit. Inquire at **Dunaway Center** (207-361-9538). **Wells Recreation Area**, Rt. 9A, Wells, has four courts.

✳ Green Space

BEACHES Three-mile-long **Ogunquit Beach** offers surf, soft sand, and space for kite flying, as well as a sheltered strip along the mouth of the Ogunquit River for toddlers. It can be approached three ways: (1) The most popular way is from the foot of Beach St. There are boardwalk snacks, changing facilities, and toilets, and it is here that the beach forms a tongue between the ocean and the Ogunquit River; (2) The Footbridge Beach access (take Ocean St. off Rt. 1 north of the village) offers restrooms and is less crowded, $15 to 25 a day weekdays, $20 weekends for parking; and (3) Moody Beach parking lot, Wells. Be sure to park in the lot provided; $20 a day. Walk west onto Ogunquit Beach, not to Moody Beach, now private above the high-water mark.

THE DEAD GRASS HAS BEEN BURNED OFF IN EARLY SPRING AT LAUDHOLM FARM

Wells Beach. Limited free parking right in the middle of the village of Wells Beach; also parking at the east end by the jetty. Wooden casino and boardwalk, clam shacks, clean public toilets, a cluster of motels, concrete benches—a gathering point for older people who sit while enjoying the view of the wide, smooth beach.

Drakes Island, Wells. Take Drakes Island Rd. off Rt. 1. There are three small parking areas on this spit of land lined with private cottages.

NATURE PRESERVES AND PARKS Wells Reserve at Laudholm (207-646-1555; wellsreserve.org), Laudholm Rd. (off Rt. 1, just south of its junction with Rt. 9; look for the blinking yellow light just south of the Maine Diner on Rt. 1), Wells. This 2,250-acre reserve on two estuaries, an area formed where ocean tides meet freshwater currents, is a National Estuarine Research Reserve with headquarters listed on the National Register of Historic Places. The reserve consists of two parts: the meadows, salt marshes, woodlands, and two barrier beaches at the mouth of the Little River; and Laudholm Farm, the former estate of railroad executive George C. Lord that began as a saltwater farm in the 1640s. Today it's a birder's mecca. A visitors center is open year-round (weekdays 10–4; also May–Oct., Sat. 10–4 and Sun. noon–4), with exhibits, restrooms, and parking. Seven miles of trails meander through fields, woods, and wetlands (bring a bathing suit if you want to swim at the beach). The Wells Reserve is open daily year-round (gates open daily 7 AM–sunset); entrance fee Memorial Day–Columbus Day is $5 adults, $1 ages 6–16; no dogs allowed. Guided trail walks and programs for adults and kids ages 6–9. The Laudholm Nature Crafts Festival is held the weekend after Labor Day. Punkinfiddle (punkinfiddle.org) in early fall is a celebration of National Estuaries Day with fiddle bands and artisan demonstrations like butter churning, apple pressing, and pumpkin rolling.

Rachel Carson National Wildlife Refuge, off Rt. 9 on the Wells–Kennebunk line. See the description in "The Kennebunks."

Dorothea Grant Common. Hidden away between Rt. 1 and the Dunaway Center, this quiet park surrounds the Ogunquit Heritage Museum at Winn House (see *To See*).

WALKS Marginal Way. In 1923 Josiah Chase gave Ogunquit this windy path along the ocean. A farmer from the town of York, just south of here, Chase had driven his cattle around rocky Israel's Head each summer to pasture on the marsh grass in Wells, just to the north. Over the years he bought land here and there until, eventually, he owned

MARGINAL WAY IN OGUNQUIT

the whole promontory. He then sold off sea-view lots at a tidy profit and donated the actual ocean frontage to the town, thus preserving his own right-of-way. There is very limited parking at the mini lighthouse on Israel's Head.

✒ & **Wells Harbor.** Here is a pleasant walk along a granite jetty and a good fishing spot. There is also a playground, and a gazebo where concerts are held.

Old Trolley Trail. An interesting nature walk and cross-country ski trail that begins on Pine Hill Rd. N., Ogunquit.

✳ Lodging

Note: Ogunquit's 2,500 "rooms" include many family-geared efficiencies, especially along Rt. 1. We do not attempt to critique them here, but all are listed on the Ogunquit Chamber of Commerce website (ogunquit .org) and in its Four Season Destination Resource Guide.

All listings are in Ogunquit, or have an Ogunquit mailing address, and are most convenient to Ogunquit, unless otherwise noted.

RESORTS ✒ & **The Cliff House** (207-361-1000; cliffhousemaine.com), 591 Shore Rd., Cape Neddick. Year-round. Opened in 1872 with a single building at the top of its spectacular location, the Cliff House now holds a spa facility and 225 rooms, many with terraces and ocean views. Renovations have done more than a face-lift at the worn resort, and each refurbished room will hold Cuddledown comforters to keep the ocean chill off. Contemporary, cool taupe, and deep blue interiors with modern furnishings fit the austere Maine coast. A "vanishing-edge" pool, set out on the terrace, and spa, open to the public as well as to guests, gives guests access to luxurious massages and facials.

This place has risen like the phoenix from its own ashes after being run down during the temporary, exclusive use of the U.S. military, which employed it as a lookout for Nazi submarines in World War II. Innkeeper Charles Weare tried to sell it for $50,000 in 1946 with an ad in *The Wall Street Journal*, but received no offers.

A fine-dining restaurant, a lobster "shack," and a cocktail bar provide close-at-hand meals, and the nearby golf courses, two indoor heated pools, tennis courts, and more take care of exercise. The most important feature, of course, is the sound of the waves hitting the rocks outside your bedroom. High-season summer rates start at $629 with no meals; starting at $229 off-season.

RESORT MOTOR INNS Our usual format places inns before motels, but in the 1960s some of Ogunquit's leading resorts replaced their old hotel buildings with luxury "motor inns."

✒ **The Sparhawk** (207-646-5562; the sparhawk.com), 85 Shore Rd., P.O. Box 936. Open mid-Apr.–late Oct. Fifty-two-unit oceanfront resort overlooks the confluence of the Ogunquit River and the Atlantic Ocean, as well as Ogunquit Beach (waves lap below the balconies). Twenty units in neighboring Ireland House (with balconies canted toward the water) are combination living room/bedroom suites. The Barbara Dean and Jacobs Houses, formerly village homes, add another 11 suites and four apartments, some with gas fireplace and Jacuzzi. Outdoor pool (heated mid-June–mid-Sept.), shuffleboard, croquet, tennis, and fitness center. One-week minimum stay July–mid-Aug.; $195–315 per night in high summer, $105–250 in spring and fall.

The Cliff House

THE CLIFF HOUSE

INNS AND B&BS ✍ ♿ **The Beachmere Inn** (207-646-2021 or 1-800-336-3983; beachmereinn.com), 62 Beachmere Place. Open year-round. Beachmere Inn consists of a rambling, updated mansion and a streamlined building that border a huge lawn overlooking Ogunquit Beach. The inn, owned by female members of the same family since 1937, has 39 rooms and 33 suites; number 35 is a blue aerie set over Marginal Way and ocean waves. All rooms have kitchenette and cable TV, and most have a private balcony, deck, or terrace. A huge indoor hot tub, cedar sauna, massage rooms, exercise rooms, and children's play area are available to guests. High-season rates, $160–395, drop in the off-season after the last weekend in October to $65–195.

The Grand Hotel (207-646-1231 or 1-800-806-1231; thegrandhotel.com), 276 Shore Dr. Open Mar.–Nov. Twenty-eight suites in this hotel, originally a condominium complex. Each has two rooms, wet bar, fridge, cable TV, a king-sized bed, and a private deck or balcony; fireplace in top-floor rooms. There's an elevator, an interior atrium, an indoor pool, and an outdoor hot tub. $180–240 in high season, $95–210 right after Labor Day, from $70 off-season.

The Trellis House (207-646-7909 or 1-800-681-7909; trellishouse.com), 10 Beachmere Place, P.O. Box 2229. Open May–Oct. This shingled, turn-of-the-20th-century summer cottage offers appealing common areas, including a wraparound screened porch. In 2015, Laurence Plotkin and Glen Porter

handsomely redecorated eight guest rooms, all with full private bath, some with a water view. $169–299, two-night minimum, might include Trellis Benedict with crabcake. The inn is handy both to the village and to Perkins Cove via Marginal Way.

Marginal Way House and Motel (207-646-8801; marginalwayhouse.com), Wharf Lane, P.O. Box 697. Open late Apr.–Oct. Just a short walk from the beach and really in the middle of the village, this delightful complex is hidden down a waterside lane; its landscaped lawn has a water view. There are old-fashioned guest rooms—number 8 has flowered wallpaper and a beach view—in the Main and Wharf Houses, each with private bath. Dockside houses six standard motel units, and there are seven (high-season weekly rental) apartments. Rates range from $55–279.

Rockmere Lodge (207-646-2985; rockmere .com), 150 Stearns Rd. Hospitality, devoted repeat guests, good books and art assembled in a shingle-style 1899 "cottage" with the sea spread at its feet. Innkeepers Andy and Bob have three beloved dogs, but no pets are allowed and no children under 12. That said, count on handsome, Victorian decor; books perhaps stocked in the bedside table; excellent breakfasts; and relaxing on the porch and in the bountiful garden. Rates range from $125–255.

Above Tide Inn (207-646-7454; above tideinn.com), 66 Beach St. Open May 15–Oct. 15. Right at the start of Marginal Way and steps from the bridge leading over to Ogunquit Beach, also steps from village shops and jutting right out into the water. Meghan and John Hubacz offer nine rooms, each with an outdoor sitting area, small fridge, TV, and shower or bath. All but one room have water views, and local artists painted the pictures hanging inside. Mid-July–Labor Day rates are $190–235; $100–140 off-season, continental breakfast included.

The Beauport Inn on Clay Hill (207-361-2400; beauportinn.com), 339 Clay Hill Rd. Open year-round. A two-minute drive from town, this quiet stone manor set by a river has vintage-1835 English oak floor-to-ceiling paneling in its great room. Each room has a gas fireplace, cable TV, and DVD; there's also a two-room suite and a fully equipped apartment. A lap pool, steam room, and Jacuzzi are

AERIAL VIEW OF BEACHMERE INN

shared by guests. $150–275 (depending on the season) includes a full breakfast.

Beach Farm Inn (207-646-8493; beach farminn.com), 97 Eldridge Rd., Wells 04090. Open Apr.–Nov. This handsome restored farmhouse has been taking in guests since the 19th century, when it was a working salt-marsh farm. The tasteful early American decor is one of the charms, as is a swimming pool that beckons from the lawn. Eight attractive bedrooms, three with private bath—others can be rented with an unattached bath for private use—and two efficiency cottages. $109–159.

COTTAGES ♂ **Dunes on the Waterfront** (207-646-2612; dunesonthewaterfront.com), 518 Main St., P.O. Box 917. Open May–Oct. Owned by the Perkins family for more than 70 years, this is really a historic property, the best of the coast's surviving "cottage colonies," as well as a great family find. The 36 units include 19 old-style white cottages with green trim, many with fireplace, scattered over well-kept grounds fronting on the Ogunquit River, with direct access to Ogunquit Beach by rowboat at high tide and on foot at low tide. All rooms have refrigerator and color TV. Minimum stay in July and Aug. in the larger cottages. $255–315 in-season, $170–195 off-season.

🐾♂ **Cottage in the Lane Motor Lodge** (207-646-7903; cottageinthelane.com), 84 Drakes Island Rd., Wells. There are 10 house-keeping cottages, all facing landscaped grounds under the pines (an artistic play structure and a pool form the centerpiece); salt marsh beyond. It's a 0.75-mile walk or bike ride to the beach. The quiet setting borders the Rachel Carson Wildlife Refuge and Laudholm Farm (see *Green Space*). A two-bedroom cottage runs $990 per week in-season, $560–750 off-season.

♂ **The Seagull Inn and Condominiums** (207-646-5164; seagullvacations.com), 1413 Post Rd. (Rt. 1), Wells. Two 3-story town houses (available year-round), 27 two-bedroom cottages, 1 one-bedroom cottage, all with a screened porch, fill what used to be an open field. Private driveway and gas grills; new cottages have ocean views. The seven remaining old cottages have been updated with bathrooms and kitchens. Two heated pools, one with hot tub, the other with a wading pool for children. Rentals by the week in summer (three-night minimum off-season), $800–1,500 for the housekeeping cottages; $2,800 a week for town houses.

MOTELS **Riverside Motel** (207-646-2741; riversidemotel.com), Shore Rd., P.O. Box 2244. Open mid-Apr.–Oct. Just across the draw-footbridge and overlooking Perkins Cove is this trim, friendly place with 42 units; also four rooms in the 1874 house. The property had been in the Staples family for more than 100 years before Geoff Scimone took over in 2009. All 4 acres are nonsmoking. All rooms have cable TV and full bath, most tiled, and all overlook the cove; fresh muffins, Congdon's Doughnuts, yogurt, and cereal served in the lobby 7:30–11 around the fire-place, with outdoor seating. $79–199, depending on season and location of room.

✳ Where to Eat

DINING OUT **Roost Café and Bistro** (207-646-9898; roostcafeandbistro.com), 262 Shore Rd., Ogunquit. Open Apr.–Dec. 1; May–Aug. open seven days a week; Sept.–Dec. open Wed.–Sun. Serving breakfast (available all day) starting at 8 AM, light fare at 3 PM at the bar, and dinner 5 PM–close. The menu is an eclectic mix, as the owners' priority is simply to "do food really well." Options range from Asian-inspired grilled swordfish with Korean BBQ and coconut scallion rice to a lobster pappardelle with house-made pasta. Reservations advised. Entrées $18–30.

♻👃 **Joshua's Restaurant** (207-646-3355; joshuas.biz), 1637 Post Rd. (Rt. 1), Wells. Open daily at 5 PM with the last seating at 9:15. The buzz about Joshua's just keeps getting better. The Mather family farm grows its own veg-etables, and chef Joshua Mather puts them to spectacular use as sides for grilled rack of lamb, pork tenderloin with plum chutney, and haddock with caramelized onion crust. An elegant, refurbished farmhouse dining room and bar. Entrées $21–35.

The New England House (207-641-0601; newenglandhousewells.com), 124 Post Road, Wells. A new mainstay in 2016, The New England House specializes in seafood, with fried clams, shrimp, fish, and a daily catch. Regulars pronounced every new dish

THE RIVERSIDE MOTEL OVERLOOKING PERKINS COVE

excellent—and never stopped coming back. $15 to $22.

✪ **Angelina's Ristorante** (207-646-0445; angelinasogunquit.com), 655 Main St., Ogunquit. Open daily 4:30–10. Reservations recommended. Owner-chef David Giarusso Jr. might be tired, but he's scrupulously polite whenever you encounter him on a busy night at this deservedly popular Italian restaurant, and that's part of why people love it here. A garden terrace feels cool in the hot summer and the bustling rooms are always comfortable, but what's most important is on the plate, and it is wonderful. Good wine list. Entrées $16–31.

MC Perkins Cove (207-646-6263; mcperkinscove.com), Perkins Cove. Lunch and dinner daily in summer, closed some days of the week off-season. Wonderful water views and live Thu.-night entertainment. Owned by the inventive chefs of Arrows, this is a casual place for fresh raw oysters, grilled steak and fish, fried trout, and other seafood with splendid touches. Choose your own "evil carbos" and sauces. The even more casual bar menu is a deal. Entrées $19–37.

Five-O Shore Road (207-646-5001; five-o shoreroad.com), 50 Shore Rd., Ogunquit Village. Open for dinner in-season nightly, light fare served until 11 PM; Thu.–Sun. in winter. Brunch served Sun. 10–2. The beef tenderloin brochette we tried remains a high point of dining out, and the skilled preparation of everything else was memorable, too. Maine lobster with crab and corn caponata and dry-rubbed pork loin with roasted tomato polenta were on a summer menu. Good wine and cocktails. Entrées $23–39.

Gypsy Sweethearts (207-646-7021; gypsy sweethearts.com), 30 Shore Rd., Ogunquit. Open Apr.–Oct. for dinner Tue.–Sun. from 5:30; weekends off-season. Meals with a Caribbean twist are served in a charming old house that is the dependable neighborhood dinner spot for demanding locals. Chef-owner Judie Clayton's green secret pumpkinseed sauce is a tangy delight on the rack of lamb. Poblano rellenos and pan-seared sea scallops with pineapple and roasted sweet potato. Many wines available by the glass. Entrées $19–32.

The Front Porch Restaurant (207-646-4005; frontporchrestaurant.net), 9 Shore Rd., Ogunquit. Closed Tue.; otherwise open 5–close except Sat. (noon–close). A popular nightspot boasts a fine fish taco with cilantro slaw, good macaroni and cheese, and burgers. Count on a crowd on summer weekends, with entertainment upstairs in the piano bar (see

LOBSTER

Note: Maine's southernmost beach resorts are the first place many visitors sample real "Maine Lobstah" the way it should be eaten: messily, with bib, butter, and a water view.

✤ **Barnacle Billy's, Etc.** (207-646-5575 or 1-800-866-5575; barnbilly.com), Perkins Cove. Open May–Oct. for lunch and dinner. What began as a no-frills lobster place (the one that's still next door) has expanded over 50 years to fill a luxurious dining space created for a more upscale waterside restaurant. Lobster and seafood dishes remain the specialty, and it's difficult to beat the view combined with comfort, which frequently includes the glow from two great stone fireplaces. Full bar; dinner entrées from $16.75, higher for a big, boiled lobster. You can also order lobster at the counter and wait for your number, dine on the outdoor deck, or order burgers.

✤ ✤ ✤ ✤ ✤ **Lobster Shack** (207 646 2941), end of Perkins Cove. Open mid-Apr.–mid-Oct., 11–8 in-season. A family-owned, old-style, serious lobster-eating place since the 1940s (when it was known as Maxwell and Perkins). The tables are wide slabs of shellacked pine with plenty of room for lobster by the pound, steamer clams, good chowder, house coleslaw; also reasonably priced burgers, apple pie à la mode, wine, and beer.

✤ **Ogunquit Lobster Pound** (207 646 2516), Rt. 1 (north of Ogunquit Village). Open Apr.–Dec. Summer hours are 4–9, fall hours (starting in Sept.) are 4:30–9. Expanded gradually over the years, this log landmark retains its 1930s atmosphere and is still all about selecting your lobster and watching it (if you so choose) get steamed in the huge outdoor pots. "Steamers" (steamed clams) are the other specialty. The large menu, however, now includes angelhair pasta, fried foods, and sirloin steaks. Beer and wine are available. Entrées $4.30 and up for lobster.

✤ ✤ **Fisherman's Catch** (207 646 8780, fishermanscatchwells.com), 134 Harbor Rd., Wells Harbor. Open May–Columbus Day, daily 11:30–9 in summer, closing earlier off-season. Set in a salt marsh, with rustic tables; a traditional seafood place with unbeatable prices. Good chowder and really good lobster stew, homemade crabcakes, lobster dinners, children's menu, beer on tap, all provided by a family that takes good care of you. Try the bread pudding with whiskey sauce. Entrées $6.99–22.99 plus.

Entertainment). The menu is served in all three spaces except during shows. Steaks, flat breads, and grilled fish, too. Entrées $10–29. Reservations not accepted.

Jonathan's Restaurant (207-646-4777; jonathansrestaurant.com), 92 Bourne Lane, Ogunquit. Open year-round. There are two entirely distinct parts to this big place. The downstairs restaurant consists of a series of nicely decorated rooms (one with a 600-gallon tropical aquarium). The mainstream fare is well made, including grilled steak, scampi Provençal, and caramelized salmon fillet. Entrées $21.95–33.95. For more about what happens upstairs, see *Entertainment*.

Varano's Restaurant (207-641-8550; varanos.com), 60 Mile Rd., Wells. Open daily at 4:30. A family-owned Italian restaurant that combines a welcoming professional staff with good food. Prosciutto and melon might be a summer appetizer, and whole-wheat vegetarian pasta keeps up the good work. Grilled lamb, house pork sausage, and lobster with black fettuccine. Entrées $14.95–31.95. Reservations not accepted.

EATING OUT **Caffé Prego** (207-646-7734; cafeprego.com), 44 Shore Rd., Ogunquit. Open daily. Amore Breakfast, with its fabulous French toast and pancakes, merged with Caffé Prego in 2017. A refreshed dining room, fantastic outdoor seating, excellent coffee, and now those elaborate feasts for breakfast, make this a vacation destination. Lunch and dinner continue in the Italian tradition, with pizza, well-made pasta, and panini vying for your allegiance. Finish with house gelato, perhaps the kiwi and the chocolate. Entrées $14–22.

A GARDEN AT THE ENTRANCE TO CAFFÉ PREGO

Oarweed Oceanside Restaurant (207-646-4022; oarweed.com), Perkins Cove. Open end of Apr.–Oct., daily at 11 AM for lunch and dinner. This seaside restaurant has outdoor seating in warm weather, but inside or out you can feast your eyes on the water—and on your plate, where you might choose a good crab roll, lobster roll, crabcakes, steamed lobster, roast chicken, or the perfectly done steamers, an essential ingredient in the shore dinner. Entrées $3.50–34.

The Greenery Café (207-360-0211), 369 Main St., Ogunquit. Open for breakfast and lunch. A justifiable popular place for its seafood Benedict, Cubans, pesto and mozzarella sandwiches, and bagels and lox, as well as the perfect blueberry pancakes.

Jake's Seafood (207-646-6771; jakes seafoodrestaurant.com), 127 Post Rd. (Rt. 1), Moody. Open daily 5 AM–9 PM Apr.–Oct., breakfast and lunch Nov.–Mar. Very popular, this spot specializes in good American cooking, fresh seafood, and ice cream.

Congdon's Donuts Family Restaurant (207-646-4219; congdons.com), 1090 Post Rd. (Rt. 1), Wells. Open 6–3 daily in summer (closed Wed.), fewer days in winter. Fresh muffins, breads, pastries, doughnuts, and a full menu for breakfast and lunch. The doughnuts are fried in lard; this place is one of the very few left that does so, and it makes a great doughnut.

Mike's Clam Shack (207-646-5999; mikes clamshack.com), 1150 Post Rd. (Rt. 1), Wells. Open daily in-season 11:30–closing. An enormous place with enormous crowds and a reputation for good fried clams.

Sandwiches, burgers, pasta, and fried seafood. $5.50–24.95.

✎ **Billy's Chowder House** (207-646-7558; billyschowderhouse.com), Mile Rd., Wells. Open daily 11:30–close mid-Jan.–early Dec. Overlooking Wells Harbor and a salt marsh, a family favorite with famous chowder and a selection of fried seafood, steamed shellfish, broiled scallops, and, of course, boiled lobster. There's also plenty of meat on the menu, including hot dog and fries. Entrées $14–32.95.

Maine Diner (207-656-4441; mainediner .com), 2265 Post Rd. (Rt. 1), Wells, near the junction of Rts. 1 and 9. Open year-round; Sun.–Thu. 7 AM–8:30 PM, Fri. and Sat. 7 AM–9 PM. This packed place can boast about its seafood chowder, made with shrimp, scallops, lobster, and clams in a milky broth. Avoid the chicken potpie. Entrées $3.50–30.95.

✎ **Village Food Market and Cafe** (207-646-2122; villagefoodmarket.com), 230 Main St., Ogunquit. This landmark grocery store has changed with the times, adding daily baked goods, soups, salads, a deli—and a new brick-oven pizzeria called Cornerstone. Call before 11 for a picnic order to avoid the line.

SNACKS **Bread & Roses Bakery** (207-646-4227; breadandrosesbakery.com), 28 Main St., Ogunquit. Over the years Mary Breen's pleasant bakery has expanded into an attractive café serving muffins and coffee, irresistible cinnamon butter puffs, and other delectable

VILLAGE FOOD MARKET

pastries. Lunch on panini, big salads, and fresh thick-crust pizza.

Scoop Deck (207-646-5150; facebook.com/thescoopdeck), Eldridge Rd. (just off Rt. 1), Wells. Open Memorial Day–Columbus Day. Mocha chip and Dinosaur Crunch (blue vanilla) are among the more than 55 flavors; the ice cream is from Thibodeau Farms in Saco. Fall flavors include pumpkin pie and apple crisp. Also yogurt, brownies, and hot dogs.

Borealis Breads (207-641-8800), Rt. 1, Wells. Open daily. Great bread and sandwiches—don't overlook the fabulous breadsticks—and the brownies and other treats are excellent. More than 100,000 pounds of whole-wheat flour for the breads is milled from wheat grown in Aroostook County.

✳ Entertainment

THEATERS **Hackmatack Playhouse** (207-698-1807; hackmatack.org), 538 School St. (Rt. 9), Berwick, stages live performances mid June–Labor Day.

Leavitt Fine Arts Theatre (207-646-3123; leavittheatre.com), 259 Main St., Ogunquit Village. An old-time theater with new screen and sound; showing first-run films since 1923 and live entertainment, including comedians.

Ogunquit Playhouse (207-646-5511; ogunquitplayhouse.org), Rt. 1 (just south of Ogunquit Village). Open May–Oct. Billing itself as "America's Foremost Summer Theater," this grand old summer-stock theater opened for its first season in 1933 and is now owned by the Ogunquit Playhouse Foundation. It continues to feature top stars in productions staged Tue.–Fri. at 8 PM, Sat. at 8:30 PM; matinees are offered several days of the week.

OTHERS **Jonathan's Ogunquit** (207-646-4777; jonathansrestaurant.com), 92 Bournes Lane, Ogunquit. Year-round, national performers. You can check the current schedule on the website.

Vinegar Hill Music Theatre (207-985-5552; vinegarhillmusictheatre.com), 53 Old Post Road, Arundel. Open June to October. Famous performers take the stage, along with excellent local musicians.

Ogunquit Performing Arts (207-646-6170) sponsors the Chamber Music Festival in June and the Capriccio annual summer arts festival; also film, music, social dances, and theater year-round.

The Front Porch Restaurant (207-646-4005; frontporchrestaurant.net), 9 Shore Rd., Ogunquit. Performances and piano and the chance to join in the show tunes; special events with live entertainment.

Hope Hobbs Gazebo at Wells Harbor Park is the site of Sat.-night concerts in summer.

✳ Selective Shopping

ANTIQUES SHOPS Rt. 1 from York through Wells and the Kennebunks is studded with antiques shops, among them is **MacDougall-Gionet** (207-646-3531; macdougall-gionet.com), open Tue.–Sun. 10–5, a particularly rich trove of formal and country furniture in a barn; 60 dealers are represented. **R. Jorgensen Antiques** (207-646-9444; rjorgensen.com) has nine rooms filled with antique furniture, including fine formal pieces from a number of countries. Open Mon.–Sat. 10–5, Sun. noon–5.

Hutchins Antiques etc. (207-646-9643; hutchinsantiquesetc.com), 166 Main St., Ogunquit. Make sure to have time to wander so you can see all the 8,000 square feet of antique, linens, vintage kitchenware, to name a few; with discounts in the off-season, starting in November.

ART GALLERIES In addition to the Ogunquit Museum of Art there is the **Barn Gallery**, home of the Ogunquit Art Association (207-646-8400; barngallery.org, ogunquitartassociation.com), Shore Rd. and Bourne Lane, Ogunquit. Open late May–early Oct., Mon.–Sat. 11–5 and Sun. 1–5. The Barn Gallery showcases work by members; also stages frequent workshops, lectures, Wed.-night films about artists, Tue.-night workshops working with a model, and concerts. Another is the **Van Ward Gallery** (207-646-0554; vanwardgallery.com), 49 Shore Rd., Ogunquit.

Beth Ellis Cove Gallery (860-338-3996; bethelliscollection.com), 294 Shore Rd., Ogunquit. Owned by the sister of the late Beth Ellis, this gallery showcases Beth Ellis' work with their layered use of color.

BARN GALLERY

BOOKS Boston book lovers drive to Wells to browse in the cluster of exceptional bookstores along Rt. 1, including **Annie's Book Stop** (207-646-3821; anniesbookstopwells .com), 676 Post Rd., Wells. Hours change with the season. Mysteries, new releases, old favorites both used and new. **Douglas N. Harding Rare Books** (207-646-8785; hardingsbooks .com), 2152 Post Rd., open year-round, is huge and excellent with some 200,000 titles, including rare finds, maps, and prints. **The Arringtons** (207-646-4124), 1908 Post Rd. (Rt. 1), specializes in military subjects as well as vintage paperbacks and postcards.

SPECIAL SHOPS Perkins Cove, the cluster of former fish shacks by Ogunquit's famous draw-footbridge, harbors more than a dozen shops and galleries.

Panache Gallery of Fine American Crafts (207-646-4878), 307 Main St., Ogunquit. In a handsome yellow building near the center of town, Panache Gallery showcases extravagant, exuberant glass work, fine jewelry and more.

Crickets Corner Toys and Kites (207-646-2261; cricketscornertoys.com), 41 Shore Rd., Ogunquit. Beach toys, games, stuffed animals, and a huge variety of kites.

Harbor Candy Shop (207-646-8078; harborcandy.com), 26 Main St., Ogunquit. Open year-round Thu.–Sun. 9 AM–9 PM, Fri.–Sat. 9 AM–10 PM. Open since 1956, this family-owned store makes turtles with Belgian chocolate and handmade caramel (made from cream and sugar and no preservatives)—they are their most popular item.

Pine Tree Farm Market and Café (207-646-7545; facebook.com/PineTreeFarm MarketCafe), 411 Post Rd., Wells. A fine place to find a good sandwich, breakfast, or wine, cheese, pickles, and more, like flowers and pumpkins in fall.

✳ Special Events

April: Big **Patriots Day celebration** at Ogunquit Beach.

June: **Ogunquit Chamber Music Festival** (first week). **Laudholm Farm Day** (mid-month). **Wells Week** (end of the month)—a weeklong celebration centering on Harbor Park Day, with boat launchings, a chicken BBQ, a sand-sculpture contest, and a crafts fair. **Métis of Maine Annual Powwow**—dance, rituals and crafts made by people of Native American ancestry, Wells.

July: **Fireworks** on July 4, sand-castle building, family fun day, and three-day **Harbor Fest** in Wells.

August: **Sidewalk Art Show**, Ogunquit.

September: **Open Homes Day**, sponsored by the Wells Historical Society. **Nature Crafts Festival** (second weekend) at Laudholm Farm. **Capriccio**, a celebration of the performing arts, **Sidewalk Sale** and **Kite Day** in Ogunquit. **Punkinfiddle** (punkinfiddle.org), a celebration of National Estuaries Day.

October: **Ogunquit Fest**, with tours and costume parade, and October Fest.

December: **Christmas parade** in Wells. **Christmas by the Sea** (second weekend) in Ogunquit.

THE KENNEBUNKS

The Kennebunks began as a fishing stage near Cape Porpoise as early as 1602, but the community was repeatedly destroyed by Native American raids. In 1719 the present "port" was incorporated as Arundel, a name that stuck through its lucrative shipbuilding and seafaring years until 1821, when it became Kennebunkport. Later, when the novel *Arundel*, by Kenneth Roberts (born in Kennebunk), had run through 32 printings, residents gave the old name to North Kennebunkport.

That the Kennebunks prospered as a shipbuilding center is obvious from the quantity and quality of its sea captains' and shipbuilders' mansions, the presence of its brick customhouse (now the library), and the beauty of its churches.

In his 1891 guidebook *The Pine-Tree Coast*, Samuel Adams Drake noted that "since the beginning of the century more than eight hundred vessels have been sent out from the shipyards of this river." He recalled: "When I first knew this place, both banks of the river were lined with shipyards . . . all alive with the labor of hundreds of workmen." But by the 1890s, Drake noted, shipbuilding was "moribund" and Kennebunkport had become "a well-established watering-place."

In 1872 this entire spectacular 5-mile stretch of coast—from Lords Point at the western end of Kennebunk Beach all the way to Cape Porpoise on the east—was acquired by one developer, the Sea Shore Company. Over the next couple of decades no fewer than 30 grand hotels and dozens of summer mansions evolved to accommodate the summer visitors that train service brought. The Kennebunks then shared the 1940s-to-1960s decline suffered by Maine coastal resorts, losing all but a scattering of old hotels.

According to the locals, the Kennebunks developed an almost countercultural feel in the 1960s and '70s. Then the tourist tide again turned, and over the past few decades, the area has grown increasingly upscale: Inns have been rehabbed and dozens of B&Bs and inns have opened. Dock Square's world-class shopping district now rivals those in Palm Beach and other swanky spots, but a walk through the historic streets of Kennebunkport is free and quite idyllic. And a meal at one of the lobster shacks is as rustic, delicious, and affordable as any on the Maine coast.

You can bed down a few steps from Dock Square's lively shops and restaurants or out at Goose Rocks, where the only sound is the lapping of waves on endless sand. Most

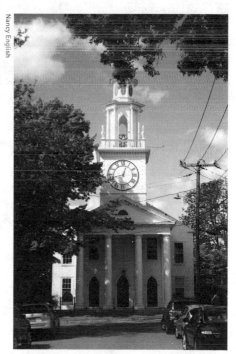

Nancy English

SOUTH CONGREGATIONAL CHURCH

The Kennebunks

© The Countryman Press

B&Bs are, however, the former sea captains' homes grouped within a few stately streets of each other, many within walking distance of both Dock Square and the open ocean.

GUIDANCE Kennebunk-Kennebunkport-Arundel Chamber of Commerce (207-967-0857, gokennebunks.com), main office, 16 Water St., Kennebunk; kiosk, 1 Chase Hill Rd., Kennebunk. Open Mon.–Fri. year-round, plus Sat. and Sun. late May–late Oct. Staff are unusually helpful, and the chamber publishes an excellent free guide.

GETTING THERE *By air:* **Portland International Jetport** is served by various airlines and taxi services.

By car: Drive up I-95 to Exit 25 and take Rt. 35 into Kennebunk, on to Kennebunkport and the Kennebunk beaches. Coming up Rt. 1, take Rt. 9 east from Wells.

By train: See *Amtrak* in "What's Where." The Downeaster service from Boston's North Station takes about two hours. Starting in 2017, Amtrak makes a seasonal stop at 12 Depot St., Kennebunk; until then, transportation is available from Wells.

GETTING AROUND Kennebunk is a busy commercial center straddling the strip of Rt. 1 between the Mousam and Kennebunk Rivers. A 10-minute ride down Summer St. (Rt. 35) brings you to Kennebunkport. Then there are the Kennebunk beaches, Cape Porpoise, Goose Rocks Beach, Cape Arundel, and Kennebunk Lower Village. Luckily, free detailed maps are readily available.

Intown Trolley (207-967-3686; intowntrolley.com), Kennebunkport, offers narrated sight-seeing tours; $16 adults, $6 ages 3–17, free for those 2 and under. The tickets are good for the day, so you can also use them to shuttle between Dock Square and the Kennebunk beaches.

PARKING A municipal fee parking lot is hidden behind the commercial block in Dock Square. You can find free parking at 30 North St., a short walk to Dock Square, and another fee lot near the bridge in Lower Village. Good luck!

WHEN TO COME One nice side effect of the Kennebunk tourist trade: This is the least seasonal resort town on the Southern Coast. Most inns and shops stay open through Christmas Prelude in early December, and many never close. Visit in the fall, when crowds thin out.

✳ To See

MUSEUMS **The Brick Store Museum and Archives** (207-985-4802; brickstoremuseum .org), 117 Main St., Kennebunk. Open year-round, Tue.–Fri. 10–4:30, Sat. 10–1. Admission $7.50 adults, $6 seniors; $3 children 6-16. This block of early-19th-century commercial buildings, including William Lord's **Brick Store** (1825), hosts a permanent exhibit documenting the region from the days of Native Americans, the arduous settlement years, and the subsequent colonial era through the period of shipbuilding glory. Changing exhibits focus on a wide variety of subjects.

♪ **Seashore Trolley Museum** (207-967-2000, trolleymuseum.org), 195 Log Cabin Rd., about 3 miles from Kennebunkport. Open daily, rain or shine, Memorial Day–Columbus Day, weekends in May and through Oct.; $10 adults, $7.50 ages 6–16, $8 seniors over 60, children under 6 free. This nonprofit museum preserves the history of the trolley era, displaying more than 250 vehicles from all over the world. The impressive collection began in 1939, when the last open-sided Biddeford–Old Orchard Beach trolley was retired. Five million passengers traveled this line in 1907. A 3-mile trolley excursion takes visitors through woods and fields. An 8,000-hour effort restored an electric locomotive that sometimes operates and is always on display; the vehicle is on the National Historic Register and is the subject of an exhibit about public transportation in the early 20th century.

Nancy English

Kennebunkport Historical Society (207-967-2751; kennebunkporthistoricalso ciety.com) has three facilities. **The Pasco Center**, 125 North St., free, is open year-round (the Benson Blacksmith Shop and Clark Shipwrights Office hours vary), **The Town House School**, 135 North St., is used for research ($10 an hour) and open year-round for abbreviated hours. Free on-site parking at both. The society also maintains **"White Columns,"** aka the Nott House, 8 Maine St. (no parking), a Greek Revival mansion with Doric columns, original wallpaper, carpets, and furnishings. Kirsten Camp, executive administrator, provides a fabulous 30-minute tour of the Nott House from 10 AM to 3 PM on the

THE CONDUCTOR DESCRIBES THE "BOWLING ALLEY" STREETCAR FROM NEW HAVEN, CONNECTICUT, DURING THE TROLLEY RIDE AT SEASHORE TROLLEY MUSEUM

EXCURSIONS

Take a scenic drive along Ocean Avenue, starting in Kennebunkport, which follows the **Kennebunk River** for a mile to Cape Arundel and the open ocean, then winds past many magnificent summer homes. Stop along **Parson's Way**, located off Ocean Ave. on the right just after the Colony Hotel, and enjoy the park benches that take advantage of the magnificent view of the mouth of the Kennebunk River and **Gooch's Beach**. Continue north and east to **Walker's Point**, former president George H. W. Bush's summer estate (it fills a private 11-acre peninsula). Built by his grandfather in 1903, its position is uncannily ideal for use as a president's summer home, moated by water on three sides yet clearly visible from pullouts along the avenue. Continue along the ocean (you don't have to worry about driving too slowly, because everyone else is, too). Follow the road to **Cape Porpoise**, site of the area's original 1600s settlement. The cove is still a base for lobster and commercial fishing boats, and the village is a good place to lunch or dine. Continue along Rt. 9 to **Clock Farm Corner** (you'll know it when you see it) and turn right onto Dyke Rd. to **Goose Rocks Beach**; park and walk. Return to Rt. 9 and cross it, continuing via Goose Rocks Rd. to the Seashore Trolley Museum and then Log Cabin Rd. to Kennebunkport.

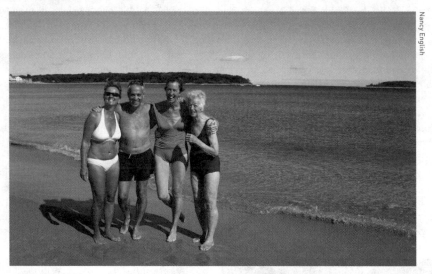

Nancy English

THESE VISITORS TO GOOSE ROCKS BEACH LAST SAW ONE ANOTHER 26 YEARS EARLIER—ALSO AT GOOSE ROCKS BEACH

hour in summer, $10; the First Families Museum, also in White Columns, is devoted to President George H. W. Bush.

HISTORIC SITES Wedding Cake House, Summer St. (Rt. 35), Kennebunk. This privately owned 1826 house is laced up and down with ornate white gingerbread. Legend has it that a local sea captain had to rush off to sea before a proper wedding cake could be baked, but he more than made up for it later.

South Congregational Church, Temple St., Kennebunkport. Just off Dock Square, built in 1824 with a Christopher Wren–style cupola and belfry; Doric columns added in 1912.

Louis T. Graves Memorial Library (207-967-2778), 18 Maine St., Kennebunkport. Built in 1813 as a bank, which went bust, it later served as a customhouse. It was subsequently donated to the library association by artist Abbott Graves, whose pictures alone make it worth a visit. You can still see the bank vault and the sign from the custom collector's office.

At the Perkins House next door, the book salesroom is full of bargains and open during the library's hours.

First Parish Unitarian Universalist Church, Main St., Kennebunk. Built between 1772 and 1773, with an Asher Benjamin–style steeple added between 1803 and 1804 along with a Paul Revere bell. In 1838 the interior was divided into two levels, with the church proper elevated to the second floor. Popular legend holds that the pulpit was carved from a single log found floating in the Caribbean Sea and towed back to Maine.

❋ To Do

BICYCLING Aquaholics (207-967-8650; aquaholicsurf.com), 166 Port Rd., Kennebunk, and **Coastal Maine Kayak** (207-967-6065; coastalmainekayak.com), 8 Western Ave., Kennebunk, rent bikes. **Kennebunkport Bicycle Co.** (207-251-3135), 34 Arundel Rd. (off North St.), Kennebunkport, rents a variety of bikes. Open seasonally. The Kennebunks lend themselves well to exploration by bike, a far more satisfying way to go in summer than by car.

Gorham Bike and Ski (207-604-1136; gorhambike.com), 65 Portland Road, Kennebunk. Bike repairs, rentals, and sales.

BOATING The *Rugosa* (207-468-4095; rugosacharters.com), at The Nonantum Resort, Ocean Ave., Kennebunkport. Several daily trips to Goat Island Lighthouse, where you can visit the tower, at high tide only. Lobstering demonstrations with traps pulled, and a cocktail cruise in the evening.

The Landing School of Boat Building and Design (207-985-7976; landingschool.edu), 286 River Rd., Arundel, offers a Sept.–June program in building and designing sailing craft. Visitors welcome if you call ahead.

CARRIAGE RIDES Rockin' Horse Stables (207-967-4288; rockinhorsemaine.com), 245 Arundel Rd., Kennebunkport. Tour Kennebunkport's historic district (25 minutes) in a spiffy white vis-à-vis carriage with burgundy-colored velvet seats and antique lanterns. Sleigh rides all winter and wagon and carriage rides at Christmas Prelude (see *Special Events*).

FISHING Stone Coast Anglers, Inc. (207-985-6005; stonecoastanglers.com), Kennebunk. Captain Paul J. Rioux specializes in chartered boat trips along the coast for up to three guests as well as guided wading trips for saltwater and game fish.

GOLF Cape Arundel Golf Club (207-967-3494; capearundelgolfclub.com), 19 River Rd., Kennebunkport, 18 holes. The local links former President George H. W. Bush frequented are open to the public daily. Three-day advance tee time reservations accepted. **Webhannet Golf Club** (207-967-2061; webhannetgolfclub.com), 26 Golf Club Dr., off Sea Rd., Kennebunk Beach, 18 holes. Open to the public but semiprivate, with limited tee times especially in July and Aug. **Dutch Elm Golf Course** (207-282-9850; dutchelmgolf.com), Arundel, 18 holes; cart and club rentals, lessons, pro shop, snack bar, putting greens. ♂ **Hillcrest Golf** (207-967-4661), Rt. 9, Kennebunk. Open daily 8 AM–dark; balls and clubs furnished.

KAYAKING Harbor Adventures (207-363-8466; harboradventures.com), Kennebunkport. Guided sea kayak tours for individuals and groups. **Coastal Maine Kayak** (207-967-6065; coastalmainekayak.com), 8 Western Ave., Kennebunk (next to Federal Jack's), offers kayak tours, rentals, a sea kayak guide course, a women's retreat, and kayak rolling sessions. The trip to Cape Porpoise Lighthouse is good for beginners and old hands.

SAILING **Schooner** *Eleanor* (207-967-8809; gwi.net/schoonersails). Two-hour sailing trips aboard a traditional, gaff-rigged, 55-foot schooner set sail from the docks at the Arundel Wharf Restaurant.

The Pineapple Ketch (207-468-7262; pineappleketch.com), 95 Ocean Ave., Kennebunkport. Daily two-hour tours and private charters at 11, 2, and sunset, mid-May–Oct., on this 38-foot ketch with red sails and a black hull. $40 per person. Book tours in-season at 207-967-4050.

SURFING **Aquaholics** (207-967-8650; aquaholicsurf.com), 166 Port Rd., Kennebunk, is the place for a surf lesson, whether you are 3 or 73. Weeklong surf camps run right into winter, and with a wetsuit on, the cold is nothing compared with the fun. Stand-up paddle clinics and tours, surf shop, and a full line of rentals.

WHALE-WATCHING AND OCEAN TOURS This is a popular departure point for whale-watching on Jefferies Ledge, about 20 miles offshore. If you have any tendency toward seasickness, be sure to choose a calm day or take anti-nausea medication. Chances are you'll see more than a dozen whales. Frequently sighted species include finbacks, minkes, rights, and humpbacks. **First Chance** (207-967-5507 or 1-800-767-2628; firstchancewhalewatch .com), 4 Western Ave. in the Lower Village (at the bridge), also offers a scenic lobster cruise.

✳ Winter Activities

CROSS-COUNTRY SKIING **Harris Farm** (207-499-2678; harrisfarm.com), 252 Buzzell Rd., Dayton. A 500-acre dairy farm with more than 20 miles of trails. Equipment rentals available, including snowshoes and ice skates. Located 1.5 miles from the Rt. 5 and Rt. 35 intersection.

SLEIGH RIDES **Rockin' Horse Stables** (207-967-4288), 245 Arundel Rd., Kennebunkport, offers 30- to 40-minute sleigh rides on a 100-acre farm.

✳ Green Space

BEACHES The Kennebunks discourage day-trippers by requiring a permit to park at major beaches. Day, week, and seasonal passes must be secured from town hall, or one of three automatic kiosks at Gooch's and Mother's Beach (credit/debit card required). You can also park in one of the town lots and walk, bike, or take a trolley to the beach.

Goose Rocks Beach, a few miles north of Kennebunkport Village on Rt. 9, is the area's most beautiful beach: a magnificent, wide, smooth stretch of silver-white sand backed by high dunes. Children here seem to mimic their less frenetic 19th-century counterparts, doing wonderfully old-fashioned things such as flying kites, playing paddleball, and making sand castles.

Kennebunk and **Gooch's Beaches** in Kennebunk are both long, wide strips of firm sand backed by Beach Ave., divided by Oak's Neck. Beyond Gooch's Beach, take Great Hill Rd. along the water to **Strawberry Island**, a great place to walk and examine tidal pools. Please don't picnic. Keep going and you come to **Mother's Beach**, small and very sandy.

Arundel Beach, near the Colony Hotel at the mouth of the Kennebunk River, offers nice rocks for climbing and good beachcombing for shell and beach-glass enthusiasts.

NATURE PRESERVES ✐ ♿ **Rachel Carson National Wildlife Refuge** (207-646-9226; fws .gov/northeast/rachelcarson). Headquarters for this almost 50-mile, 5,000-acre preserve is just south of the Kennebunkport line at 321 Port Rd. (Rt. 9) in Wells. The refuge is divided among 10 sites along Maine's Southern Coast. Pick up a leaflet guide to the mile-long, wheelchair-accessible nature trail here. Kayakers can enter the refuge traveling up the rivers, but no put-ins or takeouts allowed to avoid disturbing the wildlife. (Also see Laudholm Farm in "Ogunquit and Wells.")

Kennebunkport Conservation Trust (207-967-3465; kporttrust.org), P.O. Box 7004, Cape Porpoise, maintains a number of properties. These include the **Tyler Brook Preserve** near Goose Rocks, the 148-acre **Emmons Preserve** along the Batson River (access from unpaved Gravelly Rd. off Beachwood Rd.), the nearly 1,000-acre **Kennebunkport Town Forest**, and the **Vaughns Island Preserve**, which offers nature trails on a wooded island separated from the mainland by two tidal creeks. Cellar holes of historic houses are accessible by foot from 1½ hours before to 1½ hours after low tide. The trust also maintains historic **Goat Island Lighthouse.**

The Nature Conservancy (207-729-5181) owns 135 acres of the **Kennebunk Plains Preserve** and assists in the management of 650 state-owned acres in West Kennebunk (take Rt. 99 toward Sanford), with nearly 4 miles of shoreline on the Mousam River in Kennebunk.

WALKS **Henry Parsons Park**, Ocean Ave., is a path along the rocks leading to Spouting Rock and Blowing Cave, both sights to see at midtide. A great way to view the beautiful homes along Ocean Ave.

St. Anthony Monastery and Shrine (207-967-2011), Kennebunk. Some 44 acres of peaceful riverside fields and forests on Beach Ave., now maintained by Lithuanian Franciscans as a shrine and retreat. Visitors are welcome; gift shop. (See the Franciscan Guest House in *Other Lodging*.)

Mousam River Bridle Path is accessed at Sea Road School on Sea Road (Route 9).

HIKING **The Eastern Trail** (easterntrail.org). Download the trail guide from the website and find the parking area for this off-road and on-road trail that will someday connect with the Florida Keys; in Kennebunk, it's at the elementary school, and also off Limerick Road in Arundel.

✳ Lodging

All listings are in Kennebunkport unless otherwise noted.

INNS AND B&BS *Top dollar:* ✪ **Captain Lord Mansion** (207-967-3141 or 1-800-522-3141; captainlord.com), P.O. Box 800, at the corner of Pleasant and Green Sts. Open year-round. Sixteen rooms and suites are in the Mansion itself and four are across the lawn in the Garden House, with its own gracious common spaces. Since 1978, innkeepers Bev Davis and Rick Litchfield have worked continually to offer an exceptional experience, acquiring a loyal following in the process. All rooms have gas fireplaces, luxuriant baths and décor. Spa services are available. Rates include full breakfast, tea and many amenities; $299–599 in season (inquire about mid-week discounts), $189–449 mid-Oct.–late June.

White Barn Inn (207-967-2321; whitebarninn.com), 37 Beach Ave., P.O. Box 560C, Kennebunk 04043. Open year-round. The "barn" is an elegant dining room (see *Dining Out*) where guests have breakfast and can dine. Built in the 1860s as a farmhouse, later enlarged as the Forest Hills House, this complex lies midway between Dock Square and Kennebunk Beach. Courteous staff wear black, a sleek hotel version of the brown-robed Franciscan friars nearby (see the Franciscan Guest House in *Other Lodging*). Choose an antiques-furnished room in the farmhouse; a suite in the Carriage House with four-poster king bed, fireplace, and marble bath; a cottage suite with specially crafted furnishings, a double-sided fireplace, Jacuzzi, and steam shower. $320–860 per couple for rooms includes breakfast, tea, and use of touring bikes. The yacht *True Blue* can be rented by the day and meals arranged on board. Three waterfront cottages are also for rent. A 5.35 percent housekeeping fee is added.

Hidden Pond (207-967-9055; hiddenpond maine.com), 354 Goose Rocks Rd. Two-bedroom cottages and "bungalows" offer a private vacation home feeling in a wooded landscape. Modern and stylish, Hidden Pond caters to the wealthy, with every possible amenity, including a "WC," yoga, a spa, a shop with good cheese and wine, and a personal chef on order to make dinner in your bunga-low. A shuttle takes you to a sister property at Goose Rocks Beach, to the beach itself, and to downtown Kennebunkport and fine dining. $399–549. See *Dining Out* for Earth, the lodg-ing's restaurant.

Moderately expensive: ✍ 🦞 **Nonantum Resort** (1-888-205-1555; nonantumresort.com), 95 Ocean Ave., Kennebunkport. Open mid-April to mid-Dec. A sprawling, comfortable, nicely cared-for inn on the Kennebunk River, with boat excursions from the dock, Nonan-tum can be counted on for kids' activities, a pool, good breakfasts, well-trained staff, and comfortable rooms, many with river views. It's an easy walk to the shops and other restau-rants, too, and hosts events like Ballroom Dance Weekend and a Halloween Bash. It's owned by Mainers. $209–309, with reduced rates off-season.

Cape Arundel Inn (207-967-2125; cape arundelinn.com), 208 Ocean Ave., P.O. Box 530A. Open mid-Feb.–New Year's Eve. The most dramatic location in town, facing the open ocean with just the estate of former President George H. W. Bush interrupting the view. Rich Malconian bought this inn in 2011.

Seven rooms in the main house and six in an addition as well as a carriage house make up the accommodations; those in the addition all have picture windows and a deck facing the water, parking in back, and TV. The carriage house water-view suite (up a flight of stairs) has a deck and sitting area. Interesting art hangs in the living room, some of it by Jack Nahil, the inn's previous owner. The dining room, which is open to the public for dinner (see *Dining Out*), is deservedly well loved. $320–425 in-season, from $135 off-season, includes a continental breakfast.

🐾 ✍ **The Captain Jefferds Inn** (207-967-2311 or 1-800-839-6844; captainjefferdsinn .com), 5 Pearl St., Box 691. Erik and Sarah Lindblom are your hosts at this handsome Federal–era mansion with 16 rooms; nine have a gas fireplace, and all have air-conditioning, feather beds, and down comforters. Baxter, in the carriage house, is decorated in a "Maine camp" style—except for the two-person whirl-pool with a round stone surround. First-floor Chatham has a four-poster and two wingback chairs by the fireplace. The spacious common rooms include a sunporch where tea and cof-fee are always available. $149–379, depending on season.

✍ **Maine Stay Inn and Cottages** (207-967-2117 or 1-800-950-2117; mainestayinn.com), 34 Maine St., Box 1800A. Open year-round. The inn offers six guest rooms in the main house and 11 suites in five cottages nestled in nicely landscaped grounds. The house was built in 1860 by Melville Walker and given to his wife as a Christmas present five years later. The cottages are simple on the outside but hand-somely outfitted inside with efficiency kitch-ens, deep whirlpool tubs, and some with gas fireplaces. A breakfast, perhaps baked eggs with cheddar and Parmesan, and afternoon tea are offered by friendly owners Judi and Walter Hauer, who bought the inn in 2008. $229–379 in-season, $129–279 off-season.

Tides Beach Club (207-967-3757; tides beachclubmaine.com), 254 Kings Hwy., Goose Rocks Beach. Open late May–Oct. Twenty-one renovated rooms, some over-looking Goose Rocks Beach, are painted in pastels and outfitted with comfortable beds and high-tech amenities. Fans of the previ-ous owners' Tides-Inn-By-the-Sea will be in for a shock because the Victoriana has van-ished, traded in for cool colors and modern

THE SUNROOM AT THE CAPTAIN JEFFERDS INN, WHERE A CUP OF COFFEE OR TEA IS ALWAYS AVAILABLE

Nancy English

graphic prints. Fans of contemporary style will be thrilled. The beach across the narrow road remains its eternal self, a wide sweep of white sand banded by a ribbon of dunes. Rates $399–829 in-season.

   Seaside Inn (207-967-4461; kennebunkbeach.com), 80 Beach Ave., Kennebunk 04043. Open year-round. A modern 22-room inn set on a quiet stretch of one of Maine's best public beaches, it is the only one in the area directly on the ocean. This property has been in the Gooch-Severance family for nine generations, beginning in the 1640s when King Charles II conveyed the land to John Gooch, who ferried folks across the river. All of that seems to make this the oldest inn in the country—and the history is detailed on the website. The cheery breakfast room is an 1850 former boathouse for the 19th-century inn that stood here until the 1950s. Inn rooms feature two queen beds, air-conditioning, cable TV, phone, mini fridge, and balcony or patio. Three-day minimum in oceanfront rooms in high season. $105–259 per night, including extended continental breakfast and access to a local fitness center.

   Bufflehead Cove Inn (207-967-3879; buffleheadcove.com), Box 499, off Rt. 35. Open May–Nov. This hidden gem, sequestered on 6 acres at the end of a dirt road and overlooking an 8-foot-deep tidal cove, sits a mile from the village of Kennebunkport. Harriet Gott, a native of nearby Cape Porpoise, her husband Jim, and their son Erin offer four good-looking guest rooms, a suite, and a separate deluxe cottage. River View cottage lies off by itself with a deck, kitchen, wood-burning fireplace, and whirlpool tub. The inn's living room has a hearth and deep window seats. $155–395 includes a full breakfast on the white porch if the weather is fine, and after-noon wine and cheese.

   Kennebunkport Inn (207-967-2621 or 1-800-248-2621; kennebunkportinn.com), 1 Dock Square, P.O. Box 111. Open year-round. Owners Debbie Lennon and Tom Nill have redecorated the 33 rooms; number 303 is a "mansion room" with canopy four-poster, gas fireplace, and bathtub. The inn has four sections—the main house (originally an 1890s mansion), a 1980s Federal–style addition, a 1930s river house with smaller rooms. Guests can dine in **One Dock Prime** year-round. The cocktail lounge with a huge old bar offers

evening live music. High-season rates $259–399 per room, less off-season.

   The Captain Fairfield Inn (207-967-4454 or 1-800-322-1928; captainfairfield.com), P.O. Box 3089, corner of Pleasant and Green Sts. Open year-round. Owners Rob and Leigh Blood bought the inn in 2004, adding a wine list and small plates to serve guests afternoon or evening. Homemade cookies, included, are served in the afternoon, and the three-course breakfast features local ingredients. The lawn with two "fire tables" stretches back across the width of the block. Notable among the nine handsome rooms, the Library features a private porch and garden and double whirl-pool; Sweet Liberty has a tiled rainfall shower; and the Breakwater Room is contemporary. $259–409 in high season, $159–300 in low.

   Lower priced: **The Edgewater Inn** (207-967-3315; edgewaterinnmaine .com), 126 Ocean Ave., P.O. Box 2578. Open Apr.–Dec. A friendly little hotel with a casual atmosphere, owned and run by Peter Ciriello and Caroline Neish, The Edgewater Inn has 12 small but pleasant rooms and Coveside Cottage for rent; some also have a refrigerator and a fireplace. Portland Head, with oak fur-niture, shares a deck on the inlet on the inn's west side, where herons and other waterbirds find their own breakfast. In-season $259–309 for a double, cottage higher, includes a fantas-tic full breakfast and afternoon refreshments.

   Chetwynd House Inn (207-967-2235, chetwyndhouse.com), 4 Chestnut St., P.O. Box 130. Open year-round. In 1972 Susan Chet-wynd opened Chetwynd, Kennebunkport's first B&B. Now owned by Robert Knowles, her son, it remains a gracious 1840s home near Dock Square. The four antiques-furnished guest rooms have private bath, TV, refriger-ator, and air-conditioning; a top-floor junior suite has skylights and a river view. Generous breakfasts—with eggs cooked to order and a quarter melon with peaches, blueberries, and bananas or other fruit—are served family-style at the dining room table. $269–299 in-season.

   Harbor Inn (207-967-2074; harborinn kennebunkport.com), 90 Ocean Ave., P.O. Box 538A. Open year-round. Kathy and Barry Jones, longtime area residents, fill this fine old house with flowers and their warm friend-liness. The five rooms and two-room suite (all with private bath) feature a mix of family antiques, paintings, and prints, and the long front porch is lined with wicker. It's a short walk to the ocean, a longer but pleasant walk to Dock Square. $155–225 for rooms in-season, $125 off-season. Woodbine Cottage in-season is $225 a night or $1,500 weekly.

The Waldo Emerson Inn (207-985-4250 or 1-877-521-8776; waldoemersoninn.com), 108 Summer St. (Rt. 35), Kennebunk 04043. This special house was built in 1784 by a shipbuilder who inherited the land and original 1753 cottage (the present kitchen) from Waldo Emerson, the great-uncle of the famous poet and essayist. The building was later a stop on the Underground Railroad. The inn has four cozy guest rooms with private bath and air-conditioning, each with a wood-burning fireplace. A quilt store is on the property, and the Wedding Cake House is next door. $165–185 high season per couple includes a full gourmet breakfast and afternoon tea in one of the two handsome 18th-century parlors (one with a large-screen TV). Complimentary beach parking and bikes.

OTHER LODGING **The Franciscan Guest House** (207-967-4865; franciscanguesthouse .com), 26 Beach Ave., Kennebunk 04043. Open mid-Mar.–mid-Dec. With private bath, air-conditioning, and television, the 65 rooms here have the feeling of Maine the way it used to be. This 1908 estate on the Kennebunk River was converted to a guest house in the 1960s; the friars live in the Tudor great house. The 44-acre garden is open to the public year-round during daylight hours (no pets), and walking the riverside trails might take half an hour, past formal gardens and the Stations of the Cross, Our Lady of Lourdes, and other shrines and fountains. Maps of the trees and shrubs planted under Frederick Law Olmsted's design, and of the shrines, are available. $69–199; less off-season, with breakfast often made by the Lithuanian cook—a cross between a European and an American breakfast that might include homemade farmer's cheese, raisin bread, carrot bread, and potato bread. A moderately priced buffet dinner is served most nights in the height of summer.

🍴 🐾 ✒ ⚕ **Yachtsman Lodge and Marina** (207-967-2511; yachtsmanlodge.com), Ocean Ave., P.O. Box 560C. Open May–early Dec. This 30-room inn is great for the cruising crowd, who can sail right up the Kennebunk River to the lodge and take advantage of its 59-slip marina. The Yachtsman features rooms decorated to resemble the inside of a yacht, with private riverside patios. $179–399 includes continental breakfast in the marble-tiled breakfast room or under the pergola. Children and pets are OK, and wheelchair access is easy. Bicycles and canoes are available for guests.

✳ Where to Eat

DINING OUT ✪ **Ocean** (207-967-2125; capearundelinn.com), Ocean Ave., Kennebunkport. Open daily mid-Feb.–Dec. for dinner, closed Mon. off-season. This dining room, matching its great location facing the ocean, presents skilled cooking and fine service. Chef Pierre Gignac once ran his own restaurant, 98 Province, in Ogunquit, which was excellent, and continues his fine work in Ocean with an emphasis on classic French cuisine. Duck Magret a l'orange cannot, perhaps, be improved on; monkfish gigot comes with tomato beignets. $31–37.

✪ ⚕ **Pier 77** (207-967-8500; pier77 restaurant.com), Pier Rd., Cape Porpoise. Open daily for lunch and dinner June–Sept.; Wed.–Sun., St. Patrick's Day–May and Columbus Day–Dec.; The Ramp is open 11:30–9 Wed.–Sun. Well-made dinners upstairs and lunches downstairs in the **Ramp**, a bar filled with sports memorabilia, deserve the big following they've

Nancy English

THE RAMP AT PIER 77

earned. Duck cassoulet, chicken and dumplings, and seafood stew were on a fall menu, and pulled pork sandwiches or fried clams—perhaps dug by the man you spotted on the flats as you came inside—might be for lunch. Entrées $17–30.

White Barn Inn (207-967-2321; whitebarninn.com), 37 Beach Ave., Kennebunkport. Open for dinner year-round Mon.–Sat. (except Jan.), daily in summer. Reservations required with credit card; $25 per-person fee charged if canceled fewer than 24 hours in advance. This award-winning restaurant is set in two restored 19th-century barns with a three-story glassed rear wall, exposed beams, and extravagant seasonal floral displays. Original art, hotel silver, and fine linens are accessories to extraordinary meals. The four-course prix fixe menu changes frequently, but count on lobster among the entrées and foie gras to start. $109 prix fixe plus tax, beverage, and gratuity. The bistro menu offers à la carte dishes.

On the Marsh Bistro (207-967-2299; onthemarsh.com), Rt. 9, Kennebunk Lower Village. Open daily for dinner May–Oct.; closed Mon. and Tue. off-season. Continental dining with style overlooking a lovely salt marsh. Executive chef Jeff Savage takes pride in his high-quality ingredients. Grilled bison New York strip sirloin with chive popovers and seared scallops with lobster risotto were on a fall menu, when the bar menu listed house creton (a French Canadian pork spread) and a meatball sub. The wines are wonderful, with hundreds to choose from. Entrées $21–37.

Tides Beach Club (207-967-3757; tidesbeachclubmaine.com), Goose Rocks Beach, 6 miles northeast of Dock Square. Open late May–Oct. 1 for lunch. Under new ownership and with completely new decor, Tides Beach Club serves signature cocktails alongside its raw oysters; you might also try steamed mussels with tomato, citrus, and saffron. Of course you can also get a lobster, or a steak, or a steak with lobster. Entrées $19–42.

Salt & Honey (207-204-0195; thesaltandhoney.com), 24 Ocean Ave., Kennebunkport. Jackson Yordeon started serving lobster omelets, huevos rancheros, and braised short rib hash for breakfast, a steak sandwich for lunch, and IPA-beer-battered chicken apps and fish-and-chips for dinner in 2015. The large portions are popular and the good drinks too. Entrées $15–24.

Toroso (207-204-0454; torosorestaurant.com), 149 Port Road, Kennebunk. Owned by Shannon Bard, whose wonderful Zapoteca has been a vibrant dinner spot in Portland for years, Toroso serves tapas. These small plates can be inventive and classic; the braised octopus, lamb meatballs, and oxtail-stuffed piquillo peppers are a small sample of the long menu. Larger plates are also served, $24–29.

& **Bandaloop** (207-967-4994; bandaloop.biz), 2 Dock Square. Open daily for dinner in summer, less often in winter. Entrées and sauces can be paired as you like, but the menu always offers several entrées and specials. Seared scallops with pistachio-cilantro pesto might appeal more than the fantastic mac-and-cheese (half portion is still large); a rack of lamb with buttermilk sweet potato mash hit the spot one fall. Desserts such as dark chocolate torte or fruit crisp deserve to be enjoyed. Entrées $17–31.

Earth (207-967-6550; earthathiddenpond.com), 354 Goose Rocks Rd. Open to the public for dinner only. Local ingredients, of course. Herb-infused cocktails are served in this space mixing rustic earthiness and high style. Outdoor dining in good weather, and outdoor bonfires to keep you there after sunset. Duck breast with lily buds, swordfish with bacon and corn, a burger, and snacks of house pickle "relishes" appeared on one menu. Entrées $18–38.

50 Local (207-985-0850; localkennebunk.com), 50 Main St., Kennebunk. For anyone hungry for something grown nearby, this is the place—anyone else who simply likes to dine well will be equally satisfied. Try mussels, Taunton Bay oysters, and lobster spring rolls to start; steak frites, fish stew, and vegan noodle bowl are some entrée possibilities. Entrées $14–29.

& **Academe at the Kennebunk Inn** (207-985-3351; thekennebunkinn.com), 45 Main St., Kennebunk. Open Wed.–Sat. for dinner; daily for the more informal tavern menu, lunch on weekdays. Chef-owners Brian O'Hea and Shanna Horner O'Hea make high-quality meals at a moderate price. Braised beef short rib with garlic and Parmesan tater tots, or the famous lobster potpie were on a fall menu. Entrées $11–35.

& **Stripers Waterside Restaurant** (207-967-3625; stripersrestaurant.com), 131–133

LOBSTER

♦ ✔ ♿ **Nunan's Lobster Hut** (207-967-4362), Rt. 9, Cape Porpoise. Open for dinner weekends in May and then daily June–mid-Oct. A long telescope of a building full of old benches, with buoys hanging from the rafters, Nunan's has been feeding lobster lovers since 1953, when Bertha Nunan started working here. Her two sons and their wives are in charge, with decades of experience to guide them. The place can fill up by 5:15; people outside get a number and wait for a table. A 1½-pound lobster comes with melted butter, potato chips, a roll, and pickles. Grilled cheese and a hamburger supply other tastes, and pie, brownies, and cheesecake are on the dessert list. Beer and wine. No credit cards.

✔ **Mabel's Lobster Claw** (207-967-2562), Ocean Ave., Kennebunkport. Open Apr.–early Nov., daily for lunch and dinner. An informal favorite with locals, including former President George H. W. Bush. Reservations recommended for dinner. Specialties include stuffed lobster Savannah, lobster stew, and shore dinner (clam chowder, lobster, and steamed clams). The lunch special is a lobster roll in a buttery, grilled hot-dog roll, and the mussels marinara is great anytime. Entrées $13–30.

✔ ♿ **The Clam Shack** (207-967-3321 or 207-967-2560), Kennebunkport (at the bridge). Clams, lobsters, and fresh fish. A year-round seafood market and Mother's Day–Columbus Day takeout stand that's worth the wait. Other seafood markets include **Cape Porpoise Lobster Co.** (207-967-4268) in Cape Porpoise, where the locals get their fish and steamed lobster to go, and **Port Lobster** (207-967-2081), 122 Ocean Ave., Kennebunkport, which offers live or cooked lobsters packed to travel or ship, and lobster, shrimp, and crab rolls to go (several obvious waterside picnic spots are within walking distance). Other local businesses get their picked lobster here; it won't be fresher anywhere else.

Nancy English

THE CLAM SHACK

Ocean Ave., Kennebunkport. Open in-season daily for lunch and dinner. This upscale seafood place has a long, thin aquarium harboring little blue fish that match pale blue slipcovered chairs. But the real view is out the window where the river flows by. Pork porterhouse with onion jam and yellowfin tuna with grilled squash and poached lobster were on one menu. Entrées $20–34.

One Dock Prime (1-800-248-2621; kennebunkportinn.com), One Dock Square, Kennebunkport. Steaks are a specialty, but you will likely also find swordfish, pork chops, and sea scallops. Entrées $21–38.

EATING OUT **Old Vines** (207-967-2310; oldvineswinebar.com), 173 Port Rd., Kennebunk. Open Wed.–Mon. from 5. A popular wine bar that opened in 2009, Old Vines serves snacks and small plates with its glasses of wine from featured vineyards. More than 20 are sold by the glass; try the Noemus Rioja from Spain or Château Bousquette, a sparkling rosé from France. Small plates of spiced almonds, cheeses, and cured meats might be the start of a delicious meal centered on a soppressata panini or quiche of the day. $6–21.

🍷 🍴 **The Wayfarer** (207-967-8961; wayfarercapeporpoise.com), 1 Pier Rd., Cape Porpoise. Open Tue.–Sat. for breakfast, lunch until 2; Sun. breakfast noon. Closed Mon. New England cuisine with a twist—mac and cheese, arugula salad, lobster fettuccine, and meat loaf vie for attention. BYOB.

🍷 🍴 **Alisson's** (207-967-4841; alissons .com), 5 Dock Square, Kennebunkport. Open at 11 for lunch and 5 for dinner. Casual dining in this busy, family-run spot features standards, as well as one of the Port's best lobster rolls and clam chowder. Count on reliably good casual food. Entrées $8–22.

🍷 🍴 ♿ **Federal Jack's Restaurant & Brewpub** (207-967-4322; federaljacks.com), 8 Western Ave., Kennebunk Lower Village. Open from 11:30 for lunch and dinner, offering a variety of handcrafted ales. This is the original Shipyard Ale brewery with parking right in the thick of things. The spacious and sunny restaurant is upstairs, with a seasonal terrace dining on the river. Try the Blue Fin stout with Captain Jack's Feast—chowder, lobster, and mussels. Live acoustic music on weekends. The pub fare is the best way to go.

Cape Porpoise Kitchen (207-967-1150; capeporpoisekitchen.com), 1 Mills Rd., Cape Porpoise. Open year-round. Take-out and catering are the focus, and this is the right place to go for a fabulous BLT or many other delicious sandwiches, salads, and baked goods for a picnic on the beach. Wine, beer, cheese, and gifts, with a small seating area if the weather is bad. No restroom.

Spirit of Massachusetts Restaurant (spiritofmassachusettsrestaurant.com), 4 Western Avenue, Kennebunk. Step aboard for dinner on this 125-foot schooner—it won't set sail, but while it's tied up, you can enjoy a cocktail and a lobster spring roll or a classic lobster roll. Steamers and steamed lobster are also served.

ICE CREAM **Rococo Artisan Ice Cream** (207-251-6866; rococoicecream.com), 6 Spring St., Kennebunkport. Open May–Oct. Based on Argentinian ideas about ice cream and dairy, Rococo Ice Cream puts the flavors up front and never stops inventing them. Blue Fin Stout, Blueberry Chipotle, and Goat Cheese with Honey Whiskey and Fig give you an idea—but the proof is in the eating.

✳ Entertainment

Vinegar Hill Music Theatre (207-985-5552; vinegarhillmusictheatre.com), 53 Old Post Road, Arundel. Open June to October. Famous performers take the stage, along with excellent local musicians.

🍴 **Hackmatack Playhouse** (207-698-1807; hackmatack.org), 538 Rt. 9, Beaver Dam, Berwick. Local actors, rave reviews.

🍴 **River Tree Center for the Arts** (207-967-9120; rivertreearts.org), 35 Western Ave., Kennebunk. Encompassing the Chappell School of Music and the Irvine Gallery and School of Art, this multifaceted organization stages local concerts, productions, and happenings, as well as workshops in the visual and performing arts for all ages.

Also see **Federal Jack's** under *Eating Out* and *Entertainment* in "Ogunquit and Wells."

✳ Selective Shopping

ANTIQUES SHOPS The Kennebunks are known as an antiques center, with half a dozen shops, most on Rt. 1, representing a number of dealers. One on Rt. 9 that's sure to offer endless interest is **Antiques on Nine** (207-967-0626), 81 Western Ave., Kennebunk, overflowing with things strange and wonderful.

ART GALLERIES You'll find some 50 galleries, many seasonal; **Mast Cove Galleries** (207-967-3453) on Maine St., Kennebunkport, is touted as the largest gallery in Maine, with more than 100 artists represented. Pick up a free copy of the annual *Guide to Fine Art, Studios, and Galleries*, published by the Art Guild of the Kennebunks (207-324-4912) and available at the chamber of commerce and most galleries.

FARMS ✐ **Harris Farm** (207-499-2678; harrisfarm.com), Buzzell Rd., Dayton. July–Oct. Fresh milk, eggs, produce, and maple syrup are sold. Pick-your-own pumpkins on the last Sunday in Sept. and the first two Sundays in Oct., with hayrides offered to the pumpkin patch. A half-hour ride through beautiful, wooded forest and farms, this farm is 1 mile down Buzzell Rd. from Rt. 35.

Blackrock Farm (207-967-5783; black rockfarm.net), 293 Goose Rocks Rd., Kennebunkport. A beautifully planted perennial garden and nursery with unusual plants and trees, as well as a pick-your-own raspberry patch. Bring a picnic and feast your eyes on the stone walls, grape arbor, and sculpture.

SPAS **The Breakwater Inn & Spa** (207-967-5333; thebreakwaterinn.com), 127 Ocean Ave., P.O. Box 560C, Kennebunkport. Full-service spa with massage, facials, body wraps, steam room, and fitness center. All facilities are open to the public.

Cottage Breeze Day Spa & Boutique (207-967-2259; cottagebreeze.com), 31 Western Ave., Kennebunk. Full-service spa. With any luck, Judy will be your massage therapist, and what fine therapy it will be. Utterly comfortable treatment rooms and an array of body products.

SPECIAL SHOPS **Farm + Table** (207-604-8029; farmtablekennebunkport.com), 8 Langsford Road. A quick right turn at Cape Porpoise Kitchen brings you to a gorgeous red barn, elegantly outfitted with the home goods that furnish the serene refuge you plan on living in very soon.

KBC Coffee & Drygoods (207-967-1261; federaljacks.com), 8 Western Ave., Kennebunkport. Hidden beneath Federal Jack's, this is a source of Kennebunk Brewing Company ales (bottled or in a returnable "Growler") and brew gear as well as souvenir clothing and gifts; also good for cappuccino and homemade fudge.

Hearth and Soul (207-985-7466; hearth andsoulme.com), 35 Main St., Kennebunk. Open Tue.–Sat. "Primarily Primitives" is the motto at this quirky, charming place. Braided rugs, furniture, a folk art wall mural, and bricks of milk paint.

Daytrip Society (207-967-4440; daytrip society.com), 4 Dock Square, Kennebunkport. Essentials and fripperies in good taste, from Pendleton blankets and good Thermoses to old books and new cards. Around the corner, ✐ **Daytrip Jr.** (207-967-8345; daytripjr.com), 9 Ocean Ave., sells fine toys and games, some perfect for a long drive.

✳ Special Events

Many of the events below are listed with the Kennebunk/Kennebunkport Chamber of Commerce (207-967-0857 or 1-800-982-4421; visitthekennebunks.com), P.O. Box 740, Kennebunkport 04043.

February: **Winterfest** with hay- and sleigh rides in Kennebunk. Weekend **Paint the Town Red, #LoveKPT** events (207-967-0857).

May: **May Day Festival** on Main Street, Kennebunk.

Summer: **Farmers' Market** (kennebunk farmersmarket.org) during the growing season.

June: **The Kennebunkport Festival**, with food, wine, and works of art. LAUNCH Maritime Festival, Kennebunks.

July: Old-fashioned **July 4** picnic, fireworks, and band concert.

August: **Riverfest** (first Saturday).

October: **Presidential Road Race** (presidentialroadrace.com). **Harvest-Fest**— parades, music, and good food.

November: **Holiday Auction. Pyjama Shopping Day**.

December: **Christmas Prelude** (first full and second weekends)—Dock Square is decked out for Yuletide and there are champagne receptions, church suppers, concerts, carols, holiday fairs, and house tours.

OLD ORCHARD BEACH, SACO, AND BIDDEFORD

Old Orchard's name stems from an apple orchard, one of the first in Maine, planted in 1657 by pioneer settler Thomas Rogers. It was also one of the first Maine towns to prosper by catering to tourists.

In 1837 a canny local farmer, Ebenezer C. Staples, recognized the region's summer playground potential. Initially taking in boarders on his farm for $1.50 a week, he later opened the first hotel, the still-operating Old Orchard Beach Inn. Staples's instincts proved right: The new railroads soon brought a wave of tourists from both the United States and Canada to frolic on Old Orchard's superb 7-mile-long white-sand beach. Thanks to the Grand Trunk Railroad, Old Orchard became the closest ocean beach resort to Montreal. The area, which has a large Franco-American population, is still a popular destination for French Canadian visitors, especially when the exchange rate is in their favor.

When the first pier at Old Orchard Beach was built in 1898, it stood 20 feet above and 1,800 feet out over the water and was constructed entirely of steel. The pavilions housed animals, a casino, and a restaurant. In the decades that followed, the original pier was rebuilt many times after being damaged by fire and storms, until a wider and shorter wooden pier was built in 1980.

THE PIER AT OLD ORCHARD BEACH

Nancy English

An amusement area appeared in 1902 and grew after World War I. The 1920s brought big-name bands such as those led by Guy Lombardo and Duke Ellington to the Pier Casino, and thousands danced under a revolving crystal ball.

Fire, hard economic times, and the decline of the railroad and steamboat industries all took their toll on Old Orchard Beach over the years, but then a major revitalization plan widened sidewalks, added benches and streetlights, and passed and enforced ordinances that prevent "cruising." For families, it can't be beat, with the beach, amusement park rides, mini golf just down the road, and reasonable lodging rates.

The area is also well known for the camp meetings that began in the mid-1800s, first by Methodists, then by Baptists and the Salvation Army. These meetings continue throughout the summer in the Ocean Park community today.

Biddeford and Saco, separated by the Saco River, are often called "the twin cities."

Although it also includes the stately old seaside resort village of Biddeford Pool, the city of Biddeford is essentially a classic mill town with a strong French Canadian heritage and mammoth 19th-century brick textile mills that have largely stood idle since the 1950s. Those buildings along the Saco River, long victims of desuetude, have been revitalized—at first slowly, but rapidly in recent years—by housing, businesses, and restaurants. Run of the Mill, a brew pub with good food and a terrific terrace, was one of the first on the Saco side; in Biddeford, Lincoln Mill Hotel, led by Tim Harrington, who owns much of the Kennebunks' upscale lodgings, is scheduled to open in 2017. North Dam Mill now holds nearly 120 businesses that include Portland Pie and an auction house as well as light manufacturing such as HyperLite Moutain Gear and a clothier named Suger. Saco Island Mills feature a year-round farmers'/artisans' market, as well as public services like lawyers and social security administration. Saco is home to Maine's first green train station, where Amtrak stops five times daily on its way to and from Boston year-round.

GUIDANCE **Old Orchard Beach Chamber of Commerce** (207-934-2500; to get a free vacation planner by mail, 1-800-365-9386; oldorchardbeachmaine.com), P.O. Box 600 (1st St.), Old Orchard Beach 04064, maintains a year-round walk-in information center (open 8:30–4:30 weekdays, also Sat. and Sun., June–Aug.) and offers help with reservations.

Biddeford-Saco Chamber of Commerce + Industry (207-282-1567; biddefordsaco chamber.org), 28 Water St., Suite 1, Biddeford 04005, stocks many local brochures at its welcome center. Hours are 8–4:30 weekdays year-round and 8–noon on weekends June 15–Sept. 15; helpful, friendly staff.

GETTING THERE *By air:* **Portland International Jetport** is 13 miles north, and rental cars are available at the airport. You can also fly your own plane into **Sanford Airport**.

By hired car: **Maine Limousine Service** (207-883-0222 or 1-800-646-0068; mainelimo .com), P.O. Box 1478, Scarborough 04070, can also pick you up and bring you to the region.

By car: Exits 32, 36, and 42 off the Maine Turnpike (I-95) take you easily to Rt. 9 and the center of Old Orchard Beach and Main St. in Biddeford and Saco. You can also find the towns from Rt. 1.

By train: **The Downeaster** (1-800-USA-RAIL; amtrak.com), Amtrak's train service between Boston and Freeport, makes five stops a day year-round at Saco and seasonally, May–Oct., at Old Orchard Beach.

GETTING AROUND From many accommodations in Old Orchard Beach, you are close enough to walk to the pier, the town's center of activity. **Shuttle Bus**, the local transportation service, connects the downtowns of Biddeford, Saco, Portland, and Old Orchard Beach. Call 207-282-5408 or go to shuttlebus-zoom.com for schedules.

Saco Museum (207-283-3861; sacomuseum.org), 371 Main St., Saco. Open year-round Tue., Wed., Thu. noon–4; Fri. noon–8; Sat. 10–4; Sun. noon–4 June–Dec. 15. $5 adults, $3 seniors, $2 students, under 6 free (free to all 4–8 Fri.). Larger than it looks from the outside and very well maintained and organized. An exhibit about art and industry fills the first floor, and one room presenting a factory girl bedchamber is furnished with the artifacts of a millworker—including a racy novel. A dress-up trunk allows visitors to try on mid-1800s fashion. Original paintings include 13 portraits by deaf painter John Brewster Jr.—whose subjects seem tenacious and inured to suffering—as well as furniture, tools, and natural history specimens. Lectures and special exhibits. The institute's **Dyer Library** next door has an outstanding Maine history collection.

PARKING There are a number of privately owned lots in the center of Old Orchard Beach and one municipal lot. Most charge $5–15 for any length of time—10 minutes or all day. There are meters on the street if you don't mind circling a few times to catch an available one, but at 15 minutes for a quarter, you're better off in lots if you plan to stay long.

WHEN TO COME Biddeford is especially worth visiting during La Kermesse, the colorful four-day Franco-American festival in late June. This festival—which features a colorful parade (some marching bands wear snowshoes), concerts, dances, fireworks, and public suppers with traditional stick-to-the-ribs French Canadian food—is one of the largest ethnic events in New England. Old Orchard Beach quiets way down after Columbus Day, but there are still many places to stay and four year round restaurants for off-season visitors. The pier closes after Columbus Day weekend.

✳ Villages

Ocean Park is a historic community founded in 1881 by Free Will Baptists and well known for its outstanding religious, educational, and cultural programs. The Ocean Park Association (207-934-9068; oceanpark.org) sponsors lectures, concerts, movies, and other events throughout the summer in the cluster of old buildings known as Temple Square. Within the community you'll also find a recreation hall, shuffleboard and tennis courts, and an old-fashioned ice cream parlor. The entire community is a state game preserve, and you can find great walking trails through cathedral pines.

Pine Point. This quiet and less crowded end of the beach offers a selection of gift shops, restaurants, and lobster pounds.

Camp Ellis. At the end of a peninsula where the Saco River blends with the ocean. Residents fight a constant battle with beach erosion, and some of the homes are ever closer to the shore. Fishing trips, whale-watching, a long breakwater great for walking, interesting shops, and a couple of restaurants.

Biddeford Pool is a small yachting port

Courtesy of Saco Museum

LANDSCAPE BY WILLIAM STOODLEY GOOKIN, SACO MUSEUM

with lots of low-key charm where well-to-do families have been summering in the same big old shingled houses for generations. You'll find a few shops, a lobster pound, and a small restaurant, but not much else. Although politically part of blue-collar Biddeford, "the pool" is socially closer to fashionable nearby Kennebunkport.

✳ To Do

APPLE PICKING ⌀ **Snell Family Farm** (207-929-6166; snellfamilyfarm.com), 1000 River Rd. (Rt. 112), Buxton. Pick-your-own apples in Sept. and Oct., when the farm stand moves from its summer spot across the street over toward the farmhouse, and the greenhouse is jammed with pumpkins ready for carving. In summer and fall the farm stand is stuffed with the best produce imaginable.

BREWERIES **Run of the Mill** (see *Eating Out*) is the oldest local brewery, and offers free brewery tours by appointment. **Dirigo Brewing Company** (207-604-8663; dirigobrewing company.com), 28 Pearl St., Biddeford, opened in the summer of 2016, and started with Schöps, a Polish chocolate wheat beer, and a German Pale Ale. **Barreled Souls** (207-602-6439; barreledsouls.com), 743 Portland Road (Route 1), Saco, ferments its beer in oak barrels—the healthy yeast rises to the top and is captured and reused for the next batch. **Banded Horn Brewing Company** (207-602-1561; bandedhorn.com), 32 Main St., Biddeford, in the Pepperell Mill, has a tasting room and a stranglehold on cool, with Nordri, a red lager with bitters, or the Jolly Woodsman Coffee Stout, among its ardent offerings.

DISTILLERIES **Round Turn Distilling** (207-370-9446; roundturndistilling.com), 32 Main St., Biddeford. The tasting room in the middle of town offers an introduction to Bimini Gin, and the option to stay for a cocktail tailored to its coriander and hops top notes.

FOR FAMILIES The Rt. 1 strip in Saco and nearby Old Orchard Beach makes up Maine's biggest concentration of "family attractions." Kids go wild. Parents fear they may go broke.
⌀ **Funtown/Splashtown USA** (207-284-5139; funtownsplashtownusa.com), Rt. 1, Saco. Open daily (depending on the weather) mid-June–Labor Day, weekends in spring and fall. Water activities and a large amusement park. In addition to the 100-foot wooden roller coaster Excalibur, the park has bumper cars, New England's largest log flume, plenty of carnival rides, a hydrofighter, kiddie rides, and antique cars. Purchase discount tickets at the Biddeford-Saco Chamber Welcome Center.
⌀ **Aquaboggan Water Park** (207-282-3112; aquaboggan.com), Rt. 1, Saco. Open mid-June–Labor Day. Several water slides, including a high-thrills slide with a choice of mats or tubes, Aquasaucer, swimming pool, bumper boats, mini golf, arcade, shuffleboard, toddler area, and wave pool.
⌀ **Monkey Trunks** (603-452-8812; monkeytrunks.com), 1 Cascade Rd., Saco. A high-ropes-and-ziplines park that opened in the summer of 2011, Monkey Trunks was an immediate hit. A giant swing, a 50-foot leap, and more for $39–49, depending on height.
⌀ **Pirate's Cove Adventure Golf** (207-934-5086; piratescove.net), 70 1st St., Old Orchard Beach. Two 18-hole up-and-down mini golf courses, waterfalls, ponds.
⌀ **Palace Playland** (207-934-2001; palaceplayland.com), 1 Old Orchard St., Old Orchard Beach. Open daily June–Labor Day; arcade open through Columbus Day on weekends. For more than 60 years fun seekers have been wheeled, lifted, shaken, spun, and bumped in Palace Playland rides. There's a carousel (though it no longer contains the original 1906 horses), a Ferris wheel, a 60-foot-high (Maine's largest) water slide, and a roller coaster. You can pay by the ride or buy an all-day pass.

EXCURSIONS

From Saco there's a loop that heads up Rt. 112, past the Way-Way General Store. On the right a few miles out is the Saco Heath Preserve, worth a stop to explore. From there, continue on Rt. 112 until it intersects with Rt. 202. Turn left and stay on 202 until you see the intersection with Rt. 5. Turn left again and follow Rt. 5 along the river, back to the center of Saco.

The Yard (207-590-6745; theyardatthemill.com), 40 Main St., Biddeford. It calls itself a "beautiful park indoors"—and this year-round indoor playground for kids 9 and under is a resource on rainy, snowy, sleety days in Maine.

GOLF **Dunegrass** (207-934-4513; dunegrass.com), 200 Wild Dunes Way, Old Orchard Beach, 18 holes. **Biddeford-Saco Country Club** (207-282-5883), 101 Old Orchard Rd., Saco, 18 holes. **Deep Brook Golf Course** (207-282-3500; deepbrookgolfcourse.com), 36 New County Rd. (Rt. 5), Saco, nine holes. **Cascade Golf Center** (207-282-3524), 955 Portland Rd., Saco, driving range.

MUSEUMS **Saco Museum** (207-283-3861; sacomuseum.org), 371 Main St., Saco. Open year-round Tue., Wed., Thu. noon–4; Fri. noon–8; Sat. 10–4; Sun. noon–4 June–Dec. 15. $5 adults, $3 seniors, $2 students, under 6 free (free to all 4–8 Fri.). Larger than it looks from the outside, and very well maintained and organized. An exhibit about art and industry fills the first floor, and one room presenting a Factory Girl Bedchamber is furnished with the artifacts of a millworker—including a racy novel. A dress-up trunk allows visitors to try on mid-1800s fashion. Original paintings include 13 portraits by deaf painter John Brewster Jr.—whose subjects seem tenacious and inured to suffering—furniture, tools, and natural history specimens. Lectures and special exhibits. The institute's **Dyer Library** next door has an outstanding Maine history collection.
　　Biddeford Mills Museum (207-229-6387; biddefordmillsmuseum.org), 2 Main St., Suite 17-301G, Biddeford. Former mill workers lead reservation-only tours in the mill works and an underground canal. Daily tours run mid-June–mid-October from 10–noon. $10 donation.
　　Harmon Historical Museum (207-934-9319; harmonmuseum.org), 4 Portland Ave., Old Orchard Beach, is open June–Sept., Tue.–Fri. 11–4, Sat. 9–noon; winter hours by appointment. Home of the Old Orchard Beach Historical Society, the building is full of exhibits from the town's past. Each year, in addition to the regular school, fire, and aviation exhibits, there is a special exhibit. Pick up the timeline of the area's history and the walking map of historic sites.

TENNIS The **Ocean Park Association** (207-934-9068; oceanpark.org) maintains public tennis courts, open to the public for a fee in summer.

✳ Green Space

BEACHES Obviously, **Old Orchard Beach** is the big draw in this area, with 7 miles of sand and plenty of space for sunbathing, swimming, volleyball, and other recreation.
　　Ferry Beach State Park is marked from Rt. 9 between Old Orchard Beach and Camp Ellis in Saco. The 100-plus-acre preserve includes 70 yards of sand, a boardwalk through the dunes, bike paths, nature trails, a picnic area with grills, lifeguards, changing rooms, and pit toilets. Even in the middle of summer it isn't terribly crowded here. $6 per nonresident,

$1 ages 5–11, free under 5 or over 65 with identification. Off-season the Iron Ranger (a green pole with a green can beside the booth) collects reduced fees on the honor system.

Bay View Beach, at the end of Bay View Rd. near Ferry Beach, is 200 yards of mostly sandy beach; lifeguards, $2 per hour parking.

Camp Ellis Beach, Rt. 9, Saco. Some 2,000 feet of beach backed by cottages; also a long fishing pier and breakwater. The commercial parking lots fill quickly on sunny days.

Pine Point, off Rt. 9, Scarborough, has a small and uncrowded beach near the fisherman's co-op. The larger beach area, closer to Old Orchard, with snack bar, changing room, and bathrooms, charges fees in summer for parking in the adjacent lot.

HIKING **Saco Bay Trails** (sacobaytrails.org), P.O. Box 720, Saco 04072, publishes a trail guide for Saco, Biddeford, and Old Orchard Beach. Copies are sold for $10 in local shops and at the Biddeford-Saco Chamber of Commerce.

Saco Heath Preserve (nature.org), Rt. 112 (2 miles from I-95 Exit 36), Saco. This small Nature Conservancy preserve shouldn't be overlooked. The sign is hard to spot; look for it on the right a few miles out of Saco. A quiet, peaceful stroll through a peat bog on a mile-long wooden boardwalk and woodland trail through the 1,223-acre preserve brings visitors close to heathland plants like Labrador tea and sheep laurel. Atlantic white cedar nurtures rare-in-Maine Hessel's hairstreak butterflies.

East Point Sanctuary, off Rt. 9 (east of Goose Rocks Beach) in Biddeford Pool. A 30-acre Maine Audubon wildlife sanctuary well known to birders, who flock here during migrating seasons. Beautiful any time of year. From Rt. 9 turn right just beyond Goose Rocks Beach onto Fortune Rocks Beach Rd. to Lester B. Orcutt Blvd.; turn right, drive almost to the end, and look for a chain-link fence and AUDUBON sign. The trail continues along the golf course and sea.

LIGHTHOUSE TOUR **Wood Island Lighthouse** (207-286-3229; woodislandlighthouse .org), Biddeford Pool. Tours are offered by the Friends of Wood Island Lighthouse, departing from Vines Landing in Biddeford Pool; by phone reservation only. The tours last 1½ hours and are offered July and Aug.; donations of $10 encouraged. The 42-foot stone tower, attached keeper's house, and stone oil house can be entered on this 35-acre island where seabirds nest and others rest on their migrations. A half-mile boardwalk takes visitors from the boat landing to the lighthouse.

❋ Winter Sports

CROSS-COUNTRY SKIING ✔ **Harris Farm Cross-Country Ski Center** (207-499-2678; harrisfarm.com), 280 Buzzell Rd., Dayton. Open daily 9 AM–dusk when there's snow. This 500-acre dairy and tree farm offers 40 kilometers of groomed trails, from easy to difficult, over hills, by ponds and streams, and through the woods. Rentals include snowshoes.

❋ Lodging

INNS AND B&BS **The Atlantic Birches Inn** (207-934-5295 or 1-888-934-5295; atlantic birches.com), 20 Portland Ave., Old Orchard Beach 04064. A Victorian, shingle-style home that was built in the area's heyday. Five guest rooms in the main house are named for former grand hotels; they're cheerful, with a mix of old and new furnishings. The in-ground pool is perfect on a hot day. $131–192 in high season includes continental breakfast with fresh muffins, fruit salad, and whole-grain bread.

✔ **Old Orchard Beach Inn** (207-934-5834 or 1-877-700-6624; oldorchardbeachinn.com), 6 Portland Ave., Old Orchard Beach 04064.

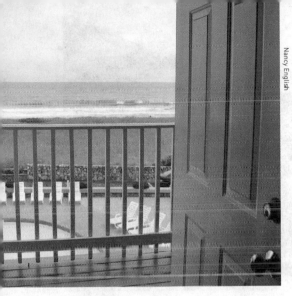

SEA VIEW MOTEL

Ebenezer Staples's original hostelry, part of this inn dates from the 1730s, and the building is on the National Register of Historic Places as Maine's oldest continuously operated inn. All 18 rooms, one a two-bedroom suite, have air-conditioning, cable TV, and private bath. $125–450 high season, $89–225 off season, with a continental breakfast that includes homemade muffins and breads.

The Nautilus by the Sea (1-800-981-7018; thenautilusatoceanpark.com), 2 Colby Ave., Ocean Park 04063. This 12-room B&B, built in 1890 as a private home, is smack up against the beach. Many rooms have beach or ocean views, with the most dramatic vista from the fourth-floor "penthouse suite," where at night you can watch the beam of Wood Island Light play across the water. Owners Jim and Charlotte Katz run this updated inn. $135–225 in-season, $105–190 off-season, with full breakfast.

OTHER LODGING **Aquarius Motel** (207-934-2626; aquariusmotel.com), 1 Brown St., Old Orchard Beach 04064. A small, family-owned and -operated 14-unit motel that's exceptionally clean and right on the beach. The patio is a great place to relax after a day of sightseeing. $159 for a double with kitchenette in-season. Family-sized units also available. Many special rates in early spring and late fall.

Ocean Walk Hotel (207-934-1716 or 1-800-992-3779; oceanwalkhotel.com), 197 E. Grand Ave., Old Orchard Beach 04064. Forty-four well-kept rooms, from studios to oceanfront suites. The top-floor rooms in one building have very high ceilings, giving them a light, airy, spacious feel. Indoor pool. $175–300 in-season, $75–200 off-season.

&. **Sea View Motel** (207-934-4180 or 1-800-541-8439; seaviewgetaway.com), 65 W. Grand Ave., Old Orchard Beach 04064. Forty-nine rooms, some with ocean views. Pretty land-scaping, with an outdoor pool and a beautiful fountain in front. The simple rooms, some with kitchenette, are modern, bright, and well maintained. $98–290 in-season, $57–125 off-season.

⨀ **The Gull Motel, Inn & Cottages** (207-934-4321; gullmotel.com), 89 W. Grand Ave., Old Orchard Beach 04064. An attractive motel with an outdoor pool, immaculate and family oriented. The inn is right on the beach, with a great porch. Cottages also available by the week. Inn rates $80–150 per night; motel rates $75–160; cottages $1,250 per week.

⨀ &. **Billowhouse** (207-934-2333 or 1-888-767-7776; billowhouse.com), 2 Temple Ave., Ocean Park 04063. This 1881 Victorian seaside guest house is Mary Kerrigan's retirement project, completely renovated yet with old-fashioned charm. There are three ground-level efficiency apartments and six kitchenette units in the adjoining motel. The four B&B units include a large three-room suite with private deck, in-room Jacuzzi, and full kitchen; a two-room suite with private deck and outside hot tub; two oceanfront rooms with private bath share a deck overlooking the ocean. $135–250 in-season, less for extended stays, breakfast included for B&B guests only; $95–155 off-season.

CAMPGROUNDS Camping is a budget-minded family's best bet in this area. There are at least a dozen campgrounds here (more than 4,000 sites in the area), many geared to families and offering games, recreational activities, and trolley service to the beach in-season. Following are a few recommendations; check with the chamber for a full listing.

Silver Springs Campground and Cottages (207-283-3880; silverspringsmaine.com), 705 Portland Rd. (Rt. 1), Saco 04072. May–mid-Oct. Thirteen cottages and 130 sites (with full RV hookups) keep Mary Ann and Bryce Ingraham busy. "Most people who come, come back," Mary Ann said. The framework for the cottages is still from the

RUN OF THE MILL

The text on the right, running vertically: Nancy English

1930s, but inside and out they are new, with interiors finished with V-match pine boards and all-new appliances. Two swimming pools and a rec hall. Camping sites $42–48, cottages $80–175 in-season. Discounts off-season.

✍ ♿ **Bayley's Camping Resort** (207-883-6043; bayleys-camping.com), 52 Ross Rd., Scarborough 04074. Just down the road from Pine Point are paddleboats, a swimming pool, Jacuzzi, fishing, game room, special programs for children and adults—and a shuttle to take you to Pine Point Beach and Old Orchard's downtown. More than 400 sites and 50 rental trailers. $47–86 depending on hookups.

✪ ✍ ♿ **Powder Horn** (207-934-4733; maine campgrounds.com), P.O. Box 366, Old Orchard Beach 04064. A 450-site campground with plenty of recreation options—playgrounds, shuffleboard, horseshoes, volleyball, rec hall and game room, activities program, mini golf, and trolley service to the beach in-season. $50–65 per night in-season, $40–50 off-season. **Hidden Pines** is a sister campground next door with basic to premium sites.

✳ Where to Eat

DINING OUT ♿ **Joseph's by the Sea** (207-934-5044; josephsbythesea.com), 55 W. Grand Ave., Old Orchard Beach. Open Apr.–Dec., hours vary. Dinners are still as polished and

well made. Wonderful grilled steaks, seared scallops, and the popular Pasta Maison—Maine shrimp, scallops, salmon, and mussels on angel-hair pasta with real cream. For once the cream is light, enhancing and not overwhelming the seafood. Entrées $18–29.

Custom Deluxe (207-494-7110; facebook.com/CustomDeluxeMaine), 140 Main St., Biddeford. Open Tue.–Fri. 11–2 and 5–9:30, Sat. 5–9:30. Thomas Malz and Megan McVey opened this ambitious place in 2015; the French dishes fit right in with the mill town history. Moules Normandie—mussels cooked with cider and served with shoestring fries—and brisket with Montreal spice were on the first menu. Entrées $11–15.

Run of the Mill (207-571-9648; therunof themill.net), 100 Main St., Saco. This microbrewery set on Saco Island in the Saco River has a fabulous outdoor deck in good weather and finely crafted ales and good food year-round. The hand-cut fries are memorable, and of course what could be better with "Basement Bitter"? Shepherd's pie and bangers and smash keep the UK close at hand. Entrées $9–20.

✍ **The Landmark** (207-934-0156; landmarkfinedining.com), 28 E. Grand Ave., Old Orchard Beach. Open at 5 for dinner Apr.–Dec.; daily June–Columbus Day; call for hours off-season. Fine dining in a 1910 Victorian house and on an outdoor terrace in fine weather. Menu specialties include a creamy lobster stew, garlicky pasta with mussels,

LOBSTER

Lobster Claw (207-282-0040), 4 Ocean Park Rd. (Rt. 5), Saco. Lobsters cooked outside in giant kettles, stews and chowders, cozy dining room, and takeout available. Twin lobster specials, also steamers, fried seafood. Lobster packed to travel.

Goldthwaite's (207-284-5000; poollobster.com), 3 Lester B. Orcutt Blvd., Biddeford Pool, is good for a lobster roll or something else at the counter; enjoy your food at a picnic table in back near the water.

GOLDTHWAITE'S AT BIDDEFORD POOL

Nanc- English

lacquered duck, and barbecued ribs, all quite good. Entrées $18–27. Early-bird specials.

Bufflehead's (207-284-6000; buffleheads restaurant.com), 122 Hills Beach Rd., Biddeford. Open year-round, daily for lunch and dinner in summer; call for hours off season. Offering indoor and outdoor seating with a terrific ocean view, this great family place makes quality food. Try the fried sole with Creole meunière sauce, or baked scallops. Entrées $11–28.

EATING OUT **Palace Diner** (207-284-0015; palacedinerme.com), 18 Franklin St., Biddeford, was lionized by *Bon Appétit* magazine in 2014—the brown butter banana bread, Palais Royale burger, challah French toast, and excellent fries are all worth the national press they are getting. Open 8 AM–2 PM daily.

Biscuits & Company (207-710-2333; biscuitsandcompany.com), 25 Alfred St., Biddeford. Excellent breakfast with thick bacon, strong coffee and perfect biscuits. Biscuits

and gravy, of course, and a vegetarian Biscuit Benedict with spinach and artichoke. Lunch on chicken on a biscuit or good salads.

Los Tapatios Mexican Restaurant (207-602-6284), 11 Adams St., Biddeford. Big plates of Mexican mainstays; the mole comes recommended, and the margaritas are just as generously made. Friendly service and a dedication to pleasing you makes your visit feel delightful. Modest prices.

Huot's Restaurant (207-282-1642; huots seafoodrestaurant.com), Camp Ellis Beach, Saco. Open mid-Apr.–mid-Sept., Tue.–Sun. 11–9. The third generation of the Huot family is carrying on the tradition of good, fresh seafood at this clean, simple spot in Camp Ellis, begun in 1935. Entrées $7–25.

Traditions (207-282-6661), 162 Main St., Saco. A cozy little restaurant specializing in pasta and traditional Italian meat and seafood dishes. Open for lunch and dinner. Entrées $8–16.

New Moon (207-282-2241; thenewmoon restaurant.com), 17 Pepperell Square. Cozy restaurant in Pepperell Square. Breakfast on the Irish Benedict with red flannel hash, and try baked stuffed lobster for dinner. Open 7:30 AM–2 PM daily, 5–9 Thu.–Sat.

Cole Road Café (207-283-4103; coleroad cafe.com), 1 Cole Rd., Biddeford. Open for breakfast and lunch Tue.–Sat. 7 AM–1 PM; breakfast only on Sun. starting at 8. Deservedly popular, this colorful, friendly place makes all the breakfast standards; specials might include blueberry-stuffed French toast with cream cheese. Joyce Rose has run Cole Road Café for 20 years. Breakfast $3–10.

Hanabi (207-284-5454; facebook.com/Saco .Hanabi), 15 Pepperell Square, Saco. Fine sushi and Korean entrées.

TAKE-OUT Near Old Orchard Beach's pier and on the main drag are an abundance of take-out stands and informal restaurants serving pizza, burgers, hot dogs, fried seafood, fried dough, pier fries, ice cream, and more. Our favorites are **Bill's** for pizza and **Lisa's** for pier fries.

Rapid Ray's (207-282-1847), 179 Main St., Saco. Open daily until around midnight. A local icon since 1953. Quick and friendly service from people who seem to know everyone who walks through the door. Burgers, hot dogs, lobster rolls, and the like at great prices.

✳ Entertainment

City Theater (207-282-0849; citytheater.org), Main St., Biddeford. This 500-seat, 1890s theater offers a series of live performances.

Saco Drive-In (207-284-1016), Rt. 1, Saco. Double features in spring and summer.

✳ Selective Shopping

Cascade Flea Market, 885 Portland Rd. (Rt. 1), Saco. One of Maine's largest outdoor flea markets, open daily in summer.

Elements (207-710-2011; elementsbooks coffeebeer.com), 256 Maine St., Biddeford. Open as early as 7 AM and as late as 11 PM but hours vary with the day; check online. New and used books line the walls and are piled in bins but this is primarily an inviting downtown space to gather or access WiFi. The light menu features coffees, beer, baked goods, soups, cheese, and tapas plates. Live music Fri., Sat. evenings.

Stone Soup Artisans (207-283-4715; stone soupartisans.com), 228 Main St., Saco. Quality crafts from more than 50 Maine artisans. Pottery and jewelry, all made in Maine.

Saco Island Farmers' Market (saco farmersmarket.com), corner of Spring and Scammon streets. This year-round farmers'/ artisans' market features organic meat and vegetables, handmade products, and live entertainment. Wed.–Sat. 7–noon, May–Oct.

✳ Special Events

January: **Annual Lobster Dip**—hundreds of participants dip into the chilly Atlantic to benefit Special Olympics of Maine in Old Orchard Beach.

February: **Winter Fest**, Biddeford.

June–Labor Day: **Fireworks** at the Old Orchard Beach square Thu. at 9:45 PM.

Late June: **La Kermesse**, Biddeford— parade, public suppers, dancing, and entertainment highlighting Franco-American culture and traditions. **Saco Sidewalk Arts Festival**, Saco.

Early July: **Greek Heritage Festival**, St. Demetrius on Bradley St. in Saco.

July 4th: **Community Parade** and art show in Ocean Park Square.

Late July: The **Lobster Bowl Shriners Football Game** in Biddeford.

August: **Ocean Park Festival of Lights** and **Salvation Army camp meetings** under the pavilion in Ocean Park. **Beach Olympics**— three days of competitions, music, displays, and presentations to benefit the Special Olympics of Maine. Annual **5K Race and Kids' Fun Run**, scholarship fund-raiser.

September: **Annual Car Show**—with a car lineup and parade, Old Orchard Beach. **River Jam Festival**, on Saco River in both Saco and Biddeford.

October: **Saco HarvestFest**.

December: **Celebrate the Season by the Sea**—a tree-lighting ceremony with horse-drawn hay-wagon rides, refreshments, a holiday bazaar, caroling, and a bonfire on the beach, in Old Orchard.

CASCO BAY

■

PORTLAND AREA

FREEPORT

L ively, walkable, and sophisticated, Maine's largest city is also a working port. Greater Portland accounts for one-quarter of Maine's total population, but Portland's most populated area is a 3½-mile-long peninsula facing Casco Bay. Visitors head down Congress Street to the Old Port, more than five square brick and stone blocks built during the city's peak shipping era and now laced with restaurants, cafés, shops, and galleries.

Portland's motto, "Resurgam" ("I shall rise again"), could not be more appropriate. The 17th-century settlement was decimated twice by Native Americans, then torched by the British. Finally it prospered as a lumbering port in the 1820s—as still evidenced by its many Federal-era mansions and commercial buildings, like the granite-and-glass Mariner's Church in the Old Port, built in 1820 to be the largest building in the capital of a brand-new state. Then, on Independence Day in 1866, a firecracker flamed up and fell in a Commercial Street boatyard, setting the city on fire and quickly destroying most of the downtown. Again the city rose like the legendary phoenix, rebuilding beautifully, this time in sturdy brick, to create the core of northern New England's shipping, rail, and manufacturing businesses.

These very buildings, a century later, were "going for peanuts," in the words of a real estate agent who began buying them up in the late 1960s, when Portland's handsome Grand Trunk Station was demolished. At that time, artists and craftspeople were renting shopfronts down by the harbor for $50 per month. They formed the Old Port Association, hoping to entice people to stroll through that no-man's-land. During its first winter, the Old Port Association strung lights through upper floors to convey a sense of security and shoveled their own streets, a service the city had ceased to provide to that area. At the end of the season they celebrated their survival by holding the first Old Port Festival, a street fair that is still held each June.

Higher up on Congress Street, the Maine College of Art (MECA) has replaced Porteus Department Store in a five-story Beaux Arts building and maintains the street-level Institute of Contemporary Art. With a student body of more than 420 and a far larger continuing-education program, MECA has had a visual impact up and down Congress Street, which is now called the Arts District.

Scattered throughout the city are members of Portland's growing immigrant community, with families from Bosnia, Russia, Somalia, Sudan, Congo, Vietnam, Puerto Rico, and Mexico, making this Maine's most diverse city.

The Western Promenade was laid out as an overlook for the West End way back in 1836; the Eastern Promenade was at the opposite end of the peninsula, along the verge of Munjoy Hill, overlooking Casco Bay. In 1879 the city gained Deering Oaks

Nancy English

TWO HORSES IN HARNESS TAKE A BREAK AT THE STANLEY THOMAS PULLEN FOUNTAIN

Park and was blessed by the design of city civil engineer William Goodwin. In 1917, with turn-of-the-century plans by Frederick Law Olmsted, a dream of James Phinney Baxter, a mayor of Portland, came true when Baxter Boulevard along Back Cove was opened to pedestrians.

Commercial Street is a departure point for the fleet of Casco Bay Lines ferries that regularly transport people, mail, and supplies to nearby Peaks Island and to the Diamond Islands, Chebeague, and Cliff Island, more than an hour's ride. The waterfront is, moreover, the departure point for deep-sea fishing, harbor cruises, whale-watching, and daysailing.

Beyond South Portland lies Cape Elizabeth, home of the vintage-1791 Portland Head Light and its museum. Nearby Scarborough to the south and both Falmouth and Yarmouth, just north of the city, also offer secluded seaside reserves for walking, boating, and birding.

GUIDANCE **Greater Portland Convention and Visitors Bureau** (207-772-5800; visit portland.com) publishes *Visit Portland Maine*, listing restaurants, sights, museums, and accommodations, including cottages. **Visitors information centers** are at 14 Ocean Gateway Pier (east of the end of Commercial St.), Portland 04101, open year-round. July–Columbus Day, the schedule is Mon.–Fri. 9–5, Sat.–Sun. 9–4. Another center is at the **Portland International Jetport** (207-775-5809), open daily 10 AM–midnight.

Portland's Downtown District (207-772-6828; portlandmaine.com), 549 Congress St., Portland 04101, offers information about performances, festivals, and special events. They publish a guide to services, attractions, dining, and lodging.

For current entertainment, weather, and dining ratings, go to pressherald.com, the *Portland Press Herald* site. *The Forecaster* (theforecaster.net)—a free weekly available in street vending boxes and at coffeehouses and shops—carries listings for galleries, music, and events. A website, portlandfoodmap.com, holds the most complete listing of Portland restaurants and is the best source for food-related events in the city.

The **Maine Tourism Association** (207-846-0833; mainetourism.com) staffs a major state information center on Rt. 1 in Yarmouth, just off I-295 Exit 17.

GETTING THERE *By air:* **Portland International Jetport** (207-774-7301; portlandjetport .org) is served by major carriers, and car rentals at the airport include National, Avis, Hertz, Budget, Enterprise, and Alamo.

By bus: **Concord Coach Lines** (207-828-1151 or 1-800-639-3317; concordcoachlines.com) stops en route from Boston to Bangor and coastal points at a modern station just off I-295 Exit 5A. **Greyhound** (1-800-231-2222; greyhound.com) offers frequent service among Portland, Boston, and Maine's coastal and inland points, using the Greyhound terminal, which unfortunately is dingy and offers little parking.

By car: From I-95, take I-295 to Exit 4 (Portland Waterfront).

By train: Amtrak service (1-800-USA-RAIL; amtrak.com). The **Downeaster** now runs five times daily between Boston's renovated North Station and Portland's clean rail–bus station on outer Congress St.; the trip takes about 2½ hours and then heads north to Freeport and Brunswick. Stops in Old Orchard Beach (seasonal), Saco/Biddeford, and Wells give another option to Portland visitors who would like to skip driving.

By ferry: **Bay Ferries Limited** (207-417-7050 USA, 1-902-742-6800 Canada; ferries.ca), 12 Ocean Gateway Pier, Portland, Maine and 58 Water St., Yarmouth, Nova Scotia B5A 1L3. The CAT is once again moving passengers from Maine to Nova Scotia on 5½ hours trips from mid-June to October 1 in 2016; the season may change, so check the website. Departures are daily at 2:30 PM; return trips from Yarmouth are daily at 8:30 AM, and a passport is required for all passengers. $592 for a roundtrip with one passenger in 2016; reduced fares for people over 59 and under 14, on Tuesdays, and during seasonal promotions.

GETTING AROUND **The Metro** (207-774-0351; gpmetrobus.net) city buses connect airport and city, and offer convenient routes around the city. $1.50 one-way, $5 day pass, or $13.50 for a 10-ride ticket; 75 cents for those over 65 or with disabilities; $1 for high school students.

PARKING Portland meters are 50 cents per half hour, but the $15 parking ticket after the meter expires makes parking expensive. Use one of the city's many parking garages. The **Fore Street Garage** (439 Fore St.) puts you at one end of the Old Port, and the **Custom House Square Garage** (25 Pearl St.) at the other. Beware private Unified Parking Partners-run lots: They boot cars that overstay their prepaid ticket.

✳ To See

MUSEUMS All listings are in Portland unless otherwise noted.

Maine Historical Society (207-774-1822; mainehistory.org), 485 Congress St. Maine Historical Society's offices are here, as are **Wadsworth-Longfellow House**, the **MHS Museum**, and **MHS Research Library**, as well as the **Maine Memory Network** (mainememory.net). The Wadsworth-Longfellow House offers a 45-minute guided tour of the house. Built in 1785 by the grandfather of Henry Wadsworth Longfellow, this was the first brick dwelling in town. Peleg Wadsworth was a Revolutionary War hero, and the entire clan of Wadsworths

Downtown Portland

© The Countryman Press

and Longfellows was prominent in the city for nearly two centuries. A small garden is hidden behind the house; another is a couple of blocks down Congress beside the granite First Parish Church (No. 425), marking the site on which Maine's constitution was drafted in 1819.

✿ ♿ **The Museum at Portland Head Light** (207-799-2661; portlandheadlight.com), 1000 Shore Rd. in Fort Williams Park, Cape Elizabeth. Memorial Day–Oct., open daily 10–4; Columbus Day–mid-Dec. and mid-Apr.–Memorial Day, open weekends 10–4. $2 adults, $1 ages 6–18. This is the oldest lighthouse in Maine, first illuminated in 1791 per order of

George Washington. It is now automated, and the former keeper's house has been transformed into an exceptional lighthouse museum.

Institute of Contemporary Art/MECA (207-879-5742; meca.edu/ica), 522 Congress St. Changing exhibits frequently worth checking; free. The ICA is a street-level gallery at the Maine College of Art (MECA), with more than 420 full-time students.

𝒪 **Maine Narrow Gauge Railroad Co. & Museum** (207-828-0814; mainenarrowgauge .org), 58 Fore St. Open May–Oct., daily 10–4, trains 10 to 3 on the hour, and seasonally for special events. A 1.5-mile roundtrip excursion along Casco Bay is offered regularly May–Oct. Leading up to Christmas, you can take the Polar Express; excursion fares are $10 roundtrip adults, $9 seniors, $6 ages 3–12. The museum sells the tickets. From the 1870s to the 1940s, five narrow-gauge lines carrying visitors linked rural Maine communities.

𝒪 ♿ **Children's Museum and Theatre of Maine** (207-828-1234; kitetails.com), 142 Free St. Open Memorial Day–Labor Day, Mon.–Sat. 10–5, Sun. noon–5; otherwise,

MUST SEE

Portland Museum of Art (207-775-6148; for a weekly schedule of events and information, 207-773-ARTS; portlandmuseum.org), 7 Congress Square. Open Tue., Wed., Thu., Sat., and Sun. 10–5, Fri. 10–9; Memorial Day–Columbus Day also open Mon. 10–5; closed New Year's Day, Thanksgiving, and Christmas. $15 adults, $10 students and $13 seniors (with ID), and 14 and under free. Free admission Fri. 5–9 PM. Maine's largest art museum is a striking building designed by I. M. Pei's firm. Featured American artists include Winslow Homer, Edward Hopper, Rockwell Kent, Louise Nevelson, Andrew and N. C. Wyeth, John Singer Sargent, and Marguerite Zorach; the museum also has interesting European works by Renoir, Degas, Prendergast, Matisse, and Picasso. Neighboring McLellan House, the lovely Federal-period home of the museum's original collection, along with the Sweat Memorial Galleries, showcases an impressive collection of 19th-century American paintings and decorative arts.

THE WATERFRONT SIDE OF THE WINSLOW HOMER STUDIO

The Portland Museum of Art bought the Winslow Homer Studio in 2006 from the artist's great grandnephew, who had enjoyed the building as a summer house and used to leave it unlocked for art lovers to visit. That informality is no more, but with a knowledgeable docent in charge, your visit will linger in memory as a glimpse of an irascible genius. The building was restored to look much the way it did when Winslow Homer lived and painted here during summers from 1884, when the studio, a former carriage house, was embellished with a second-floor porch by local architect John Calvin Stevens, until 1910 when Homer died at 74 from natural causes at the studio.

Visits require tickets and reservations ($55 for nonmembers, $30 for members; $25 for students with valid ID; two tours Thu.–Sun. are offered in fall and spring, Fri. and Mon. in the summer, lasting 2½ hours). An upscale bus takes groups of no more than 10 to the studio from the museum.

Nancy English

PORTLAND MUSEUM OF ART DOCENT CAROL PATTERSON LEADING A TOUR AT CANNON ROCK, NEAR THE WINSLOW HOMER STUDIO closed Mon. but open 9–11 for members; $10 per person (under 18 months free). Next door to the Portland Museum of Art, this fun museum features three levels of interactive, hands-on exhibits designed to help the young and old learn together. Permanent exhibits include "Have a Ball," in which kids make ramps and set balls in motion, a car repair shop and lobster boat, an ATM, a science center, a toddler area, and a black-box room that's a walk-in camera obscura.

✼ ♿ **Portland Fire Museum** (207-772-2040; portlandfiremuseum.com), 157 Spring St. (near the corner of State). Open through the year during First Friday Art Walk, the first Friday of each month, at 6; call for more hours. The only remaining firehouse in Portland with horse stalls, this wonderful old brick structure was built in 1837 and originally housed a girls' grammar school. The artifacts (including a 1938 pumper truck) chronicle the city's contentious relationship with fire, from the city's destruction by fire at the hands of the British in 1775 to the Great Fire of 1866.

Portland Science Center (207-812-3850; portlandsciencecenter.com), 68 Commercial St., Maine Wharf. $19.50 adults, $15.50 children. Opened in 2015, exhibits provide "edutainment," with subject matter mythic and compelling.

HISTORIC SITES All listings are in Portland unless otherwise noted.

✼ **Victoria Mansion**, the Morse-Libby House (207-772-4841; victoriamansion.org), 109 Danforth St. (at the corner of Park St.). Open for tours May–Oct., daily 10–3:45 (closed major holidays), Sun. 1–4:45; $15 adults, $13.50 seniors and AAA members, $5 children 6–17, under 6 free. Christmas hours and rates: day after Thanksgiving–first week of Jan., open daily; $15 adults (no senior discount), $5 students. Ruggles Sylvester Morse, a Maine native who made his fortune as a New Orleans hotelier, built this elaborately gilded, frescoed, carved, and many-mirrored mansion in 1858 as a summer home after relocating south just before the Civil War. The Italianate brownstone palazzo features a three-story grand hall with stained-glass windows, a stunning skylight, and a flying staircase with 377 balusters hand carved in black walnut. It was rescued from destruction and opened to the public in 1941.

Tate House Museum (207-774-6177; tatehouse.org), 1267 Westbrook St. Follow Congress St. (Rt. 22) west across the Fore River and turn left on Westbrook St. Open June–Oct., Wed.–Sat. 10–4, Sun. 1–4. $12 adults, $10 seniors, $5 ages 6–12, under 6 free. George Tate, mast agent for the Royal Navy, built this Georgian house in 1755 to reflect his important position. Both the interior and exterior are unusual, distinguished by clerestory windows, a gambrel roof, wood paneling, and elegant furniture.

Neal Dow Memorial (207-773-7773), 714 Congress St. Open year-round, tours given by appointment. Donation requested. Currently the headquarters of the Maine Women's Christian Temperance Union, this handsome Greek Revival mansion was built in 1829 by Neal Dow, the man responsible for an 1851 law that made Maine the first state to prohibit alcohol. He also championed women's rights and abolition.

GUIDED TOURS ✪ **Greater Portland Landmarks Center for Architecture and Preservation**, Safford House (207-774-5561; portlandlandmarks.org), 93 High St., Portland 04101. Greater Portland Landmarks fills an 1858 bow-fronted Italianate building, designed by architect Charles Alexander, which was saved from destruction by this nonprofit organization in the 1970s after a block of historic homes was demolished to widen Spring Street. Landmarks has led walking tours of Portland's historic neighborhoods, including Friday 11 AM tours of Portland's "Golden Age" in 2015. Also note the organization's excellent books and its series of walking guides, available at the observatory, the center, or online. Landmarks runs the **Portland Observatory** at 138 Congress St., high on top of Munjoy Hill. It's open late May to mid-Oct., 10–5; $10 adults, $8 seniors, $5 ages 6–16. Climb the 103 steps to the top of Captain Lemuel Moody's masterpiece and watch the ships entering Casco Bay.

THE ICONIC PORTLAND HEAD LIGHT IS IN FORT WILLIAMS PARK, CAPE ELIZABETH

✒ **Portland Discovery Land and Sea Tours** (207 774 0808, portlanddiscovery.com), 170 Commercial St., Portland. Mid-May–Oct. One trip is a narrated, 105-minute trolley tour that begins on Commercial St. in the Old Port and includes Portland Head Light. Another is the sunset lighthouse cruise. $24 adults, $17 children. Boat tours take in lighthouses.

Downeast Duck Tours (207-774-3825; downeastducktours.com), departing from Commercial St., by Casco Variety. The Duck Tour, about an hour long, takes you around Portland and into Casco Bay after the amphibious vehicle rolls into the harbor. Narrated tours run mid-May–mid-Oct., daily, with five a day before Labor Day and fewer in fall. $27 adults, $25 seniors, $20 ages 6–12, free ages 3 and under.

✳ To Do

BICYCLING **Map Adventures** (207-879-4777; mapadventures.com) makes very readable small maps of bike routes. **Portland Trails** (207-775-2411; trails.org) prints a *Map and Trail Guide*. The Maine Department of Transportation publishes a spiral-bound book with bike routes in Maine; separate tours are published in smaller books. These maps are stocked at **Cycle Mania** (207-774-2933; cyclemania1.com; 59 Federal St., Portland), which sponsors weekly group rides. Cycle Mania and **Gorham Bike and Ski** (207-773-1700; go rhambike.com; 693 Congress St., Portland) are the city bike shops that rent bicycles. They recommend you make a reservation, and they also stock DOT bike trail booklets and Portland Trails maps.

Eastern Trail (207-284-9260; easterntrail.org) is an ambitious trail system that will someday connect Casco Bay to Kittery (and Maine to Florida) with a 68.8-mile off-road greenway. Parts of the route now stretch through Scarborough Marsh, with its flocks of birds and summer scenery, up through South Portland where it is also called the **Greenbelt Trail**.

Mountain Division Trail (mountaindivisiontrail.org), Standish. Running from Standish through Gorham to Windham, the Mountain Division Trail is packed gravel with some paved sections. Four intersections take you across roads, but the 5-mile-plus trail is off-road. Horses travel on it, too.

EXCURSIONS

No one seems quite sure how many islands there are in Casco Bay. Printed descriptions range from 136 to 222. Seventeenth-century explorer John Smith dubbed them the Calendar Islands, saying there was one for every day of the year. Regular year-round ferry service runs to six of the islands, five of which invite exploration.

PEAKS ISLAND Just 3 miles from Portland and a 20-minute ferry ride, Peaks is the most accessible island. Ferry service runs regularly both in summer and off-season because many of the island's approximately 1,000 year-round residents commute to the mainland for work and school. In summer the population swells to between 5,000 and 6,000, and day-trippers are common. The 5-mile shore road around the island is great for walking or bicycling. Rent a pair of wheels at **Brad's ReCycled Bike Shop** (207-766-5631), 115 Island Ave.; when Brad isn't there, you fill out a form, place payment in the box, and return the bikes when you're through. The **Fifth Maine Regiment Museum** (207-766-3330; fifthmainemuseum.org), Seashore Ave., is a striking building erected in 1888 to house Maine's largest collection of Civil War memorabilia (local history exhibits are on the second floor). **Maine Island Kayak Co.** (207-766-2373 or 1-800-796-2373; maineislandkayak.com) offers excellent, superbly guided half-day to multiday trips in Casco Bay along the Maine coast with renowned kayaking instruction. **The Cockeyed Gull** (207-766-2800), 78 Island Ave., serves the best dinner on the island, including Korean specialties, and has a deck perched over the bay. The **Inn on Peaks Island** (207-766-5100; innonpeaks.com), 33 Island Ave., has big, airy rooms and is open year-round with its own lunch and dinner restaurant, **The Pub**. All rooms include TV/DVD, phone, ceiling fan, fireplace, whirlpool tub, and balcony, $135–300 for a double. **DownFront** (207-766-5500), 50 Island Ave., at the top of the hill from the boat, sells great ice cream, candy, clothing, souvenirs, and the "cookie colossus."

CHEBEAGUE ISLAND is the largest in Casco Bay: 4.5 miles long and 2 miles wide. Its population of 350 swells to eight times that in summer. A bike is the best way to explore. **Mack Passano** (207-846-7829), 168 South Rd., is known as the Bike Man of Chebeague and was written up in *Down East* magazine. He offers more than 100 secondhand bikes for free. **The Chebeague Island Inn** (207-846-5155; chebeagueislandinn.com), the island's dowager lodging and an elegant place for a summer

BOATING **Chebeague Transportation Company** (207-846-3700; chebeaguetrans.com) runs the ferry that travels between Cousins Island and Chebeague. Call for directions and parking details.

Casco Bay Lines (207-774-7871; cascobaylines.com), Casco Bay Ferry Terminal, 56 Commercial St. at the foot of Franklin Arterial, Portland. Founded in 1845, this business was said to be the oldest continuously operating ferry company in the country when it went bankrupt in 1980. The present, quasi-municipal Casco Bay Island Transit District now carries 870,000 passengers and 26,000 vehicles out to the bay's beautiful islands every year.

✍ *Lucky Catch* **Lobstering** (207-761-0941; luckycatch.com), 170 Commercial St., Portland. Instead of just eating them, why not land one of those tasty crustaceans yourself? Early May–late Oct., Captain Tom takes tourists and locals out to haul traps on the *Lucky Catch* five times daily Mon.–Sat., with side trips to Portland Head Light and White Head Passage. Each 80- to 90-minute cruise costs $30 per adult, $28 for seniors and $25 ages 13–18, $18 ages 2–12; children under 2 free.

✪ *Odyssey* **Whale Watch** (207-775-0727; odysseywhalewatch.com), Long Wharf, Portland. Whale-watches daily at 10 AM June–Oct. on the *Odyssey*, a 93-passenger boat. $49 adults, $39 children 12 and under.

meal, is open May–mid-Oct., with 21 rooms available at $150–370. **The Niblic** (207-846-1015) is a little store next to the boatyard where visitors can buy local crafts and snacks and drinks, as well as a good lunch. You can pick up takeout at **Doughty's Island Market** (207 846 9997). To relax and enjoy the scenery, head to **Chandler's Cove**, a white-sand beach, or the beach near **Coleman's Cove**. Golfers will want to try the **Chebeague Island Golf Club** (207-846-9478; chebeague.org), a beautiful nine-hole course founded in 1920, where nonmembers can play anytime except Mon. or Thu. morning. The **Chebeague Island Historical Society** has restored the old District No. 9 Schoolhouse, open all day in summer with a visitors center and museum. Call 207-846-5237 for details. **Casco Bay Lines** ferries dock at the southern end of the island, and **Chebeague Transportation Company** (207-846-3700; chebeaguetrans.com) runs the ferry that travels between Cousins Island and Chebeague. Call for directions and parking details.

LONG ISLAND Three miles long and approximately a mile wide, Long Island, like the others, has a thriving summer population, and rental cottages can make you a part of it. **Coveside of Long Island** (207-766-0092), 285 Beach Ave., is run by Emily Jacobs, who serves a terrific breakfast. The B&B is within walking distance of Long Island's prettiest beach, **Singing Sands**.

GREAT DIAMOND ISLAND A pleasant half-hour ferry ride from downtown, this 2-mile-long island is the site of Fort McKinley, built sturdily of brick in the 1890s, now restored as **Diamond Cove** (diamondcove.com), a resort-style development featuring 121 town houses. The **Inn at Diamond Cove** (207-775-9090; innatdiamondcove.com) is a luxury lodging that opened in 2015 following a $12 million renovation of the soldiers' barracks in Fort McKinley Park (and a fire that gutted the first renovation when it was almost done). The inn has its own dedicated transportation from the dock in Portland. $309–$569. **Diamond's Edge** (207-766-5850; diamondsedge.com) takes good care of meals; a casually elegant restaurant open late May–Oct., dinner only except mid-June–Labor Day, when lunch is also served. A popular place for weddings.

CLIFF ISLAND is a full 1½-hour ride down the bay. It is the most rustic of the islands, with 8 miles of dirt roads, no overnight accommodations, a peaceful feel, and sandy beaches.

BOWLING **Bayside Bowl** (207-791-2695; baysidebowl.com), 58 Alder St., provides excellent food and drink in a hipster setting, and the bowling is a lot of fun. Live music on weekend nights.

BREWERIES, WINERIES, AND DISTILLERIES Portland is famous for its microbreweries, and many give tours, either on a regular basis or by appointment. **The Maine Brew Bus** (207-200-9111; themainebrewbus.com), 111 Commercial St., Portland, takes care of the driving and scheduling for $50 to $75 or so, depending on the tour chosen. For information, contact individual breweries. Three fine breweries that share the same industrial neighborhood start with long-established **Allagash Brewing** (207-878-5385 or 1-800-330-5385;allagash.com), 50 Industrial Way, with world renowned Curieux, limited editions like Nancy, made with sour cherries, and classic Allagash White. Make a reservation online for a tasting. Look for Bissell Brothers in the Thompson's Point sidebar. **Foundation** (207-370-8187; foundationbrew .com), 1 Industrial Way, #5, has several unique offerings. Epiphany, Eddy, Wanderlust, and Burnside are some possible brews to sip as you wander the brewery and ask staff questions on a self-directed tour. **Oxbow** (207-315-5962; oxbowbeer.com), 49 Washington Ave., makes Farmhouse Ale and Space Cowboy, both Belgian-style ales brewed in Newcastle and easy to taste in the Portland Tasting Room. Other microbreweries include **D. L. Geary Brewing** (207-878-BEER; geary brewing.com), 38 Evergreen Dr.; **Gritty McDuff's Brew Pub** (207-772-2739; grit tys.com), 396 Fore St.; **Peak Organic Brewing Company** (207-586-5586; peak brewing.com), 110 Marginal Way; **Liquid Riot Bottling Company** (207-221-8889; liquidriot.com), 250 Commercial St; and the largest of all, **Shipyard Brewing** (207-761-0807; shipyard.com), 86 Newbury St. In East Bayside, the funky, post-industrial part of town hugging I-295, **Rising Tide Brewing Company** (207-370-2337; risingtidebrewing .com), 103 Fox St., has tours Fri. and Sat. and a tasting room to sample Spinnaker, a wheat beer made in summer, or Ursa Minor, "dark as squid ink and moody as the sea." **Bunker Brewing Co.** (207-450-5014), 122 Anderson St., makes Mockingbird, if you are in luck. **Urban Farm Fermentory** (207-773-8331; urbanfarmfermentory.com), 200 Anderson St., Bay 4, makes hard cider, kombucha, and mead, each sold by the 32-ounce growler,

THE BARREL ROOM AT ALLAGASH

with tastings on weekend evenings. **Sweetgrass Winery and Distillery** (207-761-8446; sweetgrasswinery.com), 324 Fore St., offered a tasting of four wines or spirits for $5 in 2015, with a nice glass for a souvenir. The Apple Brandy is sublime and we are all awaiting the barrel-aged bourbon with respectful impatience (release date 2018). Lamb, bitters, vanilla extract, and blankets also for sale from the Union, Maine, farm. **Cellardoor at the Point** (mainewine.com) is planned to open in 2016 on Thompson's Point, Portland's new music, circus, and brewery hotspot. The wines are made with grapes grown in Lincolnville, less than two hours up the coast. **New England Distilling** (207-878-9759; newenglanddistilling .com), 26 Evergreen Dr., Portland, is distilling Ingenium gin and Eight Bells rum. **Maine Craft Distilling** (207-798-2528; mainecraftdistilling.com), 101 Fox St., makes Chesuncook gin, Ration rum, and Queequeg spiced rum.

FOR FAMILIES 🐾 **Southworth Planetarium** (207-780-4249; usm.maine.edu/planet), University of Southern Maine, 96 Falmouth St., Portland. Astronomy shows throughout the year.

GOLF **Sable Oaks Golf Club** (18 holes, 207-775-6257), South Portland, is considered among the most challenging and best courses in Maine; **Riverside North** (18 holes, 207-797-3524) and **Riverside South** (nine holes, 207-797-5588), in Portland; **Val Halla** (18 holes, 207-829-2225), in Cumberland; and **Twin Falls** (nine holes, 207-854-5397) in Westbrook.

Willowdale Golf Club (207-883-9351; willowdalegolf.com), off Rt. 1, Scarborough, has 18 holes. **Nonesuch River Golf Club** (207-883-0007; nonesuchgolf.com), off Rt. 114, Scarborough, also has 18 holes.

RACING **Scarborough Downs** (207-883-4331; scarboroughdowns.com), off I-95 Exit 6 in Scarborough. From Apr.–Dec. Scarborough Downs, the largest facility of its kind in New

SAILING CLASS IN CASCO BAY

England, has live harness racing with betting windows; year-round thoroughbred and harness racing is available via simulcast with off-track betting.

Beech Ridge Motor Speedway (207-885-5800; beechridge.com), Holmes Rd., Scarborough. Summer stock car racing Thu.–Sat., May–Oct.

SAILING *Bagheera* (207-766-2500; portlandschooner.com), Maine State Pier, Portland. Built in 1924 of long-leaf yellow pine, oak, and mahogany, this vintage Alden sailed all over the world before making Casco Bay her home port in 2002. She can carry as many as 48 passengers. Four cruises daily, Memorial Day–Labor Day, three daily until Columbus Day. $42 for adults, $21 for children. *Wendameen*, a schooner built in 1912, is available for private charters and overnight cruises.

The *Frances* (207-749-9169; mainesailingadventures.net) offers cruises daily Memorial Day–Columbus Day, along with many theme cruises like yoga, wine, and music.

SEA KAYAKING ⚓ **Maine Island Kayak Co.** (207-766-2373 or 1-800-796-2373; maineislandkayak.com), 70 Luther St., Peaks Island. Late May–Oct. Exceptional guides, state-of-the-art equipment, and a commitment to the leave-no-trace philosophy are crucial in heavily trafficked Casco Bay. This company offers instruction in kayaking and trips throughout the summer. **Portland Paddle** (207-730-9730; portlandpaddle.net), East End Beach, Portland. Guided kayak tours and kayak and paddleboard rentals.

✳ Green Space

BEACHES ⚓ ♿ **Crescent Beach State Park** (207-799-5871), 66 Two Lights Rd., Cape Elizabeth; 8 miles from Portland on Rt. 77. A mile of sand complete with changing facilities, a playground, picnic tables, and a snack bar. Good for young children because it's protected from heavy surf.

⚓ ♿ **Wolfe's Neck Woods State Park** (207-865-4465; off-season, 207-865-6080), 426 Wolfe's Neck Rd. (take Bow St., across from L.L. Bean), Freeport. Open Apr.–Oct. Day-use fee. A 233-acre park with shoreline hiking along Casco Bay, the Harraseeket River, and salt marshes, as well as excellent birding, with ospreys the local stars.

Kettle Cove is just down the road from Crescent Beach—follow the road behind the (excellent) ice cream shop on Rt. 77. Free, but parking is limited. This spot is good for bird-watching during migration seasons.

Higgins Beach, farther down Rt. 77 in Scarborough, is an extensive strand within walking distance of lodging—but there is no parking on the street. Private lots charge a fee. The swell can kick up quite a bit here, so beware the undertow. Surfers are always here when the waves are high.

Scarborough Beach State Park (scarboroughbeachstatepark.com), 414 Black Point Rd. (Rt. 207), 3 miles south of Rt. 1 on Prouts Neck. Open Memorial Day–Sept. ($5 admission), also for walking year-round. A 243-acre park with a superb beach, but only a 65-foot stretch is technically public. Get there early because parking is minimal and open-ocean lovers like this one best.

PARKS *Deering Oaks*, Portland's 51-acre city park, designed by city civil engineer William Goodwin, has a pond, ducks, and, occasionally, a beaver and a moose, a fountain, a playground, a fine grove of oak trees, a shrub rose garden, and a refurbished urban "ravine" complete with a wading pool and spray jets for summertime frolicking. A farmers' market is held here Sat. morning May–Nov., and fabulous winter lights are designed by Pandora LaCasse.

Two Lights State Park, 66 Two Lights Rd., Cape Elizabeth, is open year-round. No swimming, but 40 acres of shore with stunning water views for picnicking and fishing.

Also see **Fort Williams Park** in *Excursions* and **Fort Allen Park** under Eastern Promenade in *Walks*.

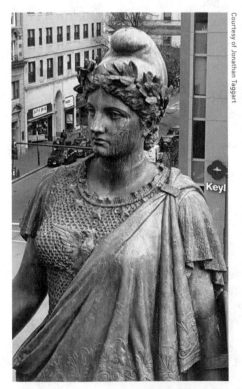

Courtesy of Jonathan Taggart

OUR LADY OF VICTORIES IN MONUMENT SQUARE

NATURE PRESERVES *Gilsland Farm Audubon Center* (207-781-2330; maineaudubon.org), 20 Gilsland Farm Rd., Falmouth (3 miles east of Portland). Open Mon.–Sat. 9–5; Sun. noon–5 in warm weather, 2–5 in cold weather. Maine Audubon's headquarters are located at this 65-acre wildlife sanctuary, along with trails, rolling fields, river frontage, and salt marsh. The education center features exhibits throughout the year and a wildlife discovery room for children.

Scarborough Marsh Audubon Center (207-883-5100), Pine Point Rd. (Rt. 9), Scarborough. Open daily mid-June–Labor Day, 9:30–5:30. The largest salt marsh (3,000 acres) in Maine, this is a great place for quiet canoe and kayak exploration. This Maine Audubon center offers canoe and kayak rentals, exhibits, a Maine Audubon Nature Store, and guided walking and canoe and kayak tours throughout the summer.

Fore River Sanctuary (207-775-2411; trails.org). Located near Maine Turnpike Exit 8, off Brighton Ave., Portland, and managed by Portland Trails. This 85-acre preserve is hidden behind a suburban

THOMPSON'S POINT

Thompson's Point (thompsonspointmaine.com) is a small peninsula jutting out into Fore River that holds a concert venue, Bissell Brothers brewery, Cellardoor winery, Big J's Fried Chicken, a skating rink, a circus school, the Cryptozoology Museum, a distillery, and an orchard of Trees of Forty Fruits that can be harvested for months, once mature. That living art project by Sam Van Aken endows one tree trunk with a bouquet of spring fruit flowers that will bear heirloom stone fruit for future generations.

Thompson's Point Summer Concert Series (thompsonspointmaine.com). Leon Bridges played the final concert of 2016. The venue has grown in popularity and events in the short few years it's been open. With food and drink at hand, it's all good. On regular weekend nights, the Circus School presents performances of juggling and trapeze artists.

Stroudwater Distillery (207-536-7811; stroudwaterdistillery.com). Brick North Building, Thompson's Point, shares the location's working class ethic, promising nothing "fussy"— as they get down to the business of distilling bourbon, rye, vodka, and gin. Tastings are offered in the handsome brick and wood public space, along with classic cocktails.

Beer brewed at Bissell Brothers Brewery (bissellbrothers.com) is so in-demand customers have to leap in line at the release time—but can still miss out. The web site advises following its "can release schedule" on social media to not be disappointed. At least in this two-floor tasting room there is lots of room to try the beers. On occasion the brewery becomes a concert venue—and an art gallery—and no doubt something new to come in 2017.

Big J's Chicken Shack (207-747-4005; bigjschicken.com). Open Wed.–Sun. 11–8 PM. Fried chicken, actually hot and "Portland hot," is made with brined juicy chicken and encased in crisp perfection—sides like mac and cheese and soft-serve ice cream complete a meal. The food is welcome in between or during tastings of wine, beer, and rum—apparently there's an app for ordering from any of the bars next door.

Cellardoor Winery (207-536-7700; mainewine.com). Open daily 12–7 PM, but check for off-season hours. An $8 glass or $8 tasting of the wines made by Cellardoor Winery introduces you to their products. A few are made with grapes grown in the vineyard behind the Lincolnville, Maine, barn; others from juice from grapes grown in New York, California, and Washington.

The International Cryptozoology Museum (cryptozoologymuseum.com). Open Mon., Wed.–Sun. 11 AM–4 PM; adults $10, 12 and under $5, 65 and older $8. What is a tatzelwurm? Come and find out—while you gaze upon the hair of abominable snowmen, the FeeJee mermaid, and a fiberglass coelacanth, among the many "hidden animals" presented for your discovery.

neighborhood where explorers might not think to look. The 2.5 miles of hiking trails offer access to Portland's only waterfall, **Jewell Falls**.

Prouts Neck Cliff Walk and Wildlife Sanctuary. Winslow Homer painted many of his seascapes in a small studio here (now owned by Portland Museum of Art). This exclusive community on Prouts Neck is not far from the Black Point Inn. Winslow Homer Road marks the start of the Cliff Path (unmarked), a beautiful stroll along the rocks, around Eastern Point, and back almost to the inn. You can also walk through the sanctuary between Winslow Homer Road (just east of St. James Episcopal Church) and Library Lane, donated by Winslow's brother Charles.

WALKS **Portland Trails** (207-775-2411; trails.org), 305 Commercial St., Portland, an organization committed to developing hiking and walking trails in the city, sells a map describing several city parks and more than 50 miles of trails as well as bus routes to take you there. The website has a page with links to every trail in Portland on an expandable map.

STROUDWATER DISTILLERY TASTING AT THOMPSON'S POINT

🍸 **The Eastern Promenade.** Follow Congress St. east to the Portland Observatory atop Munjoy Hill and then continue the extra block to the Eastern Promenade, a park-lined street high on this same bluff with sweeping views of Casco Bay. Follow it around, back toward the harbor, to 68-acre **Fort Allen Park**, which dates to 1814, set on a blustery point above the bay. Down along the bay itself, the paved **Eastern Promenade Trail** runs along the base of Munjoy Hill, good for biking and walking. The railroad museum's excursion train runs alongside it.

🐾 ♿ **The Western Promenade** is Portland's most architecturally interesting residential neighborhood. Pick up a copy of the Portland Landmarks leaflet *Guide to the Western Promenade* from the seasonal visitors bureau at Ocean Gateway.

🐾 🍸 ♿ **Baxter Boulevard.** A 3.5-mile path around the tidal flats of Back Cove connects with the Eastern Promenade Trail. It's a popular spot for dog walking, jogging, and biking. Park across from the Hannaford Bros. store.

Eastern Cemetery, Congress St. and Washington Ave. (near the Portland Observatory on Munjoy Hill). The oldest cemetery in Portland, it is listed by the National Trust for Historic Preservation. Its 6 acres hold more than 4,000 headstones dating from the mid-17th century to the early 19th; some are embellished with angels and death's heads. **Spirits Alive** (spiritsalive.org) runs guided tours here ($10 adults, $5 children under 12) in summer and a Halloween Walk Among the Shadows tour.

Portland Freedom Trail (207-591-9980; portlandfreedomtrail.org). A granite-and-bronze marker at the Eastern Cemetery on Congress St. was the first of a series of 13 markers at places in the city where abolitionists lived, preached, and harbored escaping slaves on the Underground Railroad. The website offers a Freedom Trail Map for a self-guided walking tour. The Abyssinian Church on Newbury St. was Maine's first black church when it was built in 1829 and is undergoing restoration. A pro-slavery riot erupted after a sermon criticized slavery in 1842 at First Parish Church at the head of Temple St.

Clark's Pond Trail, maintained by the South Portland Land Trust (southportland landtrust.org). Home Depot in South Portland is located at the trailhead of this plunge into the woods, a 1.1-mile trail located near the Maine Mall with a secret waterfall and turkeys and deer.

Cape Elizabeth Land Trust (207-767-6054; capelandtrust.org), 330 Ocean House Rd., Cape Elizabeth. The Cape Elizabeth Land Trust has preserved 650 acres of the town's land and developed many miles of trails on those acres and via rights-of-way that connect the scattered parcels.

✳ Lodging

HOTELS There are more than 2,000 hotel and motel rooms in and around Portland.

IN THE OLD PORT

✐ ♿ **Portland Regency** (207-774-4200 or 1-800-727-3436; theregency.com), 20 Milk St. Stay in one of 95 rooms (including suites) housed in a century-old armory. Rooms come with reproduction beds (a king or two doubles), white down comforters, cable TV, and air-conditioning; some suites feature a whirlpool tub. Downstairs gym and day spa with luxurious locker rooms, each with private sauna; also co-ed sauna and steam room, and tiled 10-person whirlpool with a waterfall. $139–329.

The Press Hotel (207-808-8800; thepress hotel.com), 119 Exchange St. A wall of manual typewriters recalls the building's origin as a newspaper office, but the reporters hammering typewriter keys never saw anything like the luxurious bedrooms and baths upstairs. This hotel is part of Marriott's Autograph Collection, a set of unique lodgings worldwide. Its **Union** is a fine dining restaurant (see below) that makes sure the burgers are top-notch. $199–600.

🐾 ✐ ♿ **Portland Harbor Hotel** (207-775-9090 or 1-888-798-9090; theportlandharbor hotel.com), 468 Fore St. Amenities include cable TV and radio, marble bath, European-style glass shower, granite counters; Jacuzzi suites feature an oval spa tub and separate sitting area with sofa bed. Fitness center. **Eve's at the Garden** serves fine dinners. $129–399, depending on view and season. Pets are allowed on the first and second floors for a $25 fee per day.

🐾 ♿ **Residence Inn Portland Downtown/ Waterfront** (207-761-1660; marriott.com), 145 Fore St. Comfortable rooms, many overlooking the harbor. There are 137 studios, 34 one-bedroom suites, and 8 two-bedroom suites. All have full kitchen and sleeping area with king bed; a hot breakfast buffet is included. Guest laundry room. One-time fee for pets. $169–349.

Hampton Inn Downtown Portland (207-775-1454; hamptoninn.com), 209 Fore St. New in 2011, this hotel was built on the site of the old Jordan's Meats factory, famous for its red hot dogs. Now the good-sized rooms, some with harbor views, are proving restful. Other perks include the free breakfast and Sebago

THE PRESS HOTEL LOBBY

Brewing Company on the first floor. $129–449 depending on season.

IN MIDTOWN PORTLAND

✎ & **Holiday Inn by the Bay** (207-775-2311 or 1-800-HOLIDAY; innbythebay.com), 88 Spring St. 04101. Portlanders love to hate this ugly, 11-story, downtown highrise, especially since it took over a beautiful neighborhood. But the harbor and skyline views are great from the inside. Amenities include an indoor pool, small fitness center, cable TV with in-room movies, free parking, laundry facility, and a restaurant and lounge. Two suites and 239 rooms range from $180 to $240 in high season.

The Westin Portland Harborview (207-775-5411; starwoodhotels.com), 157 High St. This hotel resurrects the glory of the original Eastland Hotel it took over. Gutted and completely modernized, the hotel stands across from the Portland Museum of Art. Its 289 rooms feature upscale modern furnishings. The Top of the East never looked this good; go to the top of the building for a panoramic view of the city and a drink.

BEYOND PORTLAND

✪ ✎ & **Black Point Inn** (207-883-2500 or 1-800-258-0003; blackpointinn.com), 510 Black Point Rd., Prouts Neck 04074. Open May–Nov. 1. This vintage-1878 summer hotel now has just 25 rooms. The oldest elevator in the state of Maine is still hand operated by a polite staff member. Guests use the Prouts Neck Country Club's 18-hole golf course and 14 tennis courts, as well as kayaks, boats, and bikes. Two sandy beaches, an outdoor heated pool. Rates $410-695 for double MAP (Modified American Plan) per night plus 18 percent guest service charge (covers all gratuities). Live jazz on the porch Tue. nights.

♂ ☀ ✎ & **Inn by the Sea** (207-799-3134; innbythesea.com), 40 Bowery Beach Rd., Cape Elizabeth 04107. Open year-round. A 15-minute drive from downtown Portland, this shingled beachside complex maintains a high reputation. The 61 accommodations include traditional guest rooms with gas-burning fireplace and mini fridge, two-bedroom cottages with kitchen, and suites with a bedroom and living area, mini fridge, and microwave. **Sea**

Glass, the inn's popular restaurant, serves all three meals. $200–2,000 depending on season and accommodation, plus 5 percent hotel fee.

✎ **Higgins Beach Inn** (207-883-6684; higginsbeachinn.com), 34 Ocean Ave., Scarborough 04074 (7 miles south of Portland). Open mid-May–mid-Oct. A well-cared-for 1890s three-story wooden summer hotel near sandy, gorgeous Higgins Beach. The dining room, **Garofalo's**, features seafood and pasta dishes from owner Diane's Sicilian family recipes (entrées $16–27). Upstairs the 22 guest rooms are archetypal summer hotel rooms— simple, clean, and airy—13 with private bath. $200 double with private bath, $90 with shared bath, with a minimum two-night stay in summer.

The Breakers Inn (207-883-4820; thebreakersinn.com) 2 Bay View Ave., Higgins Beach, Scarborough. One of co-author Chris Tree's favorite inns in Maine, this B&B in a 1900 private home draws praise from its guests who delight in its location. Fifteen guest rooms, some pine-paneled and some overlooking the sea, hold antiques and classic summer cottage decor, and the nights are filled with the sound of crashing waves. $150–215 depending on season; no credit cards.

INNS AND B&BS **Pomegranate Inn** (207-772-1006 or 1-800-356-0408; pomegranateinn.com), 49 Neal St., Portland 04102. In eight amazing rooms, bold, hand-painted walls by Portland artist Heidi Gerquest create an energetic atmosphere; five have a gas fireplace. Count on a fantastic breakfast from innkeeper Dana Moos, author of *The Art of Breakfast*, like egg roulade with leeks, Parmesan, and lobster. $229–329 per room in-season, $189–299 off-season, of course including breakfast.

Morrill Mansion Bed & Breakfast (207-774-6900; morrillmansion.com), 249 Vaughan St., Portland 04102. Seven bedrooms are named for local neighborhoods and old families in this elegant B&B, next to Maine Medical Center and on the edge of the West End, an easy walk to midtown. The building was completely done over by owner David Parker, and all rooms have queen beds, private bath, and cable TV/DVD. $99–239 includes a breakfast buffet with an egg custard, French toast, warm fruit crisp and yogurt, and more. Afternoon treats, perhaps whoopie pies, are served in the second-floor guest living room.

The Mercury (207-775-0224 or 1-800-600-1557; mercuryinn.com), 273 State St., Portland 04101. This small Victorian on the hill below Portland's main street, Congress, is the favorite stop for visitors who like a quiet place with all the basic comforts. Six rooms have been furnished by owners Tim Karu and Jacob Krueger with bright, clean, modern furnishings; all show the owners' concern for the environment. $110–175.

Inn on Carleton Bed & Breakfast (207-775-1910; innoncarleton.com), 46 Carleton St., Portland 04102. A beautiful building in the hands of a hospitality professional. Buddy Marcum has revitalized this town house in Portland's West End, updating the beds and the rooms with modern furniture and embellishing the classic structure to make it a fine addition to Portland's small inns. Marcum is a flight attendant; when he's working part time, his well-trained staff cater to his guests. $120–225.

West End Inn (207-772-1377 or 1-800-338-1377; westendbb.com), 146 Pine St., Portland 04102. This 1871 brick townhouse combines natural elegance with colorful decor. The most popular of the six rooms is Cliff Island, with 12-foot ceilings, private deck, and white and blue accents. All have private bath, cable TV, ceiling fan, and air-conditioning. $119–229 includes full breakfast.

Inn at Park Spring (207-774-1059 or 1-800-437-8511; innatparkspring.com), 135 Spring St., Portland 04101. At one of the most convenient locations in town, Nancy and John Gonsalves offer six well-appointed guest rooms with private bath and sitting area. The handsome Museum Room is painted yellow and furnished with two wing chairs and a four-poster queen bed. Breakfast is served in the formal dining room with floor-to-ceiling windows; a French toast croissant stuffed with marmalade and cream cheese could be on the menu. $125–225.

The Chadwick Bed & Breakfast (207-774-5141 or 1-800-774-2137; thechadwick.com), 140 Chadwick St., Portland 04102. Under the management of innkeeper E. Scot Fuller. Four rooms on the second floor have cushy beds, flat-screen TV and DVD, and private bath (but two are across the hall). A full breakfast completes the experience. The back garden and a big sitting room with capacious chairs and couches are ideal for relaxation. $100–250.

🐾 🏆 ✈ ♿ **Inn at St. John** (207-773-6481 or 1-800-636-9127; innatstjohn.com), 939 Congress St., Portland 04102. A 39-room hotel built in 1897 to accommodate railroad passengers arriving at Union Station (unfortunately long gone), this place is convenient for guests arriving by Greyhound and Vermont Transit, though it's a hike to downtown. Attractive rooms are well managed by innkeeper Paul Hood. $59–295, depending on season, includes continental breakfast.

✳ Where to Eat

DINING OUT

IN PORTLAND

♻ **Back Bay Grill** (207-772-8833; backbaygrill.com), 65 Portland St. It's always a good night for dinner at Back Bay Grill, where a lot of history hasn't made the dining room stiff, perhaps because the mural on the wall always provides such a good example of bon temps—and you can be assured of fine service and excellent wine. Scottish salmon with chanterelles in-season or braised pork chops with fava beans might be on the always appealing menu. Entrées $25–36.

Piccolo (207-747-5307; piccolomaine.com), 111 Middle St. Damian Sansonetti, from New York's Bar Boulud, and his wife and business partner, Ilma Jeil Lopez, a pastry chef with her own New York credentials from Le Bernadin, prepare exquisite Italian-inspired meals tailored to the best provisions of each season.

Fore Street (207-775-2717; forestreet.biz), 288 Fore St. Open for dinner nightly. Reservations a must in summer, but there are open tables at 5:30 when the dining room opens. Sam Hayward oversees meals full with his signature integrity. Great roast pork, turned on a spit in the open kitchen, or fish roasted in a wood-fired oven, or roast quail, or just a few chicken livers quickly sautéed, and the best steamed mussels with garlic almond butter. The local vegetable side dishes are not to be missed, nor are desserts like peach tarte tatin. Entrées $18–35.

Hugo's (207-774-8538; hugos.net), 88 Middle St. An original, adventurous menu of small plates creates an evening packed with revelations. Combinations of flavors

BACK BAY GRILL

and quirky juxtapositions, perhaps porchetta with toothwort or sweet onion agnolotti, leave diners in a reverie. Plates $22, five courses for $90.

✪ **Miyake** (207-871-9170; miyake restaurants.com), 468 Fore St. Open for lunch and dinner Mon.–Sat. In-season a variety of wild salmon allows a taste of the Pacific's best. Uni, cracked fresh from the urchin shell, and ankimo are exceptional, and the miso soup is of the highest quality. Omakase nigiri, $70, presents 10 pieces of the freshest fish possible.

♿ **five fifty-five** (207-761-0555; five fifty-five.com), 555 Congress St. Chef-owner Steve Corry makes even hamburgers an unusual pleasure. But try black pepper ice cream or other flavors the evening menu offers for real adventure. A fall menu offered paper-wrapped flounder, served with couscous and black olive tangerine butter; a steak might come with crispy potatoes. Entrées $15 (from the bar menu)–35. Reservations advised.

✪ **Emilitsa** (207-221-0245; emilitsa.com), 547 Congress St. The starter freebie, a yellow lentil purée with toasted pita, alerts you to an emphasis on vibrant flavors. Spanakopita was never so fresh, moussaka as light lamb chops and chicken livers as savory. Ask for the right Greek wines and discover how perfectly they pair. Entrées $25–36.

Caiola's (207-772-1110; caiolas.com), 58 Pine St. A short walk into the West End, Caiola's makes a burger that is a moist marvel, and the steak, pork chop, house cannelloni, and more are, too. Entrées $22–27.

Scales (207-761-0380; scalesrestaurant .com), 68 Commercial St. Owned by Dana Street of Street & Co. and Sam Hayward of Fore Street, this hopping place on the waterfront sells the city's best fried oysters, excellent ceviche and raw bar oysters, and fine seafood and steaks. A reservation is recommended.

Paciarino (207-774-3500; paciarino .com), 470 Fore St. Fabiana de Savino and Enrico Barbiero make fresh pasta daily to be lunched on with fresh tomato sauce or with pesto, or enjoyed at dinner in somewhat larger portions. The light, deft touch with fine olive oil (the gold-foil-wrapped bottle is an elixir, friends assert) and other fine imported products also for sale make a meal here utterly refreshing and *saporito*—which is "tasty" in Italian. Entrées $16–18.

Central Provisions (207-805-1085; central -provisions.com), 414 Fore St., burst into the foodie scene with culinary fireworks that haven't let up. Small plates, each crafted to make memories, like caramelized sheep's cheese, suckling pig, or orrechiete with garlic scapes, will lure you back for more. Entrées $14–24, but since you will order multiple plates, expensive.

Isa Bistro (207- 808-8533; isaportlandme .com), 79 Portland St. Closed Tuesday. Lamb merguez sliders glimmer on the menu; the tagliatelle Bolognese is perfect, and so is the braised rabbit. Three meatballs and a dish of sautéed Brussels sprouts is a perfect supper. Entrées $16–22.

Drifters Wife (drifterswife.com) 63 Washington Ave., Portland. Embraced by the food press for precise and inventive plates of such things as beef tongue with anchovy, Israeli couscous, or Atlantic mackerel with caponata, this small restaurant is set in the front of a wine shop devoted to the biodynamic and natural wines of France—the shop is called Maine & Loire. *Bon Appétit* called it one of the country's best new restaurants in 2016.

Outliers Eatery (207-747-4166; outlier seatery.com), 231 York St. Cool urban style reigns in this glimmering room, while lobster gnocchi and duck confit hash (a brunch dish) make the meals extremely satisfying. Entrées $15–29.

Vinland (207-653-8617; vinland.me), 593 Congress St. Open since the fall of 2013, David Levi features snacks of reindeer lichen, beet chips with strained yogurt, cucumber and chive, and something called Angel Egg, his spin on a deviled egg, at this Maine-sourced restaurant on Congress Square, near the art museum; main courses are determined by the season.

& **Local 188** (207-761-7909; local188.com), 685 Congress St. Open Tue.–Sat. for dinner, and Sunday brunch. A tapas bar and dinner restaurant with a great lounge and bar. The Spanish bias is evident, as is local produce and a stray influence from Turkey or elsewhere. Spanish wines are a specialty. Try the gazpacho, the garlic shrimp, grilled chorizo, or paella. Entrées $18 and up; tapas $4–14.

Ribollita (207-774-2972; ribollitamaine .com), 41 Middle St. Open for dinner

Mon.–Sat. The classics are the draw at this welcoming place, with handmade pasta in butternut squash ravioli as one example, and the creamiest flan in town. Entrées $12.50–20.

✪ **Petite Jacqueline** (207-553-7044; bistropj.com), 46 Market St. French bistro fare priced right. Quiche, roast chicken, perhaps choucroute garnie on Friday for the plat du jour, and always tarte tatin. Entrées $13–26.

The East Ender (207-879-7669; eastender portland.com), 47 Middle St. A cider-brined local pork chop and a plate of baby back ribs argued for a return visit to this friendly, comfortable place with an affection for good meat and Wed.-night half-off wine by the bottle. Entrées $16–22.

& **Street & Company** (207-775-0887; street andcompany.net), 33 Wharf St. Open for dinner daily at 5:30. Reservations recommended. The noisy, packed dining rooms here, and a comfortable bar with upholstered seats, are filled with lovers of the wonderful fish, inventive specials, and comfortable standards like lobster diavolo for two, mussels Provençal, and scallops in Pernod and cream. The raw bar serves up the best oysters in town. Entrées $18–32.

Liquid Riot Bottling Company (207-221-8889; liquidriot.com), 250 Commercial St. Open daily 11:30–1 AM. A microbrewery that experiments with fermentation both in the glass and on the plate. Pub food in a fantastically cool space.

Union (207-808-8700; thepresshotel.com), 390 Congress St. The glossy restaurant in The Press Hotel opened in 2015 to praise for scallops with crisp pork belly and roasted cod with clams, confit lamb shoulder and white anchovy tempura. Entrées $19–30.

✪ **Sonny's** (207-772-7774; sonnysportland .com), 83 Exchange St. Open daily. Sonny's bar area in an elegantly renovated old bank is perfect for an inventive cocktail, and its tables and booths are a fine place to enjoy South and Central American and Southwestern flavors. Dishes might include beef brisket enchiladas or a roasted poblano cheeseburger. Entrées $14–24.

Boda (207-347-7557; bodamaine.com), 671 Congress St. Closed Mon. "Very Thai" means fragrances and flavors turned up a notch from the typical Thai restaurant; it also means exceptional dishes anyone can love. Romelo salad with betel leaves, a range of skewered meats and vegetables, and entrées like pork hock with star anise. Entrées $12–14.

Zapoteca (207-772-8242; zapotecarestaurant.com), 505 Fore St. Eat at the lively bar or in the dining room and enjoy ceviche with crab and Maine shrimp; enchiladas stuffed with the same under green chili sauce; or a local rib eye with lime, oregano, and cilantro salsa.

The Corner Room (207-879-4747; thecornerroomkitchenandbar.com), 110 Exchange St. Harding Lee Smith runs four "Rooms." This one features fresh pasta in all shapes and sizes with lamb ragu, mushrooms, and cream, or all'Amatriciana can be counted on for lunch or dinner. Pizza and a long antipasto list of cheeses and cured meats. $15 and up.

The Grill Room (207-774-2333; thegrillroomandbar.com), 84 Exchange St. Harding Lee Smith takes care of grilled steaks with The Grill Room, where you can also order wood-oven pizza and, depending on the season, grilled swordfish, skewered scallops with rosemary and mushroom risotto, and a grilled rib eye with béarnaise and frites. The bar is a good place to meet a friend. Entrées $12–37.

Boone's Fish House and Oyster Room (207-774-5725; boonesfishhouse.com), 86 Commercial St. Fried and fresh seafood, raw oysters, a more inventive menu—local lamb flat bread and Asian-inspired dishes—upstairs where the open deck is a summer destination.

ON MUNJOY HILL

&. **The Front Room** (207-773-3366; thefrontroomrestaurant.com), 73 Congress St. Open daily for all three meals. Bustling and hectic on weekends, you can find meat loaf, roast pork chops, grilled flatiron steak, and mushroom ragu with polenta. Easy to understand why it's full, but the noise can overwhelm. Entrées $15–21.

&. **Blue Spoon** (207-773-1116; bluespoonme.com), 89 Congress St. Open for lunch and dinner Tue.–Sat., brunch on Sat. This small restaurant at the top of Munjoy Hill cooks up straightforward dishes with skill and keeps them reasonably priced. Local stuff in-season, but the juicy burger and large bowls of

mussels with lemon and garlic are mainstays. Entrées $15–20.

Lolita Vinoteca + Asador (207-775-5652; lolita-portland.com), 90 Congress St. Guy and Stella Hernandez bring years of refining small plates into bursts of fine flavor to Lolita, with its lamb kefte with figs and market fish accented with aioli. Open for lunch Sat.–Sun., dinner daily. Medium plates $14, large $24.

OUTSIDE PORTLAND

Gather (207-847-3250; gathermaine.com), 189 Main St., Yarmouth. Open Tue.–Sat. for dinner, Sun. brunch 9:30–1:30. The kitchen works on the stage of an old Masonic Hall, making Neapolitan-style pizza with house-made sausage, or local pork with milk and cheese polenta; the fried Brussels sprouts are excellent. Entrées $13–22.

&. **The Point Restaurant at The Black Point Inn** (207-883-2500 or 1-800-258-0003; blackpointinn.com), 510 Black Point Rd., Prouts Neck. Open May–Jan. 1, reservation required in the formal restaurant. Casual entrées in the **Chart Room**, no reservations accepted, range $16–31. The cocktails on the porch overlooking the coastline are always fine. Entrées $24–34.

🍸&. **Saltwater Grille** (207-799-5400; saltwatergrille.com), 231 Front St., South Portland. Open daily for lunch and dinner, with fabulous views across the bay to Portland. Entrées include marinated hanger steak with mashed potatoes, baby back ribs, and roast salmon—all in enormous portions. Entrées $19–30.

The Purple House (brescaandthehoneybee.com), 378 Walnut Hill Rd., North Yarmouth. Krista Kern Desjarlais bought this small building in North Yarmouth in 2015 for her wood-fired bakery, with once-a-month dinners by reservation only. Montreal-style bagels, boiled in water with a little honey and undergoing a slow rise, are a specialty. Cuban coffee and her other signature, fantastic ice cream.

EATING OUT

IN AND AROUND THE OLD PORT

Bao Bao Dumpling House (207-772-8400; baobao-maine.com), 133 Spring St. Cara Stadler's

Portland branch serves Vietnamese iced coffee. The boiled peanuts are a fantastic starter; the dumpling menu includes soup dumplings and other "wrapped treasures."

Eventide Oyster Co. (207-774-8538; eventideoysterco.com), 86 Middle St. Count on fresh oysters and the best choices of wine to go with them. Crab salads, grilled squid, chowders, fried oyster sides, and dinner of grilled beef brisket are all keenly tailored to taste delicious. The atmosphere is boisterous, not to mention loud. Excellent cocktails.

The Honey Paw (207-774-8538; thehoney paw.com) 78 Middle St. Closed Tue. Part of a little triumvirate in this one block of Middle Street, The Honey Paw serves eclectic noodles like ramen and ravioli with exalted flavors. Count on good wine. $14–36.

🖋 El Rayo (207-780-8226; elrayotaqueria .com), 26 Free St. (and 245 Rt. 1, Scarborough). Tacos, of course, like *al pastor*, filled with braised pork with grilled pineapple salsa, and great sides and beginners such as ceviche, fried plantains, and fundido—baked cheese with chorizo. Big burritos, daily specials; finish with *dulces suenos*, mocha milk with tequila and Kahlua. Excellent margaritas.

Vignola Cinque Terre (207-772-1330; vignolamaine.com), 10 Dana St. Open daily for dinner, Sat. for lunch and Sun. for brunch. Vignola Cinque Terre focuses on pizza, cured meats, and straightforward entrées like grilled skirt steak, pork loin, and a cassoulet with cotechino. Entrées $12–28.

Duckfat (207-774-8080; duckfat.com), 43 Middle St. Open daily 11 AM–dinner. Sister restaurant to Hugo's (see *Dining Out*), with the soul of a gourmand on a budget. Incredible fries rise from a mix of duck fat and vegetable oil. Panini are crisp cases of vegetable ratatouille or bacon, goat cheese, and tomatoes. Rich milk shakes, tender beignets, sweet dessert sandwiches of brioche and jam. Salads and iced coffee for a light lunch. Panini $6–13.50.

Sur Lie (207-956-7350; sur-lie.com), 11 Free St. Tapas and wine, wine and tapas—try the hanger steak and Lanzos Tempranillo or the fried oysters and Contadi Castaldi "Rose" with its bubbles. Happy hour paté and charcuterie with perfect garnishes are a steal. $8–14.

Pai Men Miyake (207-541-9204; miyake restaurants.com), 188 State St. Deep bowls of miso broth with pork belly and noodles might be the main attraction, but the pork buns and crab and scallop hamayaki with eel sauce will have you licking your chops. The sake list is elaborate and worth your while. $9–14.

🖋 Flatbread Pizza (207-772-8777; flat breadcompany.com), 72 Commercial St. Open daily 11:30 AM–dinner. One of a small chain of pizza joints (nine others include one in Paia Maui, Hawaii). Flatbread bakes its pies in a clay, wood-fired oven shaped like a low igloo—right in the middle of the restaurant. Kids are always sitting on a stone, mesmerized by the fire. Our favorite pizza features house maple-fennel sausage, sun-dried tomatoes, onions, mushrooms, mozzarella, and Parmesan. Outside deck overlooks the ferry terminal.

Schulte & Herr (207-773-1997), 349 Cumberland Ave. Open Tue.–Sun. 8–3. Fresh German food, from crisp potato pancakes with house lox to tangy cucumber salad and spaetzle with Emmentaler to a poppy seed cake with vanilla sauce that was authenticated by our critical German companion.

Salvage BBQ (207-553-2100; salvagebbq .com), 919 Congress St. A big space dedicated to slow-smoked meat. Brisket, ribs, and chicken can be devoured with sides of slaw, collard greens, and smoked corn in-season. Peach pie and pecan pie for dessert.

Terlingua (207-808-8502; terlingua.me), 52 Washington Ave. Open daily for lunch and dinner, Sunday brunch. Smoked meat isn't the only draw, but it's the sell-out star at this modest spot packed with meat lovers. Fine sides and chili, empanadas, seared fish and a daily tostada. The pulled-pork Benedict is for brunch.

Figgy's Take-out (207-805-0085; fig gystakeoutandcatering.com), 4 Walker St. Call in the order and pick it up or eat it in front, in good weather—you will be certain to enjoy the fried chicken, the tender biscuits, and other fixings for a fried chicken dinner worth your money. Smoked gouda and eggplant on a biscuit offer much solace to any vegetarian.

Taco Escobarr (207-541-9097; taco escobarr.com), 548 Congress St. Closed Sun. A quick, cheap meal of three crisp, puffy, or

FIGGY'S TAKE-OUT

oldest sushi place has kept its high standards. You can count on Sapporo for a great dinner.

Jewel of India (207-828-2001; thejewelof india.com), 45 Western Ave., South Portland. Owned by the same family that made its reputation in Biddeford, this branch serves the same aromatic dishes.

AROUND PORTLAND

Bonobo (207-347-8267; bonobopizza .com), 46 Pine St. Open for lunch Wed.–Fri. 11:30–2:30, Sat. noon–4; dinner Sun.–Thu. 4–10, Fri.–Sat. 4–11. A wood-fired oven bakes pizza with a thin crust made with wet dough; many organic ingredients are used. Sausage and onion is one popular pie. The house pizza, Bonobo, holds mushrooms, prosciutto, spinach, cream, fontina, and thyme. Pizza $12.50–16.50.

Oh No Café (207-774-0773; ohnocafe.com), 87 Bracket St. Home of the best breakfast sandwiches in Portland and a smoked salmon on bialy that will feed your soul. Beer and wine to purchase for take-out only.

☺ **Otto and Enzo** (207-773-7099; otto portland.com), 576 Congress St. Exceptional pizza by the slice ($3.50) or pie. This is the spot to satisfy an appetite for thin-crust, remarkable pizza, perhaps with mashed potato and bacon, grilled eggplant and tomato, or classic pepperoni. Sister restaurant **Otto** (207-358-7870), 225 Congress St., is just as convivial; same terrific pizza.

🍴 ✐ ♿ **Becky's Diner** (207-773-7070; beckys.com), 390 Commercial St. Open daily 4 AM–9 PM, this is a genuine local favorite, known for soups and pies. Breakfast on fruit salad, a granola-and-yogurt bowl, and delicious grilled, homemade corn and blueberry muffins. Also reasonably priced lunch and dinner specials, and good chowder.

🍴 ✐ **Artemisia Café** (207-761-0135), 61 Pleasant St. (just behind and to the east of Holiday Inn by the Bay). Lunch Mon.–Fri., brunch Sat. and Sun., dinner Thu.–Sat. Salads, wraps, and sandwiches, from salade Niçoise to the Tuscan grill with portobello mushrooms, pesto, and goat cheese. A friendly spot for a quiet and good brunch or dinner.

Blue Rooster Food Co. (207-747-4157; blue roosterfoodcompany.com), 5 Dana St. Open

soft tacos wrapped around braised chicken or carne asada is a welcome thing. The hot salsa is guaranteed to raise your temperature.

Tiqa (207-808-8840; tiqa.net), 327 Commercial St. Tiqa serves Middle Eastern- and Mediterranean-inspired dishes like kibbeh nayyeh from Lebanon, kabobs and kefta, and Maine lobster paella. A big terrace for outside dining or an aperitif; wines from the Middle East as well as elsewhere. Entrées $18–35.

Slab (207-245-3088; slabportland.com), 25 Preble St. Thick, soft, irresistible Sicilian slab pizza devised by baking fanatic Stephen Lanzalotta. You can get a salad, or chickpea hummus, or meatloaf or caponata, and fantastic Italian pastry. Thursday night concerts at the outside picnic tables.

☺ **Empire Chinese Kitchen** (207-747-5063; portlandempire.com), 575 Congress St. A good Chinese restaurant that opened in the summer of 2013, Empire Chinese Kitchen serves dumplings, garlic string beans, dim sum, Peking duck buns, and lobster longevity noodles. Up to $19.

Benkay (207-773-5555; sushiman.com), 2 India St. A sushi bar with Western- and Japanese-style tables, one in the shape of a dory.

Sapporo Restaurant (207-772-1233; sappororestaurant.com), 230 Commercial St. Open for lunch and dinner daily. Portland's

PORTLAND'S BEST COCKTAILS

Every self-respecting bar has a cocktail list with some ambition, and gems are scattered around Portland, such as Boda's "The Fuge's Dilemma" made with a bourbon infused with 11 tigers—bitter and medicinal—or the perfect Old Fashioned at Eventide. But we depend on Hunt & Alpine Club (207-747-4754; huntandalpineclub.com), 75 Market St., for repeated brilliance from the diabolic cocktail shaker of John Myers—like the Modern, with scotch, sloe gin, lemon, and bitters; or their perfect version of the classic Penicillin, with scotch, ginger, honey, and lemon. The Scandinavian menu includes smoked trout deviled eggs and chewy brown bread and butter to go with the oysters. At The Bearded Lady's Jewel Box, (207-747-5384; the beardedladysjewelbox.com), 644 Congress St. (and probably no sign on the door), where you are one of the jewels, Nan'l Meiklejohn devises the cocktail list. If a TransEurope Express with scotch, Punt e Mes vermouth, yellow chartreuse, Campari, bitters, and a green chartreuse rinse isn't your go-to choice, there will be something even stranger and just as delicious on the cocktail menu. The food is not the point; It's best to eat before you get there.

Nancy English

HUNT AND ALPINE CLUB

11 AM–2 AM. A sandwich shop with a few stools and benches around its small perimeter. Blue Rooster serves bacon-wrapped hot dogs with cheese sauce and crispy onions, along with a pastrami Cuban and the Godfather—mortadella, salami, Swiss, and provolone. Check out the twist on poutine made with tater tots.

Portland Patisserie (207-553-2555; portlandpatisserie.com), 46 Market St. Excellent croissants and pain au chocolat, crêpes savory and sweet, salads (including Niçoise), quiche, pâté de campagne on

baguette, wine, beer, coffee, macarons, and other desserts.

BEYOND PORTLAND

✪ **158 Pickett Street Café** (207-799-8998), 158 Benjamin Pickett St., South Portland. Breakfast and lunch Tue.–Sun. They make the bagels so exactly right: chewy, slightly sour, utterly delicious, and golden brown. A variety of original soups in winter, local salads in summer, and sandwiches like ham and Brie with roasted grapes on baguette, Anestes Fotiades's favorite (and see portlandfoodmap .com, his work of art).

Enio's Eatery (207-799-0207), 347 Cottage Rd., South Portland. A well-respected couple who have worked in many kitchens and local establishments over the years offer a fine wine list and calamari, lamb, halibut, and excellent desserts.

🦞 **The Lobster Shack at Two Lights** (207-799-1677; lobstershacktwolights.com), 225 Two Lights Rd., Cape Elizabeth (off Rt. 77 at the tip of the cape, near Two Lights State Park). Open Apr.–late Oct., 11–8. Dine inside or out at this local landmark built in the 1920s, set below the lighthouse and next to the foghorn, where Herb and Martha Porch sell amazing quantities of lobster, chowder, fried Maine shrimp, scallops, clams, and lobster and crabmeat rolls. BYOB.

Elsmere BBQ and Wood Grill (207-619-1948; elsmerebbq.com), 448 Cottage Rd., South Portland. A former gas station with reclaimed wood and concrete rehab, Elsmere serves Texas BBQ slow-cooked on a custom-built smoker along with local craft beer.

🍴🦞 **The Good Table** (207-799-4663; the goodtable.net), 526 Ocean House Rd. (Rt. 77), Cape Elizabeth. Open Tue.–Sun. for breakfast, lunch, and dinner 8 AM–9 PM in summer, from 11 AM in winter, with 3 PM Sun. closing year-round. Beloved by its loyal regulars, the restaurant serves home-style standards, but the specials board is where the best meals can be found.

Ken's Place (207-883-6611), 207 Pine Point Rd., Scarborough. Open daily for lunch and dinner Apr.–Oct. You can depend on David Wilcox to make sure things are running smoothly here, and that the kitchen is scrupulous about changing the oil and serving the freshest seafood. Great fried clams.

COFFEE **Coffee by Design** (207-772-5533; coffeebydesign.com), 620 Congress St. and 67 India St., is a friendly local chain in a cheerful spot with plenty of tables and its own roasted beans in the coffee and espresso. **Arabica** (207-899-1833; arabicacoffeeportland .com), 2 Free St. We like this place's high ceilings and its cinnamon toast. The coffee is the best in town. **Crema** (207-210-6473), 9 Commercial St.—also owned by the owners of Arabica—makes perfect espresso with their own

perfectly roasted beans. Of course, people who flock to **Bard Coffee** (207-899-4788; bard coffee.com), 185 Middle St., would say their own favorite spot, with its expert espresso, is even better. **The Speckled Ax** (207-660-3333), 567 Congress St., provides a traditional glass of seltzer with a wood-oven-roasted espresso, which beat out Bard in one newly returned-from-Italy Mainer's opinion.

Perhaps best of all is **Tandem Coffee and Roastery** (207-899-0235), 122 Anderson St., where the coffee is transformed into America's favorite breakfast drink: come by at noon on Friday for free public cuppings. **Tandem Coffee + Bakery** (207-805-1887; tandemcoffee .com) 742 Congress St. A former gas station turned into a laundromat is now a coffee shop starring baker Briana Holt, who thinks up such incredible scones and bakes such perfect pies (like a raspberry custard) that you won't be able to resist.

DOUGHNUTS **The Holy Donut** (207-874-7774; theholydonut.com), 194 Park Ave. and 7 Exchange St., Portland, makes Maine potato doughnuts with unique flavors like chocolate sea salt and Allen's coffee brandy. The potato is mashed and added to the dough, which helps create the moist consistency of the doughnuts.

BAGELS **Union Co. Bagels** (207-747-4400; unionbagel.com), 147 Cumberland Ave. With organic flour, these are hand-rolled, boiled, and baked über authentic NYC bagels.

Nancy English

KEN'S PLACE

PASTRY AND PIES Standard Baking Co.
(207-773-2112; standardbakingco.com),
75 Commercial St. (below Fore Street restaurant). Artisanal French and Italian breads are
exceptional, and so are the rolls, baguettes,
brioches, and pain au chocolat. **Ten Ten Pié**
(207-956-7330) 171 Cumberland Ave., Portland. "Unlike any other bakery in Maine," one
customer crows, and what else could be true
when the offerings range from bento boxes of
cold ramen salad with marinated egg and
savory pies to lingonberry pinwheels and
macarons. **Scratch Baking** (207-799-0668;
scratchbakingco.com), 416 Preble St., South
Portland. The best bagels for those of us who
like slow-rise, crisp crust often sell out on
weekends; sandwiches on the other breads
baked here; extraordinary cookies, cakes,
pies. **Little Bigs** (207-747-4233; littlebigs
maine.com), 340 Main St., South Portland;
supplies Mainers with its own version of a
cronut—along with Nutella- and banana-filled
doughnuts, and savory pies like a breakfast
calzone and potato-crusted egg pies. **Two Fat
Cats** (207-347-5144; twofatcatsbakery.com),
47 India St., Portland. Cupcakes, terrific blueberry pie, red velvet cake, and many other
delectables.

ICE CREAM AND GELATO **Beal's Ice
Cream** (207-828-1335; bealsicecream.com),
12 Moulton St., is in the middle of the Old
Port (and has four other locations), making 17
percent butterfat premium ice cream. **Mount
Desert Island Ice Cream** (207-210-3432;
mdiic.com), 51 Exchange St., just up the
street, makes its own terrific ice creams,
some spiked with hot chili—but who can
resist the salted caramel? **Gorgeous Gelato**
(207-699-4309; gorgeousgelato.com), 434
Fore St., calls itself the only authentic gelato
in Portland and uses cream and whole milk in
its brilliantly flavored confections. Mariagra-
zia Zanardi and her husband, Donato
Giovine, from Milan, make gelato with "70
percent less fat" than premium ice cream.
Gelato Fiasco (207-699-4314; gelatofiasco
.com), 425 Fore St., moved in across the street
in late 2011. Time to take a stroll and com-
pare them all.

✳ Entertainment

All listings are in Portland unless otherwise
noted.

Cross Insurance Arena (207-775-3458;
crossarenaportland.com), 1 Civic Center
Square. An arena with 6,733 seats, the center
hosts year-round concerts, ice-skating spec-
taculars, Portland Pirates hockey games, and
more.

MUSIC **Portland Symphony Orchestra** (207-
773-6128; portlandsymphony.com), Merrill
Auditorium, 20 Myrtle St. (just off Congress
St. behind City Hall). The winter series runs
Sept.–May; in summertime, outdoor pops
concerts at different locations along the
shores of Casco Bay.

PORTopera (207-879-7678; portopera.org),
Merrill Auditorium. This critically acclaimed
company puts on an opera in mid-summer.

Portland Ovations (207-773-3150; portland
ovations.org). A series of orchestra, jazz, and
musical theater performances staged in fall
and winter at Merrill Auditorium.

Port City Music Hall (207-899-4990;
portcitymusichall.com), 504 Congress St.
Contemporary, popular music.

PROFESSIONAL SPORTS The **Portland Sea
Dogs** (1-800-936-3647; portlandseadogs.com),
a Double-A baseball team and Boston Red Sox
affiliate, play in Hadlock Stadium on Park
Ave. (next to the Expo). The **Maine Red Claws**
(207-210-6655; nba.com/dleague/maine), an
NBA Development League affiliated with the
Boston Celtics, had their first season in 2009–
10, playing in the Portland Expo Building on
Park Ave.

THEATER **Portland Stage** (207-774-0465;
portlandstage.com) is based in the city's old
Odd Fellows Hall (25A Forest Ave.), now an
elegant, intimate, 290-seat theater. This Equity
group stages a variety of shows Oct.–Apr.

Portland Players (207-799-7337), Thaxter
Theater, 420 Cottage Rd., South Portland. An
excellent community theater; the Players put
on productions Sept.–June.

Lyric Music Theater (207-799-1421), Ced-
ric Thomas Playhouse, 176 Sawyer St., South
Portland. Four musicals each winter.

St. Lawrence Arts Center (207-775-5568; stlawrencearts.org), 76 Congress St. An umbrella performance space for musicians, filmmakers, dance companies, and other artists. **The Good Theater** (207-885-5883), a resident theater company, performs four stage productions and one musical each season. The schedule changes constantly, so call to see what's doing.

✳ Selective Shopping

All listings are in Portland unless otherwise noted.

Angela Adams (207-774-3523; angela adams.com), 131 Middle St. This store sells the swirling, colorful carpets and handbags designed by Angela Adams: Pricey rugs are coveted nationwide. Sales held at the end of each retail season.

Ferdinand (207-761-2151; ferdinandhome store.com), 243 Congress St. Just steps from Angela Adams, Ferdinand is stuffed with low chic—T-shirts with charming animals and inexpensive pins, earrings, and jewelry, all infused with owner Diane Toepfer's eccentric aesthetic.

Sea Bags (207-780-0744; seabags.com), 24 Custom House Wharf, sells fashionable, eco-friendly tote bags made in Portland, from recycled sails.

ANTIQUES **Allen and Walker** (207-772-8787), 684 Congress St. A mix of 1960s modern and older antiques, with some Japanese pottery.

ART GALLERIES **Art Walks** are held the first Friday of every month, when galleries citywide hold open houses.

Greenhut Galleries (207-772-2693 or 1-888-772-2693; greenhutgalleries.com), 146 Middle St. Greenhut Galleries represents many of Maine's top artists and sculptors.

Susan Maasch Fine Art (207-478-4087; susanmaaschfineart.com), 4 City Center. Established and new artists.

BOOKSTORES **Longfellow Books** (207-772-4045; longfellowbooks.com), 1 Monument Way, is Portland's literary hot spot, stocking a full range of titles and hosting frequent

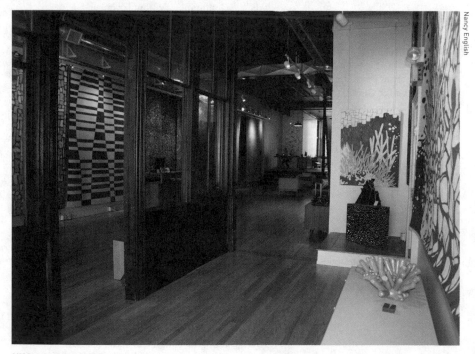

Nancy English

ANGELA ADAMS'S STORE

readings by local and national authors. **Sherman's Maine Coast Book Shops** (207-773-4100; shermans.com), 49 Exchange St., opened this fifth Maine location in 2015 with book signings and toys.

Print (207-536-4778; printbookstore.com), 273 Congress St. A new bookstore at the base of Munjoy Hill is part of a welcome trend of new bookstores in town. Look for author readings with a focus on community, a diverse stock of great books and a very comfortable place to browse.

Antiquarian-book lovers should check out **Carlson-Turner Books** (207-773-4200; carlsonturnerbooks.com), 241 Congress St. **Yes Books** (207-775-3233), 589 Congress St., founded by Pat Murphy, is considered by some to be the best used bookstore in Maine.

FOOD Micucci Grocery (207-775-1854; micuccigrocery.com), 45 India St. Order prosciutto and Parmigiana at the counter, shop for wine, olive oil, and maybe an Italian pastry while you wait.

Maine's Pantry (207-228-2028; maines pantry.com), 111 Commercial St. Many of the best food products made in Maine can be found here—like Stanchfield Farms' high-quality jams and jellies, and Captain Mowett Blue Flame hot sauce.

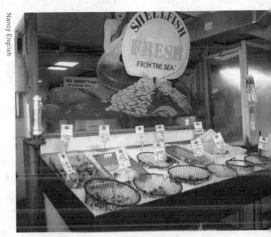

HARBOR FISH OYSTERS

Len Libby's Candies (207-883-4897; lenlibby.com), 419 Rt. 1, Scarborough. The candies made here are good, but the real draw is the enormous moose named Lenny—made with 1,700 pounds of milk chocolate, the only life-sized chocolate moose in the world, put together in 1997.

Browne Trading Market (207-775-7560; brownetrading.com), 260 Commercial St. Open Mon.–Sat. 10–6. Formerly a fish wholesaler serving upscale restaurants throughout the United States, now selling its own smoked salmon, trout, shrimp, scallops, mussels, fresh seafood, and caviar, along with a wide assortment of cheeses and wine.

Harbor Fish Market (207-775-0251 or 1-800-370-1790; harborfish.com), 9 Custom House Wharf. Open Mon.–Sat. 8:30–5:30. The epicenter of fish, lobster, crabs, oysters, clams, eels, and squid, to name a few, which you can ship anywhere you like.

SPECIAL SHOPS Portmanteau (207-774-7276; portmanteauonline.com), 3 Wharf St. Nancy Lawrence began by stitching canvas bags but has long since established a reputation for the distinctive tapestry handbags, totes, backpacks, luggage, and cloaks fabricated in her store.

Leroux Kitchen (207-553-7665; leroux kitchen.com), 161 Commercial St. Everything you could possibly need to make a gourmet meal, from marble mortars and pestles to Henckels knives, Viking cookware to wines and prepared foods.

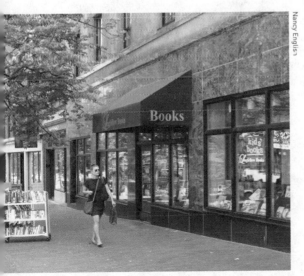

LONGFELLOW BOOKS

Vena's Fizz House (207-747-4901; venas fizzhouse.com), 345 Fore St., Portland. This emporium of bar gadgets, glassware, and specialty drink ingredients deserves a visit when nonalcoholic drinks are served, whenever it's open; on Wed.–Sat. after 4 (and all day Sunday), you can order alcoholic craft cocktails to sample the stuff you might want to bring home from the biggest collection of bitters you are likely to encounter. A short food menu offers lobster BLT, nuts, and pickles.

Cabela's (cabelas.com), Haigis Pkwy., Scarborough 04070. Located at I-95 Exit 42. Cabela's, a nationwide outdoor retail chain, opened this new 130,000-square-foot showroom in spring 2008.

✳ Special Events

Mid-March: **Maine Jewish Film Festival** (mjff.org).

June: **Old Port Festival** (second Sunday)—a celebration that began in the 1970s with the revival of the Old Port; includes a parade, various performances, street vendors, and special sales.

July: **July 4th Portland Stars and Stripes Extravaganza.** The Portland Symphony and a guest perform on the Eastern Promenade before the fireworks.

Mid-July: **Yarmouth Clam Festival**—arts and crafts, plenty of clams, performances, more. **Maine Brewer's Festival Summer Session** (mainebreweersguild.org), now at Thompson's Point. More than 50 Maine microbreweries show off their beers.

August: **Cumberland Crafts Fair**, Cumberland Fairgrounds. **Sidewalk Art Festival**, Congress St.

September: **Cumberland County Fair**, Cumberland.

October: **Harvest on the Harbor**, Portland.

Post-Thanksgiving–Christmas: **Victorian Holiday Portland**—with tree lighting, the arrival of Father Christmas, costumed carolers, and special events through Christmas.

FREEPORT

Think of Freeport, and you'll likely think of shopping. This is one coastal town that welcomes visitors every day of the year, even on Christmas morning, when the famous L.L. Bean store is open for business. A 24-hour, 365-day-a-year superstore, L.L. Bean has been a landmark since the famous boot was developed back in 1912. But it was with the influx of seconds and factory stores in the early 1980s that the reputation of Freeport as a shopping mecca took hold.

The retail facades, however, belie a rich and varied history dating back more than 200 years. The first known residents of the area were several tribes of the Wabanaki. Attempts by colonists to settle in the area resulted in a series of wars throughout the 1600s and early 1700s. By 1715 epidemics of European diseases and the settlers' persistence ended the Native American hold on the area, and a peace treaty with the Penobscots was signed in 1725.

Originally a part of North Yarmouth, Freeport was granted a charter, separating it from the town in 1789. A longtime legend (somewhat controversial, because there is no documented evidence of the occurrence) holds that in 1820 the papers separating Maine from Massachusetts were signed in the historical Jameson Tavern.

During the War of 1812, shipbuilding became an important industry, with one famous boat inspiring Whittier's poem, "The Dead Ship of Harpswell." In the 1880s shoe factories sprouted up in Freeport, adding another industry to its economy.

When an electric trolley was built to connect Portland and Yarmouth with Brunswick and Lewiston, it passed through Freeport. Many trolley companies built parks to encourage ridership; likewise, a developer built the Casco Castle Hotel to draw tourists to South Freeport. The hotel burned down, but a stone tower remains (on private property) and can be best viewed from Winslow Memorial Park or the harbor.

Despite the proliferation of shops, the village has retained the appearance of older days—even McDonald's has been confined to a gracious old house, with no golden arches in sight. The Freeport Historical Society operates a research library and museum in a historic house in the midst of the retail sector.

GUIDANCE **FreeportUSA** (207-865-1212; freeportusa.com), P.O. Box 452, Freeport 04032, operates a visitors center in a relocated historic hose tower on Depot St. Brochures, information, and restrooms can be found here.

The Maine Tourism Association's welcome center in Kittery stocks some Freeport brochures, and there is another state information center on Rt. 1 just south of Freeport, in Yarmouth, at Exit 17 off I-95.

GETTING THERE Excellent bus service on **Concord Coach Lines** (see *Getting There* in "Portland Area") runs from Boston to Brunswick. The Amtrak **Downeaster** (1-800-USA-RAIL; amtrak.com) offers service through to Brunswick with stops in Freeport, with five round-trips daily.

✳ Villages

South Freeport has been a fishing center from its beginning, when it was known as Strout's Port. Between 1825 and 1830 up to 12,000 barrels of mackerel were packed and shipped from

Courtesy of Freeport USA

DOWNTOWN FREEPORT

here each year. Later the area specialty became lobster packing. Offering a very different feel from the chaotic shopping frenzy of downtown Freeport, the harbor features great seafood. From here you can take a cruise to explore Eagle and Seguin Islands in summer.

Porter's Landing. Once the center of commercial activity, this now quiet residential neighborhood nestles amid rolling hills, woods, and streams. The village is part of the Harraseeket Historic District on the National Register of Historic Places.

✳ To See and Do

🦞 🐾 ✍ ♿ **Desert of Maine** (207-865-6962; desertofmaine.com), 95 Desert Rd., Freeport. Open daily, early May–mid-Oct., 9–5. Admission runs $10.50 adults, $7.75 ages 13–16, $6.75 ages 4–12. Narrated tram tours and self-guided walks through 40 acres of sand that was once the Tuttle Farm. Heavily farmed, then extensively logged to feed the railroad, the topsoil eventually gave way to the glacial sand deposit beneath it, which spread . . . and spread until entire trees sank below the surface. Children love it, especially the gem hunt, when you sluice for gems from a bag of "tailings" guaranteed to contain small or large gemstones or fossils (from $6 to $8.50). Camping available (see *Lodging*).

BREWERY The excellent **Maine Beer Company** (207-221-5711; mainebeercompany.com), 525 Rt. 1, has a tasting room for a special introduction to their beer, with a view of the brewery through wide glass windows.

CANOEING The **Harraseeket River** in Freeport is particularly nice for canoeing. Start at Mast Landing, the northeastern end of the waterway; there are also launching sites at Winslow Memorial Park on Staples Point Rd. and at South Freeport Harbor.

MUST SEE

L.L. BEAN (1-877-755-2326; llbean.com), 95 Main St. Open 24 hours a day, 365 days a year, as are the three other stores listed below (but not the outlet). With a kids' department, a camping department, a pond stocked with brown or brook trout, and a trail "rock" to test new hiking boots, the building resembles a fancy shopping mall more than it does a single store. Back in 1912 Leon Leonwood Bean developed his boot, or Maine Hunting Shoe, a unique combination of rubber bottom and leather top. "You cannot expect success hunting deer or moose if your feet are not properly dressed," Bean wrote in his very first catalog. Ninety out of the first 100 boots he built literally fell apart at the seams, so Bean refunded the purchasers' money and began a company tradition of guaranteed customer satisfaction, including all-night hours for the outdoorsmen who passed through in the wee hours. Bean himself died in 1967.

L.L. BEAN BIKE, BOAT & SKI STORE

L.L. Bean Hunting and Fishing Store (1-877-755-2326, llbean.com), 95 Main St. All the fishing equipment is here, along with archery gear and hunting rifles. Bean also sells used guns, and will buy guns in good condition. Fish and game mounts are hung around the store, giving the place a hunting lodge atmosphere.

L.L. Bean Bike, Boat & Ski Store (1-877-755-2326, llbean.com), 95 Main St. When the weather warms up, the bike and boat displays bloom; when it gets colder it's time for all the ski equipment, snowshoes, toboggans, and sleds to take a bigger share of the space.

L.L. Bean Home Store (1-877-755-2326, llbean.com), 12 Nathan Nye St., Freeport. Opened in the summer of 2009, the Home Store stocks attractive, inexpensive quilts based on vintage designs, good-quality flannel and cotton sheets, towels, hooked-wool pillows, and furniture like a wicker side table.

CHOCOLATE **Wilbur's of Maine** (207-865-4071; wilburs.com), 174 Lower Main St. Chocolate Factory Tours ($4.50) on many Saturdays allow some hands-on education and of course, consumption of the delicious products. Check the website for the schedule.

GOLF **Freeport Country Club** (207-865-0711; harrisgolfonline.com), 2 Old County Rd., Freeport. Nine holes, golf clinics, driving range, pro shop, and snack bar.

MUSEUM ✐ **Harrington House** (207-865-3170; freeporthistoricalsociety.org), 45 Main St., Freeport. Hours vary depending on season; check the website under VISIT US. Donations appreciated. Built of local brick and granite, this 1830 house and its garden are maintained by the Freeport Historical Society as a museum, research library, and archive.

SPECIAL LEARNING PROGRAMS **L.L. Bean Outdoor Discovery Schools** (1-888-552-3261; llbean.com/adventure), Rt. 1, Freeport. You can get your toes wet—literally, if you're kayaking—with L.L. Bean's Discovery Series. For a fee, participants can take a shuttle bus from the downtown store to enjoy 1½ hours of (Memorial Day–Columbus Day) fly casting, kayaking, archery, and clay shooting—and, when the snow permits, until March, cross-country skiing and snowshoeing.

The L.L. Bean Outdoor Discovery Schools also offer half-day or longer tours and classes that cover the basics—such as "Introduction to Stand-Up Paddleboarding." A two-night Casco Bay Island Kayak Camping Trip includes lobster dinner.

✳ Green Space

✐ **Winslow Memorial Park** (207-865-4198; freeportmaine.com), Staples Point Rd., South Freeport. Open Memorial Day–Sept. A 90-acre municipal park with a sandy beach and large grassy picnicking area; also boating and 100-site oceanside campground ($20–27 per night for nonresidents). Facilities include restrooms with showers. $2 nonresident admission fee.

✐ **Mast Landing Audubon Sanctuary** (207-781-2330; maineaudubon.org), Upper Mast Landing Rd. (take Bow St. south), Freeport. Maintained by Maine Audubon, this 140-acre sanctuary offers trails through apple orchards, woods, meadows, and along a millstream. Several paths radiate from a 1-mile loop trail. You might even get lucky and see mink, deer, or porcupines.

✿ ✐ **Bradbury Mountain State Park** (207-688-4712; bradburymountain.com), Rt. 9, 528 Hallowell Rd., Pownal (6 miles from Freeport: from I-95, take Exit 20 and follow signs). Open year-round. $4.50 nonresidents ages 12 and older, $1 ages 5–11, under 5 free. The summit, accessible by an easy (even for young children) 0.5-mile hike, yields a splendid view of Casco Bay and New Hampshire's White Mountains. Facilities in the 800-acre park include a small playground, a softball field, hiking trails, toilets, and a 35-site overnight camping area.

✐ **Pettengill Farm** (207-865-3170; freeporthistoricalsociety.org), Pettengill Rd., Freeport. Managed by the Freeport Historical Society (which conducts periodic guided tours), the grounds are open anytime. A saltwater farm with 140 acres of open fields and woodland that overlooks the Harraseeket Estuary, with a totally unmodernized vintage-1810 saltbox house.

✐ ♿ **Wolfe's Neck Woods State Park** (207-865-4465), 425 Wolfe's Neck Rd. (take Bow St., across from L.L. Bean), Freeport. Open Apr.–Nov. A 233-acre park with shoreline hiking along Casco Bay, the Harraseeket River, and salt marshes, with excellent birding. Ospreys nest here, and an eagle is nearby. Guided nature walks and scattered picnic tables and grills. Day-use fee for nonresident adults. Next door, Wolfe's Neck Farm (207-865-4469; wolfesneckfarm.org), 184 Burnett Rd., has bicycles and kayaks to rent, animals to admire, dinners and ice cream, and a campground.

✳ Lodging

All listings are in Freeport unless otherwise noted.

INNS AND B&BS ✻ ✑ ♿ **Harraseeket Inn** (207-865-9377 or 1-800-342-6423; harraseeket inn.com), 162 Main St. The Gray family—Nancy, her son Chip, and daughter Penelope (all former Maine Guides)—have a passion for Maine expressed through meticulous and warm innkeeping. Two blocks north of L.L. Bean, their inn began as a five-room B&B in the 1800 Federal house next door. Many of the rooms feature antiques and reproductions, canopy bed, and Jacuzzi; 20 have a fireplace. The inn has formal dining rooms (see *Dining Out*) and the casual and popular Broad Arrow Tavern (see *Eating Out*). A glassed-in pool overlooks the gardens. Rates in-season are $190–325, full buffet breakfast and afternoon tea included.

Hilton Garden Inn Freeport (207-865-1433; hiltongardeninn.com), 5 Park St. Reliable and with all the best amenities, this Hilton Garden Inn has 99 rooms, indoor pool, hot tub, exercise room, restaurant, and bar. A gas fireplace burns in the lounge, where you can enjoy a drink. The inn is a five-minute walk to the shops.

✻ ✑ **White Cedar Inn** (207-865-9099 or 1-800-853-1269; whitecedarinn.com), 178 Main St. Open year-round. This restored Victorian is the former home of Arctic explorer Donald B. MacMillan, who traveled nearly to the North Pole with Admiral Peary—until frostbite set in. Seven bedrooms come with private bath, down comforters, and air-conditioning; some have a fireplace. Owners Rock Nadeau and Monica Kissane, who are constantly updating the inn's rooms, serve a full breakfast at small tables in the sunroom. Doubles $135–225.

Brewster House (207-865-4121; brewster house.com), 180 Main St. The bright, warm colors of the tasteful and well-appointed rooms and immaculate bathrooms at Brewster House will put any traveler at ease. Scott and Mary Gile bought this established business in 2013. As low as $169 for the rooms and $279 for a two-bedroom suite, including breakfast that might be blueberry-stuffed French toast.

The James Place Inn (207-865-4486 or 1-800-964-9086; jamesplaceinn.com), 11 Holbrook St. Victoria and Robin Baron have furnished their pretty B&B with charm, luxury, and beautiful furnishings. Single guests enjoy a stay in the Rose Room, with a stunning spool bed and a single whirlpool bath. All seven rooms have air-conditioning and cable TV; one features a kitchenette. Full breakfast at the café tables on the deck or in the pretty glassed-in breakfast room. $149–199.

✻ **Applewood Inn** (207-865-9705; applewoodusa.com), 10 Holbrook St. Jay and Jennifer Yilmaz have five rooms in well-kept, modern buildings for nightly rentals, one with a full kitchen. Local artists are the creators of much of the engaging decor. Breakfast included in the $165–300 in-season rates; longer-term rentals available. The family also operates several AJ Dogs stands and an ice cream stand on Freeport's busy Main Street.

✺ ✻ ✑ ♿ **Royalsborough Inn at the Bagley House** (207-353-6372 or 1-800-765-1772; royalsboroughinn.com), 1290 Royalsborough Rd., Durham 04222. A 10-minute drive from downtown Freeport in a serene country setting, this is the oldest house in town, built as a public house in 1772. The town's first worship services were held here, and this was the site of the first schoolhouse. Marianne and Jim Roberts have furnished eight rooms with antiques, plus down and alpaca comforters. $140–180 double in-season includes full breakfast and afternoon refreshments.

MOTELS **The Village Inn** (207-865-3236; reservations only, 1-800-998-3649; freeport villageinn.com), 186 Main St., has rates starting at $75 and is within easy walking distance of all the shops. The very basic decor is perfectly clean, and the owners since 1986, Lewis and Jackie Corliss, are down-home Mainers who can tell you the history of their transformed town or help you get your disabled car fixed, as they did for us.

On Rt. 1 south of Freeport near the Yarmouth town line are a number of modern motels. Among these is the ✻ **Best Western Freeport Inn** (207-865-3106 or 1-800-99-VALUE; freeportinn.com), 31 Rt. 1. Set on 25 acres of lawns and nature trails, this place offers an upscale motel ambience at reasonable prices. Outdoor swimming pool and playground. Pets are allowed in 22 of the 80 rooms. Doubles are $125–214. The Freeport Café serves breakfast all day (seasonal hours).

CAMPGROUNDS ✹ 𝒮 ⅁ **Cedar Haven Campground** (207-865-6254; reservations only, 1-800-454-3403; cedarhavenfamily campground.com), 39 Baker Rd. Open May–Oct. Fifty-eight mostly wooded sites, each with fireplace and picnic table. Water and electricity hookups, five with sewer and cable TV as well. Ten tent sites. Store with wood, ice, and groceries; mini golf, playground, and pond for swimming. Two miles from Rt. 1 and downtown Freeport. $31–50 per night.

✹ 𝒮 ⅁ **Desert Dunes of Maine Campground** (207-865-6962; desertofmaine.com), 95 Desert Rd. Located next to a kitschy attraction with a natural glacial sand deposit (see *To See and Do*), this campground offers 50 wooded and open sites with hookups, hot showers, laundry, convenience store, propane, fire rings, picnic tables, horseshoe pits, nature trails, and swimming pool. Campsites are $30–39 per night.

✳ Where to Eat

All listings are in Freeport unless otherwise noted.

DINING OUT ⅁ **Harraseeket Inn Maine Dining Room** (207-865-9377 or 1-800-342-6423), 162 Main St. Open year-round for dinner and Sun. brunch 11:30–2. Continental cuisine and elegant service in three formal dining rooms. The chefs use fresh, in-season,

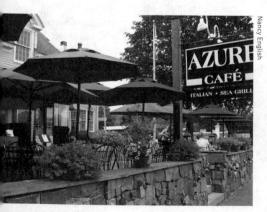

AZURE CAFÉ

Nancy English

and often organic ingredients from local gardeners and farmers. Entrées $24–38. The Harraseeket is also known for its Sunday brunch, which can feature caviar, oysters on the half shell, lobster, and a crêpe station.

❍ **Azure Café** (207-865-1237; azurecafe .com), 123 Main St. Alfresco dining in good weather allows careful surveillance of the shoppers, but warm, handsome rooms and a bar inside make sure you can enjoy the good food year-round. The focus is Italian, with ravioli stuffed with butternut squash and ricotta, or grilled filet mignon skewers glazed with roasted garlic balsamic. Maine seafood risotto marries the best of both coastlines. Steamed lobster is sold for the best price in town, guaranteed. The classic pasta dishes are worth exploring. Entrées $13–32.

Mediterranean Grill (207-865-1688; mediterraneangrill.biz), 10 School St. Open daily in summer for lunch and dinner, closing earlier off-season. A Turkish dinner awaits you here: everything from falafel and stuffed eggplant to kebabs, moussaka, and lamb shanks. Choose from Turkish wines as well as the usual from California, and baklava to end. Entrées $16–23.

EATING OUT 𝒮 ⅁ **The Broad Arrow Tavern** (207-865-9377), Harraseeket Inn, 162 Main St. Open 11:30–10:30, with drinks until midnight. A ground-floor dining room overlooking the terrace, this place is packed with fans of the delicious food, unstuffy pub atmosphere, and collection of stuffed animals on the wall (moose, fish, deer). The open kitchen has a wood-fired oven and grill, and serves up everything from pizzas, sandwiches, and grilled steak to a Caesar salad.

Tuscan Brick Oven Bistro (207-869-7200; tuscanbrickovenbistro.com), 140 Main St., has a wood-fired oven fennel sausage and burrata pizza, a daily risotto, and classic Italian entrées from gnocchi to spicy zuppa di pesce. Entrées $11–34.

Petrillo's (207-865-6055; petrillosfreeport .com), 5 Depot St., is where all the locals go for a good burger; a brunch pizza with eggs, spinach and prosciutto; or a fine plate of seafood linguine. Entrées $8–21.

❍ **Jacqueline's Tea Room** (207-865-2123; jacquelinestearoom.com), 201 Main St. Open 10:30–3 Tue.–Sat. Make a reservation for

STEAMERS AND A POUND-AND-A-HALF LOBSTER AT HARRASEEKET LUNCH & LOBSTER

tea with all the trimmings; four courses and unlimited tea, with tea sandwiches of smoked salmon or cucumber, delicate, crumbling scones with clotted cream and lemon curd, and cakes, tarts, and English toffee. Tea is chosen from a list of 100-plus teas (also available to purchase) and served in a cup teapots during a leisurely two hours.

Conundrum (207-865-0303; conundrum winebistro.com), 117 Rt. 1, South Freeport. This bistro, set right under the Big Indian, serves good burgers and other casual meals in an intimate red room along with varieties of pâté and cheese (also sold in the neighboring shop, Old World Gourmet; see *Snacks and Takeout*), which you can order as entrées. The wine selection is amazing, and you can enjoy a taste before deciding on a glass, or half glass, to drink. Entrées $10–27.

✐ & **Gritty McDuff's** (207-865-4321), 187 Lower Main St. The only brewpub in Freeport, this branch of the popular Portland pub offers outdoor dining, lobster, seafood, pizza, and pub food. Great ales brewed right here, and a tasty lamb burger with feta, too.

✪ ✐ **Harraseeket Lunch & Lobster Co.** (207-865-4888), foot of Main St., South Freeport (turn off Rt. 1 at the giant wooden Indian, then turn right at a stop sign a few miles down). Open May–Columbus Day. At this traditional lobster shack in the middle of the Harraseeket boatyard, order lobsters and clams on one side, fried food on the other, and eat at picnic tables (of which there are never enough at peak hours) overlooking a boat-filled harbor. Lobsters are fresh from the pound's boats; homemade desserts. There is also a small inside dining room. Be aware that it is a busy place; you may have to wait to eat.

SNACKS AND TAKEOUT **Old World Gourmet** (207-865-4477), Rt. 1 (next to the Big Indian). Imported cheese, pâté, prepared food, and wine are ready to fill picnic baskets or take over dinner duty.

Royal River Natural Foods (207-865-0046; rrnf.com), 443 Rt. 1. A great place to buy vegetarian snacks for the road, such as organic fruits and local vegetables, freshly made soups, pasta and green salads, sandwiches, and muffins, which you can eat in the café, too.

✳ Selective Shopping

OUTLETS 🐾 As noted in the chapter's introduction, Freeport's 74-plus downtown factory outlets, with more on the edges of town, constitute what may have become Maine's mightiest tourist magnet. *Boston Globe* writer Nathan Cobb called it "a shoppers' theme park spread out at the foot of L.L. Bean, the high church of country chic."

A $45 million open-air commercial center, Freeport Village Station, opened in 2009 on more than 3 acres of L.L. Bean–owned land in the middle of town; it holds factory outlets for Calvin Klein, Talbots, Nike, Coach, Izod, PacSun, Van Heusen, Brooks Brothers, and the L.L. Bean Outlet itself.

L.L. Bean Outlet Store, 1 Freeport Village Station. Seconds, samples, and irregular merchandise of all kinds. You never know what you'll find, but it's always worth a look. Unlike the main store, the outlet is open only during the hours for Freeport Village Station: Mon.–Sat. 9–9, Sun. 10–6.

Thomas Moser Cabinetmakers (207-865-4519 or 1-800-708-9041; thosmoser.com), 149 Main St. Open Mon.–Sat. 10–6, Sun. 11–5. Fine furniture inspired by Shaker, Arts and Crafts, Japanese, Danish, and art deco designs. This family business has been a Freeport institution for more than 35 years.

& **Cuddledown of Maine Factory Store** (207-865-1713 or 1-888-235-3696; cuddledown

.com), 554 Rt. 1. Comforters, pillows, gift items, all filled with goose down. The annual sale in mid-July is worth the trip.

Brahms Mount (207-869-4025; brahms mount.com), 115 Main St. The specialty here is beautiful fabrics—linen and cotton blankets and throws, scarves, pillows, and towels. Sold throughout the country at exclusive stores, they are on display here in all their sumptuous glory.

SPECIAL SHOPS

All listings are in Freeport unless otherwise noted.

Brown Goldsmiths (207-865-4126; brown goldsmiths.com), 11 Mechanic St. Open Mon.–Sat. Original designs in rings, earrings, and bracelets.

Maine Distilleries (207-865-4828; maine distilleries.com), 437 Rt. 1, south of Rt. 295 Exit 20. Using Maine potatoes grown on his farm in Fryeburg, Donnie Thibodeau and his brother, neurosurgeon Lee Thibodeau, teamed up with a professional brewer and former Olympic ski coach Bob Harkins to open Maine's first vodka distillery in 2005.

✪ ❀ ⚲ ♿ **Mangy Moose** (207-865-6414 or 1-800-606-6517; themangymoose.com), 112 Main St. Moose, moose, and more moose. Susan Culkins has put together a fun store filled with clothing, books, art, and mounts—meaning stuffed moose, mountain lion, bobcat, caribou, and bear heads. A beautiful rustic quilt with machine-embroidered pinecones was reasonably priced, but the moose antler chandelier rang up at $6,000.

Sherman's Maine Coast Book Shops (207-869-9000; shermans.com), 128 Main St. A branch of the Maine bookseller (also in Bar Harbor, Camden, Boothbay Harbor, and Portland), featuring Maine books and gifts, cards, and toys.

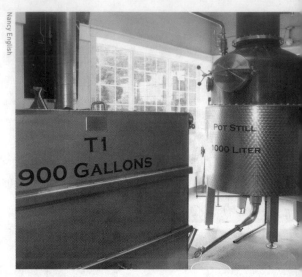

Nancy English

COLD RIVER VODKA

✳ Special Events

Mid-February: **L.L. Bean Kids Winter Fun Week; Winter Festivities and Flavors of Freeport** (freeportusa.com).

Early June: **L.L. Bean Paddlesport Weekend.**

Summer: Frequent musical and comedy performances in the **L.L. Bean Discovery Park.**

Fall: **Pettengill Farm Days**—living history demonstrations, horse-drawn wagon rides, inside/outside house tours, children's days, fresh-pressed cider. **Fall in the Village Art and Music Festival.**

December: **Sparkle Weekend** (first full weekend)—caroling, horse-drawn wagons, Santa arriving in a Maine yacht, and **Tuba Concert.**

MIDCOAST

■

BRUNSWICK AND THE HARPSWELLS

BATH AREA

WISCASSET AREA

BOOTHBAY HARBOR REGION

DAMARISCOTTA/NEWCASTLE/
WALDOBORO AND PEMAQUID AREA

MONHEGAN ISLAND

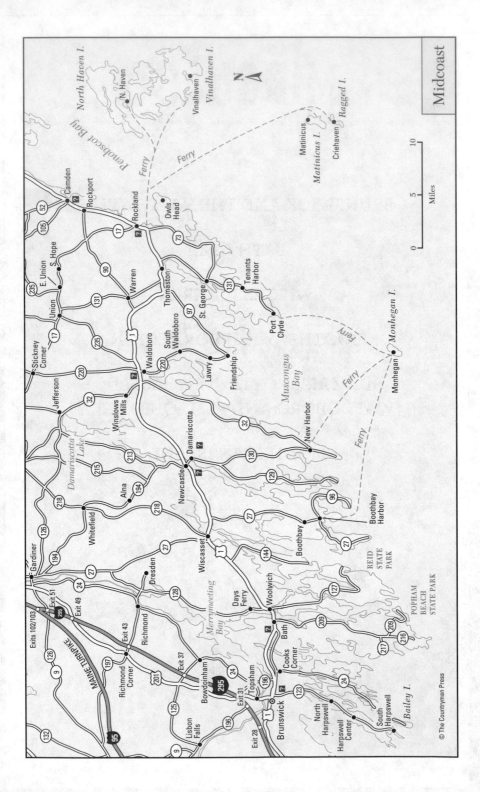

Midcoast

MIDCOAST

Beyond Casco Bay the shape of Maine's coast changes—it shreds. In contrast with the sandy arc of shoreline stretching from Kittery to Cape Elizabeth, the coast between Brunswick and Rockland comprises a series of more than a dozen ragged peninsulas extending like so many fingers south from Rt. 1, creating countless big and small harbors, coves, and bays. Scientists tell us that these peninsulas and the offshore islands are mountains drowned by the melting of the same glaciers that sculpted the many shallow lakes and tidal rivers in this area.

The 52 miles of Rt. 1 between Brunswick and Rockland are generally equated with Maine's Midcoast, and its depth is greater than the name suggests. South of Rt. 1 this coastline wanders thousands of miles, around the tips of a dozen peninsulas, from Harpswell, south of Brunswick to Phippsburg and Georgetown, the Boothbays to Pemaquid.

Communities at the tips of these peninsulas, from Potts Point and Popham Beach to Pemaquid Point, have catered to summer visitors since steamboats began off-loading them in the mid-19th century. Each peninsula differs in character from the next, but all offer their share of places to stay and eat in settings unlike any along Rt. 1.

Monhegan Island, ten miles out to sea, has drawn explorers for at least four centuries and its amazing natural beauty and light continue to draw artists, birders, and hikers from throughout the country.

North of Rt. 1, this Midcoast region also extends inland. Above Bath, for instance, five rivers meld to form Merrymeeting Bay, and north of Newcastle the tidal Damariscotta River widens into 13-mile-long Damariscotta Lake. This gently rolling river- and lake-laced backcountry harbors a number of picturesque villages and reasonably priced lodging places.

We hope that no one who reads this book simply sticks to Rt. 1.

BRUNSWICK AND THE HARPSWELLS

Brunswick is Maine's premier college town, home to **Bowdoin College** with its venerable campus and museums. It's also essentially car-free, with train and bus service from Boston and Portland to a station that's steps from lodging, dining, shops, and galleries.

The Civil War began and ended in Brunswick, or so say local historians. A case can be made. Harriet Beecher Stowe was attending a service in Brunswick's **First Parish Church** when she is said to have had a vision of the death of Uncle Tom and hurried home to begin penning the book that has been credited with starting the war. Joshua Chamberlain, a long-time parishioner in this same church, was the Union general chosen for the honor of receiving the surrender of the Confederate infantry at Appomattox.

Brunswick began as an Indian village named Pejepscot, at the base of the Androscoggin River's Great Falls. In 1688 this became a Massachusetts outpost named Fort Andross, on a site subsequently occupied by a series of mills. Its (roughly) 16,000 residents are a mix of Franco-Americans whose great-grandparents were recruited to work in mills, Bowdoin-related families and retirees, and professionals who commute to work in Portland or Augusta (Brunswick is halfway between).

Brunswick's Maine Street is the state's widest, laid out in 1717 with a grassy "mall"—a long strip of greenery, the scene of concerts and farmers' markets. Set just a bit above and beyond downtown, the handsome Bowdoin campus is visitor friendly. It's the July and August venue for the **Bowdoin International Music Festival**, and for the **Maine State Music Theatre.** Both the **Bowdoin College Museum of Art** and the **Peary-MacMillan Arctic Museum** are must-sees.

South of Brunswick one peninsula and several bridge-linked islands stretch seaward, defining the eastern rim of Casco Bay. Collectively they form the town of Harpswell—better known as **The Harpswells** because it includes so many coves, points, and islands (notably Orrs and Bailey)—which claims 216 miles of shoreline, more than any other town in Maine. Widely known for their seafood restaurants, these are Maine's most convenient peninsulas, yet seem much farther Downeast.

GUIDANCE ☀ (ᵞ) **Brunswick Visitor Center** (207-721-0999; brunswickdowntown.org), 16 Station Ave, just off upper Maine St. (look for the railroad tracks). Open daily year-round, 10-6:30 in summer. From Rt. 1 take Pleasant St. (see intro) and turn right at the "?". It's a place not only to pick up local info, but also to board **Amtrak's Downeaster** or a **Concord Coach** to Portland or Boston.

Harpswell Business Association (harpswellmaine.org) publishes a useful guide map pinpointing lodging and the many restaurants, boat excursions, and galleries on the peninsulas south of Brunswick. Check out the website.

GETTING THERE *By bus:* **Concord Coach** (concordcoachlines.com) offers 2½-hour service from Boston's Logan International Airport and South Station.

By car: The I-295 (formerly I-95) exit for Brunswick and coastal points north is Exit 28 to Rt. 1. Continue straight ahead up Pleasant St., which forms a T with Maine St. Southbound on I-295 take Exit 31A.

By train: **Amtrak's Downeaster** (1-800-USA-RAIL; amtrak.com) offers regular daily service from Boston to Brunswick via Portland, Freeport, and other points between.

By air and limo: **Mid-Coast Limo** (1-800-937-2424; midcoastlimo.com) makes runs by reservation from Portland International Jetport. **Mermaid Transportation** (1-800-696-2463; gomermaid.com) picks up at Boston and Manchester airports as well.

PUBLIC RESTROOMS **Brunswick Visitor Center**, 16 Station Ave. See *Guidance*.

WHEN TO COME Brunswick is lively year-round, but the museums and several good restaurants are closed Mondays.

✳ To See

The Harpswells, including Orrs and Bailey Islands: Given its great seafood restaurants and scenic coves, we try to spend the night along the way. From Main Street, follow Rt. 123 south past Bowdoin College 9 miles to the picturesque village of **Harpswell Center**. The white-clapboard Elijah Kellogg Church faces the matching Harpswell Town Meeting House, built in 1757. The church is named for a former minister who was a prominent 19th-century children's book author. Continue south through West Harpswell to **Potts Point**, where multicolored 19th-century summer cottages cluster on the rocks like a flock of exotic birds that have wandered in among the gulls.

Retrace your way up Rt. 123, and 2 miles north of the church turn right onto Mountain Rd., leading to busier Rt. 24 on Great (also known as Sebascodegan) Island. Drive south along **Orrs Island** across the only remaining Cribstone Bridge in the world, a National Historic Civil Engineering Landmark. (Its granite blocks are laid in honeycomb fashion—without cement—to allow tidal flows.) This bridge brings you to **Bailey Island**, with its restaurants, lodging places, picturesque **Mackerel Cove**, and rocky **Land's End**, with a statue honoring all Maine fishermen. To find the **Giant Stairs** (see *Walks*), turn off Rt. 24 at Washington Ave. and park at the Episcopal chapel. Otherwise continue on Rt. 24 and take Cundy's Harbor Rd. 4.3 miles to another picturesque fishing harbor with good places to eat.

Pejepscot Historical Society Museums (207-729-6606; pejepscothistorical.org). Founded in 1888 and named for an ancient Indian settlement, this is one of Maine's oldest historical societies. It maintains three downtown Brunswick museums: the **Joshua L. Chamberlain Museum** (see sidebar on page 138); The **Pejepscot Museum & Research Center**, 159 Park Row, open summer, Tue.–Fri. 10–4; winter, Wed.–Fri (free admission), a massive, cupola'd mansion that displays changing exhibits on Brunswick, Topsham, and Harpswell history; and the adjoining **Skolfield-Whittier House** (open late May–mid-Oct. for tours Wed.–Sat. 10 and 4), a high-Victorian mansion filled with the photos and paintings of three generations.

The First Parish Church United Church of Christ (207-729-7331; firstparish.net), Maine St. at Bath Rd., Brunswick. Open July–mid-Aug. for Tue. noon organ concerts and tours, and year-round for Sun. services. Designed in the 1840s by Richard Upjohn, architect of New York City's Trinity Church. It's open-beamed, with deeply colored stained-glass windows and a vintage 1883 tracker organ. The large sanctuary window was donated by Joshua Chamberlain, one of the first people to be married here.

✳ To Do

BICYCLING The **Androscoggin River Bicycle Path**, a 2.6-mile, paved bicycle/pedestrian trail, begins at Lower Water St. in Brunswick and runs along the river to Grover Lane in

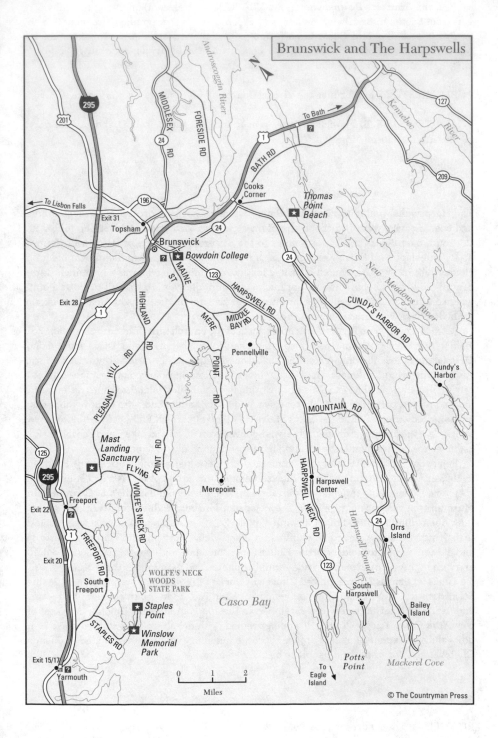

Brunswick and The Harpswells

MUST SEE

Bowdoin College (207-725-3100; bowdoin.edu), Brunswick. Tours begin at the admissions office. Visitors may park in lots off Bath Rd., College St., and Sills Dr.

Maine was part of Massachusetts when the college was founded in 1794, and the school is named for a Massachusetts governor. Nathaniel Hawthorne and Henry Wadsworth Longfellow were classmates here in 1825. The college has been co-ed since 1971; roughly 50 percent of its 1,700 students are female. Bowdoin ranks high among the nation's liberal arts colleges both in status and cost (though financial aid is substantial).

Bowdoin College Museum of Art (207-725-3275; bowdoin.edu/artmuseum), Park Row. Open year-round, Tue.–Sat. 10–5, Thu. until 8:30, Sun. 2–5. Closed Mon. and holidays. Free. The entrance to this 1894 copper-domed building designed by McKim, Mead & White is through a discreet glass pavilion facing the street. Thirteen galleries house changing exhibits, and a rotunda with murals by Abbott Thayer, Kenyon Cox, and John LaFarge is hung with early pieces from the museum's extensive collection. Check the website for current exhibits, which frequently feature contemporary artists.

Peary-MacMillan Arctic Museum (207-725-3416; bowdoin.edu/arctic-museum) Hubbard Hall, open year-round, Tue.–Sat. 10–5, Sun. 2–5. Closed Mon. A colorful, well-displayed collection of clothing, trophy walruses and seals, polar bears and caribou, and other mementos showcases expeditions to the North Pole by both Robert Peary and Donald Baxter MacMillan (class of 1898), who assisted Peary on his 1909 expedition and went on to dedicate his life to exploring Arctic waters and terrain until 1954. Displays include an interactive touch screen, photo blowups, and artifacts to tell the story, also changing exhibits about the Arctic. See the Admiral Peary & Eagle Island sidebar on page 140.

Courtesy of Bowdoin College

BOWDOIN COLLEGE MUSEUM OF ART

Cooks Corner. It connects with Topsham along the way via a bicycle lane on the Merrymeeting Bridge.

BOATING **Casco Bay Lines** (207-774-7871) offers a daily seasonal excursion from Cook's Lobster House on Bailey Island. It takes an hour and 45 minutes to circle around Eagle Island and through this northern end of Casco Bay.

Check **harpswellmaine.org** for an extensive list of fishing and sailing in Casco Bay.

JOSHUA LAWRENCE CHAMBERLAIN

Joshua Lawrence Chamberlain (1828–1914) was Maine's greatest Civil War hero, a college professor who became one of the most remarkable soldiers in American history. Thanks to the Ken Burns PBS series, *The Civil War*, and to the film *Gettysburg*, Joshua Chamberlain has been rediscovered. This scholar-soldier also presided as president of Bowdoin College after serving four terms as governor of Maine.

The Pejepscot Historical Society (pejepscothistorical.org) maintains Chamberlain's old home at 226 Maine St., across from the Bowdoin campus, open late May–mid-Oct., Tue.–Sat. 10–4, Sun. 1–4. Weekends until mid-Nov. Guided tours are on the hour; the last begins at 3. $12 adult, $10 senior, $6 children, $30 family. It's a fascinating house, with many original furnishings as well as Chamberlain's uniforms, medals, saddle sword, bullet-dented boots, and the ornate chair he used as governor and college president. Here you learn that the Bowdoin graduate was teaching rhetoric and languages (he was fluent in eight) at his alma mater when the war began.

Of all his military achievements, Chamberlain is best remembered for his valor and leadership on the second day of the Battle of Gettysburg, July 2, 1863. A lieutenant colonel commanding an inexperienced and understrength regiment, the 20th Maine Volunteer Infantry, he defended Little Round Top, a key position on the extreme left of the Union line. Repeatedly attacked by a much larger Confederate force, he refused to retreat; when there was no more ammunition and most of his men were dead or wounded, he ordered an unorthodox bayonet charge that routed the Southern troops.

Courtesy of Pejepscot Historical Society

Had the Confederates taken Little Round Top, they could have outflanked the Union army and won the battle—and with it, possibly, the war. He ended the war as a major general and was chosen by General Ulysses S. Grant to accept the surrender of the Confederate Army of Northern Virginia at Appomattox. As the Confederate regiments marched into the Union camp to lay down their arms, Chamberlain had his troops salute them, a gesture of respect that infuriated some Northerners but helped reconcile many Southerners to their defeat.

Late in life Chamberlain wrote *The Passing of the Armies*, an account of the final campaign of the Union's Army of the Potomac. Filled with vivid descriptive passages, the book is still in print.

JOSHUA LAWRENCE CHAMBERLAIN

Atlantic Seal Cruises (207-865-6112) picks up at Cook's Lobster. We can recommend Capt. Thomas Ring's Eagle Island and Casco tours. See description in Freeport section.

Sail Casco Tours (277-833-731; sailcasco.com). Capt. Ian Marshall's charter sails aboard his 38-foot *Island Packet*, based in Harpswell, and is a local favorite.

Sea Escape Charters (207-833-5531; seaescapecottages.com) offers Bailey Island–based fishing charters for mackerel and stripers in Casco Bay, also scenic cruises aboard the 35-foot ketch *Tevake* and 70-foot schooner *Alert*.

GOLF Brunswick Golf Club (207-725-8224), River Rd., Brunswick. Incorporated in 1888, an 18-hole course known for its beauty and challenging nature. Snack bar, lounge, and cart rentals. **Mere Creek Golf Club** (207-721-9995) is a nine-hole course at Brunswick Landing (former Brunswick Naval Station) and is open to the public.

SEA KAYAKING ☀ **H2outfitters** (207-833-5257; h2outfitters.com). Based just north of the Cribstone Bridge on Orrs Island, this is one of Maine's oldest kayaking outfitters. No rentals. Lessons for all abilities, from beginners to instructor certification; guided day trips and overnight excursions, also a variety of international kayaking vacations.

Seaspray Kayaking (207-443 3646; seaspraykayaking.com), 320 State Rd., West Bath. Sited on the New Meadows River, Seaspray offers rentals and guided tours and trips.

SWIMMING ⚓ **White's Beach** (207-729-0415), Durham Rd., Brunswick. Open mid-May–mid-Oct. A pond in a former gravel pit (water no deeper than 9 feet). Facilities include a small slide for children. Sandy beach, lifeguards, picnic tables, grills, and a snack bar. Inquire about campsites.

⚓ **Thomas Point Beach** (207-725-6009), off Thomas Point Rd., marked from Rt. 24, Cooks Corner. Open Memorial Day–Labor Day, 9 AM–sunset. Admission fee. The beach is part of an 85-acre private preserve on tidal water overlooking the New Meadows River and Thomas Bay. It includes groves for picnicking (hundreds of picnic tables plus a main lodge snack bar, playground, and arcade), tent and RV sites. It's the scene of the **Maine Highland Games** in August and **Bluegrass Festival**, Labor Day weekend.

⚓ **Coffin Pond** (207 725 6656), River Rd., Brunswick. Open mid-June–Labor Day 10–7. Admission fee. A strip of sandy beach surrounding a circular, spring-fed pond. Facilities include a 55-foot-long water slide, a playground, and changing rooms.

WALKS Giant Stairs, Bailey Island. Turn off Rt. 24 at Washington Ave., park at the Episcopal church, and walk down to Ocean St.; follow the path along the water and follow the small sign to the well-named "stairs."

Brunswick-Topsham Riverwalk. A 1.25-mile walking loop links the Frank J. Wood ("Green") Bridge to the "swinging" footbridge across the Androscoggin River, built in 1892 by the firm that built the Brooklyn Bridge.

Brunswick-Topsham Land Trust (207-729-7694; btlt.org), 108 Maine St., Brunswick. The land trust has preserved more than 2,300 acres in the area. A half dozen properties include nature loops at **Skolfield Nature Preserve**, Rt. 123, Brunswick (4 miles or so south of town), the **Bradley Pond Farm Preserve** in Topsham, a 2.5-mile trail system in a 162-acre preserve; and **Crystal Spring Farm Trail**, a 2.5-mile trail on the 160-acre farm on Pleasant Hill Rd. in Brunswick.

Town of Harpswell Walking Trails. By far the most famous of these leads to the **Giant Stairs** (see above), but there are half a dozen more options. Stop by the town offices on Mountain Rd. (between Rts. 24

ON BAILY ISLAND, THE GIANT STEPS FORM A WELL-NAMED CLEFT IN THE CLIFFS

Christina Tree

ADMIRAL PEARY AND EAGLE ISLAND

In the 1890s the North Pole was the equivalent of the moon in the 1960s. The race was on among nations to be the first to reach it. On April 6, 1909, Robert E. Peary (1856–1920) was the man who claimed that honor for America. Peary was a naval engineer who had sailed south to help survey a possible Nicaraguan canal route in the 1880s, but eventually became obsessed with the Far North. On his own time and financing, he began leading Greenland-based expeditions in 1886. Working with native Inuit and their dog teams, Peary pushed steadily north in subsequent expeditions. He designed the *Roosevelt*, a steam and sail vessel with a shallow draft, to navigate among icebergs, and on its second voyage it is said to have sailed to

ADMIRAL ROBERT E. PEARY GREETS THE CROWDS IN NOVA SCOTIA ON HIS RETURN FROM THE NORTH POLE

within 150 miles of the North Pole. The remaining distance was covered on sled and foot during the following spring. Dismissing their support team, Peary, along with his African American assistant Matthew Henson and four Inuit, finally reached the geographic pole, taking measurements and photographs to document the feat. Controversy continues to dog the accuracy of their final position, but this saga entranced the world.

It was on Eagle Island that Josephine Peary finally received the news of her husband's triumph. Peary had bought the 17-acre Casco Bay island soon after graduating from Bowdoin because its rocky headland resembles the prow of a ship. The shingled summer home he built there is positioned atop that bluff, facing northeast. Peary designed the three-sided living room hearth, made from island stones and Arctic quartz crystals, and stuffed many of the birds on the mantel. The player piano is one octave short because it had to fit aboard the *Roosevelt*.

The **Eagle Island State Historic Site** (207-624-6080; pearyeagleisland .org) is open mid-June–Labor Day, 10 AM–5 PM. The house offers a rare glimpse into era as well as life. A nature path circles the island (trails open July 15, after bird-nesting season), and there are also picnic sites and a small beach. See *Boating* for transport from Bailry Island. There are guest buoys and a dock.

Also see the **Peary-MacMillan Arctic Museum** (Must See).

EAGLE ISLAND STATE HISTORICAL SITE

and 123) and pick up pick a copy of the *Harpswell Guide* to local trails, landings, and other spots worth finding.

Swan Island (207-547-5322; mefishwildlife.com). At the head of Merrymeeting Bay, the island is 4 miles long and less than a mile wide, a haven for wood ducks, mergansers, bald eagles, wild turkeys, and more. It was the site of an Indian village in 1614, when Captain John Smith stopped by. It's open by self-access year-round; limited transport and tours are offered seasonally by reservation. No pets allowed. Managed by the Maine Department of Inland Fisheries and Wildlife, which requires reservations for overnight camping. The landing is in Richmond Village.

✳ Lodging

IN AND AROUND BRUNSWICK

✪ ♨ (ɕ)) **Middle Bay Farm Bed & Breakfast** (207-373-1375 or 1-800-299-4914; middlebay farm.com), 287 Pennellville Rd., Brunswick 04011. Open year-round, this handsome clapboard farmhouse dates to the 1830s and overlooks a tidal cove. Sited at the end of a country road, it's minutes from downtown Brunswick and also from seafood restaurants in the Harpswells. In the early 1900s it was a summer boardinghouse (Helen Keller is said to have stayed here). Phyllis Truesdell is a warm and skilled hostess who makes guests feel invited. There's a living room with a baby grand, a gracious dining room, and a big country kitchen. The four spacious guest rooms are decorated with many bright and tasteful touches; our current favorite is the Star Room, with its stenciled floor and writing desk. All have private full bath, water view, sitting area, and cable TV/VCR hidden in an armoire. There's also a porch from which to survey lawn, sky, and water. The neighboring Sail Loft Cottage houses two rustic suites, each with a living area, kitchenette, and two small bedrooms. The 5 landscaped acres are on a rise above Middle Bay tidal cove; kayaks and canoes are available. $170–190 in-season, $150–175 off-season, includes a full breakfast.

✪ 🐾 🎿 ⚬ (ɕ)) **Brunswick Inn** (207-729-4914 or 1-800-299-4914; thebrunswickinn .com), 165 Park Row, Brunswick 04011. This 1840s Greek Revival home with long windows and a pillared porch offers the charm of a gracious country inn, but within easy walking distance of both the Bowdoin campus and downtown restaurants. It's buffered from traffic by the town's wide green mall. Innkeeper Eileen Hornor has hung common spaces and guest rooms with well-chosen art by local artists (most of it for sale), added a flowery patio, and decorated the double parlors invitingly. On cool days wood fires glow in the parlors, the breakfast room, and the Great Room at the rear of the house, a space with comfortable seating and a full-service bar (open to the public Tue.–Sat. evenings). The 16 guest rooms are divided among the original house, a contemporary carriage house with its own common space, and a self-contained "Garden Cottage" in which pets are welcome. Each room is equipped with phone, desk, and clock-radio; TV on request. $179–329, from $129 off-season. Includes a full breakfast.

⚬ ⚬ (ɕ)) **The Brunswick Hotel & Tavern** (207-837-6565; thebrunswickhotelandtavern .com), 4 Noble St., Brunswick 04011. Handy to the Bowdoin campus and the Brunswick Station, this is a three-floor, 48-room, four-suite

BRUNSWICK INN

HARPSWELL INN

facility obviously geared to Bowdoin parents, alums, and hopefuls. Rooms are comfortably, sleekly furnished, most with two queens. Decor is notably masculine, featuring earth colors and pictures of polar bears (the college mascot). The **Tavern** serves all meals. Rooms run $179–329 EP, but check for packages.

The Daniel (207-373-1824; the danielhotel.com), 10 Water St., Brunswick. This is a contemporary inn with elevator-accessed guest rooms and suites. **Coast Bar + Bistro**, open for lunch and dinner, gets good reviews. Handy to the Androscoggin River Recreation Path (a great place to walk and jog), it's minutes by car and a pleasant stroll from downtown. Rates from $249 in high season, from $124 in low, including continental breakfast with fresh baking.

Black Lantern Bed & Breakfast (207-725-4165 or 1-888-306-4165; blacklantern bandb.com), 57 Elm St., Topsham 04086. Open year-round. Longtime local B&B owners Tom and Judy Connelie offer comfortable rooms, a view of the Androscoggin River, direct access to the bike path (also good for jogging) along its banks, as well as a dock with good access for kayakers. Just across the river from downtown Brunswick, this hospitable old house has three cheerful guest rooms, all with private bath, two with river views, and the third with a gas fireplace. $125–140, $95–115 off-season, includes a full breakfast.

IN HARPSWELL

Harpswell Inn (207-833-5509 or 1-800-843-5509; harpswellinn.com), 108 Lookout Point Rd., Harpswell 04079. Open year-round. Innkeepers Richard and Anne Moseley have deep ties to Harpswell and delight in sharing local secrets and history. Their gracious three-story white-clapboard B&B was built as the cookhouse for an adjacent boatyard and subsequently became the Lookout Point House, one of no fewer than 52 summer hotels and boardinghouses to be found in Harpswell during the steamboating era. The eight guest rooms vary widely and come with and without hearth, deck, and water views; the three suites have kitchens, decks, and more (check the website). The large living room has a massive stone fireplace, ample seating, and plenty to read. Lawns slope to the shore with plenty of comfortable spots from which to view the resident blue heron and Middle Bay. In high season $145–190 for rooms, $239–259 for suites (less off-season), with a very full breakfast, including Anne's blueberry cake if you're lucky. Off-season discounts. Richard, a professional chef, caters for groups of 50 inside and 150 with an outdoor tent. Pets are accepted in four cottages, available for weekly rental.

☙ ☕ ♨ ♂ ((•)) **The Driftwood Inn** (207-833-5461; thedriftwoodinnmaine.com), 81 Washington Ave., Bailey Island 04003. Open late May–mid-Oct.; the dining room (which is open to the public) is open June–Labor Day. Sited on a rocky point within earshot of a foghorn and walking distance of the Giant Stairs Driftwood is classically "Maine rustic," meaning naturally air-conditioned, shared baths (some are now private), and heated by fireplaces. Innkeeper David Conrad's family has owned Driftwood for more than 60 years, and this 1905 complex is one of the last of its breed along Maine's coast. Breakfast and a full-course dinner are open to the public. The cottages contain a total of 16 doubles (some have queens) and eight singles (nine with half-bath); there are also six housekeeping cottages. We recommend Rooms 6 and 7 in Driftwood, pine-walled with a firm queen bed,

Christina Tree

THE DRIFTWOOD INN

a half-bath, and windows on the water. Prices vary with the view and bath facilities. There is a small saltwater swimming pool set in the rocks. $80–145 per couple (no minimum stay). Housekeeping cottages, available by the week, are $705–770. No credit cards. Pets in the cottages ($25 fee). Inquire about group lodging at the Sewall Mansion in Bath.

Log Cabin, An Island Inn (207-833-5546; logcabin-maine.com), 1951 Harpswell Island Rd., Bailey Island 04003. Open Apr.–Oct. Built decades ago as a lavish log summer home with a huge hearth (a moose head, of course, hangs above), it offers nine rooms—four with kitchen, two with hot tub, all with private bath, fridge, coffee machine, and waterside deck—and access to the heated swimming pool. Breakfast is included for high-season rates from $189-339. Dinner is still served to guests only.

✪ ☙ **The Captain's Watch B&B** (207-725-0979; captainswatchbandb.com), 926 Cundy's Harbor Rd. and Pinkham Point Rd., Harpswell 04079. Open most of the year. Donna Dillman offers four spacious guest rooms with water views in a former Civil War–era inn with an octagonal cupola, set on a 250-foot-high bluff. Upstairs rooms are handsome, furnished with antiques (two share access to the cupola); a first-floor barnboard-sided room with a king bed and picture window is equally attractive. Full breakfasts are served in the paneled dining room or, weather permitting, on the deck. Walk down to the picturesque working harbor. $150–185 includes breakfast.

Quahog Bay Inn (207-725-9995; quahog bayinn.com), 5 Lobster Lane, Harpswell. Jane Waddle is the innkeeper at this bayside complex of self-contained one- and two-bedroom units with full kitchens, and is sited above a working wharf. Morning coffee, juice, and muffins are included in the rates, $157–295, depending on the unit and season. Fresh lobsters and rental kayaks are available.

♂ ♿ **Bailey Island Motel** (207-833-2886; baileyislandmotel.com), 1951 Harpswell Island Rd., Bailey Island 04003. Owners Rita and Paul Dube have recently renovated the 11 comfortable rooms, all with cross-ventilation from windows. A continental breakfast buffet is included in the rates, $159–169 in summer, from $119 spring and fall. Kayaks are complementary and this is a spot from which to

LOBSTER

Note: The peninsulas stretching south from Brunswick into Casco Bay have been a destination for lobster lovers since steamboatin' days.

✪ ✎ **Dolphin Marina & Restaurant** (207-833-6000; dolphinmarinaandrestaurant.com), 515 Basin Point Rd., South Harpswell (marked from Rt. 123, also accessible by water). Open 11:30–8 Apr.–Nov., daily in summer; Thu.–Sun. in shoulder months. The prime seafood destination-dining spot in the Harpswells, this snazzy restaurant sits at the very tip of Basin Point, walled in windows with sweeping views of Casco Bay. The fish chowder and lobster bisque are a specialty of the Saxton family, who opened their marina coffee shop in 1966. It grew so popular that lines eventually snaked around the building, and several years ago they built this larger, beautifully designed restaurant. The current menu has expanded, too, but the draw is still the daily hauled and handpicked lobster and crab and broiled seafood that have been luring patrons from Brunswick (45 minutes) and beyond for decades. All dinners continue to include a blueberry muffin, and no one passes on dessert. Nightly specials. Fully licensed.

✪ **Morse's Cribstone Grill** (207-833-7775), Rt. 24 at the Cribstone Bridge, Bailey Island. Open seasonally for lunch and dinner. Cathy and Sheldon Morse are local lobster dealers and their restaurant is a local favorite—glass-walled and right on the water. How can you beat fresh lobster meat cooked and picked in-house, mixed with just the right amount of mayonnaise, and served in a buttered and grilled roll—while watching cormorants and gulls on an island just offshore? Nothing fancy here, just steamers, lobster, broiled and fried scallops, haddock, chowders, stews, and fresh greens topped with chicken, haddock, sea scallops, or lobster. Wine and beer.

Cook's Lobster & Ale House (207-833-2818; cookslobster.com), 68 Garrison Cove Rd., Bailey's Island. Open in season 11:30–10. First opened as a take-out stand in 1955, this landmark seafood restaurant has been recently revamped to offer more deck seating and a raw bar as well as an expanded pub featuring local brews, small plate and salad options and frequent live music. What hasn't changed are the wooden booths and time-polished tables, the many ways of eating lobster and local seafood and the site, surrounded on three sides by water. At lunchtime try to get there before noon, when the Casco Bay liner arrives with its load of day-trippers.

launch. Walk next door to lunch or dinner at Morse's Cribstone Grill or across the way to Cook's Lobster House.

Check **harpswell.org** for cottage rentals on Orrs and Bailey Islands.

✳ Where to Eat

DINING OUT

IN BRUNSWICK

Note: This is a college town, and the quality of the food is higher than prices imply.

✪ **Henry & Marty** (207-721-9141; henryandmarty.com), 61 Maine St. Open for dinner Tue.–Sun. Reservations recommended. Filling two warmly colored and decorated storefronts with a welcoming ambience, whether you come for a glass of wine and thin-crust pizza or for paella Valencia. This is a long-established favorite with a full bar that's an oasis for single diners ($14–28).

Tao Restaurant (207-727-9002; tao-yuan.me), 22 Pleasant St. Open for dinner Tue.–Sat. Cordon Bleu–trained chef-owner Cara Stadler brings experience in top Shanghai and European restaurants to a menu inspired by seasonal, local produce. Dine on a spicy greens salad followed by barley miso glazed eggplant or tea-smoked lamb. Entrées $11.80–13.80, but plates are small, meant to be shared; ordering three or four per person is recommended. A three-course pre-theater dinner menu is $48.

✪ ✿ **The Great Impasta** (207-729-5858 thegreatimpasta.net), 42 Maine St. Open

Gurnet Trading Co (207-729-7300; gurnettrading.com), 602 Gurnet Rd. (Rt.24), Brunswick. Open daily 9–6, closing Sun., 5. Its touristy look belies the quality of this seafood market/café run by a seventh-generation fishing family. A wide choice of chowders (try the whole belly clam), fried seafood, rolls, and entire steamed shore dinners to take out (call ahead) or just as the riverside tables. We feasted on the day's special: a toasted bun stuffed with lobster, just the right amount of mayo, $11.95 including tax. Inquire about Zach's lobster bakes.

LOBSTER DEALER SHELDON MORSE BESIDE MORSE'S CRIBSTONE GRILL

Holbrook's Lobster Wharf (207-729-9050), Cundy's Harbor. Open Memorial Day–mid-June on weekends, then daily until Labor Day, 11–8. A nicely sited lobster landmark with a harbor view. Tables are topped with umbrellas and banked in flowers, and lobster is available right off the boat in all the usual ways. BYOB.

Erica's Seafood (207-833-7354; ericasseafood.com), Basin Point, South Harpswell. Mother's Day weekend–Columbus Day, 11–7. Just before Dolphin Marina (see above), this shop and takeout place with picnic tables offers lobster (hauled off the wharf here) with a view; also chowders, seafood rolls, and the basics, homemade whoopie pies.

Libby's Market (207-729-7277), 42 Jordan Ave., Brunswick. This small variety store is worth finding for the town's best lobster and crab rolls. The owner's lobsterman husband hauls daily, so the meat hasn't sat in a fridge. It's just the right temperature and mix, served in a choice of sizes and toasted buns. There are picnic tables, but better to take it to enjoy with a view.

daily (except Sun.) for lunch and dinner. A great stop even if you're simply traveling up or down Rt. 1, but arrive early to get a booth (plaques honor booth regulars). Specialties include pasta dishes like seafood lasagna and *Frutti di Mare* risotto (native scallops and Gulf shrimp sautéed with white wine, over creamy cheese risotto). Wine and beer served. Entrées $14–26.

EATING OUT

IN BRUNSWICK

✪ ✺ ✿ **Frontier Café & Cinema Gallery** (207-725-5222; explorefrontier.com), 14 Maine St. (Fort Andross). Open Tue.–Thu. 11–9, Fri., Sat. 11–10, Sun. 11–9. A theater, gallery, café, and pub is a winning combination. Long windows along two walls overlook the Androscoggin River, its dam, and frequently ospreys, sometimes eagles and peregrine falcons. There are coffees and teas, draft beers, and a full bar. The widely ranging menu might include fish-and-chips, Thai green curry, steak, rice-battered fried fish tacos as well as "marketplates" representing different parts of the world. Owner Michael "Gil" Gilroy, who traveled the world for his previous work, has used largely salvaged and recycled materials to turn this raw factory space into his vision of a cultural crossroads. Check the website for current events; also see *Entertainment*. Parking is okay in the big lot up front; also look for the rear entrance lot just before the bridge.

✪ **Scarlet Begonias** (207-721-0403), 16 Station Ave. Open Mon.–Sat., lunch–dinner.

The first and still one of the most popular Brunswick bistros, now in Brunswick Station. Doug and Colleen Lavallee, and now their son, are still in the kitchen serving up some great sandwiches, chunky, fresh-herbed pastas, salads, also fabulous pizzas. A savory bean and ham soup with half of a grilled sandwich hit the spot on a rainy day. Wine and beer.

✪ **El Camino** (207-725-8228), 15 Cushing St. Open for dinner Tue.–Sat. An unpromising exterior disguises a hip, funky interior, the setting for highly inventive Mexican food, with a dedication to using chemical-free seafood and meats as well as organic—local wherever possible—produce. The chips are warm, the selection of beers large, and the margaritas famous. Vegans as well as vegetarians have options.

Enoteca Athena (207-721-0100; enoteca athena.com), 97 Maine St. Open Mon.–Sat. from 3:30. Chef-owner Tim O'Brien recently closed his popular Tavern Athena and has focused his effort on this space, featuring fresh-made pastas, Greek and Italian wines, and a reasonably priced Mediterranean menu that now includes entrées like chianti-braised lamb shank as well as many imaginative small plates and platters.

✪ **Lemongrass Vietnamese Restaurant** (207-725-9008; lemongrassme.com), 212 Maine St. Open Tue.–Sun. 11–9. A bright, inviting space with local art is the setting for fresh, delicious, authentic Vietnamese cuisine. The specialties are pho (noodle soups) and goi salads with a tangy sauce and choice of tofu, fish, or meat toppings.

𝒮 **Sea Dog Brewing** (207-725-0162; seadogbrewing.com), Great Mill Island, 1 Main St., Topsham. Open Mon.–Sat. 11–1 AM Sun. 11:30–1 AM. Music Thu.–Sat. Housed in a picturesque (former) paper mill, vintage 1868. A big, friendly brewpub with seasonal outdoor dining overlooking the churning Androscoggin. This is a good bet for families. Specialties include fried scallops, grilled or teriyaki sirloin, potato-crusted haddock, and cioppino (seafood stew). There is a wide choice of house beers and ales.

Bangkok Garden Restaurant (207-725-9708), 14 Maine St., Fort Andross. Open daily except Sun. for lunch and dinner. This attractive restaurant is the local pick for classic Thai curries and seafood dishes.

✪ 𝒮 **Wild Oats Bakery and Café** (207-725-6287), Tontine Mall, 149 Maine St. Open Mon.–Sat. 7–5, Sun. 8–5. Set back from Maine St. with tables on the terrace and inside. A town meeting place serving coffees and teas, from-scratch pastries and breads, healthy build-your-own sandwiches, and salads. For those too impatient to stand in line, there are freshly made salads in the cooler. Outside seating, too, weather permitting.

Fat Boy Drive-In (207-729-9431), 111 Bath Rd. Open for lunch and dinner, late Mar.–mid-Oct. This is no 1950s reconstruct, just a real carhop-staffed drive-in that's survived because the frappés, hot dogs, and burgers are so good and reasonably priced.

Miss Brunswick Diner (207-729-5948), 101 Pleasant St. (Rt. 1 northbound). Open daily 5 AM–9 PM. A convenient road-food stop, a remake of a diner that originally stood in Norway (Maine) but has now been here several decades; the neon lights, booths, and jukebox are all new, but the food is what it claims to be: "home cooking at a down-home good price."

Gelato Fiasco (207-607-4002), 74 Maine St. Open daily 11 AM–11 PM. Owners Josh and Bruno make a couple dozen flavors of their irresistible ice cream from scratch daily.

IN THE HARPSWELLS

The Driftwood Inn (207-833-5461; see *Lodging*). Open seasonally; non-guests must reserve by 4:40. The pine-walled, many-windowed dining room in this rustic resort sits almost atop the water; dinner is served promptly at 6 when the bell rings. The menu offers a wide choice of local seafood as well as rib eye. Salad and rolls included in $18–21; BYOB. There's also a child's and breakfast menu.

BIGS—Bailey Island General Store (207-833-2400). The local gathering spot with an open grill, popular for breakfast and pizza. Also good for screen repair and bait.

✳ Entertainment

MUSIC **Bowdoin International Music Festival** (207-373-1400; bowdoinfestival.org), Brunswick. Famed in classical music circles since 1964, this late June–early Aug. festival brings together talented young performers and internationally acclaimed musicians for a series of both classical and contemporary works. Most concerts are staged in state-of-the-art Studzinski Recital Hall on the Bowdoin campus. Additional concerts are staged throughout the local community.

Music on the Mall (207-729-4439). July–Aug., concerts at 6 PM Wed. on Brunswick's grassy downtown mall and in the **Harpswell Bandstand by the Sea**, Thu. in June and Aug., and Sun. at 2 PM in Sept.

Also see First Parish Church under *To See*.

THEATER ♪ **Maine State Music Theatre** (207-725-8769; msmt.org), Bowdoin College, Brunswick. June–late Aug., matinees and evening performances. Special children's shows. Air-conditioned Pickard Theater is housed in Memorial Hall, an 1873 memorial to the Bowdoin students who fought and died in the Civil War—ordered built, of course, by Joshua Chamberlain. This highly professional Equity company strives for a mix of classics and new scripts and frequently gets rave reviews.

FILM **Evening Star Cinema** (207-729-6796 or 1-888-304-5486; eveningstarcinema.com), Tontine Mall, 149 Maine St., Brunswick. First runs but also alternative film: foreign, art, and documentary.

Frontier Café & Cinema Gallery (207-725-5222; explorefrontier.com), 14 Main St., Fort Andross. Check the website for frequent films and lectures in the 75-seat cinema (seats

are recycled from the Biddeford Theater, converted into swivel/rocking chairs and coffee tables). Visual storytelling, and special events, too (also see *Eating Out*).

✳ Selective Shopping

ART

IN BRUNSWICK AND TOPSHAM

Second Friday Art Walks (207-798-6985; artwalkmaine.org/brunswick), May–Nov., are major events, with open houses at many studios as well as galleries and art venues.

Bayview Gallery (207-729-5500), 58 Maine St., features traditional Maine landscapes. **Icon Contemporary Art** (207-725-8157), 19 Mason St., just off the Rt. 1 end of Main St., is open year-round, Wed. 1–5, Sat. 1–4. A serious contemporary gallery with changing exhibits of sculpture, original drawings, and paintings.

Spindleworks (207-725-8820; spindleworks.org), 7 Lincoln St., an artists' cooperative for people with disabilities that produces some striking handwoven fiber clothing and hangings, quilts, accessories, paintings, prints, T shirts, rag rugs, and more.

IN THE HARPSWELLS

The Gallery at Widgeon Cove (207-833-6081; widgeoncove.com). Open most of the year, but call before coming. This waterside gallery features Georgann Kuhl's landscapes, striking works composed of thousands of individual pieces of her handmade papers, and the gold and silver jewelry and sculptures of Condon Kuhl; it's worth a detour. **Ash Cove Pottery** (207-833-6004), farther down the road, displays a variety of hand-thrown and -glazed functional stoneware by Susan Horowitz and Gail Kass. On Rt. 24 (north of Mountain Rd.) the former Gunpoint Church now serves as a gallery for **Sebascodegan Artists** (named for the island on which it stands), a cooperative with 20 members. It's open July 4–Labor Day, Mon.–Sat. 10–5.

FARMERS' MARKET Brunswick May–Nov., Tue. and Fri. 8–2 on "the Mall"—the park-like green strip on upper Maine St. Local produce and products.

Christina Tree

PICKARD THEATER AT BOWDOIN COLLEGE

SPECIAL STORES

IN BRUNSWICK

✪ **Gulf of Maine Books** (207-729-5083), 134 Maine St. A laid-back, full-service bookstore with a wide-ranging inventory, particularly rich in Maine titles, poetry, also great cards. The owners (they have been called "curators") are photographer Beth Leonard and Gary Lawless, founder of Blackberry Press (note the full line here), which has reissued out-of-print Maine classics. Lawless is a poet with an international following.

Cabot Mill Antiques (207-725-2855; cabotiques.com), 14 Maine St. (at Rt. 1), Fort Andross. Open daily 10–5. A vast, 160-dealer space with quality antiques; flea markets on summer weekends.

Wyler's & Local (207-729-1321), 148/150 Maine St., is a great mix of quality pottery, glassware, jewelry, and clothing. It now also includes "Local," good for gourmet items and a deli, making it a great picnic source.

Wilbur's of Maine Confections (207-729-4462; wilburs.com), 143 Maine St. Open daily. We dare you to pass up a "Double Decadence" (a dark chocolate truffle with hazelnuts). The chocolate is handmade in Freeport, and there's a large inventory of other candies.

IN HARPSWELL

Black Sheep Wine Shop (207-725-9284; blacksheepwine.com), 105 Mountain Rd., Harpswell. With more than 600 different labels, a range of prices (at least 90 under $12 a bottle), friendly service, and frequent tastings, dinners, and classes, this has become a destination for wine lovers. Also a selection of Maine-crafted beers.

Island Candy Company (207-833-6639) 1795 Harpswell Islands Rd. (Rt. 24), Orrs Island. Open 11–8 in summer; fewer days and hours off-season. Closed in snow season. Melinda Harris Richter makes everything from lollipops to truffles.

Christina Tree

BRUNSWICK FARMERS' MARKET ON THE MALL

✱ Special Events

Check the Thu. edition of Brunswick's *Times Record* for current happenings.

June–Aug: See *Entertainment* for details about the **Bowdoin International Music Festival** and **Maine State Music Theatre.**

🎵 *July–August:* **Music on the Mall in Brunswick** concerts are Wed. evenings.

July: **Bailey Island Fishing Tournament** (to register, phone Cook's Lobster House at 207-833-2818). **Harpswell lobster boat races.**

August: **Topsham Fair** (first week)—a traditional agricultural fair complete with ox pulls, crafts and food competitions, a carnival, and livestock; held at Topsham Fairgrounds, Rt. 24, Topsham. **Maine Highland Games** (third Saturday), Thomas Point Beach, a daylong celebration of Scottish heritage with piping, country dancing, sheepdog demonstrations, and Highland fling competitions. **Brunswick Outdoor Arts Festival**.

September: **Annual Thomas Point Bluegrass Festival** (Labor Day weekend; thomaspointbeach.com) is huge. Also see brunswickdowntown.org for a **Taste of Brunswick.**

BATH AREA

O ver the years some 5,000 vessels have been built in Bath. Think about it: In contrast to most communities—which retain what they build—here an entire city's worth of imposing structures have sailed away. Perhaps that's why, with a population of fewer than 9,000, Bath is a city rather than a town. The granite city hall, with its rounded, pillared facade and cupola—with a Paul Revere bell and a three-masted schooner for a weather vane—seems meant for a far larger city.

American shipbuilding began downriver from Bath in 1607 when the 30-ton pinnace *Virginia* was launched by Popham Colony settlers. The tradition continues with naval vessels regularly constructed at the Bath Iron Works (BIW).

With around 5,700 workers, BIW currently employs fewer people than worked in Bath's shipyards in the 1850s. At its entrance a sign proclaims: **THROUGH THESE GATES PASS THE WORLD'S BEST SHIPBUILDERS**. This is no idle boast, and many current employees have inherited their skills from a long line of forebears.

Obviously, this is the place for a museum about ships and shipbuilding, and the **Maine Maritime Museum** has one of the country's foremost collections of ship models, journals, logs, photographs, and other seafaring memorabilia. It includes a 19th-century working shipyard and offers tours of BIW as well as river and coastal cruises.

Both BIW and the Maine Maritime Museum are sited on a 4-mile-long reach of the Kennebec River where the banks slope at precisely the right gradient for laying keels. Offshore, the channel is 35 to 150 feet deep; the open Atlantic is 18 miles downriver.

Bath's 19th-century prominence as "City of Ships" is reflected in the blend of Greek Revival, Italianate, and Georgian Revival styles in the brick storefronts along Front Street and in the imposing wooden churches and mansions in similar styles along Washington, High, and Middle Streets. Front Street offers a healthy mix of shops and restaurants, and the riverfront itself has once more become a focal point.

Today BIW, with its 400-foot-high towers at the end of Bath's Front Street, still dominates the city's economy, but Bath now styles itself "Maine's Cool Little City." Its downtown hums with newfound energy, a visitor-friendly mix of culture and commerce. Take the plunge from Rt. 1 down the steep northbound exit ramp just before the soaring Sagadahoc Bridge. Pick up walking and parking maps at the visitors center in the former rail station

Christina Tree

BATH'S FRONT STREET

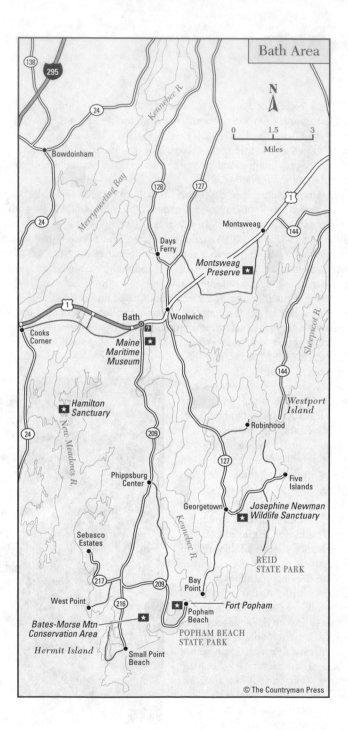

Bath Area

and explore shops and restaurants along Front Street, then settle into an Adirondack chair in Waterfront Park.

Save a day or two to explore the peninsulas south of Bath. **Phippsburg Peninsula**'s perimeter is notched with coves filled with fishing boats, and **Popham Beach** near its southern tip is a grand expanse of sand. **Reid State Park** on **Georgetown Island**, just across the Kennebec River, is the Midcoast's other major sandy strand. North of Bath, Merrymeeting Bay is a major flyway, well known to birders.

GUIDANCE The **Visitors Center** (207-443-1513; visitbath.com) in the rehabbed Bath Railroad Station, 15 Commercial St. (from Rt. 1 take Historic Downtown Bath exits). Open May–Oct., daily in high season, otherwise Mon.–Fri. with a manned info desk, restrooms, and brochures; pick up the Bath map/guide.

BATH'S CITY HALL

GETTING THERE By car: Rt. 1 barrels by the city, with views only from high on the Sagadahoc Bridge, too late if you're heading north. Take the downtown exit just south of the bridge. From points south take I-95 to I-295 to either Exit 28 (Brunswick) or Exit 31 (Topsham) and the connector (Rt. 196) to Rt. 1. We prefer Exit 28 (it's less confusing), but if it's a peak traffic time, try your luck with 31.

By bus: **Concord Coach** (1-800-639-3317; concordcoachlines.com), en route to and from Boston, stops in Bath at Coastal Plaza off Rt. 1.

By air and limo: **Mid-Coast Limo** (1-800-937-2424; midcoastlimo.com) makes runs by reservation from Portland International Jetport.

GETTING AROUND **Bath Trolley** operates a loop throughout the city, daily July–Labor Day, weekends in the shoulder seasons.

PUBLIC RESTROOMS Bath Railroad Station **Visitors Center** (see *Guidance*) and **Waterfront Park**.

WHEN TO COME Bath itself remains lively year-round, but the Popham and Georgetown areas are June–Columbus Day destinations.

✳ To See

Bath Historic District. In the 18th and 19th centuries Bath's successful families built impressive mansions. **Sagadahoc Preservation, Inc.** (207-443-2174; sagadahocpreservation .org. Check the website for the excellent *Self-Guided Walking and Driving Tours* page and events or find them at the Old Winter Street Church, 880 Washington St.

MUST SEE

MAINE MARITIME MUSEUM (207-443-1316; www.mainemaritime museum.org), 243 Washington St., Bath (watch for the turnoff from Rt. 1). Open daily year-round 9:30–5 except Thanksgiving, Christmas, and New Year's Day. $15 adults, $14 seniors, and $10 ages 6–12, good for 2 day's admission. Docking and mooring available. Sited just south of Bath Iron Works on the banks of the Kennebec River, this extensive complex—10 riverside acres—includes the brick-and-glass **Maritime History Building** and the **Percy & Small Shipyard**,

the country's only surviving wooden shipbuilding yard (its turn-of-the-20th-century belts for driving machinery have been restored). Museum exhibits focus on the era beginning after the Civil War, when 80 percent of this country's full-rigged ships were built in Maine, almost half of those in Bath.

The pride of Bath, you learn, were the Down Easters, a compromise between the clipper ship and the old-style freighter that plied the globe from the 1870s through the 1890s, and the big multimasted schooners designed to ferry coal and local exports like ice, granite, and lime. A fine example of the latter, the six-masted *Wyoming* was the largest wooden sailing vessel ever built. A full-scale steel sculpture suggests its mammoth size and height.

BATH-BUILT DOWN EASTERS PLIED THE GLOBE

The museum's permanent collection of artwork, artifacts, and documents totals more than 21,500 pieces, and there is an extensive research library. Permanent exhibits include *Distant Lands of Palm and Spice*, a fascinating, occasionally horrifying glimpse of where and why Maine ships sailed—including the 18th-century West Indies sugar and slave trade and the imperialistic exploration around Cape Horn, the Pacific, and Asia

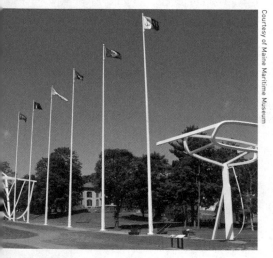

THE SIZE OF A SIX-MASTER SHIP BUILT HERE IS SUGGESTED BY THIS SCULPTURE

Patten Free Library (207-442-5141), 33 Summer St., Bath. Open Tue.–Fri. Set in landscaped grounds is one of the most inviting libraries we know. Artwork includes a half model of the six-masted *Wyoming* and the colorful mural of exotic creatures by Dahlov Ipcar in the children's room. Note the *Spirit of the Sea* sculpture by William Zorach in the adjoining park.

Maine's First Ship (207-443-4242; mfship .org). Open July–Labor Day Wed.-Sat., 9–3. Otherwise look for the OPEN flag on a long wooden "Historic Freight Shed" at the head of Commercial St. You can watch the ongoing reconstruction of the pinnace *Virginia*, built in 1607 at the mouth of the Kennebec by members of the Popham Colony—who climbed aboard and sailed back to England in 1609.

in the 19th and early 20th centuries. You hear the wind whistling in the rigging and follow the individual stories of multiple captains. Other permanent exhibits include a wealth of figureheads, ship models, and ships' portraits. Major changing exhibits are mounted each year.

Beyond the Maritime History Building exhibits are housed in half a dozen buildings, widely scattered on the museum grounds. One of our favorites, *Lobstering and the Maine Coast*, recently updated and expanded to chronicle changes in the industry over

THE MAINE MARITIME MUSEUM'S EXHIBITS INCLUDE A KID-FRIENDLY PILOTHOUSE, MARINE PAINTINGS, AND FIGUREHEADS

the past century. It includes a collection of lobstering boats and interactive activities for kids. The Donnell House, the late-Victorian home of a prominent Bath family, is open seasonally.

Exhibits aside, this museum involves visitors in the significance of its surroundings. A seasonal trolley tour highlighting the history of the neighboring General Dynamics' Bath Iron Works is not to be missed. You can also choose from half a dozen regularly offered seasonal cruises (see *To Do*) with historic narrations down the Kennebec and around into Sheepscot Bay. There's plenty for children, too, from a hands-on pilothouse and elaborate pirate-boat climbing structure to summer camps. Check the website for frequent lectures, workshops, concerts, and special events.

✳ To Do

BIRDING **Hamilton Sanctuary**, West Bath. A Maine Audubon Sanctuary (maineaudubon .org) sited on a peninsula in the New Meadows River, offering a 1.5-mile trail system and great bird-watching: common eiders, snowy egrets in the cove, and shorebirds in the mudflats at low tide. In spring there are bobolinks, red-winged blackbirds, meadowlarks, and several species of warblers. Take the New Meadows exit off Rt. 1 in West Bath; turn left on New Meadows Rd., follow it 4 miles to the sanctuary.

Thorne Head Preserve, Bath. Follow High St. 2 miles north to the end and you will find easy, wooded paths in this 96-acre Kennebec Estuary Land Trust's preserve with views of the Kennebec River, rich in common warblers and vireos. The trust publishes a widely available guide to all nine of its preserves; see kennebecestuary.org.

Also see *Green Space*.

BOATING **Maine Maritime Museum** (mainemaritimemuseum.org; see *Must See*) offers an extensive choice of regularly scheduled one- to three-hour narrated tours down the Kennebec River to view coastal islands and lighthouses and to Merrymeeting Bay.

River Run Tours (207-304-2628; riverruntours.com), based in Woolwich. Captain Ed Rice offers tours and charters for up to 15 people throughout this area.

Seguin Island Light Station (seguinisland.org). Sited 2.5 miles off the mouth of Kennebec River, this 186-foot granite lighthouse stands on a bluff on a 64-acre island. It was commissioned by George Washington in 1795; the current tower and keeper's house are vintage 1859 and maintained by **Friends of Seguin Light Station** (72 Front St., Bath; 207-443-4808). Buildings are open Memorial Day–Columbus Day, Tue.–Fri., weather permitting. The island has no dock. Visitors off-load into a dinghy, and the uphill hike is steep. What you see is a keeper's house and museum and the view from the tower. Plan to bring a picnic and stay a few hours, exploring hiking paths. Check the website for charter runs from Bath and Boothbay Harbor. The shortest, most frequent service is the **Seguin Island Ferry** (207-841-7977) from Popham Beach.

CANOEING AND KAYAKING This area's many coves and quiet stretches of smaller tidal rivers lend themselves to kayaking, and outfitters have multiplied in recent years. **Seaspray Kayaking** (207-443-3646; seaspraykayaking.com), with bases at Sebasco Harbor and 320 State Rd., on the New Meadows River, offers rentals and tours.

FISHING Surf fishing is popular at Popham Beach. Nearly 20 boats offer fishing on the river. See **visitbath.com** for a list of fishing charters.

GOLF **Bath Country Club** (207-442-8411; thebathgolfclub.com), Whiskeag Rd., Bath, has 18 holes and a pro shop; lessons available. **Sebasco Harbor Resort Golf Club** (207-389-9060) is a recently renovated, waterside nine-hole course open to the public. Reservations advised. Also see the Brunswick chapter.

EXCURSIONS

The Phippsburg Peninsula. From the Maine Maritime Museum, drive south on Rt. 209, down the narrow peninsula that's the town of Phippsburg. Pause at the first causeway you cross. This is Winnegance Creek, an ancient shortcut between Casco Bay and the Kennebec River; note the **Winnegance General Store** (*Eating Out*). Continue south on Rt. 209 until you come to **Bisson's Center Store** on your right. Turn left on Parker Head Rd. into the tiny hamlet of Phippsburg Center. This is one of those magical places, far larger in memory than in fact—perhaps because it was once larger in fact, too, as you can see in the **Phippsburg Historical Society** (open July–Sept., Mon.–Fri. 2–4). A **giant linden tree** was planted in 1774 between the white clapboard Congregational church (1802) and its small cemetery. Note the year of the striking Georgian mansion next door (now **The 1774 Inn**). Also look for the stumps of piers on the river shore beyond, remnants of a major shipyard. Continue along the peninsula's east shore on Parker Head Rd., past a former millpond where ice was once harvested. At the junction with Rt. 209, turn left and note the entrance to **Popham Beach State Park** with its 3 miles of sand. Rt. 209 ends shortly beyond at Fort Popham, a granite Civil War-era fort (with picnic benches) at the mouth of the Kennebec River, 15 miles below Bath. It's a favorite spot for fishermen and a destination for eating seafood by the water at **Spinney's Restaurant** and **Percy's General Store** (see *Eating Out*). This is also a departure point for excursions to **Sequin Island Light**. A pedestrian wooded road leads to World War I and II fortifications that constitute **Fort Baldwin Memorial Park**, a six-story tower yields views up the Kennebec and out to sea.

Along the shore at **Popham Beach**, note the pilings, in this case from vanished steamboat wharves. Around the turn of the 20th century, two big hotels served the passengers who transferred here from Boston to Kennebec River steamers, or who simply stayed a spell to enjoy the town's spectacular beach.

Returning back up Rt. 209, consider two detours. The first is a left on Rt. 216, which runs south to Small Point with limited beach access and camping on **Hermit Island** at its end. Note access to the **Morse Mountain** preserve (great walk, great beach) near the start.

A few curves north on Rt. 209, turn left on Sebasco Rd. (Rt. 217) to find **Sebasco Estates** and **Anna's Water Edge**, the reason many drive out this way from Bath.

Arrowsic and Georgetown Islands. Just east of the Sagadahoc Bridge (at the Dairy Queen that's been there forever), turn south on Rt. 127. Cross a shorter bridge and you are on Arrowsic Island.

Christina Tree

Note Robinhood Rd., which leads to two of the area's top restaurants (see *Dining Out*). Farther down Rt. 127, in Georgetown Center, look for **Georgetown Pottery**. South of **Georgetown Country Store** (good for sandwiches), turn right to find the **Georgetown Historical Society and Cultural Center** (207-371-9200; georgetownhistoricalsociety.org) at 20 Bay Point Rd.; check the website for a schedule of lectures and events. Continue on Rt. 127 to **Reid State Park**, the big draw (see *Swimming*). The road ends at the **Five Islands Lobster Co.** (see *Eating Out*).

POPHAM BEACH VILLAGE

SWIMMING 🐾 If you're traveling with a dog, it's important to know that they're allowed only in picnic areas—not on the beaches.

⚓ **Popham Beach State Park** (for current parking and tide updates, 207-389-9125), Rt. 209, Phippsburg; 14 miles south of Bath. One of the best state park swimming and walking beaches in Maine: 3 miles of sand at the mouth of the Kennebec River, a small part of the park's 519 acres. Facilities include bathhouses, showers, and picnic areas with grills. Also a sandbar, tidal pools, and smooth rocks. It can be windy; extra layers are recommended. Day-use fees are charged mid-Apr.–Oct.: $8 adults ($6 Maine residents), $2 seniors, $1 ages 5–11, under 5 free.

⚓ **Reid State Park** (207-371-2303), Rt. 127, Georgetown (14 miles south of Bath and Rt. 1). Open daily year-round. A 766-acre preserve with rock ledges, woodlands, and salt marshes as well as sand beaches. Good for year-round walking and birding. The bathhouse and snack bar overlook 2 miles of sand in three distinct beaches that seldom become overcrowded, although the limited parking area does fill by noon on summer weekends. You can choose surf or slightly warmer sheltered backwater. Little River, around the corner from Half-Mile Beach, is a tidal estuary that warms on sunny days, good for children. Entrance fee $8 adults ($6 Maine residents), $2 over age 65, $1 ages 5-11.

⚓ **Charles Pond**, Rt. 127, Georgetown (about 0.5 mile past the turnoff for Reid State Park; 15 miles down the peninsula from Rt. 1). The best all-around swimming hole in the area, this long and narrow pond has clear water and is surrounded by tall pines.

⚓ **Sewall Pond**, Arrowsic. This large pond is visible from Rt. 127, but the beach is on the far side. Heading south, turn left on Old Post Rd.; the parking area is a mile or so on your left. It's another 0.25 mile to the pond.

⚓ **Pleasant Pond** (207-582-2813), **Peacock Beach State Park**, off Rt. 201, north of Richmond. Open Memorial Day–Labor Day. A sand-and-gravel beach with lifeguards on duty. Water depth drops off gradually to about 10 feet in a 30-by-50-foot swimming area removed from boating and enclosed by colored buoys. Picnic tables and BBQ grills.

SPECIAL LEARNING PROGRAMS **Shelter Institute** (207-442-7938; shelterinstitute .com), 873 Rt. 1, Woolwich. A year-round resource center for those who want to build or retrofit their own energy-efficient home; a wide variety of classes.

Halcyon Yarn (see *Special Shops*) offers classes in fiber arts, including weaving, knitting, felting, spinning, crocheting, and rug hooking.

Rock Gardens Inn (see *Lodging*) offers widely respected, weeklong art workshops.

✳ Green Space

⚓ **Fort Baldwin Memorial Park**, Phippsburg. The short, narrow road around a one-lane corner to Point Sebago leads to the site of the **Popham Colony**. An interpretive panel details the extent of the 1607–08 settlement here. Climb the six-story tower (steep stairs, but the railing is sturdy) for a view up the Kennebec and, downriver, out to sea. There are also remnants of fortifications from World Wars I and II.

⚓ **Fort Popham Historic Site** (207-389-1335), Hunniwell's Point at Popham Beach. Open Memorial Day–Sept. Picnic sites are scattered around the ruins of this 1861 granite fort, built to guard the Kennebec during the Civil War. Beach and ocean fishing access.

Josephine Newman Wildlife Sanctuary, Georgetown. Bounded on two sides by salt marsh, these 119 acres maintained by Maine Audubon provide good birding along 2.5 miles of walking trails. Look for the sign on Rt. 127, 9.1 miles south of Rt. 1.

Bates-Morse Mountain Conservation Area consists of some 600 acres extending from the Sprague to the Morse River and out to Seawall Beach. A 2-mile hike over a hill accesses an unspoiled beach. Pack a picnic, a towel, and some water—but no dogs and please, no radios. Seawall Beach is an important nesting area for piping plovers and least terns. Look for the small sign on the left to Morse Mountain Rd. soon after Rt. 216 veers off from Rt. 209. Parking is limited; don't park on the road or you will get a ticket.

Montsweag Preserve, Montsweag Rd., Woolwich. A 1.5-mile trail takes visitors through woods, fields, and a salt marsh, and along the water. This 45-acre preserve is owned by The Nature Conservancy. From Rt. 1, take a right onto Montsweag Rd. 6.5 miles from Bath, then 1.3 miles and a left into the preserve.

Note: The **Phippsburg Land Trust** protects a constantly evolving number of preserves and offers guided walks throughout summer and fall. See phippsburglandtrust.org.

Also see *Swimming* and *Birding.*

✳ Lodging

RESORTS 🐕 🐾 🗝 ⚐ ((ᵞ)) **Sebasco Harbor Resort** (207-389-1161 or 1-800-225-3819; sebasco.com), 29 Kenyon Rd., Sebasco Estates. Open May–Oct. This 550-acre, 133-room, family-geared waterside resort dates back to 1930, featuring a nine-hole golf course, tennis courts, a large swimming pool, kayaking, and full children's and adult programs. Scenic excursions, lobster cookouts, and live entertainment are also offered. The newest additions are Harbor Village Suites and the Fairwinds Spa Suites ($219-499), handy to the full-service **Fairwinds Spa**. Lodging is otherwise divided among the main lodge, a lighthouse-shaped annex ($199-399), and 22 widely scattered and differing cottages ($249-559, based on two people). Add $48 per person MAP (breakfast and dinner); children 12 and under eat free from the children's menu. Weddings and family reunions are specialties. Informal dining is at **The Ledges,** more formal at **The Pilot House**. A spa menu is also available. Golf is $30 for nine holes (walking). Pets are accepted in some cottages ($25 per night).

✪ ⚐ **Rock Gardens Inn** (207-389-1339; rockgardensinn.com), Sebasco Estates. Open late June–mid-Sept. A hidden gem, sited on its own narrow peninsula between a cove and bay, within the Sebasco Harbor Resort grounds. Accommodating just 60 guests, it offers access to all of Sebasco's facilities as well as to its own pool and dock with kayaks. Rock Gardens dates back to 1911, and Ona Barnet has preserved the old-style atmosphere of the dining room with its painted tables and the library with its well-thumbed books. Traditions include a weekly lobster bake and cocktail party. The 10 cottages (accommodating three to eight) and three inn rooms are tastefully furnished and constantly updated. Request a water view. Aug. is family-geared. In June, July, and Sept., a series of Sebasco Art Workshops features some well-known teachers. In high season $130–200 per person MAP plus 15 percent for service; children's and weekly rates. A four-course dinner (BYOB) as well as breakfast is included; five-night minimum in July and Aug., but check for cancellations.

B&BS

IN BATH

✪ ♨ 🐾 ⚐ 🗝 ((ᵞ)) **The Inn at Bath** (207-443-4294 or 1-800-423-0964; innatbath.com), 969 Washington St. Open year-round. Elizabeth Knowlton is the hospitable keeper of this restored

COVESIDE BED AND BREAKFAST

MORNING VIEW FROM "ALICE'S ROOM" AT COVESIDE BED & BREAKFAST, GEORGETOWN

1840s Greek Revival home in the city's historic district. There are twin living rooms with marble fireplaces and eight luxurious guest rooms with private bath, including a two-bedroom suite. Four rooms have a wood-buring fireplace and all have air-conditioning, cable, DVDs, and are thoughtfully furnished but differ in decor. For rooms in season, $170–190, $215–240 for suites, from $150 off-season, with a breakfast that includes homemade granola, fresh fruit, and always a hot entrée, perhaps quiche. $25 per additional guest. Children (over 5) and dogs are welcome for a $10 fee.

(((•))) **The Kennebec Inn** (207-443-5324; kennebecinn.com), 696 High St. South of Rt. 1 but an easy walk to downtown shops and restaurants, this is a graceful 1850 captain's mansion backing on landscaped lawns with an in-ground pool. There's an elegant parlor with working hearth and four guest rooms divided between the house and (attached) carriage house—all with private baths and thoughtfully, traditionally furnished. $175–205 high season, $149–169 off season, includes a full breakfast served at the dining room table. Innkeepers Ken and Rachel Parlin invite guests to cook their own lobsters on the grill outside.

(((•))) **Benjamin F. Packard House** (207-443-6004 or 1-888-361-6004; benjaminfpackard

.com), 45 Pearl St. This striking Italianate house was built solidly to house a local shipbuilder in 1790 and remained in the same family until 1985. Amy and Mark Hranicky are enthusiastic hosts. They have created an extensive, brick-floored garden as an alternative to the more formal gathering room with its working hearth. The four guest rooms include two that work well as a family suite. $140–180 in-season, from $100 off-season, includes an exceptional breakfast with home baking and local ingredients.

(((•))) **Pryor House** (207-443-1146 or 1-866-977-7969; pryorhouse.com), 360 Front St. Don and Gwenda Pryor offer three crisp, attractive guest rooms with air-conditioning and private bath in this late-Federal-style home. The Tall Chimney Room features a small deck and big Jacuzzi. Common space is inviting. Breakfast, which may be tomato basil quiche, banana crêpes, or blueberry French toast, is included ($150–170). Guest pets are possible but carefully screened.

Mulberry House (207-389-2302; mulberryhousemaine.com), 1009 Washington St. Owners Diane and Bill Racine, spent a year de-cluttering and restoring this 1874 painted lady (formerly the Moses Galen House) to reveal the 1901 interior design by Maine's most noted architect of that era, John Calvin Stevens. "I want to let the beauty of the house speak for itself," Diane says. Detailing includes glorious stained glass windows, (including one by Tiffany), fine woodwork, and a deftly tiled dining room hearth. There are two airy big bedrooms and one smaller, 2 baths at present ($175–185). The third-floor surprise is a screening room with 16 vintage wooden seats and a projector that works off an Apple computer. Diane is an artist and is organizing artists' workshops, other groups. The snag is it's just open May–Oct and only on weekends. Bill is a busy local accountant and the couple say they want to share his showplace but keep their sanity.

   (⬩) **Hampton Inn** (207-386-1310; bathbrunswickarea.hamptoninn.com), 140 Commercial St. This four-story, 94-room inn is right downtown. Elevator-accessed rooms come with a king or two queens; facilities include a lap pool and Jacuzzi as well as a fitness center and laundry room. $129–299, breakfast included.

ON THE PHIPPSBURG PENINSULA SOUTH OF BATH

✪ **The 1774 Inn at Phippsburg** (207-389-1774; 1774inn.com), 44 Parker Head Rd., Phippsburg. Open May–Oct. This imposing

1774 INN AT PHIPPSBURG

cupola-topped, foursquare mansion was built by the Kennebec River in 1774 and served as home to Maine's first U.S. congressman. It has been beautifully restored by Bills Jacqueline Hogg and John Atkinson. Guests can choose from four splendid Federal-style guest rooms furnished with antiques, three smaller but thoughtfully decorated rooms in an ell, and the open-timbered but luxurious "Woodshed" with its own porch and steps out into the garden. Grounds slope to the river. The paneling is original throughout, and rooms are furnished with an eye to elegance and comfort. $280–320 includes a full breakfast served by the hearth in the original kitchen.

   ✪ **EdgeWater Farm** (207-389-1322 or 1-877-389-1322; ewfbb.com), 71 Small Point Rd., Phippsburg 04562. Year-round. This circa-1800 farmhouse, set in 4 acres of gardens and fruit trees, offers six guest rooms with private bath, kitchen privileges, and access to a large dining/living room. It's well suited to small-group gatherings. There's also an apartment that sleeps seven to 13, and an indoor pool. $140–225.

ON THE GEORGETOWN PENINSULA

✪ (⬩) **Coveside Bed and Breakfast** (207-371-2807 or 1-800-232-5490; covesidebandb .com), Georgetown (Five Islands). Open Memorial Day–mid-Oct. Tucked into a corner of a quiet, lobster-filled cove is a rare retreat created by Carolyn and Tom Church. The seven guest rooms are divided between a century-old farmhouse and a matching shingled cottage with its own common space and screened porch. All of the many-windowed rooms face the water; those in the cottage have French doors opening onto decks. Some have a gas fireplace and/or a Jacuzzi, but really any room here is special. All have high, angled, or cathedral ceilings with fans, and there's a sense of uncluttered spaciousness and real comfort. Weather permitting, the multicourse breakfast is served on the brick terrace from which the lawn slopes away beneath high trees to the shorefront. Carolyn and Tom are consummate hosts who go way beyond the norm in helping guests with local dining and sightseeing. Beach passes, a canoe, and bikes are free to guests, and there's exercise equipment in a rec room with TV. $150–235.

Christina Tree

⚲ **The Mooring** (207-371-2790; the mooringb-b.com), 132 Seguinland Rd., Georgetown. Open May–Oct. Paul and Penny Barabe, the great-granddaughter of Walter Reid, donor of the land for his namesake state park, share their home as a B&B. The five guest rooms all have private bath; there are gracious common spaces, and a wicker-furnished porch overlooks the lawns and water. Weddings for up to 125 are a specialty. $150-210 includes a full breakfast.

⚲ **Grey Havens Inn** (207-371-2616 or 1-855-473-9428; greyhavens.com), 96 Seguinland Rd. Open early May–Oct. The donor of the land for neighboring Reid State Park also built this turreted, gray-shingled summer hotel, opened in 1904. A huge parlor window—said to be the first picture window in Maine—as well as most of the 13 guest rooms and the long veranda command views of Sheepscot Bay. Rooms and baths have been renovated; the spacious old parlor with its tongue-and-groove paneling has been whitened and lightened with bright, contemporary furnishings. The restaurant, **"Blue,"** is open to the public for dinner (see *Dining Out*). Rooms are $215–395 mid-June–mid-Oct., $175–350 in shoulder weeks. Weekends tend to be booked for weddings.

OTHER LODGING 📷 ⚲ **Hermit Island Campground** (207-443-2101; hermitisland .com), 6 Hermit Island Rd., Phippsburg 04562; winter mailing address: 42 Front St., Bath 04530. This 255-acre almost-island at Small Point offers 275 nicely scattered campsites, 51 on the water. Only tents, small to medium pop-ups, and small pickup campers are permitted. Owned since 1953 by the Sewall family, Hermit Island also has a central lodge with a recreation room and snack bar where kids can meet. Beyond the camping area are acres of private beach and hiking trails through unspoiled woods and meadows. From $37 per night. Repeat customers mail in their summer reservations for a week or longer on Jan. 1, but shorter stays can be booked, beginning in March, by phone. No pets.

✽ Where to Eat

DINING OUT Also see "Brunswick and the Harpswells."

IN BATH

◎ **Solo Bistro** (207-443-3373; solobistro.com), 128 Front St. Open Tue.–Sat. from 5 nightly for dinner (reserve), also Sat., Sun. 10:30–2 for brunch. The best restaurant in Bath. Pia Neilson's decor is Scandinavian, simple and sleek, and the chef's way with locally sourced ingredients is inspired. The menu changes monthly, but there's always a wide choice, from a bistro burger and enticing vegan dish to a choice of fish and meat. Live jazz Fri. Entrees: $18–30 and nightly prix fixe for $25, Wed. for $18.

◎ **Kennebec Tavern and Marina** (207-442-9636; kennebectavern.com), 119 Commercial St. Open lunch–dinner until 9 weekdays, 10 Fri. and Sat. A spacious, casual oasis with booths and tables overlooking the Kennebec River, and a seasonal waterside deck. The usual choice of seafood, chicken, and steak.

Christina Tree

THE OSPREY RESTAURANT AT ROBINHOOD MARITIME CENTER

Easy access from Rt. 1. Entrées $12–36. It fits under both *Dining Out* and *Eating Out*.

☙ **Beale Street Barbeque and Grill** (207-442-9514; mainebbq.com), 215 Water St. Open for lunch and dinner. No reservations. The feel, with deep booths and soft lighting, is that of a neighborhood restaurant, but the food is authentic Tennessee: pulled pork and ribs, smoked hot sausage and chicken and sausage jambalaya, also plenty of fresh seafood. From $11 for a pulled pork bulkie to $30 for a BBQ sampler. Also fits under both *Dining Out* and *Eating Out*.

ON THE GEORGETOWN PENINSULA

"Blue" at Grey Havens Inn (207-371-2616), Seguinland Rd. (marked from Reid State Park). Open seasonally, Tue.–Sun. 5–9 in high season, Wed.–Sun. in shoulder months. White-clothed tables are well spaced in this large, classic, tongue-and-groove-paneled dining room with views out across Sheepscot Bay. The restaurant offers traditional fine dining. Nightly blackboard specials. Entrées $20–32, but you can also dine on mussels and a salad or on tasty burgers.

The Osprey (207-371-2530; robinhood marinecenter.com), 340 Robinhood Rd. (just off Rt. 127, near Reid State Park). Open mid-June through Aug., weekends only in shoulder months, 11 AM–11 PM. Reserve. This casual yachtsmen's haven with water views is squirreled away in the Robinhood Marine Center. Inside and outside seating with water views. Owner Tiffany Lee offers a largely seafood menu; also microbrews and light fare.

EATING OUT

IN BATH

☙ ⅙ **Mae's Cafe** (207-442-8577; maescafeand bakery.com), 160 Center St. (corner of High). Open 8–3, serving until 2. Breakfast omelets and specials like lobster Benedict are available all day, and the lunch menu has a loyal following. Try a crab melt or a flat-bread pizza with sautéed lobster, onion, spinach, and mozzarella. The bakery case is filled with delectable cakes—most patrons walk away with at least a cookie. Fully licensed.

Byrnes Irish Pub (207-443-6776; byrnes irishpub.com), 38 Centre St. Open 11 on, from 10 on Sundays. Single-malt whiskeys and a

WINNEGANCE GENERAL STORE & CAFE

selection of Maine and imported beers are the draw, but this is also a good place to eat. Frequent live music.

✪ **Starlight Café** (207-443-3005), 15 Lambard St. Open weekdays 7–2; also Sat. June–Christmas. This bright, funky eatery and bakery is a real find. Large, luscious sandwiches. Create your own by picking bread, meat, cheese, veggies, and daily specials. Limited indoor seating, but it's a short walk to a bench by the Kennebec River.

✪ **The Cabin** (207-443-6224), 552 Washington St., across from the Bath Iron Works. The exterior is a bit shabby, but inside it's a great local spot boasting "the only real pizza in Maine." Booths, patio seating in warm weather, pitchers of beer, and terrific pizza. The menu includes pasta and subs. Best in the evening, after the BIW closes for the day.

Live Edge Deli & Lounge (207-442-7116), 102 Front St. Open weekdays from 10:30; lounge opens at 4 PM. Good for a quick and delicious lunch: freshly made soups, salads, and make-your-own sandwiches or choose from the blackboard list. Also prepared hot meals.

☙ **J. R. Maxwell & Co.** (207-443-2014), 122 Front St. Open year-round for lunch and dinner daily. Bath's shopping street place to eat. Lunch on crabcakes and blueberry pie or dependably good burgers. Dinner choices are vast, plus nightly specials. $9–25.

Winnegance General Store & Cafe (207-443-3300), 38 High St., Bath. Open Mon.–Wed. 6–6, Thu.–Sat. 6 AM–8 PM, Sun. 6–4. South of town on Rt. 209, just before the Winnegance River. Recently restored and wildly popular.

Local chefs Shawn Shutt and Holly Snowden get raves for breakfasts like scallop, shrimp, and lobster with cheddar omelets and lunch staples like crabmeat tacos served on a bed of mixed greens (we could only eat one of the two). Wine and beer. Limited seating inside, outside picnic tables. Also check out **Schutty's** (207-798-9167), 410 State Rd., West Bath. The couple's seasonal, wildly popular food truck widely known for fresh seafood with flair. Open seasonally Mon.–Sat. 11–8, Sun. 11–4.

�@ **Best Thai II** (207-443-8655; bestthai maine.com), 23 Elm St. Open Tue.–Sun. for lunch and dinner, closed Mon. Our favorites are the volcano noodle soup and mango fried rice; plenty here to please. Beer and wine.

ON THE PHIPPSBURG PENINSULA

✪ ✿ �@ **Anna's Water's Edge** (207-389-1803), Black's Landing Rd., Phippsburg. Open Memorial Day–Labor Day, 11:30–8:30 but call in June and Sept.. Reservations accepted. Well marked from Rt. 209. Sited on a commercial fishing wharf 16 miles south of Bath, but worth the drive on a summer evening,

it's a great place for a full shore dinner, with a full menu ranging from sandwiches to surf and turf. Standout chowder and crabcakes. Nightly specials. Liquor served.

✪ ✿ **Spinney's Restaurant** (207-389-1122), 987 Popham Rd (end of Rt. 209). Open daily 8 AM–9 PM, June–Oct.; call for hours in May and Oct. Our kind of beach restaurant with tables on the glassed-in porch and water views, also on a sand-side deck and outside tables for take-out. Glen and Diane Theal specialize in fresh fish and seafood, fried, steamed, and broiled; good lobster and crabmeat rolls. Fully licensed.

Percy's General Store (207-389-2010), Popham Beach. Seasonal. Locals head for the back room with its water-view booths, good for breakfast on through lobster rolls, fried clams, and lobster dinner specials.

North Creek Farm (207-389-1341; north creekfarm.org), 24 Sebasco Rd., Phippsburg. Open year-round 9–6:30. Suzy Verrier's nursery and extensive perennial gardens are also the setting for a great little eatery with limited inside seating and picnic benches. The tables by the woodstove are inviting off-season, as are

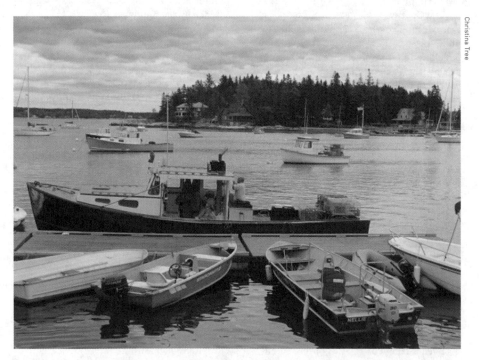

Christina Tree

VIEW FROM FIVE ISLANDS LOBSTER

the freshly made soups. Homemade pies are another draw. The store sells her organically grown produce, eggs, cut flowers, wine and beers, cheese, gardening implements, and gifts

ON THE GEORGETOWN PENINSULA

✪ ✿ **Five Islands Lobster Co.** (207-371-2990; fiveislandslobster.com), Georgetown. Fourteen miles south of Rt. 1 at the end of Rt. 127 on Five Islands wharf. Open seasonally, 11:30–8. It's hard to beat the view from this end of the-road commercial lobster wharf. A genuine, old-style lobster pound, it's all outdoors and all about steamed lobsters and clams with corn and potatoes, lobster rolls, fried clams, and fried seafood. Onion rings are also a specialty. BYOB.

Five Islands Farm (207-371-9383; five islandsfarm.com), Rt. 127, Five Islands. Open mid-May–Dec., Wed.–Mon. 10:30–6. Heidi Klingelhofer's small, shingled emporium overflows with flowers and is a seasonal trove of Maine cheeses, wines, local produce, and specialty foods. Cheese is Heidi's passion, and she carries one of the largest selections of Maine artisan cheeses available.

Also see *Dining Out*.

✳ Entertainment

✪ ✿ **Chocolate Church Arts Center** (207-442-8455; chocolatechurcharts.org), 804 Washington St., Bath. Gallery and box office open Tue.–Thu. Call ahead. The church is an 1847 Stick Gothic beauty with a soaring, graceful interior and amazing acoustics, converted to a 375-seat theater. Sept.–June presentations include plays, concerts, and a wide variety of guest artists, many of them big names. The website also lists summer events.

Gazebo Series band concerts. July and Aug., Tue. and Fri., 7 PM, Library Park, Bath.

Music on the Dock (visitbath.com). July–Aug., "Saturdays at Six," concerts at Waterfront Park.

See **Solo Bistro, Byrnes Irish Pub**, and the **Kennebec Tavern** for live music.

MARKINGS GALLERY IN BATH INCLUDES HANDCRAFTED CLOTHING

✳ Selective Shopping

IN BATH

Bath's Front Street, lined with mid-19th century redbrick buildings and anchored by **Renys** (#46), is a trove of genuine bargains. In a quick visit we unearthed turtlenecks, kitchen mitts, stationery, nail files, and a set of pillowcase for a total of $21.50. This is one of the best stores in this standout Maine chain (renys.com). **Now You're Cooking** (#49) is a major kitchen supply store with a wide following and cooking classes. **Markings Gallery** (#50), owned by local artists and craftspeople, is exceptional not only for the quality of what it shows but also for the careful blend of clay, glass, jewelry, woodworking, mixed media, and more. **House of Logan** (#66) is the city's classic clothier. **Mustard Seed Bookstore** (#74) is a serious independent bookstore that's also serious about tea (plenty of comfortable seating) and **Springer's Jewelers** (#76) is a vintage emporium with mosaic floors, chandeliers, and ornate glass sales cases. We always stop by **Bohemian Rose** at #106 (casual to formal women's ware) and **Lisa-Marie's Made in Maine** (#170), filling three storefronts. **Open Door Books** (#178) has a great selection of used, rare, and out-of-print books and **Island Treasure Toys** (#182) caters to kids of all age.

ELSEWHERE IN BATH

Halcyon Yarn (207-442-7909 or 1-800-341-0282; halcyonyarn.com), 12 School St. Warehouse open Mon.–Sat. 10–4, Wed. until 8. A destination and mecca for knitters, spinners, and rug hookers with yarns distributed worldwide. Inquire about workshops.

Centre St. Arts Gallery (207-442-0300), 11 Centre St., is a cooperative gallery showing the work of 20 local artists as well as juried shows, also offering classes and workshops.

Bath Farmers' Market (bathfarmersmarket.com) is held Sat. mornings; check website for precise times and venue. The Winter Market is at the Freight Shed, Commercial St.

BEYOND BATH

✪ **Georgetown Pottery** (georgetownpottery.com) 813 Rt.1 (207-443-8722) in Woolwich (12 miles north of Bath) and on Rt. 127 in Georgetown (207-371-2801), 9 miles south of Rt. 1. Both showrooms are open daily. Jeff Peters has been handcrafting his distinctive style of pottery since 1972. The extensive selection includes dishes, mugs, and other practical pieces in a variety of hand-painted and deeply colored designs, from casseroles to ikebana "Zen pots." The new Rt. 1 facility includes the adjoining Portage Co. store featuring Maine-crafted furnishings and more. We still prefer the original Georgetown store in which you can watch potters at work.

Old Post Office Gallery (207-371-2015; leapetersonart.net), 833 Five Islands Rd. (Rt. 127), Georgetown. Open late May–mid-Sept., Fri.–Mon. Owned by several artists and displaying work by a select number, including great local landscape cards by Lea Peterson.

Saltbox Pottery (207-443-5586; saltbox pottery.com), 4 Shaw Rd., Woolwich. Open May–Dec., Mon.–Sat. 10–5:30. Traditional-style stoneware, wheel-thrown and functional. We couldn't resist a butter dish.

Montsweag Flea Market (207-443-2809), Rt. 1, Woolwich. Open Wed. and Fri.–Sun., 6:30–3. A field filled with tables weighted down by every imaginable collectible and curiosity. Wednesday is Antique Day; on weekends look for collectibles, crafts, and good junk. Come early.

✳ Special Events

Details for most events are at visitbath.com.

Three days surrounding the Fourth of July: **Bath Heritage Days**—a grand celebration with an old-time parade of antique cars, marching bands, clowns, guided tours of the historic district, crafts sales, art shows, musical entertainment in two parks, food, bed races, bucket relays, and fireworks over the Kennebec.

Saturday of Columbus Day weekend: **Autumn Fest**. Scarecrow-making, open houses.

December: **Old-Fashioned Christmas** (all month), with competitions and special events.

WISCASSET AREA

Sea captains' mansions and mid-19th-century commercial buildings line Rt. 1 in this historic village, and on summer weekends motorists have time to study them as they inch along. When the bridge across the Sheepscot River was rebuilt and widened, it was supposed to ease the traffic snarl, but Wiscasset is the only village through which cars heading up and down the Midcoast on Rt. 1 must all file slowly, stopping at pedestrian crossings.

It's an obvious stop. The places to eat are varied and good, antiques stores abound, and the historic buildings are worth visiting.

Still the shire town of Lincoln County, Wiscasset is half as populous as it was in its shipping heyday which, judging from the town's clapboard mansions, began after the Revolution and ended around the time of the Civil War. Lincoln County Courthouse, built in 1824 on the town common, is the oldest functioning courthouse in New England.

From Wiscasset, Rt. 27 runs northwest to Dresden Mills, and from there it's just a few miles to the haunting Pownalborough Court House. Rt. 218 veers northeast, paralleling the Sheepscot River through backcountry to Alna, home of the Wiscasset, Waterville & Farmington Railway and Head Tide Village. Rt. 144 heads south down the spine of the quiet Westport Island.

GUIDANCE Wiscasset Area Chamber of Commerce (207-882-9000, wiscassetchamber .com) publishes a walking guide and maintains a useful website.

GETTING THERE *By bus:* **Concord Coach** (1-800-639-3317; concordcoachlines.com).

By car: Note the shortcut around traffic northbound: Turn right on Lee St., continue to Fore St. and Water St., and either park or continue north (right) on Rt. 1.

By air and limo: **Mid-Coast Limo** (1-800-937-2424; midcoastlimo.com) makes runs by reservation from Portland International Jetport.

PUBLIC RESTROOMS are in the Waterfront Park, corner of Water and Fore Sts.

✱ To See

IN WISCASSET VILLAGE

Nickels-Sortwell House (207-882-7191; historicnewengland.org), 121 Main St. (Rt. 1). Open June 1–Oct. 15, Fri.–Sun. Tours every half hour, 11–4. Admission $8, $7 seniors, $4 students. This classic Federal-era mansion in the middle of town was built by a shipowner and trader. After he lost his fortune the house became a hotel, and in 1895 a Cambridge, Massachusetts, mayor purchased it; it's now maintained by Historic New England with furnishings from varied periods.

Castle Tucker (207-882-7169; historicnewengland.org), 2 Lee St. Same nonprofit owner as the Nickels-Sortwell House, same season, tour hours, and admission price, but open Wed.–Sun. Castle Tucker was built in 1807 by Judge Silas Lee, who overextended his resources to present his wife with this romantic mansion. Highlights include a freestanding elliptical staircase, Victorian furnishings, and original wallpapers.

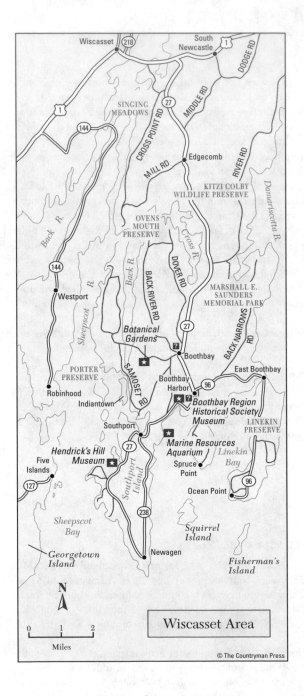

Wiscasset Area

N

0 1 2
Miles

© The Countryman Press

EXCURSIONS

Take a scenic drive across Rt. 218 to picturesque Sheepscot Village. The 32-acre Bass Falls Preserve, maintained by the **Sheepscot Valley Conservation Association** (207-586-5616), is 1.2 miles east of Rt. 218; from the parking lot, a mile-long trail leads down to the river. Back on Rt. 218 continue north past the **Alna Meeting House** to Head Tide Village, another quiet cluster of old homes around the **Old Head Tide Church** (1858). Note the swimming hole beneath the milldam. The **Alna Store** on Rt. 218 just south of **Head Tide** is a great source of sandwiches and hot specials.

Old Lincoln County Jail and Museum (207-882-6817; lincolncountyhistory.org), 133 ederal St. Open June–Sept., Sat., Sun. noon–4. $5 adults; free 16 and under. The museum consists of a chilling 1811 jail (in use until 1930) with damp, thick, granite walls (some bearing interesting 19th-century graffiti), window bars, and heavy metal doors. The jailer's house (in use until 1953) displays tools and changing exhibits.

IN DRESDEN

🚂 **Pownalborough Court House** (207-882-6817; lincolncountryhistory.org), 28 Court House Rd., off Rt. 128. Open June–Sept., Sat. 10–4, Sun. noon–4; in July, Aug. also open Tue.–Fri. 10–4. $5 adults; free under 15. Worth the drive. Maine's only surviving pre–Revolutionary War courthouse, this striking three-story building, which includes living quarters upstairs for the judge, gives a sense of this countryside along the Kennebec in 1761, when it was built to serve as an outpost tavern as well as a courtroom. The courthouse is on the second floor, and the third floor is a museum of rural life. Bring a picnic (there are tables). Take Rt. 27 north for 8 miles to Dresden Mills, then Rt. 127 south for 3.7 miles to Rt. 197 and on to Rt. 128, where you head north for 1.3 miles.

IN EDGECOMB

🚂 **Fort Edgecomb State Memorial** (207-882-7777), 66 Old Fort Rd.; the turnoff from Rt. 1 is just across the Sheepscot River. The fort is open Memorial Day–Labor Day, daily 9–6. Nominal donation. This 27-foot, two-story octagonal blockhouse, built in 1808, overlooks a narrow passage of the Sheepscot River. For the same reasons that it was an ideal site for a fort, it is today an ideal picnic site, and tables are provided.

Christina Tree

AT THE WISCASSET, WATERVILLE, AND FARMINGTON RAILWAY MUSEUM

FOR FAMILIES 🅞 🚂 **Wiscasset, Waterville, and Farmington Railway Museum** (207-882-4193; wwfry.org), 97 Cross Rd., Sheepscot Station, Alna (just off Rt. 218, 4.5 miles north of Wiscasset). Check the website for museum hours and trains, which run most weekends, six times a day in summer, less off-season. Volunteers preserve the history of this 2-foot narrow-gauge railroad. The museum's pride is Engine No. 9, an 1891 two-footer locomotive, billed as the oldest in the United States. Volunteers have built replicas of the engine house and shop, original station, and freight shed, which now houses the gift shop and museum. It's a 37-minute roundtrip run on 2.6 miles of track. Trains are usually pulled by a diesel locomotive, but on special occasions a vintage-1904 steam engine is used. Rides are $7 per adult, $6 seniors, $4 ages 4–12.

✎ **Monkey C Monkey Do** (207-882-6861; monkeycmonkeydo.com), 698 Bath Rd. (corner of Rt. 1 and Rt. 144), Wiscasset. Open daily mid-June–Labor Day, weekends Memorial Day Weekend–Columbus Day. Eight ziplines and a great swing with 30 obstacles to navigate at heights of 12–40 feet. Also Guerilla Tactics Laser Tag. Reservations recommended.

✳ Green Space

The **Back River Trail at Eaton Farm** (chewonki.org/about/nature_trails.asp). This is a 4.5-mile coastal trail. From Rt. 1 turn right onto Old Ferry Rd in Wiscasset (at Norm's Used Cars). Take the third right onto Ready Point Rd., which is 0.5 mile past Chewonki Neck Rd. Follow Ready Point Rd. until you see a well-marked sign on the right for Eaton Farm Trail. There is ample parking there and a kiosk for hikers.

Sunken Garden, Main St., Wiscasset. Down a few steps, easy to miss, but a wonderful little garden surrounded by a stone wall. Planted by the Sortwell family in the foundation of an old inn, the property was donated to the town in 1959.

Sherman Lake Rest Area, Rt. 1 between Edgecomb and Newcastle. Pick up the fixings in Wiscasset and picnic at this scenic rest area. Since the dam broke, this "lake" is now a tidal river. It's still a lovely spot, though, complete with restrooms.

✎ **Morris Farm** (207-882-4080; morrisfarm.org) 156 Gardiner Rd. (Rt. 27), Wiscasset. A 60-acre organic working farm, with trails open to the public during daylight hours; phone to check on current programming: day camps and farm tours and store.

✳ Lodging

INNS AND B&BS **Squire Tarbox Inn** (207-882-7693 or 1-800-818-0626), 1181 Main Rd. (Rt. 144; turn off Rt. 1 south of Wiscasset), Westport 04578. Open mid-Apr.–Dec. "A good country inn must be tasted," maintains Swiss chef Mario De Pietro, and food is indeed what draws most patrons to this handsome Federal-style farmhouse. Boards and timbers in the low-ceilinged dining room date to 1763, while the parlor and four largest guest rooms, all with working fireplace, are in the "new" (1825) section of house. The remaining seven, more rustic guest rooms, are in the converted 1820s Carriage Barn, off a sitting room with a gas fireplace, books, and games. De Pietro and his wife, Roni, perpetuate the inn's reputation for hospitality as well as food, encouraging guests to follow walking paths on their 13 acres, row on the saltwater pond, or explore Westport Island on a mountain bike. $139–199 per couple; off-season $120–199 per couple, including breakfast with freshly baked croissants, homemade muesli, and a hot dish prepared with fresh-laid eggs from the house hens. Also see *Dining Out*.

✪ 🐾 ✎ ((ᵖ)) **Snow Squall Inn** (207-882-6892 or 1-800-775-7245; snowsquallinn.com), 5 Bradford Rd., Wiscasset 04578. Open more or less year-round. Melanie Harris, a trained yoga instructor and massage therapist, and Paul Harris, a professional chef, who met in Bermuda, offer spaciously comfortable accommodations in this 1850s house (named for a clipper ship) with ample common space, gardens, and lounges with hearths and TV. The four guest rooms in the main house have a private bath, king or queen bed, phone, and air-conditioning. Each of the three suites in the Carriage House has two bedrooms (1½ baths) and a private entrance, good for families. $117–170 for rooms, from $160-181 per couple for suites, less off-season. A full breakfast is included. Inquire about massage and yoga.

🐾 ((ᵖ)) **Marston House** (207-882-6010 or 1-800-852-4137; marstonhouse.com), Main St., P.O. Box 517, Wiscasset 04578. Open May–Oct. The front of the house is Paul and Sharon Mrozinski's antiques shop, specializing in 18th- and early-19th-century textiles and painted furnishings. In the Carriage House behind—well away from the Rt. 1 traffic noise—are two exceptional guest rooms, each with private entrance, working fireplace, and private bath. Breakfast is served in the flowery gardens or in your room. $155 per couple, $130 per night for two nights or more.

OTHER 🐾 ✏ > (((•))) ♂ **Wiscasset Motor Lodge** (207-882-7137; wiscassetmotorlodge.com), 596 Bath Rd. (Rt. 1), Wiscasset. Open mid-Apr.–late Oct. In 2016 new owners Eric and Saundra Neperud revamped and substantially increased the appeal of this roadside lodging. There are 13 units in the two-story motel, another 12 in the "cottages" (evolved from individual cabins), renovated with woodwork from trees on the eight-acre property. Bed arrangements vary; $125-180 for rooms based on double occupancy, $10 per extra person. $210-225 for a two-room suite for four. Rates include full breakfast, including a from-scratch entrée with house baking, served in the lounge, which doubles as a daytime game area and evening space to bring in prepared food. Pet-friendly rooms offer access to a wooded trail and the grounds include badminton croquet and a fire pit.

✏ **Chewonki Campground** (207-882-7426; chewonkicampground.com), 235 Chewonki Neck Rd., Wiscasset 04578. Sited on 50 waterside acres. The website lets you check out actual, unusually spacious sites for RVs and tents. For tentative tenters a couple are already rigged, ready to rent. Amenities include saltwater pools, a tennis court, a camp store, a rec hall, lawn games, and kayak rentals. Not far enough off Rt. 1 or the local airport to eliminate all traffic noise. Sites are $48–80 in-season, less in shoulders.

✳ Where to Eat

DINING OUT Squire Tarbox Inn (207-882-7693; squiretarboxinn.com), 1181 Main Rd. (Rt. 144; turn off Rt. 1 south of Wiscasset), Westport (see *Lodging*). Open daily (except Mon.) Memorial Day–Oct.; Thu.–Sat. in Apr., May, Nov., and Dec. Reserve. Dinner is served 6–8:30 PM in an 18th-century former summer kitchen with a large colonial fireplace and ceiling timbers that were once part of a ship. In warm-weather months there's an attractive screened and canopied deck. Swiss chef-owner Mario De Pietro now shares the kitchen with his Swiss-trained daughter Lara. Ingredients are increasingly farm-to-table in classic

dishes like rosemary-roasted rack of lamb or sautéed sliced veal with Swiss-style rösti potatoes. Much of the fruit and veggies come from the inn's extensive organic farm. Entrées $23.50–30. A 15 percent gratuity is added.

✏ **Little Village Bistro** (207-687-8232), 65 Gardiner Rd. (Rt. 27) open Tue.–Sat. 4:30–9. Reserve! Tony Bickford, a top Boothbay Harbor chef, has opened his own little restaurant and it's a winner. Just about everything is locally sourced and made from scratch. The reasonably priced menu includes comfort food like slow-braised Bolognese and vegetarian dishes like pea and goat cheese tortellini with wild mushrooms (both $14), as well as crab-stuffed haddock and crispy seared duck breast (both $24) and rack of lamb ($29).

✪ ♿ **Le Garage** (207-882-5409; legaragerestaurant.com), 15 Water St., Wiscasset. Open Wed.–Sun., 11 AM–dinner, from 8:30 Sun (brunch). A former 1920s garage with a glassed-in porch overlooking the Sheepscot River (request a table on the porch). Frequently less crowded for lunch (seafood crêpes are the specialty) than restaurants on the main drag. Owned by Lee Rust's family; chefs change but specialties remain seafood chowders, stews, Newburgs, and creamed finnan haddie. Entrées $21–26.50, also a pub menu.

EATING OUT ✪ ✏ **Sarah's** (207-882-7504; sarahscafe.com), Main and Water Sts., Wiscasset. Open daily year-round, 11–8, with an outdoor deck for summer dining. The extensive menu includes good pizza (try the Greek pizza with extra garlic), salads, sandwiches in pita pockets or baked in dough, vegetarian dishes, Mexican fare, and lobster more than 15 different ways. Well known for their soup and bread bar.

Montsweag Roadhouse (207-443-6563; montsweagroadhouse.com), 942 Rt. 1, Woolwich, nearer to Wiscasset than Bath. Open 11–1 AM. Serving food until 9, until 10 Fri. and Sat. This distinctive red building is an old apple storage barn, a restaurant since the 1930s but now with a pleasantly split personality. Come on a weeknight and it's a quiet, spacious family-geared place with booths and a large, reasonably priced menu and full bar. On Fri. and Sat. this place hops with live bands.

Treats (207-882-6192), 80 Main St., Wiscasset. Open Mon.–Sat. 8–6, Sun. 10–4. A food store known for baked goods plus terrific

LOBSTER

🦞 **Red's Eats** (207-882-6128), Rt. 1 and Water St., just before the bridge, Wiscasset. Open 11:30–10 in July, Aug., until 9 in shoulder months. The lines can be an hour long and the seating is at picnic benches, but the lobster rolls—packing an entire lobster into one small hot-dog roll—continue to get rave reviews. Whether or not this is "Maine's #1 Lobster Roll" is a matter of taste. The lobster is cold, fresh from the fridge, served with a choice of drawn butter or mayo. Fried clams are the other specialty but there are also crabcakes, hot dogs, fried zucchini, and more. It's been operated by members of the Gagnon family since 1977.

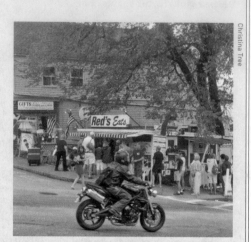

Christina Tree

RED'S EATS

Sprague's Lobster (207-882-1236), 22 Main St., Wiscasset. Open seasonally, 11–7. No lines, no legend, but a great view from picnic tables on a pier beside the river. This is the other great place for lobster any way; also really good clam fritters.

🦞 **The Sea Basket** (207-882-6581), 303 Bath Rd. (Rt. 1), Wiscasset. Open Wed.–Sun. 11–8. A long-established road stop known for fresh seafood; a lot of it is fried, but with an eye to keeping it heart healthy. Known for lobster stew, lobster rolls, and sea scallops.

soups and sandwiches, with an eat-in table. The town's picnic source.

✳ Selective Shopping

ANTIQUES SHOPS Antiques are everywhere in Wiscasset. On and just off Water Street, in or attached to attractive old homes, more than 20 shops by our last count. Pick up a map (available in most shops) and browse the day away; many specialize in nautical pieces and country primitives. **Wiscasset Village Antiques** (207-882-4029; avalon antiquemarket.com), Rt. 1, 2 miles south of Wiscasset Village. Open daily 9–7 in-season. More than 100 dealers. See the Bath chapter for details about the Montsweag Flea Market, south of Wiscasset on Rt. 1, open seasonally on Wed. and weekends.

ART GALLERIES **Wiscasset Bay Gallery** (207-882-7682; wiscassetbaygallery.com), 67 Main St., Wiscasset. Changing exhibits in spacious exhibit rooms. Specializes in 19th- and 20th-century Maine and New England marine and landscape paintings.

Maine Art Gallery (207-882-7511; maine artgallery.org), 15 Warren St. Open June–Nov., Tue.–Sat. 10–4, Sun. 11–4. Housed in a vintage-1807 brick schoolhouse, a nonprofit gallery since 1954. Frequently changing exhibits. Worth finding.

OTHER **Sheepscot River Pottery** (207-882-9410; sheepscot.com), 34 Rt. 1, Edgecomb, just north of Wiscasset; home base for one of Maine's major potteries.

Old Salt Books and Gifts (207-882-4700), 49 Water St., Wiscasset. Maine products, gifts, cards, young adult books, more. The newest occupant of the Old General Store.

Big Al's Supervalues (201-882-6423; bigalssupervalues.com), south of Wiscasset Village on Rt.1. An odd-lots trove of everything you don't need and a few things you might. Toys, gadgets, Maine souvenirs, party supplies, etc. Free coffee.

BOOTHBAY HARBOR REGION

The water surrounding the village of Boothbay Harbor is more than just a view. You must cross it—via a footbridge—to get from one side of town to the other, and you can explore it on a wide choice of excursion and charter boats and in sea kayaks. It is obvious from the very lay of this old fishing village that its people have always gotten around on foot or in boats. Though parking has increased in recent years, cars still feel like an intrusion. In the peninsula's other villages—Boothbay, Southport, and East Boothbay—roads are walled by pines, permitting only occasional glimpses of water.

Boats are what all four of the Boothbays have traditionally been about. Boats are built, repaired, and sold here, and sailing and fishing vessels fill the harbors. Excursions range from an hour-long sail around the outer harbor to a 90-minute crossing (each way) to Monhegan Island. Fishermen can pursue giant tuna, stripers, and blues, and nature lovers can cruise out to see seals, whales, and puffins.

In the middle of summer Boothbay Harbor itself is chockablock full of tourists licking ice cream cones, chewing freshly made taffy and fudge, browsing in shops, looking into art galleries, listening to band concerts on the library lawn, and, of course, eating lobster. You get the feeling it's been like this every summer since the 1870s.

Boothbay Harbor is just a dozen miles south of Rt. 1 via Rt. 27, which runs down the middle of the peninsula. The coastline is, however, a different story, measuring 100 miles

Christina Tree

BOOTHBAY HARBOR

Downtown Boothbay Harbor

0   0.25
Mile

N

as it wanders down the Sheepscot, around Southport Island, and up into Boothbay Harbor, out around Spruce Head, around Linekin Bay, out Ocean Point, and back up along the Damariscotta River.

Thanks to the fervor of developers from the 1870s on, this entire coastline is distinguished by the quantity of its summer cottages, many of which can be rented by the week for less than you might think. Still, thanks to the Boothbay Region Land Trust, there are now over 30 miles of accessible waterside preserves, with trails meandering through hundreds of acres of spruce and pine, down to smooth rocks and tidal pools. It was this landscape that inspired Rachel Carson, who first summered on the peninsula in 1946 and built a cottage on the Sheepscot River in 1953, to write much of *The Edge of the Sea* (1955) and then *Silent Spring* (1962), the book that changed global thinking about human beings' relation to basic laws of nature.

GUIDANCE **Boothbay Harbor Region Chamber of Commerce** (207-633-2353; boothbay harbor.com), 192 Townsend Ave. (Rt. 27), southbound, just before the light but north of Hannaford Supermarket at the junction with Rt. 96. Open weekdays 8–5 year-round, also weekends 10–4 June–Columbus Day. Pick up the chamber's annual *Visitor & Resource Guide* and (indispensable) map detailing local parking lots. The chamber also keeps cottage listings and tracks availability for cottages weekly and for lodgings daily.

Boothbay Information Center (207-633-4743; boothbay.org/bcc), Rt. 27, Boothbay, after the fire station. Open daily 9–9 (until 6 on Sun.) late June–Columbus Day, also Fri.–Sun. Memorial Day–late June. A friendly walk-in center that does its best to help people without reservations find places to stay. It keeps an illustrated scrapbook of options, also a cottage rental list.

GETTING THERE *By car:* Take I-295 from Portland, getting off at Exit 28 (Brunswick) or Exit 31 (Topsham). Follow signs to Rt. 1 north through Bath and Wiscasset, turning onto Rt. 27 into Boothbay and Boothbay Harbor.

GETTING AROUND **The Rocktide Trolley** (on wheels) runs every 30 minutes daily, 10–5, mid-June–Labor Day. From the east side of town, starting at the Rocktide Inn, to Brown's Wharf Inn, across to the heart of the Boothbay Harbor Region, up onto 27 north, stopping at the Meadow Mall, the Flagship Inn, and the Boothbay Region YMCA.

PARKING Finding a spot in the center of Boothbay Harbor can mean circling the block a couple of times. Still, we had little trouble on an August weekend, armed with a local map showing parking lots (see *Guidance*). Boothbay Harbor offers free street parking and a dozen public parking lots.

PUBLIC RESTROOMS In Boothbay Harbor restrooms are open Memorial Day–Columbus Day by the small park at the Town Landing; also during office hours at the town hall, Howard Street. Locations are marked on the chamber of commerce map.

WHEN TO COME Some lodgings and restaurants stay open year-round, but those bright warm days on the water can't be beat.

✳ To See

✪ ✐ **The By-Way.** Don't miss Boothbay Harbor's old-fashioned harborside boardwalk area. Walk from the By-Way down to the footbridge across the harbor.

A TOUCH TANK AT THE MAINE STATE AQUARIUM

FOR FAMILIES ✪ ✐ **Maine State Aquarium** (207-633-9559), McKown Point Rd., West Boothbay Harbor. Open Memorial Day weekend–Sept. daily 10–5; in Sept., Wed.–Sun. $7 adults, $5 seniors, $3 ages 3–12. This octagonal waterside aquarium offers tanks filled with sea creatures found in Maine waters such as striped bass, cod, alewives, and a 17-pound lobster. Dip your hands into the touch tank and view "cat sharks," dogfish, and alewives (larger than we'd thought). Presentations several times a day in summer, but get there early to ensure a good view.

✐ & **Boothbay Railway Village** (207-633-4727; railwayvillage.org), Rt. 27 (about 3 miles north of Boothbay Harbor). Open daily 9:30–5, June–mid-Oct.; special rides for Halloween and Thanksgiving, plus a Polar Express in early Dec. Regular admission $10 adults, $5 ages 2–18. A 2-foot narrow-gauge railway with a coal-fed steam engine wends its way through a miniature village made up of several restored buildings, including vintage railroad stations, the Boothbay Town Hall (1847), and the Spruce Point chapel (1923). Displays include a general store, a doll museum, and a 1920s-era home with an authentic 1929 GE refrigerator and period furniture. More than 55 antique autos (1907–49) are also on display. Many special events, including a weekend antique auto meet (more than 150 cars) in late July.

LIGHTHOUSES ✪ ✐ **Burnt Island Lighthouse Program** (maine.gov/dmr/burntisland). This 1821 lighthouse, a mile out from the inner harbor, remains an active light station owned by the Maine Department of Marine Resources. Visitors are greeted by docents in 1950s dress portraying the island's last lighthouse keeper and his family, guiding them around their '50s furnished home and up into the light. See *Boating/Balmy Days Cruises* for frequent excursions in July/Aug.

Hendrick's Head Light, Southport Island. Built in 1829, privately owned but can be viewed from Hendrick's Beach. The story goes that a keeper here found a floating bundle after a shipwreck. He adopted the baby inside, the wreck's only survivor.

The Inn at the Cuckolds Lighthouse (innatcuckoldslighthouse.org). Just half a mile off the outer tip of Southport Island, this vintage-1892 station is now a luxurious, two-suite bed & breakfast. Check the website for visuals and a schedule of weekly tours and periodic events. Also see *Lodging*.

Ram Island Light is a distinctive landmark off Ocean Point. Built in 1883, it's now automated and the island itself is maintained by a nonprofit trust.

MUSEUMS ✔ **Boothbay Region Historical Society Museum** (207-633-0820; boothbay historical.org), 72 Oak St., Boothbay Harbor. Open year-round, Thu.–Sat. 10–2. Free. Seven rooms are filled with vintage lobster traps, Native American artifacts, ships' bells, a Fresnel lens from Ram Island, and genealogical resources. The gift shop stocks books, maps, coins, photos, and more.

✔ **Hendricks Hill Museum** (207-633-1102; hendrickshill.org), 419 Hendricks Hill Rd., Rt. 27, Southport Island. Open July and Aug., Tue., Thu., and Sat. 11–3. The house looks much as it did in 1810, with a period kitchen including a beehive oven, pictures of Southport's grand hotels, as well as other village memorabilia, wooden boats, and farm implements. Farther down the road stop by **Southport Memorial Library**, which has an impressive monarch butterfly collection.

✲ To Do

BIKE RENTALS **Tidal Transit Co.** (207-633-7140; kayakboothbay.com), 18 Granary Way by the footbridge, Boothbay Harbor, rents bikes in-season.

BOATING ✔ **Balmy Days Cruises** (207-633-2284; balmydayscruises.com), Pier 8, Boothbay Harbor, offers cruises to Monhegan Island every morning Memorial Day weekend to Columbus Day weekend and weekends in shoulder seasons. The crossing takes 90 minutes each way, and you have close to four hours on the island. Bring a picnic and hit the trail. Here are also harbor tours, party fishing, and tours to **Burnt Island Lighthouse** (see *Lighthouses*).

✔ **Cap'n Fish Boat Cruises** (207-633-3244; mainewhales.com), Pier 1 (red ticket booth), Boothbay Harbor. Mid-May–mid-Oct. Daily cruises include whale-watching, lighthouses, trap hauling, and more.

Coastal Maine Botanical Gardens (207-633-6508), (see *Must See*). Electric boat *Beagle* offers hourly cruises from the Garden landing.

West Harbor Recreation (207-370-0678), West Boothbay, offers both power and sailboats.

SAILING **Boothbay Harbor Yacht Club** (207-633-5750), 156 Western Ave., West Boothbay Harbor 04575. Moorings available for sailing/cruising to visitors. Launch service 8–2, heads, showers, laundry, dining room/lounge access. Closed Mon. Free WiFi access at mooring, ice available, plus other amenities.

Daysails are offered by **Schooner** *Lazy Jack* (207-633-3444; sailschoonerlazyjack.com), ✿ **Schooner** *East Wind* (207-633-6598; schoonereastwind.com), **Friendship Sloops** *Sarah Mead* (207-380-5460) and *Bay Lady* (207-633-2284; balmydayscruises.com).

✿ **Linekin Bay Resort** (207-633-2494; linekinbayresort.com), 92 Wall Point Rd., Boothbay Harbor. Overnight moorings (all chain), onshore facilities. Qualified sailors can rent 19-foot Rhodes sailboats, and sailing lessons are offered for all abilities. Also see *Lodging*.

MUST SEE

Coastal Maine Botanical Gardens (207-633-8000; mainegardens .org), 132 Botanical Garden Dr., off Barter's Island Rd., Boothbay. Gardens and buildings open April 15–Oct. 31 daily 9–5, until 6 in July/Aug. $16 adults, $14 seniors 65 and over, $8 ages 3–17, $39 for a family of four, under 3 free. Also "Gardens Aglow," mid-Nov. through Dec., 4–9.

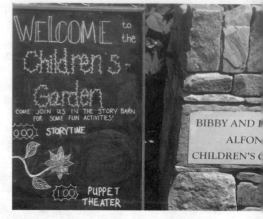

CHILDREN'S GARDEN

These 270 shorefront acres were slated for development in the 1990s when a small group of local residents dedicated themselves to turning the property into a distinctively Maine garden, some mortgaging their homes to launch the project. Much of what they had to work with was ledge and boulders so they set themselves "hardscaping" as well and landscaping. At present 30,000 plants represent more than 1,300 species and numerous rocks have been shaped into benches and water spouting sculptures as well many landscape features. Given the up and down lay of this land, there are hairpin turns, many nooks and crannies, and perpetual sense of discovery.

Plan to spend at least two hours, quite possibly a day. Begin with the website, which offers an update of what's in bloom as well as events and a mapped lay of the land. From the **Visitors Center**, with its gift shop and the **Kitchen Garden Café** (11–4) paths radiate out to themed gardens. The **Children's Garden** begins with spouting whales and a maze lawn, includes a lupine meadow, Mr. McGregor's garden, a story barn, tree house, a shallow

LERNER GARDEN VITA WITH DAISIES

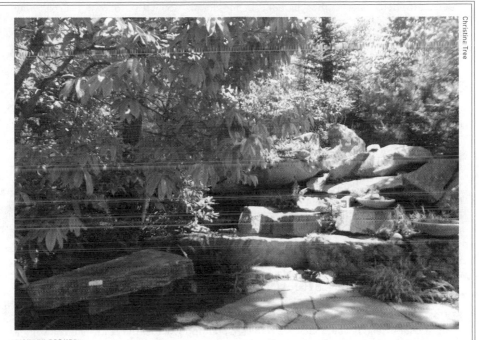

A SHADY CORNER

pond, and much more. Everywhere adults too are invited to slow down and look, smell, listen to birds (not recordings). The **Garden of the Five Senses** adds the scent of lavender and other aromatic plants, the texture of lamb's ears and creeping thyme, the noise of flowing water and frogs and wooden boards underfoot, and the tastes of herbs like Russian tarragon. A downward-sloping path brings you to the **Meditation Garden**, centered on a magnificent stone basin. From here the path can connect with the **Shoreland Trail**, along which you can find the **Fairy House Village** and **The Landing**, where you can rent **kayaks** to paddle along the Back River or board the electric-powered tour boat *Beagle* for a one-hour cruise out into the Sheepscot River. Wooded trails loop back to the Giles Rhododendron Garden set off by a

ENTRANCE TO THE LERNER GARDEN OF THE FIVE SENSES

waterfall. Free shuttles ease the way from multiple parking lots, and guided Cart Tours are available by reservation. Pets are allowed only in the parking area; there is a dog walk and water spigot. Count on the café for meals made with produce picked just outside the door in summer.

SPORTFISHING See boothbayharbor.com for details about the following: **Breakaway Sportfishing** (207-350-5118), **Redhook Charters** (207-633-3807), **Sweet Action Charters** (207-318-4898), and **Charger Charters** (207-380-4556). **Oak Street Provisions** (207-633-1290), 43 Oak St., Boothbay Harbor, rents tackle and bait, sells fishing licenses.

GOLF **Boothbay Harbor Country Club** (207-633-6085; boothbayharborcc.com), Country Club Dr. (off Rt. 27), Boothbay. Open Apr.–Nov. Eighteen holes, expansive new clubhouse and restaurant; open to the public through short-term memberships and member inns; carts and clubs for rent.

RECREATIONAL FACILITY ✒ **Boothbay Region YMCA** (207-633-2855; brymca.com), Townsend Ave., Rt. 27 (on your left as you come down the stretch that leads to town). An exceptional facility open to nonmembers (user fee charged) with two new swimming pools and other programs for children. Tennis, racquetball, gymnastics, aerobics, soccer, swimming in a heated six-lane indoor pool, saunas, exercise and weight-lifting rooms, and a fieldhouse with a three-lane track.

SEA KAYAKING ✒ **Tidal Transit Company** (see *Bike Rentals*) offers guided tours as well as hourly, half-day, and full-day rentals (basic instruction included); their rentals are also available at the landing at the Maine Coastal Botanical Garden.

SWIMMING Beaches are all private, but visitors are permitted in a number of spots:
   Hendricks Head Beach. Follow Rt. 27 toward Southport, across the Townsend Gut Bridge to a circle (white church on your left, monument in the center, general store on your right); turn right and follow Beach Rd. to the beach; roadside parking and calm, shallow water.
   🐾 **Grimes Cove** has a little pebble beach with rocks to climb at the very tip of Ocean Point, East Boothbay. Follow Rt. 96 to the end.

BOOTHBAY OFFERS PLENTY OF WAYS TO GET OUT ON THE WATER

HENDRICKS HEAD BEACH

🐚 **Barrett Park**, Lobster Cove (turn off Atlantic Ave. at the Catholic church, east side of Boothbay Harbor), is a town park with restrooms and two rocky Linekin Bay beaches.

🐚 **Knickerkane Park**, Barter's Island Rd., Boothbay. Paths lead from the parking lot to a small island with picnic tables and swimming. The road in is a bit rough, but that seems to keep crowds away from this small beach with a dock.

Ocean Point, East Boothbay. Route 96 ends at a small beach with a float to swim out to. Look for the parking lot just before, which also accesses the rocky shore stretching east.

TENNIS Public tennis courts are located across Rt. 27 from the YMCA, which also has indoor courts.

WALKS **Ocean Point**, at the tip of the East Boothbay peninsula, offers beautiful views of the ocean and several windswept islands, but parking can be tricky. Leave your car in the lot operated by the Linekin Preserve or other designated parking area and walk, though be mindful of NO TRESPASSING signs. Explore the rocky beach and its tidal pools. On a clear day you can see both Ram Island and the Cuckolds lighthouses.

Also see *Green Space*.

✳ Green Space

Boothbay Region Land Trust (207-633-4818; bbrlt.org), 137 Townsend Ave., Boothbay Harbor. Open Mon.–Fri. 9:30–4:30. The trails are open year-round and free, donations appreciated. Download maps from the website or pick up a copy of the spiral-bound, illustrated *Take a Hike*, published by the land trust—a guide to 22 preserves with a total of more than 30 miles of trails. The 1,700 acres of land under the trust's protection include several islands. In the **Porter Preserve** (23 wooded acres, including a beach) on Barters Island, an osprey peered at us from its nest atop a marker along a ledge just offshore, and another ledge was so thick with seals that they seemed like some kind of brown growth—until a dog barked and the entire ledge seemed to heave and rise, then flop and splash off in different directions.

✳ Lodging

The chamber of commerce lists more than 100 lodging places in its regional guide and keeps a list of vacation rentals. See *Guidance*.

RESORTS ♂ ♔ ✐ **Spruce Point Inn Resort & Spa** (207-633-4152 or 1-800-553-0289; sprucepointinn.com), 88 Grandview Ave., Boothbay Harbor. Open mid-May–mid-Oct. Boothbay Harbor's premier full-service resort is sited on 57 acres at the tip of a peninsula jutting into Boothbay Harbor. Roughly 100 rooms are divided between the handsome 1940s inn and "lodges," self-contained town houses and cottages scattered over landscaped grounds. There are no fewer than 22 types of rooms, varying widely in size and decor. Public rooms in the inn include an attractive library and two restaurants; elegantly casual **Bogie's** and oceanfront **88** for fine dining. We loved swimming in the cold saltwater pool and warming back up again in the hot tub, both on the edge of the bay. Amenities also include a heated freshwater pool, clay tennis courts, lawn games, a fitness center, a full-service spa, and a private pier. Guests can also take advantage of kayaks, bicycles, and sails on the Friendship Sloop *Sarah Mead*. Organized children's programs are offered in July and Aug. EP high-season rates for rooms in the inn are $220–525, cottages $295–1,200, cottage rooms $195–320, modern lodge rooms $340–435, and town houses $675–745. A resort fee is added.

♂ ✐ ♿ **Newagen Seaside Inn** (207-633-5242 or 1-800-654-5242; newagenseasideinn .com), 60 Colony Rd. (Rt. 27), Southport Island, Cape Newagen. Open mid-May–mid-Oct. When the original resort opened in the 1920s, owner Joshua Brooks—founder of the Eastern States Exposition—had both electricity and Rt. 27 extended to this southern tip of Southport Island to serve it. In 1943 the original inn burned in a fire said to be set as a signal to German U-boats. Brooks then had the present large, admittedly plain-faced facility built, painted, and open within three months. Rachel Carson frequented the inn and its splendid grounds; her ashes were scattered here. Even if you don't stay here, be sure to find your way to the property's pine-shaded shore. Rooms and suites in the main inn have

all been recently renovated, another junior suite added in the Little Inn annex, and a gorgeous new ocean-view cottage added. There's also a new pool and a brand-new restaurant, open for both lunch and dinner (see *Dining Out*). Amenities include tennis courts, bicycles, lawn games, rowboats, and the Pine Room, which houses two funky 1940s-era candlepin bowling lanes, pool table, and table tennis. Weddings fill the place on weekends but midweeks are quiet and good value. Rooms and suites $255–305, depending on room and season. Cottages, $355–415. Rates include full breakfast.

✐ ♿ **Ocean Point Inn** (207-633-4200 or 1-800-552-5554; oceanpointinn.com), 191 Shore Rd., P.O. Box 409, East Boothbay. Open Memorial Day–Columbus Day. This 110-year-old resort has a great location, longtime owners, and an enthusiastic following. All rooms have private bath, air-conditioning, cable TV, mini refrigerator, and phone; most have water views, and some have a fireplace. Guests relax in the heated pool with a hot tub or the Adirondack chairs overlooking the ocean. There's an oceanfront dining room (see *Dining Out*). $99–349 in-season, continental breakfast included; full-buffet breakfast is extra.

Ocean Gate Resort (207-633-3321 or 1-800-221-5924; oceangateinn.com), Southport 04576. Several multistory buildings with water views are ranged along the shore, and attractive cottages come with and without views on this 45-acre wooded property. A breakfast buffet and use of canoes and kayaks is included in the rates: $119–384. Facilities include a heated pool, miniature golf, fishing pond, tennis, and more.

♺ ♂ ♔ ✐ (((•))) **Linekin Bay Resort** (207-633-2494; linekinbayresort.com), 92 Wall Point Rd., Boothbay Harbor. Open July & Aug. for all-inclusive resort program, shoulder seasons for weekend weddings and weekday B&B. Billed as the last all-inclusive sailing resort on the East Coast, Lineken Bay has undergone extensive renovations under new owners. High-season rates still include all three meals, served family-style in the open-timbered central lodge, use of fleet of Rhodes 19 sailboats (with or without lessons by skilled young instructors), a Kids Camp, and use of canoes, kayaks, rowboats, standup paddleboats, and tennis and fishing gear. Facilities include a

FIVE GABLES INN

heated bayside saltwater pool, tennis court, and rec room. At present 160 guests can bed down in a mix of four waterside lodges and 22 wooded cabins. High-season rates: $370–460 per night for the first two people, $15–115 per extra family members depending on age. **West Lodge the Deck Bar & Grill** is open 11–9 with moorings for patrons who come by water. Shoulder season weekends are reserved for weddings but midweek is B&B ($150–250 per couple).

INNS AND B&BS ✪ ✐ ♿ ((φ)) **Topside** (207-633-5404 or 1-888-633-5404; topsideinn.com), 60 McKown St., Boothbay Harbor. Open May–Oct. This spacious captain's house sits atop McKown Hill with sweeping water views from its windows and the Adirondack chairs on its long, sloping lawn. Some 20 rooms are divided between the light-filled and unfussily elegant main house and two "guest houses," two-story former motel units that Mark and Buzz have transformed so completely that "Leeward," especially, is a tempting choice over the house. Common space includes a book-stocked living room as well as a guest pantry (fridge, coffee, and snacks) and multiwindowed dining room. Breakfast, which includes house granola, fruit, and freshly baked breads, perhaps deviled eggs with salmon or shrimp creole with grits and a fried egg, is included in $179–239. Downtown Boothbay Harbor is a quick, short

walk downhill (the uphill return seems steeper).

✪ ((φ)) **Five Gables Inn** (207-633-4551 or 1 800 451-5048; fivegablesinn.com), 107 Murray Hill Rd. (off Rt. 96). East Boothbay. Open Memorial Day weekend–mid-Oct. Steve and Susan Plansteiner are the owners of this special inn. Fifteen of the 16 rooms offer views of Linekin Bay; most have queen-sized beds (many with handmade quilts), and five have a working fireplace. The smaller third-floor gable rooms offer some of the best water views. Beach towels are provided for swimming off the dock. There's a wraparound porch with tables for breakfast and rockers for reading, and a spacious living room/dining area with enough room for guests to find their own corner or space around the hearth that invites conversation. Breakfast and afternoon tea is included in $145–265 double.

Blue Heron Seaside Inn (207-633-7020; blueheronseasideinn.com), 65 Townsend Ave., Boothbay Harbor. Boothbay natives Laura and Phil Chapman have restored this elegant harbor-side home as a B&B with six rooms outfitted with refrigerator/freezer, private bath, air-conditioning, and cable TV, with access to decks overlooking the harbor. Guests can use the inn's kayaks. $195–285 in-season includes a full breakfast, perhaps Vickery French toast with baked apples. Then walk out the door and you are right in the village.

Harborage Inn (207-350-0702; harborage inn.com), 75 Townsend Ave. Open May–Oct. Troy and Emery Chapman have totally

TOPSIDE INN

Christina Tree

VIEW OF BOOTHBAY HARBOR

renovated this iconic 19th-century inn, which has been in Troy's family for more than 40 years. Continuous harbor-view balconies overflow with flowers and the 11 rooms (2 suites) are uncluttered and comfortable, most with water views. Guests find a welcoming croc of iced passion tea and the blackboard menu listing the next morning's tantalizing breakfast menu. Amenities include a harborside hot tub $197-289. Midweek and last minute discounts.

MOTELS Boothbay Harbor has number of large, inviting motels, many on the harbor.

   ♿ **Flagship Inn & Suites** (207-633-5094; boothbaylodging.com), 200 Townsend Ave. (Rt. 27), Boothbay Harbor. Open year-round. This completely renovated, affordable motel offers 82 rooms and family suites. Amenities include a swimming pool, hot tub, and cable TV. $74–149, depending on the season. On-site restaurant.

   🍴 **Mid-Town Motel** (207-633-2751; midtownmaine.com), 96 McKown St., Boothbay Harbor. Open May–Oct. Billed as "a true 1950s classic," this is a pleasant, spanking-clean motel with either a queen or a double and twin in each room and an easy walk to downtown shops and the waterfront. $98 July–Labor Day, from $89 off-season.

   The Inn at the Cuckolds Lighthouse (innatcuckoldslighthouse.com). Sited half a mile off the outer tip of Southport Island, this vintage-1892 station is now a luxurious,

two-suite B&B open late May–late Sept. $1,450–$1,750 per night. Two-night minimum. Check the website for open house days on which public tours are offered.

COTTAGES The following are variations on old-style cottage colonies, still a good option, especially with children and/or pets.

   🐾 ((ᵖ)) **Harborfields on the Shore** (207-633-5082; harborfields.com), 24 McKown Point Rd., West Boothbay Harbor 04575. A friendly, quiet family resort on a 10-acre harborfront property. Cozy cottages feature woodstoves, full kitchens, and great views of the harbor. Floats for boating, swimming, and fishing are available, as are moorings and a small tidal beach. Pets welcome. From $1030 per week in high season.

   Thompson Cottages (207-633-5304; thompsoncottages.com), 7 Thompson's Hill Rd., Southport 04576. Three 1-bedroom cottages and one 3-bedroom cottage come fully equipped, located on Townsend Gut. Alice and Dick Thompson have been hosting guests here since 1968. From $735 per week.

   Note: Contact the chambers of commerce for lists of rental cottages. The Boothbays offer one of the coast's largest concentrations of vacation rentals.

CAMPING 🐾 ⚓ ♿ **Gray Homestead Campground** (207-633-4612; graysoceancamping.com), 21 Homestead Rd., Southport Island 04576. Open mid-May–Columbus Day. You can't beat the location—301 acres on the east coast of Southport Island. Forty-two sites for tents and RVs. Stephen Gray's family has been here since 1800. $41–57 per night for RVs; from $38 for tent sites.

✳ Where to Eat

DINING OUT ✪ ⚓ **Ports of Italy** (207-633-1011; portsofitaly.com), 47 Commercial St., Boothbay Harbor. Open for dinner daily from 4:30, Apr.–mid-Oct. This is a long-standing local favorite. Sante Calandri carries on the tradition of genuine northern Italian cuisine. The pasta is homemade, the upstairs dining room is attractive, and there's a seasonal porch as well as free parking. Specials aside, the menu rarely changes. We can never pass up the tagliolini alle vongole, angel hair tossed with clams, white wine, and olive oil—unless it's for saltimbocca di vitello, veal scaloppini with fresh sage and prosciutto in a white wine sauce. Entrées $18–32.

& **Harborside Tavern** (207-633-4074; harborsidetavern.com), 12 Bridge St., Boothbay Harbor. Open 7:30AM–10PM. Locally well known chefs Fiona Dunlap and Greg Warlo have transformed the former Andrew's Harborside into a casually sleek new harbor view restaurant with some of the very best food in town. Who knew that a fish taco could be so crisp, fresh, light with just the right spices? Dinner entrées ($20–29) might be seared scallops or smoked ribs.

The Thistle Inn (207-633-3541; thistleinn.com), 55 Oak St., Boothbay Harbor. Open year-round for dinner. Reservations recommended. No water views, but attractive dining rooms and seasonal deck. The focus is on local seafood and produce, a place to feast on Glidden Point oysters, pan-seared scallops, or yellow fin tuna. Entrées $18–32. Pub menu also available.

&& **Newagen Seaside Inn** (207-633-5242), 60 Newagen Colony, Southport. Open seasonally for lunch; usually closed Sat. night. Given its location at the tip of Southport Island, this is also a good place to come for lunch, maybe flat bread with foraged mushrooms, caramelized onion, bacon, and Parmesan cream sauce. The dinner menu is dictated by available local ingredients. Walk off your meal by the water. Entrées $17–36.

OLIVER'S IN SOUTHPORT

HARBORSIDE TAVERN

The Rocktide Inn (207-633-4455; rocktideinn.com), 35 Atlantic Ave., Boothbay Harbor. Open daily for breakfast and dinner; drinks 4–11 in high season. Closed Columbus Day–mid-June. Come by boat or car for dinner (jackets required in the formal dining room, not in the casual dining room) or a Rocktide martini in the On the Rocks Lounge. The view of the sunset is magnificent, and locals rate the dinners highly. Entrées $12–30.

EATING OUT ✪ **The Boathouse Bistro & Tapas Bar** (207-633-0400, theboathousebistro.com), 12 By-Way, Boothbay Harbor. Open mid-March–Christmas for lunch and dinner. Three different atmospheres—all casual—on each of the three floors, and the view improves as you climb (the top deck is open). Lunch on hot tapas like a lobster crepe and dine on Italian seafood stew.

✪ **Oliver's** (207-633-8888), 36 Cozy Harbor Rd., Southport. Open May–Sept., daily 11:30–8; no reservations. A nicely designed, casual restaurant on a hidden cove, accessible by land and water. It replaces and incorporates pieces of a much-loved local 1940s store. Eat at a shaded picnic table on the pier, in the zany, screened interior, and ideally—if you can nail a table—upstairs on the second-floor porch. The menu covers the basics and includes pleasant surprises. The blackened fish taco also comes with salsa and creamy avocado coleslaw. Beer and wine are served.

McSeagull's (207-633-5900; mcseagullsonline.com), 14 Wharf St., Boothbay Harbor.

Open daily 11:30–closing. Wharfside dining so popular it can get packed in high season. It's a local gathering place off-season because it's good. The book-sized menu ranges from pizzas to grilled as well as fried seafood platters. Try the northern white beans stewed in lobster stock, served with poached lobster.

🦞 **Lobsterman's Wharf** (207-633-3443), Rt. 96, East Boothbay (adjacent to a boatyard). Open mid-May–Columbus Day, serving 11:30–9, until 10 on weekends. The large menu includes all the usual seafood, lobster stew, and crabcakes, as well as spinach salad and pastas. Entrées $7–30.

♻ **Baker's Way** (207-633-1119), 89 Townsend Ave., Boothbay Harbor. Open 6 AM–9 PM daily. Just the place for fried apple dumpling, you think, and then you smell lemongrass cooking and wonder where you are. There are two worlds here: a full bakery, very popular with locals, and a restaurant that serves traditional Vietnamese foods. Available 11 AM–closing, appetizers include steamed buns with ground pork, onion, garlic, peas, eggs, and scallions, and fresh spring rolls. Try the stir-fried squid—or chicken or shrimp—and dine in the back garden. BYOB.

Waves Restaurant (207-315-6021), 43 Commercial St., Boothbay Harbor. Open daily 7–11, 12–3, and 4–10. Still the same wooden booths that regulars loved all those years when this was Ebb Tide, but the food has a creative spark under owners Jie and Ian Ronan. Try the fried haddock sliders at lunch and crabby haddock at dinner. Beer and wine are also served.

🦞 **Lobsterman's Wharf** (207-633-3443), 224 Ocean Pt. Rd. (Rt. 96), East Boothbay. Open mid-May–Columbus Day, serving 11:30–9, until 3 PM on Mon. Surrounded by boatyards and marinas, with a back deck on the Damariscotta River, this place has much improved its food under new ownership. Try the Seafood Nage, a bowl of seafood, scallops, lobster, large shrimp, and mussels, for less than the going price of lobster.

Carriage House Restaurant (207-633-6025), 388 Ocean Point Rd. (Rt.96). Open in season Tue.–Sun., 5pm–11pm. Closed for 15 years before Chef Kelly Dunn, an award-winning chef originally from Ocean Point,

recently reopened it as a causal dining spot with a reasonably priced menu that includes a great fish chowder for starters, grilled ribeye and lobster pappardelle as well as an innovative burger and pizza of the day. The bar features signature cocktails.

Watershed Tavern (207-633-3411), 301 Adams Rd., Boothbay. Attached to the Boothbay Craft Brewery, the multi-level tavern features its own handcrafted beers and a basic menu of pizza and typical tavern fare. Inquire about brewery tours.

The **Blue Moon Café** (207-633-2220; bluemoonboothbayharbor.com), 54 Commercial St., Boothbay Harbor. Open for breakfast and lunch daily, 7:30–2:30; Sun. brunch 7:30–noon. This little café with a seaside deck makes perfect crabcakes, and the side salad is filled with fresh greens. We needed a hot, fish-studded chowder in a hurry and got it, served in a china bowl, on the waterside deck.

Bet's Fish Fry, Boothbay Center common. Open seasonally Tue.–Sat. 11–2, 5–7. "Free beer tomorrow." This takeout is a great place to grab a scrumptious fried haddock sandwich. One is more than enough for two.

GENERAL STORES **The East Boothbay General Store** (207-633-7800), 255 Ocean Point Rd., East Boothbay. Open mid-May–mid-Oct. Tucked into a bend of Rt. 96, this is a popular stop to grab an apple Brie bacon wrap for breakfast, or a sandwich from the deli, to eat in or to bring down to Ocean Point. Wine, beer, a variety of cheeses, and soft serve.

Southport General Store (207-633-6666), 443 Hendrick's Hill Rd., Southport. Pick up deli sandwiches or pizza and head for the shore.

Trevett Country Store (207-633-1140), 381 Barters Island Rd., Boothbay. Open daily 7 AM–8 PM, a mile up the road beyond the botanical gardens. Several knowledgeable friends had recommended this as the area's best lobster roll, but we were disappointed. The setting is great: Tables on the deck overlook the Barter's Island bridge.

SNACKS 🦞 **Down East Ice Cream Factory** (207-633-3016), the By-Way, Boothbay Harbor. Homemade hard ice cream and frozen yogurt, and a make-your-own sundae bar; all sorts of

LOBSTER

The Lobster Dock (207-633-7120; thelobsterdock.com), 49 Atlantic Ave., Boothbay Harbor, at the east end of the footbridge. Open 11:29–8:01 (later on Fri. and Sat.) Memorial Day weekend–early Oct. This is our in-town place for a lobster roll, either hot with drawn butter or cold with a dab of mayo. Also lobster and shore dinners, steamed clams, mussels, steaks, and prime rib.

Robinson's Wharf (207-633-3830; robinsons wharf.com), Rt. 27, Southport Island (just across Townsend Gut from West Boothbay Harbor). Open daily year-round, 11:30–9. There's plenty of room inside, but on a sunny day sit on the dock at one of the picnic tables and watch the boats unload their catch. Lobsters and lobster rolls, fried shrimp, clams, scallops, fish chowder, lobster stew, and homemade desserts.

Cabbage Island Clambakes (207-633-7200; cabbageislandclambakes.com). Late June–early Sept., the boat departs Pier 6 at Fisherman's Wharf daily, carrying passengers to 6-acre Cabbage Island in Linekin Bay. This is a traditional clambake with lobsters, clams, corn, and potatoes steamed in seaweed, then served on picnic tables. In bad weather a circa-1900 lodge seats up to 100 people by a huge fireplace. About $62 per person plus tax, including boat ride.

Shannon's Unshelled 11 Granary Way, Boothbay Harbor. Open seasonally, 11–6. Sited by the Footbridge and a sensation since the day it opened: nothing but lobster rolls and chips. That's a whole unshelled lobster with sea-salted butter on the side. Shannon tries to keep the price under $20.

Christina Tree

THE LOBSTER DOCK

toppings, including real hot fudge. Open 10:30–10:30 in the height of summer; hours vary off-season.

Daffy Taffy and Fudge Factory (207-633-5178), the By-Way, Boothbay Harbor. Open 10–10 in the height of the season, fewer hours off-season. No credit cards. Watch taffy being pulled, designed, and wrapped—then chew! The fudge is made with fresh cream and butter.

Oak Street Provisions (207-633-1290; oakstreetprovisions.com), 43 Oak St., Boothbay Harbor, offers fresh seafood, meats, beer, wine, and specialty foods.

DOWNEAST ICE CREAM IN BOOTHBAY HARBOR

✳ Entertainment

The Opera House at Boothbay Harbor (207-633-5159; boothbayoperahouse.com), 86 Townsend Ave., Boothbay Harbor. This vintage-1894 theater is a nonprofit performance center, staging roughly 100 events annually. Check the website for current concerts, lectures, community events, and more.

Carousel Music Theater (207-633-5297; carouselmusictheater.org), 196 Townsend Ave. (Rt. 27), Boothbay. July 4–Columbus Day, 7:30 PM. Patrons are asked to come at 6:30 and have a drink, order supper, and then sit back with dessert and coffee to watch a musical revue.

Lincoln Arts Festival (207-633-3913; lincolnartsfestival.org). Concerts throughout the summer in varied locations.

Thursday evening band concerts on the library lawn, Boothbay Harbor.

✳ Selective Shopping

ART GALLERIES **First Friday Art Tours** (artwalkmaine.org/boothbay). June–Oct. On the first Fri. of each month more than a dozen local studios hold open houses.

Gleason Fine Art (207-633-6849; gleason fineart.com), 31 Townsend Ave., Boothbay Harbor. Tue.–Sat. 10–5. Museum-quality paintings by the likes of Fairfield Porter, James

Fitzgerald, and Scott Kelley, and more of the best contemporary artists in Maine.

Studio 53 Fine Art Gallery (207-633-2755), 53 Townsend Ave., Boothbay Harbor. Open seasonally. A multi-floor contemporary gallery with frequently changing shows; inquire about harpsichord concerts.

Boothbay Region Art Foundation (207-633-2703; boothbayartists.org), 1 Townsend Ave., Boothbay Harbor. Open May–late Oct., Mon.–Sat. 10–5, Sun. noon–5. Six juried shows are held each season in this long-established gallery with two floors full of varied art.

ARTISANS **Abacus Gallery** (207-633-2166; abacusgallery.com), 12 McKown St., Boothbay Harbor. We love this shop, which since its 1971 opening has spawned sister stores in four Maine towns. Check out the jewelry, whimsical wooden sculptures, hand-painted furniture, and unusual gifts.

Boothbay Harbor Artisans (207-633-1152; mainecraftcoop.org/boothbay), 4 Boothbay House Hill Rd., Boothbay Harbor. A cooperative crafts market featuring quilts, soap, stained glass, pottery, maple syrup, jewelry, and more.

A Silver Lining (207-633-4103; asilver lining.com), 17 Townsend Ave., Boothbay Harbor. Working metalsmiths. Original, exceptional sculpture and jewelry in brass, sterling, and gold.

IN HER BOOTHBAY HARBOR SHOP, ALISON EVANS SHOWCASES HER HAND-MOLDED AND GLAZED DINNERWARE

SHERMAN'S MAINE COAST BOOK SHOPS

Edgecomb Potters (207-882-0400 or 1-800-343-5529; edgecombpotters.com), Rt. 27, Edgecomb. Open year-round. One of Maine's largest, most famous pottery stores (with branches in Portland and Freeport). A two-tiered gallery filled with deeply colored pots, vases, and table settings, lamps, bowls, cookware, and jewelry. There's also a sculpture garden and a small seconds corner.

SPECIAL SHOPS **Sherman's Maine Coast Book Shops** (1-800-371-8128; shermans.com), 5 Commercial St., Boothbay Harbor. This two-story emporium is the flagship for Maine's oldest, largest bookstore chain. Plenty of stationary, souvenirs, and much more

The Palabra Shop (207-633-4225; palabrashop.com), 53 Commercial St., Boothbay Harbor. Open in summer, Sun.–Thu. 9–6, opening later on weekends. Owned by the same family for more than 50 years, a warren of 10 rooms offering everything from kitschy souvenirs to handcrafts and jewelry to a few antiques.

✳ Special Events

April: **Fishermen's Festival**—contests for fishermen and lobstermen, cabaret ball, crowning of the Shrimp Princess, tall-tale contest, boat parade, and blessing of the fleet.

June: **Windjammer Days**—parade of windjammers into the harbor, fireworks, band concert, parade of floats and bands up Main St., visiting U.S. Navy and Coast Guard vessels, live music on the waterfront, food, children's activities, and two crafts shows.

July: **Antique Auto Days**, Boothbay Railway Village, Rt. 27. **Boothbay Region Fish and Game Saltwater Fishing Tournament**, Boothbay Harbor (207-633-3788). **YMCA Southport Regatta** entails a variety of ways of circling Southport Island.

Early September: Boothbay Region Harbor Fest (boothbayharborfest.com).

Mid-September: **Clawdown**—participating restaurants compete with "lobster bites." Reserve ahead (207-633-2553); this is always a sellout.

October: **Fall Foliage Festival**—foliage cruises, crafts sales, live entertainment, steam train rides.

November: **Early-bird sale**. Stores open early to tempt shoppers. Stroll the streets in your pajamas as part of the pajama parade and then watch the fast-paced fun of the bed races.

Early December: **Harbor Lights Festival**. Mr. and Mrs. Claus arrive by boat; parade, crafts, holiday shopping.

DAMARISCOTTA/ NEWCASTLE/WALDOBORO AND PEMAQUID AREA

Damariscotta is a small region of large, quiet lakes, long tidal rivers, and almost 100 miles of meandering coastline, all within easy striking distance of Rt. 1. It encompasses the Pemaquid Peninsula communities of Bristol, Pemaquid, New Harbor, and Round Pond, as well as Lake Damariscotta and the towns of Waldoboro and Nobleboro. At the region's heart are the villages of Damariscotta and Newcastle, linked by the Main Street Bridge. Mellow brick buildings evoke the 19th century era in which these towns formed one of New England's busiest shipbuilding centers, when 30 shipyards turned out 400 boats at a time. Now blessedly bypassed by Route 1, Damariscotta's downtown is an appealing mix of specialty shops and restaurants, set on a mini-peninsula surrounded by the headwaters of the Damariscotta River.

The river's musical name is an Algonquian word loosely translated as "plenty of alewives," and in spring spawning alewives can indeed be seen climbing more than 40 feet up through a series of pools linking Great Salt Bay to the fresh water in Damariscotta Lake.

Fourteen miles stem-to-stern, Damariscotta Lake seems longer, changing character as it wanders north through three towns, its largely wooded shoreline patched with rolling farmland. Great Bay, the north basin, is wide and deep, good for catching smallmouth bass and trout, while South Arm is skinny and shallow, great for swimming.

The area's first residents also found an abundance of oysters here, judging from the shells they heaped over the course of 2,400 years on opposite banks of the river just below Salt Bay. Of late, the local oyster industry is once again thriving.

Christina Tree

Native Americans also had a name for the peninsula jutting 10 miles seaward from this spot: Pemaquid, meaning "long finger." Its protected harbors loomed large on 16th- and 17th-century maps, the nearest mainland havens for Monhegan and a busy fishing center for European fishermen. It was from these fishermen that the Pemaquid Native American Samoset learned the English with which he welcomed the Pilgrims at Plymouth in 1621. It was also from these fishermen that Plimoth Plantation, the following winter, secured supplies enough to see it through to spring.

The site of Maine's "Lost City" is a mini peninsula bordered by the Pemaquid River and Johns Bay. A round stone tower at its entrance re-creates part of a fort built here in 1692. In recent decades more than

DAMARISCOTTA WATERFRONT

Damariscotta/
Newcastle/Waldoboro
and Pemaquid Area

© The Countryman Press

NEW HARBOR

100,000 artifacts have been unearthed in the adjacent meadow, many of them now on display in a small state-run museum.

Pemaquid Light, marking the far tip of this peninsula, is pictured on Maine's quarter because it looks just like a lighthouse should. It stands atop dramatic but clamber-friendly rocks composed of varied seams of granite schist and softer volcanic rock, ridged in ways that invite climbing, and pocked with tidal pools that demand stopping.

While there is plenty to see and to do (and to eat) in this area, it's all scattered just widely enough to disperse tourist traffic. The villages are small. Downtown Damariscotta, with easy off/on access to Rt. 1, is a few waterside streets built of mellow old local brick; it's the region's compact shopping, dining, and entertainment hub.

GUIDANCE **Damariscotta Region Chamber of Commerce** (207-563-8340; damariscotta region.com). The chamber office is open year-round weekdays 8:30–4:30 at 67 Main St., Newcastle.

Waldoboro Business Association (waldoborobusiness.org) publishes a handy map/guide to this low-profile but lively town at the head of the Medomak River.

GETTING THERE *By bus:* **Concord Coach** (concordcoachlines.com) stops in Damariscotta and Waldoboro en route from Portland to Bangor.

By car: Most inns on the peninsula will pick up guests in Damariscotta, but you do need a car—or a boat—to get around. The obvious way is up Rt. 1.

PARKING in Damariscotta is much better than it first looks. Large lots are sequestered behind buildings on both sides of Main Street.

❋ Villages

Damariscotta/Newcastle. The twin villages of Newcastle (pop. 1,752) and Damariscotta (2,218 residents) are connected by a bridge and form the commercial center of the region.

Damariscotta's Main Street is the commercial hub here, lined with 1840s brick buildings and filled with shops and restaurants. Damariscotta Mills, with its fish ladder and access to Lake Damariscotta, is a few miles up Rt. 215.

Waldoboro (pop. 1,337). An inscription in the cemetery of the Old German Church (see *Historic Churches*) relates the deceptive way in which landholder General Samuel Waldo lured the town's first German settlers here. The church and much of the town overlook the tidal Medomak (pronounced with the emphasis on *med*) River. Bypassed by Rt. 1, this village includes some noteworthy art galleries. The **Waldoborough Historical Society Museum** (waldoborohistory.us), 1664 Main St., is on Rt. 220, just south of Rt. 1.

Round Pond, Bristol. The name evokes the shape of the village's harbor, said to have been a pirate base. This was once a major shipbuilding, and later on a quarrying, center. It remains a working fishing harbor with competing places to eat lobster and a famous Independence Day parade.

New Harbor, Bristol. A photogenic working harbor. Take South Side Rd. to Back Cove and walk out on the wooden pedestrian bridge for a great view. Note the memorial to Samoset, who is said to have sold land here, creating the first deed executed in New England. The village itself is far bigger than it looks at first.

Pemaquid Beach, Bristol. Just off the beaten track to Pemaquid Point Lighthouse, this is a tranquil seasonal community with a public beach (see *Swimming*), a reconstructed 17th-century fort, and a museum displaying artifacts from its early-17th-century settlement (see *Must See*).

South Bristol. Chances are you will have time to enjoy the view at "The Gut," the narrow channel spanned by a busy swing bridge. Rt. 129 continues south to Christmas Cove, a long-established summer colony.

Jefferson, the village at the head of Damariscotta Lake, also at the junction of Rts. 126, 32, and 206. Old farmhouses, a general store, and summer homes along the river now form the core of the village, and **Damariscotta Lake State Park**, with its sandy beach, is on the fringe. Be sure to drive west a couple of miles on Rt. 213 to **Bunker Hill**, with its old church commanding a superb panorama down the lake.

�֎ To See

Alewives Fish Ladder, Rt. 215 in **Damariscotta Mills** at the intersection of Austin Rd. Look for parking just south of the bridge; a walkway beyond the bridge leads into the site. Originally built in 1807 and recently rebuilt, this is a stone-lined series of stepped pools and raceways. For roughly a month beginning in early May, alewives—also known as river herring—climb the 50 feet from Salt Bay up to Damariscotta Bay while gulls, cormorants, ospreys, and eagles circle. On an early June morning the swarming fish were so thick you could smell them.

Frances Perkins Center (207-563-3374; francesperkinscenter.org), 170A Main St., Damariscotta. Exhibits in this small museum (Open June–Aug., Tues.–Sat., 10–2 and by appointment) trace the life of Frances Perkins (1880–1965), the first woman to serve in a U.S. presidential cabinet. The title of her biography by Kristin Downey is *The Woman Behind the New Deal.* As Franklin

Christina Tree

ALEWIVES FISH LADDER

MUST SEE

☼ ♦ **Pemaquid Point Lighthouse** (lighthousefoundation.org), Rt. 130 (at the end), Pemaquid Point. The tower is open Memorial Day–Columbus Day 10:30–5, but closed on rainy days. Pemaquid Point is owned by the town, which charges a per-person entry fee during summer. The lighthouse, built in 1824 and automated in 1934, is a beauty. It's just a 39-step climb to the top of the tower, but the light looms high above the rocks below and the real place to appreciate it is gained by climbing down, not up. The rocks offer a wonderfully varied example of geologic upheaval, with tilted strata and igneous intrusions. The tidal pools are exceptional, but take care not to get too close to the dangerous waves. The rocks stretch for half a mile to Kresge Point. **The Fishermen's Museum** (207-677-2494) in the former lighthouse keeper's home (May–late Oct., daily 9–5) displays photographs, ship models, and other artifacts related to the Maine fishing industry and lighthouses. Donations requested. The complex also includes the Pemaquid Art Gallery, picnic tables, and public toilets.

☼ ♦ **Colonial Pemaquid State Historic Site** (207-677-2423; friendsofcolonialpemaquid.org), Pemaquid Beach. Marked from Rt. 130, this 8-acre complex is open Memorial Day–Labor Day, 9–6; nominal fee. This small peninsula at the mouth of the Pemaquid River offers a glimpse into many layerings of history, beginning with a circa-1610 seasonal English fishing station that evolved into a year-round fur-trading outpost circa 1630–50. The foundations of homes, a customhouse, and a tavern are now on view and a period house has been reconstructed. The 17th-century tools and pottery, Spanish oil jars, and wampum found in these cellar holes are displayed in the museum.

Fort William Henry, the crenellated stone tower reconstructing the 1692 fort, displays exhibits on the early explorations of Maine and on the French and Indian Wars. It also enshrines the "Rock of Pemaquid," suggesting that settlers alighted on it long before the Pilgrims stepped onto that rock in Plymouth. The neighboring square clapboard Fort House contains a library. Picnic tables command water views. For a schedule of frequent summer lectures, tours, and reenactments, check the website.

FORT WILLIAM HENRY

Christina Tree

Roosevelt's pick for his Secretary of Labor, Perkins initiated and implemented some of the New Deal's most effective programs, including social security, the minimum wage, maximum work hours, and the ban on child labor. She is buried in the Glidden Cemetery in Newcastle, near the 57-acre riverside farm, a National Historic Landmark, that has been in her family since the 1750s. The website lists scheduled tours of the Homestead, and special events.

Thompson Ice House, (thompsonicehouse.com) Rt. 129 in South Bristol. Open July and Aug., Wed., Fri., Sat. 1–4. A 150-year-old commercial icehouse displays traditional tools for cutting ice from an adjacent pond and a video on how ice continues to be harvested here. Small blocks of this ice costs $1 in the outside cooler. On the Sunday closest to July 4, an ice cream social here features hand-churned ice cream made with the ice.

✎ **Old Rock Schoolhouse**, Bristol (halfway between Bristol Mills and Round Pond; follow signs from Rt. 130 to Rt. 132). Dank and haunting, this 1835–99 rural stone schoolhouse once was one of 20 one-room schoolhouses scattered through town. Open in summer, Wed. and Sun. 1–3; costumed volunteers offer to teach all comers.

Chapman-Hall House, 270 Main St., Damariscotta. Open June–early Oct., weekends noon–4, volunteer-dependent. Built in 1754, this is the oldest homestead in the region. The house has been restored with its original kitchen and an herb garden. $5 admission.

HISTORIC CHURCHES This particular part of the Maine coast possesses an unusual number of fine old meetinghouses and churches, all of which are open to the public.

Old German Church (207-832-5100), Rt. 32, Waldoboro. Open daily during July and Aug., 1–4. Built in 1772 with square-benched pews and a wineglass pulpit; note the inscription in the cemetery: "This town was settled in 1748 by Germans who immigrated to this place with the promise and expectation of finding a prosperous city, instead of which they found nothing but wilderness." Bostonian Samuel Waldo—owner of a large tract of land in this area—had not been straight with the 40 German families he brought to settle it. This was the first Lutheran church in Maine and is the setting of one of Andrew Wyeth's most famous Helga paintings.

St. Patrick's Catholic Church (207-563-6038), Academy Rd., Newcastle (Rt. 215 north of Damariscotta Mills). Open year-round daily, to sunset. This is the oldest surviving Catholic church (1808) in New England. It's an unusual building: brick construction, very narrow, and graced with a Paul Revere bell. The pews and stained glass date to 1896 and there's an old graveyard out back. It's used for daily Mass, but a spacious, new addition with a clerestory roof and glass-walled sanctuary is now used on Sunday.

St. Andrew's Episcopal Church (207-563-3533), Glidden St., Newcastle. A charming half-timbered building on the bank of the Damariscotta River. Set among gardens and trees, it was the first commission in this country for Henry Vaughan, the English architect who went on to design the National Cathedral in Washington, DC.

Old Walpole Meeting House, Meeting House Rd., off Rt. 129, South Bristol. Open Sun. during July and Aug. for 3 PM services. A 1772 shingled meetinghouse with box pews and a pulpit with a sounding board.

Harrington Meeting House, 278 Harrington Rd., Pemaquid. Open during July and Aug., Mon., Wed., Fri., 2–4:30. Donations accepted. The 1775 building with its original box pews has been restored and serves as a museum of Old Bristol. A nondenominational service is held here once a year, usually on the third Sun. in Aug.

OTHER (📶) **Skidompha Library** (207-563-5513; skidompha.org), 184 Main St., Damariscotta. Open Tue.–Sat. from 9 AM; until 7 PM Thu. and 1 PM on Sat., otherwise until 5 PM. This stunning library forms the heart of town, the scene of many programs geared to visitors as well as regulars. There are also frequent authors' nights and classic films.

EXCURSIONS

Damariscotta Lake. From Newcastle, Rt. 215 winds along past the Alewife Fish Ladder in Damariscotta Mills. Continue by St. Patrick's Church through farm country on Rt. 213 when 215 jogs west (note the scenic pullout across from the Bunker Hill Church, with a view down the lake) to Jefferson. Lunch at **Damariscotta Lake Farm** or pick up a sandwich at the **Jefferson General Store** and take it to **Damariscotta Lake State Park** (see *Swimming*). In the middle of Jefferson, you'll find the dockside (below a twin file of cottages) **Damariscotta Lake Watershed Association** (dlwa.org), a source of local maps, books, and a summer sailing program for kids.

Sheepscot Village and Alna Head Tide. From Rt. 215 beyond St. Patrick's Church (see above) turn left at "Cowshit Corner" (there's a sign) onto W. Hamlet Rd. and then right on Old Country Rd. through rolling, open country to the picturesque village of Head Tide. (You can also reach this point directly from Rt. 1 on Sheepscot Rd. in Newcastle.) This is a cluster of old buildings around the river and its reversing falls. Cross the river and turn north on Rt. 218 to the **Alna Store** (207-586-5515), good for hot specials as well as sandwiches, local meat, and eggs. Continue on to **Head Tide**, another scenic village with a beautiful church and overlook at a small dam. Cut back to the store and turn down Dock Rd. (it's on the corner) and then right (south) on Rt. 194, which becomes Rt. 215. This is a lovely loop, one of the best in the area for bicycling.

Pemaquid Peninsula. Follow Rt. 129 south from Damariscotta, across the South Bristol Bridge to Christmas Cove. Backtrack and cross the peninsula via **Harrington Meeting House** Rd. to **Colonial Pemaquid** and **Pemaquid Beach** (glorious at sunset). Turn south on Rt. 130 to **Pemaquid Point Lighthouse** and return via Rt. 32 and **Round Pond**; take Biscay Rd. back to Damariscotta or continue on Rt. 32 into Waldoboro.

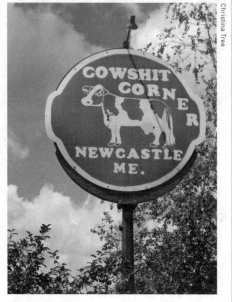

Christina Tree

COWSHIT CORNER

Fawcett's Antique Toy & Art Museum (207-832-7398), 3506 Rt. 1., Waldoboro. Memorial Day–Columbus Day, open Thu.–Mon. 10–4, then weekends noon–4 until weekend before Christmas. $5 admission. Comic book and antique toy lovers alert: This is a major collection of original cartoon art, billed as the finest Lone Ranger collection in the world, also antique Disneyana, space toys, and the like. Antique toys bought and sold.

✳ To Do

BIRDING ✐ **Audubon Camp, Hog Island** (hogisland.audubon.org). The center, 0.25 mile offshore at the head of Muscongus Bay, is a venue for nature and ornithology programs, including seasonal sessions sponsored by Audubon's Project Puffin, which reintroduced Atlantic puffins to nearby islands. Five miles of spruce trails, wildflower and herb gardens, and mudflats surround rustic bungalows. The dining room is in a restored 19th-century farmhouse. For puffin-watching and birding cruises, see Hardy Boat Cruises (below). Also see *Green Space*.

BOATING ♂ **Hardy Boat Cruises** (Stacie and Captain Al Crocetti: 207-677-2026 or 1-800-278-3346; hardyboat.com), Shaw's Wharf, New Harbor, May–Oct. The 60-foot Maine-built *Hardy III* offers daily (twice daily in high season) 50-minute-long runs to **Monhegan Island** (for a detailed description, see "Midcoast Islands"). Pick a calm day. It doesn't matter if it's foggy, but the passage is no fun if it's rough. Another cruise circles **Eastern Egg Rock**, one of only five Maine islands on which puffins breed, with narration by an Audubon naturalist. There are also seal-watching, a lighthouse (Pemaquid Light), and harbor cruises. Nominal fee for parking roughly 0.25 mile back up the road.

    ♿ **Damariscotta River Cruises** (1-888-635-4309; damariscottarivercruises.com), Schooner Landing, Main St., Damariscotta. Check the website for daytime and evening (drinks and live music) cruises aboard the former navy launch *Teciani*, "The River Tripper."

    Lake Pemaquid Camping (lakepemaquid.com), Egypt Rd., Damariscotta, rents canoes, kayaks, and paddle- and motorboats.

FISHING Damariscotta Lake is a source of bass, landlocked salmon, and trout. See Mill Pond Inn under *Inns and B&Bs*.

GOLF **Wawenock Country Club** (207-563-3938), Rt. 129 (7 miles south of Damariscotta), Walpole. Open May–Nov. A nine-hole course with 18 tee boxes and a full-service clubhouse.

HIKING **Monhegan Island**, easily accessible from New Harbor (see *Boating*), is webbed with coastal shore and cliff trails beloved by hikers and birders. A day trip gives you a sampling, but it's best to spend the night for a full exploration.

KAYAKING **Midcoast Kayak** (207-563-5732; midcoastkayak.com), 47 Main St., Damariscotta, offers a variety of guided paddles in and around Muscongus Bay, as well as rentals. **Maine Kayak** (1-866-624-6352; mainekayak.com) offers guided trips, rentals, and packages from a variety of bases, including New Harbor. Both outfitters are geared to coastal paddling, but we have used a rental to explore **Damariscotta Lake**. There's boat access off Rt. 213 and spruce-topped islands to paddle to. You can also launch at the Jefferson General Store near Damariscotta State Park and paddle up Davis Stream.

SWIMMING ✪ **Pemaquid Beach Park** (207-677-2754), Rt. 130, Pemaquid. A town-owned area open Memorial Day–Labor Day, 9–5. Nominal admission, 12 years and older. A quarter mile of fine, white sand. Bathhouse, restrooms, refreshment stand, and picnic tables. This is also a great place to walk and watch the sunset in the evening.

    ♿ **Damariscotta Lake State Park** (207-549-7600), Rt. 32, Jefferson, 9 miles north of Rt. 1. A sandy beach with changing facilities, picnic tables, and grills at the northern end of the lake. There's a new pavilion for group events and plenty of tree shade. $4 per Maine resident, $6 per out-of-stater; $2 out-of-state seniors.

    Ice House Park, Damariscotta Mills. A sign reads NO FOUL LANGUAGE AND NO ALCOHOLIC BEVERAGES, but nothing prohibits kids from jumping off the bridge. Just up from the fish ladder, this is a neighborhood place, good for getting wet when you need to.

    On Pemaquid Peninsula the big freshwater swimming holes are at **Biscay Pond** (from Rt. 1, take Biscay Rd. 3 miles) and **Bristol Mills Swimming Dam** on Rt. 130, 5 miles south of Damariscotta.

✳ Green Space

NATURE PRESERVES **Damariscotta River Association** (207-563-1393; draclt.org), 110 Belvedere Rd., 0.25 mile north of Rt. 1 in Damariscotta. Open year-round. DRA headquarters at Salt Pond Farm offers hay fields, salt- and freshwater marshes, and woods laced with walking/skiing paths. This is also the site of seasonal Friday farmers' markets, a summer concert series, special programs, and tours. DRA properties total more than 1,200 acres in over a dozen easily accessible places, including **Great Salt Bay Preserve Heritage Trail**, which loops around Glidden Point and leads to the **Glidden Midden**, oyster shells piled 30 feet deep and said to date back 2,400 years, Pick up a map at the trailhead across from the *Lincoln County News*, 116 Mills Rd., Newcastle Rt. 215 (you can park on the far edge of the lot). The **Whaleback Shell Midden State Historic Site** (Business Rt.1, just beyond Round Top Farm) offers a view across the river off what's left of the area's second major shell heap. **Dodge Point Preserve** is a 506-acre property on Newcastle's River Rd. (2.6 miles south of Rt. 1), which includes a sand beach as well as a freshwater pond, a beaver bog, and trails.

∂ **Rachel Carson Memorial Salt Pond**, Rt. 32, north of New Harbor. The pond is on the opposite side of the road from the parking lot. There's a beautiful view of the open ocean from here, and at low tide the tidal pools are filled with tiny sea creatures. Look for blue mussels, hermit crabs, starfish, and green sea urchins. Here Rachel Carson researched part of her book *The Edge of the Sea*. Inland from the pond, the preserve includes fields and forest.

∂ **Todd Wildlife Sanctuary and the Hocomock Trail**, Bremen (take Keene Neck Rd. off Rt. 32). A visitors center (207-529-5148) is open June–Aug., daily 1–4. The nature trail leads down to the beach. This is a great family picnic spot, accessible with short legs.

Hidden Valley Nature Center (hvnc.org), 131 Egypt Rd., Jefferson (0.5 mile south from Rt. 215). Nearly 1,000 acres of diverse land, 25 miles of trails to Little Dyer Pond, good for cross-country skiing and snowshoeing. Three cabins and several campsites, ongoing programs.

The Pemaquid Watershed Association manages eleven preserves scattered the length of the peninsula. Download trail maps from pemaquidwatershed.org. Our favorite is the 120-acre **La Verna Preserve** on Rt. 32, half way between Round Pond and New Harbor, with 2.5 miles of trails leading to the rocky shore.

✳ Lodging

INNS AND B&BS 🐾 ♿ **Bradley Inn** (207-677-2105 or 1-800-942-5560; bradleyinn.com), 3063 Pemaquid Point, New Harbor. Open Apr.–Dec. Warren and Beth Busteed are energetic innkeepers who have established a culinary reputation for this turn-of-the-20th-century inn (see *Dining Out*), the area's only inn serving dinner. The 14 guest rooms and two suites are divided among the main house, the Carriage House, and a cottage, all nicely furnished and each with private bath. Clunker bicycles are free, and the inn is less than a mile from Pemaquid Lighthouse and Kresge Point. Amenities include a spa with sauna and treatment rooms. High-season rooms are $225–475 (for a Carriage House suite); off-season from $160; $50 pet fee; special birding and spa weekends.

IN NEWCASTLE/DAMARISCOTTA

✪ 🐾 ((ꜛ)) *∂* **Mill Pond Inn** (207-563-8014; millpondinn.com), Rt. 215, Damariscotta Mills. Open year-round. Enter the red door of this much-expanded 1780 gray-clapboard house and you immediately feel at home. Sherry and Bobby Whear have been welcoming guests since 1986, and many have returned time after time. The five individually decorated and shaped rooms (check the website) include two 2-bedroom suites, one with its own entrance.

$150–175 per couple ($20 for a second room) includes breakfast, maybe a crabmeat omelet with veggies from the garden. Less off-season. The alewives begin running in May and by mid-June you can take a dip off the dock or ask Bobby for a ride in his antique motorboat. A registered Maine guide, realtor, bartender, and co-host of *Wuzzup?*—a weekly series on Lincoln County TV (lctv.org)—Bobby enjoys tuning guests into local secrets. No credit cards.

🐾 (ᵞ) **Newcastle Inn** (207-563-5685 or 1-877-376-6111; newcastleinn.com), 60 River Rd., Newcastle 04553. Open year-round. Julie Bolthuis offers 14 tasteful and comfortable rooms, all with private bath, some with water views, several with four-poster beds, eight with gas fireplace, and two with Jacuzzi. An inviting little bar with French doors opens onto a wide deck with water views—the breakfast venue, weather permitting. The grounds overlook the Damariscotta River. $150–295, includes a three-course breakfast. Per diem charge for dogs.

Alewives & Ales (207-563-1561; alewives andales.com), P.O. Box 809, 22 High St., Damariscotta. This Federal-style mid-19th-century house on a quiet street south of town is a B&B with three guest rooms. Host Mimi McConnell tells us that the name honors Damariscotta's spring alewife migration, and brewing "ale" is her husband Ray's hobby. A very full breakfast, served at the dining room table, is included in rates of $150–200; less off-season.

(ᵞ) **Oak Gables** (207-563-1476 or 1-800-335-7748; oakgablesbb.com), 36 Pleasant St., Damariscotta. Open year-round. The setting is 9 acres on the Damariscotta River with a heated swimming pool and boathouse (with a ping-pong table). Martha Scudder's gracious house has four second-floor guest rooms, shared bath ($120–185 with breakfast), and a river-view efficiency suite on the ground floor ($185 in-season), also available by the week. Inquire about weekly rentals for the riverside three-bedroom cottage and a two-person studio. Well-behaved children welcome.

ON THE PEMAQUID PENINSULA SOUTH OF DAMARISCOTTA

✪ 🐾 🖋 ♿ (ᵞ) **Gosnold Arms** (207-677-3727; winter, 561-575-9549; gosnold.com), 146 Rt. 32, New Harbor 04554. Open mid-May–mid-Oct. Sited at the entrance to a working harbor steps from Shaw's Wharf, this friendly inn has been owned by the Phinney family for more than three decades. It rambles on along the water, with rockers on the porch and ample

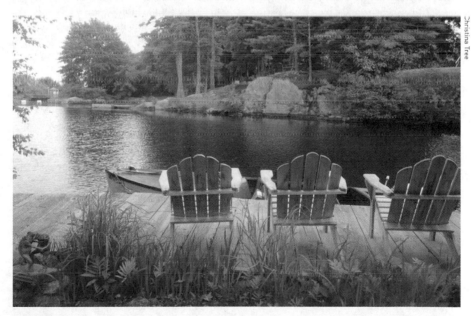

MILL POND INN

rainy-day space. There are 10 simple but comfortable guest rooms upstairs (all private bath, eight with water views) and 20 cottage units, six with deck or sunporch, smack-dab on this working harbor. The Hillside units at the back of the property are good for families. Breakfast on the enclosed porch is served buffet-style, the better to catch the boat to Monhegan (island-bound guests are permitted to park here). Inn rooms $118–152, cottages $138–216. Rates include breakfast; 15 percent less in June and Sept.

✪ ⟨⟨ɐ⟩⟩ **The Inn at Round Pond** (207-809-7386; theinnatroundpond.com), 1442 Rt. 32, Round Pond. The mansard-roofed third floor was added to this 1830s home a century or so ago when it became the Harbor View Hotel. Sue and Bill Morton have created a delightful B&B with soothing colors, comfortable antiques, and original art. There are four delightful suites and a Garden Cottage hideaway for all guests to share, fitted with books, puzzles, and wicker. A full breakfast is included in $175–185, less off-season.

♂ ⟨⟨ɐ⟩⟩ **The Hotel Pemaquid** (207-677-2312; hotelpemaquid.com), 3098 Bristol Rd., New Harbor 04554. Open mid-May–mid-Oct. A vintage-1888 summer hotel a short walk from Pemaquid Point but without water views. There's a Victorian-style lobby and living room with armchairs and a big stone hearth. The 30 rooms are divided among the main house and new annexes. Most rooms have private bath (four rooms in the inn itself share two baths). Coffee is set out at 7. From $108 off-season (private bath) to $291 in Aug. for a Carriage House suite sleeping four, with a living room, kitchen, and deck.

IN WALDOBORO

SpinnAcres Alpaca Farm Retreat (207-832-2288; spinnacres.com), 828 Gross Neck Rd. (off Rt.32). Lisa and Andrew Lane's renovated farmhouse is set in five acres, overlooking Broad Cove. The four guest rooms vary in size and shape, three with a full, one with a half bath. The six resident alpacas have their own fenced in quarters but guests are welcome to take them on walks in the surrounding fields and abutting 14-acre conservation area. From the dock guests can launch their own kayaks or cruise down to Round Pond on the couple's

small lobster boat. Midcoast Kayak also offers tours from a nearby put-in on the Medowmak River. $95–$175-includes bountiful breakfasts like Lisa's deep Belgian waffles with Andrew's blueberry sauce.

COTTAGES ⚓ ♂ Check with the Damariscotta area chamber and **Newcastle Square Vacation Rentals** (207-563-6500; mainecoast cottages.com).

⚓ ♂ **The Thompson House and Cottages** (207-677-2317; thompsoncottages.net), New Harbor. Open May–Nov. Merle and Karen Thompson are the third generation of a family that's been offering hospitality since they began taking guests in 1920. There are still two sparkling-clean rooms in the 1874 house ($80), but the big attractions are the housekeeping cottages (maximum of five people), many with ocean views and facing New Harbor or Back Cove, all with fireplace (wood supplied). $1,150–1,850 per week in-season.

⚓ **Ye Olde Forte Cabins** (207-677-2261; yeoldefortecabins.com), 18 Old Fort Rd., Pemaquid Beach. Nostalgia buffs take note: Eight classic 1922 cabins stepped roof-to-roof along a wide central lawn sloping to a private beach on John's Bay. There's a cookhouse equipped with everything you need to make meals, along with immaculate men's and women's shower houses. From $115 per day ($575 per week) in high season for a cabin with private bath and double bed to $216 per day ($820 per week) for oceanfront cabins with private shower sleeping four. Guests bring kayaks, canoes, and fishing rods. Moorings available.

⚓ 🐾 ♂ **Moody's Motel** (207-832-5362; moodysdiner.com), Waldoboro. Open May 15–Oct.15. Moody's Diner is a Rt. 1 icon; less well known is the vintage motor court squirreled away behind the eatery in a quiet hilltop meadow. P. B. and Bertha Moody built the first cabins in 1927. Still in the family, there are 18 spanking-clean cottages, each with a screened porch, bath with shower, cable TV, and heat; five have kitchens. The grounds include lawn games and swings. From $72 for a one-bedroom unit with twins; to $92 for kitchenette units. Pet fee.

CAMPING ♂ ♿ **Lake Pemaquid Camping** (207-563-5202), Damariscotta. Off Biscay Rd. More than 200 tent and RV sites, also cabin

LOBSTER

Muscongus Bay is a particularly prime lobster source, and genuine lobster pounds are plentiful around the harbors of the Pemaquid Peninsula.

☙ **Harbor View Restaurant at the Pemaquid Fisherman's Co-Op** (207-677-2642; pemaquid lobstercoop.com/PRestaurant.html),32 Co-Op Rd. off Pemaquid Harbor Rd., Pemaquid Harbor. Open Memorial Day–Columbus Day, 11–8. Maine's oldest continuously run fishermen's cooperative supplies the lobster and this is the place to feast on them—along with steamed clams and mussels, and shrimp. Indoor and outdoor tables with a great view across Johns Bay to Colonial Pemaquid.

Broad Cove Marine (207-529-5186; broadcovemarine.com), 371 Momak Rd. (look for the BCMS sign on Rt. 32), Bremen. Open daily in-season 10–7. You can't get closer to a working harbor. Lobster and clams, live and cooked, oysters on the half shell, and lobster and clam rolls as fresh as they come. Dockside deck on the Medomak River.

☙ **Shaw's Wharf** (207-677-2200), Rt. 32, New Harbor. Open early May–mid-Oct., daily for lunch and supper. This is a popular, long-established lobster pound on one of Maine's most picturesque harbors. It's also the departure point for the Hardy Boat Cruises and can get busy. Pick your lobster out of the pool below and feed on it upstairs at picnic tables, either inside or out. Chowders and stews, a wide choice of sandwiches, dinner salads, sides, and seafood dinners are also on the menu—but there's no corn. Excellent fish chowder. Fully licensed.

On the dock at Round Pond, two competing lobster shacks are both open daily for lunch through dinner in-season:

Muscongus Bay Lobster Company (207-529-5528). Sheltered picnic tables on the deck. Sample the area's oysters on the half shell, as well as the freshest crabmeat, lobsters, corn, and fixings.

Round Pond Lobster (207-529-5725). Really no-frills, but locals swear by it. BYOB.

Christina Tree

BROAD COVE MARINE, BREMEN

and cottage rentals on 7-mile Lake Pemaquid. Facilities include tennis, a pool, 18-hole mini golf, game room, laundry facilities, sauna, Jacuzzi, snack bar, store, and a marina with boat rentals.

✳ Where to Eat

DINING OUT

IN DAMARISCOTTA/NEWCASTLE

✪ ❀ ✐ **Damariscotta River Grill** (207-563-2992; damariscottarivergrill.com), 155 Main St. Open for lunch, dinner, Sunday brunch. A brick-walled, two-floor, middle-of-Main-Street gem. Head upstairs to a seat by the window or at the copper bar (note the stellar collection of hockey pucks). Begin either meal with an order of oysters on the half shell, served with the house horseradish. Rick Hirsch and Jean Kerrigan have long been committed to turning local ingredients into memorable dishes like lobster cakes on sweet corn sauce. It's a big menu with dishes of all sizes to share. Children's menu. Award-winning wine list. Entrées $18.81–27.98. Check out the new Prep Kitchen selling food and wine on the ground floor (entrance from the parking lot).

✐ **King Eider's Pub** (207-563-6008; kingeiderspub.com), 2 Elm St. Open year-round 10:30 AM–11 PM. The downstairs pub is a good foggy-evening spot for light grub and a boutique brew. Crabcakes as well as oysters are the specialty in the pleasant upstairs restaurant. The dinner menu is large, ranging from burgers to char-grilled steaks. Entrées $20–27.99.

✐ **Newcastle Publick House** (207-563-3434; newcastlepublickhouse.com), 52 Main St., Newcastle. Open daily 11–11, midnight Fri., Sat. Housed in a landmark brick building at the junction of Rts. 1 and 125, this is an informal family-friendly pub with a focus on local ingredients. Here you can feast on the town's famed oysters, then dine on shepherd's pie or wild mushroom fettuccine or a veggie burger. Draft beer selections. Entrées $14–23, also pub menu and pizzas.

Savory Maine (207-563-2111; savorymaine dining.com), 11 Water St. Open daily 11–8. Almost downtown but hidden away down by the river, this vintage-1825

schoolhouse-turned-church-turned-restaurant with a deck is a delightful spot. Owner Grace Goldberg is dedicated to using wild, organic, and local ingredients. Lunch on a DLT (dulse, lettuce, and tomato) and dine on scallops Florentine or the gnocchi of the day with seasonal veggies. Wine and beer. Most dinner entrées $18–29.

ON THE PEMAQUID PENINSULA

Bradley Inn (207-677-2105; bradleyinn.com), Pemaquid Point Rd., New Harbor. Call to check, but generally open Thu.–Tue. in-season; Thu.–Sun., Nov.–Mar. Fine dining is what these two attractive dining rooms are about. The rooms are decorated in nautical antiques and soothing colors; tables are well spaced and candlelit. The locally sourced à la carte menu might include wild salmon with crab-fried brown rice, kale chips, and a soy ginger glaze. Entrées $25–37. The inviting bar features house cocktails and grilled flat breads.

✐ **The Anchor** (207-529-2600; theanchor restaurant.com). Andrea and Dan Reny are the new hands-on proprietors. (Dan has run neighboring Muscungus Bay Lobster for a decade.) The bar area has been expanded, but this is still a tiered dining room overlooking the harbor, and it's still wise to request a table on the waterside tier. The menu focuses on local seafood. At lunch we ordered a crab and avocado wrap and our request to wrap it in lettuce was graciously granted. Dinner entrées include steak and duck, but go for the lobster and shrimp ravioli. $18–29 dinner entrées and a reasonably priced bar menu that includes lobster "popcorn" and Medomak River softshell clams as well as local oysters.

EATING OUT

IN DAMARISCOTTA

Schooner Landing (207-563-7447; schooner landingmaine.com), Schooner Wharf, Main St. Open May–Sept. daily for lunch and dinner, just weekends in Apr. and Oct.; the pub remains open for live music on weekends through winter. Harborside on the Damariscotta River, informal and draft brews. Eat inside or out. Pemaquid oysters are the feature, fresh on the half shell, baked, stewed, or fried. Plenty of lobster and other seafood,

OYSTERS

The Damariscotta River has long been known for the quality of its oysters, judging from the shell heaps piled along its banks by the area's indigenous residents over thousands of years. By the mid-1800s, however, the wild oyster beds had all but disappeared due to over-harvesting. Maine's current, thriving oyster industry dates only to the 1970s and the University of Maine's Damariscotta-based Darling marine biology laboratory, which determined this river bed to be once more perfect for seeding and producing the highest quality oysters.

Maine waters are cold enough to require up to four years to reach maturity developing a firmer meat, deeper cup and thicker shell (easier for shucking) than those which take as little as a year to develop in warmer waters. The tidal Damariscotta River is nutrient rich and exceptionally clean, producing oysters with a distinctively sweet, briny taste.

In 1986 Chris Davis was the first to put his research at the Darling Center to practical use, rallying friends to help found the Pemaquid Oyster Company (pemaquidoystersidgmail.com) and leasing beds off Clark's Cove near the river's mouth, developing many of the current oyster-farming tools now in use.

Barb Scully is, however, the best locally known pioneering oyster farmer. A former marine biologist with the states' Marine Resources Department, Scully founded Glidden Point Oyster Farm in 1987, planting her oysters as much as 40 feet deep, waiting four years to harvest them by diving to collect them by hand, selling them directly to customers for $1–2 apiece, depending on the size and grade, at her Glidden Point's Sea Farm Store (207-633-2599), 707 River Road, Edgecomb (5 miles south of Newcastle), open daily in season 8–5:30.

Ryan McPhearson now owns Glidden Point Oyster Farm but continues the slow, painstaking process developed by Scully, allowing them to grow slowly in deep water, still harvesting many by hand, known to oyster connoisseurs around the country.

A number of local farmers currently grow the same species of oyster but each has its own distinctive taste reflecting the depths and locations at which they are planted and the way they are harvested.

"Oyster Tours & Seal Cruises" offered by Damariscotta River Cruises (888-635-4309), based at Damariscotta's Schooner Landing, are a great way to see, hear about and taste the fruits of local oyster farming as well as spotting wildlife and taking in the beauty of the river.

THERE'S AN ART TO SHUCKING AN OYSTER

sandwiches, burgers, and beers. Check out free oyster Fridays, music, and other events.

Weatherbird Café (207-563-8993), 72 Courtyard St. If you are browsing the shops and want a quick but delicious lunch, this bakery and market serves up deli sandwiches on fresh-baked breads and panini.

✪ 🦞 **Larson's Lunch Box** (207-563-57550), 430 Upper Main St. (Business Rt. 1). May–late Oct., daily except Wed. 11–4. Beloved by locals, this roadside stand is known for its fresh and generous crab and lobster rolls. Billy and Barbara Ganem have installed a serious restaurant kitchen and also pride themselves on from-scratch clam chowder, sweet potato fries, and cookies. Burgers, too. Picnic tables.

🍴 **Best Thai** (207-563-1440), 74 Main St. Open Tue.–Sat. for lunch and Tues.–Sun. for dinner. The decor and presentation convey the message that this is the best Thai food around.

S. Fernald's Country Store (207-563-8484), 50 Main St. Owner Sumner Richards presides over the soda fountain and limited seating and takes pride in the '50s feel of this local gathering place.

Que Rico (207-650-8664), 67 Main Street parking lot. Open seasonally, Mon.-Sat., 11–10. Look for a rosy-orange taco stand near the Newcastle side of the Main Street Bridge.

It's billed as "authentically Mexican" and the soft, white corn tacos and flour tortillas and quesadillas as well as gluten-free options are stuffed with a wide variety of options, washed down with a Mexican soda at a picnic table overlooking the river.

Also see **Weatherbird Café** under *Special Shops.*

ON OR JUST OFF RT. 1

✪ 🦞 🍴 ♿ **Moody's Diner** (207-832-7785; moodysdiner.com), Rt. 1, Waldoboro. Open daily 6 AM–9:30 PM. A clean and warm, classic 1927 diner run by several generations of the Moody family along with other employees who have been here so long they've become part of the family. Renovated and expanded, it retains all the old atmosphere and specialties, including killer pies and family-style food— corned beef hash, meat loaf, and stews—at digestible prices. You can buy T-shirts and other Moody's paraphernalia, but you can also still get chicken or turkey potpie and a great crabmeat roll. Prices haven't soared with fame.

🍴 **Bullwinkle's Family Steakhouse** (207-832-6272), Rt. 1, Waldoboro. Locally loved and a good bet for road food. Steaks are the specialty, along with baby back ribs, seafood baskets, and subs.

Christina Tree

MOODY'S DINER, WALDOBORO

QUE RICO, NEWCASTLE

✪ ♂ **The Narrows Tavern** (207-832-2210), 15 Friendship St., Waldoboro. Open 11:30 AM–1 AM, dinner until 9. Check the tavern's Facebook site for frequent music. A welcoming village pub with picnic-style tables at which patrons mix; the TV is unobtrusive, and the brick walls are hung with local art. Standout fish chowder as well as salads, pastas with fresh veggies and fish, and burgers with sweet potato fries. Great pies. Selection of wine by the glass as well as brews.

Rising Tide Co-op (207-563-5556; risingtide.coop), 323 Main St., Damariscotta. A long-established local food co-op with a first-rate deli and café.

ON THE PEMAQUID PENINSULA: RT. 130

♂ **Cupboard Café** (207-677-3911), 137 Huddle Rd., New Harbor. Open Apr.–Dec., Tue.–Sat. 8–3, Sun. 8–noon. A family-run log eatery specializing in from-scratch baking (try the cinnamon buns) within striking distance of Pemaquid Light and the beach. Luncheon options include blackboard specials as well as salads, burgers, and sandwiches. Chicken pie is a signature dish.

The Contented Sole (207-677-3000) at Colonial Pemaquid. Open seasonally for lunch and dinner, this large wharf-side restaurant managed by the Bradley Inn is hidden down by the water, away from the tourist flow. Full menu from pizza and fish tacos to lobster scampi and steak. Fully licensed.

ON THE PEMAQUID PENINSULA: ALONG RT. 129 TO CHRISTMAS COVE

Harborside Café (207-644-8751), South Bristol. Open year-round for breakfast, lunch, supper. Just north of the drawbridge at "the Gut," this is a general store with a restaurant and a coffee bar. It offers local favorites, including pizza, omelets all day, sandwiches, fried seafood, chowder, and fresh fruit pies.

Island Grocery (207-644-8552; islandgrocery.net), 12 West Side Rd., South Bristol. Open mid-June–Labor Day. Just off Rt. 129, serving the seasonal community. Beth Fisher has created a bright combination store-café with fresh-baked muffins, scones, and yummy frozen custard.

Coveside Restaurant & Marina (207-644-8282; covesiderestaurant.com), Christmas Cove, South Bristol. Open seasonally, 11–9. Geared to customers arriving by yacht (call for moorings) and to the neighboring summer colony, not worth driving all the way to Christmas Cove—but a great amenity if you get there. Check to make sure they are open.

ELSEWHERE

🍴 **Morse's Sauerkraut** (207-832-5569; morsessauerkraut.com), 3856 Washington Rd. (8 miles north of Rt. 1 on Rt. 220), Waldoboro. Open year-round, check website for hours. Since 1918 sauerkraut has been made from fresh cabbage and sold on the premises, which now include a deli and market and a restaurant featuring build-your-own-sauerkraut dishes. Maine natives James Gammon and Cody LeMontagne are carrying on the tradition, also offering a selection of European deli meats, cheeses, delicacies, and pastries.

Borealis Breads Bakery and Sandwich Shop (207-832-0655), 1614-1702 Rt. 1, Waldoboro. Open Mon.–Fri. 8:30–5:30, Sat. and Sun. 9–4. Maine's most popular bread, made from all-natural ingredients, including local grains, and baked here on a stone hearth; more than a dozen kinds. Take-out soups, sandwiches, and more.

ICE CREAM ⊘ 🍴 **Round Top Ice Cream** (207-563-5307), 526 Main St. (Business Rt. 1), Damariscotta. Open early Apr.–Columbus Day, 11:30–9, until 8 off-season. You'll find delicious Round Top Ice Cream, made with 15 percent butterfat, offered at restaurants throughout the region, but this is the original shop just up the road from the farm where it all began in 1924. The ice cream comes in 60 flavors, including fresh blueberry.

✳ Entertainment

Lincoln Theater (207-563-3424; lcct.org), entrance off Main St., Damariscotta. The biggest hall east of Boston in 1875, later boasting the largest motion-picture screen in the state. A second-floor theater has been restored (with elevator access) by the Lincoln County Community Theater, which stages its own productions here. Also first-run films and special programs.

🍴 **Colonial Pemaquid State Historic Site** (207-677-2423; friendsofcolonialpemaquid .org) is a venue for frequent reenactments, lectures, and other special events (see *Must See* on page 192).

✳ Selective Shopping

ANTIQUES **Robert Foster** (207-563-8110; fosterauctions.com) holds frequent auctions at his gallery, 811 Rt. 1, Newcastle. **The Art of Antiquing** (207-529-5300), 4 Back Shore Road, Round Pond (just of Rt. 32) is open seasonally, Wed.–Sun. 10–5, specializing in fine domestic and European antiques.

ART

IN DAMARISCOTTA UNLESS OTHERWISE NOTED

Twin Villages Art Walk, June–Oct., third Fri. 4–7. Twenty venues.

River Gallery (207-563-6330), Main St. Open in-season Mon.–Sat. 10–3; features 19th- and early-20th-century landscapes.

Damariscotta Pottery (207-563-8843), Elm St. Extension (around back of the Weatherbird). Open year-round except Sun. Majolica ware, decorated in bright floral designs. You won't see this advertised. It doesn't have to be. Watch it being shaped and painted.

The Stable Gallery (207-563-1991; stable gallerymaine.com), 26 Water St. Open daily mid-May–mid-Oct. A cooperative showing works of member artists and a variety of craftspeople.

Gifts at 136 (207-563-1011), 136 Maine St. An exceptional selection of Maine-made sculpture, pottery, jewelry, artwork, artisan chocolates, too.

Watershed Center for Ceramic Arts (207-882-6705; watershedceramics.org), 19 Rick Hill Rd., Newcastle. An old brickworks serves as a studio in which artists use the local clay to create work. Inquire about two-week workshops, studio tours, and Salad Days.

Sheepscot River Pottery (207-882-9410), 115 Main St. The big shop is on Rt. 1 in Edgecomb, but this gift shop features the distinctive hand-painted dinnerware, plates, lamps, and more.

IN WALDOBORO

Philippe Guillerm Gallery (207-701-9085; guillermsculptures.com), 882 Main St., Waldoboro Village. Open Apr.–Nov., Tue.–Fri. 10–4. Paris-born and -bred Philippe Guillerm has devoted the past 25 years to sailing—collecting exotic and local woods and sculpting them into amazing shapes, from whimsical violins to human forms. The gallery in a former bank building is also—beyond the teller's window—his working studio. Also changing art exhibits.

Tidemark Gallery (207-832-5109; tidemarkgallery.com), 929 Main St., Waldoboro Village. Open Wed.–Sat. 10–5. A quality contemporary gallery with frequently changing shows and varied media.

IN NEW HARBOR AND PEMAQUID POINT

Pemaquid Craft Co-op (207-677-2077), 2565 Bristol Rd. (Rt. 130), New Harbor. Open May–Oct., daily 10–6, then Fri.–Sun. until Dec. 24. Fifteen rooms filled with work by 50 Maine crafters.

North Country Wind Bells (207-677-2224; mainebuoybells.com), 544 Rt. 32, Chamberlain. Open daily June–Labor Day, weekdays off-season. North of New Harbor on the pretty coastal road to Round Pond. Buoy wind bells, wilderness bells, and lighthouse bells are made and sold, along with garden and home accessories.

SPECIAL SHOPS

IN DAMARISCOTTA

✪ 🐚 ✎ **Renys** (207-563-3177; renys.com), Main St. First opened in Damariscotta in 1949, family-owned Renys has since become a small-town Maine institution, with 14 stores from Wells to Ellsworth as well as many inland. Corporate headquarters are south of town. Main Street hosts two stores: The original sells quality clothing, while Renys Underground offers everything from tea to TVs, bedding, china, and toys; a wide assortment of canned and boxed foodstuffs at amazing savings; a wide assortment of shoes, sandals, and boots; beach equipment; and all manner of staples and things you didn't realize you needed. The antithesis of Walmart, Renys has been the subject of two Maine musicals. The biggest sales of the year here begin at 6 AM on the first Saturday of November.

✪ ✎ **Sherman's Maine Coast Book Shop & Café** (207-563-3207), 158 Main St. With its name change in 2016, this became the sixth store in Maine's largest bookstore chain. According to owner Jeff Curtis, the quality of this beloved, formerly independent bookstore will remain. The internet café has been expanded.

Weatherbird on Main (207-563-1177), 132 Main St. An exceptional women's clothing store, expanded from the corner it previously occupied at Weatherbird's Courtyard Street store (see *Eating Out*).

ELSEWHERE

✎ **Granite Hall Store** (207-529-5864), Rt. 32, Round Pond. Open daily May–Dec. 10–8:30. This distinctive, mansard-roofed building was constructed as a dance hall in 1879 at the center of a busy little port. Check out the movie screen and piano upstairs, relics of its silent-movie days. Sarah Herndon has preserved this sense of the past but filled it with reasons to explore, from the penny candy up front to Scottish scarves, Irish hats, and Maine-made woolens, books, and cards, plus an ice cream take-out window.

Alewives Fabrics (207-563-5002), Rt. 215, Damariscotta Mills. Open daily, year-round. Two miles north of Rt. 1, this is an excellent fabric store. The selection is outstanding, including Marimekko, batik, and Asian. Also quilting supplies. We stopped because we were looking for and found pillow forms.

PHILIPPE GUILLERM GALLERY, WALDOBORO

Christina Tree

FARMERS' MARKET **The Damariscotta Farmers Market** (damariscottafarmersmarket.org) is held mid-May–Oct., Fri. 9–noon at Round Top Farm, 526 Main St. (Business Rt. 1); also Mon. late June–late Sept. at **Rising Tide Co-op** (see *Eating Out*).

❋ Special Events

Note: See damariscotta.com for details.

February: Annual **ice harvest** at the Thompson Ice House, South Bristol. Sunday of Presidents Weekend.

May–early June: Alewives climb the fish ladder in Damariscotta Mills to spawn in Damariscotta Lake, and an **Alewives Festival** featuring smoked and grilled alewives is held the Sunday of Memorial Day weekend (*To See*).

July: Annual July 4 **fireworks** in Damariscotta and Wiscasset and a famously unorthodox **parade** in Round Pond. **Great Salt Bay Music Festival** at Damariscotta River Association.

Early August: **Olde Bristol Days**, Old Fort Grounds, Pemaquid Beach—parade, fish fry, chicken BBQ, bands, bagpipers, pancake breakfast, boat race, much more.

September: **Pemaquid Oyster Festival** at Schooner Landing, Damariscotta.

October: **Annual Pumpkinfest & Regatta** (Columbus Day weekend) has become one of the biggest events of the year; it includes a parade of river-worthy pumpkins.

November: **Early Bird Sale at Renys** (first Sat.) and at stores throughout town. Free coffee, doughnuts, and bargains. From 6 AM.

December: **Coastal Christmas Fest**.

MONHEGAN ISLAND

This island is endless and wonderful in its variety. It's possessed of enough beauty to supply a continent.
—Artist George Bellows, on first seeing Monhegan

Ten miles off Pemaquid Point and barely a mile square, Monhegan is a microcosm of Maine landscapes, from 160-foot sheer headlands to pine woods, from wildflower-filled inland meadows to the smooth, low rocks along Lobster Cove. "Backed like a whale" is the way one mariner in 1590 described the island's shape: headlands sloping down to the small off-island of Manana, a blip on Monhegan's silhouette.

Monhegan is known for the quality and quantity of its artists and the grit of its lobstermen, who fish October through June. The island's first recorded artist arrived in 1858, and by the 1870s a hotel and several boardinghouses were filled with summer guests, many of them artists. In 1903 Robert Henri, a founder of New York's Ashcan School and a well-known art teacher, discovered Monhegan and soon introduced it to his students, among them George Bellows and Rockwell Kent. The island remains a genuine art colony. Jamie Wyeth owns a house built by Rockwell Kent, and Rockwell Kent passed his studio on to James Fitzgerald. More than 20 artists regularly open their studios to visitors.

The island continues to draw artists in good part because its beauty not only survives but also remains accessible. Prospect Hill, the only attempted development, foundered around

Christine Tree

VIEW FROM FISH BEACH

1900. It was Theodore Edison, son of the inventor, who amassed property enough to erase its traces and keep the island's cedar-shingled cottages (which still number around 130) bunched along the sheltered harbor, the rest preserved as common space and laced with footpaths.

In 1954 Edison helped organize Monhegan Associates, a nonprofit corporation dedicated to preserving the "natural, wild beauty" of the island. Ironically, this was one of the country's few communities to shun electricity until relatively recently. A number of homes and one inn still use kerosene lamps. Vehicles are limited to a few trucks for those with businesses and golf carts for those with medical needs. Visitors come to walk, to paint, to bird, and to relax.

Captain John Smith is said to have discovered the island in 1614. Native American artifacts on display in the Monhegan Museum may date back as far as 8,000 years. The island's present settlement has been continuous since 1790; it's been a "plantation" since 1839. The year-round population of around 60 swells in summer to a little more than 600, not counting roughly 100 seasonal employees, 300 overnight guests, and up to 300 day-trippers. At this writing the number of working lobstermen is down to nine. The one-room white-clapboard school serves grades K–8.

Monhegan has three inns, a B&B, several nightly rental units, and a limited number of weekly rental cottages. Fog and a frequently rough passage insulate it to some degree, but on summer days a high tide of day-trippers from Boothbay Harbor and New Harbor, as well as from Port Clyde, washes over this small, fragile island. More worrisome still are skyrocketing real estate prices. Monhegan Island Sustainable Community Association (MISCA) is now dedicated to ensuring affordable housing for year-round residents.

GUIDANCE *A Visitor's Guide to Monhegan Island, Maine*, a free 10-page leaflet, comes with every boat ticket to the island in the hope that visitors will read about the dangers and rules as well as the obvious beauty of the cliff-side trails on the island's backside. The *Monhegan Associates Trail Map*, also available on the boats, is well worth $1 (see *Hiking*), and the free Studio Locations sheet (see the chapter intro) is also handy if you want to

THE VILLAGE ON MONHEGAN

FISH BEACH

meet resident artists. Also check **monheganwelcome.com, monhegan.com,** and **monhegan associates.org.**

GETTING THERE **Monhegan Boat Line** (207-372-8848; monheganboat.com) operates both the sleek *Elizabeth Ann* and the beloved old *Laura B* from Port Clyde; reservations a must. Service is three times daily in-season, less frequent in spring and fall, and only Mon., Wed., and Fri. in winter. It's a 50- or 70-minute trip, depending on which boat you catch. Mid-May–Columbus Day weekend **Hardy Boat Cruises** (1-800-278-3346; hardyboat.com) offers a 50-minute run from New Harbor with two daily roundtrips early June–Sept. **The Ocean House** in Port Clyde and the **Gosnold Arms** in New Harbor are within walking distance of these two services, taking the sting out of making morning boats. The *Balmy Days II* (1-800-298-2284, balmydayscruises.com) also offers seasonal roundtrips from Boothbay.

EQUIPMENT AND RULES Come properly shod for the precipitous paths. Hikers should wear long pants and socks against poison ivy; bring sweaters and windbreakers. Wading or swimming anywhere but Swim Beach (on the harbor) can be lethal. During one of our visits a young man was washed away by a rogue wave. Kayaking is also dangerous. Flashlights are a must for overnight visitors. Hiking boots and rain gear are also good ideas. Public phones are few; cell phone reception has improved, thanks to a tower that now dwarfs the lighthouse. Smoking is prohibited beyond the village. So is camping. Do not bring bicycles. Dogs must be leashed at all times. And *please* don't pick the flowers.

PUBLIC RESTROOMS The two public pay toilets are on a lane behind the Monhegan House.

GETTING AROUND Several trucks meet each boat as it arrives and provide baggage service. Otherwise visitors have no access to motorized transport.

Christina Tree

DUSK ATOP BURNT HEAD

WHEN TO COME The spring migration season brings birds and birders. June can be rainy and foggy—but also glorious and always flowery, with wild strawberries to be found along hiking paths. July and Aug. are prime time, but Sept. is best for hiking; birds and birders return.

✳ To See

Monhegan Island Light, built of granite in 1850 and automated in 1959, caps a hill that's well worth climbing for the view alone. The **Monhegan Art & History** (207-596-7003; monheganmuseum.org) is a real gem. In July and Aug., it's open daily 11:30–3:30; in late June and all Sept. it's 1:30–3:30. $5 per adult. A spellbinding display of island art, including prints by George Bellows and Rockwell Kent, and annual special exhibits in the neighboring gallery. Flora, fauna, some geology, lobstering, and island history are interpreted through artifacts, including documents dating back to the 16th century. The neighboring **Art Gallery** houses annually changing exhibits. There's also a gift shop.

The **Kent-Fitzgerald-Hubert House**, Horn's Hill. Open seasonally, check jamesfitzgerald .org for hours. Built by Rockwell Kent, it later served as a home and studio for James Fitzgerald (1899–1971), one of the most distinctive and prominent artists for whom Monhegan has been a home and inspiration.

Monhegan Memorial Library (207-596-0549), 1 Main St. Open May–Oct. A welcoming shingled cottage walled with books. There's a large children's section, and visitors can borrow books. Note special events.

✳ To Do

ART WALKS **Open studios.** In contrast to the once-a-month art walks popular in many communities, on Monhegan more than 20 resident artists welcome visitors to their studios on most summer days. Pick up the ubiquitous map/guide and schedule, or look for shingles hung outside houses, listing the hours they're open. Don Stone is the current dean of Monhegan painters, and his studio on the way to Burnt Head is open by chance or appointment. Stop by the **Lupine Gallery** (see *Selective Shopping*) to spot work by resident artists you may fancy. Everywhere you'll see artists at work and soon your own fingers may begin itching. Google **Monhegan Island Workshops** for a choice of teachers and dates. Don't miss the great paintings in the island's museums (see *To See*).

BIRDING Positioned in the middle of the Atlantic flyway, Monhegan is one of the best birding places on the East Coast. Your local Audubon Society may have a trip going in May or mid- through late Sept.

HIKING Pick up a current Monhegan Associates Trail Map before setting out on the island's network. Day-trippers are advised to take the **Burnt Head Trail** (No. 4) and loop back to the village via the **Whitehead Trail** (No. 7), descending by the lighthouse, or vice versa. This way you get a sense of the high bluffs and the unusual rocks in Gull Cove.

Beyond this well-trod loop, trails are marked with few guideposts. It's easy to get turned around in **Cathedral Woods** (justly famed and known for its "fairy houses"), which, along with **Pulpit Rock**, should be reserved for an unhurried day. The path along the southern outer tip of the island, from Burnt Head to Christmas Cove, is ledgy and unsuitable for children and shaky hikers. The relatively flat trail from the village to **Lobster Cove** at the southern tip of the island is a favorite and has recently been improved. It can, however, be the muddiest and slipperiest of all after rains. Be sure to bring a flashlight if you are setting out toward evening, just in case you get lost—the fate of our brother-in-law, who wandered around all through the night.

❋ Lodging

ON MONHEGAN ISLAND

Note: Lodging is limited but remarkably varied.

INNS ✪ **Island Inn** (207-596-0371; islandinn monhegan.com). Open Memorial Day–Columbus Day weekend. This shingled, cupola-topped, gabled, classic 1907 summer hotel with a long, rocker-lined veranda is steps from the ferry dock and overlooks the boat-filled harbor and Manana Island. The public rooms are a winning mix of old-fashioned and chic, with a comfortable living room and book-stocked side porches. The nicely decorated dining room has the harbor view (see *Dining Out*). The 28 rooms and four suites are divided between the main inn and Pierce Cottage (with remodeled suites) behind it. Eight rooms still share 4 baths. In high season (July–Labor Day), from $185 per couple (shared bath, meadow view) to $435 for the top suite. Otherwise $148–367, depending on room and week. $10 charge for one-night stays. Children under 5 are free. All rates include a full breakfast, served buffet-style, usually featuring lobster scramble.

Artists should inquire about 4-bedroom Zimmie's Artist Cottage, available to working artists either singly or as a group, $400–600 per person per week, $2,000 for the whole house.

✏ **Monhegan House** (207-594-7983; monheganhouse.com), P.O. Box 345. Open Memorial Day–early Oct. Holden and Susan Nelson have revived Monhegan's oldest continuously operating summer hotel, adding two suites with bath and a deck. This is the island's oldest **inn** and set in the middle of the village. The 28 rooms are on four floors. No closets, and most baths and showers (plentiful and immaculate) are in a wing off the middle of the second floor. For couples and families we recommend the third floor; for singles the bargain-priced fourth-floor rooms have the best views (coveted by artists). The downstairs lobby is hung with art, warmed by a gas fireplace, and equipped with books and games. Children are welcome and free under age 3. A full breakfast is included in the rates ($125–199 in high season, $199–229 for suites; $88–149 in low). Head in for breakfast before 8 AM, because it's open to the public and very popular. Dinner is also excellent (see *Dining Out*).

✪ ⚘ ❀ ✏ (((•))) **The Trailing Yew** (207-596-6194; trailingyew.com). Open mid-May–mid-Oct. This quirky institution has a loyal following among artists and writers (ourselves included). New England's last genuine 19th-century-style "summer boardinghouse," it's the place for the many solo travelers

THE TRAILING YEW

drawn to Monhegan. Now owned by the Chioffi family and friends, the inn's 32 rooms, lit with kerosene lamps, are divided among the main house and adjacent annexes and cottages on the grounds. We try to reserve an upstairs room in Seagull, an 1840s captain's house with water views. The Mooring Chain (good only for groups) is up the road. With the exception of The Cabin, baths are shared and have electricity (guests are asked to charge electronic devices in the office). In shoulder seasons it's advisable to bring a sleeping bag. Dining is at 6:30; guests gather beforehand in Adirondack chairs on the porch and lawn, again around shared tables, and the conversation is usually lively (BYOB). Dinner is open to the public: $32 for four courses, tax and gratuity included. $140 per person solo, $240 double includes breakfast and dinner; sliding scale for ages 2–12. $10 pet fee. No credit cards.

B&BS ✪ ✹ **Shining Sails** (207-596-0041; shiningsails.com), P.O. Box 346. Open pretty much year-round. Lobsterman John Murdock and his wife, Winnie, offer two rooms and five exceptional apartments in their welcoming village home overlooking the water. All five water-view units have a deck, the better to savor the sunset and stars. All rooms are tastefully decorated, featuring original island art. On foggy days a woodstove warms the living room, where an ample continental breakfast is served daily, May–Columbus Day. The Murdocks are helpful hosts and this place is so justly popular, it's advisable to book far in advance for July and Aug., but there are always some openings. $150–230 per night with breakfast, $110–165 off-season. Four apartments are also for rent at the Inn at Fish & Maine.

GUESTHOUSES AND DAILY RENTALS
Hitchcock House (207-594-8137; hitchcock house.com), Horn's Hill. Hidden away on Horn's Hill with a delightful garden and a large, sheltered deck, which serves as common space for guests. In the house itself Barbara Hitchcock offers two appealing housekeeping units, both with decks with views down across the meadows to the village and water. There are also two upstairs guest rooms, each with a small fridge and a hot pot,

sharing one bath; a "cabin" in the garden has a full kitchen, living room, and bath. July–Labor Day weekend efficiencies are $125 per night, $815 per week; rooms are $90 per night, $555 per week, less off-season.

Tribler Cottage (207-594-2445; tribler cottage.com). Open mid-May–mid-Oct. On the edge of the meadow, at the base of Lighthouse Hill, this remains in the same family that has been welcoming visitors since the 1920s. Richard Farrell offers two housekeeping apartments. Hillside apartment has a sundeck and living room with fireplace; both apartments have a gas heater. $140–160 per couple per night based on three-night stay; $945–1,085 weekly.

WEEKLY RENTALS Cooking facilities come in handy here: You can buy lobster, good fresh and smoked fish, and a limited line of vegetables (bring meat and staples). **Shining Sails Cottage Rental** (207-596-0041; shiningsails.com) manages more than two dozen rental cottages, available by the week. **Brackett Rentals** (207-594-9151; brackettrentals.com) offers upward of 20 units. Also check with Maryann Body (207-596-0175). It's wise to get in your bid in early for the summer.

✳ Where to Eat

Note: Restaurants are BYOB, but wine is readily available in island stores.

DINING OUT **The Island Inn** (207-596-0371). Open to the public Memorial Day–Columbus Day for breakfast and dinner, also for lunch July 4–Labor Day. This classic, turn-of-the-20th-century dining room has contemporary decor and water views. Lunch on incredibly light mini-crab cakes on a bed of mixed greens and a beer from The Barnacle, the inn's gift shop. Reserve a table overlooking the water for dinner. We can vouch for pan-seared scallops. Entrées $19–34.

Monhegan House Open nightly late June–Labor Day, then weekends. The attractive, many-windowed dining room at the back of the inn overlooks the village and meadow. Breakfasts feature house-made breads and

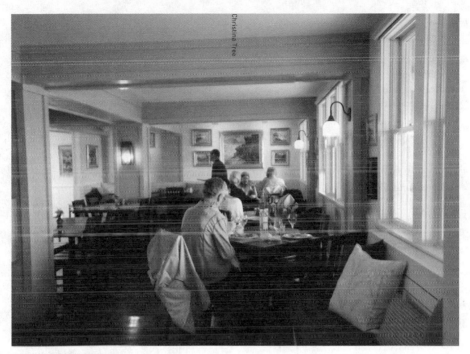

LUNCH AT THE ISLAND INN

omelets. The dinner menu changes nightly and always includes a vegetarian option; it might offer a house-made onion and lavender sausage, haddock en papillote, honey-brined chicken, or cumin-scented scallops. Entrées $22–27.

EATING OUT ✪ The **Fish House Market**, Fish Beach. Open daily. The seasonal source of the freshest of seafood for anyone with cooking facilities. Better yet, anyone can enjoy Damariscotta oysters, steamed clams, the island's best crab and lobster rolls, and daily specials to eat at picnic tables on Fish Beach with the island's best view of the sun setting behind Manana Island (BYOB).

The Barnacle. Sited beside the ferry wharf and owned by the Island Inn, the Barnacle offers limited seating on the deck and inside. Sandwiches, soups, and pastries; also espresso and prepared sandwiches. Wine and beer sold.

The Novelty, behind Monhegan House. Pizza, soups and sandwiches, quiche, salads, and hot wraps. Freshly made cookies are great hiking fuel as you set off up Horn's Hill.

Hand-dipped ice cream and frozen yogurt hit the spot on the way down. Wine, beer, splits of champagne. Outside shaded seating.

Black Duck Emporium. Open Memorial Day–Columbus Day in the former general store. Sited at the center of the village, next to the post office, this is the current island gathering place, good for snacks and pastry as well as coffee, tea, books, kitchenware, pottery, and jewelry.

Monhegan Brewing (monheganbrewing .com), Lobster Lane. Open May–Oct., daily in summer 11–6, fewer hours, days in shoulder months. Matt Weber is a longtime Maine craft brewer and this seven-barrel system brewery gets good reviews. The selection of ales, malts, and stouts changes; Matt's specialty is a "big" IPA. Also house-made ginger beer. Brews are available in 32 oz. "growlettes" and 22 oz. "bombers".

L. Bracket & Son (207-594-2222), 2–4 Main St. Open year-round, 7–5:30. The island's general store stocks basic groceries and produce, also wine, beer, and a respectable selection of cheese. Take-out and eat-in (there's a 4-stool counter), lunch 11–3.

✳ Entertainment

Check monhegan.com for frequent evening concerts, jams, art lectures, and poetry readings in venues such as the schoolhouse, church, and library.

✳ Selective Shopping

The Lupine Gallery (207-594-8131; lupine gallerymonhegan.com), 48 Main St. Open early May–Columbus Day, 11–4:30. Bill Boynton and Jackie Bogel offer original works by 100 artists who paint regularly on the island. This is a very special gallery, showcasing the work of many professional artists within walking distance. Sited just uphill from the ferry dock, it's a good place to judge which studios you want to visit. Great cards, prints, and art books, also artists' supplies and framing.

Black Duck Emporium. Open Memorial Day–Columbus Day. This longtime island gift store has expanded to fill the former general store, offering cappuccino and pastries as well as imaginative T-shirts, books, kitchenware, pottery, and jewelry.

Winterworks. Open more or less daily Memorial Day–Columbus Day, by the ferry dock. A former fish house is now the island co-op, filled with work produced by the island's craftspeople: good quality knitted goods, jewelry, and Christmas decorations.

PENOBSCOT BAY REGION

ROCKLAND/THOMASTON AREA

VINALHAVEN, NORTH HAVEN, AND MATINICUS

CAMDEN/ROCKPORT AREA

Isleboro

BELFAST, SEARSPORT, AND STOCKTON SPRINGS

EAST PENOBSCOT BAY REGION

Bucksport/Orland Area; Blue Hill Peninsula;
Stonington and Isle au Haut; Castine

Penobscot Bay

202

Bucksport

179

1A

182

1A

175

Ellsworth

1

Searsport

166

15

Trenton

Belfast

Castine

Blue Hill

102

Bar Harbor

1

175

Lincolnville

Southwest
Harbor

N

0   5   10
Miles

© The Countryman Press

PENOBSCOT BAY REGION

Penobscot Bay is an impressive 15 miles wide and 40 miles deep, spotted with more than 200 islands. For centuries it was a heavily trafficked highway, filled with fishing boats, ferries, and the coastal schooners trucking lime from Rockland and Rockport, granite from Vinalhaven and Stonington, lumber that came down the Penobscot River from Bangor.

Today more than half of Maine's Windjammers fleet are century-old schooners, rebuilt to carry passengers instead of freight, sailing out of Rockland or Camden with the prevailing winds "downeast," anchoring in island or eastern shore harbors. Beloved by yachtsmen, the bay can be savored for an hour or two under sail as well as by excursion boats. Given the many small, off-shore islands, East Penobscot Bay is also one of Maine's great places to kayak.

Car-carrying Maine State Ferries serve the islands of Isleboro (3 miles off Lincolnville Beach), and both North Haven and Vinalhaven and roughly 12 miles off Rockland. Isle au Haut, 6 miles south of Stonington, is accessible by passenger ferry. Each island is described in this section.

By road it's roughly 100 miles around the bay, from Tenant's Harbor south of Rockland on the Southwest to Stonington on its southeast shore. From Rockland Route 1 arcs north to Belfast and Searsport, following the bay as it narrows into the Penobscot River. Just south of Bucksport, at the confluence of river and bay, an observatory 45-stories high atop of the Waldo-Hancock Bridge offers a memorable view.

From the summits of Mt. Battie (accessible by road) and Megunticook in Camden you get a sense of the full sweep of water and islands, and on from Caterpillar Hill, (Rt. 15 on the Blue Hill peninsula), the panorama is back across the bay to the Camden Hills. But such vantage points are rare. Beyond Bucksport Rt. 1 turns due east to Ellsworth, bypassing the Blue Hill peninsula and its "hinged" islands that compose the towns of Deer Isle and Stonington along the eastern shore of the Bay.

Penobscot Bay remains home to many hundreds of lobster and fishing boats. A growing number of these too are fitted for passengers, offering excursions, and taxi service. One way or another, sampling the beauty of this splendid bay is well worth the effort, and easier than it's been in decades.

ROCKLAND/ THOMASTON AREA

Long billed as the "Lobster Capital of the World," Rockland is now better known as home of the Farnsworth Museum, with its exceptional collection of Maine-based paintings, and for the galleries, shops, attractions, and restaurants lining its mile-long, floridly brick Main Street. Departure point for ferries to the islands of Vinalhaven, North Haven, and Matinicus, it is also home port for the majority of Maine's windjammers, as well as for several daysailers and excursion boats.

In the past couple of decades this city of nearly 7,300 has been transformed almost completely. Never a "tourist town" like Camden or Boothbay, Rockland is fiercely proud of its working waterfront. Its sardine-packing and fish-processing plants are, however, gone, and the huge harbor, protected by a nearly mile-long granite—and walkable—breakwater, is now sparkling clean and equipped to accommodate pleasure boats. Old waterside industrial sheds have disappeared, replaced by offices and restaurants. The harborside walking trail lengthens with every edition of this book. A former newspaper plant is now the chamber of commerce visitors center and the Maine Lighthouse Museum.

Still, Rockland prides itself on its grit. The city's industrial base still includes FMC Bio-Polymer (processing carrageenan from seaweed) and homegrown Fisher Snowplow. The harbor, Maine's second largest after Portland, remains home to a sizable fishing and lobstering fleet along with tugs and U.S. Coast Guard and commercial vessels.

Initially known for its shipbuilding, the city became synonymous in the late 19th century with the limestone it quarried, burned, and shipped off to be made into plaster. When wallboard replaced plaster, Rockland quickly switched to catching and processing fish. In the 1990s, with fishing on the decline, city entrepreneurs once more looked to widen their base. Initially MBNA, the national credit card company, seemed a gift from the gods, tidying the southern rim of the harbor into an office "campus" and building a public boardwalk along its rim. In 2005, however, the firm sold out and disappeared.

Truly amazing is the way Rockland's resurgence has continued to be powered by the economic engines of fine art, food, and cultural attractions. The vacated office space was filled, and restaurants moved in to take advantage of waterfront views.

A century ago summer people heading for Bar Harbor, as well as the islands, took the train as far as Rockland, switching here to steamboats. Today a similar summer crowd rides the bus to the ferry terminal or flies into Knox County Regional Airport on Owls Head, just south of town, transferring to rental cars, air taxis, or windjammers to charter boats as well as ferries.

Southwest of Rockland, two peninsulas separate Muscongus Bay from Penobscot Bay. One is the fat arm of land on which the villages of Friendship and Cushing doze. Nearer is the skinnier St. George Peninsula with Port Clyde at its tip, departure point for the year-round passenger ferry service to Monhegan Island.

GUIDANCE Penobscot Bay Regional Chamber of Commerce (207-596-0376 or 1-800-562-2529; camdenrockland.com), 1 Park Dr., Rockland. Open daily Memorial Day–Columbus Day, Mon.–Fri. 9–5 and Sat., Sun. 10–4; then weekdays and 10–4 Sat. The chamber's visitors

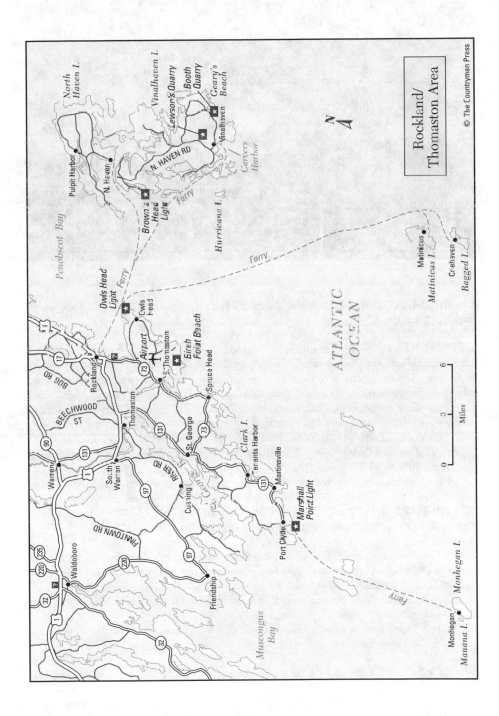

Rockland/
Thomaston Area

© The Countryman Press

PORT CLYDE

centers (the second is in Camden at 2 Public Landing) serve the Rockland area, which includes Owls Head, Thomaston, the peninsula villages, and the islands.

GETTING THERE *By air:* **Knox County Regional Airport** (207-594-4131) at Owls Head, just south of Rockland. Frequent daily service is via **Cape Air** (1-866-227-3247; capeair.com) to Boston's Logan Airport, with baggage connections to major carriers. **Penobscot Island Air** (penobscotislandair.net) offers both scheduled and charter service to Vinalhaven, North Haven, and Matinicus. Rental cars are available at the airport. Also see *By taxi* under *Getting Around*; all offer service to Portland International Jetport (see "Portland Area"). **Mid-Coast Limo** (1-800-937-2424; midcoastlimo.com) also serves Boston's Logan Airport.

By bus: **Concord Coach** (1-800-639-3317; concordcoachlines.com) stops in Rockland at the Maine State Ferry Terminal.

By boat: For moorings contact the harbormaster (office, 207-594-0312; dock, 207-594-0314).

GETTING AROUND *By taxi:* **Schooner Bay Limo & Taxi** (207-594-5000), **Hit the Road Driver Service** (207-230-0095; cell, 207-691-0295), and **Joe's Taxi** (207-975-3560) will get you there.

By ferry: Frequent service from the **Maine State Ferry Service Terminal** (207-596-2022 or 1-800-491-4883) to Vinalhaven, North Haven, and, less frequently, to Matinicus (see "Midcoast Islands"). **Monhegan Boat Line** (207-372-8848) serves Monhegan from Port Clyde.

Note: Rockland can be accessed and thoroughly enjoyed without a car.

PARKING Try to park in a free, all-day municipal lot off Tillson Ave. Note that street parking is limited to two hours and strictly enforced.

WHEN TO COME Rockland stages a series of festivals that draw weekend crowds from mid-July through September. The biggest is the Maine Lobster Festival, first weekend in August. The Farnsworth Museum, major galleries, restaurants, and lodging all remain open year-round.

✱ Villages and Islands

Friendship (pop. 1,200). Best known as the birthplace of the classic Friendship sloop, first built by local lobstermen to haul their traps (originals and reproductions of this sturdy vessel hold races here every summer), Friendship remains a quiet fishing village. The **Friendship Museum** (207-832-4852), housed in a former brick schoolhouse at the junction of Rt. 220 and Martin Point Rd., is open late June–Labor Day, Mon.–Sat. 1–4 and Sun. 2–4, also weekends March–Columbus Day. Displays feature Friendship sloops.

St. George is a town composed of several distinct villages along Rt. 131 on the St. George Peninsula, a 15-mile-long land finger between the tidal St. George River and the Atlantic. The most visible of these is **Tenants Harbor**, a fishing village with a terrific sculpture of St. George and the Dragon in front of the town office. There's a good little library and, beyond, rock cliffs, tidal pools, old cemeteries, and the kind of countryside described by Sarah Orne Jewett in *The Country of the Pointed Firs*. Jewett lived just a few bends down Rt. 131 in Martinville while she wrote the book.

Port Clyde marks the end of Rt. 131 and the tip of the peninsula. The departure point for the year-round ferries to Monhegan, it's tranquil and picturesque—with the exception of ferry departures and arrivals, when it's chaotic. The Ocean House Hotel is a great place to spend the night before boarding the ferry. Linda Bean (as in L.L. Bean) owns the working wharf (207-372-6543). She also owns the Dip Net restaurant, the Port Clyde General Store, and the neighboring Seaside Inn and gallery. This is a great spot for kayaking (see *To Do*), and Marshall Point Light (see *Lighthouses* on page 225) is around the bend.

Thomaston (pop. 2,800). Passing through Thomaston on Rt. 1 you'll notice the handsome brick downtown and line of handsome captains' homes, evidence of early-19th-century wealth from shipbuilding. In the 1840 census, three of the nation's seven millionaires lived in town. To dramatize its history Thomaston has installed 25 plaques along Main, Knox, and Water Sts., each with a photo taken at that spot a century ago with text in both English and French. Leaflet guides to this **Museum in the Streets** are available at the library. The **Thomaston Historical Society** (207-354-2314; thomastonhistoricalsociety.com) at the foot of Knox St. is open June–Aug., Tue.–Thu. 2–4. The state prison has moved to Warren but left behind its popular Maine State Prison Showroom (see *Selective Shopping*). Montpelier, home of the General Knox Museum (see *To See*), is just north of town at the junctions of Rts. 1 and 131.

Union (pop. 2,350) is 15 miles west of Rockland via Rt. 17, a little less if you follow Rt. 131 north along the St. George River. It's sited between Round Pond and Seven Tree Pond and surrounded by gentle hills and farm country. The **Union Fair** in August has been held since 1892. This place is also a good spot to swim, eat, and explore the **Matthews Museum of Maine Heritage** (matthewsmuseum.org) at the fairgrounds, open Wed.–Sat. in July and Aug., noon–4.

Islands. An overnight or longer stay on an island is far preferable to a day trip. From Rockland you can take a Maine State (car) Ferry to **Vinalhaven** and **North Haven**. Together these form the Fox Islands, divided by a narrow passage. Vinalhaven is Maine's largest offshore island, with its largest year-round population and lobstering fleet. A number of shopping, eating, and lodging options cluster around Carver's Harbor, a 10-minute walk from the ferry. North Haven offers fewer and more seasonal places to eat, shop, and stay, but a more open landscape. **Matinicus**, also accessible from Rockland, is the most remote of Maine's island communities, and quietly beautiful. Tiny **Monhegan**, accessible from Port Clyde, offers the most dramatic cliff scenery and the most hospitable welcome to visitors.

MUST SEE

⊙ & Farnsworth Art Museum and Wyeth Center (207-596-6457; farnsworthmuseum.org), 16 Museum St., Rockland. Open year-round. Memorial Day weekend–Oct. 31, daily 10–5, also Wed. and First Fridays 5–8 (free); Nov.–Dec. 31, closed Mon.; Jan.–Memorial Day weekend, Wed.–Sun. 10–5. Admission to the museum and Farnsworth Homestead (see below) is $12 adults, $10 senior citizens and students over 17; no charge under 17; free for all Wed. 5–8. Add $5 to include a visit to the Olson House (see below). This exceptional art museum was established by Lucy Farnsworth, who amazed everyone when, on her death at age 97 in 1935, she left $1.3 million to preserve her house and build a library and art gallery to honor the memory of her father. From the beginning the collection included paintings of Maine by Winslow Homer, George Bellows, and a (then) little-known local summer resident, Andrew Wyeth.

Since the early 1990s the Farnsworth has more than doubled its space and now occupies 3 acres in the middle of downtown Rockland. The collection numbers over 14,000 objects housed in five buildings with 28 galleries. The museum remains Maine-focused. A permanent exhibit traces the evolution of Maine landscape paintings with Hudson River School artists such as Thomas Cole and 19th-century marine artist Fitz Henry Lane; American impressionists Frank Benson, Willard Metcalf, Childe Hassam, and Maurice Prendergast; early-20th-century greats like Rockwell Kent and Charles Woodbury; and such modernists as John Marin and Marsden Hartley. Rockland-raised painter and sculptor Louise Nevelson is also well represented. In recent years contemporary art holdings have been significantly expanded to include works by Alex Katz, Neil Welliver, Janet Fish, Bernard Langlais, and Robert Indiana, along with such photographers as Eliot Porter and Rockland native Kosti Ruohomaa.

Gardens connect the main museum with the Wyeth Center, a two-story exhibit space in a former church, displaying works by N. C. Wyeth (1882–1945) and Jamie Wyeth (born 1946). Exhibits vary. Andrew Wyeth's paintings are shown in the main museum.

Farnsworth Homestead (207-596-6457), 21 Elm St., Rockland. Open late May–mid-Oct., Tue.–Sun. 11–5. Tours on

TURKEY POND BY ANDREW WYETH, 1944

✷ To See

The Olson House (207-596-6457), Hawthorn Point Rd., Cushing. Open Memorial Day–Columbus Day, daily 11–4. $10 adults, $8 seniors and students over 17. Administered by the Farnsworth Art Museum, this house served as a backdrop for many works by Andrew Wyeth, including *Christina's World*. It's been intentionally left unrestored except for interpretive materials. On Pleasant Point, accessed by quiet back roads, this saltwater farm makes a good bicycle destination. Built in the late 1700s, it was remodeled in 1872 but remained in the same family, ultimately passing to Alvara and Christina (1892–1968) Olson. Owned by the Farnsworth since 1991, it evokes the familiar painting.

MUSEUMS AND HISTORIC HOMES ♪ **General Henry Knox Museum** (Montpelier) (207-354-8062; knoxmuseum.org), 30 High St., Thomaston. Guided tours Memorial Day–Columbus Day, Thu.–Fri. 10–4; more days open on website. Admission $10 adults, $8 seniors,

CENTER FOR MAINE CONTEMPORARY ART, OR CMCA

the hour. Free with museum admission. Built in 1850 for successful businessman William A. Farnsworth and his growing family, this was the nearly lifelong home of his daughter and museum founder Lucy Copeland Farnsworth. The Greek Revival-style Farnsworth Homestead has a richly decorated Victorian interior, with original furniture, carpets, wallpaper, paintings and prints, gas lighting fixtures, and many of the family's original belongings.

CMCA, Center for Maine Contemporary Art (207-701-5005; cmcanow.org), 21 Winter St. Rockland. Admission $6 adults, 12 and under free. Exhibitions are splendidly presented in this new modern building by Toshiko Mori, which opened in June 2016, with 7,700 square feet of exhibition space, spacious and lofty under north-facing high windows. Changing exhibitions and regular gallery talks, workshops, and film showings. The outdoor sculpture garden joins the sidewalk in an open embrace, designed to tempt passers-by in. Winter Street itself is undergoing urban redesign, creating an intimate promenade to the sea, or from the sea to CMCA and its near neighbor, the Farnsworth.

$4 ages 5–14 (family: $18). A 1926 re-creation of the grand mansion built (on another spot) in 1794 by General Henry Knox (1750–1806), the portly 5-foot-6-inch, 300-pound Boston bookseller who became a Revolutionary War hero, then our first secretary of war. He married a granddaughter of Samuel Waldo, the Boston developer who owned all of this area and for whom the county is named.

✒ **Owls Head Transportation Museum** (207-594-4418; owlshead.org), 117 Museum St., Owls Head. Off Rt. 73, 2 miles south of Rockland, adjacent to the Knox County Regional Airport. Open daily year-round (except Christmas, Thanksgiving, and New Year's Day) 10–5. Check the website for frequent special-event days. On non-event days admission is $10 adults, $8 seniors, free under 18. One of the country's outstanding collections of antique planes and automobiles. In the exhibition hall you can take a 100-year journey through the evolution of transportation, from horse-drawn carriages to World War I fighter planes; from a 16-cylinder Cadillac to a Rolls-Royce; from the Red Baron's Fokker triplane to a vintage 1923 popcorn wagon from Old Orchard Beach.

EVERYTHING AT THE OWLS HEAD TRANSPORTATION MUSEUM WORKS

⌀ **Project Puffin Visitor Center** (207-596-5566; projectpuffin.org), 311 Main St., Rockland. Open daily June–Oct. 10–5 (until 7 Wed in July and Aug.), then weekends until Dec.; call for off-season hours. Free. Live-streaming mini cams and audio provide a virtual visit with nesting puffins. A joint project of National Audubon and Maine Audubon, this is a must-stop, with exhibits cleverly designed for children, like the "burrow" into which they can crawl and observe puffins feeding their chicks in a similar burrow.

Sail, Power & Steam Museum (207-701-7627; sailpowersteammuseum.org), 75 Mechanic St., Sharps Point South. Open May–Nov.; check the web or call for hours. $5 adults, $3 ages 7–16. Free over 65. Nineteenth-century sail and steam vessels are the focus of this evolving museum, sited in the historic, still-working Snow Family Shipyard. It's the brainchild of Captain Jim Sharp, who helped restore Maine windjammer *Stephen Taber* and Arctic explorer Donald MacMillan's schooner *Bowdoin* (now owned by the Maine Maritime Academy). The growing collection includes half models, marine paintings and prints, and a vintage-1674 brass navigational instrument owned by Nathaniel Bowditch.

⌀ **The Coastal Children's Museum** (207-975-2530; coastalchildrensmuseum .org), 75 Mechanic St. at Sharps Point South. $5 admission, under 2 free. Wed.–Sat. 10–4, Sun. 1–4. More than 16 hands-on, interactive displays include a touch tank, a full-sized sailboat, and a lobster trap you can crawl through.

✳ To Do

BICYCLING Side Country Sports (207-701-5100; sidecountrysports.com), 41 Main St., Rockland. Rent bikes year-round (and skis and snowboards) for one, five, or seven days.

CAPTAIN JIM SHARPE AT HIS SAIL, POWER & STEAM MUSEUM

LIGHTHOUSES

Penobscot Bay boasts the largest concentration of Maine's 68 lighthouses. Three in the Rockland area are accessible by land.

Rockland Breakwater Light (207-542-7574; rocklandlighthouse.com). Wear sensible shoes for the glorious but uneven almost-mile-long granite breakwater (turn off Rt. 1 onto Waldo Ave. just north of Rockland, then right onto Samoset Rd.; follow this to the end). The squat brick light- and foghouse attached to a gabled keeper's house is currently under renovation as a museum. It's open Memorial–Columbus Day weekends, Sat. and Sun. 10–5, weather and volunteers permitting.

Owls Head Light State Park, a classic, white conical tower 20 feet high, built in 1825 atop sheer cliffs, nonetheless has safe trails down one side to the rocks below—good for scrambling and picnicking. Now this light is also the headquarters of the American Lighthouse Foundation. Open Memorial–Columbus Day weekends, Sat.–Sun. 10–4, weather and volunteers permitting. From Rockland or the Owls Head Transportation Museum, take Rt. 73 to North Shore Dr. After about 2 miles you come to a small post office at an intersection. Turn left onto Main St., and after 0.25 mile make a left onto Lighthouse Dr. Follow signs to Owls Head Light State Park.

Just north of the village of Port Clyde (turn off Rt. 131 onto Marshall Point Rd.) is the **Marshall Point Lighthouse Museum** (207-372-6450; marshallpoint.org), open Memorial Day–Columbus Day, Sun.–Fri. 1–5 and Sat. 10–5; during May, weekends 1–5. Built in 1885, deactivated in 1971, this is a small light on a scenic point; part of the former lighthouse keeper's home is now a lively museum dedicated to the history of the town of St. George in general and the light station (established in 1832) in particular. Even if the lighthouse isn't open, this is a great spot to sit, walk, and picnic.

Goose Rocks Lighthouse (207-867-4747; beaconpreservation.org) is a freestanding "sparkplug-style" light 10 miles off Rockland in the Fox Islands Thorofare between Vinalhaven and North Haven, built in 1890. It offers two bedrooms and a bunk room, bath, kitchen with an Aga stove, and dining "snug," as well as balconies. "Keeper stays" are available with a donation.

✔ **Maine Lighthouse Museum** (207-594-3301; mainelighthousemuseum.com), Maine Discovery Center, 1 Park Dr., Rockland. Open daily Memorial Day–Oct., Mon.–Fri. 9–5, Sat. and Sun. 10–4. Check the website for winter hours. $5 adults, $4 seniors. Billed as the country's largest exhibit of lighthouse lenses and lifesaving artifacts, the display showcases more than a dozen Fresnel lenses. Most of these were amassed by Kenneth Black, former commander of the Rockland Coast Guard Station. Black realized that with the automation of lighthouses, historic lenses and other mechanical gear would largely be scrapped. He created the Shore Village Museum—known as "Mt. Lighthouse"—in a former Civil War veterans' hall, where he delighted in demonstrating the working foghorns. He lived to see the collection installed in this spacious hall, named in his memory. Note the LEDs locating Maine's working lighthouses. Exhibits include flashing lights, search-and-rescue gear, buoys, bells, rescue boats, and half models.

American Lighthouse Foundation (207-594-4174; lighthousefoundation.org), and Keeper's House Interpretive Center & Gift Shop, 186 Lighthouse Road, Owls Head. This is a nonprofit umbrella for the organizations supporting many lighthouses in need of preservation and/or renovation since automation. Thanks to these "Friends" groups, a number of lights have also become visitor-friendly. The foundation maintains a helpful information center picturing and mapping lights; gift items benefit restoration efforts. Check the ALF website for the latest about individual lighthouses.

WINDJAMMERS

In three days aboard a windjammer you can explore islands and remote mainland harbors that would take hundreds of miles of driving and several ferries to reach. Two-, three-, four-, five-, and six-day cruises are offered late May–mid-Oct. and run from $365 for two-day to $1,995 for nine-day trips. This includes all meals and—for our money—the most relaxing way to experience Penobscot Bay. All these vessels are inspected and certified each year by the Coast Guard. Most are members of the Maine Windjammer Association (1-800-807-WIND; sailmainecoast.com). Also see *Windjammers* in "What's Where" and "Camden/Rockport Area."

Schooner *American Eagle* (207-594-8007 or 1-800-648-4544; schooneramericaneagle .com), North End Shipyard, Rockland. One of the last classic Gloucester fishing schooners to be launched (in 1930), this 92-foot vessel continued to fish (minus her original stern and masts, plus a pilothouse) off Gloucester until 1983, when Captain John Foss brought her to Rockland's North End Shipyard and spent the next two years restoring and refitting her. The *Eagle* was built with an engine (so she still has one) as well as sails, and she offers some comfortable below decks spaces. The *Eagle* sails farther out to sea (to see whales and seabirds) than other windjammers and also offers a July cruise to Canada and a Labor Day sail to Gloucester (MA) to participate in a race. Most cruises are four to six days, accommodating 26 guests in 14 double cabins.

Schooner *Heritage* (207-594-8007 or 1-800-648-4544; schoonerheritage.com), North End Shipyard, Rockland. Captain Doug Lee likes to describe the graceful, 95-foot, 30-passenger vessel he designed and built as "the next generation of coasting schooner rather than a

Fred LeBlanc

THE LADONA, LEFT, AND AMERICAN EAGLE, TWO SCHOONERS OUT OF ROCKLAND'S WINDJAMMER FLEET

Georges River Bikeways is the name of a free map/guide that traces routes along the river and in its watershed area from Thomaston north into Liberty. Check with the Georges River Land Trust (207-594-5166), 328 Main St., Rockland.

BOATING Check with the chamber of commerce for a complete list of current excursions. Also see the Maine State Ferry Service under *Getting Around*. The ferry rides to both North Haven and Vinalhaven are reasonably priced and a good way to get out on the water. Both islands make good day trips, but Monhegan is far more walkable. See the Midcoast Islands chapter for details about all three islands.

Monhegan Boat Line (207-372-8848; monheganboat.com) in Port Clyde offers frequent 50-minute service to the island using its two boats, the *Elizabeth Ann* (built in 1995 for this replica." He notes that schooners were modified over the years to suit whatever cargo they carried. Here headroom in the cabins and the top of the companionways was raised to accommodate upright cargo, and the main cabin is an unusually airy, bright space in which to gather. Lee is a marine historian who, with his wife and co-captain, Linda, designed and built the *Heritage* in Rockland's North End Shipyard. Their two daughters, Clara and Rachel, sometimes sail as crew. Both captains are unusually warm hosts.

Schooner *Stephen Taber* (207-594-4723 or 1-800-999-7352; stephentaber.com) was launched in 1871 and is the oldest documented U.S. sailing vessel in continuous use. She is 68 feet long and accommodates 22 passengers. Cabins have windows; two are singles, four have full-sized double beds, and six have twins; all have sink with running water. Heads and showers are on deck. Captain Noah Barnes is the first second-generation windjammer captain, taking over the helm from his parents (both licensed captains), who restored the vessel and sailed her for 25 years. The *Taber* continues to have an enthusiastic following, known for her exceptional food, also for wine-tasting and other special-interest cruises.

Schooner *Victory Chimes* (207-594-0755 or 1-800-745-5651; victorychimes.com). "There was nothing special about this boat in 1900 when she was built," Captain Kip Files is fond of telling his passengers at their first breakfast aboard. "But now she's the only three-masted American-built schooner left. And she's the largest commercial sailing vessel in the United States." The *Chimes* is 132 feet long, accommodating 40 passengers in a variety of cabins (four singles, two quads, one triple, 12 doubles).

Schooner *Ladona* (207-596-4723 or 1-800-999-7352; windjammervacation.com) was built in East Boothbay as a racing yacht in 1922. Eighty-two feet long, she took special honors in the 1923 Bermuda Race and served in the Coast Guard during World War II. Eighteen months of rebuilding have transformed this schooner, which now holds six cabins, three with queens, two with two twins and one single, and a capacity of 16 guests. Captain J.R. Braugh, co-owner with Captain Noah and Jane Barnes (who also owned the *Stephen Taber*) sails amid the 2,200 islands of the cruising ground, stopping for a lobster bake and barbeque on one island, and excursions on others, and its small capacity lends to the calm tranquility on board.

Schooner *Isaac H. Evans* (207-594-7956 or 1-877-238-1325; isaacevans.com). A trim 22-passenger schooner dating (in part) to 1886, built for oystering in Delaware Bay, now back in service with owner-captain Brenda Thomas. There are 11 double berths, some side-by-side, some upper-lower bunks. One-, two-, three- and four-day and weeklong cruises are offered. Specializes in family trips; children 6 and over welcome on all cruises.

♻ ♂ Schooner *J&E Riggin* (207-594-1875 or 1-800-869-0604; mainewindjammer.com) was built in 1927 for the oyster-dredging trade. A speedy 90-footer, she was extensively rebuilt in the 1970s before joining the windjammer trade. Captains Jon Finger and Anne Mahle take 24 passengers in nine double and two triple cabins. Mahle is an outstanding chef, author of the cookbook *At Home, At Sea*. The *J&E Riggin* welcomes families with children ages 6 and up on a special family cruise

run, with both open top and lower enclosed decks) and the smaller *Laura B* (built in 1943 for World War II duty). The same boats are also used for seasonal "Puffin/Nature" cruises to Eastern Egg Rock and to view the area's lighthouses.

Captain Jack Lobster Boat Adventure (207-542-6852; captainjacklobstertours.com), 130 Thomaston St., Rockland. Memorial Day–Columbus Day. Lobster-boat tours that may include an onboard lobster dinner.

Daysails and longer: **Summertime Cruises** (1-800-562-8290; schoonersummertime .com), 115 South St., Rockland. Captain Bill Brown offers three- and six-day cruises on a 53-foot pinky schooner for up to six passengers throughout the summer, plus day sails in spring and autumn.

A Morning in Maine (207-691-7245; amorninginmaine.com), Rockland Middle Pier. A classic coastal ketch with an overall length of 55 feet, captained by marine biologist Bob Pratt, offers sails ranging from a few hours to overnights for up to 21 people.

Johanson Boatworks (207-596-7060 or 1-877-456-4267), 11 Farwell Dr., Rockland, offers sailboat charters. **Bay Sailing** (207-831-8425; bay-sailing.com), the Pier at the Pearl, Rockland, offers yacht charters, boat rentals, and an ASA sailing school.

SEA KAYAKING **Breakwater Kayak** (207-596-6895; breakwaterkayak.com), behind Landings Restaurant on Commercial St., Rockland. Two-hour to multiday guided kayaking tours.

Port Clyde Kayaks (207-372-8100; port clydekayaks.com), Port Clyde. Based at an outfitting shop near the Port Clyde wharf. Guided tours take you across Port Clyde Harbor to Marshall Point Light and among the nearby Georges Islands.

FISHING, HUNTING, AND CANOE-ING **Saltwater Fishing & Guide Service** (207-542-8915), **Cramer Guide Services** (207-233-3979), and **Ten Mile Guide Service** (207-542-8777).

Maine Outdoors (207-785-4496; main eoutdoors.biz), 69 Beote Rd., Union, offers fishing and other paddling adventures.

OWLS HEAD LIGHT

GOLF **Rockland Golf Club** (207-594-9322; rocklandgolf.com), 606 Old County Rd., Rockland. Open Apr.–Oct. This 18-hole public course gets high marks from pros; complete with a modern clubhouse serving meals from 7 AM.

✳ Green Space

BEACHES ⚓ **Johnson Memorial Park**, Chickawaukee Lake, Rt. 17, 2 miles north of downtown Rockland. Restrooms, picnic area, a sand beach, and warm water add up to the area's best swimming, good for small children.

⚓ **Birch Point Beach State Park**, also known as Lucia Beach, off Ash Point Rd. in Owls Head. Sandy, with smooth boulders for sunning, wooded walking trails, and picnic benches. Marked from Rt. 73 (Dublin Rd. to Ballyhac Rd.).

Drift Inn Beach in Port Clyde, down Drift Inn Rd. by the Harpoon Restaurant, just off Rt. 131; a small beach in a great spot.

WALKING/PICNICKING **Rockland waterfront**. The area's most spectacular stretch of the **Rockland Harbor Trail** begins on the Samoset Hotel property just over the Rockport line and runs 1.7 miles out along the Rockland Breakwater to the lighthouse.

Harbor Park at the public landing marks the beginning of the trail south along the water past Sandy Beach Park (picnic benches) to Mechanic St. and on to Snow Marine Park. Along the way you'll find benches, flowers, and a gazebo.

Owls Head Light State Park. This classic lighthouse is set into a beautiful point with walks and views on both the bay and harbor sides, picnic tables. See *Lighthouses* for directions.

Waldo Tyler Wildlife Sanctuary, Buttermilk Lane (off Rt. 73), South Thomaston, is a birding spot on the Weskeag River.

The Georges River Land Trust (207-594-5166), 8 N. Main St., Rockland, publishes a map/guide to the Georges Highland Path, a foot trail through the hills of the Georges River watershed. Maps are available at the chamber of commerce.

✳ Lodging

HOTEL **250 Main Hotel** (207-594-5994; 250mainhotel.com), 250 Main St., Rockland. Twenty-six rooms, some with panoramic views, bring contemporary style to a former sardine capital of the Maine coast, now shifting far from those blue-collar roots. A boat-building company, Lyman Moore, contributed the high design in the interior. Ten-foot ceilings and balconies in the water-view rooms are prized, but sleepers may suffer from a noisy street. Continental breakfast doesn't skimp on fresh fruit and pastries; from 4 to 6 there's a free glass of wine. $159 to 400, depending on season.

Rockland Harbor Hotel (207-594-2131; rocklandharborhotel.com), 520 Main St., Rockland. This renovation of the old Navigator Hotel is a convenient spot and perfect for ferry travel in the early morning. A variety of rooms suit singles and big families. All of the rooms look out over the ferry waiting area and water. WiFi and hot breakfast are included. $109 in January to $290 during the Lobster Fest.

INNS AND B&BS

IN ROCKLAND

((ᵢ)) **Berry Manor Inn** (207-596-7696 or 1-800-774-5692; berrymanorinn.com), 81 Talbot Ave., P.O. Box 1117. This expansive 19th-century shingle-style mansion is a sumptuous retreat. The 12 guest rooms, divided among the second and third floors of the mansion and the second floor of the carriage house, all have a queen- or king-sized bed, flat-screen TV,

phone, air-conditioning, and luxurious bath; almost all have a gas fireplace. A two-room, two-bath suite in the carriage house has a separate living room. $125–305 for rooms, $420 for the suite mid-June–mid-Oct., less off-season, including a multicourse breakfast and a guest pantry stocked with goodies that include homemade pies.

((ᵢ)) **LimeRock Inn** (207-594-2257 or 1-800-546-3762, limerockinn.com), 98 Limerock St. P. J. Walter and Frank Isganitis are the innkeepers of this 1890s Queen Anne–style mansion on a quiet residential street with a wraparound front porch and two living rooms to relax in. The eight guest rooms, all with private bath, are opulently furnished with antiques. The turret room is over the top, but our favorite is the airy Island Cottage room at the back of the house, opening on the garden. Amenities include a 24-hour guest pantry and computer. $169–249 ($129–169 off-season) includes a full breakfast.

✿ ✹ ♿ ((ᵢ)) **Granite Inn** (207-594-9036 or 1-800-386-9036; oldgraniteinn.com), 546 Main St. An 1840s mansion built of local granite, set in a flower garden across from the Maine State Ferry Terminal (also the Concord Coach stop). Ideal if you come without a car and are bound for an island, but innkeepers Edwin and Joan Hantz have added plenty of other reasons to stay here. Joan is a graphic artist with an eye for blending contemporary furnishings and antiques. There are eight guest rooms, including two suites. Two front second-floor bedrooms—the largest—overlook the water and ferry terminal. The two-room suites (the second bedrooms have twin beds) represent good value for families or couples who don't mind sharing a bath. $95–215 per night includes a breakfast featuring fresh fruit, from-scratch baked goods, bacon or sausage, and a hot entrée, maybe lemon crêpes with wild blueberry compote.

✪ ♿ (ᵢ) **The Captain Lindsey House** (207-596-7950 or 1-800-523-2145; lindseyhouse.com), 5 Lindsey St. This was built in 1837 as one of Rockland's first inns, and the feel is that of a small, boutique hotel. With richly paneled public rooms and nine spacious guest rooms (one handicap accessible), it's both a gem and the most convenient lodging to the Farnsworth Museum and Main Street shops. Run by schooner captains Ken and Ellen Barnes, who a lso restored and operated the windjammer *Stephen Taber* for more than 25 years, each guest room is different, but all have air-conditioning, TV, and private bath. $131–228 includes a full buffet breakfast, served in the garden, weather permitting.

🐾 ✎ **Ripples Inn at the Harbor** (207-594-2771 or 1-800-375-5771; ripplesinnattheharbor.com), 16 Pleasant St. Open year-round. Sandi Dillon provides rooms that are not overly fussy but nicely decorated with an eye to comfort. There are four rooms and a family suite (accommodating four) with a whirlpool tub and private entrance. In addition to the usual common spaces, "The UN-common Room" has a microwave, fridge, and TV. $100–240 (for a two-bedroom suite) with full breakfast.

ON SPRUCE HEAD AND ON THE ST. GEORGE PENINSULA

🐾 (ᵢ) **Craignair Inn** (207-594-7644 or 1-800-320-9997; craignair.com), Clark Island Rd., Spruce Head 04859. Main building open year-round. Michael and Joann O'Shea offer 20 guest rooms that are divided between the main house (Room 12 is a corner room with a queen and three windows with water views) and the Vestry, a former chapel set in gardens in the rear with water views from the second floor. The dining room overlooks the water and is open to the public for dinner (see *Dining Out*). Walk across the causeway to the Clark Island shoreline and a granite quarry that's good for swimming. In high season from $90 for a room with shared bath to $200 for a private room with water view, $80–140

off-season, including a full breakfast. $20 extra for a pet.

🐾 (ᵢ) **East Wind Inn** (207-372-6366 or 1-800-241-8439; eastwindinn.com), 21 Mechanic St., P.O. Box 149, Tenants Harbor 04860. Open May–Oct. This tall, distinctive, 19th-century building, an inn since the 1920s, when patrons arrived by steamboat, offers expansive waterside grounds and superlative views from the veranda and a sunny dining room, as well as from six updated suites and two bedrooms, all with private bath, and 10 rooms in the Meeting House annex. In 2012 Randy Deutsch took over from longtime innkeeper Tim Watts and has sustained the inn's traditional ambience while adding updated comforts. From $172 in high season; $148–200 off-season, including a full breakfast. See the inn's restaurant and Quarry Tavern in *Dining Out*.

✎ (ᵢ) **Weskeag Inn** (207-596-6676 or 1-800-596-5576), Rt. 73, P.O. Box 213, South Thomaston 04858. Open year-round. Handy to the Owls Head Transportation Museum and to Knox County Regional Airport (pickups provided, perhaps in one of Gray Smith's antique cars). A handsome and hospitable 1830s home overlooking the Weskeag estuary in the tiny village of South Thomaston. The lawn (available for weddings) sweeps to the river's edge. Six attractive guest rooms have private bath; two share or are rented as a suite. Our pick would be the third-floor rooms with dormers and water views. $135–150 in-season, $100–112 off-season, including breakfast.

🦞 ✎ (ᵢ) **Ocean House Hotel** (207-372-6691 or 1-800-269-6691; oceanhousehotel.com), P.O. Box 66, Port Clyde 04855. Open May–Oct. This friendly old village inn is the logical place to spend the night before or after taking the neighboring ferry to Monhegan. Built to board local mariners in the 1820s, it's earned a loyal following under longtime ownership by the Murdock family. Second- and third-floor rooms include one apartment. This is a good place for a single traveler, thanks to the single rates and the ease of meeting fellow guests, but families are welcome. Rooms from $110, $125–145 with private bath, less solo, full breakfast included. No credit cards.

Mill Pond House Bed & Breakfast (207-372-6209; millpondhouse.com), 453 Port

EAST WIND INN, TENANTS HARBOR

Clyde Rd., Tenants Harbor 04860. Leslie Kor-pinen's rambling 1860s farmhouse is a homey, attractive B&B with three second-floor guest rooms, from $70 single (shared bath) to $105 double (private bath), morning muffins and fruit included.

MOTELS ♿ (('·)) **Trade Winds Motor Inn** (207-596-6661 or 1-800-834-3139; tradewinds maine.com), 2 Park Dr., Rockland 04841. Open year-round. This locally owned, 120-unit motel is composed of several wings, obviously added over the decades. Units vary from "non-view" basics (from $74 off-season) to balcony rooms ($134–154) and "deluxe suites" ($214–234 in high season). Amenities include a health club, pool, and restaurant.

❊ Where to Eat

DINING OUT

IN ROCKLAND

✪ **Primo** (207-596-0770; primorestaurant .com), 2 S. Main St. (Rt. 73). Open May–Jan., daily in summer, otherwise Wed.–Mon. 5:30–9:30; call first. Reservations are a must. This very special restaurant, rated among the best in Maine, grows much of what it serves. "Primo" was chef and co-owner Melissa Kelly's grandfather, a butcher. Kelly follows tradition by raising her own pork and making several kinds of sausages as well as preparing cuts of meats and overseeing the gardens, greenhouses, and beehives on the 4-acre, intensely cultivated property. With two James Beard Foundation Best Chef: North-east Awards, the second for Primo, she knows how to make your dinner, from mushroom pizza ($18) to sautéed pork scaloppine with prosciutto in sage-mushroom Madeira. The house cannoli are crisp, rich, and excellent. Delectable pastas are $32–34, entrées $33–45. The menu, along with a pizza and small plates, is also available upstairs, a lively space with a long copper bar and $1-per-oyster nights.

Suzuki's Sushi Bar (207-596-7447; suzuki sushi.com), 419 Main St. Open Tue.–Sat. for dinner. Where better to sample the full variety of the ocean's yield than a sophisticated

Japanese restaurant? Keiko Suzuki's extensive menu includes raw nigiri dishes and spicy sushi rolls, entrées such as shrimp with shiitake and many delectable salads and vegetarian dishes. Entrées $10–30.

In Good Company (207-593-9110; ingoodcompanymaine.com), 415 Main St. Open from 4:30 except Mon. No reservations. A wine bar in a living-room-like setting, serving salads, cheeses, nibbles, and light meals such as cedar-planked salmon and cold-sliced beef tenderloin. $5–20.

✪ ❧ **Café Miranda** (207-594-2034; cafemiranda.com), 15 Oak St. Open year-round 5–9:30. Reserve for dinner. In 1993 Kerry Altiero was the first chef in Rockland to offer the hip kind of dining for which the city has since become known. His small restaurant has, however, neither expanded (unless you count seasonal café tables) nor moved from its side street. Single diners sit up at the counter watching an amazing variety of food emerge from the brick oven, with more than 40 entrées on the menu, including a kale dish roasted with mushrooms, garlic, and feta, followed by mussels roasted with curry. Entrées $19–28.

The Pearl (207-593-8629), 273 Main St., Rockland. The site on top of the water and the

KERRY ALTIERO USES HIS WOOD-FIRED OVEN IN CREATIVE WAYS AT CAFÉ MIRANDA

fresh oysters are all about Maine at its oceanfront best, with seafood from crab cakes and lobsters to a swordfish special.

✪ **Rustica** (207-594-0015; rusticamaine.com), 315 Main St. Open Mon.–Sat. 11–3 and 5–10, Sun. 11–8; Tue.–Sat. off-season. No reservations. High quality at reasonable prices, a pleasant atmosphere, and decent wine

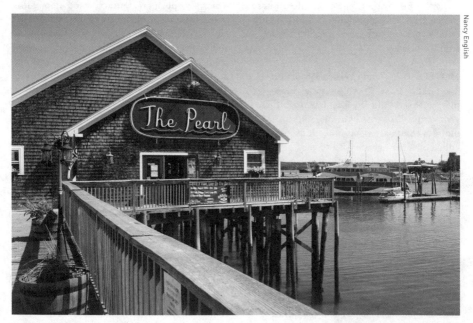

THE PEARL IN ROCKLAND

LOBSTER

McLoons Lobster Shack (207-593-1382; mcloonslobster.com), 315 Island Rd., South Thomaston. Open 11–7 Memorial Day to Columbus Day. Corn chowder and lobster stew along with the lobster just off the boats you watch pull in and unload.

Miller's Lobster Co. (207-594-7406; millerslobster.com), 83 Eagle Quarry Rd., Spruce Head. Open 11–7 Late June to early Sept. Lobsters (of course), steamers, a view of the sea, and fresh blueberry pie.

are a winning combination for this "cucina Italiana." Chef-owner John Stowe serves up hearty soups, wild mushroom pasta, and three cheese lasagna (house-made pasta layered with portobello, crimini, and shiitake mushrooms, Swiss chard, and three cheeses, served on a bed of marinara). Entrées from $12 for pizzas; $17–21 for pasta and entrées such as veal Marsala and pan-roasted cod.

Salt Water Farm (207-236-0554; saltwaterfarm.com), 24 Central St. In the Union Hall Building's spacious first floor, Salt Water Farm is both a restaurant and a cooking school, sourcing supplies from the local water and farms. Celery root and little neck clam chowder, a crab melt, baked beans, and lemon meringue pie were on one menu, which changes often. $13–22.

Archer's on the Pier (207-594-2435; archersonthepier.com), 58 Ocean St. Open Mon.–Sat. 11–10, and for jazz brunch on Sun. Chef-owner Lynn Archer, the dynamo powering the Brass Compass Café, runs Archer's at a prime site overlooking both the harbor and bay (formerly the Boathouse). Plenty of seafood: $31 in 2013 for twin lobster dinner; $27 for duck confit with butternut risotto. Lunch includes the lobsters along with slow-roasted beef and gravy on toast.

ELSEWHERE

✪ **The Slipway** (207-542-1829; theslipway
maine.com), 24 Public Landing, Thomaston. Open May–Oct., lunch and dinner except Tue. Scott Yakovenko enjoys an enthusiastic following at this waterside venue (formerly the Harborside). We recommend the fried oysters, crisp and still juicy, grilled scallops

and grilled swordfish with pesto, topped off with perfect blueberry pie, a dessert staple made by Scott's mother. The chef's specialty remains a seafood-studded bouillabaisse. The dining room is good looking, but best views are from the porch and seasonal deck and wharf. Entrées $18.50–24.

Thomaston Café and Bakery (207-354-8589; thomastoncafe.com), 154 Main St., Thomaston. Open year-round Wed.–Sat. 7:30–2, Sun. brunch 11–2. Dinner Fri. and Sat. 5:30–8. Lunch on fresh-made soups, great sandwiches, fish cakes with home fries, salads. The dinner menu might include lobster ravioli with brandied lobster cream sauce. Entrées $17–25.

The East Wind Inn's **Wan-e-set Restaurant** and **Quarry Tavern** (207-372-6366 or 1-800-241-8439; eastwindinn.com), 21 Mechanic St., Tenants Harbor. Open May–Oct., tavern open year-round except for time off in January: call first. Local specialties prepared with creativity.

Craignair Inn & Restaurant (207-594-7644), Clark Island Rd., off Rt. 73, Spruce Head. Open May–Oct. for dinner; Fri., Sat. in spring and fall. Walk the shore before dining by a water-view window. Signature dishes include Craignair crabcakes served with risotto with Dijon rémoulade and fresh vegetables ($18), seared scallops and black Japonica rice ($23), and crispy pan-seared duck breast with cranberry orange reduction. Wines are limited but reasonably priced.

EATING OUT

IN ROCKLAND

Atlantic Baking Co. (207-596-0505), 351 Main St. Open Mon.–Sat. 1–6, Sun. 8–4; Tue.–Sat.

in winter. Sited across from the Farnsworth Museum, this busy place seduces passersby with the aroma of fresh-baked bread. There's a blackboard sandwich menu and plenty of help-yourself salads and such in deli cases. Yummy soups and breads. The plastic and Styrofoam do seem at odds with the from-scratch, PC ethos of the place.

Home Kitchen Café (207-596-2449; homekitchencafe.com), 650 Main St. Fresh and vibrant ingredients, attentive and skillful cooking turn out invigorating breakfast omelets—bacon, roasted red pepper, and Cooper cheese, for instance—and a good haddock sandwich. Many items to choose from, and both breakfast and lunch are served all day.

✪ **The Brass Compass Café** (207-596-5960), 305 Main St. Open Mon.–Sat. 5–3, Sun. 6–3. Lynn Archer's friendly eatery is a find. Seafood stews, sandwiches, and salads, generous portions, good value. Yummy onion rings and fries. The house special is a lobster club, with one and a quarter lobsters, bacon, lettuce, and tomato on Lynn's toasted, fresh-made white bread.

✪ ((ᵖ)) **Rock City Café** (207-594-4123), 316 Main St., open 7–7, until 9 Thu.–Sat. Rock City Coffee—chai and teas, too—along with bagels, scones, and pastries baked on premises. The soups and wraps are exceptional, and sandwiches come on Borealis sourdough. We feasted on a summer-veggie grilled panini loaded with roasted eggplant, squash, red onion, and tomatoes. Local beer and wine. In sleek new quarters, still the town meeting and gathering place. Live music, weekends.

Claws (207-596-5600; clawsrockland maine.com), 743 Main St., Rockland. A takeout place with a covered deck overlooking Rockland Harbor, this is a seasonal fresh seafood place open from Mid-May to the beginning of Oct. Some of the lobster is picked here and about 7 ounces go into the lobster roll. The place won the award for best lobster mac' and cheese at the Lobster Lollapalooza in 2016; the picnic tables are the best spot in town to crack open a lobster for dinner.

Sunfire Mexican Grill (207-594-6196), 488 Main St. Open for lunch Tue.–Sat. 11–3, for dinner Wed. and Sat. 5–8. This is exceptional Mexican fare, all the basics but with very fresh veggies (try the mango avocado salad) and just the right taste. Beer, wine.

Nancy English

CLAWS FOR AN OUTDOOR LOBSTER DINNER

⚓ **Rockland Café** (207-596-7556; rockland cafe.com), 441 Main St. Open daily 5:30 AM–9 PM. This is a reliable family eatery, good for fish-and-chips, soups, salad, clam rolls, and daily specials. Warning: The crabcakes are more like crab pancakes. Look for the green-and-white-striped awning.

⚓ **Trackside Station** (207-594-7500; tracksideme.com), 4 Union St. Open daily for lunch and dinner. Ironically this is just off the beaten track and as a result it's either briefly mobbed or relatively empty. The vintage railroad station makes an attractive dining space. It's decorated with blowup photos from Rockland's past. We lunched happily on a fresh crabmeat cheese melt.

⚓ **Wasses Wagon**, 2 N. Main St. A local institution for hot dogs.

✴ Entertainment

The Strand Theatre (207-594-0070; rockland strand.com), 345 Main St., Rockland. Vintage 1923, a beautifully restored classic downtown 350-seat theater offering films, concerts, and live performances including a summer Wed. evening series of Bay Chamber Concerts, also streamed performances ranging from the Metropolitan Opera to the Super Bowl.

The Farnsworth Art Museum (207-596-6457; farnsworthmuseum.org) in Rockland stages a year-round series of Sunday films and other weekly cultural events.

✳ Selective Shopping

ART AND CRAFTS GALLERIES

IN ROCKLAND

Arts in Rockland (AIR; artsinrockland.com) publishes a widely available downtown map of the two dozen galleries hosting **First Friday Receptions** (5–8) during the seasonal **Art Walks**. Galleries include the oldest (since 1982) and prestigious **Caldbeck Gallery** (caldbeck.com), at 12 Elm St.; goldsmith Thomas O'Donovan's **Harbor Square Gallery** (harborsquaregallery.com), filling three floors of a former bank building (374 Main St.) with art but also featuring fine jewelry. The **Dowling Walsh Gallery** (dowlingwalsh.com) is another highlight. Others to check: **Art Space Gallery** (207-594-8784; artspacemaine.com), 342 Main St. Also check out **Playing with Fire! Glassworks and Gallery** (playingwith fireglassworks.com), 497 Main St.

Archipelago Fine Arts (thearchipelago .net) at the Island Institute (386 Main St.) represents roughly 300 artists and craftspeople on "hinged" as well as real islands. Changing exhibits. The **Island Institute** (207-594-9209; islandinstitute.org) is a nonprofit organization focusing on the human dimension of Maine's 15 surviving year-round island communities (a century ago there were 300). The monthly *Working Waterfront* newspaper, as well as the glossy *Island Journal*, focus on shared concerns ranging from fisheries to schools to mapping.

The Museum Store at the Farnsworth Art Museum (207-596-5789; shop.farnsworth museum.org) is itself a standout trove of quality gifts including jewelry, books, and toys as well as art books, cards, and prints.

SPECIAL SHOPS

ALONG MAIN ST. IN ROCKLAND

Hello Hello Books (207-593-7780; hellohello books.com), No. 316. In the rear of the Rock City Café but with its own side-street entrance. Open daily except Tue. Lacy Simons offers a wide but obviously selective stock of used and new books. The **Black Parrot** (207-594-0138; No. 328) specializes in its colorful fleece-lined reversible garments but carries a mix of clothing, toys, cards, and more. The

Grasshopper Shop (207-596-6156; No. 400) is a major link in a small Maine chain featuring clothing and a widely eclectic and colorful inventory. **Fiore Artisan Olive Oils and Vinegars** (207-596-0276; No. 503) is all about extra-virgin unfiltered olive oils and aged balsamic vinegars from the world over; sample them in the tasting room.

SOUTH FROM THE JUNCTION OF RTS. 1 AND 73, WHICH BEGINS AT THE SOUTHERN END OF MAIN ST., ROCKLAND

Rock City Coffee Roasters (207-594-5688; rockcitycoffee.com), 252 Main St. Roasted on the spot, the source of this widely distributed brew.

✪ **Trillium Soaps** (207-593-9019; trillium soaps.com), 216 S. Main St. A find for all of us with dry skin. Using organic olive oil, Peter and Nancy Digirolamo make small batches on the spot in some two dozen varieties, like rosemary-lime, clove, and bay rum. Also moisturizing bath soap including palm and coconut. Reasonably priced.

✪ **Jess's Market** (207-593-5068; jess market.com), 118 S. Main St. This is definitely the place in Rockland to buy lobster and a wide variety of very fresh fish, clams, mussels, oysters, and crab. Also the best takeout crab rolls.

Breakwater Vineyards (207-594-1721, breakwatervineyards.com), 35 Ash Point Dr., Owls Head (turn off Rt. 73 onto North Shore Dr.). Open Memorial Day–Columbus Day weekends, Wed.–Sun. noon–5. This 32-acre estate, with expansive views across the harbor and bay to the Camden Hills, has some 3,000 vines of hardy vinifera grapes. Bill and Jean Johnson currently offer oaked and unoaked Chardonnays, a dry Riesling, a Pinot Noir, and a blueberry wine.

Art of the Sea Galleries (207-594-9396; artofthesea.com), 5 Spruce Head Rd. (Rt. 73), displays nearly 100 museum-quality, full-rigged ship models; also half models and hundreds of nautical paintings and prints.

ALONG RT. 131 TO PORT CLYDE

Check out **St. George Pottery** (4.5 miles south of Rt. 1), George Pearlman's combination studio and contemporary ceramics gallery.

Noble Clay (529 Port Clyde Rd.) in Tenants Harbor, open year-round, displays Trish and Steve Barnes's white-and-blue-glazed porcelain pottery with whimsical and botanical designs. **Mars Hall Gallery** (marshallgallery .net), 621 Port Clyde Rd., Tenants Harbor, is well worth a stop. **Ocean House Gallery** (207-372-6930; oceanhousegallery.com), end of Port Clyde Rd., is a seasonal gallery in the inn. **The Store Upstairs** over the Port Clyde General Store is worth a look: kitchenware and gadgets, oilcloth, children's books and toys, gifts.

IN THOMASTON

Maine State Prison Showroom (207-354-9237), 358 Main St. (Rt. 1), Thomaston, at the south end of town. Open daily 9–5. A variety of wooden furniture—coffee tables, stools, lamps, and trays—and small souvenirs, all carved by inmates. Prices are reasonable, and profits go to the craftsmen.

    Oyster River Winegrowers (207-354-7177; oysterriverwinegrowers.com). The Tasting Room, 12 Oyster River Rd. (Rt. 131 north), Thomaston, is open May–Halloween, usually noon–6. Brian Smith is an experienced vintner who is just beginning to harvest his own vines. In the meantime he's souring Merlot grapes from the Finger Lakes and Petite Syrah from California.

IN UNION

Savage Oaks Vineyard & Winery (207-785-2828; savageoaks.com), 174 Barrett Hill Rd. (north of the junction of Rts. 17 and 131). Tasting room open Mother's Day–Oct., then weekends until Christmas, 11–5. Elmer (Buddy) and Holly Savage have been growing grapes on their 95-acre farm for a decade. A variety of red and white wines are available for sampling, along with three blueberry wines made from their 15 acres of wild blueberries.

    Sweetgrass Farm Winery & Distillery (207-785-3024; sweetgrasswinery.com), 347 Carroll Rd., marked from Rt. 17 west of Union village. Tasting room open daily Mother's Day through Dec., 11–5. Keith and Constance Bodine produce fruit wines and highly respected spirits using Maine-grown apples, cranberries, blueberries, and rhubarb. Best sellers and prize winners are many: We love Back River gin and the apple brandy. The property also includes the **Carroll Farm Trail**, part of the Medomak Valley Land Trust; visitors are welcome to hike, snowshoe, and ski.

❋ Special Events

June: **Summer Solstice Night**, a Main Street Rockland street fair.

    July: **Thomaston Fourth of July** festivities include a big parade, footraces, live entertainment, a crafts fair, BBQ, and fireworks. The **North Atlantic Blues Festival** (midmonth), Harbor Park, Rockland (northatlanticbluesfestival.com) is huge. **Maine Windjammer Parade of Sail** (midmonth), Rockland Harbor. **Friendship Sloop Days** (last weekend) includes a regatta and festivities in Rockland and a parade, BBQ, and children's activities in Friendship.

    August: **Maine Lobster Festival** (first weekend, plus the preceding Wed. and Thu.), Harbor Park, Rockland (mainelobsterfestival .com). This is probably the world's biggest lobster feed, prepared in the world's largest lobster boiler. Patrons queue up on the public landing to heap their plates with lobsters, clams, corn, and all the fixings. King Neptune and the Maine Sea Goddess reign over the event, which includes a parade down Main Street, concerts, an art exhibit, and more. **Maine Boats, Homes & Harbor Show** (midmonth), Harbor Park, Rockland. **Union Fair and State of Maine Wild Blueberry Festival** (third week; unionfair.org)—a real agricultural fair with tractor- and ox-pulling contests, livestock and food shows, a midway, and the crowning of the Blueberry Queen.

    November–December: **Rockland Festival of Lights** begins on Thanksgiving—parade, Santa's Village, sleigh rides.

VINALHAVEN, NORTH HAVEN, AND MATINICUS

The Fox Islands Thorofare, a rowable stretch of yacht-filled water, separates Vinalhaven and North Haven, two islands of more than a dozen out in Penobscot Bay. The two differ deeply, even geologically. It's said that they were once oceans apart. Frequent Maine State Ferry service links both islands to Rockland but no ferry stops at both.

Maine's largest off-shore island, Vinalhaven is the size of Manhattan but home to fewer than 1,200 residents (Maine's largest year-round island community) plus an equal number of widely scattered summer people. Life eddies around the village of Carver's Harbor at the island's southern end. Vinalhaven was once a world-known source of granite, and two former quarries are now swimming holes. There are also wildflower-filled moors, wooded coastal paths, and sheltered paddling places.

There is, however, no yacht club or golf course, and yachtsmen will be hard-put to find a guest mooring among the fishing boats in Carver's Harbor, home to one of the world's largest lobstering fleets. In recent years three 1.5-megawatt wind turbines have been installed on the north side of Vinalhaven, capable of generating all the electricity needed for both islands.

North Haven is half as big, with just 355 year-round residents, some 1,500 in summer. Founded well over a century ago by Boston yachtsmen, its summer colony includes some of the country's wealthiest and most influential families. The former general store by the ferry dock is now Waterman's Community Center, with a 140-seat state-of-the-art theater, the venue for summer lectures, concerts, and plays.

The village of North Haven offers gift shops and galleries, seasonal restaurants, and gracious year-round lodging and dining. Beyond the village a 10-mile loop beckons bicyclists through rolling, open fields, spotted with buttercups and idyllic farmhouses, most of them summer homes. Sheltered Pulpit Harbor is a favorite mooring for windjammers and yachtsmen. There's also a public golf club and a private yacht club, the North Haven Casino, home to the island's distinctive dinghies.

GUIDANCE Town offices on **North Haven** (207-867-4433) and **Vinalhaven** (207-863-4471) field most questions. The Vinalhaven Chamber site is vinalhaven.org. On-island, pick up a free copy of *The Wind*, the island's newsletter. For North Haven, check northhavenmaine .org.

GETTING THERE **Maine State Ferry Service** (in Rockland: 207-596-5400). The islands are serviced by different ferries; from Rockland it's a 75-minute ride. Day-trippers rarely have a problem walking on; the bike fee is nominal. Each ferry takes a set number of cars, and only a handful of these spaces can be reserved; otherwise, cars are taken in order of their position in line. For the morning boats, it's wise to be in line the night before. It doesn't make sense to bring a car unless you plan to stay awhile.

Note: **Concord Coach Lines** (concordcoachlines.com) stops daily at the Rockland Ferry Terminal.

Penobscot Island Air (207-596-7500; penobscotislandair.net) will fly you in from Portland or Boston as well as Rockland to either Vinalhaven or North Haven.

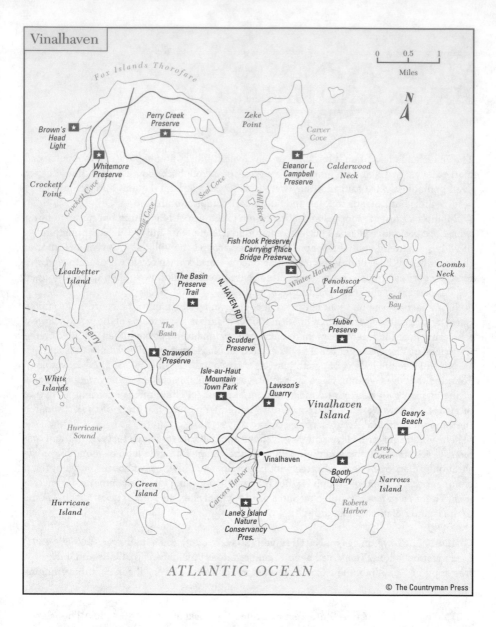

GETTING AROUND *By boat:* Shuttle service between North Haven and Vinalhaven is possible through **J. O. Brown & Sons Boatyard** (207-867-4621) in North Haven. Try calling from the phone on the boat landing on the Vinalhaven side of the Thorofare. On Vinalhaven the **Tidewater Motel** rents cars and Vinalhaven Taxi (207-720-0056) gets you around. Also see *Bicycling.*

Note: Day-trippers to North Haven will find shopping and food within steps of the ferry dock, but on Vinalhaven it's 0.4 mile from the ferry to the village and another mile or so to the quarries and Lanes Island Nature Preserve. A bike comes in handy.

WHEN TO COME Only June–Aug. can you count on all visitor-geared facilities being open on both these islands. September, however, is beautiful.

✳ To See

The Vinalhaven Historical Society Museum (207-863-4410; vinalhavenhistoricalsociety .org), 41 High St. Open Mon.–Fri., also Sat., July & Aug. 11–4, mid-June–mid-Sept. Within walking distance of the ferry, worth the uphill climb. An outstanding community museum housed in the former church, built in 1838 in Rockland and floated over on a barge in 1878. It has also served as a theater and skating rink. Displays feature the island's granite industry.

The first order for Vinalhaven granite was shipped to Boston in 1826 to build a jail, but production skyrocketed after the Civil War, when granite was the preferred building material for the country's building boom. On an island map, 40 red pins mark the sites of major quarries, but there are also countless "motions," or backyard pits.

Museum displays also depict island life and other industries, such as fishing and lobstering (in the 1880s the Basin, a large saltwater inlet, was used as a giant holding tank, penning as many as 150,000 lobsters until prices peaked). Knitting horse nets (to keep off flies) in intricate designs were yet another island industry that's now an art form.

The Victorian-era village of Carver's Harbor straddles a causeway and narrow land strip between the harbor and Carver's Pond. A boomtown dating from the 1880s, when Vinalhaven was synonymous with granite, the village is built almost entirely of wood, the reason why many of the best of its golden-era buildings are missing. The strikingly Victorian Star of Hope Lodge, owned by artist Robert Indiana, is one of two surviving Second Empire mansard buildings (there were once four) marking the center of town. The 6 foot eagle on the town landing is limestone. Still, it appears to be a fitting memorial to the island's granite industry and craftsmen. Also on the town landing, the recently restored Old Fire Engine House displays "Old Rueben," a vintage-1888 fire truck. You'll also find amazing antique equipment and public restrooms. A Galamander, a huge wagon used

GEARY BEACH, VINALHAVEN

SWIMMING AT LAWSON'S QUARRY

to carry stone from island quarries to schooners, stands in the small park at the far end of Main St. For some reason the neighboring Vinalhaven Public Library (207-863-4401; vinalhavenpubliclibrary.org), 6 Carver St., is sheathed in pink granite from Jonesboro, Maine.

ON NORTH HAVEN

North Haven Village itself is charming, with several shops, galleries, and a choice of places to eat. Pulpit Harbor, the island's second, much smaller community several miles away, is the site of the general store and the North Haven Historical Society's North Island Museum (open Sun. in July and Aug., 2–4:30 Tue., Wed. 9–12). A general store, period kitchen and living room, special exhibits.

✳ To Do

BICYCLING If you take care to keep to the roadside, both North Haven and Vinalhaven are suited to bicycling. Bike rentals are available at Bikesenjava (see *Bicycling* in "Rockland") near the ferry terminal. A more limited selection is available at Tidewater Motel on Vinalhaven and Nebo Lodge on North Haven.

In North Haven we recommend the North Shore Rd. In Vinalhaven we recommend the Granite Island Rd. out along the Basin or following Main St. the other direction out to Geary's Beach (see *Green Space*). The North Haven Rd. is an 8-mile slog up the middle of

Vinalhaven, but the rewards are great: Browns Head Light, the Perry Creek Preserve, and views of North Haven.

GOLF **North Haven Golf Club** (207-867-2054), open June–Sept. A waterside course, nine holes.

SEA KAYAKING **Tidewater Motel** in Carver's Harbor, Vinalhaven, rents kayaks and will transport you to put-ins like the Basin, a long tidal inlet that's great for spotting seals.

SWIMMING On Vinalhaven, ✪ **Lawson's Quarry**. From the middle of Carver's Harbor, turn (uphill) at the Bank Building and continue up and up High St., past the historical society, and then turn right on North Haven Rd. for 0.5 mile. For Booth Quarry begin at the east (uphill) end of Main St., 1.5 miles past the Union Church (E. Main St.).

✳ Green Space

ON VINALHAVEN

The **Vinalhaven Land Trust** (207-863-2543; vinalhavenlandtrust.org) maintains 17 preserves mapped on its website and in handouts available at 12 Skoog Park near the ferry dock. Our favorites include: Lane's Island Preserve, a 15-minute walk from town, 40 acres of fields, marsh, moor, and beach with trails along the beach and up into the meadows facing open ocean; Grimes Park, beside the ferry terminal, a 2-acre point of rocky land with two small beaches; and Geary's Beach—explore the trails, lunch at the picnic tables, and enjoy a view of Isle au Haut and Matinicus.

✳ Lodging

ON VINALHAVEN

✪ 🐾 ✑ (((•))) **Tidewater Motel and Gathering Place** (207-863-4618; tidewatermotel.com), 15 Main St., Carver's Harbor. Open except Jan.–Feb. "I don't want to leave this room," we wrote about Room 16, an aerie with a deck overlooking a harbor full of lobster boats, all turned into the wind like gulls. Phil and Elaine Crossman's waterside motel spans a tidal stream connecting the harbor with Carver's Pond. The water swooshing under rooms once powered a gristmill, granite-polishing mill, and blacksmith shop. The 19 units come in varied sizes and shapes, including suites and efficiencies, one fit for reunions or a small conference. Rooms have harbor-side decks and all have a microwave, coffeemaker, small fridge, full bath, and small TV. The Crossmans also loan bikes and rent kayaks,

meet the ferry, and help guests around the island. All the town's eating options are within steps. Elaine Crossman is a noted artist, and Phil is the island chronicler. His genuinely funny book of essays, *Away Happens*, captures island life. $185–210 for rooms, from $115 off-season. $8 for each additional person over two; kids 10 and under are free, and families with more than one older kid are only charged for one; morning coffee, juice, and muffins are included. Inquire about Millstream Cottage.

🐾 **Libby House** (207-863-4696; libbyhouse1869.com), Water St. Open June–Sept. This proud home was built in 1869 by T. E. Libby, namesake of an island ferry (he was responsible for bringing the Maine State Ferry Service to Vinalhaven). It's on the edge of the village, on the way to Lane's Island Preserve. Guests share the long sunporch with its rocking chairs and upright piano, as well as a living room with a fireplace and access to the dining room and kitchen fridge. The four

VIEW FROM THE TIDEWATER MOTEL

guest rooms (private baths) are furnished with comfortable antiques. There's also a downstairs two-bedroom apartment with a full kitchen. Longtime host Philip Roberts asks guests to remove their shoes on entering. $110–140 for rooms, $160 for the apartment. Pets accepted Sept.–June.

ON NORTH HAVEN

✪ 🐾 ⚲ ♿ (ᵖ) **Nebo Lodge** (207-867-2007; nebolodge.com), 11 Mullins Lane, P.O. Box 358. Open May–Oct. Built handsomely in 1912 as an inn but privatized in 1956, it was reopened in 2006 by a dedicated local group of women who included now U.S. Representative Chellie Pingree and her daughter Hannah. Their goal was to preserve it both as a place for residents to dine together and as an island entrée for visitors. The inn building offers nine crisp guest rooms, four with shared bath, many with tufted wool rugs, throw pillows, and linens by nationally known designer and island native Angela Adams. Two third-floor rooms are the brightest and most attractive, both with private bath. The sitting room is delightful, with a rosy Angela Adams rug. There's a strong commitment here to all things green and local. The dining room with its working fireplace is justly busy (see *Dining Out*). Your cell phone may not work, but there is wireless Internet. All rooms have a small fridge. Bikes are available, and the innkeeper can arrange a boat trip. High season (July–Columbus Day) $160–$295, $350 for garden unit. There is a wheelchair-accessible garden unit with kitchenette in a neighboring house. Rates include a continental breakfast. Pets are accepted on a case-by-case basis; cleaning fee. Check the website for frequent special events.

COTTAGE RENTALS **Davidson Realty** (207-863-2200; maineislandliving.com) specializes in summer rentals. High-season weekly vacation rentals range from $700 for a village house to $4,000 for a summer mansion overlooking the Fox Islands Thorofare. Also check vinalhaven.org.

✳ Where to Eat

ON VINALHAVEN

Salt (207-863-4444; saltvh.com), 64 Min St. Open Thu.–Sun. for dinner, Sun. brunch, Fri.–Sat. off-season. A limited menu focused on local seafood and Maine-raised meat, house-made specialties from pâté to pastries.

The Haven (207-863-4969), 49 Main St. Open May–Dec. Tory Pratt is the island's favorite caterer and the back, harbor-side dining room (reservations recommended) offers superb seafood dishes, also pasta and steak. Entrées $17–25. Inquire about the more casual café.

⌒ **The Harbor Gawker** (207-863-9365), Main St., middle of the village. Open mid-Apr.–mid-Nov., Mon.–Sat. 11–8. Lobster rolls, crabmeat rolls, and baskets of just about anything. Owned by the Morton family since 1975, this is a great, casual spot with views of the millrace and Carver's Pond. Order at the counter: from-scratch soups and chowders, seafood baskets, and blueberry pies, along with ice cream and a dairy bar. It's a big menu, from hot dogs through salads and wraps to quesadillas and lobster dinners.

Surfside (207-863-2767), Harbor Wharf, W. Main St. Donna Webster opens at 3:30 AM for the lobstermen, breakfast until 10:30. A great harbor-side breakfast spot with tables on the deck and specials like a crabmeat or lobster omelet, or a tomato herb cheese omelet with fish cakes.

Homeport Family Restaurant (207-963-2318), 62 West Main St. Open 5–2. A cheery new place for breakfast/lunch. Lobster omelets and house baking, lunch soups and sandwiches; the reuben and BLT get rave reviews.

Greet's Eats (207-863-2057), West Main St. near the ferry dock. Greta McCarthy's food truck gets raves for lobster rolls and burgers.

ON NORTH HAVEN

Nebo Lodge (207-867-2007; nebolodge.com), 11 Mullins Lane, North Haven Village. Open July and Aug., Tue.–Sat.; Fri. and Sat. in May, June, and Sept.–mid-Oct. Reserve. This is a very special inn (see *Lodging*) right in the

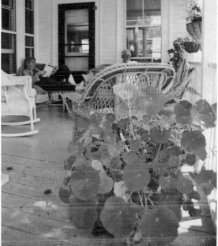

NEBO LODGE, NORTH HAVEN

village with a menu that changes nightly. Chef Amanda Hallowell is committed to using as much locally grown produce as possible. A "first taste" might be fried green tomatoes with chive dressing or the house-made pickle plate with locally produced chèvre and rye bread. On a June evening we dined on roast organic duck, raised at Turner Farm, with rhubarb crème brûlée and cardamom-ginger ice cream. The à la carte menu ranges from $8 for an appetizer to $36 for Lobster Bohemienne and includes "light suppers" such as hand-ground burger. The full bar offers classic cocktails as well as island originals like the "Oystertini." Free transport across the Thorofare is offered to patrons coming from Vinalhaven. Inquire about roundtrip "dinner cruises" from Rockland Harbor and Stonington.

Cooper's Landing (207-867-2060). Open July and Aug. for lunch and dinner; check in June and Sept. Mickey Campbell runs this handy little restaurant, which offers seating inside and out at the summer heart of the village. Burgers, veggie options, lobster and crab rolls, fish cakes, chowder and salads, and wine and beer. The low-cal chocolate shake, made from unsweetened chocolate and hemp milk, comes highly recommended.

Calderwood Hall (207-867-4700), North Haven Village. You can't miss it, the large distinctive village building that's been many things. Currently it houses seasonal market (Tues.–Sat., 9–6) selling fresh produce, pre-made sandwiches and provisions, and pizza restaurant (Wed.–Sun., 5–9) eat-in or take-out with a gradually expanding menu, also cocktails and, as of 2017, **North Haven Brewing Co.** (housed in the basement) brew on tap.

✳ Entertainment

Waterman's Community Center (207-867-2100; watermans.org), North Haven Village. This exceptional center right at the ferry dock includes a theater, the venue for frequent productions, concerts, and presentations. Check the calendar for contra dance, workshops, and children's activities. Open daily year-round 7–4 for coffee, tea, muffins, sodas, and bagels in an airy, nonprofit community center with couches, tables, board games, and newspapers.

Smith Hokanson Memorial Hall at Vinalhaven High School (207-863-4800) in Carver's Harbor is the stage for lectures, theater, and a variety of community activities.

✳ Selective Shopping

IN CARVER'S HARBOR ON VINALHAVEN

New Era Gallery (207-863-9351; neweragallery.com), Main St. Open Memorial Day–Dec. Painter and printmaker Elaine Austin Crossman's gallery shows work by some of Maine's most prominent painters, sculptors, photographers, and fiber artists. Note the widely celebrated three-dimensional traditional knotted netting sculptures by Stephanie Crossman; also check out the sculpture garden and special exhibits.

✐ **Go Fish** (207-863-4193), Main St. Open seasonally, Tue.–Sat. 10–4:30. A great kids-geared shop with books, healthy toys, games, penny candy, original island T-shirts, and much more.

Five Elements Gallery & Studio (207-863-2262), 50 Main St. Original jewelry in dichroic glass, worth a look.

Second Hand Prose, Main St. Open Mon.–Sat. 9–4:30. Run by Friends of the Library and featuring secondhand books. Good selection of Maine and maritime titles.

IN NORTH HAVEN VILLAGE

North Haven Gift Shop and Gallery (207-867-4444). Open Memorial Day–mid-Sept., 9:30–5. Eva Hopkins now manages her family's gift shop, an island institution since 1954. It meanders on and on, filled with pottery, books, accessories, jewelry, and much more, including bags by the island's famous young designer, Angela Adams. Gallery exhibits change frequently. Hopkins keeps running accounts for summer families and knows the names of members of as many as six generations of a family when they walk in.

Hopkins Wharf Gallery (207-867-4647). Open July and Aug. 10–5; by appointment in spring and fall. Owned by David Hopkins (brother of Eric) and David Wilson, this is a contemporary gallery featuring work by island-related artists. It's also a source for works by longtime North Haven summer resident Frank Benson.

✳ Special Events

Year-round: **North Haven Arts Enrichment Presentations** include exceptional plays, concerts, and lectures performed in Waterman's Community Center in North Haven Village at the ferry landing. For details, phone 207-867-2100; watermans.org.

Christina Tree

FOURTH OF JULY PARADE, VINALHAVEN

Summer season: **Concerts**, primarily classical, chamber, and jazz, are staged on both islands, sponsored by Fox Islands Concerts.

July 4: **Parade** in Vinalhaven.

July–August: **Saturday Farmers' Market** at the ball field, North Haven Village, features crafts as well as produce. **Saturday Flea Market**, 10 AM in the field next to the Galamander, Carver's Harbor, Vinalhaven. **Union Church Baked Bean Supper** (every other Thu. in summer), Vinalhaven. Check vinalhaven landtrust.org for the schedule of frequent morning walks and evening talks.

For details about other regular occurrences on both islands, consult *The Wind*, a weekly newsletter published on Vinalhaven.

Matinicus

Home to some 30 hardy souls in winter, most of whom make their living lobstering, Matinicus's population grows to about 200 in summer. Maine's outermost island, it lies 23 miles at sea beyond the outer edge of Penobscot Bay. Quiet and unspoiled, it's a haven for birds, with some 650 species identified. Walking trails thread the meadows and shore, and there are two sand beaches—one at each end of the 750-acre island. Matinicus Rock is offshore, a protected nesting site for puffins, a lure for birders in June and July. Matinicus and neighboring Ragged Island (better known as Criehaven, the name of its seasonal village) are the setting for Elizabeth Ogilvie's trilogy: *High Tide at Noon, Storm Tide,* and *Ebb Tide.*

GETTING THERE The flying time via **Penobscot Island Air** (207-596-7500) from Owls Head is 15 minutes, but flights may be canceled because of weather—and the fog can hang in there for days. That's when you contact matinicusexcursions.com; it's an hour's ride. Inquire about puffin watching trips. The **Maine State Ferry** (207-596-2022) takes 2¼ hours to ply between Matinicus and Rockland, four times a month May–Oct., and once a month the rest of the year. At this time there is no overnight lodging, but check for rentals.

Camden/Rockport Area

0 1 2
Miles

Pripet

MAIN RD

Islesboro I.

N

East
Northport   Bayside

DURHAM
STATE
FOREST

Northport

Islesboro

MAIN RD

52

PRIEST RD

BEECH HILL RD

Pitcher
Pond

Grindel
Pt.

Spruce
Head

Dark Harbor

+ Ducktrap
Mtn.

Ferry

WARREN
ISLAND
ST PK

Warren I.

Pendleton
Pt.

BELMONT RD   SLAB CITY RD

Ducktrap

Lincolnville Beach

Job I.

52

173

Bald Rock
Mtn.
+

1

173

Lincolnville
Center

YOUNGTOWN RD

CAMDEN HILLS
STATE PARK

Penobscot Bay

235

Lake
Megunticook

Mt.
Megunticook
+

Fernald's Neck
Nature
Conservancy
Preserve

52

Mt.
Battie
+

Curtis I.

105

Hope

HOWE HILL RD

COBB RD

Camden

Bald
Mtn. +

Conway
House

235

BARNSTOWN RD

Goose R.

BEECH ST

Rockport

Ragged
Mtn. +

Camden
Snow
Bowl

Alford
Lake

S.
Hope

PARK ST

90

W.
Rockport

17

ROCKVILLE ST

1

235

17

MT. PLEASANT
ST

MILL ST

E. Union

© The Countryman Press

Smack on Rt. 1, Camden is the most popular way station between Kennebunkport or Boothbay Harbor and Bar Harbor. Seemingly half its 19th century captains' homes are now B&Bs. Shops and restaurants line a photogenic harbor filled with private sailing and motor yachts. It's also a poor man's yacht haven—open year-round—with a thriving fishing industry. The ski area would make a good winter vacation destination as well as a summer tour.

Here, in 1936, artist Frank Swift refitted a few former fishing and cargo schooners to carry passengers around the islands in Penobscot Bay. He called the boats windjammers. Half a dozen members of Maine's current windjammer fleet are still based here (the rest are in neighboring ports), and several schooners offer daysails. You can also get out on the water in an excursion boat or a sea kayak.

From the water you can see two aspects of Camden not apparent from land. The first is the size and extent of the Camden Hills. The second is the size and number of the palatial old waterside "cottages" along Beauchamp Point, the rocky promontory separating Camden from Rockport. Here, as in Bar Harbor, summer residents were wise and powerful enough to preserve the local mountains, seeding the creation of the present 6,500 acre Camden Hills State Park, one of Maine's more spectacular places to hike.

Camden's first resort era coincided with those colorful decades during which steam and sail overlapped. As a stop on the Boston–Bangor steamboat line, Camden acquired a couple of big (now vanished) hotels. In 1900, when Bean's boatyard launched the world's first six-masted schooner, onlookers crowded the ornate neighboring steamboat wharf to watch.

In contrast with Boothbay and Bar Harbor, Camden has always been a year-round town and never overdependent on tourism. Camden's early business was, of course, building and sailing ships. By the mid-1800s half a dozen mills lined the series of falls on the Megunticook River, just a block or two from the waterfront. The vast wooden Knox Woolen Company—the "Harrington Mill" portrayed in the movie *Peyton Place*—made the felts used by Maine's paper mills to absorb water from paper stock. It operated until 1988, and now holds a hodgepodge of restaurants, businesses, and homes.

Culturally enriched by its sophisticated populace—workaday residents, retired diplo-

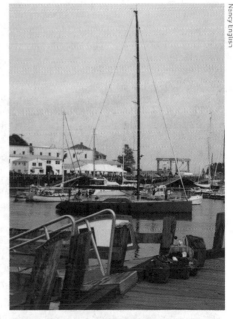

LUGGAGE AWAITS DEPARTURE TIME ON THE WHARF IN CAMDEN HARBOR

Nancy English

mats, military and intelligence officers, and summer people alike—Camden (along with Rockport) offers a bonanza of music, art, and theatrical productions, all of surprising quality. There are also world-renowned programs in filmmaking, computer science, woodworking, and photography.

Ironically, only a small fraction of the thousands of tourists who stream through Camden every summer takes the time to discover the extent of its beauty. The tourist tide eddies around the harborside restaurants, shops, and galleries and continues to flow on up Rt. 1 toward Bar Harbor. Even in August you are likely to find yourself alone atop Mount Battie (accessible by car as well as on foot) or Mount Megunticook (highest point in the Camden Hills), or in the open-sided Vesper Hill Children's Chapel, with its flowers and sea view. Few visitors see, let alone swim in, Megunticook Lake or set foot on the nearby island of Islesboro.

A decade or two ago you could count on your fingers the number of places to stay here, but Camden has since become synonymous with B&Bs. A total of some 1,000 rooms can now be found in hotels, motels, inns, and cottages as well as the B&Bs between Camden and neighboring Lincolnville and Rockport.

GUIDANCE **Penobscot Bay Regional Chamber of Commerce** (207-596-0376 or 1-800-562-2529; camdenrockland.com), 2 Public Landing (and also at its home base, 1 Park Dr., Rockland). Open daily Memorial Day through the Columbus Day weekend, Mon.–Fri. 9–5 and Sat., Sun. 10–4; then weekdays and 10–2 Sat. The chamber's visitors centers serve the Rockland and Camden area, which includes Owls Head, Thomaston, the peninsula villages, and the islands.

GETTING THERE *By air:* **Knox County Regional Airport**, at Owls Head, about 10 miles from Camden, offers daily flights to and from Boston. **Bangor International Airport** and **Portland International Jetport** offer connections to all parts of the country.

CAMDEN HARBOR

Nancy English

By bus: **Concord Coach Lines** (1-800-639-3317; concordcoachlines.com) stops on Rt. 1 at the Maritime Farms, just south of Camden, en route from Bangor to Portland and Boston and vice versa.

By limo: **Mid-Coast Limo** (207-236-2424 or 1-800-937-2424; midcoastlimo.com) makes runs from Portland International Jetport by reservation. **Schooner Bay Limo** (207-594-5000; schoonerbaytaxi.com) goes to Portland and elsewhere.

By car: Our preferred route, to bypass Rt. 1 traffic, is to take I-295 to Gardiner, then follow signs to Rt. 226. When this road ends, take a right onto Rt. 17, which winds through pretty countryside to Rt. 90, and then intersects with Rt. 1 leading into Camden.

PARKING is a problem in July and August. In-town parking has a stringently enforced two-hour limit (just 15 minutes in a few spots, so be sure to read the signs). There is parking just a two- to five-minute walk away; the chamber recommends parking on Chestnut St., Union St., Mechanic St., and Washington St. The chamber has a map that highlights all-day parking areas.

WHEN TO COME Camden and Rockport are open year-round with a thriving fishing industry; the ski area makes this area a good winter destination as well as a summer tour. But for sailing and swimming, summer is the time to come, and fall foliage contrasts beautifully with the blue water.

❋ Villages

Rockport's harbor is as picturesque as Camden's, and the small village is set high above it Its quiet, subdued charm provides a nice respite from the hustle of Rt. 1. Steps (you have to look closely for them) lead down to Marine Park, a departure point in 1816 for 300 casks of lime shipped to Washington, DC, to help construct the Capitol. In the small park you'll see the restored remains of a triple kiln, a saddleback steam locomotive, and a granite sculpture of André the Seal, the legendary performer who drew crowds every summer in the early and mid-1980s. The village (part of Camden until 1891) includes the restored Rockport Opera House, site of Bay Chamber Concerts, the Maine Media Workshops program, and restaurants and shops.

Lincolnville's landmarks—the Lobster Pound Restaurant, Maine State Ferry to Islesboro, and the Whale's Tooth Pub, formerly a customhouse with a big fireplace—serve as centerpieces for proliferating shops, restaurants, and B&Bs. The beach offers a nice swimming spot on hot days.

❋ To See

LIGHTHOUSE Curtis Island Light. A public park, the island is nevertheless accessible only by boat, and the lighthouse is not open to the public. The best views are from sightseeing cruises out of Camden Harbor, but if you walk down to where Bayview St. connects with Beacon, there's a good lookout.

MUSEUMS ✐ ♿ **Old Conway Homestead and Cramer Museum** (207-236-2257; conway house.org), Conway Rd. (off Rt. 1 at the Camden–Rockport town line). Open July and Aug., Wed.–Sat. 1–4; admission charged. Open June and Sept. by appointment. Administered by the Camden-Rockport Historical Society, this restored early-18th-century farmhouse features antiques from several periods. The barn holds collections of carriages, sleighs, and

EXCURSIONS

Drive or, better yet, bicycle around **Beauchamp Point**. Begin on Chestnut St. in Camden and follow this peaceful road by the lily pond and on by the herd of **belted Galloway cows** (black on both ends and white in the middle). Take Calderwood Lane through the woods and by the **Vesper Hill Children's Chapel**, built on the site of a former hotel and banked with flowers, a great spot to get married or simply to sit. Continue along Beauchamp Ave. to Rockport Village to lunch or picnic by the harbor, and return via Union St. to Camden.

early farm tools; don't miss the Victorian privy, blacksmith shop, and 1820 maple sugar house, where sugaring demonstrations are held each spring. **The Cramer Museum** displays local memorabilia and changing exhibits.

Schoolhouse Museum (207-789-5445), Rt. 173, Lincolnville Beach. Open Mon., Wed., and Fri. 1–4, June–Oct., other times by appointment. Admission is free. A small museum detailing the history of Lincolnville, with exhibits that change often and include stereoptics and tintypes, early settlers' tools, and Native American artifacts. The museum also publishes *Ducktrap: Chronicles of a Maine Village*, an excellent book on local history, and *Staying Put in Lincolnville, Maine*, both by local author Diane O'Brien.

OTHER SITES Cellardoor Vineyard (207-763-4478; mainewine.com), 367 Youngtown Rd., Lincolnville, 11–6 daily, May–Oct., and **Cellardoor Winery at the Villa** (207-236-2654), aka The Yellow House, Rt. 1 (at Rt. 90), Rockport; noon–5 daily in winter, 11–6 Apr.–Oct. Vines in this 7-acre Lincolnville vineyard were completely removed in 2008 and 2009. Some were dead and others didn't produce the best wines, according to Bettina Doulton, who purchased the business in 2007. New grape varietals planted, better suited to the climate, include Seyval Blanc, Frontenac Gris, and Marquette. To supplement the crop, the business buys grapes from the West Coast to make, for instance, its excellent Viognier.

✳ To Do

BICYCLING 🚲 **Camden Hills State Park**, Rt. 1, Camden, has a 10-mile (roundtrip) ride through the woods on a snowmobile trail. Bikes are not allowed on hiking trails. The **Camden Snow Bowl** also offers a number of rides through woods and swamps, as well as riding on ski trails. It's a hearty ride, but the views from the top are terrific.

🚲 **Georges River Bikeways**. The Georges River Land Trust (207-594-5166) puts out a pamphlet highlighting several good biking routes, with many scenic spots within the Georges River watershed.

Maine Sport Outfitters (207-236-7120 or 1-800-722-0826; mainesport.com), Rt. 1, Rockport, rents Raleigh hybrids as well as bike trailers and car racks for a day or extended periods. Rentals include helmets, locks, water bottles, and cable. **Map Adventures** (1-800-891-1534; mapadventures.com) makes a very readable small map of bike routes and trails in the Camden Hills, stocked here.

BOATING See also **Windjammers**.

Yacht charters are offered spring to autumn along the Maine coast. Most charters run for a week, although sometimes it's possible to charter a boat just for a long weekend, with or without crew. For more information, contact **Johanson Boatworks** (207-596-7060 or 1-877-4-JOHANS), which rents everything from J-40 sloops to Ericson 38s. **Rockport**

Charters (207-691-1066; rockportcharters.com) offers, with advance notice, 20-passenger, three-hour wildlife charters to see puffins, eagles, ospreys, and more. Leaving from both Camden and Rockland, as well as Rockport, Captain Robert Iserbyt also provides transportation for workers out to North Haven.

It would be a shame to be in Camden and not spend some time on the water. The two-hour sailing excursions are a wonderful way to get a taste of what the harbor has to offer if your time is limited. Remember to bring a jacket, because the air can get chilly once you're offshore, even on a sunny day. Wander down the wooden boardwalk and check the offerings, which include:

♪ **Schooner *Appledore II*** (207-236-8353; appledore2.com), an 86-foot schooner (the largest of the daysailing fleet), has sailed around the world and now offers several trips daily, including sunset cruises. Licensed bar.

Schooner *Surprise* (207-236-4687; camdenmainesailing.com), a traditional, historic, 57-foot schooner, offers entertaining, informative two-hour sails. Captain Jack and wife Barbara Moore spent seven years cruising between Maine and the Caribbean, educating their four children on board in the process.

Schooner *Olad* (207-236-2323; maineschooners.com), a 57-foot schooner, offers two-hour sails and charters.

Schooner *Heron* (207-236-8605 or 1-800-599-8605; woodenboatco.com), runs lobster lunch, midafternoon, and evening sails (BYOB, with hors d'oeuvres served) out of Rockport for a maximum of 36 passengers. With typically eight to 20 passengers on the regular sails, this 65-foot schooner, built in 2003 in Camden by its owners, is available for private trips.

♪ ***Betselma*** (207-236-4446), a motor launch, provides one-hour coastal and two-hour island trips (owner Les Bex was a longtime windjammer captain) out of the harbor and down the coast.

♪ ***Lively Lady Too*** (207-236-6672 or 418-839-7933; livelyladytoo.com), a traditional lobster boat, takes passengers on two-hour ecotours that can include watching lobster traps being hauled and swinging in close to an island for bird-watching. A monitor shows video of the ocean floor.

Schooner *Lazy Jack II* (207-230-0602). Two-hour sails and private charters from Camden Harbor with Captain Sean O'Connor.

♪ **Maine State Ferry** from Lincolnville Beach to Islesboro (207-734-6935). At $10 roundtrip per passenger, $27.50 per vehicle, and $8.50 per bicycle, this is the bargain of the local boating scene. An extra $12 each way secures your reservation. (See *Getting There* under "Islesboro.")

BOWLING **Oakland Park Bowling Lanes** (207-594-7525), 714 Commercial St., Rockport. Susan and Joe Plaskas have updated this old-fashioned bowling alley with refinished lanes, air-conditioning, and tile flooring, retaining the 1950s decor. Video games and air hockey too.

GOLF **Goose River Golf Club** (207-236-8488; gooseriver.com), Simonton Rd., Rockport. Nine holes, but you can play through twice using different starting tees. Cart rentals; clubhouse. Tee times recommended any time of the week; you can request up to a week in advance.

♪ **Golfers Crossing Miniature Golf** (207-230-0090). Water hazards and obstacles complete this mini golf experience on Rt. 1 in Rockport.

Samoset Resort Golf Course (clubhouse, 207-594-1431), Rockport, has an 18-hole, par-70 course with seven oceanside holes and ocean views from 14 holes. A renovation includes a redesigned 18th hole featuring a stone seawall, a remodeled 185-yard, par-three 5th hole, and renovations to hole 4. The clubhouse has a pro shop, locker rooms, and the **Clubhouse Grille**. Carts are available.

HIKING **Bald Rock Mountain.** This 1,100-foot mountain in Lincolnville once had a ski area at the top. Great views of Penobscot Bay and the Camden Hills. You'll find the trailhead 1.25 miles down a dirt road from the gate on Ski Lodge Rd. (off Youngtown Rd.). The climb is about 0.5 mile long and moderate. Ask about overnight camping at the Camden Hills State Park headquarters on Rt. 1 in Camden.

Georges Highland Path is a 40-mile trail network created and maintained by the Georges River Land Trust (207-594-5166; grlt.org). Trails wind through the Oyster River Bog, a magnificent semi-wilderness area with a 7.2-mile trail that links the Thomaston Town Forest with the Ragged Mountain section. A map put out by the trust details distances and hiking times and shows where the trailheads are.

Coastal Mountain Hiking (207-236-7731), Camden, offers guided hikes and packed lunches.

See also **Beech Hill** and **Camden Hills State Park** in *Green Space.*

SEA KAYAKING **Ducktrap Sea Kayak Tours** (207-236-8608; ducktrapkayak.com), Lincolnville Beach, offers two-hour and half-day guided tours in Penobscot Bay. Most patrons are first-time kayakers. Group and family tours, rentals, and lessons.

Maine Sport Outfitters (207-236-8797 or 1-800-722-0826; mainesport.com), on Rt. 1 just south of Rockport, offers courses in kayaking, guided excursions around Camden Harbor and out into Penobscot Bay, and island-based workshops. They also rent kayaks and canoes (also see *Special Learning Programs*).

SPECIAL LEARNING PROGRAMS ✒ **Camden Yacht Club Sailing Program** (207-236-4575; off-season, 207-236-7033), Bayview St., Camden, provides sailing classes for children and adults, boat owners and non-boat owners, during late June, July, and Aug.

🦞 **Maine Media Workshops College** (207-236-8581; mainemedia.edu), 70 Camden St., Rockport. This nationally respected year-round school for photography, cinematography, television production, and related fields offers a choice of 200 programs that vary in length from one week to three months for every skill level. The faculty includes established, recognized professionals from across the country; the students come from around the world. Housing is provided for most of the students, and the school helps arrange accommodations for others. Also a gallery with changing exhibitions, open to the public.

Maine Sport Outfitters (207-236-8797; mainesport.com), Rockport. This Rt. 1 complex is worth a stop whether you're up for adventure sports or not. The place has evolved from a fly-fishing and canvas shop into a multitiered store that's a home base for a wide variety of local kayaking tours and multiday kayaking workshops geared to all levels of ability, based at facilities on Gay Island.

Center for Furniture Craftsmanship (207-594-5611; woodschool.com), 25 Mill St., Rockport. June–Oct. Hands-on one- and two-week workshops for novice, intermediate, and advanced woodworkers and cabinetmakers. Twelve-week intensive courses are also offered three times a year. A nine-month comprehensive course runs from Sept. to June.

SWIMMING ✒ Saltwater swimming from Camden's **Laite Memorial Park and Beach**, Upper Bayview St.; at **Lincolnville Beach**, Rt. 1 north of Camden; and in Rockport at **Walker Park**, across the road from Marine Park. Freshwater swimming at **Megunticook Lake**, Lincolnville (**Barret Cove Memorial Park and Beach**; turn left off Rt. 52 northwest of Camden), where you'll also find picnic grounds and a parking area; **Shirttail Beach**, Camden (Rt. 105); and at the **Willis Hodson Park** on the Megunticook River, Camden (Molyneaux Rd.). At the **Penobscot Bay YMCA** (207-236-3375), Union St., visitors can pay a day-use fee that entitles them to swim in the Olympic-sized pool (check hours for family swimming, lap swimming, and other programs); use the weight rooms, rock climbing gym and sauna; and play basketball in the gym.

TENNIS There are two public tennis courts at the **Camden Snow Bowl** on Hosmer Pond Rd. (first come, first served). In addition, **Samoset Resort** (207-593-1545), Rockport, has outdoor courts, as does the **Rockport Recreation Park** (207-236-9648).

WALKING The Camden-Rockport Historical Society (207-236-2257) has prepared a brochure (available at the chamber of commerce and the Cramer Museum) with a 2.5-mile walk past historic buildings. The brochure includes historical details and a sketch map. An expanded bicycle or car tour encompassing two towns is also included.

WINDJAMMERS ⚓ Windjammer cruises are offered late May–mid-Oct. Nine traditional tall ships sail from Camden, Rockport, and Rockland on three- to six-day cruises throughout Penobscot Bay. For brochures and sailing schedules, contact the **Maine Windjammer Association** (1-800-807-WIND; sailmainecoast.com).

Angelique (1-800-282-9989; sailangelique.com), Camden, is a 95-foot ketch that was built expressly for the windjammer trade in 1980. Patterned after 19th-century English fishing vessels, she offers 15 passenger cabins, a pleasant deck-level salon with piano, below-decks showers, and rowboats and paddleboards made by Capt. Dennis Gallant for exploring the coast.

Lewis R. French (1-800-469-4635; schoonerfrench.com), Camden, was launched on the Damariscotta River in 1871 and is the oldest documented vessel in America's windjammer fleet. Before becoming a passenger vessel, the *French* carried cargo such as lumber, fire wood, bricks, granite, lime—even Christmas trees—along the coast. She had three major rebuilds, the most recent in 1976 when she was brought into passenger service. Sixty-five feet long, the *French* accommodates 21 passengers in 13 private cabins with freshwater sinks and portholes that open. Hot, freshwater shower on board. Captain Garth Wells enjoys

WINDJAMMER *GRACE BAILEY*

getting his guests actively involved in the experience of sailing an authentic 19th-century schooner.

Mary Day (1-800-992-2218; schoonermaryday.com), Camden, was the first schooner built specifically for carrying passengers. At 90 feet, she's among the swiftest; Captains Barry King and Jen Martin have extensive sailing experience. Features include a fireplace and parlor organ and hot, freshwater showers on the deck. The *Mary Day* accommodates up to 28 passengers, and meals include a New England boiled dinner, baked goods made in the galley's woodstove, and a lobster bake on every cruise.

Grace Bailey, Mercantile, and Mistress (207-236-2938 or 1-800-736-7981; mainewind jammercruises.com), Maine Windjammer Cruises, Camden. For years known as the *Mattie*, *Grace Bailey* took back her original name following a thorough restoration in 1990. Built in 1882 in New York, the 81-foot *Grace Bailey* once carried cargo along the Atlantic coast and to the West Indies. She has belowdecks showers. *Mercantile* was built in Maine in 1916 as a shallow-draft coasting schooner; 78 feet long, she has been in the windjammer trade since its beginning in 1942. There are belowdecks showers. *Mistress*, the smallest of the fleet at 46 feet, carries just six passengers. A topsail schooner built in 1960 along the lines of the old coasting schooners, she is also available for private charter. All three cabins have private heads, but there is no shower on board.

❄ Winter Sports

CROSS-COUNTRY SKIING **Camden Hills State Park** (207-236-3109) marks and maintains some trails for cross-country skiing, and there's a ski hut on Mount Battie (see *Green Space*).

Tanglewood 4-H Camp (207-789-5868 or 1-877-944-2267), 1 Tanglewood Rd., off Rt. 1 near Lincolnville Beach. Ungroomed, scenic cross-country trails that wend through woodlands and along streams. Maps with a description of trails are at the kiosk at the trailhead on the loop of the road.

DOWNHILL SKIING ✈ **Camden Snow Bowl** (207-236-3438; camdensnowbowl.com), Hosmer Pond Rd., Camden. With an 850-foot vertical drop, 11 trails for beginners through experts, a new chairlift and a new conveyor lift following a $6.5 million investment, Camden Snow Bowl has a base lodge, rental and repair shop, ski school, and cafeteria, plus the Jack Williams Toboggan Chute. In early February the Snow Bowl hosts the annual U.S. National Toboggan Championship Races at the toboggan chute with outlandishly costumed teams making mad runs down the chute at 40-plus miles an hour, bottoming out on the ice-covered Hosmer Pond. $39 full-day adult weekend pass, $29 students.

❄ Green Space

✈ ♿ **Camden Hills State Park** (207-236-3109; off-season, 207-236-0849), 280 Belfast Rd., Rt. 1, Camden. $6 nonresident adults, $4 Mainers, $1 ages 5–11; free under 5 and over 65 for residents, $2 nonresidents 65 and older. In addition to Mount Battie, this 6,500-acre park includes Mount Megunticook, one of the highest points on the Atlantic seaboard, and a shoreside picnic site. You can drive to the top of Mount Battie on the road that starts at the park entrance, just north of town. At the entrance pick up a Camden Hills State Park brochure, which outlines 19 trails with distance and difficulty level. In winter many of the trails convert to cross-country ski runs, given snow. There are 106 campsites available May 15–Oct. 14.

Warren Island State Park, also administered by Camden Hills State Park, is just a stone's throw off the island of Islesboro. The park features picnic tables, trails, and tent sites. Accessibility is the problem: You can arrange to have a private boat carry you over from the mainland, rent your own boat in Camden, or paddle out in a sea kayak. Because of this, the island boasts a peace and quiet often hard to find on the mainland in high season.

MERRYSPRING NATURE CENTER

Marine Park, off Russell Ave. (just after you cross the bridge), Rockport. A nicely landscaped waterside area with sheltered picnic tables. Restored lime kilns and a locomotive remind visitors of the era when the town's chief industry was processing and exporting lime. During a stroll you're likely to see several painters capturing the picturesque harbor on canvas.

Merryspring Nature Center (207-236-2239; merryspring.org), Camden. Open to the public year-round during daylight hours. A 66-acre private preserve with walking trails; herb, daylily, demonstration, and rose gardens; raised beds; and an arboretum. The Goose River borders the preserve, accessible via Conway Rd. from Rt. 1 in Camden. Birders frequent the gardens on the lookout for barred owls and warblers. If you're lucky you'll see white-tailed deer, ermine, porcupine, raccoon, rabbit, and even moose. Weekly talks in summer. Free to members, $5 for nonmembers.

Fernald's Neck Preserve (207-236-7091; coastalmountains.org). Owned by the Coastal Mountains Land Trust, located at the end of Fernald Neck Rd. off Rt. 52, past Youngtown Rd., Lincolnville and Camden. Open dawn until 7:30 PM, no pets allowed. The preserve's 326 acres cover most of a wooded peninsula that juts into Lake Megunticook. Signs showing walking trails are at the trailhead kiosk and trail intersections. Trails lead to stunning water views. Trails can be boggy: Wear boots or old shoes.

Camden Harbor Park and Amphitheatre (207-236-3440), Atlantic Ave., Camden. The amphitheater, designed by Fletcher Steele in 1929, has been nominated as a National Historic Landmark; it's a magical setting for summertime concerts or weddings, and a good place to sit, think, or read anytime. Across the street Harbor Park covers a manicured slope down to the water, with the Megunticook River waterfall in its midst. Picnic on one of the benches overlooking Camden Harbor.

The Beech Hill Preserve (207-236-7091; coastalmountains.org), Beech Hill Rd., Rockport. The Coastal Mountains Land Trust cares for 295 acres on this hilltop preserve, bare of trees and the perfect place to drink in the intricate coastline of Midcoast Maine. More than 100 species of birds stop here at some point in the year, feasting on the organic blueberries that attract people,

CAMDEN AMPHITHEATRE

too—although access is limited to the annual free picking days. The berries are harvested and sold to support the preserve. A sod-roofed stone house at the top of the hill called Beech Nut is on the National Register of Historic Places. A trail map is available by download, or with a call to the land trust.

Curtis Island, in the outer harbor. A small island with a lighthouse that marks the entrance to Camden, this is a public picnic spot and a popular sea kayaking destination.

✳ Lodging

All listings are in Camden unless otherwise noted.

Camden Accommodations (207-236-6090 or 1-800-344-4830; camdenac.com), 43 Elm St., is a vacation rental agency with more than 85 private properties in the Camden area.

Camden Bed & Breakfast Association (camdeninns.com), Camden. The brochure lists 13 members with descriptions of each and contact information.

RESORT ✏ & **Samoset Resort** (207-594-2511 or 1-800-341-1650; samoset.com), 220 Warrenton St., Rockport 04856. Open year-round. The original Samoset lodge burned down in 1972; a renovation in 2011 brought this resort closest yet to its luxurious beginnings. Set on 230 oceanfront acres, the Samoset holds 178 rooms and suites, many with ocean views, balcony, or patio, all with private bath, TV, and air-conditioning; and four cottages, including the two-bedroom Flume Cottage perched on a rocky outcropping above the water. The Samoset has a world-class 18-hole golf course and golf pro shop, outdoor tennis courts, fitness center, spa, sauna, and indoor and heated, handicapped-accessible outdoor pools. Samoset takes wonderful care of families with young children with a children's program. The dining room, Enoteca (see *Eating Out*), has floor-to-ceiling windows overlooking the water. Rooms $249–479, off-season $129–329.

INNS & **Inn at Ocean's Edge** (207-236-0945; innatoceansedge.com), P.O. Box 258, Lincolnville 04849. Look for the entrance off Rt. 1 a couple of miles north of the Camden line. Open May–Oct. This modern hotel features a main inn with three common areas and 18 guest rooms; the Hilltop building with 12 rooms, each with a balcony, sits up the hill.

Almost every room features a water view, and all have a Jacuzzi, gas fireplace, TV, VCR, stereo. The Spa building holds two luxury suites. Steps lead down to a private shingle beach. Breakfast might include Grand Marnier French toast. An elegant heated pool, spa with treatment rooms, sauna, and whirlpool are available to guests. $205–495 includes breakfast. Children 14 and up welcome.

Camden Harbour Inn (207-236-4200 or 1-800-236-4266; camdenharbourinn.com), 83 Bayview St. This luxury inn names its rooms for former Dutch ports and colonies, and each room's decor takes flight from the places evoked—like Java, with an orange-red headboard and green-gold pillows. Views of the harbor, some fireplaces, thick feather beds, TV/DVD, CD player, and much more. You can arrange a lobster picnic on the beach, too. Natalie's is the site of breakfast (included in rates of $225–1,090) and fine dining (see *Dining Out*).

✏ & **Whitehall** (207-236-3391; whitehall maine.com), 52 High St. (Rt. 1). Open mid-May–Oct. This old inn has been spruced up by new corporate owners Lark Hotels, though the vintage-1904 Steinway looks much the way it did on the summer evening in 1912 when a young local woman, Edna St. Vincent Millay, read her poem "Renascence" to assembled guests. One of the guests, swept away by Millay's verse, paid for her Vassar education. Thirty-six guest rooms in the main inn and several two-bedroom suites have private bath, air-conditioning, and flat-screen TV; all come with an iPad for the visit stocked with local information. See *Dining Out* for the Pig + Poet restaurant. Rooms $159–509.

Hartstone Inn (207-236-4259 or 1-800-788-4823; hartstoneinn.com), 41 Elm St. Open year-round. Mary Jo and Michael Salmon and their innkeepers are in charge of three properties: the first building on Rt. 1, the

THE LOBBY OF WHITEHALL

Hideaway House, and the Manor House. Some of the 11 guest rooms and 12 suites (all with private bath) offer a fireplace and canopy bed. Dinner is served in the main inn (see *Dining Out*). In high season $125–285 double with full breakfast and afternoon tea and cookies; low season $105–185. Spa services offered. Guests can take a group cooking class between Nov. and May.

Cedarholm Garden Bay Inn (207-236-3886; cedarholm.com), Rt. 1, Lincolnville Beach 04849. The pleasures of privacy and setting make a stay extraordinary. Down a road set in the midst of the landscaped grounds are the four cottages, Osprey, Puffin, Tern, and Loon, each with fireplace, Jacuzzi, queen (or king) bed, wet bar with microwave oven, small fridge, and a fabulous view of the ocean from a private deck. Two upper cottages, closer to Rt. 1, have a private bath, wet bar, and mini fridge. Continental breakfast includes muffins baked with berries grown here, in-season. All guests have access to a shared deck right on the beach. Upper units begin at $175 per night; luxury cottages, $300–495 per night.

B&BS ✪ ✿ **The Hawthorn Inn** (207-236-8842; camdenhawthorn.com), 9 High St. (Rt. 1). Open year-round. Owners Ted and Lisa Weiss offer 10 guest rooms at this Victorian mansion. The inn is a short walk from Camden Village and its harbor. The luxury rooms in the Carriage House have a double Jacuzzi, TV/DVD, fireplace, and private deck or patio. Breakfast could include blueberry walnut

pancakes. A landscaped garden spreads out beyond the two-tiered deck and terrace, where breakfast is served in fine weather. Children are welcome; some rooms accommodate more than two people. $175–295 in high season.

The Camden Maine Stay (207-236-9636; camdenmainestay.com), 22 High St. (Rt. 1). Open year-round. Innkeepers Claudio and Roberta Latanza welcome guests to this 1802 Greek Revival house, one of the best known in Camden's High Street Historic District. Stay in one of four standard rooms and four suites with names like the Common Ground Room, which has a cathedral ceiling and private deck over the garden. The 2-acre property is embellished with impeccable gardens. Breakfast in the formal dining room or on the sunporch. Afternoon tea included. $155–270 double room rate, in-season; $120–260 off.

Norumbega (207-236-4646 or 1-877-363-4646; norumbegainn.com), 63 High St. (Rt. 1). Open year-round. With one of the most imposing facades of any B&B anywhere, this turreted stone "castle" has long been a landmark just north of Camden, and new owners Phil Crispo, a CIA-trained chef, and Sue Walser have sunk their resources and

LIBRARY SUITE AT NORUMBEGA

DINING ROOM AT NORUMBEGA

energy into an extensive renovation to keep it that way. Inside you'll find an ornate staircase with fireplace and love seat on the landing, a formal parlor, and a dining room with a blue-tiled fireplace. Nine guest rooms and two suites named for European castles come with king or queen bed, private bath, antiques, and TV. Doubles $209–629, including full breakfast. The inn serves dinner to its guests and has a liquor license.

The Blue Harbor House (207-236-3196 or 1-800-248-3196; blueharborhouse.com), 67 Elm St. Open year-round. This friendly 11-room inn serves cocktails and hors d'oeuvres to guests (by reservation, starting at $10 per person); breakfast, included in the rates, is served on the spacious sunporch and might include quiche Florentine for a main course. Fresh Scottish shortbread was baking for the afternoon snack on our visit. Rooms are pleasantly decorated with hand-made quilts; all have private bath, telephone, air-conditioning, and TV/VCR. The Captain's Quarters has a kitchenette. Doubles $95–205.

The Camden Windward House (207-236-9656 or 1-877-492-9656; windwardhouse .com), 6 High St. (Rt. 1). Open year-round. Kristen and Jesse Bifulco have added a cozy wine bar upstairs with a second-floor deck overlooking Mount Battie; they have been entertaining guests since 2005. The five guest rooms and three suites all have private bath, air-conditioning, cable TV, and clock-radio with CD player. The Quarterdeck Room with skylights has its own entrance, fireplace, TV/DVD, library, sofa, Jacuzzi whirlpool tub, and

separate shower. Ironed linens and feather beds make for blissful sleep. Breakfast, perhaps orange yogurt pancakes and sausage, is a choice of several dishes from a menu. $125–280 high season, $99–199 low.

A Little Dream (207-236-8742; littledream .com), 60 High St. (Rt. 1). Open year-round except March. Raised up on a hill over busy Rt. 1, this place feels wonderfully secluded, with seven guest rooms including a carriage house suite called the Isle Watch. Overlooking the harbor and Curtis Island, it has a gas fireplace, king canopy bed, soaking tub, and covered porch complete with porch swing. If you stay here or in Treetops July 4, you can view three separate fireworks displays from your rooms. $159–295 double includes breakfast, perhaps lemon ricotta pancakes. Foreign guests are always welcome: Innkeeper JoAnna Ball speaks Italian, German, and French. Her husband, Bill Fontana, is a sculptor.

🐾 🖋 **Inns at Blackberry Common** (207-236-6060 or 1-800-388-6000; blackberryinn .com), 82 Elm St. Open year-round. Cyndi and Jim Ostrowski's two buildings hold some of the prettiest interiors in town. Settees covered in silk damask, ornate Oriental rugs, and decorative swords set the style. Stay in the Bette Davis room, where the movie star slept after the cast party for *Peyton Place*, with a queen brass bed and antique lighting fixture. In-house dinners offered Nov.–June on Sat. nights. $129–249 in-season, $149–189 off, including a full breakfast served in the dining room or in the courtyard.

The Inn at Sunrise Point (207-236-7716 or 1-800-435-6278; sunrisepoint.com), Sunrise Point Rd., P.O. Box 1344. Open May–Oct. Set on a 4-acre waterfront estate just over the town line in Lincolnville, this small, luxurious B&B is now run by Daina Hill. Five cottages named for Maine painters and writers— among them Winslow Homer and Richard Russo—have an incredible view, fireplace, private deck, and Jacuzzi. The Wyeth Loft Suite offers a king bed, gas fireplace, small deck, and TV/DVD; an attached bedroom can be rented. Count on fine linens on all the sumptuous beds. Three rooms and the loft are $300–445, cottages $330–595, full breakfast, perhaps poached eggs with asparagus and chive oil, included.

The Belmont (207-236-8053 or 1-800-238-8053; thebelmontinn.com), 6 Belmont St. Open mid-May–Oct. This inn, with a peaceful location a few blocks off Rt. 1, has been undergoing a renewal under the ownership of Anita Zeno. An 1890s Edwardian house with a wraparound veranda and a blue ceiling, the Belmont has six guest rooms with private bath and several with a gas fireplace. Full breakfast, afternoon tea always available. $199–289 per night in-season.

⏧ **The Victorian by the Sea** (207-236-3785 or 1-800-382-9817; victorianbythesea.com), Lincolnville Beach 04849. Open year-round. Jeanne and Rob Short own this 1889 shingle-style Victorian "cottage" overlooking the water, away from Rt. 1. Seven guest rooms each have a queen bed, private bath, and fireplace. The Victorian Suite, with a turret room, chaise lounge, and fireplace, overlooks Penobscot Bay. The $165–250 in-season rate includes full breakfast with, perhaps, blueberry buttermilk scones.

OTHER LODGING 🦞 ☀ ⏧ **High Tide Inn** (207-236-3724 or 1-800-778-7068; hightideinn.com), Rt. 1. Open May–late Oct. Set far enough back from Rt. 1 to preclude traffic noise, this no-frills, easygoing complex appeals to singles and couples (who tend to choose one of the five rooms in the inn) and families (who often opt for a cottage, two-bedroom deck house, or motel unit, five with connecting sleeping rooms). Most of the very clean 31 rooms have breathtaking views—especially for the price. The complex fills 7 quiet acres of landscaped grounds that slope to the water and more than 250 feet of private ocean beach. Continental breakfast with just-baked popovers and muffins. Pets allowed in only four of the cottages. $89–195.

☀ ⏧ ♿ **Lord Camden Inn** (207-236-4325 or 1-800-336-4325; lordcamdeninn.com), 24 Main St. Open year-round. This inn is named for the British nobleman who championed the American cause in the House of Lords during the Revolutionary War. Occupying a restored 1893 brick Masonic hall, the 36 rooms offer cable TV, private bath, telephone, air-conditioning, and elevator. Most rooms have two double beds and private balcony overlooking the town and harbor or the hills beyond. June–Nov. rates include a full breakfast with a make-your-own waffle stand; continental breakfast off-season. $99–289.

CAMPING ⏧ ☀ ♿ **Megunticook Campground by the Sea** (207-594-2428; megunticookcampgrounds.com), 620 Commercial St., Rockport 04856. Open May 15–early or mid-Oct. Wooded, oceanfront campground with 100 sites and 10 rustic camping cabins. Facilities include a store, recreation hall, fishing, heated pool, and oceanfront picnic area and gardens for Sat.-night lobster bakes. $35–45 in-season. **Camden Hills RV Resort** (207-236-2498), 30 Applewood Rd. in Rockport, is a sister park.

✳ Where to Eat

DINING OUT ✪ **Francine Bistro** (207-230-0083; francinebistro.com), 55 Chestnut St., Camden. Open Tue.–Sat. 5:30–10; reservations recommended. Small, intimate, and sometimes noisy. Chef-owner Brian Hill has been earning high praise since 2003. Chewy, moist bread with a marvelous crust is one mark of excellence. The dry-aged steak has an astonishingly good flavor, as does the venison, and the seared line-caught Chatham cod is both moist and crisp. Count on Hill to seek out the best ingredients in Maine. Excellent wine list. Entrées $24–30.

Long Grain (207-236-9001), 31 Elm St. Reservations recommended. Customers extoll the crab fried rice, coconut soup with chicken or tofu, and the Thai beef salad, Nua Nam Tok, aromatic with lime; house noodles in organic farmers greens are simply fantastic. $9.20–15.

Natalie's (207-236-7008; camdenharbourinn.com), at the Camden Harbour Inn, 82 Bayview St., Camden. Open daily for dinner 5:30–9 and employing the coast's best seafood and farm products to make French-inspired meals—perhaps seared duck breast with turnip purée and black mission figs or halibut with crushed cauliflower and royal trumpet mushrooms. Fine wine list. Three-course prix fixe dinner $68; bar menu $18–35.

Fresh (207-236-7005; freshcamden.com), 1 Bay View Landing. For once, the server's recommendation of the crabcakes was founded in reality—they are excellent. Good

LOBSTER

Graffam Brothers Seafood (207-236-8391), 211 Union St., Rockport. Open late spring to sometime in Oct. Across the street from the fish store are picnic tables where you can enjoy lobsters, clams, and more. This takeout-only spot serves hand-cut French fries, lobster rolls made with freshly picked lobster, and lobster dinners, with hot dogs, chicken fingers, and salads for alternatives.

wine, lobster risotto, fish-and-chips, burgers; sidewalk seating is delightful in good weather. $18–28.

✪ ♦ ♿ **Chez Michel** (207-789-5600), Lincolnville Beach (across from the beach). Open Apr.–mid-Nov., dinner Tue.–Sun., lunch and dinner on Sun. This restaurant serves French food and has been winning repeat loyal customers since 1989. The mussels marinière with garlic, onion, and white wine is a great appetizer, and even better for dinner (with salad, potato, and French bread). New England-style fisherman's chowder with haddock, Maine shrimp, clams, and scallops, and steak au poivre are always good. Raspberry pie in-season inspires requests with reservations. Entrées run $17–24.

Pig + Poet (207-236-3391; whitehall maine.com), 52 High St. Chef Sam Talbot, a good-looking TV "personality," collaborated on a menu that includes grilled clams with nori butter and porchetta with egg and Poet hot sauce—in honor of Edna St. Vincent Millay, who in life and in her poetry burned the candle at both ends. A Sazerac or a Hemingway daiquiri could sustain the tradition. $15–32.

Hartstone Inn (207-236-4259 or 1-800-788-4823; hartstoneinn.com), 41 Elm St., Camden. Open year-round. The menu for the five-course, prix fixe dinner ($55) changes nightly—with only one available each night. Menus are on the website, so you can choose what you prefer, perhaps finding seared duck breast with sweet potatoes or grilled swordfish with pesto.

40 Paper (207-230-0111; 40Paper.com), 40 Washington St., has won praise for many of its more than 40 cocktails; carbonara made with bucatini and whatever local vegetables are in season may be starring on an ever-changing menu with an Italian focus.

EATING OUT

IN CAMDEN

The Drouthy Bear (207-542-7741; drouthy bear.com), 50 Elm St. A Scottish pub with Scotch eggs and kedgeree, bangers and mash, and ploughman's platter. Mushy peas on the side and a long list of good ale—for the drouthy among us, otherwise known as thirsty.

♦ ♿ **Peter Ott's** (207-236-4032), 16 Bayview St. Open year-round for casual dinner, with a large menu that features grilled sirloin steak and salmon with maple chipotle glaze. Entrées are served with the salad bar unless you choose something lighter. $17–31.

♦ ♿ **Camden Deli** (207-236-8343; camdendeli.com), 37 Main St. Open 7 AM–10 PM daily. Breakfast and more than 40 sandwich choices combining all the regular deli meats and cheeses as well as some less expected

Nancy English

PETER OTT'S WATERSIDE DINING

Nancy English

VIEW FROM THE BACK DECK OF CAMDEN DELI

IN ROCKPORT

18 Central Oyster Bar & Grill (207-466-9055; 18central.com), 18 Central St., Rockport. Open in the summer of 2016 by Patrick and Jessica Duffy, 18 Central served food that was excellent from the start, with raw and broiled oysters, country paté to start, and halibut, steak, a perfect burger and fried chicken for dinner. Entrées $25–29. Closed Wednesdays.

Sweet Sensations and 3 Dogs Café (207-230-0955; mainesweets.com; 3dogscafe.com), 309 Commercial St. (Rt. 1). Open daily and early in summer; shorter hours in winter. The café and bakery offer dinosaur cookies, meringues, and much, much more. Lunch is soup, salad, and sandwiches—perhaps the Vinalhaven, a BLT with applewood-smoked bacon on organic whole wheat bread. Lunch $7–14.

Enoteca (207-593-1529), at Samoset Resort. Open daily for breakfast, dinner, and Sunday brunch, year-round. Brick oven–fired pizza and an Italian American menu, with a large fireplace indoors and an outdoor firepit on the terrace (open until mid-Sept.) and floor-to-ceiling windows overlooking the water.

TAKEOUT The Market Basket (207-236-4371), Rts. 1 and 90, Rockport. Open Mon.–Fri. 7–6:30, Sat. 8–6:30, Sun. 9–4. This specialty food store offers a wide variety of creative salads, French bread, soups, entrées, sandwich specials for takeout, more than 500 wines from around the world, and more than 75 varieties of cheese. Baked goods like double choc olate mini cakes are another reason to visit.

Scott's Place (207-236-8751), Elm St. (Renys parking lot), Camden. Open 10:30–4, Mon.–Sat. Since 1974 this tiny building in the parking lot of a small shopping center has served thousands of toasted crabmeat and lobster rolls, chicken sandwiches, burgers, veggie burgers, hot dogs, and chips. Prices are among the best around, and it's open year-round.

✳ Entertainment

Bay Chamber Concerts (207-236-2823; bay chamberconcerts.org), 58 Bay View St., Suite

choices, such as a pressed Cubano or a Monte Cristo, for lunch. The back dining room overlooks the waterfall in downtown Camden, and another dining room upstairs, with a deck open in summer, does, too.

🍴 ♿ **Camden Bagel Café** (207-236-2661), 25 Mechanic St. Open Mon.–Sat. 6:30 AM–2 PM, Sun. 7:30–2. Bagels with substance are baked here, some in whole wheat. The plain interior makes a good refuge as you enjoy a bagel with cream cheese or with an egg and bacon for breakfast. Soups and chili when things cool down.

🍴 ♿ **The Waterfront Restaurant** (207-236-3747; waterfrontcamden.com), Bayview St. Open for lunch and dinner; you can watch the activity in the harbor. Popular and with a well-trained staff, this place fills up fast and doesn't take reservations. Dinners include a shore dinner (clam chowder, corn on the cob, steamers, mussels, and a lobster) and steaks. $18–24.

1, Camden 04843. This renowned organization has presented outstanding concerts since 1961. In July and Aug., they sponsor Thu.-evening chamber music concerts in the Rockport Opera House with its gilded interior, and Wed.-evening concerts at the beautifully restored Strand in Rockland. The series celebrated its 50th year in 2010. Winter-season selections include classical and jazz music concerts and dance performances.

Camden Civic Theatre (207-236-2281; camdencivictheatre.com), Main St., Camden. A variety of theatrical performances are presented in the restored Camden Opera House, a second-floor theater with plum seats and cream-and-gold walls. Tickets are reasonably priced.

Everyman Repertory Theatre (207-236-0173; everymanrep.org), Rockport. Noel Coward's *Blythe Spirit* was performed in June 2012 at this nonprofit, professional theater dedicated to fine acting, inspired playwrights, and reasonable ticket prices.

✳ Selective Shopping

Avena Botanicals (207-594-0694; avena botanicals.com), 219 Mill St., Rockport. Open in summer Mon.–Fri. 9–5, off-season Mon.-Thu. 9–5, Fri. 9–1. Walk in the botanical garden in growing season, when you can drink in the scents serenaded by the chorus of crickets and honeybees. At the apothecary you can purchase creams, salves, teas, and tinctures, during the same hours, year-round. Check the website for the summer schedule of free herb walks with Deb Soule, the herbalist founder.

ART GALLERIES **Bay View Gallery** (207-236-4534; bayviewgallery.com), 33 Bayview St., Camden. One of the largest galleries in the Midcoast area. Original paintings and sculptures by contemporary artists working in Maine. Custom framing.

A Small Wonder Gallery (207-236-6005; smallwondergallery.com), 1 Public Landing (across from the chamber of commerce), Camden. A small gallery with well-chosen, limited-edition graphics, watercolors, hand-painted tiles, and more.

ARTISANS **Windsor Chairmakers** (207-789-5188; windsorchair.com), Rt. 1, Lincolnville Beach. Filling two floors of an old farmhouse are Windsor chairs and tables, highboys, and four-poster beds, all offered in a selection of finishes. A gallery in a wing of the connected farmhouse shows a line of Shaker-style furniture. Visitors can tour the workshop to see furniture being made.

Maine Artisans (207-789-5376), Rt. 1, Lincolnville Beach. Open daily May–Oct., this charming store sells work by weavers, potters, and sock makers, among others.

The Foundry (207-236-3200; remsen.com), 531 Park St., West Rockport (next to the Baptist church). Richard Remsen makes 20-inch-long fishing lures out of handblown glass that are outfitted with metal hardware.

Michael Good Gallery (207-595-2580; michaelgood.com), 325 Commercial St. (Rt. 1), Rockland. Original and extraordinary pottery, jewelry, sculpture, and accessories.

BOOKSTORES ♿ **Down East** (207-594-9544), Rt. 1, Rockport. The headquarters for Down East Enterprises (publishers of *Down East, Fly Rod & Reel*, and *Shooting Sportsman* magazines, as well as a line of New England books) is located in a handsome old mansion that includes a bookshop, open 8–5 Mon.–Fri. year-round.

Sherman's Maine Coast Book Shops (207-236-2223 or 1-800-803-5949; shermans.com), 14 Main St., Camden. Another in the fine chain of Sherman's bookstores on the Maine coast, Camden's branch has expanded in its new, sun-filled location and is packed with books, toys, puzzles, cards, and gifts.

♫ **The Owl and Turtle Bookshop** (207-236-7335), 33 Bayview St. One of Maine's best bookstores. Maine authors and Maine history, children's books, and signings by such exemplary local authors as Tess Gerritsen. The café serves its own blend of local coffee and is the perfect place to rejuvenate yourself after an afternoon in town.

SPECIAL SHOPS
All shops are in Camden and open year-round unless otherwise noted

♫ **The Smiling Cow** (207-236-3351; smiling cow.com), 41 Main St. Seasonal. Three generations ago a mother and five children converted this stable into a classic gift shop, one with unusual warmth; members of the fifth generation are now employed inside. We like the Maine-themed items like fragrant, locally made soaps.

The Cashmere Goat (207-236-7236; thecashmeregoatknit.com), 20 Bayview St. Drop-in classes will get you started on the project that the soft, irresistible cashmere will inspire you to undertake. Alpaca fiber, wool, and cotton, too.

🐾 **Heavenly Threads** (207-236-3203), 57 Elm St. (Rt. 1). Open Mon.–Fri. 10–4, Sat. 10–1, closed Mon. off-season. Wealthy summer folks and locals both donate to this extremely clean shop full of surprising finds, maybe Calvin Klein for under $5. Proceeds benefit Coastal Hospice, Rockland Soup Kitchen, and more.

Glendarragh Lavender (207-236-8151; mainelavender.com), 22 Main St. Just standing inside this store is calming; the lavender grows on a 26-acre farm near town and is sold here in many forms, ready to soothe, salve, and sustain you.

Ducktrap Bay Trading Company (1-800-560-9500; ducktrapbay.com), 20 Main St. Many of these pieces—decoys, wildlife and marine art, scrimshaw, and paintings—have earned awards for their creators.

Danica Candleworks (207-236-3060), 569 West St. (Rt. 90), West Rockport. In a building with a Scandinavian-inspired exterior especially pretty when it snows, you'll find a candle factory and a shop that sells high-quality hand-dipped and scented candles and accessories.

❋ Special Events

February: **U.S. National Toboggan Championships**—teams from all over the country compete in two-, three-, and four-person races, often in costume (Camden Snow Bowl); **Winterfest**; and **Camden Conference**.

March: **Maine Maple Sugar Sunday.**

Mid- to late July: **Annual Open House and Garden Day**, sponsored by the Camden Garden Club. Very popular tour of homes and gardens in Camden and Rockport held every year for five decades. **Summer HarborArts**, a juried arts and crafts show (third Saturday and Sunday), Camden Harbor Park. **The North Atlantic Blues Festival**, Rockland.

August: Merryspring's **Annual Kitchen Tour**—see uniquely designed kitchens in Camden, Rockport, and Lincolnville, plus demonstrations and tastings. **Union Fair** and **Blueberry Festival** (late month), Union Fairgrounds (see "Rockland/Thomaston Area").

Labor Day weekend: **Camden Windjammer Festival**, Camden Harbor. A celebration of the windjammer industry featuring a parade of boats, music, nautical history, fireworks, and the Schooner Bum Talent Contest.

September: **VinFest**, Cellardoor Winery, Lincolnville.

October: **Fall HarborArts**, a juried arts and crafts show, Camden Harbor Park—75 artisans displaying work for sale. **Lincolnville Fall Festival**, Lincolnville. **PopTech**, Camden.

December: **Christmas by the Sea** (first weekend)—tree lighting, Santa's arrival, caroling, holiday house tour, refreshments in shops. Rockport Garden Club **Holly Berry Fair**.

Islesboro

A 14-mile-long, string-bean-shaped island just 3 miles off Lincolnville Beach (a 20-minute ferry ride), Islesboro is a private kind of place, best visited with a car or a bicycle.

There are three distinct communities on the island. The town of Islesboro with the necessary services (town office, post office, health center, and fire department) sits in the center between Dark Harbor and Pripet. Dark Harbor (described by Sidney Sheldon in his best seller *Master of the Game* as the "jealously guarded colony of the super-rich") has long been a summer resort village, where huge "cottages" peek from behind the trees along the road to Pendleton Point. Pripet is a thriving year-round neighborhood of boatbuilders and fishermen.

GETTING THERE Take the car-carrying **Maine State Ferry** (207-789-5611 or 207-734-6935); $10 round-trip per passenger, $27.50 per vehicle, and $8.50 for a bicycle, with reservations from the mainland or island available for a fee. The ferry lands mid-island at Grindle Point. The crossing is a 3-mile, 20-minute ride, the schedule depending on the season. If you go for a day trip only, pay close attention to when the last ferry leaves the island to avoid being stranded. At the landing you'll find a clean ferry terminal with public restrooms. When you board the Maine State Ferry, ask for a map and schedule. The detailed and informative island map shows a full view of the island as well as business locations, a ferry schedule, a brief description of the island, and a historical society events calendar.

GUIDANCE The **Islesboro town office** (207-734-2253), 150 Main Rd., is a great source of information, with friendly service both on the phone and in person.

WHEN TO COME Only in summer will visitors be able to visit a bookstore, one café, and a historical society museum with a gallery.

✳ To See and Do

The old lighthouse on **Grindle Point** (built in 1850, now automated) and keeper's cottage now house the seasonal **Sailors' Memorial Museum** (207-734-2253), open July–Labor Day, 9:30–4:30, closed Wed. and Sun. Look for summer musical and theatrical performances at the **Free Will Baptist Church**. Check out the **Up Island Church**, a fine old structure with beautiful wall stencils and fascinating old headstones in the adjacent graveyard.

The layout of the island makes at least a bicycle necessary to get a real feel for the place. But the roads are narrow and have no shoulder. Bicyclists should use great caution. Even so, after both driving and biking the island, we prefer biking. In Dark Harbor you'll see huge "cottages" and impressive architecture. In summer you'll also find the **Dark Harbor Shop** (207-734-8878), with souvenirs, gifts, ice cream, and a deli. "We haven't changed in 40 years—change comes slowly to Islesboro," said owner Bill Warren, laughing. Open daily the Fri. of Memorial Day weekend to Labor Day. A picnic area and town beach at Pendleton Point have spectacular views. The trip down the other side of the island will take you past the **Islesboro Historical Society** (207-734-6733) in the former high school, a beautiful stone building which houses an annual arts and crafts show.

BELFAST, SEARSPORT, AND STOCKTON SPRINGS

Belfast's long, Victorian brick Main Street slopes steadily downward, away from Rt. 1, toward the confluence of the tidal Passagassawakeag River and Belfast Bay and the site of the largest boatyard downeast.

With just 7,100 residents and a small-town feel, Belfast is a city and the seat of Waldo County. Magnificent Greek Revival and Federal homes, proof of early prominence, line High and Church Streets. Lower blocks suggest a checkered commercial history that included a sarsaparilla company, a rum distillery, and a city-owned railroad. Now it's a bustling, hip small town with exceptional food and drink.

High above downtown Belfast, Rt. 1 crosses the Passagassawakeag River into East Belfast, threading a string of shops, restaurants, and a mix of 1940s motor courts and motor inns with water views.

In Searsport Rt. 1 becomes, suddenly and briefly, a mid-19th-century brick-and-granite downtown. Visit the Penobscot Marine Museum to learn that more than 3,000 different vessels have been built in and around Penobscot Bay since 1770. Searsport alone launched eight brigs and six schooners in one year (1845), and for many years boasted more sea captains than any other town its size, explaining the dozens of 19th-century mansions lining Rt. 1.

If you have the time, take the scenic route to this region from Augusta, poking through the communities of Unity, Thorndike, and Brooks, detouring to Liberty then down to Belfast. Rt. 1 continues to shadow the shore as it narrows into what seems more like a broad river.

GUIDANCE The Belfast Area Chamber of Commerce (207-338-5900; belfastmaine.org), P.O. Box 58, Belfast 04915, maintains an information center at 14 Main St. near the waterfront; open daily June–mid-Oct., 9–4; mid-Oct.–May, Mon.–Fri. 9–4.

GETTING THERE *By car:* The most direct route to this region from points south and west is via I-95, exiting in Augusta and taking Rt. 3 to Belfast. Exit 113 on I-95 accesses a connector to Rt. 3, offering motorists bound for the Midcoast a way around Augusta. If you're coming up Rt. 1, take the first turnoff for downtown Belfast.

By bus: **Concord Coach Lines** (1-800-639-3317; concordcoachlines.com) stops in both Searsport and Belfast.

PUBLIC RESTROOMS At the public landing at the bottom of Main Street, open May–mid-Oct.

Nancy English

BUSKING ON THE MAIN STREET IN BELFAST

WHEN TO COME The town chugs along through winter, with most inns and restaurants open throughout the year; still, the summer season gives the ocean a friendlier look and fills the farm stands. Come to Belfast anytime to enjoy the downtown.

WOODWORKING AND CARPENTRY TOOLS OVERFLOW THE SHELVES AT LIBERTY TOOL COMPANY

Nancy English

✳ Villages

Brooks. In the center of this quiet county, surrounded by hills, this town has the most scenic golf course around.

Liberty, straddling Rt. 3, is home to Lake St. George State Park and to the extraordinary **Liberty Tool Company** (207-589-4771; jonesport-wood.com), Main St. Open June–mid-Oct., daily, fewer days off-season, closed Jan. and Feb. and reopening in Mar. with a big sale on the first Saturday. Antique and used tools and every other thing that you can imagine—clocks, lanterns, books, postcards. Tools for sale can be looked at Sat. morning, or call 1-888-405-2007. The octagonal Liberty post office, located across the street from Liberty Graphics, dates to 1867 and houses the Liberty Historical Society (207-589-4393), open weekend afternoons in July and Aug. **Liberty Graphics** (207-589-4035; libertygraphicstshirts.com), Main St., open daily in summer, fewer days off-season, sells T-shirts, including organic cotton versions, printed with water-based designs from nature and designs by Frank Lloyd Wright.

Northport. A low-key community with pleasure boats in the harbor and golf clubs, as well as a mid-19th-century former Methodist campground with hundreds of gingerbread cottages on the bay.

Unity. Home to a rural college, a raceway, and the fairgrounds for the popular late-Sept. Common Ground Fair.

Stockton Springs. Rt. 1 now bypasses this former shipbuilding town. Follow East St. down to Fort Point.

✳ To See

MUSEUMS **Davistown Museum** (207-589-4900; davistownmuseum.org), 58 Main St., Liberty. Skip Brack, meticulous owner of Liberty Tool Company, has sorted out the finest antique tools of his collection to create this museum above Liberty Graphics. Its specialty is a collection of signed shipbuilders' edge tools. Contemporary Maine artists, 108 in total, exhibit their work in this space, and a permanent collection is also on display, most in the top floors. As the website states, the art and artifact combination at Davistown Museum "is unique among Maine's museums and galleries." Native American artifacts. Children can make a sculpture out of odds and ends gathered from the tool store. Suggested donation $3.

Belfast Historical Society and Museum (207-338-9229; belfastmuseum.org), 10 Market St., Belfast. Open mid-June–mid-Oct.; in summer Tue.–Sat. 11–4, from Labor Day Fri.–Sat. 11–4; by appointment year-round. A ship model of the *Charlotte W. White* has been restored for display. A self-guided "Museum-in-the-Streets" walking tour is installed downtown.

MUST SEE

Penobscot Marine Museum (207-548-2529; penobscot marinemuseum.org), Rt. 1, Searsport. Open May–mid-Oct., Mon.–Sat. 10–5 and Sun. noon–5. $12 adults; children 7–15 are $8. Family rate $30. (The library is open Mon.–Fri. 9–1.) The 13 buildings include eight on the National Register of Historic Places. The museum shop is at the entrance to the complex on Rt. 1. More than 50 small craft, one of the largest collections in New England, are on display, including peapods, dories, canoes, and lobster boats. A meticulously restored ship captain's home re-creates prosperous Maine coast life in the 19th century, while a commercial fishing exhibit in Searsport's original town hall shows the working side of the maritime community. Other artifacts show the changing faces of Maine, from the Wabanaki natives to the shipbuilders of the 1800s. The galleries in the **Captain Jeremiah Merithew House** hold a world-class collection of paintings by father, son, and grandson marine artists Thomas Buttersworth (Sr. and Jr.) and James Buttersworth, whose depictions of ships in storm and calm are luminous and exciting. The museum displays scrimshaw-carved whales' teeth, ship models, and artifacts of the China trade. Tours include scheduled visits to the adjacent First Congregational Church to view glorious stained-glass windows and a 100-year-old organ with over 1,000 pipes. Three children's activity areas include a "marine science lab," a ship's capstan, and a large-scale model of a square-rigger's mast and sails that kids can manipulate. Other exhibits focus on the working-class people who made their living in the granite, lime, ice, lumber, and tourism industries.

Safe Harbor Church, Rt. 1, Searsport. Phone 207-548-6663 or pick up the key across the street and check out the fabulous stained-glass windows in this church, built in 1815. It's now maintained as a meditation space and holds regular services.

Bryant Wood Stove Museum (207-568-3665; bryantstove.com), 27 Stovepipe Alley (junction of Rts. 220 and 139), Thorndike. Open year-round, Mon.–Sat. 8–4:30. What began as a stove shop has evolved into a fascinating museum. The front room is crammed with restored woodstoves (for sale). Walk through these to the doll circus, with its array of mechanical, musical dolls from Barbie to Disney characters and everything in between. The back room houses a collection of player pianos, nickelodeons, and vintage automobiles. Worth the drive.

✳ To Do

BERRY PICKING **Staples Homestead Blueberries** (207-567-3393 or 207-567-3703), 302 Old County Rd., Stockton Springs. Turn at the ball field on Rts. 1/3, then drive 3 miles to the T at County Rd.; turn right. Open 8–5 daily while its certified organic berries are in-season (Aug.). Friendly owners Basil and Mary Staples will instruct you in the mysteries of blueberry raking, then let you go to it, or you can pick by hand.

BEER **Liberty Craft Brewing** (207-322-7663; libertycraftbrewing.com), 7 Coon Mountain Lane, Liberty. Queen Bee Honey Lager, imperial porter, and golden pilsner are a few of the ales on tap at this destination brewery with a pub food menu.

BOATING Community rowing in 32-foot Cornish rowing gigs is a summer tradition: Sign up with "Come Boating" (comeboating.com) and enjoy the free sport at the town dock.

Schooner *Timberwind* (207-619-0654), Thompson's Wharf, Belfast. Day sails and sunset cruises. Built in Portland in 1931 as a pilot schooner, this pretty 96-foot vessel was converted to a passenger vessel in 1969; it moved to Belfast from Rockland in 2015.

Belfast Bay Company Lobster Boat Trips (207-323-1443; belfastbaycompany.com). Take the *Clara K* from Belfast to visit Castine or Holbrook Island Sanctuary. $45–75.

COOKING CLASSES (207-505-5231; belfastbreezeinn.com) 192 Northport Ave. Sandi Knapp, of the **Belfast Breeze Inn,** offers cooking classes in the summer along with music performances and a dinner show.

GOLF **Country View Golf Club** (207-722-3161) in Brooks is the most scenic in the area: nine holes, par 36, cart and club rentals, lessons, clubhouse. **Northport Golf Club** (207-338-2270), Northport. A fully irrigated nine-hole course, pro shop, snack bar, driving range, and rentals.

KAYAKING **Water Walker Sea Kayaks** (207-338-6424; touringkayaks.com), Belfast. Ray Wirth, a Registered Maine Guide and ACA-certified open-water instructor, offers tours ranging from several hours in Belfast Harbor or around Sears Island to full-day trips to other islands to overnight trips.

SWIMMING **Lake St. George State Park** (207-589-4255), Rt. 3, Liberty. Open May 15–Oct. 15. A great way station for travelers going to or from Down East. A deep, clear lake with a small beach, lifeguard, bathhouse, 38 campsites, and a boat launch. **Swan Lake State Park**, Rt. 141, Swanville (north of town; follow signs), has a beach with picnicking facilities. **Belfast City Park**, Rt. 1, Belfast (south of town), holds a swimming pool, tennis courts, picnicking facilities, and a gravel beach. **Sandy Point Beach** is off Rt. 1 north of Stockton Springs (it's posted HERSEY RETREAT; turn toward the water directly across from the Rocky Ridge Motel).

TRAINS **Belfast and Moosehead Lake Railway** (brookspreservation.org), Upper Bridge Station, High St., Belfast. Train rides leave the station twice a day on weekends in summer, taking passengers over 7 miles of track and bridges along the harbor and river.

WINE **Winterport Winery** (207-223-4500; winterportwinery.com), 279 S. Main St., Winterport. Open May–Dec., Tue.-Sat. 11–5; Mar.–Apr., Fri.–Sat. 11–5; closed Jan.–Feb. Taste the wine and ales from Penobscot Bay Brewery. A line of ice cream made with Half Moon Stout is worth sampling. (See **The Bacon Tree** in *Eating Out*.)

✳ Green Space

Also see Lake St. George State Park and Belfast City Park under *Swimming*.

Moose Point State Park, Rt. 1, south of Searsport. Open May 30–Oct. 15. A good spot for picnicking; cookout facilities are in an evergreen grove and an open field overlooking Penobscot Bay. Also check out **Mosman Park** in downtown Searsport with its playground and picnic benches by tidal pools and the public landing.

Fort Pownall and Fort Point State Park, Stockton Springs (marked from Rt. 1; follow the 3.5-mile access road). The 1759 fort built to defend the British claim to Maine (the Penobscot River was the actual boundary between the English and French territories) was burned twice to prevent its being taken; only earthworks remain. The adjacent park, on the tip of a peninsula jutting into Penobscot Bay, is a fine fishing and picnic spot.

Sears Island. After decades of debate about the future of this island (it was slated to be a container port, nuclear power plant site, LNG port, and more), it's open to the public. There are 940 acres and about 5 miles of shorefront to explore, just as migratory birds do. Good

EXCURSIONS

Rt. 3, past Lake St. George and Sheepscot Pond, through the China Lakes region, is the most direct path between Belfast and Augusta, but take time to detour down Rt. 173 to **Liberty** to see the octagonal post office and the **Liberty Tool Company** and **Davistown Museum** (see *Museums*). For a leisurely tour of the villages between Belfast and Augusta, head north from East Belfast on Rt. 141 to Monroe. Ask for directions to **Stone Soup Farm** to see their gardens, then check out **Monroe Falls**, just off Rt. 139, and maybe have a picnic. Head out on Rt. 139, through Brooks, and then on toward Thorndike, where you'll want to stop at the **Bryant Museum**. Follow Rt. 139 into Kennebec County to Fairfield to meet up with I-95, or detour yet again onto Rt. 202, which will bring you through the China Lakes region to Augusta.

for walking, biking, kayaking, and fishing; visit the sand beaches to view the Camden Hills. It's connected to the mainland by a causeway. Off Rt. 1, take Sears Island Rd.

Carleton Pond Waterfowl Production Area, Troy. Part of the Maine Wildlife Refuge System. One thousand acres are accessible by canoe or kayak. Unstaffed. Contact the Maine Coastal Islands Wildlife Refuge Rockport office (207-236-6970), P.O. Box 495, Rockport 04856, for information and for regulations on duck and geese hunting.

✳ Lodging

RESORTS ✵ **Point Lookout** (207-789-2000 or 1-800-515-3611; visitpointlookout.com), 67 Atlantic Hwy., Northport (on the Lincolnville line). Open year-round. The 106 luxurious one-, two-, and three-bedroom cabins at Point Lookout, a gorgeous setting, started their existence as a corporate retreat built by MBNA in the mid-1990s. In 2008 these pine-paneled cabins were transformed into a resort. Each one holds a cable TV/DVD, a propane fireplace, and a screened porch, and more than half have cooking facilities; a small number have ocean views. **Copper Pine Café** takes care of breakfast and lunch, perhaps a panini with fresh mozzarella and tomatoes. Fitness center with massage and Zumba and yoga classes offered, plus bowling, racquetball, virtual golf, an artificial turf soccer field, a baseball field, and hiking trails. $271–350 in high season.

INNS AND B&BS

IN BELFAST

The Belfast Bay Inn (207-338-5600; belfastbayinn.com), 72 Main St. Ed and Judy Hemmingsen, former owners of the Bluenose Inn in Bar Harbor, have transformed a brick building on Main Street into a boutique hotel that pulls out all the stops. The eight luxury rooms are filled with gorgeous upholstered furniture and plush beds, art, refrigerators, cable TV/DVD; some have views of the harbor, fireplace, dining area, and/or a balcony. Breakfast in a garden courtyard. Spa services. $198–378.

The Alden House (207-338-2151 or 1-877-337-8151; thealdenhouse.com), 63 Church St. This gracious 1840 Greek Revival mansion holds Italian marble mantel, sinks, and a circular staircase inside its substantial, and walls. Larry Marshal and Rosemarie Cyr are the innkeepers overseeing the six guest rooms—five with private bath—a charming open porch, and comfortable furnishings. $129–179 includes a full breakfast served at separate tables.

The Jeweled Turret Inn (207-338-2304 or 1-800-696-2304; jeweledturret.com), 40 Pearl St. Open year-round. A handsome 1890s gabled and turreted house that's ornate inside and out, with a fireplace in the den said to be made of stones from every state in the Union at that time. This now lovely house suffered neglect before Carl and Cathy Heffentrager began transforming it in 1986, reviving its original glory by restoring the wood stairs and decking of the stone-edged verandas, where guests love to lounge in rockers and a swing. $130–169.

IN SEARSPORT

Captain A. V. Nickels Inn (207-548-1104; captainnickelsinn.com), 127 E. Main St. (Rt. 1). Open June–Dec. Brenda and Michael Liston bought this inn in 2011 and gave it a complete renovation, upgrading the eight bedrooms and suites (all with private bath) with European antiques, flat-screen TV, and more. Each room is named for a port of call. Paris, with a four-poster bed, wine-red walls, and white moldings, is our top choice. Twin parlors, a library, and a porch are fine places for relaxation. Overnight guests receive a three-course breakfast and wine and cheese in the afternoon. $165–255. Two resident terriers.

COTTAGES ✔ **Bayside Village**, built in the 1800s, has about 50 cottages on Penobscot Bay in Northport rented by the week by Bayside Cottage Rentals (207-338-5355; baysidecottagerentals.com). Margaret Lacoste's agency is open spring, summer, and fall, renting the cottages out for between $550 and $1,595 a week May–mid Oct. Originally a Methodist campground, the cottages are ornately trimmed with Victorian gingerbread, some with stone fireplace. The village offers a main common, a swim float and dock on the pebble beach, sailing lessons, and a little yacht club with children's activities in summer.

MOTELS 🐾 ✔ **Ocean's Edge Fireside Suites** (207-338-2090 or 1-800-303-5098), 159 Searsport Ave. (Rt. 1), Belfast 04915. The location of this three-story facility is terrific. All 83 units (with two queen beds, king beds, or suites) have a balcony overlooking the bay; amenities include a full-service restaurant, guest laundry, indoor "mineral" pool (no chlorine) with sauna and hot tub, and lobby computer. $89–329 in summer includes continental breakfast. Try the two-night specials in winter midweek—the pool is heated to 86 degrees.

✳ Where to Eat

DINING OUT **The Lost Kitchen** (207-382-3333) 22 Mill St., Freedom. Open Wed.–Sat., May 1 to New Year's Eve. Sixteen miles west of Belfast and worth the drive, The Lost Kitchen wows its visitors with a short, excellent menu. A neighboring farm's chickens are roasted with a magic that leaves the skin crisp and the meat moist; the chef, Erin French, knows exactly what she is doing. The mill

building that houses this restaurant received equally painstaking attention during its renovation. Reservations open April 1 and close soon afterward, so call them for a summer dinner. Entrées $26–42.

Meanwhile in Belfast (207-218-1288; meanwhile-in-belfast.com), 2 Cross St. With owners from Salerno on Italy's Amalfi Coast, you can count on the best wood-fired oven pizzas with thin, crisp dough, fantastic fresh mozzarella, flavorful olive oil—all the reasons Italian pizza is justifiably renowned. Travelers are seeking this pizza out; locals are devotees. $10–20.

Arata (207-338-4684; matthewkenneycuisine.com/hospitality/arata), 108 Main St. Maine vegetables in Japanese dishes from steamed buns and ramen noodles to fried oyster mushrooms. Plates $10–15.

Delvino's Grill & Pasta House (207-338-4565; delvinos.com), 52 Main St., Belfast. Open daily. The Italian classics are made well at Delvino's, where you can also dine on a blue cheese burger, fresh fish, or rib eye. Local buffalo and Maine beef are usually offered. Or try the mushroom sacchetti—pasta stuffed with portobello and porcini mushrooms and cheeses, topped with peppered cream sauce. House desserts change daily. Entrées $8–22.

The Captain's Table and **Port of Call Restaurant & Tapas Lounge** (207-548-1104; captainnickelsinn.com), 127 E. Main St. (Rt. 1), Searsport. Open June–Dec. Reservations recommended; no table is turned over at this restaurant dedicated to relaxed, fine

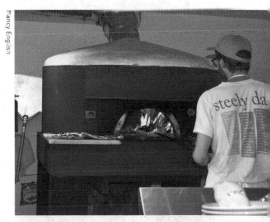

BAKING THE PIZZA AT MEANWHILE IN BELFAST REQUIRES CONSTANT ATTENTION

dining. Three- and four-course meals from a changing menu might include seared duck in a cherry reduction. $49 for four courses. Entrées from The Captain's Table (or from the bar—perhaps steak or vodka lobster, $16–26) can be enjoyed in Port of Call.

EATING OUT **Chase's Daily** (207-338-0555), 96 Main St., Belfast. Breakfast and lunch Tue.–Sat., dinner Fri. from 5:30, Sun. brunch 8–1. This high-ceilinged restaurant features enticing produce from the owners' Chase Farm in Freedom, sold in the back. The freshness of the ingredients and the great cooking combine to make the vegetarian fare wonderful. Thin-crusted Margherita pizza with fresh tomatoes and pools of melted mozzarella is great in late summer, as are soft corn tacos stuffed with black beans, spicy pepitas, feta, crema, shredded cabbage, and lime. Freshly baked bread and treats like sunken chocolate cake for dessert. Meals $7–19.

✪ **Three Tides** (207-338-1707; 3tides .com), 2 Pinchy Lane, Belfast. Open Tue.–Sat. from 3 PM, Sun. 1–8, later opening in winter. A fun spot with a serpentine concrete bar and an outdoor deck over the river, where you can drink special cocktails and eat pizzettes ($8.50), salads, and quesadillas. The oysters, mussels, steamers, and lobsters are very fresh; the lobsters are from their own lobster pound. The **Marshall Wharf Brewing Company** next door makes the exceptional microbrews; Cant Dog Imperial IPA is a "hops monster," exhilarating and bitter. An open-air terrace downstairs serves oysters raw and roasted, drinks, and French fries.

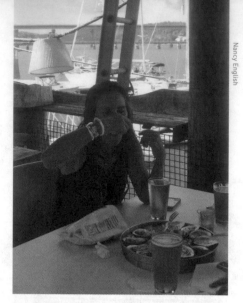

DOWNING OYSTERS AT THREE TIDES IN BELFAST

The Bacon Tree (207-223-4313; thebacon tree.com), 11 Main St., Winterport. Breakfast on perfect bacon, house-baked goods and local berries; dine on raw runa, house ravioli, or scallops. The restaurant is close to the Winterport Winery. Check online for seasonal hours.

✐ ♿ **The Ocean's Edge Restaurant** (207-338-2090), 159 Searsport Ave., Belfast. Open daily 4–9, closed Sun. off-season. Not just an amenity for the Comfort Inn to which it's attached, this spot is a local favorite given the view, the service, and the menu, which ranges from chicken and broccoli Alfredo with fettuccine to surf and turf. Entrées $10–28. Children's menu.

Darby's Restaurant and Pub (207-338-2339), 155 High St., Belfast. Open daily for lunch and dinner. A storefront café with tin ceilings and local artwork. A reasonably priced dinner might include pecan haddock with mojito sauce, or a black bean enchilada "smothered in cheddar and Ranchero sauce." Soups, salads, and sandwiches are served all day. Entrées $8–22.

✐ **Anglers** (207-548-2405), Rt. 1, Searsport. Open daily 11–8. Buddy Hall's Maine-style diner serves seafood that ranges from chowder to fried and broiled fish dinners to lobster every which way. "Land Lovers" get chicken Parmesan, BBQ ribs, and prime rib, and the Minnow Menu is for "the smaller appetite" (you don't have to be small). Entrées $7–30.

CHERRY TARTS AT CHASE'S DAILY, BELFAST

LOBSTER

✪ **Young's Lobster Pound** (207-338-1160; youngslobsterpound.webs.com), Fairview St. (posted from Rt. 1 just across the bridge from downtown Belfast), East Belfast. Open in-season 7:30–8, and year-round (winter closing at 4) for live and cooked lobsters, crabs, clams, and mussels, or take-out. A pound with as many as 30,000 lobsters and seating (indoor and outdoor) to accommodate 500 with a beautiful view of Belfast across the Passagassawakeag River. They pick the lobster meat here fresh every day for the lobster rolls.

Bay Wrap (207-338-9757; thebaywrap .com), 20 Beaver St. (off Main), Belfast. Open daily for lunch and dinner, except Sun., closing earlier in winter. An eatery with a next-door coffee shop called the Hub, where you can eat the wraps. On a foggy day we feasted on warm grilled eggplant with roasted red peppers, ricotta and feta cheeses, mint, field greens, and salsa verde ($7.95 for large).

Bell the Cat (207-338-2084), 15G Starett Drive, Belfast. Open 7:30–7:30, Sun. 9–5. Set inside a spacious upfront corner of Mr. Paperback, this is the local, very casual favorite for designer sandwiches, from breakfast sandwiches to a fat Reuben. Also good for salads, soups, and ice cream. Coffees and teas. This little café has a cult-like following—among adults.

Seng Thai (207-338-0010), 139 Searsport Ave. (Rt. 1), Belfast. Open daily (except Mon.) from 11:30. Not your ordinary Thai. Residents warn you not to try level-five spiciness. Entrées $9–14.

BAKERY Moonbat City Baking Co. (207-218-1039), 137 Main St., Belfast. Pain au chocolat and croissants are perfect at 7 AM—and gone by 9! There are other consolations. Open 7–1 Thurs. to Sun.

CHEESE Eat More Cheese (207-358-9701; eatmorecheese.me), 33 Main St. Eating more cheese is a delightful experience with Eat More Cheese's selections. Salami goes nicely, too. Sample to your heart's content.

ICE CREAM In Liberty, Maine, on Rt. 3, you will find possibly the best ice cream in the state of Maine at **John's Ice Cream Factory** (207-589-3700), 510 Belfast Augusta Rd. (Rt. 3). This is why you may very well choose to

drive to this area via I-95 to Augusta and Rt. 3. Lemon custard; mandarin orange chocolate; strawberry rhubarb; espresso anise swirl.

BEER Marshall Wharf Brewery Store and Tasting Room (207-338-1707; marshallwharf .com), 2 Pinchy Lane, Belfast. Call for hours. This is the brewery store for Marshall Wharf Brewery, making some of the best beer in Maine and selling tastes, pints, growlers, or half gallons of whatever is on tap.

✳ Entertainment

Marsh River Theater (207-722-4110; marsh rivertheater.com), Rt. 139, Brooks. Community theater performed in historic Union Hall. This group formed in the mid-1990s and has been offering performances ever since.

The Colonial Theater (207-338-1930; colonialtheater.com). The new home of the

JOHN'S ICE CREAM, LIBERTY, MAINE

DANNY MCGOVERN, BREWER AT MARSHALL WHARF

outsized carved elephants from a local land-mark, **Perry's Nut House**; three screens with nightly showings in a restored theater in downtown Belfast.

✳ Selective Shopping

ART The **Parent Gallery** (207-338-1553; neal parent.com), 92 Main St., displaying fine black-and-white photographs by Neal Parent, and pastels and oils by daughter Joanne; **Susan Tobey White Fine Art** (207-338-8990; susantobeywhite.com), 149 High St., featuring Susan Tobey White's many-peopled land-scapes. The website has information about her popular workshops. **Waterfall Arts** (207-338-2222; waterfallarts.org), 256 High St., is an arts organization offering classes, residen-cies, and exhibits in Belfast at Clifford Gallery and Fallout Shelter Gallery. **Finch Gallery** (207-338-1060; jerryfinch.com), 16 Main St., Belfast. Distinguished landscapes of the area around Belfast.

ANTIQUES Searsport claims to be the Antiques Capital of Maine. **The Searsport Antique Mall**, 149 E. Main St., open more or less daily year-round, is a cooperative of more than 70 dealers spread over two floors. **The Pumpkin Patch Antiques Center** (207-548-6047), 15 W. Main St., a 12-dealer shop in busi-ness since 1975, is run by Phyllis Sommer and is widely respected. Cindy Gallant runs the **Hobby Horse Flea Market** (207-548-2981, 379

E. Main St.), which fills a 3-acre complex with five retail stores. A flea market surrounds it every day but Tue., May–Columbus Day. Two other Searsport flea markets are held week-ends in-season. **Captain Tinkham's Empo-rium** (207-548-6465; jonesport-wood.com), 34 Main St., next to the Penobscot Marine Museum store, is where you can find antique and functional tools as well as books, records, sheet music, and other finds. Open daily in summer, Sat. year-round.

BlueJacket Ship Crafters (207-548-9974 or 1-800-448-5567; bluejacketinc.com), 160 E. Main St. (Rt. 1), Searsport. The to-scale ship models, from starting kits to cus-tom commissions, are made in Maine. Begin-ners undertaking the *Red Baron*, a Holland 32 lobster boat built in Belfast, for instance, will be able to call Charlie Cook if they need advice assembling the kits. The company began in 1904 under the name of the founder, H. E. Boucher. The radio-controlled pond yacht *Osprey* can go for a spin, a voyage that will be guided by Michael de Lesseps's expert, engaging instruction.

BOOKSTORES ✿ **Left Bank Books** (207-338-9009; leftbankbookshop.com), 109 Church St., Belfast. You'll find cozy chairs and flowers here, among books ranging from great mys-teries to Arctic explorations. This handsome and welcoming bookstore sells beautiful cards, has a marvelous children's section, and stocks treats for your dog.

Old Professor's Bookshop (207-338-2006), 99 Main St. Curated used books, rare books, and the best of the new.

Penobscot Books (207-548-6490; penobscotbooks.com), 164 W. Main St., Sears-port. Open May–Oct. and Christmas. With art, architecture, and photography books, more than 50,000 titles, this store sells to universi-ties and libraries all over the world.

Victorian House/Book Barn (207-567-3351), 290 Main St., Stockton Springs. Open every day of the year. A landmark collection of 20,000 antiquarian books and a special find for mystery-book buffs.

SPECIAL SHOPS

IN NORTHPORT

Swan's Island Blankets (207-338-9691; swans islandblankets.com), 231 Atlantic Hwy. (Rt.

1), Northport. The old looms are in use in the back room, visible through a window from the elegant showroom, near to which a few of the natural sources of dye stand in jars, ready to be used in making these soft, beautiful, expensive blankets. Organic, naturally dyed, imported merino yarn is for sale.

IN BELFAST

Belfast Co-op Store (207-338-2532; belfast .coop), 123 High St. Open daily 7:30 AM–8 PM. Everyone needs something in this store and café with its standout deli and lunches. **The Treasured Tea Leaf Tea Company** (207-930 5584) 158 High St., Belfast. Tea tastings, and more than 60 varieties to try. **Coyote Moon** (207-338-5659), 54 Main St., is a nifty, reasonably priced women's clothing and gift store. **All About Games** (207-338-9984), 78 Main St., is a great place to buy traditional board games; **The Game Loft**, 78A Main, over the store, is a youth center where kids can play nonelectronic games for free. **Colburn Shoe Store** (207-338-1934), 79 Main St., bills itself as the oldest shoe store in America, open since 1832. **Renys** (207-338-4588), Renys Plaza, Rt. 3 just north of the junction with Rt. 1, is one of Maine's chain of distinctive outlet stores. Always worth a stop (good for everything from TVs to socks).

NORTH ALONG RT. 1

Perry's Nut House (207-338-1630), Rt. 1 just north of the Belfast Bridge. Reopened and working on being what it used to be. The nut collection is in the Smithsonian. The man-eating clam cannot be located. **Mainely Pottery** (207-338-1108; mainelypottery.com), 181 Searsport Ave. (Rt. 1), features the work of owner Jamie Oates and carries varied work by 30 other Maine potters.

IN SEARSPORT

Silkweeds (207-548-6501), Rt. 1, Searsport. Specializes in "country gifts": tinware, cotton afghans, wreaths. **Waldo County Craft Co-op** (207-548-6686), 307 E. Main St. (Rt. 1), Searsport Harbor. Open mid-May–mid-Oct. daily 9–5, weekends until Christmas. A showcase for the local extension service.

✳ Special Events

May–October: **Belfast Farmers' Market**, Fri. 9–1 at 256 High St.

June–October: **Friday Night Art Walk.**

July 4: Parade, fairs, and fireworks in Searsport; **Arts in the Park**; and the **Celtic Festival.**

July–August: Free Thu.-night **street concerts** in downtown Belfast.

August: **Searsport Lobster Boat Races** and related events; **Marine Heritage Festival & Boatbuilding Challenge**; **Harbor Fest**, Belfast.

September: ❂ **Common Ground Fair** in Unity—organic farm products, children's activities, sheepdog roundup, crafts, entertainment, and terrific food.

October: First Sat., **Church Street Festival** and parade (first Sat.); **Fright at the Fort**, when Fort Knox is haunted. **Fling into Fall celebration** (Columbus Day weekend)—parade, bonfire, church suppers.

December: **Searsport Victorian Christmas**—open houses at museums, homes, and B&Bs; **New Year's by the Bay.**

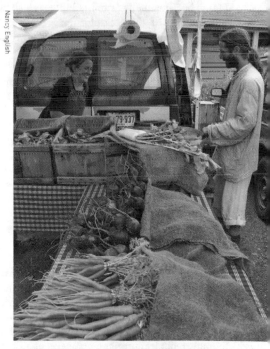

ORGANIC PRODUCE AT BELFAST FARMERS' MARKET

EAST PENOBSCOT BAY REGION

Bucksport/Orland Area, Blue Hill Peninsula, Stonington and Isle au Haut, Castine

T he dramatic Waldo-Hancock bridge at the Penobscot Narrows links two counties and Midcoast with Downeast Maine. It visually underscores the sense of turning a major coastal corner.

Bucksport/Orland Area

Whoosh and the elevator sets you 45 stories above the Penobscot River, atop one of the two obelisk-like pylons anchoring the dramatic bridge at the confluence of the Penobscot River and Penobscot Bay. The entrance to this observatory is in neighboring Fort Knox State Park and the best view of both bridge and fort is from Bucksport's waterside walkway. Cross the island of Verona and hang a left down Bucksport's recently revived Main Street.

Positioned at the head of Penobscot Bay and mouth of the Penobscot River, Bucksport was a major shipping port in 1799, the reason it was burned by the British then and was later occupied by them during the War of 1812. In the 1820s it was the largest town in eastern Maine but eventually atrophied into a small, work-a-day mill town. Its present transformation began with the 2014 closure of the paper mill, its longtime economic underpinning. Empty storefronts and historic buildings began filling with inviting places to eat, shop, and browse, complementing those already here.

GUIDANCE **Bucksport Bay Area Chamber of Commerce** (207-469-6818; bucksportbay chamber.com), 52 Main St. Open June–Oct., Mon., Thu., and Fri.; fewer days off-season. Brochures available 24 hours.

PUBLIC RESTROOMS The Bucksport Waterfront Walkway just off Rt. 1 (hang left at the light at the end of the Verona Bridge) offers clean, seasonal restrooms right near the bridge and a short way up at the town landing. This is the perfect place for man and beast alike to take a break after a long ride. Note the doggy waste bags and water bowls as well as drinking fountains.

✳ To Do

Northeast Historic Film/The Alamo Theatre (207-469-0924; oldfilm.org), 85 Main St., Bucksport (entrance on Elm). This 125-seat, vintage-1916 restored theater is open year-round, featuring first-run movies, Dolby digital sound, low prices, and real buttered popcorn. It is also a venue for concerts and live performances. The theater was restored by nonprofit Northeast Historic Film, New England's only "moving-image" archive. Stock footage, technical services, and sales of videos of life in New England are all available. The

East Penobscot
Bay Region

© The Countryman Press

MUST SEE

guide.com), Rt. 174 (off Rt. 1), Prospect. The observatory is open May through Oct., daily 9–5, until 6 in July/Aug. Combo tickets for the observatory/fort are $7 adults ($5 for Maine residents), $3 ages 5–11, $4 for seniors ($2.50 charge for Maine seniors). Nominal admission for the fort only (open in-season until sunset). West of the Waldo-Hancock bridge a traffic light eases access to the Fort Knox grounds, site of the elevator up to the observatory. The elevator whisks you to the top in a minute. Far below, Bucksport is a toy town, and from another window Penobscot Bay sweeps away to the horizon. This is the only bridge with an observatory in the country.

Massive **Fort Knox** itself was built in 1844 as a defense against Canada during the so-called "Aroostook War" with New Brunswick. The war, really a boundary dispute, was ignored in Washington, and so in 1839 the new, lumber-rich state took matters into its own hands by arming its northern forts and mobilizing the militia. The war formally ended in 1842 without a shot being fired, but Maine built this fort two years later, just in case. Though it was never entirely completed, troops were stationed here during the Civil War and again during the Spanish-American War. This is a great fort with plenty of tunnels and turrets to explore. It's a venue for re-enactments, dramas, and a variety of events—including "Fright of the Fort" nights, sponsored by Friends of Fort Knox, on the two weekends before Halloween. Check the website.

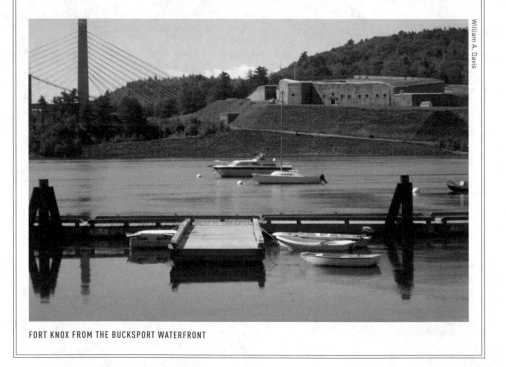

FORT KNOX FROM THE BUCKSPORT WATERFRONT

William A. Davis

theater store is open during business hours (weekdays 9–4) as well as weekends in July and Aug. during films and performances. The events line is 207-469-6910; check the website for available films.

The Bucksport Waterfront Walkway. A landscaped brick path stretches a mile from the Verona Bridge to the town landing and on up along the Penobscot River. The **Bucksport**

Historical Society Museum (207-469-3284), open July–Sept., Wed.–Fri. 1–4, Sat. 2–4, is housed in the former waterside Maine Central Railroad Station and is genuinely interesting.

Craig Brook National Fish Hatchery, (207-469-7300), 306 Hatchery Rd., East Orland (marked from Rt. 1). First opened in 1889, this is the country's oldest salmon hatchery. A visitors center (open daily 8–3) offers videos and interactive displays on Maine rivers, watersheds, and salmon. A small Atlantic Salmon Flyfishing Museum exhibits salmon industry memorabilia. There's also a boat launch on Alamoosook Lake, a picnic area and swim beach on Craig Pond, and hiking trails.

✳ Lodging

✪ ♂ ♂ (ᵧ) **Alamoosook Lakeside Inn** (207-469-6393; alamoosooklakesideinn.com), 229 Soper Rd., Orland. Open year-round. A few miles north of Rt. 1, this log lodge—built as a corporate retreat—feels much farther away. Grounds stretch along the lake and you can swim at the beach or push off in a paddleboat or kayak. Innkeeper Gina Bushong likes to help guests explore off the beaten path. The six attractive guest rooms are $95–148 per couple and $10 for each additional person, breakfast included. The lakeside dining room lends itself to weddings and retreats.

Fort Knox Park Inn (207-469-3113; fort knoxparkinn.com), 64 Main St., Bucksport 04416. Open year-round. Built as a modern annex to the old Jed Prouty Inn, it offers rooms with a choice of two double beds, a queen, or king. Request a view of Fort Knox and the dramatic bridge across the mouth of the Penobscot River, well worth the extra $10. $80–150 per couple, depending on the room and season.

(ᵧ) **Williams Pond Lodge Bed & Breakfast** (207-460-6064; williwamspondlodge.com), 327 Williams Pond Rd., Bucksport. We hear great things but honestly we have yet to visit this solar-powered, pond-side lodge deep in the woods, just seven miles north of Main St. The three guestrooms (one accommodates four) are cheerfully rustic with private baths. Guests are greeted with a fresh-baked evening dessert and breakfast is full, included along with use of canoes in $190–200 rates, discounts for three days, midweek.

✳ Where to Eat

♂ (ᵧ) **MacLeods** (207 469-3963), 63 Main St., Bucksport. Open daily. 4–close, also lunch from 11:30 Tue.–Fri. Newly lightened and brightened, still dependably pleasurable dining with entrées ($11–24) ranging from comfort food such as baked meat loaf and barbecued ribs to specials pastas, salads and lobster rolls to fresh-broiled scallops and roasted prime rib.

♂ **Harbor View Grille** (207-469-3396), 96 Main St., Bucksport. Open daily 6 AM–8 PM. Sited on the town dock, it overlooks water, Fort Knox, and the bridge. Reasonably priced seafood baskets and specials and a full road-food menu. Kids' menu, too.

♂ **Wahl's Dairy Port** (207 469-3697), 79 Main St., Bucksport. Open Apr.–late Sept., 11–8. For more than 50 years this old-fashioned ice cream stand has been dishing it up: many flavors of ice cream (Gifford's), also soft serve, frozen yogurt, sherbet, shakes, and more.

✳ Selective Shopping

Lighthouse Arts Center (TC; lighthouseart scenter.com), 86 Main St., Bucksport. Open year-round, Mon. –Sat. The street-level gallery in this recently renovated, three-story building showcases work by dozens of established, locally based and connected artists and photographers, as well as sculptors, woodworkers, jewelry-makers, and potters; a shop sells art supplies and gifts. The entrance to the arts studio space is a level down and behind the street, accessed from the Waterfront Walkway. Check the website for ongoing classes.

&. (ᵖ) **Book Stacks** (207-469-8992 or 1-888-295-0123), 71 Main St., Bucksport. Open Mon.–Sat. 9–6, Sun. 9–3. Andy Lacher's inviting, full-service bookstore is reason enough to stop in Bucksport. Aside from a wide selection of titles, periodicals, and cards, it offers WiFi, coffee, comfortable seating, and a welcoming cat. You can also pick up a pretty good bottle of wine.

H.O.M.E. (207-469-7961; homecoop.net), Rt. 1, Orland. Open daily 9–5. Homeworkers Organized for More Employment is part of the international Emmaus community, selling crafted coverlets, toys, and clothing; and a market stand with fresh vegetables, herbs, garden produce, and Christmas wreaths. Among its many good works, this non-profit offers shelter to refugees and the homeless. Well worth a stop.

Allen's Wild Maine Blueberries (207-469-7060), Rt. 15, Orland. South of Rt. 1 a huge blue processing plant looms above blueberry barrens. Turn up the driveway to find the small Wild Blueberry Patch Gift Shop selling fresh (in season) and frozen berries as well as mixes and souvenirs. During blueberry season you are also likely to find a stand open on Rt. 1, just south of the Rt. 15 turn-off.

✳ Special Events

Note: Check with **Friends of Fort Knox** (fort knox.maineguide.com) for colorful events at the fort, staged most weekends Apr.–Oct. Halloween is huge here.

July: **Bay Festival** (last weekend)—parade, plus a variety of events on the river; at the fort and along the Bucksport waterfront.

August: h.o.m.e.'s **Annual Craft & Farm Fair and Benefit Auction** (207-469-7961; homecoop.net). A Sat. blueberry pancake breakfast, poetry readings, music, fish-fry supper, street dance, BBQ, children's games, crafts, and more.

October: **Ghostport**, Bucksport. Held 10–10 Sat. before Halloween—coffin races, lunch with witches, goblins' parade, tent dance, fireworks, and much more. Shuttle runs to **Fright of the Fort** across the river at Fort Knox, held the two weekends before Halloween.

Blue Hill Peninsula

The series of peninsulas and islands defining the eastern rim of Penobscot Bay—an intermingling of land and water along ponds and tidal rivers, as well as bays—is a landscape that's exceptional, even in Maine. Scattered over an area webbed with narrow roads threading numerous land fingers are roads leading to studios of local craftspeople and artists. What you remember afterward is the beauty of clouds over fields of wildflowers, quiet coves, some amazing things that have been woven, painted, or blown, and conversations with the people who created them. Getting anywhere takes longer than you'll anticipate, so it's best to allow a few days here.

In Maine, *Blue Hill* refers to a specific hill, a village, a town, a bay, and a peninsula—also to an unusual gathering of artists, musicians, and craftspeople. A shade off the beaten path, one peninsula west of Mount Desert, Blue Hill has its own following—especially among creative people. For many decades the small town of Brooklin was a familiar byline in *The New Yorker* thanks to E. B. White, who also wrote *Charlotte's Web* and *Stuart Little* here at about the time children began to read about Blueberry Hill in Robert McCloskey's *Blueberries for Sal* and about Condon's Garage (still a South Brooksville family-owned landmark) in the 1940s classic *One Morning in Maine*. In the 1950s Helen and Scott Nearing, searching for a new place to live "the Good Life," swung a dowsing pendulum over a map of coastal Maine. It came to rest on Cape Rosier.

Energy lines or not, this peninsula is exceptionally beautiful, with views to the east toward Mount Desert as well as back across Penobscot Bay. Pause at the turnout on Caterpillar Hill, the height-of-land on Rt. 15/175 (just north of the Deer Isle Bridge), to appreciate the panorama. Then plunge down the hill to an improbably narrow, soaring suspension bridge.

MUST SEE

A dozen miles south of Rt. 1 via Rt. 15, the **Blue Hill Village** (blue hill.gov) is cradled between its namesake hill and bay. In the center of town you'll find a pillared town hall, a handsome WPA library, two Federal-era historic houses, shops, and galleries. This is the peninsula hub, but to come this far and no farther would be like walking up to a door and not opening it. The beauty of the peninsula lies beyond—down roads that wander southwest to **Brooksville** (Rt. 15 south to Rt. 176 north to Rt. 176/175) and across the **Bagaduce River** at the **Reversing Falls** (see Bagaduce Lunch in *Eating Out*); head south on Rt. 176 to **Bucks Harbor**. Rt 176 rejoins Rt. 175 and then Rt. 15; follow it south (right) over **Caterpillar Hill**, where a pullout permits space to enjoy one of the most spectacular panoramas across Penobscot Bay to the Camden Hills. From this height Rt. 15 plunges downhill. Turn left at the bottom, following Rt. 175 as it shadows **Eggemoggin Reach**, through Sargentville, winds up around the Benjamin River in Sedgwick, and down along the Reach again into **Brooklin**, home to **WoodenBoat School** (see *Special Learning Programs*). See *Selective Shopping* for stops along the way.

The 1939 bridge spans Eggemoggin Reach, a 10-mile-long passage dividing the Blue Hill Peninsula from Little Deer Isle but linking Penobscot and Jericho Bays. A century ago this was a busy thoroughfare, a shortcut from Rockland to points Downeast for freight-carrying schooners and passenger steamboats. It remains a popular route for windjammers, yachts, and, increasingly, sea kayakers.

GUIDANCE The **Blue Hill Peninsula Chamber of Commerce** (207-374-3242; bluehill peninsula.org), 10D South St. (beside Dunkin' Donuts), Blue Hill, covers the six peninsula towns, publishing a booklet guide. Its year-round information center is open Mon.–Fri. 11–3. Pick up a guide and local map (essential). Also pick up the current free copies of the **Arts Guide** and the **Bay Community Register**. **The Weekly Packet** lists what's going on each day.

GETTING THERE *By car:* From points south take I-95 to Rt. 295 to I-95 (briefly) to Exit 113: Rt. 3 to Belfast and Rt. 1 to Rt. 15 to Blue Hill. There are many shortcuts through the confusing web of roads on this peninsula; ask directions to your lodging.

By air: The nearest commercial airports are **Bangor International** (flybangor.com) and **Hancock County & Bar Harbor Airport** (between Ellsworth and Bar Harbor).

WHEN TO COME Most Blue Hill lodging is seasonal, mid-May through October.

✳ To See

Jonathan Fisher House (207-374-2459; jonathanfisherhouse.org), 0.5 mile south of Blue Hill Village on Rt. 15/176. Open July–Labor Day, Wed.–Sat. 1–4; Fri., Sat. until Columbus Day. A house built in 1814 by Blue Hill's first pastor, a Harvard graduate who augmented his meager salary with a varied line of crafts and by teaching (he founded Blue Hill Academy), farming, and writing. His furniture, paintings, books, journals, and woodcuts are exhibited. Antiques show mid-Aug. Admission $5.

Holt House, 3 Water St., Blue Hill. Open July–mid-Sept., Tue. and Fri. 1–4, Sat. 11–2. The Blue Hill Historical Society collection is housed in this restored 1815 Federal mansion near the harbor and noted for its stenciled walls. Don't pass this by if it's open: a lovely old house filled with images and tokens evoking Blue Hill's past.

Blue Hill Library (207-374-5515; bhpl.net), 5 Parker Point Rd., Blue Hill. Open daily

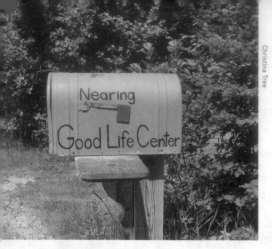

THE GOOD LIFE CENTER

except Sun. A handsome WPA building with periodicals and ample reading space; changing art shows in summer.

Bagaduce Music Lending Library (207-374-5454; bagaducemusic.org), 49 South St. (Rt. 172), Blue Hill. Open Mon.–Fri. 10–4. Relocated in new, larger quarters in 2017, this Blue Hill phenomenon features roughly 250,000 sheet music titles (instrumental, keyboard, and vocal), some more than a century old and most special for one reason or another—all available for borrowing. The collection includes more than 1,400 pieces about Maine, by Maine composers, or published in Maine. Stop by just to see the mural over the entrance.

The Good Life Center (207-326-8211; goodlife.org), 372 Harborside Rd., Harborside, on Cape Rosier. Open June–Labor Day, Thu.–Mon. 1–4, then weekends until Columbus Day; and by appointment. The grounds are open year-round. **Forest Farm** is a stone home built in 1973 by Scott Nearing when he was in his 90s (d. 1983), along with Helen, then in her 70s. The couple coauthored *Living the Good Life* and seven other books based on their simple, purposeful lifestyle. The grounds include an intensively cultivated organic garden, a greenhouse, and a yurt. Check the website for workshops.

✷ To Do

BOATING **Buck's Harbor Marine** (207-326-8839), South Brooksville, rents sail- and motor-boats. Inquire about sailing lessons.

Also see *Sea Kayaking, Canoeing*.

FISHING **Eggemoggin Guide Service** (207-359-2746; eggemogginguideservice.net), Sedgwick. Captain Pete Douvarjo offers half-day trips for striped bass and full-day float trips on the Penobscot River. Fly-fishing and handcrafted fishing rods are specialties.

SEA KAYAKING, CANOEING **The Activity Shop** (207-374-3600; activityshop.com), 139 Mines Road, Blue Hill. Old Town canoes, kayak, and bicycle rentals. The Bagaduce River north from Walker Pond is a favorite flatwater run for novices, with some popular whitewater at Blue Hill Falls, a reversing falls accessible off Rt. 175. Also see *To Do* in "Stonington and Isle au Haut" and "Castine."

SPECIAL LEARNING PROGRAMS **WoodenBoat School** (207-359-4651; thewoodenboatschool.com), off Naskeag Rd., south of Brooklin Village. A spinoff from *WoodenBoat* magazine, this seafaring institute of national fame offers summer courses that range from building your own sailboat, canoe, or kayak to navigation and drawing and painting. Accommodations available. The store is a shopping destination in its own right; open weekdays 7:30–6, Sat. 9–5.

Also see **Haystack Mountain School of Crafts** in "Stonington and Isle au Haut."

SWIMMING **Walker Pond Landing**, Sedgwick. From Rt. 175/15 south of the Caterpillar Hill lookout, turn right on Cooper Farm Road, right again on Walker Pond Road. This is a

BUCKS HARBOR IS A SAILING CENTER

joint Brooksville/Sedgwick-maintained facility with a roped-off swim area and raft, boat launch, and a sand beach with warm, shallow water; great for small children.

✳ Green Space

Blue Hill. Our friends at the Blue Hill Bookstore tell us that this was not the setting for the children's classic *Blueberries for Sal*, by Robert McCloskey—a longtime summer resident of the area. But we choose to disbelieve them. It looks just like the hill in the book and has its share of in-season blueberries. The big attraction, however, is the view of the Mount Desert mountains from the 934-foot summit. From Rt. 172 take Mountain Rd. to the parking area (on your right). It's a mile to the top via the Hayes Trail, a little longer if you loop back down to the road via the Osgood Trail through Blue Hill Heritage Trust land. A trail right from town begins behind the post office.

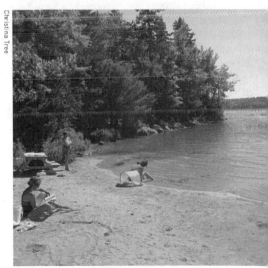

Holbrook Island Sanctuary State Park (207-326-4012; friendsofholbrook.org), Cape Rosier Road, off Rt. 176 in West Brooksville, is 1,350 acres, including 2.3 miles of shore and 115-acre Holbrook Island. Check the website for a detailed map. A network of old roads and trails leads along the shore and through marshes and forest. This is the gift of Anita Harris, who died in 1985 at age 92. Her will stipulated that her mansion and all the other buildings on Holbrook Island and

THE BEACH AT WALKER POND LANDING

in the sanctuary be demolished. Birding is exceptional, especially during spring and fall migrations. Great blue herons nest around the pond and the estuary. Bald eagles may also be seen. Guided nature walks in-season.

Blue Hill Heritage Trust (207-374-5118; bluehillheritagetrust.org) is steadily increasing the amount of preserved open space throughout the peninsula. Check the website for a current trail list (at this writing there are 20) and descriptions. Our latest discovery is Bluff Head, a quick and easy walk in the woods to a rocky outcropping high above the Bagaduce River.

✐ **Blue Hill Town Park**. Follow Water St. past the hospital to this pleasant waterside park with picnic tables and great rocks for kids.

✳ Lodging

INNS AND B&BS

IN BLUE HILL

✪ 🐾 ♿ **Blue Hill Inn** (207-374-2844 or 1-800-826-7415; bluehillinn.com), 40 Union St. The inn is open mid-May–Oct.; the Cape House, year-round. There's a grace to this classic 1830s New England inn on a quiet, elm-lined street in the village. The sitting room and library are stocked with reading material, and innkeeper Duncan Hamilton shows a sure touch and attention to detail in 11 guest rooms, some with sitting room and/or working fireplace. The handicap-accessible Cape House cottage is divided into two suites with kitchen facilities. Guests may gather for wine and hors d'oeuvres in the evening. A full breakfast with a choice of entrées is served at individual tables in the large, sunny dining

room. It's included along with afternoon tea in $195–265 double for rooms in high season, from $145 before July. Suites are $285–375 in-season; from $170 in winter.

Also see *Dining Out*.

The Farmhouse Inn (207-374-5286), 578 Pleasant St. (Rt. 15). Open almost year-round. In 2015 Bill and Ann Rioux reopened the former Blue Hill Farm Country Inn after totally renovating the 19th-century farmhouse and attached barn, reducing guest rooms from 14 to 9. An instant success as a restaurant (see *Dining Out*), its rooms are also now bright and appealing, all with private baths, common space, and game rooms. From $150 for a cozy room with a large skylight to $300 for a two-room suite, breakfast included.

ELSEWHERE ON THE BLUE HILL PENINSULA

♂ 📶 **Wave Walker Bed & Breakfast** (207-667-5767; wavewalkerbedandbreakfast.com), 28 Wavewalker Lane, Surry 04684. Open year-round. Sited near the tip of Newbury Neck with spectacular views across the bay to Mount Desert Island, this expansive house comes with 20 acres and a 1,000-foot waterfront. The four guest rooms all have views and many comfort perks. $195–290 in-season; from $115 off, three-day minimum, weekly rates. Inquire about weddings and the Guest House.

📶 **Maine Hideaway Guest House** (207-610-2244; mainehideway.com), 19 Naskeag Point, Brooklin. An attractive old house up the road from Wooden Boat and a short walk from the village offers uncluttered rooms that vary in size and shape; private and shared baths, $105–175, breakfast included.

Christina Tree

BLUE HILL INN

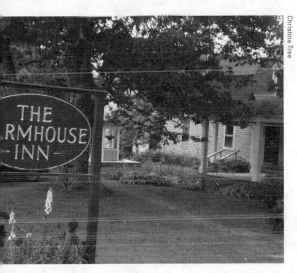

THE FARMHOUSE INN

The Brooklin Inn (207-359-2777; brook lininn.com), 22 Reach Rd., Brooklin 01416. A casual, friendly, year-round village inn up the road from the Wooden Boat School. Chip and Gail Angell are the right innkeepers for this landmark that's known for its restaurant (see *Dining Out*). The five pleasant upstairs rooms (three with private bath) are $155–195, includes full-breakfast, less off-season. Guests are shuttled from moorings.

COTTAGES AND MORE ✪ ✕ (((•))) 🐾 **Oakland House Cottages by the Side of the Sea** (207-359-8521; oaklandhouse.com), 435 Herrick Rd., Brooksville. Few rental cottages have the kind of setting and views these 10 can offer, salted through the woods and along the shorefront near the entrance to Eggemoggin Reach. Each is different, with cooking facilities, living room, and fireplace. Accommodating up to eight, they offer access to an expansive beach, a rec hall with weekly happenings, and 60 mostly wooded acres laced with trails. They are part of former Oakland House resort (check-in is still at the picturesque old hotel), and its "Barn" continues to house weekly events (open to the public) in summer. $150–326 per night in high season, less per week.

Acorn by the Sea (207-359-8521; maine hostel.com). A rehabbed annex on the Oakland House property (see above), it has six country-comfortable rooms; all share a kitchen, baths, and attractive common rooms, as well as access to the beach and trails. From $40 per room.

✪ 🦞 🐾 ✕ (((•))) **Hiram Blake Camp** (207-326-4951; hiramblake.com), Cape Rosier, Harborside. Open May–Columbus Day weekend. Well off the beaten track and operated by Deborah Venno's family since 1916, this is the kind of place where you come to stay put. The one- to three-bedroom cottages each have a living room with a wood-burning stove, kitchen, shower, porch, and view of Penobscot Bay. In July and Aug., everyone eats in the dining room, which doubles as a library with thousands of books ingeniously filed away by category in the ceiling. There are rowboats at the dock and kayaks for rent, a playground, and a recreation room with table tennis and board games; also trails. In high season, from $1,075 per week with breakfast and dinner for the one-room Acorn Cottage to $3,450 for a three-bedroom cottage (up to five guests). Rates drop during "housekeeping months" (when the dining room closes at the end of Aug.) to $800–1,700 per week plus $20 for linen. Most cottages are reserved by Jan., but it's worth checking.

Peninsula Property Rentals (207-374-2428; peninsulapropertyrentals.com), Main St., Blue Hill 04614. A range of area rentals. Also see **Maine Vacation Rentals** (207-374-2444; mainevacationrentalsonline.com), 105 Main St., Blue Hill.

OAKLAND HOUSE

❋ Where to Eat

DINING OUT

IN BLUE HILL

Arborvine (207-374-2119; arborvine.com), 33 Tenney Hill (Rt. 172), south Blue Hill Village. Open for dinner Tue.–Sun. in-season, Fri.–Sun. off-season. Few Maine restaurants are as widely acclaimed, and reservations may be necessary a couple of days in advance. Chef-owner John Hikade and his wife, Beth, restored the handsome 1820s Hinckley homestead. The several open-beamed dining rooms with fireplaces are simple and elegant. The menu presents local produce in memorable ways. For starters try Bagaduce River oysters in the half shell with a frozen sake mignonette ($12). Entrées $26–34. The reasonably priced wine list is extensive.

🍴 **Barncastle** (207-374-2300), 125 South St. Open daily year-round 3–8, until 9 Fri., Sat. This former mansion is an unlikely but delightful venue for the area's best pizza. The ambience is casual, the oven is wood-fired, and the pie comes with a choice of more than 30 toppings. The reasonably priced menu also includes crabcakes, ribs, mussels in white wine, also sandwiches and salads featuring local farm ingredients.

The Farmhouse Inn (207-374-5286), 578 Pleasant St. (Rt. 15) , Blue Hill (2 miles north of the village). Open most of the year Wed.–Sat., 3–5 happy hour with a wide selection of tapas and small plates, then a full menu. An open-raftered, nicely rehabbed barn with well-spaced tables and an attractive 10-seat bar. Many small plates to choose from. Entrées $16-18. Owner Ann Rioux is also a local caterer, ably assisted by daughter Megan Rioux.

ELSEWHERE ON THE BLUE HILL PENINSULA

⊙ **Buck's Restaurant** (207-326-8688), Buck's Harbor Market, center of South Brooksville, Rt. 176. Open seasonally except Sun. 5:30–8:30; check nights off-season. Reserve. The informal dining room behind the village market is decorated with local sculpture and art and is all about turning local ingredients into tasty dishes. The menu changes daily,

but starters might include local mussels with house-made chorizo and grilled swordfish with spicy mango and papaya relish. Entrées $18–32.

⊙ **The Brooklin Inn** (207-359-2777; brooklininn.com), 22 Reach Rd. (Rt. 175), Brooklin Village. Reservations advised. Open for lunch and nightly in summer, closed Mon. and Tue. in winter. This hospitable small-village inn religiously serves only wild fish and produce that's organic and local. Chefs tend to change, but quality has been consistent. Entrées: $22 for chicken Francaise to $30 for scallops. A three-course prix fixe is $28. There's also a downstairs pub with its own menu.

🍴 **The Lookout Inn & Restaurant** (207-359-2188; thelookoutinn.biz), 455 Flye Point Rd., Brooklin. Open for dinner Tue.–Sat. mid-June–mid-Oct.; call off-season. Owner Butch Smith was in the kitchen on our last visit, and the sautéed duck breast with raspberry mustard glaze was delicious as was the baked artichoke with kale as a starter. A bit of a local secret, this is one of Maine's oldest family-owned summer hotels and the view is across the sloping meadow to the bay. Entrées $26–30.

The Blue Hill Inn (207-374-2844), 40 Union Street. Inquire about Monday night dinners at Blue Hill's iconic inn (see *Lodging*). At this writing a Monday night $85 four-course tasting menu with paired wines is deservedly popular (reservations required).

Christina Tree

BOATYARD GRILL

BAGADUCE LUNCH HAS BEEN NAMED "AN AMERICAN CLASSIC" BY THE JAMES BEARD FOUNDATION

The fact that the inn's bountiful breakfasts are open to the public is a bit of a secret.

Also see *Dining Out* in "Stonington and Isle au Haut," and "Castine" and **Nebo Lodge Dinner Cruises** under *Boating*.

EATING OUT

IN BLUE HILL

✒ **Boatyard Grill** (207-374-3533), 13 E. Blue Hill Rd. Open June–mid-Sept., Tue.–Sat. for lunch and dinner but call. Eat inside or out in a pavilion sited in a working boatyard. Chef-owner Annelise Riggall serves up local mussels, clams, and lobster in forms that range from pizza and mac-and-cheese to a shore dinner. Daily specials and all seafood is grilled rather than fried.

✒ **The Fish Net** (207-374-5840), Blue Hill Village, 162 Main St. (Rt. 172). Open seasonally 11–8, until 9 Fri.–Sat. Known for lobster rolls; also as a place to feast on lobster and steamers or to buy a cooked lobster to take home, plus the usual fried seafood, burgers, and sandwiches. Seating inside and out with a playground for kids.

✒ **Marlintini's Grill** (207-374-2500), 89 Mines Rd. (Rt. 15/176) south of Blue Hill Village. Local favorite, open for all three meals. There's a sports bar but plenty of space to get away from it. Grilled and fried meat and seafood, hot sandwiches, and nightly specials.

The Deep Water Brew Pub (207-374-2441; arborvine.com), 33 Tenney Hill. Open seasonally, Tue.–Sun. for supper; bar open until 10.

No reservations. The attraction is beer (primarily ales) handcrafted in the solar-powered microbrewery in the barn behind Arborvine (see *Dining Out*). The casual pub, created by Tim Hikade and partner Chrissy Allen, offers a reasonably priced menu featuring burgers, ribs, and the like.

Blue Hill Food Co-op Café (207-374-2165), Rt. 172 in Green's Hill Place, but due to move in 2018 to South St. Open daily in summer 7–8, off-season, 7–7. This attractive café is part of a well-stocked market specializing in organic and local produce as well as wines, vitamins, and premade sandwiches. Organic coffees, teas, wines, and a selection of baked goods, soups, sandwiches, and specials.

Bucklyn Coffee (917-971-3246), 103 Main St. Open 8–4. That small yellow building across from the post office is the source of the best coffee in town. David Dillon is a passionate barista and the well-chosen beans make memorable espressos and lattes. Muffins and pastries are different daily, always freshly baked.

ELSEWHERE ON THE BLUE HILL PENINSULA

✪ ✒ **El El Frijoles** (207-359-2486; elelfrijoles.com), 41 Caterpillar Hill Rd. (Rt. 15), Sargentville. Open Memorial Day–Sept., Wed.–Sun. 11–8, off-season Wed. and Thu. 11–7. We love the takeoff on L.L. Bean. Michael Rossney and Michele La Vesque serve up California/Mexican food with local ingredients, right down to the black beans. Taco and burrito fillings include grilled veggies and carnitas (slow-braised, shredded pork with chilies, onions, and spices). The house special is spicy lobster. Mini burritos and a PB&J quesadilla for kids. Takeout and a few inside tables, more seating outside at covered and open picnic tables, a play structure, sandbox, and badminton court.

✪ 🦞 **Bagaduce Lunch** (207-326-4197), 145 Franks Flat Rd. (Rt. 176), South Penobscot at the reversing falls and the bridge to North Brooksville. Open seasonally, 11–3, except Wed. Owned by the Snow family for more than 70 years, this hugely popular lunch stand is a must. Fried seafood baskets are the big draw, and they will spoil you for seafood baskets anywhere else forever. Generous crab and lobster rolls. Picnic tables are scattered over the lawn that slopes to the Bagaduce River.

⚓ **Millbrook Company Bakery and Restaurant** (207-359-8344), 160 Snow's Cove Rd. (Rt. 15), Sedgwick. Open year-round, Wed.–Sun. 7:30–2. Attractive dining room, great breads, focaccia, "local chef salad" with locally sourced greens, veggies, and goat cheese, with or without marinated grilled chicken or fish. Daily specials, inside/outside dining.

Buck's Harbor Market (207-326-8683), Cornfield Hill Rd. (Rt. 176), Brooksville Village. Open year-round, 8–6. Soups, deli, baking done here (baked olives too); great picnic fare. The market also has a few tables, should you decide to stay and eat.

Tinder Hearth Wood-Fired Bread (207-326-8381; tinderhearth.com), 1452 Coastal Rd., West Brooksville. Look for the wood-fired bread and croissants in area shops. The thin-crust pizza, made from organic flour with locally sourced toppings, is available from the bakery Tue. , Wed., and Fri. 5–8 PM. Reserve ahead. Check the website for added summer days and music.

✪ **Perry's Lobster Shack** (207-667-1955) 1076 Newbury Neck Rd, Surry. Open May–mid-Oct., but call to check in shoulder months. Near the tip of a long, skinny sliver of land dangling off the peninsula proper in Surry. Picnic tables on the dock below with a view of Acadia. Great lobster and crab rolls, plus local sweet corn and homemade ice cream sandwiches. BYOB.

JUD HARTMAN GALLERY, BLUE HILL

Pugnuts Ice Cream Shoppe, (207-412-0086; pugnuts.com) 127 Surry Rd (Jct. Rt. 172), Surry. Open year-round, Tue.–Sun., 12–9 in summer, until 8 off-season. The sensational artisanal ice cream and gelato is well worth the ten-minute drive from Blue Hill. Karl Holmes and Eric Treworgy create small-batches of ice cream in flavors like caramel cashew and ginger with geranium, creamy gelato like lavender and honey. Check the website for the many possibilities, also varied cones, cakes, and more, even a yummy non-dairy good-for-you creation . Settle in at a table in the former 19th century store.

PICNIC FIXINGS Don't waste a nice day by eating inside! For picnic sites, see *Green Space*. Also see **Buck's Harbor Market** in Brooksville and the **Blue Hill Food Co-op**.

❊ Entertainment

New Surry Theatre (207-200-4720; newsurry theatre.org), 18 Union St. (upstairs in the Blue Hill Town Hall). Performances and acting classes throughout the year.

⚓ **Kneisel Hall Chamber Music School and Festival** (207-374-2811; kneisel.org), Pleasant St. (Rt. 15), Blue Hill. One of the oldest chamber music festivals in the country (founded 1924). Faculty present string and ensemble music in a series of Sun. afternoon and Fri. evening concerts, June–Aug.; inquire about Young Artist Concerts.

PUGNUTS ICE CREAM IN SURRY DRAWS PATRONS FROM ELLSWORTH TO BUCKSPORT

WERU (207-469-6600; weru.org) is a major nonprofit community radio station based in East Orland (89.9 FM) known for folk and Celtic music, jazz, and reggae.

Flash in the Pans Community Steel Band (peninsulapan.org). Mon.-night street dances, Memorial Day–Labor Day, 7:30–9 throughout the Peninsula; check website for schedule.

Bagaduce Theatre Summer Play Festival (bagaducetheatre.com), Fowler Farm, Bagaduce Rd., Brooksville. Check the website for the season's schedule of classic plays and innovative productions by a mix of professional and local actors.

✳ Selective Shopping

IN BLUE HILL

ART **Jud Hartman Gallery and Sculpture Studio** (207-374-917; judhartmangallery.com), 79 Main St. Open mid-June–mid-Sept., daily. Hartman exhibits his nationally known realistic bronze sculptures of northeastern Native Americans as well as the work of other well-known local artists.

Randy Eckard (207-374-2510; randyeckard paintings.com), 29 Pleasant St. Open July–Sept., Tue.-Sat. 11–4. Limited-edition prints of the artist's precise, luminous landscapes.

HANDWORKS GALLERY, BLUE HILL

CYNTHIA WININGS GALLERY, BLUE HILL

Liros Gallery (207-374-5370; lirosgallery .com), Parker Point Rd., specializes in fine paintings, old prints, and Russian icons; appraisals.

Blue Hill Bay Gallery (207-274-4001; bluehillbaygallery.com), 11 Tenney Hill. Open 10–5 Memorial Day–Labor Day; weekends thereafter. Changing exhibits of 19th-century and contemporary art, featuring northern landscapes and the sea.

Cynthia Winings Gallery (207-204-5001; cynthiawiningsgallery.com), 24 Parker Point Rd. Open June–Oct., Tue.-Sat., also Mon. in July and Aug. A quality contemporary gallery.

✪ **Handworks Gallery** (207-374-5613; handworksgallery.org), 48 Main St. Open Memorial Day–late Dec., Mon.-Sat. 10–5; weekends year-round. A middle-of-town space filled with stunning work by Maine artists and artisans: handwoven clothing, jewelry, furniture, rugs, and blown glass and art.

Rackliffe Pottery (207-374-2297; rackliffe pottery.com), Rt. 172. Open Mon.-Sat. 8–4; also Sun. in July and Aug., noon–4. Since 1968 Phyllis and Phil Rackliffe have produced their distinctive pottery, featuring local clay and their own glazes. Their emphasis is on individual small pieces rather than on sets. Visitors are welcome to watch.

ELSEWHERE

Flye Point Sculpture Garden & Art Gallery (207-610-0350; flyepointart.com), 436 Flye Point Rd., Brooklin. Open Wed.–Sun., 11–4, Worth the detour off Rt. 175, this bayside home/gallery showcases work by a number of sculptors and Maine artists, featuring accordian books by watercolorist Marcia Stremlau. Ask for directions to walking trails on nearby Harriman Point.

SPECIAL SHOPS

IN BLUE HILL VILLAGE

✪ **Blue Hill Books** (207-374-5632; bluehill books.com), 26 Pleasant St (Rt. 15). Open Mon.–Sat. 10–5:30, Blue Hill. A long-established, independent, full-service, two-floor, family-run bookstore with a separate room for children's titles. One of the best bookstores in Maine, with frequent readings by the many local authors.

✪ **Blue Hill Wine Shop** (207-374-2161), 138 Main St. Open Mon.–Sat. 10–5:30. A long-established shop dedicated to the perfect cup of tea or coffee, a well-chosen wine, cheese, and the right blend of tobacco. Also morning coffee and muffins.

✪ **Black Dinah Chocolatiers** (207-374-5621), 5 Main St., inside the Fairwinds Florist building, Blue Hill. Open Mon.–Sat. 8:30–5, Sun. 10–3. Handcrafted from Venezuelan and Peruvian chocolate, local butter, cream, herbs, fruits, and flowers; signature truffles and artisanal ice cream, chocolate drinks, espresso, and cookies.

ON AND OFF RT. 175 ALONG EGGEMOGGIN REACH

Sedgwick Antiques (207-359-8834), 775 N. Sedgwick Rd. (Rt. 172), Sedgwick. May–Sept., Thu., Fri. 10–4, Sat. 12–4 and by appointment. William Petry runs an old-fashioned shop with a range of furniture, rugs, ceramics, and lighting, emphasis on formal styles.

Handmade Papers Gallery (207-359-8345), 113 Reach Rd., Brooklin. Open summer, Wed.–Sun. noon–5. Virginia Sarsfield fashions exquisite lamp shades and other creations from a variety of fibers, including tufts of cattail. She also carries a selection of striking prints, featuring maritime linocuts by James Dodds, and work in a variety of media, featuring rag rugs by Hillary Hutton.

✪ **Betsy's Sunflower** (207-359-5030), 12 Reach Rd., Brooklin. A winner. Unusual but handy kitchen and garden gadgets and other

THE BLUE HILL FARMERS' MARKET

nifty things for cottages and boats; also home furnishings, toys, gifts, books, sailcloth totes, local music, and more.

ALONG RT. 176

Tinder Hearth Wood-Fired Bread, (tinder hearth.com) 1452 Coastal Rd., West Brooksville. (See *Eating Out*.)

♂ ✿ **David's Folly Farm** (207-266-6512; davidsfollyfarm.com), 1390 Coastal Rd., West Brooksville. Look for the "Open" flag. A strikingly beautiful 200-year-old working farm. Emma and John Altman practice organic, sustainable methods. Check out the farm store for meat and produce and the website for frequent special events in the barn.

✳ Special Events

Memorial Day–mid-October: **Farmers' Markets**, in **Blue Hill**, Sat. 9–11:30 AM, Blue Hill Fairgrounds, Rt. 15; at Mainescape Garden Shop, Columbus Day–Apr. Crafts, food, and baked goods as well as seasonal produce and flowers. Guest artists in July and Aug. In **Brooklin**, Thu. 3–5 beside Friend Memorial Library. **Brooksville:** Tue. 9–11, Community Center, Cornfield Rd. **Surry:** Sweet Pea Gardens (center of town), Thu. 3–6.

July: **Touring Through Time** (fourth weekend)—all the local historical sites hold open houses. **Blue Hill Bach Festival**, last weekend; (bluehillbach.org).

August: **Academy Antiques Fair** (first weekend), George Stevens Academy, Blue Hill, is big. The **Annual St. Francis Fair** (mid-month), Blue Hill Fairgrounds, is bigger, also about antiques.

Labor Day weekend: **Blue Hill Fair** (207-374-3701; bluehillfair.com) at the fairgrounds—harness racing, a midway, livestock competitions; one of the most colorful old-style fairs in New England. Best view of the fireworks is from the top of Blue Hill.

Stonington and Isle au Haut

The narrow, half-mile-long suspension bridge across Eggemoggin Reach connects the Blue Hill Peninsula with Little Deer Isle, linked in turn by causeways and bridges to Deer Isle and its wandering land fingers. This intermingling of land and water is characterized by the kind of coves, spruce- and lupine-fringed inlets usually equated with "the real Maine." It's divided between the towns of Deer Isle and Stonington, and there are the villages of Sunset, Oceanville, and Sunshine, home of the nationally respected Haystack Mountain School of Crafts. Galleries display outstanding work by dozens of artists and craftspeople who live, or at least summer, in town.

Stonington, 36 miles south of Rt. 1, remains a working fishing harbor, but with more than its share of galleries. Most buildings, scattered on smooth rocks around the harbor, date from the 1880s to the World War I boom years, during which time Deer Isle's pink granite was shipped off to face buildings from Rockefeller Center to Boston's Museum of Fine Arts. The Deer Isle Granite Museum depicts Stonington at the height of the granite boom when its population was 5,000, compared with 1,143 in 2010.

In Stonington life still eddies around Billings Diesel and Marine and the commercial pier, home base for one of Maine's largest fishing/lobstering fleets. The tourist season is

EGGEMOGGIN REACH BRIDGE

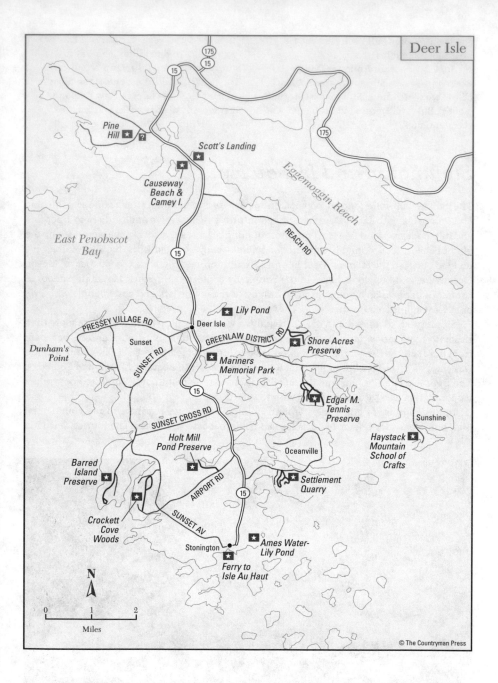

Pine Hill

Scott's Landing

Causeway Beach & Camey I.

Eggemoggin Reach

East Penobscot Bay

REACH RD

15

PRESSEY VILLAGE RD

Deer Isle

Lily Pond

GREENLAW DISTRICT RD

Shore Acres Preserve

Sunset

Dunham's Point

SUNSET RD

Mariners Memorial Park

15

Edgar M. Tennis Preserve

Sunshine

SUNSET CROSS RD

Holt Mill Pond Preserve

Oceanville

Haystack Mountain School of Crafts

Barred Island Preserve

AIRPORT RD

Settlement Quarry

15

Crockett Cove Woods

SUNSET AV

Stonington

Ames Water-Lily Pond

Ferry to Isle Au Haut

N

0   1   2
Miles

© The Countryman Press

short but busy enough to support a string of seasonal galleries and visitors-geared shops along waterside Main Street. The restored opera house stages frequent films, live performances, and readings, and the Reach Performing Arts Center is also active year-round. Hundreds of new houses have been built in recent decades, a boon to renters, and the number of nature preserves has also multiplied.

Stonington is a departure point for the mail boat to Isle au Haut, a wooded, mountainous island with more than half its acreage preserved as a part of Acadia National Park. The

STONINGTON WATERFRONT

boat makes seasonal stops at Duck Harbor, near the island's southern tip, accessing rugged, coastal hiking trails. The remaining half of the island, which supports some 70 year-round residents and an old summer colony, is vividly depicted in *The Lobster Chronicles* by Linda Greenlaw.

GUIDANCE **Deer Isle–Stonington Chamber of Commerce** (207-348-6124; deerisle.com) maintains an "Information Building" (with facilities) on Rt. 15 at Little Deer Isle, south of the bridge. Open 10–4 mid-June–Labor Day, sporadically after that for a few weeks. Pick up the current map/guide (an outside box is kept stocked) and a copy of *Island Advantages*, Stonington's weekly paper since 1882.

GETTING THERE Follow directions under *Getting There* in "Blue Hill Peninsula"; continue down Rt. 15 to Deer Isle.

PUBLIC RESTROOMS are on the public landing in Stonington.

✳ To See

✐ ❖ **Deer Isle Granite Museum** (207-367-6331), Main St., Stonington. Open July 3–Labor Day, 1–5 except Wed. This small museum features an 8-by-15-foot working model of quarrying operations on Crotch Island and the town of Stonington in 1900. Derricks move and trains carry granite to waiting ships. Photo blowups and a video also dramatize the story of the quarryman's life during the height of the boom.

✐ **The Penobscot East Resource Center** (207-367-2708; penobscoteast.org), 13 Atlantic Ave. Open seasonally, Mon.–Fri. 10–4. This is a regional fisheries research facility, but visitors are welcome in the Education Room with its touch tank and interactive "touch wall."

MUST SEE

Isle au Haut (pronounced *eye-la-HO*) is 6 miles long and 3 miles wide, a 45-minute boat ride from Stonington. Samuel de Champlain named it "High Island" in 1605, and the highest hill (543 feet) is named for him. It's a quiet, working island with a general store and an inn. More than half its land is maintained as part of **Acadia National Park**, with an 18-mile network of trails around **Duck Harbor** and along the cliffy southern tip. In summer the **Isle au Haut Ferry** offers round-trip service to Duck Harbor, allowing time to hike the dramatic Western Head and Cliff Trails. The town landing enjoys more frequent (year-round) ferry service, and a well-timed (seasonal) excursion boat also runs (see **Old Quarry Adventures**). From there it's a short walk to the ranger station (207-335-5551), where you can use the facilities and pick up a map, but then it's 6 miles over paved and unpaved roads (see *Bicycling*) to Duck Harbor. Allow four hours to enjoy the dramatic hiking trails, which are largely pine-needle-carpeted and shaded but demanding with cliffy outcroppings. Camping at Duck Harbor is mid-May–mid-Oct. in the five Adirondack-style shelters (each accommodating six people). Reserve on or as soon after April 1 as possible (207-288-8791, or download a form at nps.gov/acad). Leashed dogs permitted.

⚓ **Nervous Nellie's Jams and Jellies and Mountainville Café** (800-77-6845; nervous nellies.com), 598 Sunshine Rd., Deer Isle. Open May–Oct., 9–5, check off-season. Children of all ages love the whimsical life-sized sculptures Peter Beerits has created over the decades, including a "Nellieville" western-style village peopled by life-sized villains and heroes and a wood full of knights and dragons in Grail Castle, with owls and herons lurking in the shadows and plenty besides the sandbox to please small kids. There's no charge and at every turn the unexpected epitomizes what you come to expect when exploring this area. This all began with Anne and Peter's jams and jellies (wild blueberry preserves, blackberry-peach conserve, hot tomato chutney), cooked up every Mon.-Thu. The Mountainville Café serves tea, coffee, and scones with jams, etc. Three miles off Rt. 15.

The Salome Sellers House (207-348-2897), 416 Sunset Rd. (Rt. 15A), Sunset. Open mid-June–mid-Sept., Wed.–Fri. 1–4. Salome Sellers herself lived to be 108 years old in this snug 1803 red Cape, now the home of the Deer Isle–Stonington Historical Society, displaying ship models, Native American artifacts, and old photos; frequent summer events include music.

LIGHTHOUSES **Pumpkin Island Light**, at the entrance to Eggemoggin Reach, visible from the end of Eggemoggin Rd. on Little Deer Isle, now a private home. **Eagle Island Light** can be viewed from Sylvester Cove in Sunset or, better yet, from the Eagle Island mail boat, from which you can also see the **Heron Neck**, **Brown's Head**, and **Goose Rocks Lights**. From Goose Cove Lodge in Sunset, you can see and hear the now-automated **Mark Island Light** (its old bronze bell sits on the resort's lawn); the **Saddleback Ledge Light** is also visible on the horizon. The most extensive lighthouse cruise is offered by **Isle au Haut Ferry Service** (see *Boating*) once a month June–Sept., taking you from East Penobscot Bay through the Fox Islands Thorofare and back up along Vinalhaven and Isle au Haut.

✱ To Do

ART WORKSHOPS **Haystack** (see sidebar on page 297) is the famous draw here for artists as well as craftsmen but in summer short, plein-air classes are also available. Deer Isle-based watercolorist and Asian brush painter **Frederica Marshall** (see *Art Galleries and Artisans*) teaches year-round classes in her studio as well as seasonal outdoors workshops. This past summer we signed on for a four-day, Stonington-based workshop with **Marjory Glick** (marjory glick.com) a well-known landscape watercolorist and, it turns out, an exceptional teacher.

BICYCLING Old Quarry Ocean Adventures rents mountain bikes (see *Boating*), but we advise using two wheels only on quieter side roads and on Isle au Haut. **Isle au Haut Ferry Service** also rents bikes.

BOATING 🐾 🛶 **Isle au Haut Ferry Services** (207-367-5193; isleauhaut.com), end of Seabreeze Ave., Stonington, twice daily mid-June–mid-Sept. This is the only regularly scheduled service to Duck Harbor (see *Must See* sidebar on previous page) and it's limited to 50 daily passengers, first come/first served—so buy your ticket at least an hour before the 10 AM departure, then go get some breakfast. $39 roundtrip adults, $19.50 children, $4 pets (must be leashed). The mail boat also serves the island's town dock year-round. It takes kayaks and canoes ($23 one-way) and bicycles ($11 one-way). Check the website for frequent scenic cruises with lobster hauling, also special lighthouse tours.

    Old Quarry Ocean Adventures (207-367-8977; oldquarry.com), 130 Settlement Rd. off the Oceanville Rd., Stonington. Captain Bill Baker offers seasonal 9 AM runs to the Isle au Haut town dock (returning 5 PM), carrying bikes and kayaks gratis ($38.95 roundtrip adults, $20.50 children); guided kayaking around the island is also available. Stay aboard until noon for an ecotour. A variety of other cruises, sailboat rentals and lessons, kayak rentals and lessons, and both half- and full-day guided trips are also offered. The **Old Quarry Campground**, with platform tent sites and camp store, caters to kayakers. The waters off Stonington and Merchant's Row—the many islands just offshore—are among the most popular along the coast, but novice kayakers need a guide; bunkhouses are also available. Inquire about offshore island cottage rentals.

    Sunset Bay Co. Ferry Tour and Charter (207-701-9316), Deer Isle Yacht Club, Sylvester's Cove, Sunset. June–September. *Mailboat Kahterine* departs on a two-hour round, delivering mail and passengers to Eagle, Butter, and the smaller islands in this stretch of East Penobscot Bay. $24 per adult, $12 under age 12. Charters also available.

    Guided Island Tours (207-348-6789; guidedislandtours.com). Biologist and Registered Maine Guide Capt. Walt Reed takes up to five passengers aboard his former lobster boat on affordable tours that average two to three hours and focus on the wildlife and fisheries in the island-studded waters between Stonington and Isle au Haut.

    Charters and Dinner Cruises From Stonington the island of North Haven is a 288 mile-drive (five hours plus) to Rockland and then a 75-minute ferry ride. Both *Susan Marie* **Charters** (207-367-6318) or the *Nanatoo* **Charters** (207-367-5146) offer a 40-mintue cruise across Penobscot Bay to dinner at North Haven's classy Nebo Lodge. Both are lobster boat-style vessels, designed by their captains to comfortably carry passengers. We can't say enough for

NERVOUS NELLIE'S JAMS AND JELLIES

our cruise aboard the *Susan Marie*: Capt. Peter Buxton makes the early dinner reservations and pairs passengers for a specific date, making the evening sunset run affordable ($55 per person). Via either charter you can cruise east to Acadia as well as anywhere around the island-studded Penobscot Bay.

GOLF AND TENNIS **Island Country Club** (207-348-2379), 442 Sunset Rd. (Rt. 15A), Deer Isle, welcomes guests mid-May–mid-Oct. Nine holes; Fairway Café opens Memorial Day for lunch except Mon. Lessons, carts, also tennis courts and lessons.

KAYAKING **Sea Kayaking Driftwood Kayak** (617-957-8802; driftwoodkayak.com), 17 Hardy's Hill Road, Deer Isle. Experienced guide Peter Jones offers a variety of tours, from 2-hour sunrise/sunset paddles to two- and three-day trips. Also see **Old Quarry Ocean Adventures** under *Boating*.

SWIMMING ✪ ✐ **Lily Pond**, off Rt. 15 north of Deer Isle Village. The beach and access have been preserved and tidied by the Island Heritage Trust. Turn in at Deer Run Apartments; it's a five-minute walk to the pond. The island's freshwater swimming hole offers a shaded, grassy beach that's a great spot for small children, also for long swims. Inquire about new access from Quaco Rd.

Sand Beach in Burnt Cove, Stonington. Turn off Rt. 15A on the fire road across from Burnt Cove Market (the sign says NO ENTRANCE AFTER DARK). This is a spacious, sheltered beach with a path that leads beyond, up over a wooded knoll to a smaller strand, a favorite painting spot.

Also see **Scott's Landing** in *Green Space*.

SAND BEACH

HAYSTACK MOUNTAIN SCHOOL OF CRAFTS

Two-week residencies, summer conferences, one- and two-week workshop sessions, June–Labor Day, attract some of the country's top artisans in clay, metals, wood, fibers, graphics, and glass. From its beginnings in 1950, Haystack has been equated with cutting-edge design rather than traditional craft. Each session is limited to no more than 90 students, and the workshop topics, like the students, change every two weeks. Each group is carefully balanced to include young (minimum age 18) and old neophytes as well as master craftsmen; repeaters are kept to a third.

Visitors are welcome to tour the campus, but not workshops; guided tours are offered Wed. at 1 PM and during the "walk-throughs," in which student and faculty work is displayed (7:30 PM on the second Thu. of each session, followed by an 8:15 auction). The public is also welcome in the Gateway Building auditorium for frequent 7:30 PM slide lectures, visiting artists' presentations, and occasional concerts. The campus itself is a work of art: a series of spare, shingled buildings, studios with a central dining hall and sleeping quarters, all weathered the color of surrounding rocks and fitted between trees, connected by steps and terraced decks, floated above the fragile lichens and wildflowers on land sloping steeply toward Jericho Bay. (207-348-2306; haystack-mtn.org), Deer Isle.

✳ Green Space

Island Heritage Trust (207-348-2455; islandheritagetrust.org), 420 Sunset Rd., Deer Isle. Office open Mon.–Fri. 8–5. Detailed maps of the following walking trails are available from the office, at the visitors center (see *Guidance*), and on the website, which lists walks, talks, and events. Holdings include: **Settlement Quarry**, Stonington. A 0.25-mile walk along an old road to the top of this former working quarry for a view across Webb Cove and west to the Camden Hills. Side trails loop back through the woods; **Scott's Landing**. Trails from the causeway web this 24-acre point on Eggemoggin Reach, leading to a vintage-1807 dock and a sandy beach; **Pine Hill Preserve** on Little Deer Isle is a short, rugged climb to a bald summit with a sweeping view; and **Edgar M. Tennis Preserve**, with both wooded and shore trails with shore views, can be found off Sunshine Rd.

Crockett Cove Woods Preserve (a Maine Nature Conservancy property) consists of 100 acres along the water, with a nature trail. From Stonington, take Sunset Rd. through the village of Burnt Cove and turn left onto Whitman Rd.; a right turn at the end of the road brings you to the entrance, marked by a small sign and registration box.

⟋ **Barred Island Preserve** is a 2-acre island owned by The Nature Conservancy, accessible only at low tide by a wide sandbar; parking is on the road to Goose Cove Lodge. Owned by landscape architect Frederick Law Olmsted around the turn of the 20th century and bequeathed to The Nature Conservancy by his grandniece, this is a very special place, a good walk with small children.

MORE PUBLIC SPACES **Ames Pond**, east of Stonington Village on Indian Point Rd., is full of pink-and-white water lilies in bloom June–early Sept.

Mariner's Memorial Park, Deer Isle. This is a delightful picnic and bird-watching spot with views of Long Cove. Take Fire Rd. 501 off Sunshine Rd., just east of Rt. 15.

THE HIDDEN POINT BEYOND SAND BEACH IS A FAVORITE SPOT FOR ARTISTS

✳ Lodging

INNS AND B&BS

IN DEER ISLE

✪ 🐾 📶 **Pilgrim's Inn** (207-348-6615 or 1-888-778-7505; pilgrimsinn.com), 20 Main St. Open mid-May–mid-Oct. This gracious, four-story, hip-roofed inn stands in the middle of Deer Isle Village yet both fronts and backs on water. According to innkeeper Tina Oddleifson, it was built in 1793 by Ignatius Haskel to house his wife and nine children, and in 1889 Lizzie Haskell turned it into an inn to lodge guests arriving by steamer. Pilgrim's Inn has been lucky in its subsequent owners. The pumpkin pine floors and the 8-foot-wide original fireplaces in the common and tap rooms survive, along with working hearths and paneling in the game room and library, and the original hardware in most of the dozen guest rooms. Tasteful but unfussy furnishings underscore rather than upstage the 18th-century feel of the space, which has a view of the millpond. On the other hand, jetted tubs and bracing showers are welcome additions. Rooms vary in size, but most have water views; all have private bath and are furnished in antiques. There are also three

nicely decorated, two-bedroom cottages with kitchens and living rooms. The Whale's Rib (see *Dining Out*) is open to the public. Inn rooms $139–219 in-season, $119–199 in shoulder months, including full breakfast. $50 charge for pets allowed in cottages, which are $199–259.

✪ ✎ **The Inn at Ferry Landing** (207-348-7760; ferrylanding.com), 77 Old Ferry Rd., RR 1, Box 163. Open year-round. Overlooking Eggemoggin Reach, Jean and Gerald Wheeler's 1840s seaside farmhouse offers magnificent water views, spacious rooms, patchwork quilts, and a great common room with many windows, two grand pianos, and a harpsichord that Gerald plays and uses for summer recitals and spontaneous music sessions. The four guest rooms include a large master suite with a woodstove and skylights. $130–140 for double rooms, $185 for the suite; less off-season. Room rates include a full breakfast; minimum of two nights in high season. The Mooring, a two-story, two-bedroom, fully equipped housekeeping cottage, sleeping five, is $1,500 per week.

IN STONINGTON

✪ 📶 ♿ **The Inn on the Harbor** (207-367-2420 or 1-800-942-2420; innontheharbor

.com), 45 Main St. Open year-round. Guest rooms come with binoculars, the better to focus on lobster boats and regularly on the schooners in the Maine windjammer fleet, for which each of the 14 comfortable rooms (private bath, fridge, phone, cable TV) is named. The inn backs on Stonington's bustling Main Street, but most rooms, some with balcony, face the working harbor, one of Maine's most photographed views. Our favorite rooms: the Heritage, with working hearth; the Stephen Taber, a freestanding room retaining its tin ceiling (it used to be a barbershop); and the American Eagle suite with two bedrooms, an open kitchen, dining area, and living room. A flowery ground-floor café with espresso and expansive deck is shared by all. $151–239 summer, $67–137 off-season, includes continental breakfast.

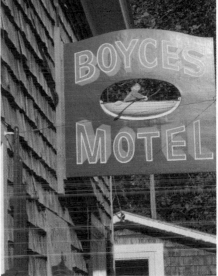

BOYCE'S MOTEL, STONINGTON

☀ ⌁ **Boyce's Motel** (207-367-2421 or 1-800-224-2421; boycesmotel.com), 44 Main St. In the heart of Stonington Village, Barrett Gray has expanded on this appealing motel, run by his family for four decades. This is a bit of a local secret, far bigger than it looks from the street. Most of the 11 units line a quiet lane that angles off Main St. They have queen or twin beds, and there are several efficiency units—one with two bedrooms, a living room, and kitchen. All are clean and comfortable, with in-room coffee, water views from some decks, free long-distance; popular with families and kayakers. $183–165 in high season, $70–135 off season; $15 per pet per stay.

INN ON THE HARBOR

ON ISLE AU HAUT

The Keeper's House (207-335-2990; keepers house.com), Robinson Point Lighthouse Station. Open June–Columbus Day. The Keeper's House, first opened as a B&B in 1986, has been renovated and reopened by Dr. Marshall Chapman. The seven-room, hip-roofed clapboard house offers four guest rooms, two baths, and another self-contained room in the small Oil House. Off the grid, the complex is powered by photovoltaics, a windmill, and a 30-kilowatt generator. There's a dock for arriving guests; the mail boat from Stonington stops on request. Sited a ways from town and a hike from Duck Harbor. Bikes are available, and the innkeeper frequently offers a lift in his Model T and rides on his vintage-1903 Friendship sloop. $350–400 (two-day minimum) includes three meals. BYOB. Inquire about weekly rental of the Woodshed Cottage.

OFF THE GRID **Deer Isle Hostel** (207-248-2308; deerislehostel.com), 65 Tennis Rd., Deer Isle. Open late May–early Sept. An authentic homesteading endeavor, a three-story 17th-century-style house built from wood harvested on the property, using mostly hand tools. Water is hand pumped and electricity is solar generated. There's an outhouse with a composting toilet and a heated outdoor shower. The hostel sleeps 10 in private as well as dorm rooms. Set in vegetable gardens and woodland. $25 per person in the dorm, $30 per person for a private room, $70 for a secluded hut for two. Rates include dinner (BYO breakfast). Check the website for guided tours, otherwise visitors are not welcome.

VACATION RENTALS Check listings at the chamber website: deerisle.com. Also see Realtors listed for Blue Hill.

✳ Where to Eat

DINING OUT **Whale's Rib Tavern at Pilgrim's Inn** (207-348-5222; pilgrimsinn.com), 20 Main St., Deer Isle Village. Open mid-May–Oct., daily 5–9 for dinner; closed Tue. in shoulder seasons. Reservations advised. Co-innkeeper Tony Lawless, a graduate of the Culinary Institute of America, maintains the reliably high-quality dining in this many-windowed old barn on the garden level of the Pilgrim's Inn, overlooking a millpond. We feasted with friends on Deer Isle clams steamed in beer and on locally raised mussels in a butter and cream sauce with roasted garlic and fried leeks, mopped up with freshly baked breads and followed by a seafood stew that included mahogany clams and calamari as well as a half lobster. Daily specials. Entrées $18–30. The wine list is respectable, and there's a choice of Maine microbrews.

Aragosta (207-367-5500), 27 Main St., Stonington. Open seasonally for lunch and happy hour (5–8) on the deck; dinner 5–9 except Wed. Known locally for farm-to-table fare, Devin Finigan is the chef-owner of Aragosta (Italian for *lobster*). Lunch and evening happy hour pub food is served on the large outdoor deck overlooking the harbor and at the small restaurant itself. Entrées: $26–40..

Cockatoo Portuguese Restaurant at Goose Cove (207-348-2300; thecockatoo restaurant.com), marked from Rt. 15 west of Stonington in Sunset, Deer Isle. Open daily in-season, noon–9. The wooded road ends in an open green expanse overlooking a beach and the ocean—but that's not the call of seagulls you hear. It's the throaty screech and chatter of Peaches and Mango, Suzen Carter's pet cockatoos. The dining room in this classic old lodge is spacious, with a many-windowed view of the water, and there's dining on the deck. It features the freshest of fish but also meat prepared in interesting ways by Azorean chefs. At lunch try a cup or bowl of Portuguese kale soup; chowder with a scallop roll; or a chorizo and pepper sandwich. The house specialty is Portuguese paella ($40 for one but our waitress says you can add a $5 plate fee to share). If it's on the menu, try the authentic bacalhau (shredded codfish with onions, crispy potatoes, and peppers, served with greens), a $15 special. Entrées $18–40 but less for nightly specials.

Also see **Nebo Lodge Cruises** (*Boating*).

EATING OUT ✪ ✐ **Harbor Café**, Stonington. Open year-round, Mon.–Sat. 6 AM–8 PM; in summer, open later on Fri. and Sat., plus Sun. 6–2. Spanking clean and friendly; booths and dependable food. Soups and salads. Seafood rolls, sandwiches and subs, fried and broiled seafood. Friday night it's a good idea to reserve for the seafood and fries with free

LOBSTER

Stonington Lobster Co-op (207-367-2286 or 1-800-315-6625), 51 Indian Point Rd. Since 1948, the largest co-op in Maine of its type, wholesale and retail.

Carter's Seafood (207-367-0900), 24 Carter Lane, off Oceanville Rd. at Webb Cove. Open Mon.–Sat. 10–5. Very fresh fish, clams, lobsters, mussels, and shrimp.

Cold Water Seafood (207-348-3084), 100 N. Main St. (Rt. 15). Open Mon.–Sat. 9–6, call off-season. Fresh fish, local steamers, fresh crab, and house-smoked mussels.

second helpings. Check out the two-for-one lobster specials. Spirits available.

♣ ✿ **The Fisherman's Friend Restaurant** (207-367-2442), 5 Atlantic Ave., Stonington. Open year-round, 11–9 in summer months, until 10 Sat.; check off-season. This vast waterfront restaurant (next to the quarryman statue) can seat more than 200 with a second-floor deck. A wide choice of fried and broiled fish, chowders and stews, burgers, and all the usual sandwiches. Lobster many ways. Children's menu.

((ɯ)) **Madelyn's Drive-in** (207-348-9444), 495 N. Deer Isle Rd. (Rt. 15), Deer Isle. A local favorite. Roadside takeout with burgers, fried seafood, hard and soft ice cream. Plenty of picnic table seating, playground for kids.

Stonington Ice Cream Co., next to G. Watson Gallery (68 Main St., Stonington). A seasonal takeout known for its lobster rolls, Gifford's ice cream, daily specials.

✿ **Harbor Ice Cream** (207-348-9949), 11 Main St., Deer Isle Village. A casual oasis good for sandwiches, wraps, Gifford's ice cream, and lobster rolls.

Espresso Bar at the Inn on the Harbor (207-367-2420), 45 Main St., Stonington. Open daily in-season. Espresso, iced drinks, homemade ice cream, and desserts. In good weather this is a must, an excuse to sit a spell on the inn's flower-filled harborside deck.

((ɯ)) **44 North Café**, 70 Main St., Stonington. Open May–Oct., Mon.–Sat. 6:30–5, Sun. 8–2. Housed in the former Eagle Gallery, this sleek new café serves up its locally roasted beans in a variety of hot and cold brews, along with Black Dinah's sipping chocolate, tea from Stonington's Tempest in a Teapot, and locally baked pastries. The beans are sold here or you can climb the stairs to the source, the Deer Isle Roastery and Café (207-348-3403), 11 Church St., Deer Isle Village.

✳ Entertainment

✪ **Stonington Opera House** (207-367-2788; operahousearts.org), School St., Stonington. Open year-round. This shingled building with its skinny, four-story "fly tower" dates to 1912 and was expanded in 2015. It stages an astonishingly full calendar of reasonably priced concerts and original theatrical productions. Movies Fri.–Sun. at 7 PM. Call for schedules of movies (digital!) and live performances.

Reach Performing Art Center (207-348-6301; atthereach.com), 249 N. Deer Isle Rd. at the elementary school, Deer Isle, a venue for theater, dance, and musical performances.

✳ Selective Shopping

ART GALLERIES AND ARTISANS *Note:* Studio crawling is a popular local pastime. Because local galleries feature work by local artists, it's frequently possible to trace a piece to its creator. Handout studio maps and post cards that picture individual artists' works are also readily available. The following is a partial listing.

IN DEER ISLE

Deer Isle Artists Association (207-348-2330; deerisleartists.com), 15 Main St. Open Memorial Day weekend–Columbus Day, daily 10–6; until mid-Dec., noon–5. A stunning, middle-of-the-village cooperative gallery with exhibits changing every two weeks.

Turtle Gallery (207-348-9977; turtlegallery.com), Rt. 15, north of Deer Isle Village. Open daily in summer, year-round by appointment. Artist Elena Kubler's gallery showcases exceptional jewelry as well as biweekly changing shows featuring fine art and contemporary crafts. It's housed in the barn in which Haystack faculty work was first displayed, back when the adjoining Centennial House was home to Francis ("Fran") Sumner Merritt, the school's founding director, and his wife, Priscilla, a noted weaver.

Greene-Ziner Gallery (207-348-2601), 73 Reach Rd. (off Rt. 15 north of the village). Open July–Sept. In a barn surrounded by meadows, iron sculptor Eric Ziner displays his ornate and whimsical creations and potter Melissa Greene, her thrown earthenware pots suggesting Greek amphorae in shape but decorated with designs evoking tribal themes. Their **Yellow Birch Farm Stand** (Tue.–Sat. 10–5) sells fruit, veggies, herbs, eggs, and dairy products.

Frederica Marshall Gallery (207-348-2782; fredericamarshall.com), 81 N. Deer Isle Rd. A widely respected watercolorist, Marshall is also a master brush painter (studied during 28 years in Japan). Note the watercolors of local landscapes using Japanese handmade paper to striking effect. The property also includes the studio in which Marshall offers classes and the forge in which her husband Herman Kidder shapes useful and imaginative work displayed in the gallery. Also see *Art Workshops*.

IN STONINGTON

✪ ♿ **Hoy Gallery** (207-367-2368; jillhoy.com), 80 Thurlow Hill. Open daily July–Columbus Day. Don't miss this big white barn set back from the street, filled with Jill Hoy's bold, bright Maine landscapes.

G. Watson Gallery (207-367-2900; gwatsongallery.com), 68 Main St. Open May–Oct., Mon.–Sat. 10–5, Sun. 1–5. This is a serious gallery, showing contemporary painting and sculpture, featuring prominent East Coast artists.

SPECIAL SHOPS The Periwinkle (207-348-5277), in the middle of Deer Isle Village. Open June–Oct., 9–5, closed Sun. Jim and Candy Eaton now run this tiny landmark shop, crammed with toys and games galore, books, cards, and other rainy-day savers, most locally made. Ask Jim about what happened to the store's vintage cash register.

✪ **Dockside Books and Gifts** (207-367-2652), 62 W. Main St., Stonington. Seasonal. Al Webber's waterside bookstore has an exceptional selection of Maine and marine books, also gifts, sweaters by local knitters, and a great harbor view from the deck.

✪ **The Dry Dock** (207-367-5528), Main St. Open daily mid-May–Oct., 9–5. Tempting clothing and craftwork; an outlet for Deer Isle granite products, and much more.

✪ **Prints & Reprints** (207-367-5821), 31 Main St. Virginia Burnett's landmark shop featuring framed art, antiquarian books, and unexpected treasures.

V&S Variety Stores (207-367-5570), Rt. 15A, Burnt Cove. The many boutiques and galleries have displaced the basic stuff of life—groceries and everything a five-and-dime once carried. It's all moved out to Burnt Cove, along with the recycle shop, gas, and plenty of parking. Beside Burnt Cove Market (the supermarket, open daily until 9 PM), this huge but homespun "variety store" stocks everything you forgot to bring.

Also see **Nervous Nellie's Jams and Jellies** under *To See*. The shop is open year-round, producing 15 flavors of jam, chutney, marmalade, and much more.

✳ Special Events

Note: The weekly *Island Advantages* (islandadvantages.com) lists and details many more current happenings. Unless otherwise noted, the contact is the chamber of commerce: 207-348-6124; deerislemaine.com.

May: **Wings, Waves & Woods**, "birding by land, by sea and by art"—puffin and pelagic trips, walks, lectures, food. **Memorial Day Parade**.

May–October: Fri.-morning (10–noon) **farmers' market** at the Island Community Center (the former elementary school) in Stonington. This is huge.

July: **Independence Day** features islandwide festivities—a parade in Deer Isle Village, fireworks at Stonington Fish Pier. **Lobster boat races** are usually the next Sat. **Fisherman's Day** (slippery cod contest, wacky boat races, and family fun) is the following week, sponsored by the Island Fishermen's Wives Association.

Castine

While the bulk of the Blue Hill Peninsula wanders away to the southeast, one fat finger of land points down along the Penobscot River toward the bay. Rt. 175, the first turnoff from Rt. 1 for the Blue Hill Peninsula, shadows the river, leading to a mini peninsula with Castine at its tip. Sited at the confluence of the Penobscot and Bagaduce Rivers, the town still looms larger on nautical charts than on road maps.

Castine has always had a sense of its own importance. According to the historical markers that pepper its tranquil streets, it has been claimed by four different countries since its early-17th-century founding as Fort Pentagoet. It was an early trading post for the Pilgrims but fell into the hands of Baron de Saint Castine, a young French nobleman who married a Penobscot Indian princess and reigned as a combination feudal lord and Indian chief over Maine's eastern coast for many decades.

Because no two accounts agree, we won't attempt to describe the outpost's constantly shifting fortunes—even the Dutch owned it briefly. Nobody denies that in 1779 residents (mostly Tories who fled here from Boston and Portland) welcomed the invading British. The Commonwealth of Massachusetts retaliated by mounting a fleet of 18 armed vessels and 24 transports with 1,000 troops and 400 marines aboard. This small navy disgraced itself absurdly when it sailed into town in 1779. The British Fort George was barely in the making, fortified by 750 soldiers with two sloops as backup, but the American privateers refused to attack and hung around in the bay long enough for several British men-of-war to come along and destroy them. The surviving patriots had to walk back to Boston, and many of their officers, Paul Revere included, were court-martialed for their part in the disgrace. The town was occupied by the British again in 1814.

Perhaps it was to spur young men on to avenge this affair that Castine was picked (150 years later) as the home of the Maine Maritime Academy, which occupies the actual site of the British barracks and keeps a training ship anchored at the town dock, incongruously huge beside the graceful, white-clapboard buildings from an earlier era.

In the mid-19th century, thanks to shipbuilding, Castine claimed to be the second wealthiest town per capita in the United States. Its genteel qualities were recognized by summer visitors, who later came by steamboat to stay in eight hotels. Many built seasonal mansions. Castine remains one of Maine's most photogenic coastal villages, the kind writers describe as "perfectly preserved." Trees that arch high above Main Street's clapboard homes and shops have managed to escape the blight that felled elms elsewhere, and Castine's post office is the oldest continuously operating post office in the country (since 1833). Current population hovers around 1,670, including the 700 Maine Maritime Academy students, but it roughly doubles in summer. Two of the hotels survive, and one baronial mansion is now an inn. The town dock is unusually welcoming, complete with picnic tables, parking, and restrooms. It remains the heart of this walking town, where you can amble uphill past shops to the impressive Historical Society museum on the common, or down along Perkins St. to the Wilson Museum.

GUIDANCE The **Castine Merchants Association** and Castine Historical Society produce a helpful map/guide, available around town. The seasonal visitors center at 1 Main St. is a welcome addition. Also check **castine.me.us.** For moorings and harbor information call 207-326-9231 or check **castineyachtclub.org.**

PUBLIC RESTROOMS are at the town landing, foot of Main St.

WHEN TO COME Museums are highly seasonal, but the Maritime Academy contributes to the sense of a college town, a pleasant place to stay through October.

✳ To See

Historic District. All of downtown Castine is on the National Register of Historic Places. Pick up the pamphlet *A Walking Tour of Castine*—it's free, available at shops—and walk out along Perkins St. and up along Maine to Battle Ave. Don't miss:

Castine Historical Society (207-326-4118; castinehistoricalsociety.org), 17 School St. Castine town common. July–Labor Day, Mon.–Sat. 10–4; Sun. 1–4. The permanent exhibit is a multimedia presentation about the 1779 Penobscot Expedition (see chapter introduction), also changing exhibits and the newly opened Grindle House.

✿ ✐ **Wilson Museum** (207-326-9247; wilsonmuseum.org), 120 Perkins St. Open daily May 27–Sept. 30, 10–5 weekdays, 2–5 weekends; free. This waterside building houses collections amassed by geologist J. Howard Wilson. These include prehistoric artifacts from North and South America, ancient artifacts from Africa and Oceana, vintage dioramas depicting life in prehistoric and Native American cultures, as well as minerals, stones, shells, early firearms, tools, farm equipment, an 1805 kitchen, and a Victorian parlor. The campus also includes a 19th-century **Blacksmith Shop** and the **John Perkins House**, a pre–Revolutionary War home, restored and furnished. Open July and Aug., Wed. and Sun. 2–5 (admission for Perkins House). Check the website for changing exhibits, demonstrations, and frequent special events.

Fort George, Battle Ave. Open May 30–Labor Day, daylight hours. The sorry tale of its capture by the British during the American Revolution (see the chapter introduction) and again during the War of 1812, when redcoats occupied the town for eight months, is told on panels at the fort—an earthworks complex of grassy walls (great to roll down) and a flat interior.

State of Maine (207-326-4311), town dock. When in port, the training vessel for Maine Maritime Academy is usually open to visitors daily from the second week in July until mid-Aug. Call to check the schedule for tours.

THE MAINE MARITIME ACADEMY VESSEL *STATE OF MAINE* IN CASTINE

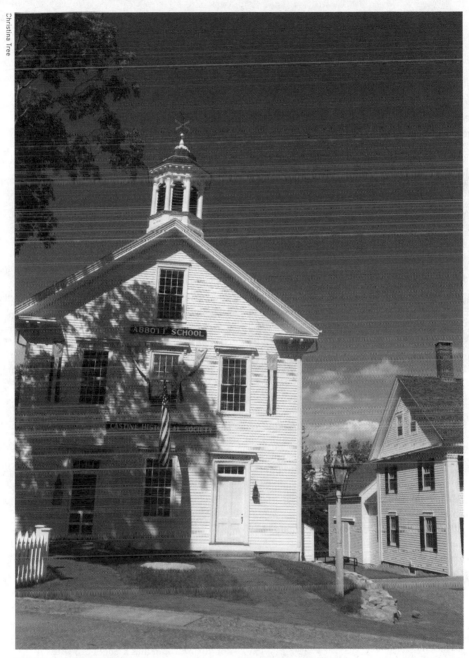

Christina Tree

CASTINE HISTORICAL SOCIETY

✴ To Do

GOLF AND TENNIS **Castine Golf Club** (207-326-8844), Battle Ave. Offers nine holes. To use the tennis courts, call 207-326-9548.

SEA KAYAKING **Castine Kayak Adventures** (207-866-3506; castinekayak.com), Sea St., beyond Dennett's Wharf. Half- and full-day trips plus a number of "unique adventures" such as sunrise and phosphorescent paddles, and "intermediate adventures" to

Christina Tree

PENTAGOET INN

the Bagaduce reversing falls and around Cape Rosier. Also overnight camping, B&B tours, and workshops ranging from beginning skills to advanced coastal navigation. This is also the area's source of **bike rentals**.

SAILING **Guildive Cruises** (207-701-1421; castinecruises.com), 15 Sea St. Daily departures in-season for two-hour excursions and sunset sails aboard a vintage-1934, 56-foot sailing yacht, limited to six passengers; Capts. Kate and Zander also offer half- and full-day charters.

SWIMMING ✵ **Back Beach**. This is a long strip of sand backed by parking. Shallow, relatively warm water, great for kids. From Battle Ave., follow Wadsworth Cove Rd. to the end.

✳ Green Space

Witherle Woods is an extensive wooded area webbed with paths at the western end

of town. The ledges below **Dyce's Head Light**, also at the western end of town, are great for clambering. The Castine Conservation Commission sponsors nature walks occasionally in July and Aug.; check local bulletin boards.

✳ Lodging

IN CASTINE

✿ 🐾 ((ᵖ)) **Pentagoët Inn** (207-326-8616 or 1-800-845-1701; pentagoet.com), 26 Main St., P.O. Box 4. Open May–Oct. A very Victorian summer hotel with a three-story turret, gables, and wraparound porch. Jack Burke and Julie VandeGraaf have restored this vintage-1894 Queen Anne–style building room by room. They've added exceptional food and created an inn with rare warmth and personality. Jack presides behind an oak bar in the **Passports Pub**, papered floor-to-ceiling in photos, paintings, and memorabilia depicting the likes of Lenin, Gandhi, and Queen Elizabeth, collected during this innkeeper's previous life in the foreign service. The 16 guest rooms are variously shaped and furnished in comfortable, period antiques—ornately carved headboards and marble-topped dressers—but good mattresses, serious showers. In all there are 16 guest rooms, most on the second and third floors of the inn, several in the neighboring 18th-century "cottage." There's a cheerful sitting room, a flowery veranda, and a garden. $135–295 during high season with full buffet breakfast. $25 for pets. Amenities include bicycles and a guest computer. (Also see *Dining Out*.)

✵ **Castine Inn** (207-326-4365; castineinn .com), 33 Main St. Open May–Oct. Vintage 1898 with a wide, welcoming hallway with an old-style check-in desk. There's a pleasant sitting room and a pub, both with frequently lit fireplaces. A mural of Castine covers all four walls of the dining room, and French doors open onto a broad veranda overlooking the garden. The village slopes away below, and the 10 rooms on this side of the building all enjoy harbor views. Most 19 second- and third-floor rooms have private bath and have been recently renovated; $125–235; full breakfast (served & open to the public).

☀ (ᵖ)) **The Manor Inn** (207-326-4861; manor-inn.com), 76 Battle Ave. Open mid-March thru Dec. This 1890s stone-and-shingle mansion, set off above the village and its own lawns, offers 14 guest rooms. These range widely in size and price, in high season from $130. $290 for spacious Pine Tree with its king canopy bed, working fireplace, and porch. Innkeepers Tom Ehrman and Nancy Watson are hands-on hosts, with Tom at the front desk or behind the bar and Nancy presiding over the kitchen. The lighthouse is an easy walk; wooded paths lead through neighboring conservation land. Rates include a full breakfast, less off season. Pets are $25 per stay. (See *Dining Out.*)

Rental cottages are available through **De Raat Realty** (207-326-8448; deraatrealty.com) and **Mainely Rentals, Inc.** (207-316-4246; mainelyrentals.com).

✳ Where to Eat

IN CASTINE

DINING OUT ✪ **Pentagoët Inn** (207-326-8616; pentagoet.com), 26 Main St. Open for dinner in-season. Reservations advised. The rose-colored dining room glows with candlelight in the evening. White tablecloths and garden flowers dress well-spaced tables, more seating on the veranda. Tables are also set for dinner in **Passports Pub** (see *Lodging*). The focus is on locally sourced seafood and produce. We split a big bowl of rope-cultured mussels followed by seared scallops. House specialties include lobster linguine and lobster bouillabaisse. Entrées $24–28; "bistro plates" $12–16. Don't pass up dessert.

The Manor Inn (207-326-4861), Battle Ave. Open for dinner April–Dec; Tue.–Sat in summer; Thu.–Sat. off-season. A former enclosed porch has been expanded into an appealing dining room overlooking the sweeping front lawn and gardens. Co-owner Nancy Watson is the chef. The crabcakes are a family recipe, served as an entrée with mustard and aioli

sauces. Other choices on the daily changing menu might include seared sesame-marinated hanger steak. Entrées $16–24. Full liquor license and pub food in the appealing **Pine Cone Pub**.

EATING OUT **Dennett's Wharf Restaurant & Oyster Bar** (207-326-9045), 15 Sea St. (off the town dock). Open daily May–Columbus Day, 11–11. An open-framed, harborside structure said to have been built as a bowling alley after the Civil War, this is the town's informal gathering place. There's a big all-day menu with plenty of salads as well as seafood and BBQ back ribs. The home brew is Wharf Rat Ale. Entrées $16–25.

MarKel's Bakehouse (207-326-9510; markelsbakehouse.com), 26 Water St. Open 7–3. A find tucked in off Main St., with a deck overlooking the bay. Fresh-baked muffins, croissants, breads, and pastries, also hot breakfast menu, lunch salads, sandwiches, and wraps, house-smoked ribs and brisket, full deli counter and dinners to go.

Dudley's Refresher (207-812-3800), Town Dock. May–Sept., Tue.–Sun. 11–sunset. The owners of El El Frijoles in Sargentville now operate this newly renamed and rebuilt (by the town) take-out on the town dock: fish tacos, burgers, salads, and such. With luck, you can dine at the shaded picnic table.

Castine Variety (207-326-9920), corner of Main and Water Sts. Open 7 AM–8 PM. The village gathering spot from early morning on. Oahu native Snow Logan offers unexpected delicacies such as "Lokomoko," Japanese chicken salad, miso soup, and combinations like fresh crabmeat and avocado; white tablecloths complement the reasonably priced dinner menu. (BYOB). "The Breeze" sign from her former facility on the dock now hangs above the ice cream take-out window.

✳ Selective Shopping

IN CASTINE

✐ **Compass Rose Bookstore & Café** (207-326-9366 or 1-800-698-9366), 3 Main St. Open Mon.–Sat. 10–6. Sharon Biggie's shop features children's titles, summer reading, nautical, and regional books. The café serves drinks, cookies, and soups.

Lucky Hill (207-326-1066), 15 Main St. Kristin Blanck features family gifts like "gurgle pots" and seriously fine paintings by husband Dan Graziano.

Gallery B. (213-839-0851; gallerybgallery.com), 5 Main St. Open seasonally, showcasing fine art, crafts.

CW Hooke & Co. (207-326-5060), 9 Main St. features fine wines (frequent tastings) also, craft beers and cigars.

✳ Special Events

May: Memorial Day parade.

June–Oct. **Farmers' Market**, Thu., 7–noon, Castine Common.

July: **Independence Day parade and fireworks**.

ACADIA AREA

ACADIA NATIONAL PARK

BAR HARBOR AND ELLSWORTH

THE QUIET SIDE OF MOUNT DESERT

EAST HANCOCK COUNTY

Acadia Area

ACADIA NATIONAL PARK

Mount Desert Island

Mount Desert (pronounced *dessert*) is New England's second largest island, one conveniently linked to the mainland. Two-fifths of its 108 square miles are maintained as Acadia National Park, laced with roads ideally suited for touring by car, more than 50 miles of "carriage roads" specifically for biking and skiing, and 120 miles of hiking trails.

The beauty of "MDI" (as it is locally known) cannot be overstated. Twenty-six mountains rise abruptly from the sea and from the shores of four large lakes. Mount Cadillac, at 1,532 feet, is the highest point on the U.S. Atlantic seaboard; a road winds to its smooth, broad summit for a 360-degree view that's said to yield the first view of dawn (which usually attracts a crowd) in the United States. Sunset, however, attracts a far larger crowd. There are also countless ponds and streams, an unusual variety of flora, and more than 300 species of birds. Mount Desert Island is almost bisected by Somes Sound, the only natural fjord on the East Coast.

Native Americans populated the island for at least 6,000 years before 1604, when Samuel de Champlain sailed by and named it L'Isle de Monts Deserts. In 1613 two French Jesuits attempted to establish a mission on Fernald Point near present Southwest Harbor. They were welcomed by the local Wabanaki chief Asticou but massacred by sailors from an English ship, and for 150 years this part of Maine remained a war zone between French and English. Finally settled in the second half of the 18th century, this remained a peaceful, out-of-the-way island even after a bridge was built in 1836, connecting it to the mainland.

In the 1840s landscape painters Thomas Cole and Frederic Church began summering here, and their images of the rugged shore were widely circulated. Summer visitors began arriving by steamboat, and they were soon joined by travelers taking express trains, bringing guests who filled the dozen huge hotels that mushroomed in Bar Harbor. By the 1880s many of these hotel patrons had already built their own mansion-sized "cottages." These grandiose summer mansions numbered more than 200 before the Depression; many are now inns.

Bar Harbor lost 67 of its 220 summer mansions and five hotels in the devastating

Nancy English

A TENACIOUS PINE ON THE ROCKY COAST OF MOUNT DESERT ISLAND

fire of 1947, which also destroyed 17,000 acres of woodland, but both the forest and Bar Harbor have recovered in recent decades.

Politically the island is divided into four townships: Bar Harbor, Mount Desert, Southwest Harbor, and Tremont. Northeast Harbor (a village in Mount Desert) and Southwest Harbor, the island's other two resort centers, also enjoy easy access to hiking, swimming, and boating within the park. Compared with Bar Harbor, however, they are relatively quiet, even in July and August, and the several accessible offshore islands are quieter still.

Mount Desert's mountains with "their gray coats and rounded backs look like a herd of elephants, marching majestically across the island," travel writer Samuel Adams Drake wrote in 1891. He was arriving by steamboat instead of traveling down the unimpressive commercial strip that is Rt. 3. Today it's harder to get beyond the clutter and crowds—but not that hard. The memorable march of rounded mountains is still what you see from excursion boats and from Little Cranberry Island.

Acadia National Park

The legacy of Bar Harbor's wealthy "rusticators" is Acadia National Park. A cadre of influential citizens, which included Harvard University's President Charles W. Eliot, began to assemble parcels of land for public use in 1901, thus protecting the forests from portable sawmill. Boston textile heir George Dorr devoted his fortune and energy to amassing a total of 11,000 acres and persuading the federal government to accept it. In 1919 Acadia became the first national park east of the Mississippi. It is now a more-than-47,000-acre preserve, with 30,300 acres and more than another 10,000 in easements encompassing almost half of Mount Desert Island.

Almost two-thirds of the park's more than 2 million annual visitors get out of their cars and hike the park's trails. Many take the free, white-and-blue Island Explorer buses. They usually begin by viewing the introductory film in the Hulls Cove Visitor Center and then drive the 27-mile Park Loop Rd., stopping to see the obvious sites and noting what they want to explore more fully. The park has much more to offer, from simple hikes to rock climbing, horse-drawn carriage rides to swimming, bicycling, canoeing, and kayaking.

Within the park are more than 45 miles of carriage roads donated by John D. Rockefeller Jr. These incredible broken-stone roads take bikers, hikers, joggers, and cross-country skiers through woods, up mountains, past lakes and streams. The paths also lead over and under 17 spectacular stone bridges. In recent years volunteers have rallied to refurbish and improve this truly spectacular network, and many trails have been reopened. Isle au Haut (see "East Penobscot Bay Region") and the Schoodic Peninsula (see "East Hancock County") are also part of Acadia National Park, but they are not located on Mount Desert Island and are much quieter, less traveled areas.

FEES The entrance fee for vehicles is $25 for a weekly pass, May–Oct. Free Nov.–Apr. For individuals on foot, the Island Explorer, or a bicycle, the fee is $12 for a weekly pass.

GUIDANCE The park maintains **Hulls Cove Visitor Center** (207-288-3338; nps.gov/acad), just north of Bar Harbor. It's open mid-Apr.–Oct. In July–Aug., hours are 8–6 daily; Sept., 8–5; during shoulder seasons, 8–4:30. The glass-and-stone building, set atop 50 steps, shows a 15-minute introductory film and sells books, guides, and postcards. Pick up a free map and a listing of all naturalist activities, and sign up for the various programs scheduled June–Sept. at the amphitheaters in Blackwoods and Seawall Campgrounds. Children of all ages are eligible to join the park's Junior Ranger Program. The park headquarters at Eagle Lake on Rt. 233 (207-288-3338) is open throughout winter, daily 8–4:30.

✳ To See

MUSEUM AND GARDENS **Robert Abbe Museum at Sieur de Monts Spring** (207-288-3519; abbemuseum.org), 2 miles south of Bar Harbor, posted from Rt. 3 (south of Jackson Laboratory). The spring itself is encased in a Florentine-style canopy placed there by park

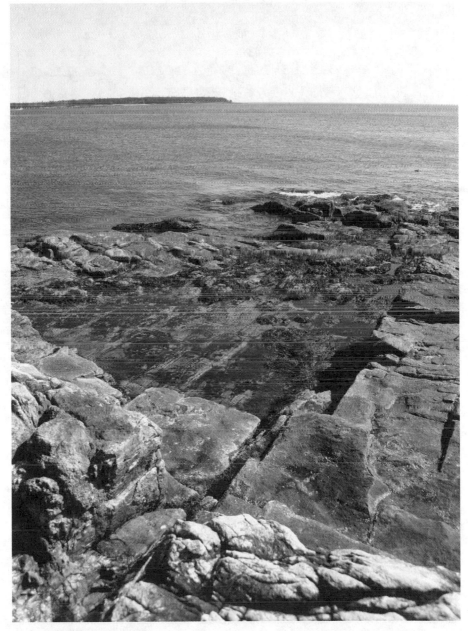

SEAWALL ON MOUNT DESERT ISLAND

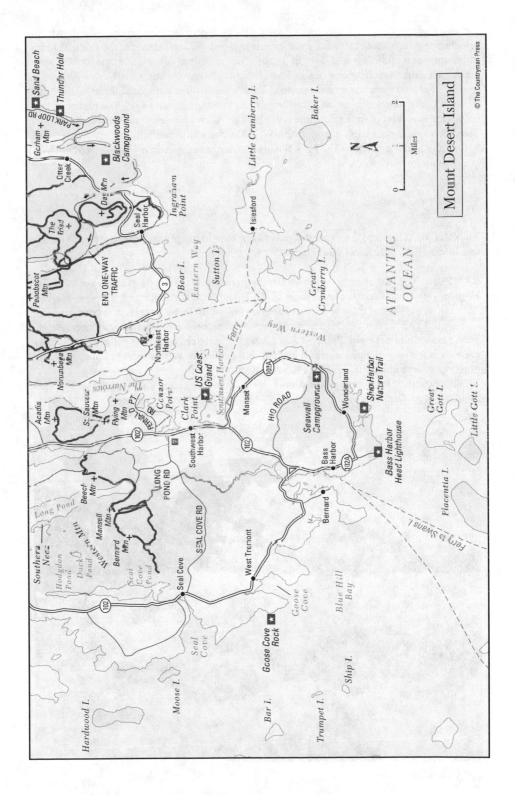

Mount Desert Island

© The Countryman Press

founder George B. Dorr, who purchased the property to prevent enterprising islanders from opening a springwater business here. It stands in a garden, and beyond is the original **Abbe Museum**, open mid-May–mid-Oct., daily 10–5. On exhibit at Sieur de Monts are Dr. Robert Abbe's original collections of stone and bone tools, representing the Native American people in Maine from the archaic periods. Admission to this octagonal building, built by Abbe in 1928 and possibly haunted by his spirit, is $3 adults, $1 ages 6–15. The rest of Abbe's collection is exhibited in the downtown Bar Harbor Abbe Museum (see "Bar Harbor"). The park museum is accessible through the **Wild Gardens of Acadia**, where 300 species of native plants are on display. The **Park Nature Center** here (open mid-May–Sept., daily 9–5) has displays on park wildlife.

✳ To Do

BICYCLING The more than 45 miles of broken-stone carriage roads make for good mountain biking. Find outfitters in Bar Harbor.

CAMPING The two campgrounds within the park are Blackwoods, 5 miles south of Bar Harbor, and Seawall, on the quiet side of the island, 4 miles south of Southwest Harbor. Both are in woods and close to the ocean. One vehicle, up to six people, is allowed on each site. No utility hookups, but both have comfort stations, cold running water, a dump station, picnic tables, and fire rings. Showers and a camping store are within 0.5 mile of each. There are also four group campsites at Blackwoods and five at Seawall, for up to 15 people, which must be reserved through the park (207-288-3338).

Blackwoods (207-288-3274, answered May–Oct. only), open all year. Reservations required May–Oct. through the National Recreation Reservation Service (1-877-444-6777;

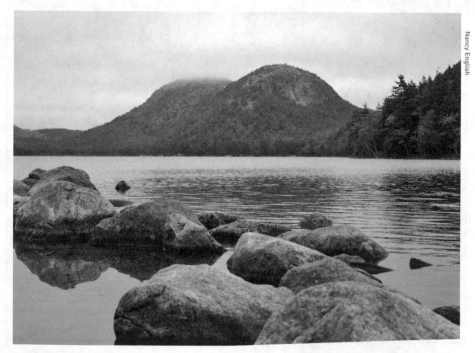

"THE BUBBLES" AT JORDAN POND

EXCURSIONS

Park Loop Road The 27-mile Park Loop Road is the prime tourist route within Acadia National Park. There is a weekly fee of $25 per car on the road in summer. The road always closes on Dec. 1, reopening mid-Apr., weather permitting.

Park Loop Road officially begins at the Hulls Cove Visitor Center but may be entered at many points along the way. Most of the road is one-way, so be alert to how traffic is flowing. Places of interest along the Loop Road include Sieur de Monts Spring, a stop that could include the Wild Gardens of Acadia, Abbe Museum, and Park Nature Center as well as the covered spring itself; Sand Beach, which is actually made up of ground shells and sand and is a great beach to walk down and from which to take a dip, if you don't mind 50- to 60-degree water (there are changing rooms and lifeguards); Thunder Hole, where the water rushes in and out of a small cave, which you can view from behind a railing; Jordan Pond House, popular for afternoon tea and popovers; and Cadillac Mountain. From Cadillac's smooth summit (accessible by car), you look north across Frenchman's Bay, dotted with the Porcupine Islands, which look like giant stepping-stones. Many visitors come at sunrise, but sunset can be far more spectacular.

recreation.gov). Cost of site is $20 per night during the reservation period; fees vary during the off-season, when you need a special use permit and must walk 0.75 mile to the campsite. The road is not plowed.

Seawall (877-444-6777), near Southwest Harbor, open late May–late Sept. First-come first-served sites, and also sites you can reserve in advance. Cost is $30 with a vehicle.

Schoodic Woods Campground (207-288-1300 or 877-444-677), open late May–Columbus Day. For Reserve at www.recreation.gov or phone 1-877-444-677. Like Blackwoods and Seawall in Acadia National Park on Mount Dessert Island, this new campground is managed by the National Park Service. Unlike the others, it accommodates RVs (33 sites with water and power hookups, $36–40). There are 50 drive-up tent/small RV sites ($30), 9 hike-in sites (22) and 2 groups sites with a shared picnic shelter. There is also a 100-seat amphitheater with ranger-led programs and a large day-use parking area. Camping is on a first-come, first-served basis.

HIKING The park is a mecca for hikers. Several detailed maps are sold at the Hulls Cove Visitor Center. Trails range in difficulty from the **Jordan Pond Loop Trail** (a 3.3-mile path around the pond) to the rugged **Precipice Trail** (1.5 miles, very steep, with iron rungs as ladders). There are 17 trails to mountain summits on Mount Desert. **Acadia Mountain** on the island's west side (2 miles roundtrip) commands the best view of Somes Sound and the islands. The **Ship Harbor** on Rt. 102A (near Bass Harbor) offers a nature trail that winds along the shore and into the woods; it's also a great birding spot.

HORSE-DRAWN CARRIAGE TOURS ✐ **Wildwood Stables** (1-877-276-3622), 0.5 mile south of the Jordan Pond House. One- and two-hour horse-drawn tours in multiple-seat carriages are offered six times a day.

RANGER PROGRAMS A wide variety of programs—from guided nature walks and hikes to birding talks, sea cruises, and evening lectures—are offered throughout the season. Ask at the Hulls Cove Visitor Center for a current schedule.

ROCK CLIMBING Acadia National Park is the most popular place to climb in Maine; famous climbs include the **Precipice**, **Great Head**, and **Otter Cliffs**. See "Bar Harbor" for guide services.

SWIMMING Within Acadia there is supervised swimming at **Sand Beach**, 4 miles south of Bar Harbor, and at **Echo Lake**, a warmer, quieter option 14 miles west of Bar Harbor (see "The Quiet Side of Mount Desert").

WINTER SPORTS More than 45 miles of carriage roads at Acadia National Park are maintained as cross-country skiing and snowshoeing trails. Request the *Winter Activities* leaflet from the park headquarters.

BAR HARBOR AND ELLSWORTH

Bar Harbor is the island's resort town, one of New England's largest clusters of hotels, motels, inns, B&Bs, restaurants, and shops—all within easy reach of the park's Hulls Cove Visitor Center and Acadia National Park.

Ellsworth is the shire town and shopping hub of Hancock County, a place with a split personality: the old brick downtown blocks along and around the Union River and its falls, and the strip of malls and outlets along the mile between the junctions of Rts. 1A and 1, and Rts. 1 and 3. If you're coming down Rt. 1A from Bangor, you miss downtown Ellsworth, which offers the restored art deco Grand Auditorium as well a sense of the lumbering-boom era in which the Colonel Black Mansion, arguably the most elegant in Maine, was built.

In Bar Harbor itself, shops and restaurants line Cottage, Mount Desert, West, and Main Sts., which slope to the Town Pier and to the Shore Path, a mile walk between mansions and the bay. On sunny days most visitors tend to be out in the park or on the water; half an hour before sunset (the time is announced each day in local publications), folks gather on and near the top of Cadillac Mountain.

GUIDANCE Bar Harbor Chamber of Commerce (year-round 207-288-5103 or 1 800-540-9990; barharbormaine.com), 1201 Bar Harbor Rd., Trenton 04605, also maintains a year-round information center on the corner of Cottage and Main Sts. in Bar Harbor.

Mount Desert Island Information Center (207-288-3411) is open daily mid-May–mid-Oct. (8:30–6 during high season) on Thompson Island, just after Rt. 3 crosses the bridge. This is the island's most helpful walk-in center, with restrooms and help with lodging reservations on all parts of the island. The in-town **Bar Harbor Information Center** is at the corner of Main and Cottage Sts., open May until the last cruise ship in Oct.

Ellsworth Chamber of Commerce (207-667-5584 or 207-667-2617; ellsworthchamber .org), 163 High St., Ellsworth 04605, is an information center in the Ellsworth Shopping Center on the Rt. 1/3 strip; look for Wendy's.

GETTING THERE *By air:* **Hancock County & Bar Harbor Airport** in Trenton (between Ellsworth and Bar Harbor) is still served by some regional flights out of Boston. Check their website (bhbairport.com) for more information. **Bangor International Airport** (207-947-0384; flybangor.com), 26 miles north of Ellsworth, offers connections to most American cities.

By private boat: For details about moorings, contact the Bar Harbor harbormaster at 207-288-5571.

BAR HARBOR VILLAGE GREEN

Downtown Bar Harbor

By bus: **Concord Coach Lines** (1-800-639-3317; concordcoachlines.com) offers unbeatable year-round service from Boston's Logan Airport and South Station (five hours) to Bangor. The **Bar Harbor Shuttle** (207-479-5911; barharborshuttle.com) stops at the Bar Harbor Villager Motel and can pick up passengers by reservation elsewhere. The 10-passenger van provides transportation to and from the airports and the bus depots in Bangor, with other stops in Ellsworth and Somesville.

By ferry: **The Schoodic Ferry** (207-801-9444; frenchmanbayresearchboating.org), College of the Atlantic Campus. Island Explorer Bus #2 leaving from the Bar Harbor Village Green will get you there, but there is no parking allowed on campus. Schoodic Marine Center, the destination, is close to downtown Winter Harbor. Late May to the Sunday before Columbus Day, this ferry travels 5 to 6 times daily between Bar Harbor and Winter Harbor. Reserve early for the July 4th Fireworks trip; or join biologists on the twice-daily research trips.

By car: From Brunswick and points south (including Boston and New York), the shortest route is I-295 to I-95 in Augusta, to Bangor to I-395 to Rt. 1A south to Ellsworth. A slightly slower route that includes some coastal views is I-95 to Augusta, then Rt. 3 east to Belfast (stop for a swim at Lake St. George State Park), and north on Rt. 1 to Ellsworth.

GETTING AROUND Jump on the **Island Explorer** buses operated by Downeast Transportation (207-288-4573; exploreacadia.com). The free, propane-powered buses travel eight routes around the island and carry bikes front and back. They will stop on request wherever it's safe. Readers have informed us that you can park at the Hulls Cove parking lot as long as you put the receipt on view in your car after buying the pass. You can get off at one trailhead and be picked up at another. Bus schedules are timed to coincide with ferry departures to Swans Island and the Cranberry Isles. The bus service starts June 23 every year and ends Columbus Day.

PARKING Note the lots on our Downtown Bar Harbor map. Much of the lodging is downtown (with parking), and the village is compact. Park and walk.

WHEN TO COME Because this is the most crowded summer place on the coast, everyone who lives nearby, from Portland north, prefers a visit in the off-season, preferably early fall. Although the Island Explorer bus schedule is reduced and the nights are chilly, the scenery is spectacular and the museums are still open. Winter is quiet indeed.

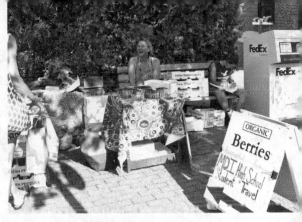

SELLING SUMMER BERRIES FOR MOUNT DESERT ISLAND STUDENTS' TRAVELS

✳ To See

IN BAR HARBOR

✪ ✎ ♿ **Abbe Museum** (207-288-3519; abbemuseum.org), 26 Mount Desert St. Open May–Oct. daily 10–5, off-season Thu.–Sat. 10–4. $8 per adult, $4 ages 6–15, under 6 free. Museum members and Native Americans, no admission fee. The downtown Abbe in the heart of Bar Harbor, facing the village green, is more than eight times the size of its original building and dedicated to showcasing the cultures of Maine's Wabanaki, the 7,000 members of the Penobscot, Passamaquoddy, Micmac, and Maliseet tribes who live in Maine and the Maritimes. The permanent collection of 50,000 objects ranges from 10,000-year-old artifacts to exquisite basketry and crafts from several centuries. The orientation gallery and time line begin with the present and draw visitors back slowly and skillfully through 10,000 years to the core, a circular three-story tower, the "Circle of Four Directions." Exhibits include a fabricated copy of the 1794 treaty between Massachusetts and the Wabanaki that deeded much of Maine to its Native people.

✎ **College of the Atlantic** (207-288-5395; coa.edu), Rt. 3. Housed in the original Acadia National Park headquarters, the **George B. Dorr Museum of Natural History** is a good stop (open Tue.–Sat. 10–5, closed Sun.–Mon.). Admission by donation. Exhibits include a tidal pool tank with marine animals that visitors can touch as well as student-created dioramas of plants and animals of coastal Maine. "Study skins" from animals and birds can be touched as well. The **Ethel H. Blum Gallery** (open Tue.–Sat. 11–4) holds changing exhibits. Founded in 1969, COA is a liberal-arts college specializing in ecological studies. Its waterside acreage, an amalgam of four large summer estates, is now a handsome campus for 350 students.

Bar Harbor Historical Society (207-288-0000; barharborhistorical.org), 33 Ledgelawn Ave. Open June–Oct., Mon.–Sat. 1–4. In winter, open by appointment. A fascinating collection of early photographs of local hotels, Gilded Era clothing, books by local authors and about Bar Harbor, and the story of the big fire of 1947.

IN HULLS COVE

✎ **Hulls Cove Sculpture Garden** (207-288-5126; jonesport-wood.com), 17 Breakneck Rd. This is the Bar Harbor branch of the Davistown Museum in Liberty. Two acres with a path and signage thread through grounds full of work by contemporary Maine artists like Melita Westerlund, who works with polychrome steel; David McLaughlin, who does assemblage art; painter Philip Barter; sculptor Obadiah Buell; and others. A picnic area, tree house, and playhouse for children are all open sunrise to sunset (Rocky Mann's studio is next door). You can also park here to walk into the Breakneck Hollow entrance to Acadia National Park and find a beaver pond.

THE GEORGE B. DORR MUSEUM

IN ELLSWORTH

Woodlawn: Museum, Garden & Park (207-667-8671; woodlawnmuseum.org), Surry Rd. (Rt. 172). Open June–Sept., Tue.–Sat. 10–5, Sun. 1–4; May and Oct., Tue.–Sun. 1–4. Audio tours $10 adults, $3 children. The stone walls are shipshape around this outstanding 1824 Federal mansion based on a design by Asher Benjamin and built by John Black, who moved in with his wife and his three youngest children (five older children had already left home). The rooms are furnished as they were when the last Mr. Black and his family lived here. Stroll the formal gardens, walk the 2 miles of walking trails open dawn to dusk year-round, or reserve the croquet court for a match.

Birdsacre/Stanwood Wildlife Sanctuary (207-667-8460; birdsacre.com), Rt. 3. Old homestead and gift shop open May–Oct., daily 10–4; sanctuary open year-round with outdoor shelters that house non-releasable (injured) hawks and owls. This 200-acre nature preserve is a memorial to Cordelia Stanwood (1865–1958), a pioneer ornithologist, nature photographer, and writer. The 1850 homestead contains a collection of Stanwood's photos.

The Telephone Museum (207-667-9491; thetelephonemuseum.org), 166 Winkumpaugh Rd., marked from Rt. 1A north of Ellsworth. Open July–Sept., Sat. 1–4. $10 adults, $5 children. The evolution of telephone service, from 1876 to 1983 (when the museum was founded), is the subject of this quirky museum. Switchboards and phones are hooked up ready for people to place calls—within the museum.

FOR FAMILIES 🐾 **Acadia National Park Junior Ranger Programs** (207-288-3338) are the best thing going here for youngsters: First complete the activities in the Junior Ranger booklet, then join a ranger-led program or walk to receive a Junior Ranger patch. Books are for 7 and younger, and 8 and older; the senior ranger book for 18 and older contains much harder activities.

🐾 **Family Nature Camp at College of the Atlantic** (see previous page) offers one- and two-week programs, summer field studies for children, and a one-week session for families who live in dorms and spend days on field trips led by naturalists in Acadia National Park.

RT. 3 ATTRACTIONS

🐾 **Mount Desert Oceanarium** (207-288-5005; theoceanarium.com), 1351 Rt. 3, Bar Harbor 04609. Open 9–5 daily, except Sun., mid-May–mid-Oct. $10–12 adults, $6–7 ages 4–12, depending on what you want to see and do. Tour the lobster hatchery and the Thomas Bay Marsh Walk.

Kisma Preserve (207-667-3244; kismapreserve.org), Rt. 3, Trenton. Open mid-May–late fall. $25 adults, under 3 free, but check if allowed. Tours are geared toward adults and more mature children. Make your reservation in advance and consider choosing an animal encounter with a wolf, moose, or primate at this 35-acre nonprofit animal preserve with native and non-native animal species. The moose is a draw for tourists who want to see one, but animals from 60 other species are also living here, many retired, injured, or abused.

♪ **The Great Maine Lumberjack Show** (207-667-0067; mainelumberjack.com), Rt. 3, Trenton. Mid-June–Labor Day, nightly at 7 rain or shine, in fall on Sat. and Sun. The 1¼-hour show includes ax throwing, log rolling, speed climbing, and more.

✳ To Do

AIRPLANE RIDES **Scenic Flights of Acadia** (207-667-6527; mainecoastalflight.com), Rt. 3, Hancock County Airport, Trenton. Sightseeing flights in a Cessna 172 take four different routes over MDI.

Acadia Air Tours (207-667-7627; acadiaairtours.com), located at both the Hancock County–Bar Harbor Airport and on the pier in downtown Bar Harbor, offers scenic airplane, biplane, and glider flights sunrise to sunset, by appointment, weather permitting. The biplane and the glider flights are extremely popular.

AMUSEMENT PARK ♪ **Wild Acadia Fun Park** (207-667-3573; wildacadia.com), 233 Bar Harbor Rd., Trenton. Open end of May–Labor Day. Water slides and splash pool, 18-hole mini golf, Indy style go-carts, 32-foot rock climbing wall, slingshot trampoline, and water wars with water balloons and catapults.

BEER AND WINE **Atlantic Brewing Company** (207-288-BEER; atlanticbrewing.com), 15 Knox Rd. in Town Hill (across from the Town Hill Market), has re-created an indoor-outdoor European brewery-pub. Daily tours and tastings, Memorial Day–Columbus Day; coffee milk stout is a wonderful thing to try, and so are the rest of the brews.

Bar Harbor Cellars (207-288-3907; barharborcellars.com), 854 Route 3, Bar Harbor. Open daily from Memorial Day to the weekend after Columbus Day. On the way into Bar Harbor from Trenton Bridge, Bar Harbors Cellars sells the wine it makes with juice it buys from around the country; the apples are local and make a good dry cider. Don't miss the chocolate room, with Monica's Chocolates from Lubec and Black Dinah chocolate bark bars.

BICYCLING The network of gravel carriage roads constructed by John D. Rockefeller Jr. in 1915 lends itself particularly well to mountain biking. In Bar Harbor, **Bar Harbor Bicycle Shop** (207-288-3886; barharborbike.com), 141 Cottage St., is the oldest bike outfitter in town and still rents only bikes: mountain, tandem, and everything that goes with them. **Acadia Bike** (207-288-9605 or 1-800-526-8615; acadiabike.com), 48 Cottage St., rents mountain and hybrid bikes and offers a full bike shop for sales and service. **Acadia Outfitters** (207-288-8118; acadiaoutfitters.com), 106 Cottage St., offers rentals of mountain and hybrid bikes, sea kayaks, and scooters.

BIRDING **The Natural History Center** (207-266-9461; thenaturalhistorycenter .com), Bar Harbor. A snowy owl on Sargent Mountain was one sighting on a bird tour

ACADIA BIKE

MUST SEE

There are five Cranberry Isles just southeast of Mount Desert, though we list only the two with year-round residents (cranberry isles.com).

LITTLE CRANBERRY The most visitor-friendly of the islands is 400-acre Little Cranberry (islesford.com), located 20 minutes offshore. The official "sight-to-see" is the incongruously brick and formal **Islesford Historical Museum** (207-244-9224; open daily mid-June–Sept., 9–noon and 12:30–3:30), built in 1928 with funds raised by Bangor-born, MIT-educated summer resident William Otis Sawtelle to house his fascinating collection of local historical objects. Acadia National Park maintains the museum (and restrooms), featuring it as part of a ranger-narrated **Islesford Historical Cruise**. We prefer to come by mail boat, taking our time to explore the island and beating the crowd to **Islesford Dock Restaurant**, the island's gathering spot and a great place to eat. Stop in at the **Islesford Dock Galley** and walk on up the road to Danny and Kate Fernald's **Islesford Artists Gallery** (207-244-3145; islesfordartists.com), specializing in Maine's many excellent island artists. At the dock look for the **Alleyway**, Cari Alley's white truck selling reasonably priced fresh lobster and shrimp rolls (her husband is a lobsterman/shrimper), hot dogs, island desserts, and more. **Winter's Work** showcases island-made crafts, and Marian Baker's **Islesford Pottery** (207-244-5686) is worth a stop. The **Islesford Market** (207-244-7667) has been open sporadically in recent years. Stop by at least to meet island-bred postmistress Joy Sprague, who sells more stamps per year from her window here than any other post office in Maine, despite the fact that Islesford has fewer than 80 year-round and some 400 summer residents. Requests for Sprague's "Stamps by Mail" come from as far as Fiji, Iceland, and Istanbul—perhaps because with each order she encloses one of her island photos and a monthly newsletter (her address is USPO, Islesford 04646). Sprague also operates **Joy of Kayaking** (207-244-4309), renting one- and two-person kayaks. For a wide choice of summer rentals, see islesford.com. To get there see *Boating*.

GREAT CRANBERRY—the largest of the islands—is a lobstering and boatbuilding island with a year-round population of around 40 that swells to 300 in summer. The **Seawich Café & Cranberry General Store** (207-244-0622) at the ferry landing offers salads, sandwiches, and daily specials. About 0.3 mile down the road is **Cranberry House**, start of the trail to Whistler Cove and home to the **Historical Society Museum** (207-244-7800) and **Hitty's Café** (207-244-7845), serving meals and ice cream on a cheerful deck. Another 0.25 mile farther on is the library in the currently inactive school. Just beyond that look for **The Whale's Rib** (207-244-5153), offering a selection of crafts and art.

offered by Rich MacDonald and Natalie Springuel, who run nature tours and adventure tours.

✐ **Downeast Nature Tours** (207-288-8128; downeastnaturetours.com), 150 Knox Rd., Bar Harbor. Michael J. Good offers guided bird-watching and nature tours daily.

BOATING American Cruise Lines (1-800-814-6880; americancruiselines.com), 741 Boston Post Rd., Ste. 200, Guilford, CT. This cruise company offers an eight-day cruise called the Maine Coast and Harbors, with stops in Bar Harbor, Castine, Belfast, Camden, Rockland, Boothbay Harbor, Bath, and Portland.

Bar Harbor Ferry Co. (207-288-2984; barharborferry.com) sails from the Bar Harbor Inn Pier, crossing Frenchman Bay to Winter Harbor several times a day; bring a bicycle and bike around Schoodic. **Lulu Lobster Boat Ride** (207-963-2341; lululobsterboat.com), Harborside Hotel and Marina, offers sightseeing (*le capitaine parle français*) on Frenchman Bay, with lobstering demonstrations and seal-watching. **Dive-in-Theater** (207-288-3483; divered.com) operates the *Seal*, an excursion boat from which passengers can watch Diver

SWANS ISLAND (swansisland.org). At the mouth of Blue Hill Bay, 6 miles out of Bass Harbor, with frequent car ferry service (see *Getting There*), this is a large lobstering and fishing island with a year-round population of 300, a library, a general store (no alcohol), seasonal restaurants, quarry pond to swim in, and fine sand beach to walk on. With a bike it's a possible day trip, but be fore-warned: The ferry dock is 4 hilly miles from **Burnt Coat Harbor**, the picturesque island center with **Hockamock Light** (built in 1872) at its entrance. Swans works better as an overnight, given its choice of places to stay and the beauty of local hiking trails (check out the shore path at the light)

Swans Island is divided into three areas: **Atlantic**, where the ferry docks; **Minturn**, by the quarry pond and grocery store; and **Swans Island Village**, with the beach and lighthouse. The island was named for James Swan, the original owner. Maili Bailey arranges seasonal rentals of cottages, houses and apartments at **Swans Island Vacation** (swansislandvacation.com). **Harbor Watch Motel** (207-526-4563; swansisland.com) is open year-round on Burnt Coat Harbor. The **Island Bake Shop** (207-526-4578) serves breakfast and lunch and is known for its pastries. **Carrying Place Market and Take-out** (207-526-4043) is another welcome place for prepared food; you can buy lobsters and clams from **Trafton's** (207-526-4427).

The Sweet Chariot Music Festival (sweetchariotmusicfestival.com) gathers folksingers from across the country and starts with a serenade of the boats in the harbor, many of them Maine wind-jammers, usually in the first week of Aug.

The **Swans Island Library** (207-526-4330) has historic displays and summer speakers; **Swans Island Lobster & Marine Museum** (207-526-4423), open mid-June–mid-Sept., displays ship mod-els, fishing equipment, and photos. **Iverstudio** (207-526-4350) offers weeklong workshops in wood-block printing.

FRENCHBORO The town of Frenchboro (frenchboroonline.com) is composed of 12 islands, but the name is usually applied to Long Island, 8 miles out of Bass Harbor, home to 70 year-round resi-dents (up from 38 in 2000), most in Lunts Harbor. Two-thirds of the island (nearly 1,000 acres) is preserved by the Maine Coast Heritage Trust as the Frenchboro Preserve. A network of hiking trails runs along the shoreline, and the birding is terrific. See *Boating* for access via the **Maine State Ferry** and **Island Cruises**. The seasonal **Lunt's Dockside Deli** (207-334-2902) serves the basics, from veggie wraps to a lobster dinner; the fish chowder is good. The **Frenchboro Historical Society** (207-334-2932), open daily in-season 12:30–5, displays old tools, furniture, and local memorabilia, and also sells crafted items. *Note:* One day a year (early in Aug.) the island welcomes visitors for the **Annual Lobster Festival**, a lobster feed with plenty of chicken salad and pies.

Ed (through an underwater camera) probe the depths of Frenchman Bay, and then get to touch what he fetches.

CANOEING AND SEA KAYAKING Most ponds on Mount Desert offer easy access. **Long Pond**, the largest lake on the island, has three access points. Boats can be launched at **Echo Lake** from **Ike's Point**, just off Rt. 102. **Seal Cove Pond** is less used and accessible from fire roads north of Seal Cove. **Bass Harbor Marsh** is another possibility at high tide. Canoe rental sources offer suggestions and directions. **National Park Canoe Rentals** (207-244-5854) on Long Pond near Somesville offers tours as well as rentals, including kayaks. In Bar Harbor, **Aquaterra Adventures** (207-288-0007; aquaterra-adventures.com), 1 West St., does guided sea kayak tours and sells gear. **National Park Sea Kayak Tours** (207-288-0342 or 1-800-347-0940; acadiakayak.com), 39 Cottage St., gives guided kayak trips on the remote, west side of MDI. **Coastal Kayaking Tours** (207-288-9605 or 1-800-526-8615; acadiafun.com), 48 Cottage St., operates guided sea kayaking tours 2½–7 hours long and multiday camping excursions. It also rents touring sea kayaks.

GOLF **Kebo Valley Club** (207-288-3000; kebovalleyclub.com), Rt. 233, Bar Harbor. Open daily May–Oct. Eighteen holes. "Eighth oldest golf grounds in America," since 1888. **Bar Harbor Golf Course** (207-667-7505; barharborgolfcourse.com), Rts. 3 and 204, Trenton. Eighteen holes.

FISHING Several charter boats offer deep-sea fishing. **Downeast Windjammer Cruises** (207-288-4585; downeastwindjammer.com) offers a four-hour fishing trip once or twice a day, with bait and tackle provided, leaving from the Bar Harbor Inn pier.

ROCK CLIMBING **Acadia Mountain Guides** (207-288-8186; acadiamountainguides.com), 198 Main St., and **Atlantic Climbing School** (207-288-2521), 67 Main St., offer instruction and guiding for beginner through advanced climbers. (Also see "Acadia National Park.")

SAILING **The *Margaret Todd*** (207-288-4585) sails from the Bar Harbor pier from late May to mid- to late Oct. This 151-foot

VIEW ACROSS BAR HARBOR GREEN AND THE *MARGARET TODD*

four-masted schooner, designed and built in 1998 by Captain Steve Pagels, cruises through Frenchman Bay three times a day in high season, less frequently in late Oct.

SWIMMING ✇ **Lake Wood** near Hulls Cove is a pleasant freshwater beach, ideal for children.

TRAINS **Downeast Scenic Railroad** (1-866-449-7245; downeastscenicrail.org), behind Maine Community Foundation, 245 Main St., Ellsworth. The Calais Branch Line is back in operation—$15 for adults and $8 children 3–12 from Memorial Day weekend to mid-Oct. **Antique rail cars** take passengers down 13 miles of Maine woods and wetlands. Ninety-minute trips leave at 10:30 AM and 1:30 PM every weekend.

WHALE-WATCHING The big operator is **Bar Harbor Whale Watch Co.** (207-288-2386; barharborwhales.com), 1 West St., Bar Harbor, which also offers seal-watching and lobstering tours. Bring a jacket, sunblock, binoculars, and a camera.

✳ Lodging

Reservations are not as crucial as they used to be, with a surge in the number of rooms here, but they're still a good idea. We cannot claim to have inspected every room in town, but we have checked out the most appealing options.

WATER-VIEW B&BS

IN AND NEAR BAR HARBOR

Ullikana Bed & Breakfast (207-288-9552; ullikana.com), 16 The Field. Open May–Oct. This is our top pick in downtown Bar Harbor, steps from both Main Street and the Shore Path, yet with an away-from-it-all feel.

Innkeepers Helene Harton and her husband, Roy Kasindorf, combine a rare flair for decorating with a genuine warmth that sets guests at ease. They bought Ullikana, a vintage-1885 Tudor style summer mansion, in 1990 and transformed it. Breakfast, perhaps a light berry-stuffed soufflé pancake or a Bulgarian feta omelet, is served on the terrace overlooking the water or in Ullikana's attractive dining room, where you will feel as if you've returned to the home you always wished for. Guest rooms all have private bath, air-conditioning; $165–295

The Shore Path Cottage (207-288-0643; shorepathcottage.com), 24 Atlantic Ave. Open May–Oct. Lisabeth Chester Oxman has taken over management of this delightful Bar Harbor "cottage" and comfortable B&B previously run by her mother, Roberta Chester, since 1973. The dining room has a kind of authentic elegance that can't be imitated. Seven guest rooms (just one without with private bath, a few with claw-foot tub) are named for the youngsters who grew up in them. The house is filled with books. Both kosher and vegetarian breakfasts are served, and solo travelers and children are particularly welcome. $140–280 in-season, $110–200 low-season.

The Bass Cottage Inn (207-288-1234 or 1-866-782-9224; basscottage.com), 14 The Field, P.O. Box 242. Open mid-May to the end of Oct., this 10-room inn has rooms with whirlpool tubs, gas fireplaces, and TVs with DVD players. Teri Anderholm oversees the cuisine, featuring Maine lobster hash and

coconut crunch muffins for breakfast to be eaten on a bright, elegant sunporch, and wine with fine hors d'oeuvres in the early evening. She and her husband, Jeff Anderholm, run things smoothly in the handsome and comfortable inn, where rates range $260–420 in-season, less before and after.

Balance Rock Inn (207-288-2610 or 1-800-753-0494; balancerockinn.com), 21 Albert Meadow. The original mansion, built in 1903 for a Scottish railroad tycoon, is augmented by a heated pool. Fourteen rooms, most with ocean view, private balcony, whirlpool bath; some with fireplace. The three suites have a kitchen, living room, and sauna. Rooms and suites, all with breakfast, range $155–635 depending on season. $40 fee for pets.

Saltair Inn (207-288-2882; saltairinn.com), 121 West St. Set on the street that overlooks Frenchman Bay and close to the center of things, Saltair Inn provides traditional accommodations with excellent extras, like the heated travertine tile floor in Sedgwick Room. Stroll down the sweep of green lawn to the seats overlooking the sea and back to enjoy breakfast on a deck close to the inn in fine weather. $95–355.

Inn at Bay Ledge (207-288-4202 summer; 207-875-3262 winter; innatbayledge.com) 150 Sand Point Road, Bar Harbor. Open end of May to mid-Oct. Twelve rooms fill this handsome long lodge set on a cliff with 450 feet of waterfront. Jeani and Jack Ochtera, owners for 28 years, have everything figured out for newcomers and a warm welcome for their return guests. With wood-paneled living areas and a breakfast porch, on the northeast side of the island, the inn's accommodations include four cottages. $180 to 450 rooms and for the cottages (May and June for lower rates).

OTHER DOWNTOWN B&BS

IN AND NEAR BAR HARBOR

Manor House Inn (207-288-3759 or 1-800-437-0088; barharbormanorhouse.com), 106 West St. Open mid-Apr.–Oct. No real water views, but a short walk from Bar Island. Nine comfortable rooms with private bath are in the vintage-1887 "Manor" with its rich woodwork. The full acre of landscaped grounds also includes Acadia Cottage with whirlpool, the

Nancy English

AN EARLY-EVENING GATHERING ON THE TERRACE AT ULLIKANA

Chauffeur's Cottage with three guest rooms and two suites, and two garden cottages with gas fireplace. $83–250 includes full breakfast and afternoon tea.

Seacroft Inn (207-288-4669 or 1-800-824-9694; seacroftinn.com), 18 Albert Meadow. Open mid-May–Oct. Bunny Brown's gracious, many-gabled old "cottage" is sequestered on a quiet street, steps from the Shore Path. Extended stays are the norm; all seven rooms have a fridge and a microwave, or a kitchen. $89–129 in-season, substantially less off-season, with housekeeping $10 extra and a complimentary coffee bar and towel exchange. A "Breakfast Basket" with fruit, muffin, juice, and yogurt is $5.

Primrose Inn (207-288-4031 or 1-877-TIME-4-BH; primroseinn.com), 73 Mount Desert St. Open mid-May–Oct. This is a spiffy 1878 stick-style "painted lady" Victorian summer cottage owned by Melissa Collier DeVos. The 15 guest rooms are bright with floral wallpaper and Victorian decor; several have a gas fireplace and private balcony. The nicest rooms in the house have a "bubble massage" Kohler bathtub. Every room has a flat-panel TV with DVD player. Rooms are $154–264, depending on season, including a great breakfast and afternoon tea.

The Maples Inn (207-288-3443; maplesinn.com), 16 Roberts Ave. Open May–Oct. Mark Dresser bought this inn in 2005 and has been decorating with his and his family's antiques; his architectural books are a resource at this pleasant 1903 house on a quiet side street within walking distance of shops and restaurants. The six rooms (all with private bath) are crisply decorated, furnished with a high, antique bed and down comforter. Red Oak, under the eaves, has its own tranquil deck. $165–205 per couple; $95–125 off-season, with a fine breakfast.

☙ **Canterbury Cottage** (207-288-2112; canterburycottage.com), 12 Roberts Ave. Open year-round. This architecturally interesting Victorian house (its original owner was the B&M stationmaster, and its architect specialized in railroad stations) has a canine welcome committee. Rooms each hold a private bath and cable TV. One has a small balcony. $145–155 double in-season, $89–99 off-season, includes full breakfast served in the pretty dining room.

POOLSIDE AT THE HARBORSIDE
HOTEL & MARINA

Cleftstone Manor (207-288-4951; cleftstone.com), 92 Eden St. Open May–Oct. Located a short drive from downtown, this 1880 mansion once owned by wealthy summer visitors has been an inn for 50 years. One smallish room called Benjamin Stanwood has a huge bathroom; four have a sofa bed. Joseph Pulitzer summered here, and a few of the original antiques are still in place, like two crystal chandeliers in the dining room. Seventeen rooms with private bath, two with whirlpools, five with fireplace. Pool and spa services are shared with neighbor **Bluenose Inn.** In-season rates $130–195, less off-season.

Anne's White Columns Inn (207-288-5357 or 1-800-321-6379; anneswhitecolumns.com), 57 Mount Desert St. Open May–Oct. Built in the 1930s as a Christian Science church, hence the columns. The 10 rooms have private bath, air-conditioning, and cable TV. $110–165 July–mid-Oct. (less off-season), including full breakfast and afternoon wine and cheese.

& **Mira Monte Inn and Suites** (207-288-4263 or 1-800-553-5109; miramonte.com), 69 Mount Desert St. Open May–mid-Oct. Bar Harbor native Marian Burns offers 13 comfortable guest rooms and four suites in her gracious 1864 mansion. Many, like Malvern, have a private balcony overlooking the deep, peaceful lawn in back or the gardens on the side. All rooms have private bath, phone, clock-radio, voice mail, and flat-screen cable TV; some have a gas fireplace. Rates include a full breakfast buffet and afternoon refreshments. $188–256 for rooms and suites; $95–165 off-season.

HOTELS AND MOTELS

IN BAR HARBOR

♪ ⚐ **Bar Harbor Inn** (207-288-3351 or 1-800-248-3351; barharborinn.com), Newport Dr. Open Mar.–Nov. With 153 units, this landmark hotel gets its share of groups, but its downtown waterside location is unbeatable. It's a genuinely gracious hotel, with a 24-hour front desk, bellhops, a restaurant, and room service. The hotel-sized lobby with seating near the fire is quite grand. The 51 guest rooms in the Main Inn were the first new hotel rooms available in town after the 1947 fire. Of these, 43 were completely rebuilt in 1998; balconies, jetted tubs, and fireplaces were added. The grounds also include a 64-unit Oceanfront Lodge with private balconies on the bay, and the Newport Building—38 equally comfortable rooms without views. All rooms have phone, cable TV, and access to the pool, Jacuzzi, fitness room, and 7 acres of manicured lawns on the water. $199–379 in-season, continental breakfast included.

Harborside Hotel & Marina (207-288 5033 or 1-800-328-5033; theharborsidehotel .com), 55 West St. Open May–Oct. Views of the harbor and Porcupine Islands in some rooms. Luxuriously furnished and accented with marble baths and marble-tiled floors, many rooms and suites are equipped with full kitchens; some have a fireplace in the master bedroom and Jacuzzi on the porch. **La Bella Vita**, a high-end Italian restaurant, lies off the main lobby (and has the same branding as The Samoset's 2011 version in Rockport). The spa is located in the neighboring Bar Harbor Club with its own restaurant. Tennis courts and a saltwater pool. Standard rooms $275–425, suites $399–1,700 in-season; off-season $99–199, $299–800.

♪ **Wonder View Inn** (207-288-3358 or 1-888-439-8439; wonderviewinn.com), 50 Eden St., P.O. Box 25. Open May–Oct. Children are welcome in the 75-unit motel built on 14 acres, the site of an estate once owned by Mary Roberts Rinehart, author of popular mystery stories. Near downtown Bar Harbor, the motel overlooks Frenchman Bay and includes a swimming pool. $109–249 in summer, less off-season. Most rooms have a balcony with an ocean view.

⚐ ♪ **Bar Harbor Villager Motel** (207-288-3211 or 1-888-383-3211; barharborvillager .com), 207 Main St. This reasonably priced motel provides immaculately clean and comfortable rooms within an easy walk of everything Bar Harbor offers, along with a turquoise, heated pool tucked into a back corner of the parking lot. The **Bar Harbor Shuttle** (207-479-5911; barharborshuttle.com) stops here, going to the airports and the bus depot in Bangor. Summer rates $89–$179, depending on season, children 12 and under free.

IN ELLSWORTH

⚐ ♪ **Twilite Motel** (207-667-8165 or 1 800-395-5097; twilitemotel.com), Rts. 1 and 3. In 2007 Chuck and Ariela Zucker took over this charming motel with flowers spilling out in between the 1950s-style, updated rooms, all with private bath and a little outdoor seating area. Children's play area, continental breakfast served in the breakfast room, and coin-operated laundry with games and books for guests to enjoy. Rates $82–123, less off-season.

COTTAGES ♪ **Acadia Cottage Rentals** (207-288-3636; acadiarental.com) offers camps, cottages, private homes, and estates for a minimum of one week (Sat.–Sat.).

♪ **Emery's Cottages on the Shore** (207-288 3432 or 1-888-240-3432; emeryscottages .com), Sand Point Rd., Bar Harbor 04609. Open May–late Oct. In the family since 1969, these 22 cottages and an apartment on Frenchman Bay offer electric heat, shower, and cable TV; 14 have a kitchen. Linens, dishes, and cooking utensils provided. Serene, private pebble beach. Telephone available for local calls. No pets. Hikers like to use these cabins as a launching place from which to set out on day trips in Acadia National Park. $560–1,075 per week late June–late Aug.; $470–820 late Aug.–Oct.; less in May and June.

PUBLIC CAMPGROUNDS **Lamoine State Park** (207-667-4778; campwithme.com), Rt. 184, Lamoine. Open mid-May–mid-Oct. Minutes from busy Rt. 3 (between Ellsworth and Bar Harbor), this 55-acre waterside park offers a boat launch and 62 campsites (no hookups, but hot showers in a bathhouse), two-night reservation minimum, $25 per night for nonresidents in-season, $15 for residents. Neighboring Lamoine Beach is great for skipping stones. *Note:* There are occasionally vacancies here in July and Aug. when Acadia National Park campsites are full, and about 20 sites are on a first-come, first-served basis.

✳ Where to Eat

DINING OUT

All listings are in Bar Harbor unless otherwise noted.

The Burning Tree (207-288-9331), Rt. 3, Otter Creek. Open June–Columbus Day 5–10; closed Tue., also Mon. after Labor Day. Reservations recommended. Admired for its fresh fish and its own organically grown produce from five gardens. Dine inside or on a lattice-enclosed porch on a wide choice of seafood, chicken, and vegetable entrées, but no red meat. You might begin with crispy kale and oven-roasted littleneck clams with garlic, pine nuts, and chèvre ($12.50), then dine on a cashew, brown rice, and Gruyère cheese terrine ($23.50) or basil-and-chèvre-stuffed organic chicken breast with homemade tomato jam ($24). Entrées $20–29.

Mache Bistro (207-288-0447; machebistro .com), 321 Main St. Kyle Yarborough has made Mache Bistro a place to count on for vibrant flavors and great cooking. His lobster-stuffed piquillo peppers get dinner started perfectly, and the swordfish with tabbouleh and heirloom tomatoes shows off the summer. Entrées $18–29.

Side Street Café (207-801-2591; side streetbarharbor.com), 49 Rodick St., Bar Harbor. Lobster stew, lobster cobb salad, great pub food like fries with chipotle dipping sauce. This year-round café is depended on by its patrons for its burgers and mac and cheese.

♿ **Café This Way** (207-288-4483; cafethisway.com), 14½ Mount Desert St. Open seasonally for breakfast and dinner. Tucked just off the village green, this is a winner. Start dinner with a smoked salmon "parcel" that wraps up goat cheese and pickled jalapeños, then try fish-and-chips made with tempura ahi tuna. Entrées $15–26. Reservations a good idea. Breakfast is just as good (see *Eating Out*).

♪ **Jordan Pond House** (207-276-3316; jordanpond.com), Park Loop Rd., Seal Harbor. Open mid-May–late Oct. for lunch and tea 11:30–6 in summer, 5:30 early and late in the season, and for dinner 6–9. Reservations advised. First opened in the 1870s, this landmark was beautifully rebuilt after a 1979 fire, with dining rooms overlooking the pond and mountains. It's best known for popovers and outdoor tea. Jordan Pond House is least crowded at dinner, when dishes such as prime rib, fresh fish, and baked scallops are served.

♿ **Havana** (207-288-CUBA; havanamaine .com), 318 Main St. Open from 5 nightly; reservations suggested. The menu changes weekly, and the accent ranges from the Caribbean to Africa and farther east. Dinners have included braised beef short ribs in soy sauce, apple cider, and brown sugar with avocado guasaca, a spicy Venezuelan spread, and local squash curry. Entrées $19–34.

Sweet Pea's Café (207-801-9078), 854 Rt. 3, Bar Harbor (just north of town). Open seasonally. Wood-fire oven-baked pizza, house-smoked bacon and pastrami, grilled beef tenderloin, and blueberry pie. The local goats at the farm out back are utterly charming.

Galyn's (207-288-9706; galynsbarharbor .com), 17 Main St. Lunch and dinner. Easy to miss among the shops near the bottom of Main St., but it's bigger than it looks, with dining rooms upstairs and down. Try the crabcake salad or lobster enchilada. Entrées from $16.

McKay's Public House (207-288-2002; mckayspublichouse.com), 231 Main St. Two floors (with live music upstairs) fill up with dedicated local customers at this year-round place. Farm stand salad, Maine étouffée, roasted organic chicken, and brandy-braised pork are possibilities. Entrées $16–21.

LOBSTER

Lobster pounds are the best places to eat lobster. The easiest to find are the clutch around the Trenton Bridge on Rt. 3. The **Trenton Bridge Lobster Pound** (207-667-2977; trentonbridge lobster.com), open Memorial Day–Columbus Day 8–8, or for live lobsters year round, has been in George Gascon's family a long time. The view and the aromas are unparalleled.

&. **Bar Harbor Lobster Bakes** (207-288-4055; barharborlobsterbakes.com), Rt. 3, Hulls Cove, is a twist on the traditional lobster pound. Reservations are a must. Choices are lobster or steak. Watch the lobsters being steamed with your potatoes and corn in the large steel cookers.

&° **Testa's** (207-288-3327; testasrestaurants .com), 53 Main St. Open 8 AM–10 PM, June–Aug., closing earlier off-season (the family moves to its Palm Beach restaurant in Nov.). In Bar Harbor since 1934. Extensive menu, including Italian and seafood specialties. Entrées $17–30.

EATING OUT

IN BAR HARBOR

The Black Friar Pub (207-288-5091; black friarinn.com), across from the Shop and Save, serves winning pub fare, like sweet potato fries, crab fritters, and fish-and-chips. Of course the big beer selection, with many Maine brews on tap, is another draw, along with the best chocolate cakes and fruit pies in town. Meals $10–17.50.

Café This Way (207-288-4483), 14½ Mount Desert St. Open for breakfast 7–11 Mon.–Sat., 8–1 Sun. The menu ranges from scrambled tofu to steak and includes omelets, eggs Benedict with smoked salmon, and many other appetizing dishes.

Lompoc Café (207-288-9392; lompoccafe .com), 36 Rodick St. Open daily with lunch 11:30–3 in the summer and 5–9:30 for dinner, until 1 for drinks. Billed as the original home of Bar Harbor Real Ale (the Atlantic Brewing Company itself has outgrown its birthplace), this is a congenial oasis with an open knotty-pine dining room, plus porch and terrace tables by a bocce court. Entrée choices include pizzas and salads; live music on weekends.

The Fish House Grill (207-288-3070; eat fishmaine.com), 1 West St., Bar Harbor. Set on a deck overlooking Frenchman's Bay, this is a reliable place for scenery and fried seafood,

a seafood marinara, and, of course, good beer. The raw bar serves the perfect oysters of Maine. Entrées $18 to 28. Sister spots line Main Street—and Cherrystones has good people-watching tables.

&° **Rosalie's Pizza** (207-288-5666), 46 Cottage St. Locals head for a booth at Rosalie's when they want excellent pizza. Calzones, salads, and baked subs are also served.

Morning Glory Bakery (207-288-3041; morningglorybakery.com), 39 Rodick St. Open weekdays 7–7, Sat.–Sun. 8–7. Smoothies, espresso, savory and sweet baked goods, soup, and sandwiches. Local meats, produce, and dairy products on the menu; the bacon and fresh eggs are local, Smith Family Farm yogurt, and Sunset Acres Farm goat cheese.

&° **Poor Boy's Gourmet** (207-288-4148), 300 Main St. Open for dinner from 4:30 nightly. Count on a decent dining experience at reasonable prices. Choices range from vegetarian entrées to a full lobster dinner—including brownie à la mode. Wine and beer.

Jordan's Restaurant (207-288-3586), 80 Cottage St. Open 4:30 AM–2 PM. Under David Paine's ownership (since 1976), this remains an old-style diner: breakfast all day, specializing in blueberry pancakes and muffins and a wide variety of three-egg omelets. The place to fuel up for a hike.

IN HULLS COVE

Chart Room (207-288-9740), Rt. 3. Open for lunch and dinner. A dependable, family-geared waterside restaurant with seafood specialties; good quiche and Caesar salads.

IN TOWN HILL

Mother's Kitchen (207-288-4403; mothers kitchenfoods.com), Rt. 102, Town Hill. Fantastic sandwiches, and everything can be served as a salad. Muffins, scones, pies, and picnic tables to dine at in good weather, if you are not hiking to the top of Precipice. Order by phone ahead of time and skip the wait.

IN ELLSWORTH

Airline Brewing Co. (207-584-2337; abcmaine. beer), 173 Main St., Ellsworth. Loving craftsmanship went into the renovation of this paneled pub. Flights of beer soar with more excellent craftsmanship: check the website for new releases. Simple, satisfying pub food.

The Cellar (207-669-6439), 112 Main St. A wide array of charcuterie and cheese to choose from for a starter, then maybe a cioppino, a salad with a crab cake, or flank steak as an entrée. Brunch and lunch too. $18–23.

🦞 🦅 **Union River Lobster Pot** (207-667-5077; lobsterpot.com), behind Rooster Brothers at the western edge of Ellsworth. Open daily June–Aug., 11:30–8:30, dinner only through Oct. Brian and Jane Langley own this pleasant riverside restaurant and serve a full menu, including ribs, but the specialty is lobster and seafood cooked four ways. Leave room for pie. Beer and wine, and an eagle overhead at a beautiful setting.

♿ **Riverside Café** (207-667-7220), 151 Main St. Open 6 AM–3 PM weekdays, 7–3 Sat., 7–2 Sun. for breakfast and lunch in expanded, bright, spacious quarters. Good food and coffees.

Dyon's (207-664-6116; dyonstapas.com), 35 Eastward Ln. A small boîte in the massive indoor tennis facility, Dyon's serves tapas or small plates and wine. The waffle falafel, crispy and warm, works well, along with tapenade and house crackers and chicken satay.

AFTERNOON TEA **Jordan Pond House** (207-276-3316; jordanpond.com), Park Loop Rd., Seal Harbor. Tea on the lawn at the Jordan Pond House (served 11:30–6 mid-July–Aug., till 5:30 mid-May–mid-Oct.) comes with freshly baked popovers and homemade ice cream. Reservations suggested.

SNACKS AND ICE CREAM **Mount Desert Island Ice Cream** (for information call 207-460-5515; mdiic.com). 7 Firefly Lane (207-801-4007) and 325 Main St. (207-801-4006), both in Bar Harbor. Ice cream—chocolate made with Callebaut chocolate, vanilla with vanilla beans—and sorbet, like lemon made with hand-squeezed lemons. Blueberry basil sorbet and salted caramel ice cream were both hits.

Morton's Moo (207-266-9671; mortons moo.com), 9 School St., Ellsworth. Devotees to Morton's Moo ice cream are intimately familiar with the high quality of the mint chocolate chip, coffee bean, and double dark chocolate ice cream, as well as many other flavors.

Rooster Brother (207-667-8675; rooster brother.com), Rt. 1, Ellsworth. Just south of the bridge. Gourmet groceries, cheese, fresh-roasted coffee blends, and takeout sandwiches.

✳ Entertainment

MUSIC **Bar Harbor Music Festival** (207-288-5744, off-season 212-222-1026; barharbor musicfestival.org), the Rodick Building, 59 Cottage St., Bar Harbor. Late June–late July. For more than 40 years this annual series has brought up-and-coming young artists to the island, with opera, jazz, new composers, the Bar Harbor Festival String Orchestra, and more. The evening concerts are staged at a variety of sites around town.

FILM **Criterion Movie Theater**, Cottage St., Bar Harbor. This vintage-1932, art deco, 700-seat nonprofit performing-arts theater is run by the Bar Harbor Jazz Festival and presents

THE CRITERION THEATER IN BAR HARBOR

COURTHOUSE GALLERY

live performances, year-round movies, and modern jazz.

Reel Pizza Cinema (207-288-3811), 22 Kennebec Place, Bar Harbor. Pizza and art, along with foreign and independent films, in a funky setting (beanbag chairs and big sofas). Films at 6 and 8:30 nightly, year-round.

The Grand (207-667-9500; grandonline .org), Main St., Ellsworth. A classic theater, recently restored, offers live performances, musical theater; live opera from the Met; art and independent films.

THEATER See **Acadia Repertory Theatre** in "The Quiet Side of Mount Desert" and **The Grand**, above.

✳ Selective Shopping

ART AND FINE-CRAFTS GALLERIES
Eclipse Gallery (207-288-9048; eclipse gallery.us), 12 Mount Desert St., Bar Harbor. Seasonal. A quality gallery specializing in contemporary handblown American glass, ceramics, and fine furniture; also showing metal sculpture.

Island Artisans (207-288-4214; island artisans.com), 99 Main St., Bar Harbor. Open May–Dec. Featuring Maine artists and crafts-people: textiles, pottery, Native American baskets. Glass, silver, and more.

Alone Moose Fine Crafts (207-288-4229), 78 West St., Bar Harbor. A long-established collection of "made in Maine" crafts, special-izing in wildlife sculpture in bronze and wood.

Courthouse Gallery (207-667-6611; court housegallery.com), 6 Court St., Ellsworth. Representing many fine contemporary artists, with a sculpture garden always open on the sloping front lawn, Courthouse Gallery holds receptions and talks worth attending.

Naturalist's Notebook (207-801-2777; thenaturalistsnotebook.com), 16 Main St., Seal Harbor. One part shop, one part exhibit hall, and one part science program, the Naturalist's Notebook offers riches for anyone alert to flora and fauna on MDI hikes, as well as books and prints by Bernd Heinrich, a past speaker.

The Hulls Cove Tool Barn (207-288-5126; jonesport-wood.com), Hulls Cove. Open Wed.–Sun. year-round, closed in Jan. Owned by Jonesport Wood Company, this store holds a huge selection of hand planes and other old woodworking tools. Books, old postcards, and more are also stocked. The store is next to the Sculpture Garden of the Davistown Museum. (See Liberty Tool Company in "Belfast, Sear-sport, and Stockton Springs" chapter.)

Rocky Mann Studio Potter and Gallery (207-288-5478; rockymann.com), Breakneck Rd., Hulls Cove. Turn off Rt. 3 at the Hulls Cove General Store. In summer open daily 10–5; off-season 11–4, closed Mon. After Christmas by appointment. Rocky Mann's ever-evolving work is worth a trip, with his raku and charming frogs and turtles, and the Acadia starry night series. Paintings and cards by Carol Shutt.

Asticou Connection (207-288-2400; asticouconnection.com), 1302 State Highway 102, Town Hill. Intricate baskets, jewelry, and fine furniture share space with fine art with an emphasis on Maine and nature.

BOOKSTORES **Sherman's Bookstore and Stationery** (207-288-3161; shermans.com), 56 Main St., Bar Harbor. Open 9 AM–10:30 PM

COLONEL BLACK MANSION

in summer, 9–6 daily in winter. A great browsing emporium; really a combination five-and-dime, stationery store, gift shop, and well-stocked bookshop.

Big Chicken Barn Books and Antiques (207-667-7308; bigchickenbarn.com), Rt. 1/3 south of Ellsworth. Open daily year-round; call for hours. Maine's largest used bookstore fills the vast interior of a former chicken house. Annegret Cukierski has 150,000 books in stock: hardbacks, paperbacks, magazines, and comics; also used furniture and collectibles.

✳ Special Events

Throughout the summer: **Band concerts**, Bar Harbor village green (check current listings); **Ellsworth Harbor Park**, concerts on Friday nights.

June: **Acadia Birding Festival**—lectures, walks, and boat tours. **Working Waterfront Celebration** (second Sunday) includes the Blessing of the Fleet. **Legacy of the Arts** (midmonth), a week of art and culture with concerts, artists' events, and, at the week's end, **Bar Harbor Chamber of Commerce Art Show**, displaying original work on the Bar Harbor village green (207-288-5103).

July: **Bar Harbor Music Festival** (see *Entertainment*).

July 4 weekend: **Independence Day**—blueberry pancake breakfast, town parade, seafood festival focused on lobster and mussels, and strawberry shortcake. Live music, kids' games, and fireworks from the pier at night. **Native American Festival**—dances and

CROQUET AT COLONEL BLACK MANSION

Nancy English

a big sale by the Maine Indian Basketmakers at the College of the Atlantic (207-288-5744).

August: **Ellsworth Antiques show at Woodlawn**, Ellsworth.

Late September: **Acadia Night Sky Festival** (acadianightskyfestival.com). **Art in the Park** on the Bar Harbor village green throughout a weekend.

October: **Woodlawn Golf Croquet Tournament**, Colonel Black Mansion, Ellsworth.

November: **Shopping in your PJs** downtown for extra discounts, with a parade and fashion show at 9 PM, prize for craziest sleepwear.

December: **Midnight Madness Sale and Village Holidays** (first Friday)—Santa arrives, lights the tree. Discounts from 8 PM to midnight. **Island Arts Association Holiday Fair** (first weekend) sponsored by YWCA (207-288-5008).

THE QUIET SIDE OF MOUNT DESERT

The Quiet Side has come to refer to the longer, thinner arm of land that's divided by Somes Sound from the part of Mount Desert that's home to Bar Harbor, the Acadia National Park visitors center, and Park Loop Road. The name generally also applies to Northeast Harbor.

Northeast is a yachting village, with a large marina geared to visiting yacht owners, summer residents, and ferries to the Cranberry Islands. A 2008 fire destroyed several Main Street buildings and some priceless art in one of Maine's oldest, most established galleries. Soon after however, the village was bright and humming again. It's flanked by a mile of mansions hidden along Somes Sound. The splendid, public Thuya Gardens are just east of town. The Mount Desert Historical Society in Somesville is well worth a stop. Some of Acadia's best hiking, as well as its best public swimming beach (at Echo Lake) and canoeing (on Long Pond), are found west of Somes Sound.

Southwest Harbor is a boatbuilding center, home of the Hinckley Company—the Rolls-Royce of yacht builders—and a substantial commercial fishing fleet. In the neighboring town of Tremont, Bass Harbor is a classic fishing village. It's also the departure point for Swans, a destination in its own right, and several other islands that were once far busier.

Ironically, back in the 1840s, Mount Desert's first summer visitors—artists in search of solitude—headed for the Bar Harbor area precisely because it was then far less peopled than the villages on this western side of the island.

STEPS ACROSS THE WATER AT ASTICOU GARDEN

Nancy English

THUYA GARDENS

Southwest Harbor and Tremont Chamber of Commerce (207-244-9264; acadia chamber.com), 329 Main St. The walk-in info center is open early May–Columbus Day, 9–5 daily.

GETTING THERE

Note: **Airport & Harbor Car Service** (207-667-5995) meets planes, buses, and boats; serves the entire area.

By boat: Contact the harbormasters in Northeast Harbor (207-276-5737) and Southwest Harbor (207-244-7913) about guest moorings.

By car: From Ellsworth: Fork right off Rt. 3 as soon as it crosses the Mount Desert narrows; follow Rt. 102/198 to Somesville and Rt. 198 to Northeast Harbor, or Rt. 102 to Southwest Harbor.

GETTING AROUND **Beal & Bunker** (207-244-3573) offers year-round mail and ferry service from Northeast Harbor to the Cranberry Islands, and the **Maine State Ferry Service** (207-244-4353 or 1-800-491-4883) services Swans Island and Frenchboro.

Island Explorer Bus Service (207-288-4573 or 1-866-282-7558), late June–Columbus Day. Free. This bus stops frequently along the routes from Southwest Harbor to Bernard, up and down both sides of Somes Sound, and into the park and Bar Harbor, connecting with service from Northeast Harbor.

✻ To See

IN NORTHEAST HARBOR

Thuya Garden and Lodge (207-276-5130). Parking is marked on Rt. 3, just east of the junction with Rt. 198. Cross the road and climb the steps, carved in granite beside the Asticou Terraces. These wind up Asticou Hill, offering a splendid view of Northeast Harbor. Thuya Lodge (open late June into Sept., 10–4:30), a botanic library and a lovely spot to read, is the former home of Joseph Henry Curtis, a landscape architect who began this exquisite system of paths and shelters around 1900 and donated the 140-acre property to the public. It is now maintained by the Mount Desert Land and Garden Preserve, to which visitors are asked to donate $3. The 2-acre Thuya Garden was designed by the Asticou Inn's longtime former innkeeper, Charles Savage, who also designed the 2.3-acre **Asticou Azalea Garden** (junction of Rt. 3 and Rt. 198), a spectacular show of azaleas and laurels mid-May–mid-June. Stroll down winding paths and over ornamental bridges. Those not wishing to climb the Asticou Terrace steps can take Thuya Drive (just past the parking lot) up to the garden and lodge. Also note the 1.4-mile **Eliot Mountain Trail** behind Thuya Garden, leading up through blueberry bushes to a sweeping view.

Great Harbor Maritime Museum (207-276-5262; greatharbormaritimemuseum.org), 125 Main St. in the Old Firehouse. Open seasonally, Tue.–Sat. 10–5. $3. The permanent

Sargent Drive, obviously built for carriages, runs from Northeast Harbor north half a dozen miles right along Somes Sound.

Route 102A loop. This isn't the quickest way between Southwest and Bass Harbors, but it's beautiful, following the shore through a section of Acadia National Park that includes the Seawall Campground and picnic area and the Ship Harbor Nature Trail down to gorgeous, flat pink rocks. A short way beyond, be sure to turn onto Lighthouse Rd. to see Bass Harbor Light, a photographer's delight.

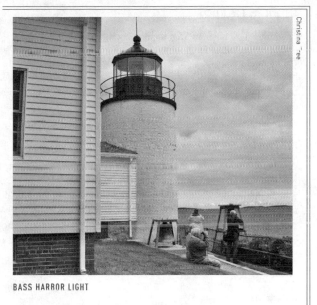

Christina Tree

BASS HARBOR LIGHT

collection is of model ships, small boats, and historical maritime artifacts from Mount Desert Island, there are also notable changing exhibits on a variety of subjects.

Petite Plaisance (207-276-3940; petiteplaisance@acadia.net), South Shore Rd. Open by appointment mid-June–Aug. as well as the first and last two days of this season. The former home of French author Marguerite Yourcenar, where she wrote most of *Memoirs of Hadrian* and also where she died, has long been a destination for her readers.

IN MOUNT DESERT

The tiny white wooden village of **Somesville** at the head of Somes Sound is a National Historic District; be sure to check out **Brookside Cemetery** and the **Somesville Museum** (207-244-5043; mdihistory.org), Rt. 102. Open mid-June–mid-Oct., Tue.–Sat. 1–4 (donation), this lively museum is maintained by the **Mount Desert Historical Society**. Two tidy buildings, one dating back to 1780, connected by a moon bridge, house many artifacts and photographs of the island's vanished hotels and the shipyards for which this village was once widely known. An heirloom garden shows off MDI plants and herbs. The MDI Historical Society's headquarters is on the other side of Somes Sound in the vintage-1892 **School House and Museum**, Rt. 3/198 between Somesville and Northeast Harbor, open June–Sept., Tue.–Sat. 10–4; Sept.–May, weekdays 10–4.

IN SOUTHWEST HARBOR

Wendell Gilley Museum (207-244-7555; wendellgilleymuseum.org), Rt. 102. Open June–Dec., 10–4 (10–5 in July and Aug.), daily except Mon.; Fri.–Sun. only in May, Nov., and Dec. $5 adults, $2 ages 5–12. Wendell Gilley was a local plumber who began hand carving birds as a hobby in the 1930s. For over more than 50 years he carved some 10,000 birds, acquiring a reputation as a master. Friend and patron Steven Rockefeller helped develop the museum, housing more than 200 of Gilley's works.

IN BASS HARBOR

Tremont Historical Society (207-244-9753), Shore Rd. near the Swans Island Ferry. Open July–Columbus Day, Mon. and Wed. 1–4. If you are lucky enough to find this restored country store open, don't pass it by. It's now filled with historic artifacts and photos and sells bargain-priced copies of novels like *The Weir, Spoonhandle,* and *Speak to the Winds,* written in the 1940s by longtime local resident Ruth Moore, vividly capturing life on the offshore islands here.

IN SEAL COVE

✎ **Seal Cove Auto Museum** (207-244-9242; sealcoveautomuseum.org), Pretty Marsh Rd. (Rt. 102), between Bass Harbor and Somesville. Open May–Oct., daily 10–5. $6 adults, $5 seniors and teens, and $2 children 12 and under. Squirreled away in a little-trafficked corner of the island across from Cove Pond and Western Mountain, this collection is a real find: more than 50 gleaming antique cars and 15 motorcycles, including the country's largest assemblage of pre-1915 cars—the lifework of a private collector.

✱ To Do

✎ **Acadia Ranger Programs.** Pick up a copy of *Acadia's Beaver Log* at Seawall Campground (Rt. 102A). The free handout *Acadia Weekly* also lists programs ranging from guided walks and cruises to evening programs.

BICYCLING The network of gravel carriage roads constructed by John D. Rockefeller Jr. in 1915 lends itself particularly well to mountain biking. The fire roads are also good for mountain biking, as is Swans Island. **Southwest Cycle** (207-244-5856; southwestcycle.com), 370 Main St., Southwest Harbor, rents mountain and touring bicycles, children's bikes, baby seats, car racks, and jogging strollers.

BOATING

FROM BASS HARBOR

Island Cruises (207-244-5785; bassharborcruises.com), Little Island Marine. Mid-June–mid-Sept. Kim Strauss offers daily (weather-dependent) lunch cruises aboard 40-foot *R. L. Gott* to Frenchboro, also afternoon cruises to see wildlife—a wide variety of birds, including several bald eagles, porpoises, and many harbor and gray seals on and around Placentia and Black Islands as well as Great and Little Gott Islands, all depicted in novels by Great Gott native Ruth Moore (1903–89). In *The Weir, Speak to the Winds,* and *Spoonhandle,* Moore describes the poignant ebb of life from these islands in the 1930s and 1940s.

    Maine State Ferry (207-244-3254) makes the 40-minute run to Swans Island several times a day, twice weekly to Frenchboro, carrying cars.

THE 1913 PEUGEOT AT SEAL COVE AUTO MUSEUM

BEES MAKING THE MOST OF A ROSA RUGOSA

FROM NORTHEAST HARBOR

Beal & Bunker (207-244-3575) offers year-round mail boat and ferry service to the Cranberries and Sutton Island. **Sea Princess Cruises** (207-276-5352; barharborcruises.com) offers seasonal regular cruises with naturalists, including Somes Sound, sunset, and Islesford historical cruises.

FROM SOUTHWEST HARBOR

Cranberry Cove Ferry (207-244-5882) offers frequent service to the Cranberries from both Manset and Upper Town Dock on Clark Point Rd., both in Southwest Harbor. **Downeast Friendship Sloop Charters** (207-266-5210; sailacadia.com) offers daysails and private charters. **Schooner** *Rachel B. Jackson* (207-288-2216; downeastsail.com) and **Friendship sloop** *Surprise* both offer daysails from Southwest Harbor.

In Southwest Harbor both **Manset Yacht Service** (207-244-4040) and **Mansell Boat Rental Company** (207-244-5625) rent power- and sailboats and offer sail lesson cruises.

CANOEING AND KAYAKING Long Pond, the largest lake on any Maine island, has three access points. Boats can be launched at Echo Lake on Ike's Point, just off Rt. 102. Seal Cove Pond is less used and accessible from fire roads north of Seal Cove. Bass Harbor Marsh is another possibility at high tide. Canoe rental sources offer suggestions and directions. **National Park Canoe/Kayak Rentals** (207-244-5854; nationalparkcanoerental.com), on Long Pond near Somesville, offers guided paddles and instruction. Guided half- and full-day paddles are offered by **Maine State Sea Kayak** (207-244-9500; mainestatekayak.com), 254 Main St., Southwest Harbor.

GOLF Causeway Golf Club (207-244-3780), Fernald Point Rd., Southwest Harbor. Nine-hole waterside course, clubhouse and pull carts, pro shop.

HIKING The highest mountains on the western side of Somes Sound are Bernard and Mansell, but both summits are wooded. The more popular hikes are up Acadia Mountain (3.5 miles roundtrip, off Rt. 102), with an east–west summit trail commanding a spectacular view of the sound and islands. Admittedly we have only climbed **Flying Mountain**, a quick hit with a great view, too. The trail begins at the Fernald Cove parking area. Don't miss **Asticou Terraces** and the **Indian Point Blagden Preserve. Ship Harbor Nature Trail** (off Rt. 102A) winds along the shore and into the woods, with

good birding. If a sunny Friday is promised, take advantage of the once-weekly service to **Frenchboro** (207-244-5785; see *Boating*) and spend the day hiking in the Frenchboro Preserve.

SAILING Mansell Boat Rentals (207-244-5625), Rt. 102A, Manset (near Southwest Harbor), offers sailing lessons; also rents small sailboats. All-day sailing trips offered with Captain Robert Wellborn; bring some wine and cheese and spend the day on the water. Also check **Hinckley Yacht Charters** (207-244-5008), Southwest Harbor, and **Manset Yacht Service** (207-244-4040) in Manset.

SWIMMING Echo Lake offers a beach with a lifeguard, restrooms, and parking

CLAREMONT HOTEL

Gracious but not stuffy, Mount Desert's oldest hotel has the grace and dignity but not the size of a grand hotel. It also has the best views on the island and has benefited from the fact that, since its 1884 opening, there have been just three owners. Upstairs the original 35 second- and third-floor rooms have been reduced to 24, all with closets and baths, furnished with refinished original pieces and graceful reproductions, all with phones and fresh flowers. Wood floors gleam around thick carpets in sitting rooms, the wraparound porch is lined with rockers, and every table in the dining room has a view. Visitors are welcome to lunch at The Boathouse (see *Eating Out*), to dine at Xanthus (see *Dining Out*), and to attend Thu.-evening lectures (see *Entertainment*). There are large suites in Phillips House, and individual cottages, each with living room and fireplace, all with kitchenette. Facilities include tennis on clay courts, three croquet courts, badminton, and water sports; bicycles and rowboats are available. The Croquet Classic in August is the social high point of the season. The McCue family, current owners, have been summering on Mount Desert since 1871. "We didn't expect to make money, just to keep it going and to improve it" is how the late Gertrude McCue explained what she and her late husband, Allen, were thinking when they bought the hotel in 1968. $145–335 B&B in the hotel; the 12 rooms on the water side are priced slightly higher than those overlooking the tennis courts. Cottages are $180–370 with a three-day minimum. A 15 percent service charge is added. ✪ ✎ ♪ ♿ (207-244-5036 or 1-800-244-5036; theclaremonthotel.com), 22 Claremont Rd., Southwest Harbor 04679. Open May–mid-Oct.

(Rt. 102 between Somesville and Southwest Harbor). Another favorite spot is known as "the bluffs" or "the ledges." Park in the Acadia Mountain parking area (about 3 miles south of Somesville on Rt. 102). A short path leads down to the lake.

TENNIS The courts at the **Northeast Harbor Marina** are open to the public, and the Mount Desert Chamber of Commerce (see *Guidance*) offers racquets and balls.

✱ Green Space

Indian Point Blagden Preserve, a 110-acre Nature Conservancy preserve in the northwestern corner of the island, includes 1,000 feet of shorefront and paths that wander through the woods. It offers a view of Blue Hill Bay and is a tried-and-true seal-watching spot. From Rt. 198 north of Somesville, turn right on Indian Point Rd., bear right at the fork, and look for the entrance; sign in and pick up a map at the caretaker's house.

Seal Cove. An unpublicized waterside park with picnic tables, a beach at low tide, a kayaking put-in. From Rt. 102 turn at the red buoy onto the waterside extension of Seal Cove Rd.

✱ Lodging

INNS AND B&BS

IN SOUTHWEST HARBOR

The Inn at Southwest (207-244-3835; innatsouthwest.com), Main St., P.O. Box 593. Open May–Oct. Built in 1884 as a Victorian-style annex to a now-vanished hotel, this delightful B&B is furnished with comfortable Arts and Crafts antiques. Of the seven guest rooms, all with private bath and named for lighthouses, the third-floor Pemaquid Point suite with its chapel-style window and window seat stands out; Egg Rock was a snug spot for a one-night visit. Dora and Daniel are the warm innkeepers, serving Belgian waffles and a lovely fruit bowl for breakfast, or perhaps eggs and sausages if you prefer. $150–215 per couple in high season.

    Lindenwood Inn (207-244-5335 or 1-800-307-5335; lindenwoodinn.com), 118 Clark Point Rd., P.O. Box 1328. This turn-of-the-20th-century sea captain's home set by the harbor among stately linden trees is open Apr.–Nov. 1. Australian-born owner Jim King has a sure decorating touch in the 15 rooms (all with private bath) in the main inn and the Rosebrook House, many with water views, balcony, and fireplace. The pool and hot tub

BRUNCH ON THE PORCH OF THE ASTICOU INN, NORTHEAST HARBOR

are appreciated after hiking or biking. A full breakfast is served in the paneled dining room. A full bar is also available. $175–295 double in-season, $125–225 in low season.

Harbour Cottage Inn and Pier One (207-244-5738 or 1-888-843-3022; harbour cottageinn.com), 9 Dirigo Rd., P.O. Box 258. Don Jalbert and Javier Montesinos have revamped this old landmark to feature creature comforts and romance. The eight standard rooms are equipped with flat-screen TV; some have whirlpool bath. The Southwester (sleeping six) and Carriage House (sleeping four), both neighboring cottages, have full kitchen. Five skillfully furnished weekly rental units with kitchens ($1,155–1,715) are clustered by the water and are collectively known as Pier One. $179–245 for standard rooms, $199–269 for suites or cottages. Rates include breakfast at separate tables in a sunny dining room and afternoon refreshments.

The Kingsleigh Inn (207-244-5302; kingsleighinn.com), 373 Main St. Open seasonally. The check-in desk is the counter of a large, open kitchen, and the living room has a wood-burning fireplace; wicker chairs fill the wraparound porch, and several rooms have decks to maximize harbor views. We like the Chelsea, Abbott, and Hawthorne Rooms more than the three-room third-floor suite. Innkeepers Pamela Parker and Bryan Stevens offer a multicourse breakfast that's a true event; afternoon tea is another. $170–205 mid-June–mid-Oct., $315 for the three-room, third-floor suite; from $145 off-season.

✒ **Penury Hall** (207-244-7102; penuryhall .com), Main St., P.O. Box 68. Open year-round.

This attractive village house with three guest rooms (private bath) was the first B&B on the island. Gretchen Strong takes her job seriously and delights in helping guests figure out what's happening on the island. Breakfast may be blueberry pancakes or a "penurious omelet" (eggs, cheese, and salsa with no meat), served with popovers on Tuesday. $165 May–Oct., otherwise from $120 includes modest use of the fridge, laundry facilities, library, music, games, and sauna. There are also two frisky, friendly black cats; cash or check preferred.

🐾 ✒ **The Birches** (207-244-5182; thebirchesbnb.com), Fernald Point Rd., P.O. Box 178. Open year-round. A very special place. Susi Homer's home, built in 1916, offers a waterfront view from its spacious living room. Formal gardens include a croquet court. The three guest rooms (private bath) are furnished in family antiques. $149–189 includes a full breakfast. Inquire about moorings and ski specials.

Moorings Inn (207-244-5523 or 1-800-596-5523; mooringsinn.com), 133 Shore Rd., Rt. 102A, Manset. Overlooking the entrance to Somes Sound, this rambling old inn stands beside the fabled Hinkley boat (as in yacht) yard. Leslie Watson, the fourth generation of her family to run the inn, has made major and tasteful renovations in the Main House, which dates in part to 1784. The inviting living room features a telescope aimed at the spread of mountains and water beyond the picture window. There are 13 rooms in the house itself,

SPACIOUS QUARTERS AT ANN'S POINT INN

ranging from a couple of small "lawn view" rooms to suites with spectacular views. Three rooms in the Lighthouse Wing have a deck, microwave, and fridge. The complex also includes six cottages, most with a living room, fireplace, and kitchenette. Bikes, canoes, and kayaks are available, and sailing lessons are offered through Mansell Boat Rentals, also on the property. $95–195 for the rooms.

IN NORTHEAST HARBOR

🦞 **Harbourside Inn** (207-276-3272; harbour sideinn.com), P.O. Box 178. Open mid-June–mid-Sept. A gracious 1880s shingle-style inn set on 4 wooded acres, with 11 guest rooms and three suites (two with kitchenette) on three floors, all with phone and private bath, some with kitchen. There are also nine working fireplaces in first- and second-floor guest rooms. This very special place has four generations of the Sweet family living on the premises. Flowers from the garden brighten every guest room. Guests mingle at breakfast over fresh-baked blueberry muffins, served on the sunporch, with all-organic ingredients. The Asticou Azalea Gardens, extensive woodland walks, shops, and the town landing with its water excursions are all within walking distance. $150–180 for a room; $250 for a suite with kitchen.

♂ **Asticou Inn** (207-276-3344 or 1-800-258-3373; asticou.com), Rt. 3. Late May–mid-Oct. The inn offers rooms with and without water views, public rooms with Oriental rugs, and a porch overlooking formal gardens and the harbor. The 48 rooms and suites, all with private bath, are divided among the main house and annexes, which include Cranberry Lodge across the road and the Topsider suites in modern water-view cottages. Facilities include a cocktail lounge, tennis courts, and a heated swimming pool. Since the 1960s the inn has been owned by a consortium of summer residents and businesspeople. New management in 2015 made it a popular destination for popovers and brunch on the porch. Along with many of the area's shingle-style "cottages," the inn was designed by Fred Savage, son of A. C. Savage, the original innkeeper. $295–375 per couple in high season, from $155 in shoulder months, plus 5 percent resort fee. Breakfast served but not included in bill. Also see *Dining Out*.

IN BASS HARBOR

🦞 **Bass Harbor Inn** (207-244-5157), P.O. Box 326. Open May–Oct. In an 1870 house with harbor views, within walking distance of village restaurants and the ferry to Swans Island, Barbara and Alan Graff offer six rooms ranging from doubles with shared baths to a fabulous top-floor studio with kitchenette. One room with half-bath has a fireplace; two open onto the side deck. $90–135 in-season, $70–115 off-season, including continental breakfast.

Ann's Point Inn (207-244-9595, anns pointinn.com), P.O. Box 398. This secluded, contemporary waterfront home packs some unusual luxuries, like a hot tub, sauna, and 32-by-12-foot indoor pool. The four large rooms have water views and extras like gas fireplace and king bed; three have private terrace. Jeannette and Alan Feuer are hospitable hosts. $295–350 includes a full breakfast with the inn's own vegetables and afternoon nibbles and evening cookies, mid-June–mid-Oct.

MOTELS ✐ ♿ **Kimball Terrace Inn** (207-276-3383 or 1-800-454-6225; kimballterrace inn.com), 10 Huntington Rd., P.O. Box 1030, Northeast Harbor 04662. Open May–late Oct. Replacing its predecessor hotel of the same name, this pleasant motor inn occupies a prime site on the harbor by the Northeast Harbor Yacht Marina. It offers 70 large rooms, 52 with sliding doors opening onto private patio or balcony. Outdoor pool and tennis courts. $155–205 in high season, from $70 single off-season.

🦞 🐾 ✐ **Harbor View Motel and Cottages** (207-244-5031 or 1-800-538-6463; harborview motelandcottages.com), P.O. Box 701, Southwest Harbor 04679. Open mid-May–mid-Oct. Lorraine and Joe Saunders have owned this 20-unit harborside motel for more than 42 years. In July and Aug., rooms with decks right on the water are $116–128, while others are $84–97 including continental breakfast, less in Sept., for solo travelers, and by the week. A third-floor apartment and seven cottages are available in high season by the week.

Seawall Motel (207-244-3020 or 1-800-248-9250; seawallmotel.com), 566 Seawall Rd., Southwest Harbor 04679. Open year-round. Twenty clean, quiet rooms with two queen beds and cable TV, right across the road from the ocean. The free, seasonal Island Express shuttle bus stops outside. From $65 in winter to $115 in high season, when rates include a generous continental breakfast.

OTHER LODGING ⚓ **Appalachian Mountain Club's Echo Lake Camp** (207-244-3747; amcecholakecamp.org), AMC/Echo Lake Camp, Mount Desert 04660. Open late June–Labor Day weekend. Accommodations are platform tents; family-style meals are served in a central hall. There is a rustic library and reading room, but more to the point are boats for use on the lake and daily hikes. Reserve on April 1. Rates for the minimum one-week stay (Sat.–Sat.) are inexpensive per person but add up for a family. All meals included.

⚓ **Bass Harbor Cottages** (207-244-3460; bassharborcottages.com), 95 Harbor Dr. (Rt. 102A), Bass Harbor 04653. Open year-round. This is a classic old farmhouse with three guest rooms and three more assorted cottages scattered in the meadow below, above the water. It's a great spot for families and kayakers. All accommodations offer housekeeping. $80–175 per couple in the inn, $100–400 daily and $800–3,000 weekly in the cottages. Sorry, no pets.

✳ Where to Eat

DINING OUT

IN THE SOUTHWEST HARBOR AREA

Red Sky Restaurant (207-244-0476; redsky restaurant.com), 14 Clark Point Rd., Southwest Harbor. Open nightly June–Columbus Day, hours vary the rest of the year; closed Jan. The toast of this restaurant town, a comfortably low-key bistro with locally sourced food to come back for again and again: appetizers like fried quail with figs, and crispy polenta with mushrooms and beet greens; entrées like round of lamb and lobster with risotto. Ingredients are all as fresh and local as possible. The raspberry sorbet tastes fresh picked. Owners Elizabeth and James Lindquist are both owners and chefs. Entrées $19–30.

Rogue Café (207-244-7101), 1 Main St. Opened in 2015, this excellent restaurant is the rebirth of Town Hill Bistro, which lost its space and was missed. Be sure to reserve, as careful management allots only a certain number of covers to ensure that the kitchen is in full command. Co-owners Maureen Cosgrove—the chef—and JJ Zeph—a suave master of everything in the front of the house—run the show. If you opt for two small plates and one large, you will be full but not sorry; the pork belly is irresistible, and the fish is fresh and perfect; indeed, it's the ingredients themselves that make the dishes stand out. Entrées $21–25.

⚐ **Xanthus at the Claremont** (207-244-5036; theclaremonthotel.com), Clark Point Rd., Southwest Harbor. Open for dinner June–Oct. Here most tables have some water view. Both decor and service are traditional, with white tablecloths and wall sconces spilling fresh flowers, the kind of place where it's appropriate (but not required) to dress up. The restaurant is named for Xanthus Smith, who painted the 1885 portrait of the inn hung here. Flash-fried PEI oysters; late summer vegetable soup and pan-roasted scallops are from a September menu. Entrées $24–29.

XYZ Restaurant & Gallery (207-244-5221; xyzmaine.com), end of Bennett Lane off Seawall Rd. (Rt. 102A), Manset. Open nightly for dinner in high season, varying hours shoulder seasons. Ask for directions when you call to reserve. Janet Strong and Robert Hoyt have made XYZ well-loved for its sharp, spicy, complex Mexican dishes (X is for "Xalapa," Y for "Yucatán," and Z for "Zacatecas"). The atmosphere is intimate (just 30 seats) and colorful with Mexican folk art. The fresh lime margaritas are legendary and chiles rellenos a fixed star. Entrées $26.

Café 2 (207-244-4344), 326 Main St., Southwest Harbor. Dinner served Tue.–Sun. 5–9, May–mid-Oct. Reserve a booth. A vintage car dealership transformed into an informal, colorful café with a patio bar offers dishes from pasta to sesame-crusted tuna or rack of lamb. The dinner salads are generous. Entrées $17–26.

IN NORTHEAST HARBOR

Asticou Inn (207-276-3344), Rt. 3. Open for dinner May–mid-Oct., also for lunch and brunch in July and Aug. Grand old hotel atmosphere with water views. Dinner includes lobster bisque and steak. Entrées $21–30.

The Fork and Table (207-276-0746), 102 Main St., Northeast Harbor. Local is the ethos, from the goat cheese terrine, the crab in the salad, even the oat shortbread. Vegan dishes included one night's wheat berries with asparagus and garlic pistou. Entrées $20–42, but small bites are served at the bar.

IN LITTLE CRANBERRY ISLAND (ISLESFORD)

Islesford Dock (207-244-7494; islesford dock.com), Islesford. Open mid-June–Labor Day except Mon. for lunch (11–3), dinner (5–9), and Sunday brunch (10–2). Another great reason to come to the Cranberry Islands (see the *Must See* sidebar on pages 324–325), this is also a spectacular place to watch the sun set behind the entire line of Mount Desert's mountains. Check the website before making the trip for any dates "closed for a private event." Owners Cynthia and Dan Lief grow herbs and vegetables behind the restaurant and secure most of their seafood and produce from close by or from Maine wonders like Tide Mill Farm far Downeast, an eighth-generation farm. The dinner menu includes the Dock burger (served with fresh-cut fries or a salad) and a crabcake sandwich, "small plates" of Maine mussels or hake sliders, as well as entrées like Gulf of Maine halibut with spinach or duck breast with oyster mushrooms. Save room for blueberry crisp. Entrées $10–42. An attached gallery showcases artists and craftsmen, all with an aesthetic connection to the islands of Maine.

EATING OUT

IN SOUTHWEST HARBOR

Common Good Kitchen Café (207-244-3007; commongoodsoupkitchen.org), 19 Clark Point Rd. Open June to Columbus Day for breakfast. The top "restaurant" in MDI on one tourism website, Common Good started out in a man's kitchen, when Bill Morrison made soup he shared with elderly locals. In 2015, his space with a big kitchen in downtown Southwest Harbor has become a morning destination for popovers with butter and jam, and good coffee—you pay what you wish. Funds raised in the summer pay for weekly winter community dinners. Needless to say, we love the idea as much as we love the food.

Eat-a-Pita (207-244-4344), 326 Main St. Open May–mid-Oct., daily from 8 AM; at dinner this spot turns into Café 2 (see *Dining Out*). A lively, bright café with a patio, soups, salads, pastas, specialty coffees, and pastries, fully licensed.

✒ **Sips** (207-244-4550), 4 Clark Point Rd. Open 7 AM–9 PM in summer, shorter hours off-season. Sips opens early for fresh-brewed coffee, espresso, and full breakfasts, from bagels with homemade spreads to crêpes and all-natural egg omelets. Lunch options include unusual sandwiches and salads. The dinner menu includes crêpes, risotto, vegetarian pastas, and polentas as well classic meat loaf and baked haddock stuffed with crabmeat. Wine and beer. Kids' menu. Entrées $10–24.

Little Notch Café (207-244-3357), 340 Main St. Open late May–Columbus Day 8–8 for coffees, breads, and light meals. The aroma of freshly baked bread is almost impossible to resist. Arthur and Katherine Jacobs specialize in soups and sandwiches like grilled tuna salad with cheddar on wheat; also great pizza. Seating inside and out, take-out.

Beal's Lobster Pier (207-244-3202; bealslobsterpier.net), Clark Point Rd. Open daily Memorial Day–Columbus Day, 11–8. The dining room on this working pier is all about lobster, crabmeat rolls, chowder, fresh fish specialties, and lobster. This is also a place to buy lobster to ship.

The Boathouse at the Claremont Hotel (207-244-3512), Clark Point Rd. Open July–Aug., serving lunch until 2 PM. This informal dockside facility on the grounds of the island's oldest hotel arguably offers the island's best view, east across the mouth of Somes Sound with Acadia's mountains rising beyond. Sandwiches, salads, and burgers; also good for drinks at sunset.

IN NORTHEAST HARBOR

✒ **The Colonel's Restaurant** (207-276-5147), Main St. Open early Apr.–late Oct. Serving breakfast 6:30–11:30, lunch and dinner 11:30–9. A big, informal eatery rebuilt after the 2008 fire. There's a deli-style storefront section as well as the more formal dining area. Still good for fresh-dough pizzas, burgers, and reasonably priced seafood dinners.

Docksider (207-276-3965), Sea St. Open Memorial Day–Columbus Day, 11–9. Bigger than it looks, with a no-frills, knotty-pine interior and amazingly efficient, friendly waitresses. The light and crispy onion rings are simply the best anywhere; one serving is enough for two. Good chowder and Maine crabcakes; also salads, burgers, clam rolls, and a shore dinner.

Milk and Honey (207-276-4003; milkand honeykitchen.com) 3 Old Firehouse Lane, Northeast Harbor. Scones, sour cream pecan coffee cake for breakfast, and sandwiches and frittata for lunch. Open daily in summer, but not till 10 on Sat. and Sun.

IN BASS HARBOR

Thurston's Lobster Pound (207-244-7600; thurstonslobster.com), Steamboat Wharf Rd., Bernard. Open Memorial Day–Columbus Day, daily 11–8:30. Weatherproofed, on a working wharf overlooking Bass Harbor, and just far enough off the beaten path not to be mobbed. Fresh and tender as lobster can be, plus corn and pie, also seafood stew, sandwiches, and blueberry cheesecake. Wine and beer.

Seafood Ketch (207-244-7463; seafood ketch.com), on Bass Harbor. Open mid-May–mid-Oct., daily 11–9. Longtime ownership by Stuart and Lisa Branch has given this place a solid reputation for homemade breads and desserts and fried seafood. Eat inside or out on the new deck. Entrées $19–30.

✳ Entertainment

MUSIC **Mount Desert Festival of Chamber Music** (207-276-3988; mtdesertfestival.org), Neighborhood House, Main St., Northeast Harbor. A series of six concerts presented for more than 48 seasons mid-July–mid-Aug.

Saturday Evening Concerts at the Claremont Hotel (207-244-5036), Claremont Rd., Southwest Harbor. Summer concerts have included the Jerks of Grass and the Gilbert and Sullivan Society of Hancock County.

THEATER **Acadia Repertory Theatre** (207-244-7260; acadiarep.com), Rt. 102, Somesville. Performances during July and Aug., Tue.–Sun. at 8:15 PM; matinees at 2 on the last Sun. of each run. A regional repertory theater group

performs in the Somesville Masonic Hall, presenting several popular plays in the course of the season. Tickets are reasonably priced.

Barn Arts Collective (207-412-9435; barn artscollective.com, 130 Tremont Road, Bass Harbor. *Middlemarch* presented as a musical; Chekhov's *Seagull*; original productions by artists in residence assembled into one production called the Hamilton Project bring crowds on summer nights to this barn in Bass Harbor.

The Claremont Hotel Thursday Evening Lecture Series (207-244-5036), Claremont Rd., Southwest Harbor. July and Aug. An impressive array of authorities speak on a variety of topic like "Writing for a Living and Other Mistakes I Have Made" by Alex Beam, as well as talks on jazz, mountain climbing, and Mount Desert history. All lectures are at 8:15 PM.

✳ Selective Shopping

IN NORTHEAST HARBOR

Naturalist's Notebook (207-276-4120, the naturalistsnotebook.com), 115 Main St. A treasure box of books, prints, art, and science for anyone fascinated by 13.8 billion years of earthly nature. The staffer will no doubt be a local naturalist, perhaps Jordan Chalfant, who studied the puffins for several lonely months on a small island far off the coast. **Island Artisans** (207-276-4045; islandartisans .com), 119 Main St. Open mid-June–mid Oct. (also in Bar Harbor), showcasing exceptional work by more than 100 area craftspeople working with textiles, pottery, baskets, paper, wood, glass, silver, metal, and stone. **Artemis Gallery** (207-276-3001; artemisgallery.com), 1 Old Firehouse Lane. Exhibits of skilled MDI artists' work. **Shaw Contemporary Jewelry** (207-276-5000; shawjewelry.com), 126 Main St., open year-round, is an outstanding gallery featuring Sam Shaw's own work but also displaying work by artists from throughout the United States and Europe, genuine eye candy, priced $20–2,000. A village anchor is the **Kimball Shop & Boutique** (207-276-3300; kimballshop.com), an upscale shop geared to summer residents' needs since 1935. Invest some time in the basement and save 50 percent. An amazing trove of home furnishings, gadgets, fine china, and gifts is next door.

McGrath's Store (207-276-5548), Main St., is an old-fashioned newspaper/stationery store with some surprises, while long-established **Wikhegan Books** (208-276-5079), 117 Main St., is a trove of early history and guidebooks as well as fiction relating to the MDI region, including the legendary Red Book directory of Northeast Harbor summer residents; also nautical titles, Eastern Woodland Indians, poetry, antiques, and much more.

IN SOUTHWEST HARBOR

Aylen & Son Fine Jewelry (207-244-7369; peteraylen.com), 320 Main St. Open mid-Apr.–Oct. Peter Aylen fashions gold, silver, pearl, and Maine gemstone jewelry; Judy Aylen creates bead necklaces and works with a variety of stones.

Carroll Drug Store (207-244-5588), just off Main St. at the north end of the village. A supermarket-sized store with a genuine general-store/five-and-dime feel.

Sawyer's Market (207-244-3315), 344 Main St. This is a great old grocery store with a good deli counter and good soups on tap. **Sawyer's Specialties** (207-244-3317), 353 Main St., sells terrific wine and a good selection of cheeses. Count on good free tastings.

IN BERNARD AND SEAL COVE

Seal Cove Pottery and Gallery (207-244-3602; sealcovepottery.com), Kelly Town Rd., Seal Cove. Marked from Rt. 102. Open Apr.–mid-Nov., 10–5. Lisbeth Faulkner and Ed Davis create handsome, functional pottery (glazes are made from scratch), worth a special trip. Davis is a fifth-generation (both sides) MDI native.

✱ Special Events

July: **Independence Day fireworks**, Southwest Harbor. **Quietside Festival and Pink Flamingo Festival,** Southwest Harbor, with pancake breakfast, 4-mile run, parade, craft fair and steel drum band, Flash in a Pan.

Early August: **Sweet Chariot Music Festival** on Swans Island. **Frenchboro Days** in Frenchboro. **Annual Art Show on the Green**, Southwest Harbor (1-800-423-9264).

September: **Mount Desert Island Garlic Festival** (207-288-0269), 20 Main St., Southwest Harbor, at Smugglers Den Campground, with local restaurants, brewers, musicians, and garlic growers.

October: **Acadia Oktoberfest**, Southwest Harbor.

Nowhere in Maine does the coast change as abruptly as along this rim of Frenchman Bay. On the western side of the bay on Mount Desert Island, Acadia National Park draws everyone from everywhere. By contrast, the northern and eastern shores of the bay are a quiet, curving stretch of coves, tidal bays, and peninsulas. Both the village and park are busier since the recent opening of the Schoodic Wood Campground. The 16,000-acre property adjacent to the national park was anonymously purchased and developed with 94 campsites, also miles of biking and hiking trails on the remaining 14,000 acres under conservation easement, all managed by the National Park Service.

In 1889 the Maine Central's Boston & Mount Desert Limited carried passengers from Boston to a terminal in **Hancock**, connecting with ferries across the bay to Bar Harbor, spawning the area's once large, now vanished, summer hotels. Seasonal ferries now link Winter Bar Harbor with **Winter Harbor**, gateway to the **Schoodic Peninsula** section of **Acadia National Park**.

This is one place that we suggest taking land over water. The 29-mile **Schoodic National Scenic Byway** offers spectacular views back across the bay to Acadia's high, rounded mountains and accesses outstanding galleries and hiking trails. It begins on Rt. 1 at the Hancock-Sullivan Bridge, continues to shadow the shore down the Gouldsboro Peninsula, and then makes its way around the loop road within the national park.

The Schoodic Peninsula is one of those just-off-the-beaten-path places that should be busier than it is—and everyone seems grateful that it isn't. **Winter Harbor** and the photogenic fishing villages of **Prospect Harbor** and **Corea** offer several good places to stay and eat. Art and crafts galleries are scattered through the area; in July and early Aug. the **Schoodic Arts Festival for All** offers more than 100 workshops and performances.

Inland there are hidden lakes and high mountains. The **Blackwoods Scenic Byway** (Rt. 182) here links Black and Schoodic Mountains, both offering long views of Mt. Katahdin as well as the Acadia peaks.

GUIDANCE **Schoodic Peninsula Chamber of Commerce** (acadia-schoodic.org). **Acadia National Park** information is available from the ranger station at **Schoodic Woods Campground** (207-288-1300) at the entrance to the park and at the Visitors Center (Rockefeller Hall) in the park at the **Schoodic Education and Research Center** (207-288-1310).

GETTING THERE *By car:* For a shortcut to Hancock from Bar Harbor, take Rt. 3 north to Rt. 204, posted for Lamoine State Park. Turn left onto Rt. 184, immediately right at the town hall onto Pinkham Rd., left after a mile or so at the sign for Rt. 1 (Mud Creek Rd.). From points south, see *Getting There* in "Bar Harbor."

By boat: The **Bar Harbor Ferry** (207-288-2984; barharborferry.com) offers frequent service Memorial Day–Columbus Day weekends across Frenchman Bay between Bar Harbor and Winter Harbor, connecting with the free *Island Explorer* that makes stops in Winter, Birch, and Prospect Harbors as well as the park. Bring your bike or rent at either side.

Schoodic Ferry (207-801-9444; frenchmabayresearchboating.org) Frequent seasonal service from the College of the Atlantic in Bar Harbor to Winter Harbor, timed to meet the bus at both ends. Captained by a biologist, the vessel briefly stops to check on-going

EXCURSIONS

Schoodic Scenic Byway (see the description in this chapter's introduction and at byways.org). Federal funding has improved signage and turnouts along this breathtakingly beautiful 29-mile stretch of coast with views back across the bay to Acadia's mountains.

Blackwoods Scenic Byway (Rt. 182; blackwoodsbyway.org). Rt. 182 is the mostly wooded, inland shortcut from Hancock to Washington County (you save 9 miles vs. Rt. 1). The 12.5 easternmost miles—between **Franklin** and **Cherryfield** (see the Washington County chapter)—is a state scenic byway, meaning better signage and turnout areas, and boat launches to access the more than 14,000 acres of woods and water now maintained by the **Donnell Pond Public Reserved**. It includes **Tunk Lake**, **Donnell Pond**, and **Spring River Lake** and hiking trails up **Schoodic Mountain** and **Black Mountain** (see *Hiking*).

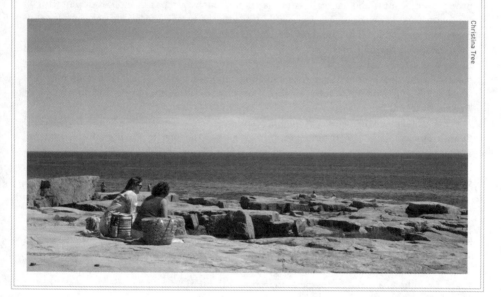

Christina Tree

research projects in Frenchman Bay and offers narration about the Bay and its islands. Check the website for early and late runs, also scenic tours.

GETTING AROUND **Island Explorer** (exploreacadia.com). Late June–Aug. This fabulous, free bus meets the Bar Harbor Ferry and makes an hourly circuit from Winter Harbor around Schoodic Point and back through Birch and Winter Harbors. Bicycles are a great way to explore the park itself.

✳ To Do

BIKING The 12.2-mile loop from Winter Harbor around Schoodic Point, the Schoodic Peninsula, is a popular bike route. Just before the entrance to the national park, bicyclists can park their cars at the **Schoodic Woods Campground** and pick up the free Schoodic Trail System map showing 4 miles of new bike trails. You can also park and unload bikes at Frazier Point Picnic Area just within the park (restrooms). Rentals available from **SeaScape Kayaking** (below). Also check out the **Down East Sunrise Trail** (sunrisetrail.org), a gravel-topped

MUST SEE

Acadia National Park, Schoodic Peninsula (nps.gov/acad). Accessed from Rt. 186 three miles east of Winter Harbor, this is a one-way shore road, 6 miles of it within the park. Stop by the ranger station at **Schoodic Woods Campground** (See *Camping*), for park information. This is also a place to park and unload a bike. **Frazer Point Picnic Area** (with comfort station) is a good first stop, another place to unload bikes if you want to tour on two wheels. It's said to have been an Indian campsite for thousands of years.

Farther along this stretch note the turnouts with views of the **Winter Harbor Light** (1856) and across Frenchman Bay to Cadillac Mountain.

A little more than 2.5 miles farther along, the unmarked, unpaved road up to **Schoodic Head** may or may not be open. Visitors are clearly encouraged to access the long views from this rocky 400-foot summit via hiking trails (see *Hiking*).

Bear right at the intersection for Schoodic Point (this portion of the road is two-way). You can pick up a map and hiking advice at the **visitors center** at the **Schoodic Education and Research Center** (207-288-1310; shoodicinstitute

PICK UP A MAP AND HIKING ADVICE AT THE NEW SERC VISITOR CENTER

.org) campus. Housed in handsome, 1930s Rockefeller Hall, the staffed center includes displays on the park's history and ecology, and on the radio and cryptologic operations carried on here between 1935 and 2002. The former U.S. Navy base is now managed jointly by Acadia National Park and SERC, a private nonprofit organization. Try your hand at typing Morse code. Check the website for year-round lectures, discussions, and ranger-led programs. Limited lodging is also available.

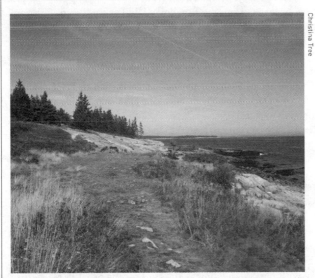

SCHOODIC POINT IS PART OF ACADIA NATIONAL PARK

Schoodic Point (plenty of parking) thrusts into the Atlantic, and on sunny days tidal pools invite clambering. On stormy days surf and spray can shoot as high as 40 feet, a popular spectacle. That surf can be deadly, so be careful. Bear right along the drive to the **Blueberry Hill Parking Area** (about a mile beyond Schoodic Point) with its views of Moose and Schoodic Islands and access to most of the area's hiking trails. Continue along the drive 2 more miles to Rt. 186 in the village of Birch Harbor.

converted railbed that begins at Washington Junction in Hancock and runs east to the Canadian border. Popular with ATVs and snowmobiles, it's also suitable for fat tire bikes.

BOATING **Bar Harbor Ferry** and **Schoodic Ferry** (see *Getting There*).

Robertson Sea Tours (robertsonseatours.com), departing from Milbridge Marina (see *To Do* in "Way Downeast"), cruises the 50 miles east of Schoodic.

CAMPING **Schoodic Woods Campground** (207-288-1300), open late May–Columbus Day. Reserve at www.recreation.gov (1-877-444-6777). Like Blackwoods and Seawall in Acadia National Park on Mount Dessert Island, this new campground is managed by the National Park Service. Unlike them, it accommodates RVs over 35 feet long (33 sites with water and power hookups, $36–40). There are 50 drive-up tent/small RV sites ($30), 9 hike-in sites (22) and 2 groups sites with a shared picnic shelter. There is also a 100-seat amphitheater with ranger-led programs and a large day-use parking area. Camping is on a first-come, first-served basis.

FISHING **Donnell Pond** is known for salmon; **Tunk Lake** and **Spring River Lake** are good for trout. Look for launch sites along Rt. 182.

KAYAKING **Hancock Point Kayak Tours** (207-422-6854; hancockpointkayak.com), 58 Point Rd., Hancock. Antonio Blasi offers guided paddling in Frenchman and Taunton Bays, also overnight camping and guided snowshoeing.

SeaScape Kayak & Bike (207-963-5806; seascapekayaking.com), 8 Duck Pond Rd., Winter Harbor. Kayak and canoe rentals, good for lakes only.

GOLF **Grindstone Neck Golf Course** (207-963-7760), Gerrishville. A nine-hole course dating to 1895 as part of this summer colony; open to the public June–Sept.

Blink Bonnie Golf Course (207-422-3930), Rt. 185, Sorrento. A nine-hole walking course with an open layout and views of Flanders Bay. Golf cart rentals.

HIKING **Acadia National Park, Schoodic Peninsula** (see *Must See* on opposite page), offers several short hikes, all best accessed from the Blueberry Hill Parking Area. The gentle 0.6-mile **Alder Trail** leads to the steeper 0.6-mile **Schoodic Head Trail** to the summit of Schoodic Head (440 feet), a vantage point also accessed by the relatively demanding 1.1-mile **Anvil Trail**. While it's not marked, another popular hike at low tide is out on Little Moose Island. Check the tide and pick up a map at the Schoodic Gatehouse.

Schoodic Mountain, off Rt. 183 north of Sullivan, provides one of eastern Maine's most spectacular hikes, with 360-degree views. Maine's Bureau of Parks and Lands (207-287-5936) has improved the parking area and trail system here. Take the first left (it's unpaved) after crossing the **Sunrise Trail** (sunrisetrail.org) on Rt. 183; bear left at the Y and in 2 miles reach the parking lot (outhouse facility). The hike to the top of Schoodic Mountain (1,069 feet) should take around 45 minutes; a marked trail from the summit leads down to sandy **Schoodic Beach** at the southern end of **Donnell Pond** (good swimming and half a dozen primitive campsites). Return to the parking lot on the old road that's now a footpath (0.5 mile). From the same parking lot, you can also follow a dirt path down to Donnell Pond or hike to the bluffs on **Black Mountain**, a mesmerizingly beautiful hike with summit views north to Tunk Lake and east across Washington County. Another trail descends to **Schoodic Beach**. This is now part of 14,000 acres known as **Donnell Pond Public Preserved Land**, which also includes Tunk and Spring River Lakes and primitive campsites. **Tucker Mountain** rewards a mile's hike with panoramic views. The trail begins on old Rt. 1, across from the Long Cove scenic turnout on Rt. 1 in Sullivan.

Also see **Frenchman Bay Conservancy** under *Green Space*.

SWIMMING **Jones Beach** on Jones Pond in West Gouldsboro offers a family playground, swimming and picnic areas, changing rooms, and a boat launch. Take Recreation Rd. off Rt. 195 just south of Rt. 1. Along Rt. 183 there's **Flanders Pond** (turn left 2.9 miles north of Rt. 1); **Little Tunk Lake** offers a sandy beach. Look for a blue FBC sign on your left at 4.7 miles (it's 0.4 mile to the beach). Ask locally about **Molasses Pond** in Eastbrook. Also see **Donnell Pond** under *Hiking*.

✳ Green Space

The **Schoodic** section of **Acadia National Park** is detailed under the *Must See* sidebar on page 348. In addition, the **Frenchman Bay Conservancy** (frenchmanbay.org) maintains many outstanding preserves; check out 13 SHORT HIKES on their website and look for their blue diamond-shaped trail sign. Outstanding: **Tidal Falls**, formerly a popular lobster pound, is now a great picnicking site from which to watch eagles, herons, seals, and kayakers playing in the whitewater of the reversing falls in the Taunton River. From Rt. 1 turn right just before the Hancock-Sullivan bridge on Eastside Rd., then left on Tidal Falls Rd. (0.7 mile down).

    Corea Heath is an excuse to drive, as everyone should, out scenic Corea Rd. (Rt. 195); look for the FBC sign beyond the junction with Rt. 186 and park in the National Wildlife Refuge lot a short distance beyond on the right. The path loops around a peat bog and beaver flowage. Great for bird-watching, as is the adjoining 600-acre wildlife refuge, formerly owned by the Navy, which includes Grand Marsh and Grand Marsh Bay.

    Also see *Hiking* and *Swimming* for more about the 14,000-acre mountain- and lake-spotted **Donnell Pond Public Preserved Land**, maintained by the **Maine Bureau of Parks and Lands**.

✳ Lodging

INNS AND B&BS ⓞ ☙ ✐ ♿ (ᵗᵖ) **Crocker House Country Inn** (207-422-6806 or 1-877-715-6017; crockerhouse.com), 967 Point Rd., Hancock Point 04640. Open daily May–Oct., weekends Nov.–New Year's Eve. Billed as "a little out of the way and out of the ordinary," this handsome, shingled inn is midway between the sections of Acadia National Parks on Mount Desert and Schoodic Point. Sited at the center of a charming 1880s summer colony, complete with a chapel, tiny post office, octagonal library, and tennis courts, it's the lone survivor among several once-larger hotels. Since 1980 it's been owned by Richard and Elizabeth Malaby, and the welcome is genuine. There are nine antiques-furnished rooms in the inn itself, two in the Carriage House, all with private bath and phone, and in addition to the inn's parlor, there's a den with TV in the Carriage House. The inn is set among flowers and trees, but water is a short walk in most directions. $145–165

mid-June–mid-Oct., $120–130 off-season, $10 more Fri., Sat. rates include a full breakfast. Moorings are available, and a few touring bikes are kept for guests. The restaurant is a major draw (see *Dining Out*).

    (ᵗᵖ) **Ironbound** (207-422-3395; ironboundinn .com), 1513 Rt. 1, Hancock 04640. Open mid-May–late-Oct. The restaurant (see *Dining Out*) remains the draw, and the five rooms are still a bit of a secret. Sited at the back of the building (away from Rt. 1) are decks overlooking acres of landscaped garden. All are brightly, comfortably furnished with king or queen beds, art, and antiques. A breakfast of fresh fruit, bagels, cream cheese, and locally smoked salmon is included in $160–190.

    (ᵗᵖ) **Acadia Bay Inn** (207-422-0127; aca diabayinn.com), 12 Miramar Ave., Sullivan. Built in the 1880s as one of the gilded era's "summer cottages", this was formerly the Island View Inn. It offers spectacular views across Frenchman Bay and the mountains in Acadia National Park. The seven, spacious, second-floor rooms share a wrap-around outside balcony and, weather permitting, a full

ELSA'S INN ON THE HARBOR

breakfast is served downstairs on a first-floor deck. The large, open living/room dining room and guest rooms have all been recently renovated by innkeepers Angie and Todd. $195–215 includes breakfast.

Acadia View Bed & Breakfast (1-866-963-7457; acadiaview.com), 175 Rt. 1, P.O. Box 247, Gouldsboro 04607. Aerospace engineers in a previous life that took them many places, Pat and Jim Close have designed and built this mansion specifically as a B&B. The Great Room, with its wood-burning fireplace, and two of the four guest rooms (private bath) all share splendid views across Frenchman Bay to Acadia. All rooms have private deck with water views. $155–185 in high season, otherwise from $135, includes a full breakfast.

✿ ♿ ✿ **Acadia's Oceanside Meadows Inn** (207-963-5557; oceaninn.com), P.O. Box 90, Prospect Harbor 04669. Open May–Oct., off-season by special arrangement. This 1860s sea captain's home and neighboring 1820s farmhouse offer a total of 15 guest rooms, most overlooking well-named Sand Cove. Sonja Sundaram and Ben Walter are passionate conservationists, and their 200 acres of woods and meadows are webbed with trails, good for spotting wildlife ranging from moose to eagles. From $169 for rooms, $189–209 for suites July–Labor Day weekend, including Sonja's multicourse breakfasts, which might begin with sweet sorrel soup. Less off-season. Also see *Entertainment*.

✿ ✿ **Three Pines B&B** (207-460-7595; threepinesbandb.com), 274 Eastside Rd.,

Hancock 04640. Open year-round. Turn in at this organic farm and follow a private road down through 40 acres of woods and meadow to the shore. Here Ed and Karen Curtis have built a shingled, timber-frame, passive solar dream house with a separate wing housing two delightful B&B guest rooms, each with a sitting room and water view. Breakfast includes eggs from the farm's chickens, and frequently home-grown vegetables and fruit, too. Farm animals also include sheep, ducks, and roosters. $100–125 per couple, $15 per extra person.

✿ ✿ ✿ ♿ **Elsa's Inn on the Harbor** (207-963-7571; elsasinn.com), 179 Main St., Prospect Harbor 04669. This gabled, mid-1800s house overlooks a working harbor. Cherrie and Scott Markwood welcome guests to six bright, spiffy guest rooms with handmade quilts, private bath, and water views, as well as a comfortable living room, veranda, and patio. In all, 16 guests can bed down. $125–175 June 15–Oct. 15, from $115 off-season, including a full breakfast. Shared space includes a back patio as well as the bright, comfy living room and long veranda with rockers.

♂ ✿ ✿ (( )) **Bluff House Inn** (207-963-7805; bluffinn.com), 57 Bluff House Rd., South Gouldsboro 04607. Open year-round. This

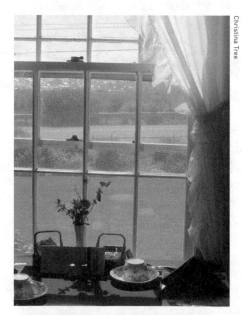

OCEANSIDE MEADOWS INN OVERLOOKS SAND COVE IN PROSPECT HARBOR

contemporary lodge offers a dining room with floor-to-ceiling windows, a screened porch overlooking the water, and a comfortable sitting area by a stone hearth. The eight guest rooms line the upstairs hall; three have water views. It's set off by itself above the pink granite shore; there's a road down to a beach from which you can launch a kayak onto Frenchman Bay. Inquire about Sat.-night lobster dinner. $125–150 in high season includes a continental breakfast. From $85 off-season.

COTTAGES **Albee Shoreline Cottages** (207-963-2336), 70 Maine St. (Rt.186), Prospect Harbor. Open Memorial Day–Columbus Day. The ten rustic, nicely shaded, and landscaped cottages, most sleeping four people. Five are directly on the shore and are classic old Maine motor court era. Each has a homey, comfortable feel and is warmed by either a gas heater, woodstove or fireplace. After 30 years, owner Richard Rieth still enjoys orienting new guests as well as welcoming back his many regulars. $95–150 per night. Weekly rentals preferred but a night or two is possible.

✳ Where to Eat

DINING OUT **Ironbound Restaurant** (207-422-3395; ironboundmaine.com), 1513 Rt. 1, Hancock Village. Open daily 5–9. Patrons of the former Le Domaine will recognize the Provençal-style dining rooms, but the vibe is now casual—a handsome bar and outdoor seating have been added. Named for an island in Frenchman Bay, Ironbound's menu is varied, moderately priced, and with locally sourced sea bass, oysters and steamers. Specialties include fish smoked next door at Sullivan Harbor Salmon. Also good: hamburgers, jerk pork ribs, tender duck breast. Music Thu.–Sat, 5–6:30.

○ **Crocker House Country Inn** (207-422-6806; crockerhouse.com), Hancock Point. Open nightly Apr.–Jan., weekends off-season, for dinner 5:30–9. The main dining room, with its 19th-century leaded-glass windows, is the setting for reliably fine dining. Frequent menu changes take advantage of local produce and fish. Staples include Crocker House scallops and farm-raised semi-boneless roast duckling with Grand Marnier ginger sauce. Entrées

$26–34, include fresh-baked bread, salad, starch, and a fresh vegetable. Don't pass on the Crocker House mousse (layered white and dark chocolate, laced with Myers's rum).

Salt Box (207-422-9900; saltboxmaine .com), 1166 Rt. 1, Hancock. Open for dinner Wed.–Sat., Sun. brunch., Wed. tasting menu. Reserve for dinner. Chef Mike Poirier has a strong local following and this is his latest restaurant, tucked into a corner of a large Rt. 1 commercial building. The menu features exotic meals made from scratch, and it's constantly changing. Check the website. Entrées $24–29; the nine-course tasting menu is $45. Cash only, on-site ATM. Wine and beer are served.

Raven's Nest Restaurant (207-963-2234; ravensnestrestaurant.com), 10 Newman St., Winter Harbor. Open seasonally Thurs.–Sun. 11–9. Built and operated by Roxanne Quimby, Raven's Nest is both a convenient source of lunch and local information (maps and brochures), plus diners have the chance to sample Roxanne's own wood-fired pizza (Thu.–Sat. evenings). Soups, sandwiches, salads, and pasta plus dinner entrées ranging from burgers to steak and lobster.

Also see **The Pickled Wrinkle** in *Eating Out* listings.

EATING OUT

HEADING EAST ALONG RT. 1

Ruth & Wimpy's Kitchen (207-422-3723), Rt. 1, Hancock. Open year-round. Look for "Wilbur the Lobster." Wimpy Wilbur is a former long-haul truck driver, and this family-run mainstay is decorated with his collection of miniature trucks, license plates, beer bottles, and more. The menu includes burgers and steaks, overstuffed sandwiches, and seafood, including lobster with all the fixings.

Chester Pike's Galley (207-422-8200), 2336 Rt. 1, Sullivan. Open 6–2 Tue.–Sat.; also 4:30–8:30 Fri., 7–2 Sun. The nicest kind of roadside diner, ideal for a Maine crabmeat and cheese omelet, strawberry rhubarb pie, or cream-cheese-stuffed French toast. There's also a sardine salad.

Tracey's Seafood (207-422-9071), 2719 Rt. 1, Sullivan. Open 11–7. The area's best lobster rolls, fresh fried clams at the best prices, as well as scallops and haddock. Take-out or eat in. Beer and wine served.

ON THE SCHOODIC PENINSULA

Fisherman's Galley (207-963-5585), 7 Newman St., Winter Harbor. Open in high season daily, 3–9, fewer days and hours in shoulder season. After almost 70 years as the full-service Fisherman's Inn Restaurant, the owners have changed the name and nature of this mid-village landmark, with an eye to the big, new campground nearby. It's now counter service for seafood fried, steamed, sandwiched, and more. Lobster dinners, steamed mussels, and clams are the specialties.

The Pickled Wrinkle (207-963-7916; the pickledwrinkle.com), 9 East Schoodic Drive, Birch Harbor. Kitchen open 11–9, pub until 11 PM daily, year-round, with frequent live music. Some of the best food around is to be found in this neighborhood gathering spot (formerly the Nautica Pub) in a small shopping plaza. "Wrinkle" is a local name for a sea snail, better known as a whelk. Patrons can sample it as a starter—it's worth splitting the order. Don't pass up the seafood chowder or onion rings, either. Kudos for the crab salad on local greens. The menu ranges from clam dinners to rib eye (Wed. only; reserve), and there are also a variety of pizzas.

&. **J. M. Gerrish** (207-963-7000), 352 Main St., Winter Harbor. Open Memorial Day–Columbus Day, 8–4 daily in July, Aug.; otherwise closed Wed. Long established as an old-style ice cream parlor beloved by generations of summer residents, this is the place for breakfast, lunch, and pastries as well as ice cream.

Wharf Gallery & Grill (207-963-8888), 13 Gibbs Lane, Corea. Open June–Sept. for lunch and dinner, weather permitting. On a sunny day you can't beat the view or experience. In the village turn left after the post office at the sharp bend in Rt. 195. Joe Young puts a sign at this spot if he's open. The real deal: reasonably priced stone crab claws, grilled cheese, lobster rolls, and much more, served on the wharf. There's also a gallery displaying work by Joe's mother, Louise, a pioneer photographer. Joe also makes and sells recycled lobster rope doormats.

🍴 🎵 **Chase's Restaurant** (207-963-7171), 193 Main St., Winter Harbor. Open all year for all three meals. A convenient local hangout on

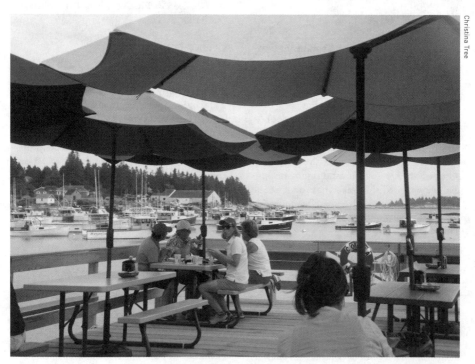

COREA WHARF OFFERS GREAT HARBOR VIEWS

Christina Tree

PHILIP BARTER STUDIO & GALLERY IS
WORTH A DETOUR

Rt. 186 near the entrance to the park. Booths,
fried lobsters and clams, good chowder; will
pack a picnic.

✴ Entertainment

Schoodic Arts for All (207-963-2569;
schoodicartsforall.org), Hammond Hall, 427
Main St., Winter Harbor. This grassroots nonprofit sponsors music, art, crafts, dance, theater, and film through most of the year. Check
the website for ongoing events such as Fri.
concerts, coffeehouses, community theater,
and a summer chorus. See *Special Events* for
the early August **Schoodic Arts Festival**.

Pierre Monteux Memorial Concert Hall
(207-422-3931; monteuxschool.org), off Rt. 1,
Hancock. In June and July the internationally
respected Pierre Monteux School for Con-
ductors, founded in 1943, hosts a series of
symphony concerts (Sun. at 5) and chamber
music concerts (Wed. at 7:30) presented by
faculty and students in the school's Forest
Studio.

Acadia's Oceanside Meadows Institute
hosts seasonal Thursday night lectures and concerts in its open-timbered restored 19th century
barn and also posts the most extensive list of
the summer's cultural events on its website:
oceaninn.com/events. For details contact Acadia's Oceanside Meadows Inn (207-963-5557).

Also check sercinstitute.com for frequent
programs at the **Schoodic Education and
Research Center** and frenchmanbay.org
for Mon.-evening concerts at **Tidal Falls** in
Hancock, sponsored by the **Frenchman Bay
Conservancy**.

Also see *Special Events*.

✴ Selective Shopping

ART

LISTED GEOGRAPHICALLY, MORE OR
LESS, HEADING EAST ALONG RT. 1

*On and off Taunton Bay Road, posted from
Rt. 1 at the Sullivan town common, just east of
the Hancock-Sullivan bridge.*

☻ **Philip Barter Studio & Gallery** (207-
422-3190; bartergallery.com), 318 Taunton Bay
Rd., Sullivan. Open mid-June to mid-October,
Tue.–Sat. 10–5, or by appointment. Posted
from Rt. 1 at Sullivan's common just east of the
bridge. Maine native Phil Barter's bold, deeply
colored paintings hang in museums and fetch
big money in the best galleries. His own studio/
gallery adjoins the small house that he built and
in which he and his wife Priscilla raised seven
children. It's easily the most colorful gallery in

Christina Tree

PHILIP BARTER IN THE BARTER FAMILY GALLERY, SULLIVAN

AT COREA WHARF CHECK OUT OWNER JOE YOUNG'S
RECYCLED LOBSTER ROPE DOORMATS. WINTER WORK
FOR MANY LOBSTERMEN, YOU SEE THESE IN STORES UP
AND DOWN THE COAST BUT RARELY BY THE LOBSTERMEN
THEMSELVES

Maine, but remote enough to keep browsers and buyers to a trickle. Here, in addition to dozens of distinctive Barter mountains, houses, and harbors, there are off-the-wall pieces and wood sculptures.

Lunaform (207-422-0923; lunaform.com), 66 Cedar Lane, marked from Rt. 1 at the Sullivan common. Open year-round, Mon.–Fri. 9:30–4:30; closed 11:30–1. Striking handmade, steel-reinforced concrete garden urns (some are huge) as well as pots and planters are made in this former granite quarry.

WORKS OF HAND GALLERY, WINTER HARBOR ANTIQUES

The Granite Garden Gallery (207-664-3424; stonedesignsmaine.com), 228 Whales Back Rd. Obadiah Bourne Buell shapes sculpted items of all sizes from local rock and granite from the water-filled quarry that's now part of his sculpture garden. The sculptor may or may not be there but the gallery is usually open. Call ahead.

ALSO WORTH A DETOUR

✪ **Hog Bay Pottery** (207-565-2282; hogbay .com), 245 Hog Bay Rd. (Rt. 200, 4 miles north of Rt. 1), Franklin. Open Apr.–Nov.; call off-season. This shop/studio is a find, the kind of place patrons return to again and again. Susanne Grosjean's bright, multicolored, hand-dyed and -woven, award-winning rugs complement distinctive table- and ovenware by Charles Grosjean (great seconds).

Spring Woods Gallery (207-442-3007; springwoodsgallery.com), Rt. 200, 0.25 mile off Rt. 1, Sullivan. Open May–Oct., Mon.–Sat. 10–6. This gallery features work by *National Geographic* cartographer and illustrator Paul Breeden, paintings by Ann Breeden, as well as work by other members of the Breeden family. The garden alone is worth a stop.

ON THE PENINSULA

Lee Art Glass Studio (207-963-7280; leeart glass.com), Rt. 186, 3 miles south of Rt. 1. Open June–Oct., Mon.–Sat. 10–4. It's difficult to describe this fused-glass tableware, which incorporates ground enamels and crocheted doilies or stencils. Wayne Taylor has acquired the secret of creating these distinctive pieces, which he makes and sells in a former post office in South Gouldsboro.

✪ **Works of Hand & Winter Harbor Antiques** (207-963-7900), 424–426 Main St., Winter Harbor. Open June–Oct., daily 10–5. Set back in a flowery, visitor-friendly garden, Roger Fisher's two-floor gallery showcases work by more than 50 artists and craftsmen in a wide range of media, and a selection of author-signed books. Check out the jewelry and the adjoining antiques shop.

Littlefield Gallery (207-838-2156; littlefieldgallery.com), 145 Main St., Winter Harbor. Open seasonally, 11–6. Sited just before the turnoff for the park, this is an exceptional contemporary Maine gallery, housing a mix of

AWARD-WINNING SULLIVAN HARBOR SALMON IS SMOKED, SAMPLED, AND SOLD IN ITS RT. 1 SHOP, HANCOCK

paintings and pieces by prominent sculptors. Changing shows, receptions.

U.S. Bells and Watering Cove Pottery (207-963-7184; usbells.com), Rt. 186, Prospect Harbor. Open weekdays 9–5, Sat. 9–2, and by appointment. Richard Fisher designs and casts bells that form musical sculptures, and Liza Fisher creates wood-fired stoneware and porcelain.

✪ **Chapter Two** (207 963 7269), 611 Corea Rd., Prospect Harbor. Open year-round, Thu.–Mon. 11–4.; daily July, Aug. Rosemary's hand-hooked designs and Gary's extraordinary accumulation of books are a winning combination. Many local products, from jewelry to soap; frequent workshops.

Hurdy Gurdy Man Antiques & Salty Dog Gallery (207-963-7575, saltydoggallery.net). 175 Main St., Prospect Harbor. Open Wed.–Sun., 10–5. Look for the lobster boat crashing into this building above the entry-way, a clue to the whimsical mix of antiques, collectibles vintage clothing and gifts inside. Owner Dean Kotlula's serious gallery is upstairs, a display of fine art maritime photography.

SMOKED SALMON ✪ **Sullivan Harbor Salmon** (1-800-422-4014; sullivanharborfarm .com), 1542 Rt. 1, Hancock Village. Open 9–5 Mon.–Sat.; weekdays only off-season. Maine's premier, award-winning artisanal smoked salmon. Only salmon from within 60 nautical miles is used, and it's processed within hours of harvesting. In the smokehouse attached to

the Rt. 1 store, it's cured in small batches, hand rubbed with a blend of salt and brown sugar, then rinsed in springwater and slowly smoked over a smudge fire of hickory shavings. No preservatives or additives. The store also sells day boat scallops from Nova Scotia, smoked mussels, rainbow trout, salmon bacon, pâtés, and Maine-made items. Tasty samples.

Grindstone Neck of Maine (207-963-7347; grindstoneneck.com), 311 Newman St. (Rt. 186), Winter Harbor. A source of smoked mussels, oysters, scallops, and seafood spreads as well as salmon.

WINE AND SPIRITS ✪ ♿ **Bartlett Winery and Spirits of Maine** 175 Chicken Mill Pond Rd. (207-546-2408; bartlettwinery.com), just off Rt. 1, Gouldsboro. Open for tastings ($5) June into Oct., Tue.–Sat. 11–5 and by appointment. Before Bob and Kathe Bartlett could open Maine's first winery back in 1982, they had to get the law changed. "Prohibition began in Maine," Bob Bartlett will remind you. An architect by training, he designed this low-slung winery sequestered in firs. Over a dozen wines, which utilize Maine fruit and honey as well as regional pears and peaches, continue to win top honors in national and international competitions, as do such spirits as Rusticator Rum, pear eau de vie, and Calvados-style apple brandy. Call before coming for handicap directions.

Shalom Orchard Organic Farm and Winery (207-565-2312; shalomorchard.com), 158 Eastbrook Rd. (Rt. 200 north of Rt. 182). The peaceful old hilltop farm includes a 1,000-plus apple orchard, also blueberries, cherries, and raspberries that are all made into organic wines. The farm store sells eggs, meat, and homespun yarns as well as tanned pelts and fleece from Rambouillet sheep.

SPECIAL SHOPS ✑ **Darthia Farm** (207-963-2770; darthiafarm.com), 51 Darthia Farm Rd. off Rt. 186 (east), Gouldsboro. Open June–late Sept. Mon.–Fri. 8–5, Sat. 8–noon. A 150-acre organic farm on West Bay with resident sheep, pigs, and turkeys, where much of the farm-work is powered by drafthorses. Cynthia and Bill Thayer's farm stand is justly famed for its vinegars, jams, salsas, and cheeses; Hattie's Shed, a weaving shop also at the farm, features coats, jackets, scarves, shawls, and Cynthia Thayer's well-respected, locally set novels.

✪ **Winter Harbor 5&10** (207-963-7927; winterharbor5and10.com), 349 Main St., Winter Harbor. Open daily, year-round. Peter Drinkwater will tell you it isn't easy operating a genuine, old-style five-and-dime these days. While it sells some souvenirs, this is the genuine article with just about everything you come looking for; also the local stop for keys, photo developing, digital printing, UPS, a copier, fax, and newspapers.

✳ Special Events

Late June–Labor Day: **Winter Harbor Farmers' Market**, Tue. 9–noon, corner of Rt. 186 and Main St.

July–August: **Frenchman Bay Conservancy Mon.-night concerts** at Tidal Falls Preserve, Hancock (207-422-2328; frenchmanbay.org; also see *Green Space*).

Late July–mid-August: ♿ The **Schoodic Arts Festival** (schoodicarts.org), held annually the first two weeks in August, is a destination extravaganza with dance, theater, visual arts, writing and crafts workshops, and evening performances staged throughout the area, but otherwise the venue is Hammond Hall—renovated, heated, and handicap-accessible. **Sullivan Daze** (first Saturday) is a daylong celebration in Sullivan. The **Winter Harbor Lobster Festival** (second Saturday; acadia.schoodic.org) is the biggest day of the summer here: crafts fair, lobster-boat races, a parade, live music, and a huge lobster feed.

Christina Tree

WINTER HARBOR 5&10

WAY DOWNEAST

THE BOLD COAST

AROUND PASSAMAQUODDY BAY

Eastport; Calais and the Downeast Lakes
Region; St. Andrews, New Brunswick; Grand
Manan Island, New Brunswick

Way Downeast

WAY DOWNEAST

Travel down east as far as you can in this country and you get to a coastline that harbors some of the most dramatic cliffs and deepest coves—certainly the highest tides—on the eastern U.S. seaboard. Lobster boats and trawlers far outnumber pleasure craft and pickups outnumber cars.

This is Washington County, created in 1789 by order of the General Court of Massachusetts. It's as large as the states of Delaware and Rhode Island combined, yet home to roughly 32,000 people, widely scattered among fishing villages, logging outposts, Native American reservations, and saltwater farms. Many people—not just some—survive here by raking blueberries, fishing, lobstering, clamming, digging sea worms, harvesting sea cucumbers, diving for sea urchins and making Christmas wreaths. It's the world's largest source of wild blueberries.

A fraction of Maine's visitors get this far, but those who do find a distinctly different landscape: vast blueberry barrens that turn crimson in Autumn and 700 miles of bleakly beautiful, little-developed coastline that's increasingly accessible. On **Machias Seal Island** you can watch puffins, auks, and arctic terns close-up or view them from excursion boats off **Petit Manan Wildlife Refuge**. In late summer there are whales in Passamaquoddy Bay and the Gulf of Maine, visible both from land and close up on boats from Lubec, Eastport, and Campobello Island. Seals ride the tides in narrows and tidal rivers. Dramatic hiking trails rim the cliffs along the **Bold Coast** in Cutler and on up to **West Quoddy Light** and along the rocky shores of Campobello Island. In recent years more than a million acres of former commercial woodland have been preserved as trail- or water-accessed conservation land. Varied local and national nonprofits and the state together have created many hundreds of miles of trails leading to quiet coves and sweeping vistas of open water. Fishing guides lead the way to landlocked salmon and smallmouth bass in the vast chain of Downeast Lakes. Bald eagles are everywhere.

The few towns along this stretch of Rt. 1 are shadows of the thriving shipbuilding and sardine-canning ports they were in the 19th century, but all still offer a wealth of discoveries and a Maine you thought had disappeared decades ago. Rt. 1, however, offers few glimpses of the area's natural beauty. Follow the **Bold Coast Scenic Byway** down Rt. 187 to the fishing villages of Jonesport and Beals Island, Rt. 191 from Machias to Lubec via Cutler and out 189 to Lubec and out 190 to Eastport.

You don't drop off the end of the world beyond **Calais** or **Campobello Island**, despite the boundary drawn across the face of **Passamaquoddy Bay** in 1842. From Calais it's 19 miles to **St. Andrews**, the Bar Harbor of New Brunswick. In summer it is lovely crossing the bay, either via passenger or car-ferries. We also include the magnificent island of **Grand Manan**, which lies 12.5 miles off Maine's Bold Coast but is in New Brunswick, accessible by a 20-mile car-ferry ride from Blacks Harbour, New Brunswick.

With the border tightening after 9/11, the international flow of tourists ebbed for several years, but it's on the rise again, with an ever-increasing number of websites and pamphlets promoting a "Two Nation Vacation," encompassing Passamaquoddy Bay.

For exploring purposes, we divide this area into two distinct regions.

(1) The **Bold Coast,** Steuben to Lubec via the Rt. 1 towns of Milbride and Machias, with many detours along the coastline and across the bridge to **Roosevelt Campobello International Park**.

N

Weston

Forest
City

Danforth

2A

1

NEW
BRUNSWICK

785

Baskahegan
Lake

169

Brookton

Lambert
Lake

Vanceboro

4

1

Topsfield

6

Carroll

Waite

West
Grand Lake

Big
Lake

St. Croix R.

3

St.
Stephen

Calais

760

1

St.
George

127

Princeton

1

Woodland
(Baileyville)

Baring

Robbinston

St.
Andrews

Grand
Lake
Stream

STUD MILL RD

Alexander

Crawford

9

Meddybemps
Lake

Meddybemps

191

MOOSEHORN
N.W.R.

Passamaquoddy
Bay

Ferry

Deer I.

Wesley

192

191

Lake
Cathance

P

214

Pembroke

190

Eastport

Campobello
I.

Ferry

Machias R.

P

Dennysville

Sunrise Trail

86

P

Lubec

ROOSEVELT
CAMPOBELLO
'INT'L PK

9

191

Cobscook
Bay St Pk

MOOSEHORN
N.W.R.

189

W.
Lubec

North
Head

GREAT HEATH
PUBLIC RESERVE
LAND

Nanraguagus R.

193

P

Marshfield

P

P

Whitneyville

1A

E. Machias

Machias

Whiting

1

Quoddy
Head
St Pk

Seal
Cove

Columbia Falls

P

Jonesboro

191

Cutler

CUTLER COAST
PUBLIC RESERVE
LAND

Grand
Manan I.

Harrington

182

Addison

1

187

CROSS I.
N.W.R.

Cherryfield

1A

187

ROQUE BLUFFS
STATE PARK

Machias
Seal I.

Steuben

Milbridge

Jonesport

1

186

Beals

195

Great
Wass I.

ATLANTIC OCEAN

PETIT MANAN NAT'L
WILDLIFE REFUGE

Prospect Harbor

ACADIA
NATIONAL PARK

© The Countryman Press

0   5   10

Miles

(2) Around Passamaquoddy Bay Region, from Eastport to Calais and St. Andrews, New Brunswick.

GUIDANCE DownEast & Acadia Regional Tourism (1-888-665-3278; downeastacadia .com) is the umbrella tourism promotion for Hancock and Washington Counties. Also see the chambers of commerce for specific regions.

((ᵞ)) **The Maine Tourism Association** maintains a full-service visitors center (207-454-2211) at 39 Union St. (the Wabanaki Cultural Center), Calais. Open June–Oct., daily 8–6, otherwise 9–5:30.

Tourism New Brunswick (800-561-0213; tourismnewbrunswick.ca) covers the Canadian side of Passamaquoddy Bay.

Fundy Acadia Regional Adventures (fundyacadia.com) is good for vacation planning for enterprises in Washington County and Charlotte County, New Brunswick.

THE RESTORED RR STATION 98 SERVES AS A VISITORS CENTER FOR THE MACHIAS AREA

GETTING THERE *By air:* See "Bar Harbor" and "Bangor Area" for scheduled airline service.

By bus: **Concord Coach** (1-800-639-3317; concordcoachlines.com), best service to Bangor from Augusta, Portland, and Boston. **West's Coastal Connection** (1-800-596-2823; west busservice.com) offers daily service year-round between Bangor Airport and Calais, with stops in Machias and Perry, flag-down stops (call ahead) between.

By car: **The Bold Coast Scenic Byway** designates 125 miles of Rt. 1 from Milbridge to Eastport with detouring loops along Rt. 187 and Rt. 191/189 to Cutler and Lubec.

Practical Tips: From points south take I-95 to Rt. 295 to I-95 to Bangor. For the westernmost towns take Rt. 1A to Ellsworth, then Rt. 1. For coastal points east of Harrington, you save 9 miles by cutting inland on Rt. 182 from Hancock to Cherryfield, but for most easterly points from Bangor, take the Airline Highway (Rt. 9) from which many roads connect to coastal communities. Rt. 9 runs for 90 miles, straight through the blueberry barrens and woods, to Calais.

GETTING AROUND The Quoddy Loop (quoddyloop.com) refers to a rewarding way of touring the Passamaquoddy Bay area on both sides of the border by both land and water. See **East Coast Ferries** (eastcoastferriesltd.com) in **The Bold Coast** section for details about car/passenger service from Campobello Island to Deer Island and on across the bay to the New Brunswick mainland. We suggest spending the night in St. Andrews, known as "the Bar Harbor of New Brunswick" (see sidebar on page 396). It's just 19 miles rom Rt. 1 once you've crossed the border in Calais.

Inquire about ferry service from Eastport to Lubec and to Deer Island.

CROSSING THE BORDER Passports or NEXUS cards are required for re-entry to the United States from Canada by land. For details check **getyouhome.gov**. Children 15 and under need a birth certificate. For questions about pets and what you can bring back and forth, see **cbp.gov**. U.S. Immigration in Lubec (207-733-4331) can also answer questions about the crossing there and in Calais. Canadian citizens are also required to present a passport or a NEXUS card.

Note: Do not bring a radar detector into Canada; they are illegal in the Maritime Provinces. Also, if you're driving a vehicle other than your own, you must have the owner's written permission. The Calais crossing has been eased since the opening of the International Avenue crossing on Rt. 1 north of town. There is also a Milltown crossing.

TIME CHANGE Cross the bridge from Lubec and you lose an hour. Atlantic Canada is an hour ahead of Maine during daylight saving months, especially significant if you are catching a Canadian ferry.

THE BOLD COAST

Including Milbridge, Machias, Lubec, and
Campobello, New Brunswick

The Bold Coast takes its name from the stretch of high cliffs between Cutler and Quoddy Head State Park but now brands a far larger area.

GUIDANCE **The Machias Bay Area Chamber of Commerce** (207-255-4402; machias chamber.org). A walk-in information center in the town's newly restored Station 98 at the eastern end of Main Street, across from Helen's Restaurant; open Wed.–Fri. 10–3 weekdays, by chance Mon., Tue. A prime source of local and regional information. Note the historical videos of Machias.

In *Milbridge* (milbridge.org) the first village most visitors hit, in this area **Schooner Gallery** (107-546-2791) stocks local information, open and staffed May–Mid.-Oct., daily 9–5.

For **Lubec** check the websites **visitlubecmaine.com**, **cobscookbay.com**, and **westquoddy .com**. The **West Quoddy Head Lighthouse Visitor Center** (207-733-2180; westquoddy.com) at the lighthouse is open daily Memorial Day weekend to mid-Oct., 10–4. Also check: visit-lubecmaine.com.

The **Campobello Welcome Center** (506-752-7040) is open daily May–Columbus Day. Also New Brunswick tourist information at 1-800-561-0123; also see: visitcampobello.com.

WHEN TO GO **The Down East Birding Festival** (downeastbirdfest.org) is held Memorial Day weekend, and the best months to view puffins on Machias Seal Island are May–early July. **Milbridge Days**, last weekend in July, and the **Wild Blueberry Festival** in Machias, third weekend in Aug., are the big summer events. September brings the clearest weather. From mid-Sept. to early Oct., the blueberry barrens turn red, adding their brilliance to Maine's fall foliage.

GETTING AROUND
By land: **The Bold Coast Scenic Byway** (boldcoastbyway.com) begins on Rt. 1 in Milbridge and loops down Rt. 187 to **Jonesport** (continue across the bridge to Beals Island and continue to the hiking trails on Grand Wass). Beyond **Machias**, the byway detours from Rt. 1 down Rt. 191 to **Cutler** and on up toward **Lubec**. If time permits, bear right on Boot Cove Rd. in South Trescott and follow the unpaved road along the real "Bold Coast" to **West Quoddy Light**.

By water: **Lubec-Eastport passenger ferry service** runs late June to mid-Sept., Tue.–Sun.; contact **The Wharf** (207-733-4400), 69 Johnson St., Lubec.

East Coast Ferries Ltd. (506-747-2159 or 1-877-747-2159; eastcoastferriesltd.com) runs a seasonal car ferry from Campobello Island to Deer Island. From there the free ferries run by the New Brunswick Department of Transportation (506-453-3939) cross Passaquoddy Bay to L'Etete, NB, handy to St. Andrews and to Blacks Harbour. The harbor is a departure point for ferries to Grand Manan. The ferry is a tug with long, hydraulically operated arms linked to a barge. Passengers and bikes, cars, and even buses board on ramps lowered to the beach. It's 100 miles shorter from Campobello to St. Andrews by water than land, but the two trips may take the same amount of time. On a beautiful day, however, there's no comparison. At this writing the ferry from Eastport is suspended but inquire.

✳ To See

Steuben, the first town in Washington County, is known as the site of the **Maine Coastal Islands Refuge**.

Milbridge (visitmilbridge.com). A Rt. 1 town of fewer than 1,300 residents, with a wandering coastline, is the administrative home of Jasper Wyman and Sons, one of the oldest wild blueberry processors. **McClellan Park** (207-546-2422), overlooking Narraguagus (pronounced *nair-a-GWAY-gus*) Bay, offers picnic tables, fireplaces, campsites, restrooms, and drinking water. The **Milbridge Historical Museum** (207-546-4471; milbridgehistorical society.org) is open in summer Tue. and Sun. 1–4. It's a delightful window into the past of this spirited community. **Milbridge Days**, in late July, features a codfish relay race.

Cherryfield (pop. 1,230). A few miles up the Narraguagus River, Cherryfield bills itself as the Blueberry Capital of Maine (there are two processing plants in town), but its very early, stately houses (see *Lodging*) were built with the proceeds of lumbering. The **Cherryfield-Narraguagus Historical Society**, 88 River Rd., is generally open summer Saturdays, 1–4. The small village is known for its antiques stores.

Columbia Falls (pop. 560) is a picturesque village with one of Maine's most notable houses at its center: **Ruggles House** (207-483-4637; 0.25 miles off Rt. 1; open June–mid-Oct., Mon.–Sat. for guided tours, 9:30–4, Sun. noon–4; $5 adults, $2 children 6–12) is a Federal-style mansion built by wealthy lumber dealer Thomas Ruggles in 1818. It is a beauty, with a graceful flying staircase, a fine Palladian window, and superb woodwork. Legend has it that a woodcarver was imprisoned in the house for three years with a penknife. South of Ruggles House veer left at the fork. Also note: Behind the town offices is where you can find the **Wreaths Across America Museum** (wreathsacross america.org). Housed in the back of the former elementary school and open daily 9–4, this museum is dedicated to the U.S. military and chronicles the story of the movement, begun by local wreath-maker Morrill Worcester, to place Christmas wreaths on veterans' graves in some 1200 locations around the world. Just off Rt. 1 note the sign for the **Wild Salmon Research Center** (207-483-4336; mainesalmonrivers.org), open weekdays 8–4.

Jonesport (townofjonesport.com; pop. roughly 1,400) is at the tip of a 12-mile-long peninsula facing Moosabec Reach, which is, in turn, spanned by a bridge leading to **Beals Island** (pop. 600, known for the design of its lobster boats). Both communities are all about fishing. Together these towns are home to eastern Maine's largest lobstering fleet, and the bridge is a popular

Christina Tree

CHERRYFIELD IS AN ANTIQUES CENTER

viewing stand for the July 4 lobster boat races. Beals Island, populated largely by Alleys and Beals, is connected to **Great Wass Island**, a hiking destination with trails through a 1,579-acre Nature Conservancy preserve with good picnicking on the rocky shore. The neighboring **Downeast Institute for Applied Marine Research and Education** (207-497-5769; downeastinstitute.org; open to the public year-round, daily 9–4) produces millions of seed clams annually for local clam flats, also thousands of lobsters; check out the lobster tanks in the Education Center.

Back in Jonesport, the **Peabody Memorial Library** offers WiFi, restrooms, and art exhibits. It's home to the **Jonesport Historical Society** (207-497-2395) with computer access to visual and oral histories of over 65,000 residents (present, past, and related). Heading north from the village on Rt. 187, be sure to stop if the open sign is out at Ronnie Peabody's **Maine Coast Sardine History Museum** and farther along at Buzz and Helen Beal's **Maine Central Model Railroad** (call ahead: 207-497-2255; Mon.–Sat. 10–6), where 380 cars traverse 3,000 feet of tracks that wind through hand-built miniature replicas of local towns and scenery.

Jonesboro (pop. roughly 800), judging from Rt. 1, is just blueberry barrens, a church, and a post office. The beauty of this town is its shoreline, which wanders in and out of points and coves along the tidal Chandler River and Chandler Bay on the way to **Roque Bluffs State Park**, 6 miles south of Rt. 1. A public boat launch with picnic tables is five minutes south of Rt. 1 on Roque Bluffs Rd. (right on Evergreen Point Rd.).

Machias (pop. 2,221). Early in the 19th century, Machias was second only to Bangor among Maine lumber ports. The opera house, two newspapers, three hotels, and trotting park are long gone, but Machias remains a must-stop. The Machias River runs down along the back of Main Street and over the **Bad Little Falls**. Look for picnic tables in the park by the falls and for **Burnham Tavern** (207-255-6930; burnhamtavern.com), 14 Colonial Way (open mid-June–Sept., Mon.–Fri., 10–3). A 1770s gambrel-roofed tavern, it's filled with period furnishings and tells the story of British man-of-war *Margaretta*, captured on June

JONESPORT

"THE DIKE" IN MACHIAS USUALLY OFFERS INTERESTING SHOPPING

12, 1775, by townspeople sailing the small sloop *Unity*. This was the first naval battle of the American Revolution. Unfortunately, the British retaliated by burning Portland.

At the opposite eastern end of downtown, across from **Helen's Restaurant**, note the Machias Chamber's **1898 Station** (information center) and the access point to the multi-use **Sunrise Trail** along the Middle River. The neighboring "**Dike**," a land bridge between Machias Bay and Middle River, is a Thurs.–Sat. venue for vendors selling everything from fish to antiques. The **University of Maine at Machias** (207-255-1200), just south of downtown, enrolls roughly 1,000 students on a 43-acre campus; check maine.edu for art gallery hours and use of the fitness center and pool. Machias is best known for its **Wild Blueberry Festival** (third weekend in August), but the summer organ concerts in its 1836 Congregational church are also a major attraction.

Machiasport (pop. 1,071). Take Rt. 92 at Bad Little Falls Park in Machias. This picturesque village is home to the **Machiasport Historical Society** which maintains the Federal-style **Cooper House** (open July and Aug., Tue.–Fri. 12:30–4:30, free). **Cooper House** displays old tools and maritime exhibits and period rooms. Neighboring **Fort O'Brien** consists of earthen breastworks with cannons and includes the grass-covered remains of the ammunition powder magazine used during the American Revolution and the War of 1812. Continue on down this road to the fishing village of Bucks Harbor and on to **Jasper Beach**, so named for the wave-tumbled and polished pebbles of jasper and rhyolite that give it its distinctive color. The road ends with great views and a beach to walk in the part of town known as **Starboard**.

Cutler (pop. less than 650). From East Machias, follow Rt. 191 south to this small, photogenic fishing village that's happily shielded from a view of the U.S. Navy communications station's 26 antenna towers (800 to 980 feet tall), which light up red at night and can be seen from much of the county's coast. A portion of this former base is now Beachwood Bay Estates, a housing development with an enterprising general store. The **Little River Lighthouse** (see *Other Lodging*) at the mouth of its harbor has been restored. This area was initially about lumbering, not fishing. In 1835 Massachusetts investors built a dam across the upper part of the harbor and a tidal mill to turn spruce into laths and shingles. However, fires destroyed what was left of the original forest in the 1850s and the area's economy shifted to fishing. Cutler is a departure point for **Bold Coast puffin cruises** to **Machias Seal Island**, 9.7 miles offshore (see *Puffin-Watching and Other Birding* sidebar on page 373). Beyond the village, Rt. 191 follows the shoreline through moorlike blueberry and

LUBEC HISTORICAL SOCIETY MUSEUM

WEST QUODDY LIGHT

cranberry country, with disappointingly few views from the road but splendid panoramas from the **Bold Coast Trails** (see *Hiking* sidebar on page 374).

In South Trescott bear right onto Boot Cove Rd. Instead of continuing north on Rt. 191 and follow the coast, keeping an eye out for the **Hamilton Cove Preserve**, with a walk to a cobble beach. Continue on to **West Quoddy Light** (next page), one of the jewels of the entire Maine coast. Take time to hike and/or get out on the water.

Lubec (pop. 1,508). The direct route from Machias to **Quoddy Head State Park** (207-733-0911) in South Lubec is via Rt. 1 to the marked Rt. 189 turnoff. The 532-acre park is open mid May–mid-Oct., sunrise to sunset, with a staffed visitors center (&) in the **Light Keepers' House** (207-733-2180; westquoddy.com), open Memorial Day–mid-Oct., 10–4. Displays tell the story of the lighthouse, which dates back to 1858, and of local industries; there's also a gift shop and a gallery with changing art exhibits. Despite its name, the red candy-striped **West Quoddy Head Lighthouse** marks the easternmost tip of the United States (see the *Must See* sidebar on pages 370–371 for the **East Quoddy Head Lighthouse**). There are benches for those who come to be among the first in the United States to see (fog permitting) the sunrise, a pleasant picnic area, and a fine view of **Grand Manan Island**. Best of all is the spectacular 2-mile **Coastal Trail** along the cliffs to Carrying Place Cove. Between the cove and the bay, roughly a mile back down the road from the light, is an unusual coastal, raised-plateau bog with dense sphagnum moss and heath.

MCCURDY'S HERRING SMOKEHOUSE, LUBEC

MUST SEE

CAMPOBELLO ISLAND Campobello Island, New Brunswick, is easily accessible from Lubec via the FDR Memorial Bridge. You have to pass through Canadian and U.S. Customs, but there's rarely a wait. Franklin D. Roosevelt's "Beloved Island" (the family summered here for six decades) is 9 miles long with some 925 year-round residents living primarily in the fishing villages of Wilson's Beach, Welshpool, and North Road. Granted to Captain William Owen in the 1760s, much of the island remained in the family until 1881, when a large part was sold to Boston developers who built three large (long-gone) hotels. Another major real estate development in the 1980s and '90s by the same Arkansas-based company that developed Whitewater (the Clintons were not involved in this one) failed.

⚓ **Roosevelt Campobello International Park** (506-752-2922; fdr.net), Welshpool, Campobello Island, New Brunswick. Open Sat. before Memorial Day weekend–mid-Oct., daily 9–5 EDT (10–6 Canadian Atlantic Daylight Time). This manicured 2,800-acre park with a Visitor Centre and shingled "cottages" is the number one sight to see east of Bar Harbor. The house in which Franklin Delano Roosevelt summered as a boy has disappeared, but the airy 34-room **Roosevelt Cottage**, a wedding gift to Franklin and Eleanor, is sensitively maintained just as the family left it, charged with the spirit of the dynamic man who was felled by polio here on August 25, 1921. (They are quick to tell you that he had contracted it several weeks before at a Boy Scout jamboree in New York.) The house is filled with many poignant objects, such as the toy boat FDR carved for his children. During his subsequent stints as governor of New York and then as president of the United States, FDR returned only three times. Neighboring **Hubbard Cottage**, with its oval picture window, gives another slant on this turn-of-the-20th-century resort. Afternoon "**Tea with Eleanor**" is offered here twice daily (free but tickets required); you can also reserve ($12) a seat for tea at the Wells-Sober Cottage. For information about **Road Scholar programs** (roadscholar.org) offered in the Victorian cottages and nearby Campobello venues, contact the Atlantic Leadership Center (207-853-6036). The park's **Visitor Centre** offers excellent historical exhibits and a 15-minute introductory film. Beyond stretch more than **8 miles of trails** to the shore and then inland through woods to lakes and ponds. There are also 15.4 miles of **carriage road drives** modified from the network that the wealthy "cottagers" maintained on the island. Detailed trail maps and advice are available at the Visitor Centre. A short but rewarding walk leads to **Friar's Head**. We recommend the coastal trails from **Southern Head to the Duck Ponds** and from **Raccoon Beach to Liberty Point**. Seals frequently sun on the ledges off Lower Duck Pond, and loons are often seen off Liberty Point. Along this dramatic shoreline at the southern end of the island, also look for whales July–Sept. The international

ROOSEVELT COTTAGE

Christina Tree

In **downtown Lubec**, Water Street is transitioning from sardine cannery row to a lively lineup of shops, restaurants, and galleries. Don't miss **McCurdy's Herring Smokehouse** (207-733-42197), 50 Water St., restored to evoke the era in which Lubec was home to 20 canneries. Stop by the old town landing with its public boat launch, breakwater, and a view of **Mulholland Point Light** just across on Campobello Island. The tide rushes in and out through the narrows here, and frequently you can see seals playing and fishing in the water. **Lubec Channel Light**, for obvious

HEAD HARBOUR LIGHT, CAMPOBELLO

park has acquired the **Adams Lodge** (now housing **Fireside Reastaurant**). Neighboring 1,049-acre **Herring Cove Provincial Park** (506-561-7010), open mid-May–mid-Nov., also offers trails, a beach, a **restaurant** (open 8–8), and a **golf course** with nine holes, a clubhouse, and rentals. There's also a **campground** with 76 campsites, 40 hook-ups.

Head Harbour Light, as it's known in Canada (in the US it's **East Quoddy Head Lighthouse**) is a 51-foot-high tower built in 1829, at the northern tip of the island. Its wooden, shingled exterior, painted white with a distinctive red cross, has recently been restored, thanks to its "Friends." The cast-iron lantern is vintage 1887. This is a popular whale-watching station but demanding to reach and accessible only at low tide, then only if you are physically fit. Beware the incoming tide. There's a great viewing spot from just across the narrow channel. From the international park take a right at the fork on Rt. 774 and follow it to the end. There's WiFi and Internet access at the **Campobello Public Library & Museum** (open Tue.–Fri.), car-ferry service via Deer Island to mainland New Brunswick, and direct passenger ferry service to St. Andrews (see *Getting Around*).

WHALE-WATCH CRUISES Campobello is a prime departure point for seasonal whale-watching. Both **Capt. Riddle's Whale Watch Cruises** (1-877-FINBACK; finback.com), tickets: 727 Friar's Bay Rd., and **Island Cruises** (1-888-249-4400; bayoffundywhales.com), from **Head of Harbour Wharf**, offer several cruises.

Campobello Sightseeing Tours (506-752-1901). These reasonably priced, 2.5 hour tours of the island get rave reviews from customers we talked to and we've seen their van in the island's most beautiful but challenging-to-find spots. They also meet boats and pick-up in Lubec to transfer between island places.

reasons better known as "the Sparkplug," can be viewed from **Stockford Park**, along the water south of the bridge. **SummerKeys** (see *Special Programs (Adults)*) offers musical, writing, art, and photography workshops and a series of free Wed.-evening concerts all summer long. The **Lubec Historical Society Museum** (207-733-2274), 135 Main St. (Rt. 189), fills the old Columbian Store with photos and memorabilia from the days when Lubec was home to 14 sardine canneries. See *Hiking* sidebar on page 374 for trails that access scenic stretches of the town's widely wandering shoreline.

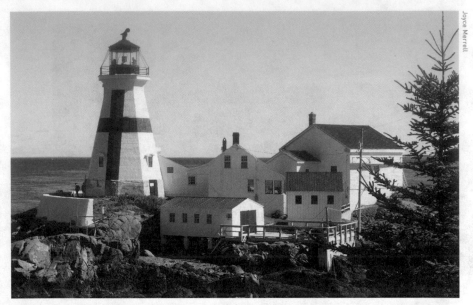

Joyce Merrell

GUIDED TOURS OF THE HEAD HARBOR LIGHTSTATION ON CAMPOBELLO ISLAND ARE OFFERED EARLY JUNE TO LATE AUGUST

✳ To Do

BICYCLING **Down East Sunrise Trail** (sunrisetrail.org). An 85-mile railbed, paralleling Rt. 1 as far as East Machias then turning inland, has been surfaced to serve wide-wheel bicyclists, ATVs, and pedestrians. Best access: from Cherryfield off Rt. 193 at Matthews Grocery; in Columbia Falls: off Rt. 1 on Tibbettstown Rd. north; in Machias: at the boxcar just south of the Dike (causeway); in East Machias: off Rt.1 on Willow St. next to the gas station and on Rt. 191, 7 miles north of Rt. 1. Ideal for mountain bikes. **Bicycle rentals** are available from **The Wharf** (207-733-4400), Lubec.

BOATING AND PADDLING **Robertson Sea Tours Adventures** (207-483-6110; cell phone, 207-461-7439; robertsonseatours.com). Captain Robertson offers a variety of cruises on a 30-foot lobster boat from Milbridge, including whale-watching and island lobster bakes. The focus is on the 50 miles of coast west to Schoodic.

Coastal Cruises (207-598-7473; cruisedowneast.com), 117 Kelley Point Rd., Jonesport. Captain Laura Fish and her brother Harry, whose family has been in this area since 1773, are themselves seasoned guides to Moosabec Reach and its islands. Their cabin cruiser *Aaron Thomas* accommodates up to six passengers on three- and five-hour cruises. Special charters and dive trips are also offered.

✪ **Bold Coast Charter Co.** (see *Puffin-Watching and Other Birding* sidebar on opposite page). Puffins up close are Captain Andy's specialty, but he also offers coastal sightseeing cruises and nature/hiking tours.

✪ **Sunrise Canoe and Kayak Tours** (207-255-3375; sunrisecanoeandkayak.com), at 68 Main St. (Rt. 1 just north of the Dyke), Machias. Rob Scribner offers kayak rentals and guided tours out in Machias Bay. Conditions permitting, tours visit petroglyphs, The Bold Coast, and the Wass Island Archipelago. Shuttles and logistical support offered.

Wharf Rentals (207-773-4400), 69 Johnson St., Lubec, offers full- and half-day kayak and bike rentals.

Also see *Getting Around* for ferries across Passamaquoddy Bay and whale-watching.

PUFFIN-WATCHING AND OTHER BIRDING

This region is said to have every northern forest habitat, from thick stands of boreal softwood to marsh and bog wetlands, clam flats, rocky cliffs, meadows, and blueberry barrens. Thinly populated, it also has two national wildlife refuges and is home (or a migratory stop) for hundreds of species, many now rare (see mainebirdingtrail.com/Downeast). The Annual Down East Spring Birding Festival, Memorial Day weekend (downeastbirdfest.org), with an associated Road Scholar (roadscholar.org) program, is growing year by year; more than 171 species of birds are usually spotted. By far the area's most famous bird is the puffin, and the place to see it is Machias Seal Island, 9.7 miles off Cutler.

PUFFINS CAN BE VIEWED UP CLOSE ON MACHIAS SEAL ISLAND

Puffins are alcids, seabirds that come to land only to breed. Just about 12 inches tall, these colorful "sea parrots" converge in spring on 15-acre Machias Seal Island, a rodent-free outcropping of rocks with crevices seemingly designed for birds to lay and nurture eggs. On the June day we visited, Captain Andy Patterson estimated it was home to 3,000 pairs of nesting puffins, 2,000 pairs of razorbills, 300 arctic terns, and 800 common murres. Visitors are strictly limited to formal groups and herded into blinds, which tend to be surrounded by birds. It's an unforgettable sight—and sound (a chorus of puffins sounds just like a chainsaw). The birds are pretty much gone by late August. Although it's just 9 miles off Cutler, Canada maintains and staffs a lighthouse station as well as the wildlife refuge. Reservations are usually required well ahead of time with any of the two outfits that have landing permits for the island.

Bold Coast Charter Company (207-259-4484; boldcoast.com), Cutler, offers the only U.S.-based access to the island itself, so bookings are necessary far in advance. Captain Patterson's five-hour puffin-watching trips (weather permitting) are late May–mid-Aug. His partially enclosed 40-foot passenger vessel *Barbara Frost* also cruises The Bold Coast, the stretch of high, rocky bluffs east of Cutler. Sea Watch Tours offers tours to Machias Seal Island from Grand Manan.

Also see *Boating and Paddling.* For any of these trips, come prepared with windbreakers, hats, and mittens for the early-morning ride out, usually in fog.

CAPTAIN ANDY ABOARD *BARBARA FROST*

HIKING

The number of coastal hiking options is constantly increasing. *Explore Maine's Cobscook Bay & Bold Coast Region*, a free overview map/guide to two-dozen trails is available locally and at www.cobscooktrails.org.

Our favorite hikes in the area include:

Pigeon Hill and Petit Manan. From Rt. 1 in Steuben turn onto Pigeon Hill Rd.; after some 5 miles, look for a small graveyard on your left. Stop. The well-trod path up Pigeon Hill begins across the road. The climb is fairly steep in places, but it's nonetheless a pleasant 20-minute hike, and the view from the summit reveals the series of island-filled bays that stretch away to the east, as well as mountains inland. Drive another mile down Pigeon Hill Rd. and past the sign announcing that you have entered a 2,166-acre preserve, part of **Maine Coastal Islands Refuge** (fws.gov/northeast/mainecoastal), which includes two other parcels and 47 offshore islands. There are two loop trails, and you can drive to the parking lot for the second. This is a varied area with pine stands, cedar swamps, blueberry barrens, marshes, and great birding (more than 250 species have been identified here). Maps are posted at the parking lots. A 0.5-mile shore path hugs the woods and coastline.

Great Wass Island. The Maine chapter of The Nature Conservancy owns this 1,579-acre tract at the southern tip of the Jonesport-Addison peninsula. Trail maps are posted at the parking lot (simply follow the island's main road to its logical end). The interior of the island supports one of Maine's largest stands of jack pine and is a quite beautiful mix of lichen-covered open ledge, wooded path, and coastal peatland. Roughly a third of the 5-mile loop is along the shore. Little Cape Point is a great picnic spot. Wear rubber-soled shoes.

Western Head, off Rt. 191, 11 miles south of East Machias, is maintained by the Maine Coast Heritage Trust, Brunswick (207-276-5156). Take the first right after the Baptist church onto Destiny Bay Rd. and follow it to the sign. The 3- to 4-mile loop trail is through mixed-growth woods and spruce to the shore, with views of the entrance to Cutler Harbor and high ledges with crashing surf, large expanses of open ocean, as well as the high, sheer ledges of Grand Manan to the northeast and Machias Seal Island to the southeast.

Bold Coast Trails. Look for the trailhead marked CUTLER COAST UNIT TRAILS some 4 miles east of Cutler Harbor on Rt. 191. Maine's Bureau of Parks and Lands (207-287-4920) has constructed inner and outer loop trails (one 5 miles, one 10 miles) from the road to the rugged cliffs and along the shore overlooking Grand Manan Channel. The Coastal Trail begins in deep spruce-fir forest, bridges a cedar swamp, and 1.5 miles from the parking lot climbs out of the woods and onto a promontory, continuing to rise and dip along the cliffs to Black Point Cove, a cobble beach. (Note: The cliffs are high and sheer, not good for children or shaky adults.) Bring a picnic and allow at least five hours. The trail continues from Black Point Cove to Fairy Head, site of three primitive campsites.

Hamilton Cove Preserve, Lubec. Boot Head Road (2.4 miles south of Quoddy Head State

FISHING Sea-run Atlantic salmon, long the draw for fishermen to the Narraguagus and Machias Rivers, are currently illegal to catch and will be until stocks have been replenished. Landlocked salmon are, however, still fair game and can be found in **Schoodic Lake** (8 miles north of Cherryfield), **Bog Lake** in Northfield on Rt. 192 (10 miles north of Machias), **Gardner Lake** in East Machias (look for the new boat ramp and parking area), and **Cathance Lake** on Rt. 191 (some 18 miles north of East Machias with a nice boat landing). Trolling lures, streamer flies, or bait from a boat are the most popular ways to catch landlocked salmon. Brook trout can be caught in May and June in local rivers and streams, but in warm weather they move to

Park). Maine Coast Heritage Trust (mcht.org) maintains this 1,250-acre preserve that includes cobble beaches, sheer cliffs, and rocky promontories. From the parking lot follow the coastal trail to a viewing platform.

Quoddy Head State Park, Lubec (follow signs from Rt. 189). The candy-striped lighthouse and visitors center (see *To See*) are as far as most people come, but the Coastal Trail, along the cliffs, is one of the most dramatic in Maine. The views from the trail and from well-placed benches are back to the lighthouse, down the coast, and across to the sheer cliffs of Grand Manan 7 miles offshore.

Roosevelt Campobello International Park offers a wide range of hiking trails; the most difficult, the 2.4-mile trail from Racoon Beach to Liberty Point, offers the area's most spectacular panoramas of Grand Manan and the Bay of Fundy. Pick up the Park's Trail Guide (www.fdr.net).

THE BOLD COAST TRAILS IN CUTLER

deeper water such as **Six Mile Lake** in Marshfield (6 miles north of Machias on Rt. 192), **Indian Lake** along Rt. 1 in Whiting, and **Lily Lake** in Trescott. Brown trout are found in **Simpson Pond** in Roque Bluffs (park in Roque Bluffs State Park), as well as in the lakes listed above.

Saltwater or tidewater fishing is usually for striped bass or mackerel. For information about licenses, guides, and fish, check **Inland Fisheries and Wildlife Department** (maine .gov/ifwl)

The East Machias Aquatic Research Center and Atlantic Salmon Hatchery (207-255-0676), 13 Willow St., East Machias (just off Rt. 1 near the Rt. 191 jct.) welcomes visitors daily

8–4, but is best equipped to handle them Fri., Sat. when volunteers assist. **The Wild Salmon Resource Center and Pleasant River Hatchery** (207-483-4336), 201 Main St., Columbia Falls, is also open pretty much every day.

GOLF **Great Cove Golf Course** (207-434-7200), 387 Great Cove Rd., Roque Bluffs, offers nine holes, water views, a clubhouse, rental clubs, and carts.

Barren View Golf Course (207-434-7651), Rt. 1, Jonesboro. This new course offers nine holes with views of the blueberry barrens and boasts Maine's largest sand trap. Facilities include a clubhouse plus rental carts and clubs. Also see the *Must See* sidebar on page 370.

HIKING The number of coastal hiking options is constantly increasing. See *Green Space*.

PICNICKING **McClellan Park**, in Milbridge, 5 miles south of town at Baldwin Head, overlooks the Atlantic and Narraguagus Bay (from Rt. 1, follow Wyman Rd. to the park gates). It's a town park on 10.5 acres donated in 1926 by George McClellan, a one-time mayor of New York City. There's no charge for walking or picnicking.

Roosevelt Campobello International Park's large natural area on Campobello Island, **Quoddy Head State Park** in Lubec, and **Roque Bluffs State Park** also all have picnic areas.

SPECIAL PROGRAMS (ADULT) ✪ **SummerKeys** (207-733-2316; in winter, 973-316-6220; summerkeys.com), 6 Bayview St., Lubec. Mid-June–Labor Day. In 1992 New York piano teacher Bruce Potterton began offering weeklong programs in Lubec. The program has ballooned to cover a wide variety of instruments, but especially piano for beginners to advanced students. Plein-air summer art workshops are now also offered, along with writing and photography. Lodging is at local B&Bs.

Road Scholar (formerly Elderhostel; roadscholar.org) offers weeklong programs on varied subjects on Campobello Island, geared to groups of 24 with lodging in the International Park cottages. Varied programs are also based at the Cobscook Community Center in Trescott.

SWIMMING ✦ **Roque Bluffs State Park**, Roque Bluffs (6 miles off Rt. 1). The pebbly ocean beach is frequently windy, but a sheltered sand beach on a freshwater pond is good for children—though the water is cold. Tables, grills, changing areas with toilets, and a playground. A 6-mile trail network leads inland and along Englishman's Bay.

Sandy River Beach in Jonesport (off Rt. 187), marked by a small sign, is a rare white-sand beach—but the water is frigid. On Beals Island, the Backfield Area, Alley's Bay, offers equally bracing saltwater swimming.

Gardner Lake, Chases Mills Rd., East Machias. Freshwater swimming, a picnic area, and a boat launch. **Six Mile Lake**, Rt. 192 in Marshfield (north of Machias), is also good for a dip.

WHALE-WATCHING **The Wharf** (207-733-4400; theinnatthewharf.com), 69 Johnson St. Lubec is the departure point for the 26-passenger *Tarquin*, specializing in whale-watching in Passamaquoddy Bay. Also see the *Must See* sidebar on page 370.

Downeast Charter Boat Tours (207-733-2009; downeastcharterboattours.com), 31 Johnson St., Lubec. Capt. Ralph and 25-foot lobster yacht *Lorna Doone* take you out into Passamaquoddy Bay and beyond to check out the Old Sow whirlpool. Watch for whales, seals, eagles, and more.

✳ Green Space

McClellan Park, in Milbridge, 5 miles south of town at Baldwin's Head, overlooks the Atlantic and Narraguagus Bay (from Rt. 1, follow Wyman Rd. to the park gates). It's a town park on 10.5 acres donated in 1926 by George McClellan, a one-time mayor of New York City. There's no charge for walking or picnicking.

Middle River Park and **Machias River Preserve**, both maintained by Downeast Coastal Conservancy (207-255-4500), have recently greatly expanded river access right in Machias. Access to 100-acre Middle Park is via Kilton Lane (across from Helen's Restaurant) and parking for the 900-acre preserve is on Rt. 1A.

Also see *Hiking* and *Swimming*.

✳ Lodging

INNS AND B&BS

LISTED GEOGRAPHICALLY, HEADING EAST

♣ **The Englishman's Bed and Breakfast** (207-546-2337; englishmansbandb.com), 122 Main St., Cherryfield 04622. This is a beautifully restored four-square 1793 Federal-style mansion (on the National Register) set above the Narraguagus River, with a wide back deck and screened gazebo. Kathy and Peter Winham offer two guest rooms (1½ baths) in the house itself and a delightful Carriage House unit with a fridge, microwave, toaster, and hot plate. A full breakfast is served by the 18th-century hearth in the dining room. Teas and cream teas are also available on request. Per-couple rates: $80–100 for rooms; $95–155 for the Carriage House (pets permitted); less for singles.

✿ 🐾 (((•))) **Pleasant Bay Bed & Breakfast** (207-483-4490; pleasantbay.com), 386 West Side Rd., P.O. Box 222, Addison 04606. Open year-round. We can't say enough about this special place! After raising six children and a number of llamas in New Hampshire, Leon

A BENCH WITH A VIEW AT PLEASANT BAY B&B

PLEASANT BAY BED & BREAKFAST

✪ 🍴 🐾 ⚓ **Micmac Farm Guesthouses and Gardner House** (207-255-3008; micmacfarm .com), 47 Micmac Lane, Machiasport 04655. Open Memorial Day to Columbus Day weekends. This classic Cape, built by Ebenezer Gardner above the Machias River in 1776, is the oldest house in Machias and a real treasure. Ebenezer Gardner was born in Roxbury, Massachusetts, and went to Nova Scotia in 1763, but because he sided with the Americans in the Revolution he had to move back down the coast. The house he built there is now home to Anthony Dunn, Bonnie, his wife, and their small daughter; in summer they occupy a separate wing and offer guests the large downstairs bedroom off the library. Very private—with a deck overlooking the river and a bath with whirlpool tub—it's furnished in family antiques, a desk, and a life's collection of books. $125 includes breakfast. Three comfortable, well-designed guesthouses ($95 daily, $595 per week). Children and pets are welcome in the cabins and kayaks can easily be launched here.

The Inn at Schoppe Farm (207-255-4648; schoppefarm.com), 21 Schoppee Dairy Road, Machias. David and Julie Barker are Machias natives who spent many years away but returned to buy this landmark farm, set on a 40-acre meadow rise above the Machias River. There are two spacious, well-furnished rooms and a two-bedroom suite, all with AC, a fridge, coffee-maker, private entrance, and river view.

and Joan Yeaton returned to Joan's girlhood turf, cleared this land, and built this gracious house with many windows and a deck and porch overlooking the tidal Pleasant River. A living room is well stocked with puzzles and books for foggy days; there's also a more formal library with fireplace and a big screened porch. But the heart of the house is the open kitchen and dining area, overlooking grounds that slope to the water. Amazing breakfasts—maybe individual herbed egg soufflés, sourced from the house hens and herb garden—are served at a common table overlooking the water. There are horses and angora goats and wooded trails through more than 100 acres of woods and meadow, down to the bay. The four upstairs guest rooms with views include one family-sized room with private bath and a lovely two-room suite with a living room, kitchenette, and deck overlooking the water. There are moorings for guests arriving by water. $60–115 per couple ($15 per child); $160 for the suite.

Chandler River Lodge (207-434-2540; chandlerriverlodge.com), 654 Rt. 1, Jonesboro 04648. Open year-round, this comfortable old house welcomed guests in decades past, and it's nice to see it restored. Set back in its grounds from Rt. 1, it offers four rooms, one with a king-sized bed and spa bath, the others with queens and private bath, although one is down the hall. $100–200 in-season includes a continental breakfast. There is no common space, as the first floor is a restaurant (see *Dining Out*).

MICMAC FARM GUESTHOUSES, MACHIASPORT

Breakfast is not included in the rates ($110–135) but there's no obvious choice just across the Dyke. The Barkers also operate Helen's (see *Dining Out*)

○ **Riverside Inn** (1-888-255-4344; riversideinn-maine.com), Rt. 1, East Machias 04630. Open year-round. The heart of this vintage-1805 house—actually the first thing guests see—is the kitchen. Innkeepers Ellen McLaughlin and Rocky Rakoczy will probably be there preparing for the evening meal (see *Dining Out*). We recommend one of the two suites (one with a living room, bedroom, and kitchen facilities; the other with two bedrooms) in the Coach House, nearer the river and with decks. The Downeast Sunrise (recreation) Trail passes below the inn, by the river. There are also two nicely decorated upstairs guest rooms with private bath in the house. $89–135 includes a full breakfast.

Talbot House Inn (207-259-2203; thetalbothouseinn.com), 509 Main St., East Machias. Open except Jan.–March. Liz and Michael Henry spent four years restoring this tall Victorian mansion set in lawns high above the junction of Rts. 1 and 1919. The formal dining room is a gathering place for breakfast and high teas (by reservation). Common space also includes a living room with a piano, TV, and board games. All five guestrooms have AC and are furnished with antiques and have private baths, TVs, coffeemakers, and combination locks. $85–115 per couple includes a full breakfast.

West Quoddy Station (1-877-535-4714; quoddyvacation.com), 823 South Lubec Rd. The former U.S. Coast Guard station within walking distance of Quoddy Head State Park has been transformed into six attractive units, nicely furnished with antiques, fitted with phones and TV; upstairs units have a sea view. From $80–190 per day and $750 per week for a one-bedroom to $2,200 per week for the five-bedroom Station House. Less off-season.

♿ ((ᵖ)) **Peacock House** (207-733-2403; peacockhouse.com), 27 Summer St., Lubec 04652. Open May–Oct. A gracious 1860s house on a quiet side street, home to four generations of the Peacock family, owners of the major local cannery. There are three carefully, comfortably furnished guest rooms and four suites, one handicap accessible. The most

luxurious suite, the Peacock, is especially spacious and has a gas fireplace. Innkeeper Mary Beth Hoffman has the right touch. Children ages 10 and up are welcome. Rates, which include a full breakfast served at the dining room table, are $105–150.

Whiting Bay Bed & Breakfast (207-733-2402; whitingbaybb.com), 1 Cobscook Way, Whiting 04691. A contemporary house on the water's edge, designed and built by owner Brenda Gay. Open year-round but check off-season. The three rooms vary in size: A sunny room has a double bed and shared bath $119-129; the master bedroom features a private bath and a king-sized bed; a suite, which can sleep a family, also has private bath. $169 double. A full breakfast is included.

Home Port Inn Bed and Breakfast (207-733-2077 or 1-800-457-2077; homeportinn.com), 45 Main St., Lubec. Open mid-May–mid-Oct. Happily, this long-established inn is flourishing under innkeeper Suzannah Gale. The large, raspberry-colored living room is a great space to read or watch TV, and each of the seven guest rooms (private bath) has been tastefully decorated. We like Room 5, melon-colored with a canopy bed. $99–135 per couple; $30 per extra person.

○ **Inn on the Wharf** (207-733-4400; theinnonthewharf.com), 69 Johnson St., Lubec 04652. Open May–Oct. 20. Victor and Judy Trafford have transformed the town's last surviving sardine-processing plant into a well-designed contemporary waterside inn with in-your-face views of Passamaquoddy Bay. There are 12 spacious suites and 3 two-bedroom, two-bath apartments (suitable for four) with full kitchens. The suites share a common gathering space with a guest kitchen, dining area, and two-level bayside deck. This remains a working wharf with lobster boats and in the basement of the building harbors holding tanks for their catch. Suites $120, apartments $180 daily; inquire about weekly rates for these and the three neighboring rental cottages. This wharf also rents bikes and kayaks and is departure point for whale watching tours.

○ ✐ **The Owen House** (506-752-2977; owenhouse.ca), 11 Welshpool St., Welshpool, Campobello, New Brunswick, Canada E5E 1G3. Open late May–mid-Oct. This delightful inn is reason enough to come to Campobello. Built in 1835 by Admiral William Fitzwilliam

THE OWEN HOUSE

Owen, son of the British captain to whom the island was granted in 1769, this is probably the most historic house on the island, and it's a beauty, set on a headland overlooking Passamaquoddy Bay. Joyce Morrell, a watercolor artist who maintains a gallery here, inherited the house from her parents and, with an able assist from Jan Meiners, maintains the B&B beautifully. The nine guest rooms (seven with private bath) are furnished with friendly antiques, handmade quilts, and good art. Room 1 is really a suite with a single bed in the adjoining room; Room 2, the other front room, is a favorite. Guests gather around the formal dining room table for a full breakfast and around one of several fireplaces in the evening. Paths lead through the 10-acre property to the water, and the Deer Island ferry leaves from the neighboring beach. From $110 (Canadian) for the shared-bath third-floor rooms to $210 for the water-view suite; $115–178 for a private room with bath, plus 13 percent tax.

COTTAGES Summer rentals with water views in this area abound. We describe only those that offer one-night lodging but heartily recommend renting for a week, something we have done many times here, taking advantage of local seafood, wild blueberries, and other produce. Check chamber listings under *Guidance*.

Robinson's Log Cottages (207-726-9546; robinsonscottages.com), 231 King St., off Rt. 86, Edmunds Township 04628. Open spring–Thanksgiving. These are fourth-generation sporting-camp-style cottages on the Dennys River, fully equipped, heated, most with stone fireplace, canoes, and direct access to the multiuse Sunrise Trail, good for mountain biking. $90–115 per night, from $511 per week. Inquire about the Guide Service.

MOTELS Machias River Inn (207-255-4861; machiasmotorinn.com), Rt. 1 next to Helen's Restaurant, Machias 04654. This family-owned, '50s motel has recently had a make-over. All rooms come with cable TV, Keurig coffee, fridge, microwave, table, and phone. Request one of the rooms, efficiency suites or the two-bedroom apartment with decks overlooking the Machias River. From $84 for a non-waterfront room in winter to $165 for river-view apartment or suite in August, less in early and late summer as well as shoulder seasons. The Inn rents bicycle rentals for use on the Sunrise Trail (access across the road) and you can grill or boil up a lobster by the river launch as well as launch your kayak.

Blueberry Patch Motel & Cabins (207-434-5411; blueberrypatchmotel.com), 550 Rt.1., Jonesboro. Open May–Nov. The classic line of five cabins, set well back and facing away from Rt. 1, as well as the eight-unit motel nearer the road, have all had a total makeover in recent years and are now an appealing waystop. The Alley family are obviously caring hosts: The immaculate units have cheerful bedspreads as well as flat screen TVs, AC, heat, and coffeemakers, and there are freshly made blueberry muffins for breakfast. There's also an attractive pool. In-season rates: $770–90 (for a cottage with full kitchen).

The Eastland Motel (207-733-5501; eastlandmotel.com), 385 County Rd., Lubec 04652. Open year-round. Current owners have breathed new life into this classic motel. Rooms are brightly, thoughtfully furnished and spanking clean, each fitted with a fridge, microwave, coffeemaker, and TV, as well as phones with free service in the US. $90 double includes a continental breakfast with fresh fruit and homemade doughnuts. Dogs are $10; from $68 off-season.

CAMPGROUNDS **McClellan Park**, marked from Rt. 1, Milbridge. Open Memorial Day–Columbus Day. This waterside town park is free for day use; a nominal fee is charged to stay at one of the 14 campsites (showers available). For details, call the town hall at 207-546-2422.

Also see **Cobscook Property Management** under *Lodging* in "Eastport."

OTHER LODGING **Little River Lighthouse** (207-259-3833; littleriverlight.org). This 1847 lighthouse is set on a 15-acre trail-webbed island at the mouth of Cutler Harbor. Three guest rooms in the 1888 keeper's house can be reserved mid-June through Aug, $150–225 per night (two guests maximum per room). Transport is included but it's BYO linens, towels, sleeping bag, food, beverages, and bottled water.

✳ Where to Eat

DINING OUT ✪ ✪ **44 Degrees North** (207-546-4440; 44-degrees-north.com), 17 Main St., Milbridge. Open daily 11–9 in season, Mon.–Sat. 11–8 in winter. Bright, attractive, and affordable, this is a great road-food stop. Soups and salads, burgers and slow-roasted prime rib, Bourbon Street chicken, grilled swordfish, beer-batter-fried shrimp, pasta, daily specials, homemade pies, and a full bar (blueberry martinis). However, if you order grilled or baked fish and don't like it dry, say so. Children's menu.

Chandler River Lodge (207-434-2540; chandlerriverlodge.com), Rt. 1, Jonesboro. Open by reservation for dinner July–Sept., Wed.–Sat. 5–8; off-season, Thu.–Sat.; closed Mar.–Apr. Chef-owner Beth Foss is well known locally, having honed her skills at her family-owned Bluebird Ranch Restaurant in Machias. Two candlelit dining rooms with white-clothed tables are the setting for a fine dining menu. Entrées $18–38.

✪ ✪ **Helen's Restaurant** (207-255-8423; helensrestaurantmachias.com) 111 E. Main St., Machias. Open 6 AM–8 :30 PM, Fri. and Sat. until 9; Sun. 7–3. The town's landmark restaurant since 1950 burned to the ground in 2014, but energetic owners David and Julie Barker managed to reopen for the 2015 season. The new Helen's is airier, filled with natural and recessed light, with nicely designed open spaces, which means that most tables now have water views. Improvements also include a bar and heated floor, but the menu is thankfully unchanged. The fish chowder is made daily with haddock, onions, Maine potatoes, butter, and cream. Options range from a (local) crabmeat salad to a hot roast beef sandwich on homemade bread; also from hot dogs, burgers, and pot roast to rib-eye steak and lobster dinners. Whatever you do, don't pass up a piece of pie. Fully licensed. Children's plates.

Riverside Inn (207-255-4134; riverside inn-maine.com), 622 Main St. (Rt.1), East Machias. Open for dinner by reservation Wed.–Sat., 5–8 (closed Jan.–March). Chef-owner Rocky Rakoczy has a wide following and the menu choices are surprisingly wide, given the size of the dining area; request a river-view table on the winterized wraparound porch. House specialties include seafood Meritage and beef Wellington. Entrees $27.95–$34.95, including salad and herbed bread.

🍴 ✪ **Blue Bird Ranch** (207-255-3351), Lower Main St. (Rt. 1). Open year-round for all three meals. Family-owned with a diner atmosphere and good food. Plenty of fried fish and steak choices, fresh-made chowders and seafood stews, burgers and sandwiches, pies and puddings. Fully licensed.

Frank's Dockside (207-733-4484), 20 Water St., Lubec. Open year-round for lunch and dinner, daily except Wed. in

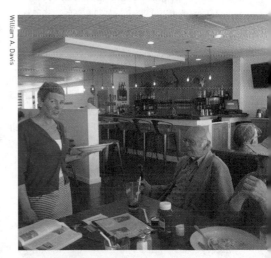

HELEN'S RESTAURANT, MACHIAS

William A. Davis

THE VIEW FROM FISHERMAN'S WHARF MARKET & RESTAURANT, LUBEC

summer. Check days off-season. Seafood chowders, soups, and baskets at lunch; Italian menu at dinner, plenty of pasta and veal dishes plus chicken Leanna, baked with seasoned crabmeat. There's a welcoming feel and reliably good taste to this place, with its cheery dining room and back deck overlooking the water. Moderately priced.

Water Street Tavern & Inn (207-733-2477; watersttavernandinn.com), 12 Water St., Lubec. Open 7 AM–8 PM. A prime spot with a great water view. It's a frequently changing and varied menu: From Southwest chicken egg rolls to scallop po'boys and turkey with cranberries at lunch; tavern pie, duck with a berry sauce, and Brazilian seafood stew at dinner. Moderately priced. Inquire about rooms and the Narrows Suite.

Fisherman's Wharf Seafood & Restaurant (207-733-4400; theinnonthewharf.com), 68 Johnson St., Lubec. Open May–Oct., 11:30–8. Reservations suggested for dinner in high season. Walled in windows overlooking the water, as well as a deck. Lobster, steamers, and local seafood are the specialties. Dinner entrées $16–30.

Fireside Restaurant, (506-752-6055) 610 Rt. 774, Campobello Island. Open seasonally Sun.–Wed. 12–5, Thu.–Sat. 12–9. Owned and managed by the Roosevelt International Park, this large log lodge was the centerpiece of a vintage-1913 estate and sits atop a bluff with views across the bay. Reserve if you want a seat near the window or hearth. The interior and the atmosphere are casual, comfortable for families. Specialties include local salmon and scallops but there's plenty to choose from. Don't pass up the raspberry cobbler. Entrees: $15–28.

Herring Cove Clubhouse (506-752-1092), Herring Cove Road (end). May–Oct., 8 AM–9 PM daily. A lovely setting with a water view, good for fried fish, soups, salads, tortilla chips with lobster salsa, and house-made pies including wild berry and coconut cream. Local brews. Moderately priced.

EATING OUT

LISTED GEOGRAPHICALLY, HEADING EAST

✿ **Vazquez Mexican Food**, 38 Main St., Milbridge. Open May–late July (closed Sun.). Chimichangas, chorizo, tacos, and much more are served up by a Mexican family who know how to cook. While it still shelters picnic tables, this enterprise has evolved from a backstreet bus serving Mexican blueberry harvesters.

○ **Milbridge House Restaurant** (207 546-4454; milbridgehouse.com), 20 Main St. Open Tue.–Sun., 6–2. This middle-of-the-village diner is a find! Serious breakfasts and a big lunch, local produce and seafood—scallop, crab, and lobster stew—house-made coleslaw, and baking. Don't pass on the pie.

○ **Bayview Takeout** (207-497-3301) is just over the bridge from Jonesport on Beal's Island (by the co-op). The best bet around for a lobster or crab roll, deep-fried seafood, and ice cream.

IN MACHIAS

⸙ **Salt Water Café** (207-255-8855), 4 Colonial Way. Open year-round, Mon.–Sat. 11–2. A spacious, window-side café in Whole Life Natural Market, with espresso bar and baked goods, also full menu including grilled panini, many veggie choices, daily soups, and specials.

BAYVIEW TAKEOUT, BEAL'S ISLAND

Christina Tree

Skywalkers Bar & Grille (207-259-6001), 86 Main St., corner of Rt. 1, south of the Dike. Open daily 11:30 AM–1 AM. A Tex-Mex menu plus extensive cocktail and beer selections, live music Fri. and Sat. nights, open mic Wed. nights.

Riverside Take-Out (207-263-7676), 273 Main St. (Rt. 1, north of the Dike). Open 11–7, weather permitting. A local favorite for all the basics and known for its monster haddock burger, crab and lobster rolls, fried seafood, and homemade blueberry iced tea.

IN LUBEC

Lubec Brewing Company (207-733-4555), 41 Water St. Open Thurs.–Sun., 2:30–8:30. A popular craft brewery and tap room with frequent live entertainment. The beer is brewed from organic barley with four or five brews on tap, maybe Quoddy Red Ale or Johnson Bay IPA; a flight of four is $10. Casual seating and a friendly atmosphere (board games encourage families). The menu changes daily, with light dishes like eggplant cannelloni, haddock cakes, and thin-crust pizza. Larger entrées $13–16.

Sunrise (207-733-0906), 52 Water St. Open seasonally, daily, 6–2. Formerly Atlantic House Coffee Shop and now under the same ownership as Lubec Brewing, this is the town's breakfast place: fresh-baked breads and pastries, house-made homefries, good coffee, and friendly staff. Check out the back deck.

Cohill's Pub (207-743-4300), 7 Water St., Lubec. Open daily 11–8. An Irish themed pub with local beers on tap and good shepherd's pie.

ON CAMPOBELLO ISLAND, NEW BRUNSWICK

Family Fisheries (506-752-2470), Rt. 774, Wilson's Beach. Open from 11:30 through at least 8:30 daily off-season; until 9 local time (an hour later than Lubec) June–Oct. Basic fried seafood menu. Eat-in or take-out, BYOB.

⸙ **Jocie's Porch** (506-752-9816), 724 Rt. 774, Welshpool. Open seasonally 7–7. Robert Calder presides at this spacious way station on Friar's Bay (Jocie is his daughter), a good stop any time of day for fresh-roasted coffee, gluten-free pies and sweets, or soup and a sandwich. Open Mon.–Thu. 9–6, Fri. 9–7, Sat. 9–5. Closed Sun.

✻ Entertainment

MUSIC **Machias Bay Chamber Concerts** (207-255-3889), Center Street Congregational Church, Machias. A series of six chamber music concerts, July–early Aug., Tue. at 7:30 PM. Top groups such as the Kneisel Hall Chamber Players and the Vermeer Quartet are featured.

Mary Potterton Memorial Piano Concerts (summerkeys.com), Lubec Congregational Christian Church. Mid-June–Aug., Wed. at 7:30 PM. Free. Featuring SummerKeys faculty and guest artists. See *Special Programs*.

Summer outdoor movies at Station 98 (see Guidance), Machias. June–Sept., alternating Saturdays. Films are projected on an antique box car. Also see *Saltwater Bar & Grill* in Machias and *Lubec Brewing Company*.

✻ Selective Shopping

LISTED GEOGRAPHICALLY, HEADING EAST

✪ **A&M Chain Saw Sculptures** (207-546-3462), 232 Rogers Point Rd., Steuben. Arthur Smith's wooden animals are truly amazing and exhibited in widely respected galleries for many times the price that he sells them for from his roadside house-gallery. Marie Smith is responsible for painting the sculptures.

Riverlily (207-546-7666; theriverlily .com), 14 Main St., Milbridge. Open May until Christmas, Mon.–Sat., 10–5. Recently relocated from Cherryfield to this historic downtown building, PJ and Jeff Trowell's shop is a must-stop, chock-full of things you didn't realize you needed, from kitchen gadgets and toys to hats, scents and a wealth of cards and wide variety of books.

Schooner Gallery (207-546-3179; schoonergallery.com), Milbridge. Open May–mid-Oct., 9–5. A quality contemporary art gallery with changing exhibits, also an information center and gift store.

Milbridge Farmers' Market, 29 Main St. parking lot, June–Oct., Sat. 9–noon.

RIVERLILY, A MUST STOP IN MILBRIDGE

IN CHERRYFIELD

4 Main Street Antiques (207-546-2664), 4 Main St. Open mid-June–mid-Oct., Tue.–Sat. 10–5. Two floors, an eclectic mix including furniture, large architectural and garden items.

Catherine Hill Winery (207-546-3426; cathillwinery.com), 661 Blackwoods Rd. (Rt.182). Open Wed.–Fri. and Sun. Now with a shop in Bar Harbor, but the wine is made here and has names like "Black Fly Special."

Intervale Farm (207-546-2589; intervale blueberryfarm.com). In Cherryfield head north on Rt. 193 for 2.2 miles; it's No. 199. A family farm growing and packing certified organic wild blueberries, jam, and chutney.

ON AND OFF RT. 1

✪ **Columbia Falls Pottery** (207-483-4075 or 1-800-235-2512; columbiafallspottery.com), 150 Main St., Columbia Falls (0.5 mile off Rt. 1). Open June–Oct., daily 10–5; otherwise call ahead. Striking bright, sophisticated pottery featuring lupines and other wildflowers; custom Delft-style bird- and sea-themed tiles, lamps, and tide clocks by April Adams; sculpture by Dana McEacharn.

Wild Blueberry Land (207-483-3583), Rt. 1, Columbia Falls. The blue geodesic dome suggests a squashed blueberry and houses an

Christina Tree

WILD BLUEBERRY LAND, RT. 1, COLUMBIA FALLS

assortment of berries—fried, in freshly made pies, jam, syrup, juice, frozen (will ship), and actual blueberries beyond the usual season.

Nelson Decoys Gallery and Gifts (207-497-3488), Cranberry Lane, Jonesport. Open May–Dec., sells prizewinning decoys, local art, and Maine-made gifts.

IN MACHIAS

Machias Bay Antiques and Fine Art (207-255-0686), 1 Water St. Specializing in 17th-through 19th-century American furniture and decorative arts, vintage and contemporary Maine paintings.

Columbia Falls Pottery (207-255-2716), 4 Water St. Open Tue.–Sat. 10–5, less off-season. See the Columbia store for details about this shop's appealing pottery and tiles. This in-town branch showcases the work made in Columbia Falls.

✪ **Woodwind Gallery** (207-255-3727), 23 Main St. Open July–Aug., Tue.–Sun., closed Sun. off-season. Holly Garner Jackson's gallery showcases some 40 local sculptors and artists. Work includes glass, pottery, photography, paintings, and metal; art supplies too. This is also home base for the **Maine Blackfly Breeder's Association** and an info source for all things cultural in the area.

Machias Hardware Co. (207-255-6581), 25 Main St. An old-fashioned hardware store that's also an unexpected source of reasonably priced herbs and spices in 2-ounce and 1-pound packages. Also local products such as those by Look's Gourmet Food.

((♪)) **Whole Life Natural Market** (207-255-8855), 80 Main St., Machias. Open year-round; summer hours Mon.–Sat. 9–6, Sun. 10–2. Finally, a first-class market featuring organic and local produce and environmentally safe products, beauty aids, wine, books, and supplements. There's also a resource/lending library and café with wireless Internet.

Machias Valley Farmers' Market (machiasvalleyfarmersmarket.com), Rt. 1 across from Helen's Restaurant, May–Oct., Fri., Sat. 9–1.

BACK ON AND OFF RT. 1, HEADING EAST

Connie's Clay of Fundy (207-255-4574), Rt. 1, East Machias. Open year-round. Connie Harter-Bagley's combination studio-shop is filled with her distinctive glazed earthenware in deep colors. Bowls, pie plates, platters, lamps, and small essentials like garlic jars and ring boxes, also "healing spiritual jewelry."

Maine Sea Salt Company (207-255-3310; maineseasalt.com), 11 Church Lane, Marshfield, 2 miles up Rt. 192 from downtown Machias. Salt is produced in shallow pools of seawater inside greenhouses. Tours are offered daily. Open 8–6 most days, salt tastings.

Look's Gourmet Food Co. (207-259-3341 or 1-800-962-6258), Rt. 191 south of East Machias. Retail shop open year-round, weekdays 8–4. Said to be the first company

Christina Tree

APRIL ADAMS AT COLUMBIA FALLS POTTERY

to successfully can crabmeat and the first to bottle clam juice, Look's now produces a whole line of specialty products under both the Atlantic and Bar Harbor labels.

A2Z General Store (207-259-3800), Beachwood Bay Estates, Rt. 191, Cutler. Open 10–2. This much-needed general store has opened in the former Cutler Naval Base. In addition to groceries, pizza, sandwiches, and gas, it carries local products.

IN LUBEC

✪ **Monica's Chocolates** (207-733-4500 or 1-866-952-4500; monicaschocolates.com), 100 County Rd. (Rt. 189). Open daily. Monica Elliott, a native of Peru, pioneered (so to speak) chocolate-making in Lubec, where she now creates truffles, crèmes, and bonbons with her father's special recipes.

Northern Tides Art and Gift Gallery (207-733-2500), 24 Water St., Lubec. Mark and Deb Lindsay's attractive shop features original prints, locally woven, carved, and otherwise produced art and crafted work.

Campobello Island Gift Shop (506-752-2233), Rt. 774, Welshpool. The specialty of the house is New Brunswick and Celtic folk music, but there's plenty of everything else, from souvenirs (especially lighthouse stuff) to books and local crafts, especially jewelry.

CHRISTMAS WREATHS More than half of Maine's Christmas wreaths are made in Washington County. You can order in the fall and take delivery of a freshly made wreath right before Christmas. Prices quoted include delivery. **The Wreath Shoppe** (207-483-4598), Harrington (wreaths decorated with cones, berries, and reindeer moss), and **Sunrise County Evergreens** (wreath.com) in Milbridge, are a couple among dozens of purveyors. The big ones are **Whitney Wreaths** (whitneywreath.com) and **Worcester Wreaths** (worcesterwreath.com).

❋ Special Events

Memorial Day weekend: **Down East Birding Festival**—guided hikes, cruises, lectures (downeastbirdfest.org).

June: ♿ **Bay of Fundy International Marathon** (bayoffundymarathon.com) from West Quoddy Lighthouse in South Lubec, across the FDR Memorial Bridge to Campobello in Canada and out to Head of Harbor Lighthouse.

Margaretta Days (margarettadays.com), held on the second Sat., celebrates Machias's role in the American Revolution with a parade, re-enactments, and more.

July: **Independence Day** celebrations in **Jonesport/Beals Island** (lobster boat races, easily viewed from the bridge); **Cherryfield** (parade and fireworks); and **Steuben** (firemen's lobster picnic and parade); **Lubec** goes all-out with a grand parade, contests, and fireworks; **Cutler** and **Machias** also celebrate. Campobello celebrates **Canada Day** (July 1) in a big way. Also see the **Eastport** section for the state's biggest celebration. **Milbridge Days** (last weekend; visitmilbridge.com) includes a parade, dance, lobster dinner, and the famous codfish relay race. **Campobello** stages a five-day **Fog Fest**, end of July.

August: **Wild Blueberry Festival and Machias Craft Festival** (third weekend) in downtown Machias—concerts, food, a major crafts fair, and live entertainment.

September: **Lights Across the Border** is a day of activities at all the area's lighthouses. **Harvest Fair** (third Sat.) pumpkin chucking, ghost tours, beer and wine tastings.

AROUND PASSAMAQUODDY BAY

During the 1890s Maine towns along Passamaquoddy Bay were all about sardine fishing and canning, but this region's summer hotels and cottages, attracting as many Americans as Canadians, were all in New Brunswick—on Campobello Island and in St. Andrews.

In the era of sail and steam the border made little difference and the bay was a busy highway. The grand old Algonquin Resort still sits enthroned like a queen mother above St. Andrews, a bustling summer resort that's just 19 miles beyond Calais. The resort town, settled by American loyalists, offers a wealth of lodging, dining, a stunning botanical garden, and a wealth of ways to get out on the Bay of Fundy as well as Passamaquoddy Bay.

At this writing, ferry service is suspended from Eastport but inquire about water links across the bay.

Eastport

The force of the tides in Passamaquoddy Bay on Eastport's eastern and northern shores is so powerful that in the 1930s President Roosevelt backed a proposal to harness this power to electrify much of the northeast coast, including Boston. More modest attempts continue.

The sardine-canning process in Maine began in Eastport in 1875 and a boom era quickly followed, but today the population of this island "city" has dropped to below 1,300 (from more than 5,000 in 1900). Still, Eastport—which once rivaled New York in shipping—remains a "city" and a working deepwater port, the deepest on the U.S. East Coast. Large freighters regularly dock, loading cows bound for Russia and pulpwood for China. Federal-style homes here are reminders that by the War of 1812, this was already an important enough port for the British to capture and occupy it.

Today there are many gaps in the old waterfront, now riprapped in pink granite to form a walkable seawall. With its flat, haunting light, Eastport has an end-of-the-world feel and suggests an Edward Hopper painting. It's a landscape that draws artists, and there are a number of galleries in the handsome brick storefronts along Water Street, which is anchored on its southern end by the Tides Institute and Museum of Art.

Eastport consists entirely of islands, principally Moose Island, which is connected to Rt. 1 by Rt. 190 via a series of causeways linking other islands. Frequently there are whales to be seen off land as well as from the whale-watching boats and always there's Old Sow, a whirlpool between Eastport and Deer Island, said to be the largest in the Western Hemisphere.

Moose is one in a cluster of islands that include Deer Island and Campobello Island in Passamaquoddy Bay. Together with Lubec, they form a narrow passage through which tides funnel into the backwater of Cobscook Bay between Eastport and Lubec (Eastport is just 3 miles north of Lubec by boat but 43 miles by land). *Cobscook* is said to mean "boiling water" in the Passamaquoddy tongue, and tremendous tides—sometimes ranging more than 25 feet—boil in through this passage and slosh up deep inlets. In Pembroke tides funnel through a narrows at 6 to 8 knots, alternately filling and draining the smaller bays beyond. For several hours the incoming tide actually roars through these "Cobscook Reversing Falls."

EASTPORT

Thanks to the extreme tides and currents, marine life is more varied than in other places. Nutrients that elsewhere settle to the bottom shoot here to the surface and nourish some forms of life that exist nowhere else. The fact that you can see only a short distance down into the water around Eastport is due not to pollution but to this nutrient-rich life.

Rt. 190 runs through the center of Sipayik (pronounced *zeh-BAY-igh*), the **Pleasant Point Indian Reservation**, home to some 2,000 members of the Passamaquoddy Indian tribe. The three-day Indian Ceremonial Days in early August fully celebrate Passamaquoddy culture.

Unfortunately, the 20 miles of Rt. 1 between Whiting (turnoff for Lubec) and Perry (turn-off for Eastport) offer few glimpses of Cobscook Bay. We recommend the short detour into **Cobscook Bay State Park** and, time permitting, into the village of **Pembroke** to find your way to the **Reversing Falls Park**.

GUIDANCE **Eastport Chamber of Commerce** (205-853-4644; eastportchamber .net), operates a **Visitors Center** in the Eastport Port Authority Building (restrooms) at the head of the breakwater. Open daily, 9–5; manned weekdays 10–3 Memorial Day and Columbus Day weekends.

GETTING AROUND **Artsipelago** (artsipelago.net), published by the **Tides Institute and Museum of Art** (tidesinstitute.org), is a free map/guide to cultural and specifically local sites and festivals on both sides of Passamaquoddy Bay.

Inquire about Lubec-Eastport Ferry and service to Deer Island.

✳ To See

✪ **The Tides Institute and Museum of Art** (207-853-4047; tides.institute.org), 43 Water St., Eastport. Open seasonally Tue.–Sun. 10–4. In 2002 the city's ornate, vintage-1887 bank building came up for sale and seemed in danger of demolition. Still evolving, it now houses changing art and photography exhibits as well as a permanent collection and a small shop featuring archival and original broadsides produced on its letterpress. TIMA, as it's known, is also an impressive cultural center committed to fostering art and culture in both US and Canadian towns around Passamaquoddy Bay. Check the website for talks by the visiting artists who utilize its downtown **Studio Works** space. Check for art installations and performances in the **Free Will North Church** (82 High Street) and cultural talks in **Seaman's Church** (26 Middle Street), both recently acquired. In all the institute has preserved and repurposed a half dozen Eastport buildings. Pick up a copy of Artsipelago, (artsipelago.net) an excellent detailed, free cultural guide to this two-country bay region.

FISHERMAN STATUE, EASTPORT

◎ **Raye's Mustard Mill and Pantry** (207-853-4451 or 1-800-853-1903; rayesmustard .com), Rt. 190 (Washington St.), Eastport. Open daily 9–5 in summer, 10–4 off-season. Closed Sun. off-season. In business since 1900, this company is the country's last stone-ground mustard mill. Washington County's sardines were packed in this mustard and are sensational. Sample many varieties. Mill tours year-round, daily.

Quoddy Dam Museum, 72 Water St., Eastport, open Memorial Day–Sept., usually open daily 10–4. A 14-by-16-foot concrete model of the **Passamaquoddy Tidal Power Project** (see the introduction). The storefront also houses a crafts cooperative and information center. Inquire here about the nearby **Barracks Museum** (borderhistoricalsociety.com), originally part of Fort Sullivan and occupied by the British during the War of 1812.

Seawall Walk. This flowery walk runs behind the commercial blocks, from the Waco Diner to the Quoddy Tides office. Note the amphitheater, scene of seasonal concerts and happenings, including Fri.-night movies.

Waponahki Museum and Resource Center (tribal office 207-853-4500; wabanaki.org), 59 Passamaquoddy Rd. off Rt. 190, Pleasant Point in the Sipayik Youth Center. Open Mon.–Thu. 1–4 and alternate Saturdays. Baskets, beaded artifacts, historical photos, and crafts.

Reversing Falls Park. Turn off Rt. 1 at Rt. 214 into the village of Pembroke; follow the slight jog in the road, then Leighton Point for 3.3 miles, and turn right onto Clarkside Cemetery Rd. (the sign may or may not be there), then left at the T. This last road turns to dirt before it ends at a parking area for a town park with two short trails to the water. Try to time your visit to coincide with the couple of hours before the height of the incoming tide, which funnels furiously through the gap between Mahar's Point and Falls Island. As the salt water flows along at 6 to 8 or more knots, it strikes a series of rocks, resulting in rapids. At low water this is a great place to hunt for fossils, and it's well worth finding anytime.

Old Sow. Billed as the largest tidal whirlpool in the Western Hemisphere, this is 230 feet in diameter, sited between the tips of Moose and Deer Islands. It's said to be produced by 70 billion cubic feet of water rushing into Passamaquoddy Bay, much of which finds its way around the tip of Deer Island and an underwater mountain at this narrow point. The area's smaller whirlpools are called Piglets. See *Boating* for viewing.

✳ To Do

BIRDING **Moosehorn National Wildlife Refuge** (see *Green Space*) is a prime spot for spotting bald eagles. Vast tidal flats in Eastport are good places to watch migrating plovers, sandpipers, and other shorebirds. For details about the late-May **Down East Spring Birding Festival**, see downeastbirdfest.org, and for puffin-watching on Machias Seal Island see boldcoast.com.

BOATING **Eastport Windjammers/Harris Whale Watching & Fishing** (207-853-2500; eastportwindjammers.com), 104 Water St., Eastport. Mid-June–Oct. Butch Harris offers frequent, daily 2½ to 3 hour cruises for up to 45 people aboard *Pier Pressure*, the new lobster-style excursion boat he built after the Eastport Pier collapsed, badly damaging his windjammer. Tours include a look at Old Sow and Campobello Island's Head Harbour Lighthouse Station (also known as East Quoddy Light), as well as whale, seals, and eagle spotting. Sunset cruises and fishing charters also offered.

Fundy Breeze Charters (207-853-4660), 109 Water St., Eastport. Captain Skip Harris can take six passengers max at a time on whale watches, lighthouse tours, and cruises around Machias Seal Island to see the puffins. He specializes in deep-sea fishing charters.

WALKS **Shackford Head State Park** (posted from Rt. 190 near downtown Eastport) is a 90-acre peninsula with several trails, including a roughly 0.7-mile path from the parking lot to a 173-foot-high headland overlooking Campobello Island and Lubec in one direction and Cobscook Bay in the other. Another 0.25-mile-long trail leads down the headland and permits access to the shore. Views are of the bay with its floating salmon pens. Look for fossils at low water.

SPECIAL LEARNING PROGRAMS **Eastport Arts Center** (see *Entertainment*) offers a variety of arts workshops ranging from outdoor painting to storytelling and soap making. **The Tides Institute** (see *To See*) offers workshops in printmaking, letterpress, and photography and more in its StudioWorks space.

✳ Green Space

The Quoddy Regional Land Trust (207-733-5509) publishes *Cobscook Trails* (see *Hiking* sidebar on page 374).

Moosehorn National Wildlife Refuge (fws.gov/northeast/moosehorn) consists of two divisions. Trails in the first—the Baring section (Unit 1)—are maintained; see "Calais." The second division, the Edmunds, is threaded by Rt. 1 between Dennysville and Whiting. Some 7,200 acres are bounded by Whiting and Dennys Bays and the mouth of the Dennys River. North Trail Rd. is 2.5 miles long and leads to a parking area from which canoes can be launched into Hobart Stream. South Trail Rd. covers 0.9 mile and leads to a parking area for a 10-mile unmaintained trail network.

✪ **Cobscook Bay State Park** (207-726-4412), S. Edmunds Rd., just off Rt. 1 between Dennysville and Whiting. The 880-acre park includes a 2-mile nature trail with water views and a 0.5-mile Shore Trail. Wildlife and birds are plentiful. The campground is open mid-May–mid-Oct.; there are 150 campsites, most of them for tents and many with water views. It also offers a boat-launch area, picnic benches, and a hiking and cross-country ski trail. Birding is superb.

Gleason's Point State Park, Perry. On Rt. 1 look for Shore Rd., across from the New Friendly Restaurant. After a short way turn right on Gleason Cove Rd. This is a great place for walking, sunbathing, and picnics (tables provided).

❋ Lodging

IN EASTPORT

INNS AND B&BS ✪ ✿ (ɡʎ) **Kilby House Inn** (207-853-0989 or 1-800-853-4557; kilbyhouseinn.com), 122 Water St. Open year-round. This Queen Anne–style house is on the quiet end of the waterfront, an easy walk from shops and restaurants. The double parlor with a fireplace and grand piano invites you to sit down and read. Innkeeper Gregg Noyes's passions include playing the Estey reed organ, refinishing antiques, and sharing Eastport and Kilby family history. He clearly relishes his role as full-time innkeeper after many years of also teaching. The four pleasant antiques-furnished upstairs guest rooms (private baths) include a sunny master with a four-poster canopy bed and water view. The interior of the neighboring coach house has been crafted with a woodworker's eye to detail as well as comfort. Guests gather around the dining room table for very full breakfasts. $95–110; the Carriage House is a gem, an open-plan cottage with a full kitchen, $145 per night, $850 per week.

✿ ✿ ✦ ♿ **Todd House** (207-853-2328), 1 Capen Ave. Open year-round. A restored and expanded 1775 Cape, the oldest house in Eastport, with water views. In 1801 men met here to charter a Masonic order, and in 1861 the house became a temporary barracks. Three large double rooms with kitchenettes, also one double room with twin beds. Our favorites are the ground-floor Cornerstone Room and the Masonic Room, with a working fireplace. Grandmotherly innkeeper Ruth McInnis presides in the living room, welcoming well-behaved children and pets; her own pets include three cockatiels. $70–110 in-season.

❀ ✦ **The Milliken House** (207-853-2955 or 1-888-507-9370; eastport-inn.com), 29 Washington St. Mary Williams is the owner of this 1840s house, which retains Victorian charm with a large double parlor, ornate detailing, and some original furniture. There are six guest rooms, all with private bath. $90–100 year-round includes a full breakfast.

The Commons (207-853-4123; thecommonseastport.com), 51 Water St., P.O. Box 255. Two second-floor, two-bedroom upscale units in a lovingly restored 1887 brick waterfront building in the walkable waterfront historic district. $900–1,150 per week.

Cobscook Property Management (207-853-6179; cobscookpm.com), based in Eastport, offers a wide selection of weekly and monthly rentals.

Note: A number of weekly cottage rentals are available, check eastportchamber.net

❋ Where to Eat

IN EASTPORT UNLESS OTHERWISE NOTED

✪ ✿ **Quoddy Bay Lobster Co.** (207-853-6640), 7 Sea St. Open daily in-season 10–6, Sun. 11–4. It's well worth finding your way down to this fish store/eatery. The rewards are fresh fish and lobster rolls drizzled with butter, great homemade chowder and coleslaw, and fried clam rolls so thick you have to eat them with a fork. Try a grilled seared scallop roll with garlic pepper seasoning (scallops are the local specialty). This family

Christina Tree

THE CARRIAGE HOUSE AT KILBY HOUSE INN

operates four fishing boats, and both the quality and prices reflect a lack of middlemen. Picnic tables, sheltered pavilion overlooking Passamaquoddy Bay, limited seating in the fish store.

1887 Landmark Grill & Ale House (207-853-7074), 32 Water St., Eastport. Open seasonally, Thu.–Sun. for lunch and dinner, Mon., Tue. for dinner from 4. Pleasant ambiance and a menu ranging from burgers, salads, and pizzas to steak and seafood, specials.

⚓ **Eastport Chowder House** (207-853-4700), 167 Water St. Open seasonally, daily 11–9. A good location on what's said to be the site of the country's first fish and sardine cannery. The downstairs pub on Cannery Wharf is informal, and it's possible to get take-out (and thus park in line) for the ferry that departs from the adjacent beach. The restaurant is barnlike and can be noisy; the outside deck is a blessing. The reasonably priced menu runs from fried haddock and eggplant Parmesan to lobster.

WaCo Diner (207-853-4046; wacodiner.com), 47 Water St. Open year-round; 6 AM–8 PM in summer. Billed as the oldest diner in Maine, a local landmark with a great view from its Schooner Room and a deck.

⚓ **The Happy Crab Downeast Grill and Sports Bar** (207-853-9400), 35 Water St. Open daily 11:30–8:30. There are two sides to this place, one family-geared with a selection of burgers, pizza, seafood baskets, and sandwiches, all made with the specially flavored house mayo. The other is a sports bar with a pool table, popular dining with a deck.

(((•))) **Moose Island Bakery** (207-853-3111; mooseislandbakery.com), 75 Water St. Open year-round, 7–5. Cream puffs, carrot cakes, coffees, drinks, a great deck with water views.

(((•))) **Dastardly Dick's** (207-853-2090), 62 Water St. Open 7–3 (or later); Sun. 9–1. Espressos, teas, frappés, smoothies, snacks, and sweets, a welcome gathering spot in the middle of town.

Rosie's Hot Dog Stand at the breakwater. Local institution open seasonally for decades.

✪ ✿ ⚓ **The New Friendly Restaurant** (207-853-6610), Rt. 1, Perry. Open daily 11–8. Great road food. A homey restaurant with booths. Fish stews and chowders, basics like liver and onions, not-so-basics like crab salad and plenty of lobster in a lobster sandwich.

Desserts include Grape-Nuts pudding as well as pies. Beer and wine served.

More Food: Part of the appeal of a vacation rental around here is the plethora of local seafood, produce, and locally made staples; check out the **Eat Local made Co-op** (207-853-7138), 49 Water St., open year-round Thu.–Sat., as well as the **Eastport Farmers' Market** (207-853-0800), 149 Water St., Sat. 11–1.

✳ Entertainment

Eastport Arts Center (207-853-5803; eastportartscenter.com), 36 Washington St., Eastport. The vintage-1837 Washington Street Baptist Church has been restored and fitted with a new heating system as home to six arts organizations, including the **Northern Lights Film Society** (Thu.-evening films at 7 on a large screen, great sound) as well as frequent performances by the **Passamaquoddy Bay Symphony Orchestra** and other concerts, performances by **Stage East** (stageeast.org), a terrific community theater, plus puppetry, and more. Check the website for the current schedule.

The Tides Institute (tidesinstitute.org) sponsors artist talks at its downtown **StudioWorks**, installations and performance at **Free Will North Church** and cultural talks at **Seaman's Church**, as well as **Music on the Rocks** concerts every other Wednesday in the Sutherland Amphitheater, Eastport waterfront.

✳ Selective Shopping

IN DOWNTOWN EASTPORT

ART **The Commons** (207-853-4123; thecommonseastport.com), 51 Water St. Open year-round; in summer, Mon.–Sat. 10–6, Sun. 1–5, otherwise Mon.–Sat. 10–6. An outstanding gallery displaying the work of more than 90 Passamaquoddy Bay area artists and artisans: botanical and wildlife paintings, fabric art, carved burl bowls, jewelry, hand-knit sweaters, wooden ware, pottery, ash, and Passamaquoddy sweetgrass baskets.

🐚 **The Eastport Gallery** (207-853-4166; eastportgallery.com), 74 Water St. Open early

June–Oct. 1, daily 10–5, Sun. noon–5. Eastport's oldest art gallery, a cooperative representing local artists.

Crow Tracks (207-853-2336; crowtracks.com), 11 Water St. Open year-round. R. J. LaVallee carves a variety of birds, whales, and fantasy figures, from decoys to Christmas ornaments.

✪ **Breakwater Gallery** (207-853-4773; eastportbreakwatergallery.com), 93 Water St. Cynthia Morse is a talented artist and her husband, Michael Morse, is a talented (not your traditional) bird carver. This is a serious gallery, with paintings, sculptures, much more.

SPECIAL SHOPS **Port O'Call** (207-853-0800; portocalleastport.com), 54 Water St. An enticing shop with a great mix of cards, alpaca gifts, PJs, jewelry and bags, books, and toys.

Quoddy Crafts. Sharing space with the Quoddy Dam Museum (see *To See*), a local crafts outlet worth checking out.

S. L. Wadsworth & Sons (207-853-4343; slwadsworth.com), 42–44 Water St. Opened in 1818 by Samuel Wadsworth, son of General Peleg Wadsworth and uncle of poet Henry Wadsworth Longfellow, this is billed as the country's oldest ship chandlery. It remains marine-geared but also carries hardware and "nautical gifts." Buy a rod and fish from the breakwater (you don't need a license).

Sweeties Downeast (207-853-3120; sweetiesdowneast.com), 80 Water St. Sweet!

Seaside Salts (207-853-7008), 103 Water St. These salts are mined in the foothills of the Himalayas and turned into lamps that are good for you.

ALONG RT. 1, HEADING NORTH FROM PERRY

✪ **Tide Mill Farm** (207-733-2551; tidemillfarmorganicfarm.com), 91 Tide Mill Rd., Edmunds. This 200-year-old working farm on Whiting Bay and Crane Mill Stream has been in the Bell family since 1765. It is set on 1,600 acres with 6 miles of shorefront. Bob Bell maintains the property as a working organic farm. The seventh through ninth generations raise organic produce and animals, with milk, vegetables, and eggs available in summer

THE 45TH PARALLEL IS A GREAT ECLECTIC MIX OF ANTIQUES AND GIFTS FROM AROUND THE WORLD

season. Check the website for current open farm days and farm stand hours.

Mainely Smoked Salmon Company (207-853-4794; mainelysmokedsalmon.com), 555 South Meadow Rd., Perry. Hot and cold smoked salmon.

✪ **45th Parallel** (207-853-9500), "Halfway between the Equator and the North Pole," Rt. 1, Perry. Open seasonally. Filled from floor to 12-foot-high ceilings with an eclectic mix of gifts and home decor accents and furnishings: stained glass and antique beds, a stuffed lion, drawer pulls and lamps, jewelry, bird feeders, much more.

✳ Special Events

Memorial Day weekend: **Down East Birding Festival**—guided hikes, boat tours, presentations (downeastbirdfest.org).

July: **Independence Day** is celebrated for an entire week in Eastport, with parades, a military flyover, and fireworks. Eastport's is the first flag in the United States to be raised on July 4 at dawn (eastport4th.com).

Mid-August: **Annual Indian Ceremonial Days**, Pleasant Point Reservation—a celebration of Passamaquoddy culture climaxing with dances in full regalia (wabanaki.com).

September: **Eastport Salmon and Seafood Festival** (Labor Day weekend; eastportsalmon fest.com) celebrates Eastport's salmon industry with great food, boat tours of area fish farms, walking tours, live entertainment, games, concerts. **Eastport Pirate Festival** (eastportpiratefestival.com), a weeklong celebration climaxing the following weekend.

December: **New Year's Eve** is huge in Eastport, the first American city to welcome in the new year. But first, at 11 PM ET/midnight AT, the Canadian New Year is celebrated with a giant maple leaf drop and singing of "O, Canada." At midnight is the giant sardine drop, along with singing "Auld Lang Sine." Kiss the sardine for good luck!

Calais and the Downeast Lakes Region

Calais (pronounced *Callus*), the largest community in Washington County, is positioned at the head of navigation on the St. Croix River.

The city's present population is fewer than 3,000, half what it was in the 1870s when its fleet of sailing vessels numbered 176 and the brick downtown was rebuilt after a fire. The wooden residential district retains many older, handsome sailing-era houses. At the center of town, the **Wabanaki Cultural Center**, showcasing the history and culture of the Passamaquoddy Nation, hidden away downstairs in the Visitors Center, is a must-see. Exhibits are drawn from the Passamaquoddy reservations north of Calais, divided between Princeton and Peter Dana Point on Big Lake.

Calais is just across the St. Croix River from St. Stephen, New Brunswick, and the two communities are inextricably linked, celebrating a nine-day International Homecoming Festival together in August. This is, of course, a major border crossing. In summer months (during daylight saving time) it's an hour later in St. Stephen than in Calais.

Signs are in French as well as English, gas is priced by the liter, and for Americans (at this writing), everything is cheaper. To come as far as Calais and not continue along NB1 to St. Andrews makes as little sense as going to Lubec and not crossing the bridge to Campobello (see the introduction to this chapter and sidebar at the end).

There is also the magnificent island of Grand Manan, accessible by ferry from Blacks Harbour, 35 miles beyond St. Andrews. It's Canada's southernmost island, a rugged outpost at the mouth of the Bay of Fundy. All you birders, hikers, and lovers of beautiful, unspoiled, out-of-the-way places, take notice.

GUIDANCE (ᵅ) **Maine Tourist Information Center** (207-454-2211), 39 Union St., Calais. Open year-round; June–Oct. 15, daily 8–6, otherwise 9–5:30. This center, staffed by the Maine Tourism Association, has information for all of Maine as well as the local area; public restrooms. Note the three-dimensional map of Washington County and the Passamaquoddy

William A. Davis

WABANAKI CULTURAL CENTER, CALAIS

Bay area, the diorama of a local shipyard, and the touch tank for kids. Also **visitstcroix valley.com**.

Tourism New Brunswick (800-561-0123; tourismnewbrunswick.ca)

St. Stephen Provincial Visitor Information Centre (506-466-7390), 5 King St., St. Stephen, New Brunswick.

St. Andrews Visitor Information Centre (800-563-7397; townofstandrews.ca), 24 Reed Ave., St. Andrews.

Grand Manan Tourism Association (grandmanannb.com)

GETTING THERE *By car:* The direct route to Calais from Bangor and points west of Washington County is Rt. 9, the Airline Highway. From the Machias area, take Rt. 191. The slower but more scenic **Bold Coast Byway** (boldcoastbyway.com) follows Rt. 1.

CROSSING THE BORDER See the "Way Downeast" introduction. *Note:* If the crossing in the middle of town is backed up, there are two alternatives: Rt. 1 north of town and the Milltown crossing.

✳ To See

Wabanaki Cultural Center (207-454-2126), 39 Union St., Calais. Open daily, same hours as the Maine Tourist Information Center (it's downstairs). Created in 2004 to celebrate the 400th anniversary of the settling of nearby St. Croix Island, the first European settlement north of Florida, but focused on telling the story Maine's native tribes. The numerous exhibits are about the local Passamaquoddy tribe and include a vintage 1872 canoe, exquisite basketry, and more.

St. Croix International Historic Site Overlook, (207-454-3871; usnps.gov/stcrois island) 8 miles south of Calais in Red Beach. A **visitors center** (restrooms) is open mid-May–Columbus Day weekend, 9–4:30 (closed Tue.–Wed. through June). The island itself is a ways offshore. A path leads to a bronze replica of the settlement. Along the way you encounter half a dozen haunting, life-sized bronze statues, here an elaborately dressed Frenchman, there a young Passamaquoddy girl. The French expedition came for the fur trade, and its leader, Pierre Dugua, Sieur de Monts, retained Samuel de Champlain as his mapmaker and chronicler. They chose a 6½-acre island for their settlement in June 1604 and set about building a storehouse and dwellings, despite the black flies. The waters teemed with fish, and the Native inhabitants were friendly—but the first snow came in early October, the river froze, and 35 of the 79 settlers died. Finally, on June 15, supply vessels arrived, and Dugua sailed eventually to Port Royal, Nova Scotia, seeding French culture in Canada.

Dr. Holmes Cottage/Museum (stcroixhistorical.com), 527 Main St. Open July through mid-Aug. The oldest existing house in Calais, restored to its 1850 look. Pick up a *Walking Tour Guide to the Calais Residential Historic District*, which includes several Gothic Revival gingerbread houses on S. Main St.

Whitlock Mills Lighthouse. The northeastern-most lighthouse in the country is best viewed from the Pike Woods Rest Area on Rt. 1, 3 miles south of Calais.

✳ To Do

BIRDING **Moosehorn National Wildlife Refuge** is a prime birding center with some 190 species recorded, as well as resident bald eagles (see *Green Space* and *Grand Manan* sidebars).

ST. ANDREWS, NEW BRUNSWICK

During the 1890s the Maine towns along Passamaquoddy Bay were all about sardine fishing and canning. The summer hotels—attracting as many Americans as Canadians—were on Campobello Island and on the New Brunswick mainland at St. Andrews. The canneries and most of the hotels are long gone now, but the grand old Algonquin Resort sits enthroned like a queen mother above St. Andrews.

Street names like Queen, King, and Princess Royal date to the town's 1783 founding by American colonists who so strongly opposed breaking with the mother country that they left the new United States . . . and settled in what they thought was Canada, only to find out when the border was finally determined that they were actually in Maine! Loyally they moved again and an appreciative British government responded by granting them a superb site. British army engineers dug wells, built a dock, constructed a fort, and laid out the town on its present grid. Each loyalist family was also given a house lot twice the usual size. The result is an unusually gracious-looking town. The focal point remains Market Wharf, where the first settlers stepped ashore—now the cluster point for outfitters offering whale-watching, sailing, and kayaking tours—and Water Street, lined with shops.

St. Andrews is the Bar Harbor of New Brunswick, but with distinctly Anglo-Canadian attractions like the **Kingsbrae Horticultural Garden** (506-529-3335; kingsbraegarden.com) a 27-acre floral extravaganza. Built on the grounds of several long-gone estates, it weaves long-standing cedar hedges, flower beds, and old-growth forest into magnificent designs. There are display gardens with rare and native plants, a fantasy garden with animals made from moss, demonstration gardens, a woodland trail through the old-growth forest, a therapy garden, bird and butterfly gardens, and much more. Housed in the original manor home, the gracious art-hung café is a pleasant place for lunch and afternoon tea. Come evening it's **Savour in the Garden** (506-529-4055; chefalexhaun. com), set for fine dining (by reservation) with white-clothed tables, candles reflected in the long windows, and delicacies prepared by celebrated Chef Alex Haun. Wednesdays are Pump Nights: light menu, patio dining, and live music

St. Andrew's grandest surviving estate is **Ministers Island Historic Site** (506-529-5081; ministersisland.net), built around 1890 on an island accessed by a "tidal road" at low tide; otherwise by shuttle boat or kayak. Built for Sir William Van Horne, the driving force in construction of the Canadian Pacific Railway, the 50-room mansion has 17 bedrooms, a vast drawing room, a bathhouse, and a gigantic livestock barn.

Be sure to visit **Huntsman Marine Science Centre** (506-529-1200; huntsman marine.ca), Lower Campus Rd. (off Rt. 127), a nonprofit aquaculture and research center that showcases the bay's sea creatures, big and small. It features a 20,000-square-foot aquarium and a display dramatizing the magnitude of the Fundy tides. **Ross Memorial Museum** (506-520-5124; rossmemorial museum.ca), an 1824 mansion at King and Montague Streets, displays an exceptionally fine decorative art collection.

St. Andrews is a true resort town. The 18-hole, waterside **Algonquin Resort Golf Course** (algonquinresort.com) is legendary. The other big draw

Christina Tree

THE ALGONQUIN RESORT IS ONE OF NORTH AMERICA'S GREATEST HOTELS

KINGSBRAE GARDENS

is whale watching in Passamaquoddy Bay and beyond via fast hurricane boats (fundytiderunners.com), traditional tours, and sailing vessels (jollybreeze.com). You can also kayak or canoe (easternoutdoors.com) and swim in relatively warm water at Katy's Cove (506-529-3433).

Open year-round, The Algonquin Resort (506-529-8823; in the U.S., 1-855-529-8693; algonquinresort.com) is the last of the truly grand 19th-century coastal resorts in northeastern America. The 233-room (including suites), Tudor-style hotel is staffed in summer by about 200 employees—some in kilts. Amenities include tennis courts and an outdoor pool. The hotel was recently totally renovated, and new amenities include an indoor water slide, full spa, and a fitness center. Rack rates from $189.

Other St. Andrews lodging options include **Kingsbrae Arms Relais & Chateaux** (506-529-1897; kingsbrae.com), a luxurious 1897 shingled mansion adjoining Kingsbrae Gardens, and the **Treadwell Inn** (1-888-529-1011; treadwellinn.com) and **St. Andrews Motor Inn** (506-529-4571; standrewsmotorinn.com), both on Water St. overlooking the bay.

Rossmount Inn (506-529-3351; rossmountinn.com), east of town, is a boxy three-story hilltop period piece with 18 charmingly furnished rooms, a swimming pool, and walking trails up Chamcook Mountain, the highest point on this side of Passamaquoddy Bay. Thanks to Swiss-born and -trained chef-owner Chris Aerni, the many-windowed dining room is the premier place to dine. Another favorite is **Niger Reef Tea House** (506-529-8006; nigerreefteahouse.com), 1 Joe's Point Rd. Good for either lunch or dinner, it occupies a 1926 waterside summer cottage that served for many years as a meetinghouse for the Daughters of the Empire, local equivalent of the Daughters of the American Revolution.

The **St. Andrews Block-house** (506-529-4270), erected during the War of 1812, is in neighboring Centennial Park. Last but not least, the town's best WiFi and caffeine source is **Honeybeans** (506-529-4888), 157 Water St. Open year-round, Mon.–Sat. 7:30–6. Serious teas as well as locally roasted beans. Angela and Matthew Honey also serve up scones and other fresh-baked treats.

ST. ANDREWS SHOPS

FISHING The Downeast Lakes are famed for their abundance of landlocked salmon, square-tailed trout, and some of the finest smallmouth bass fishing in Maine. Best May–mid-June. When ice is out in spring, trolling starts on **West Grand Lake**, **Big Lake**, and **Pocumcus Lake**. **Grand Lake Stream** itself, fast-flowing water linking West Grand and Big Lakes, is one of the country's premier fly-fishing spots for landlocked salmon. Fishing licenses covering three days to a full season (also necessary for ice fishing) are available, along with lodging and supplies, in the village of Grand Lake Stream (grandlakestream .org), the focal point of the region and base for the state's largest concentration of fishing guides (grandlakestreamguides.com). Princeton, on the way to Grand Lake Stream, also offers access to Big Lake and Grand Falls Lake. Both once ran freely into the St. Croix River, but thanks to a series of 19th-century industrial dams, they're now known for their shallows and flowage, great for trout as well as moose-watching and canoeing. Within **Moosehorn National Wildlife Refuge** (see *Green Space*), several lakes and streams are open for fishing.

GOLF **St. Croix Country Club** (207-454-8875), River Rd., Calais. A tricky nine-hole course on the banks of the St. Croix River.

PADDLING **Cobscook Hikes & Paddles** (207-726-4776; off-season, 207-454-2130). Registered Maine Guides Stephen and Tess Forek, based in Robbinston, offer guided two- and three-hour kayaking paddles from Whiting to Calais. All fishing camps offer boat rentals.

OUTDOOR PROGRAMS **Washington County Community College** (207-454-1060), 1 College Dr., Calais. Year-round programs open to the public: hiking, kayaking, camping, cross-country skiing; inside climbing wall also available.

SWIMMING **Red Beach** on the St. Croix River is named for the sand on these strands: pulverized deep red granite. There is also swimming in dozens of crystal-clear lakes. Round Pond in Charlotte has a free beach and boat launch. North of Calais, follow the Charlotte Rd. 8 miles to the pond.

✳ Green Space

Moosehorn National Wildlife Refuge (207-454-7161; moosehorn.fws.gov). This area is the northeast end of a chain of wildlife and migratory bird refuges extending from Florida to Maine and managed by the U.S. Fish and Wildlife Service. The 23,000-acre refuge is divided into two sections some 20 miles apart. The larger, 17,200-acre area is in Baring, 5 miles north of Calais on Rt. 1. Look for eagles, which nest each spring at the intersection of Charlotte Rd. and Rt. 1. The Edmunds Division is found by heading south on Rt. 1 from Calais, between Dennysville and Whiting (see "Eastport"). This 7,200-acre area lies on the border of the tidal waters of Cobscook Bay. Volunteer-dependent programs—guided hikes, bike tours, and van tours, which sometimes take you down roads you wouldn't be able to explore on your own—are offered late June–Aug.

Downeast Lakes (downeastlakes.org). Evolving preservation efforts safeguard some 370,000 forested acres, one of the largest wilderness areas in the East. It's best explored by canoe or kayak with a guide (readily available at local lodging places), but there are also trails. Look for loons, bald eagles, herons, ruffed grouse, and many kinds of warblers as well as fish.

WALKS

IN THE CALAIS AREA

Calais Waterfront Walkway. A 1.5-mile path follows a former railbed along the river, beginning at city landing parking lot. It's the northern terminus of the East Coast Greenway, with land from Key West, FL, embedded in it (there's a piece of Red Beach granite embedded at the Key West end). A good venue from which to appreciate the daily 25-foot tidal changes.

Devil's Head. A trail leads to a promontory, said to be the highest point east of Cadillac Mountain; great views. Look for the sign on Rt. 1 south of Heslin's Motel.

✳ Lodging

IN THE CALAIS AREA

🐾 🌊 ((ᵠ)) **The International Motel** (207-454-7515 or 1-800-336-7515; theinternational motel.com), 626 Main St. The best lodging views in town are from the 19 Riverview units in this 61-unit motel owned and operated by three generations of the Thomas family. From $75, $80–90 per couple for water views, $150 for efficiency units with whirlpool tubs. Dogs accepted but not in Riverview rooms. Meals are next door at the Wickachee (see *Where to Eat*).

🐾 🌊 **Calais Motor Inn** (1-800-439-5531; calaismotorinn.com), 663 Main St. A friendly, locally owned 70-unit motel with a licensed restaurant (see *Where to Eat*). $79–89 per couple in-season, from $69 off-season.

✳ Where to Eat

Z Crumbs Café & Bake Shoppe (207-454-8996), 257 Main St., Calais. Open 7:30–7 Tue.–Fri., 9–5 Mon. An inviting café with varied seating, homemade soups and chowders, a wide choice of paninis, several kinds of grilled cheese, as well as sandwiches and pastries. All breads baked from scratch on site.

🌊 **Wickachee** (207-454-3400), 282 Main St. (Rt. 1), Calais. Open year-round 6 AM–10 PM. Steak and seafood, a big salad bar, specials. Spacious, clean, and friendly.

Nino's, Calais Motor Inn Restaurant (207-454-7111), 293 Main St. (Rt. 1), Calais. Open for lunch and dinner. A large, comfortable dining room, known for steak and seafood.

✳ Selective Shopping

✪ **Calais Bookshop** (207-454-1110), 405 Main St., Calais. This is Washington County's only genuine bookstore and it's a treasure. Carole Heinlein stocks new, used, and rare titles and serves a wide circle of loyal patrons. Maine titles make this a destination for far and near, but so does the pile of well-chosen novels, both current and classic.

Artemis's Attic (207-454-7000), 297 Main St., Suite B, Calais. Open year-round except Sun., Mon. A great barn of a place filled from floor to ceiling by 30 vendors: with antiques big and small, vintage clothing and jewelry, fleece, much more.

Urban Moose (207-454-8277), corner of North and Main Sts., Calais. Open May–Dec. An enticing, smaller version of the owner's 45th Parallel, south on Rt. 1 in Perry.

Marden's (207-454-1421), 189 Main St. and Rt. 1, Calais. Two representatives of the chain of Maine discount centers, which has been doing business in the state since 1964. Big-time bargains can be found here, from furniture to fabrics, housewares to clothing.

✳ Special Events

August: **International Festival**, Calais and St. Stephen, NB—a week of events on both sides of the border, including pageants, a parade, entertainment, and more.

October: **Scarecrow Fest.** Scarecrows are draped on lampposts all month; last Saturday Fest features casket races and cadaver-throwing.

GRAND MANAN, NEW BRUNSWICK

Grand Manan (grandmanannb.com) is Canada's southernmost island, far enough at sea to be very much its own place, a rugged outpost at the mouth of the Bay of Fundy.

Right whales, the rarest of whales, gather offshore in summer months, feeding on krill and other nutrients in the tide-churned waters. Some 360 species of birds have been identified on the island itself. Birders find their way along 45 miles of hiking trails that in many places hug cliffs varying from 100 to almost 400 feet. From mid-June to early Aug. Seal Cove is also departure point for tours to see puffins up close on Machias Seal Island (seawatchtours .com; 1-877-662-8552).

Fishing boats line Grand Manan wharves the way they used to in New England. The hundreds of herring smokehouses, for which the island was known, are long gone, but salmon farming remains big, along with harvesting lobster and clams, periwinkles, and that Grand Manan delicacy: dulse (rolandsdulse.com), a mineral-rich seaweed that's sold worldwide.

The island's population (2,460) clusters in the sheltered harbors and coves along its gentle Bay of Fundy shore. In contrast, the northern and southern "heads" of the island are soaring cliffs, and the western shore is a mirror image of Maine's Bold Coast, clearly visible 10 miles offshore from Blacks Harbour. Trails and boats lead to isolated beaches and coves.

Grand Manan is all about getting out and enjoying the island's rare beauty, which you don't see by simply driving the 15-mile length of grandiosely numbered Rt. 776, the island's one main road. Begin by visiting the Swallowtail Light in North Head and be sure to walk the spectacular cliff paths at Southwest Head Light. Take a kayak or a whale-watch tour.

Grand Manan remains as out-of-the-way and unspoiled as it was during the 20 summers (1922–42) that Willa Cather spent here, working on some of her most famous novels, including *Death Comes for the Archbishop*. Her beautiful cottage at Whale Cove (whalecovecottages.ca) remains much the way she knew it. The novelist's typewriter and desk are in The Grand Manan Museum (506-662-3524; grandmananmuseum.ca), which also showcases one man's collection of more than 300 mounted birds and documents the island's smoked herring industry in paintings, photographs, memorabilia, and much more.

Coastal Transport (506-662-3724; coastaltransport.ca) operates ferries on the 20-mile sail between Blacks Harbour (35 miles from Calais, ME) and the mainland. Car ferries run year-round, every two hours beginning at 7:30 AM in high season. Plenty of comfortable seating, food, and computer plug-ins plus WiFi. Roundtrip reservations are strongly advised for vehicles. Pedestrians and bicyclists have no problem getting on, and for an overnight you might not want to leave your car parked (free) in the ferry lot. Whale-watching and sea-kayaking tours, and rental bikes within walking distance of the ferry terminal in North Head. The Compass Rose (compassroseinn.com) is a gem of an inn within walking distance of the ferry, and the Marathon Inn (marathoninn.com) is also in North Head. A car, however, is essential for longer stays. There's camping at The Anchorage Provincial Park (1-800-561-0123) and at Hole in the Wall Park & Campground (1-866-662-4489; grandmanancamping.com).

GUIDANCE The Grand Manan Tourism Association maintains a seasonal information center at 130 Rt. 776 in North Head. It also publishes *Grand Manan Trails* and *Grand Manan Guide*, available in most island stores. The island website is excellent.

Note: Prices are in Canadian dollars.

INDEX